Business Innovation and the Law

Business Innovation and the Law

Perspectives from Intellectual Property, Labour, Competition and Corporate Law

Edited by

Marilyn Pittard, Ann L. Monotti and John Duns

Faculty of Law, Monash University, Australia

Edward Elgar

Cheltenham, UK • Northampton, MA, USA

Published by
Edward Elgar Publishing Limited
The Lypiatts
15 Lansdown Road
Cheltenham
Glos GL50 2JA
UK

Edward Elgar Publishing, Inc.
William Pratt House
9 Dewey Court
Northampton
Massachusetts 01060
USA

A catalogue record for this book
is available from the British Library

Library of Congress Control Number: 2012948159

This book is available electronically in the ElgarOnline.com Law Subject Collection, E-ISBN 978 1 78100 162 2

ISBN 978 1 78100 161 5

Typeset by Columns Design XML Ltd, Reading
Printed and bound by MPG PRINTGROUP, UK

Contents

Contributors

Richard (Rick) Bales

Rick Bales is Professor of Law and Director of the Advocacy Center at Northern Kentucky University, Salmon P. Chase College of Law. He has authored or co-authored five books, on employment arbitration, alternative dispute resolution in the workplace, employment law, labour law, and arbitration law, including *Collective Bargaining in a Free Society* (Westlaw, 2009, with Timothy Heinzs and Dennis Nolan). He has published more than 70 scholarly articles, including many co-authored with Chase students. In 2010, Rick received the Frank Sinton Milburn (the outstanding University-wide professor) Award. He spent July 2010 as a Fulbright Specialist in Kuala Lumpur, Malaysia, where he conducted a mediation training workshop for Malaysian judges and trial lawyers.

Noel Byrne

Dr Noel Byrne worked as an avionics engineer and engineering manager throughout the 1960s and left engineering to study law in late 1969. He taught intellectual property law at Queen Mary College, University of London, where he was Senior Fellow in Intellectual Property law until his early retirement in September 2001. He is legal adviser on intellectual property law and related areas of law (including competition law, technology licensing agreements, research and development contracts) to a number of major companies and biotechnology research centres. Noel's publications include two editions of the book *Licensing Technology: Negotiating and Drafting Technology Transfer Agreements* (Jordan), the third edition of which was co-authored with Amanda McBratney in 2005.

Simon Deakin

Simon Deakin is Professor of Law at the University of Cambridge and Fellow in Law, Peterhouse, Cambridge, specialising in labour law, private law, company law, law and economics, and EU law. He is a programme director in the Centre for Business Research, an interdisciplinary research unit based in the Judge Business School at Cambridge. His books include *Markesinis & Deakin's Tort Law* (6th edn, Oxford University Press 2008, with Basil Markesinis and Angus Johnston), *Labour Law* (5th edn, Hart Publishing 2009, with Gillian S. Morris), *The Law of the Labour Market: Industrialization, Employment, and Legal Evolution* (Oxford University Press 2005, with Frank Wilkinson) and *Hedge Fund Activism in Japan: The Limits of Shareholder Primacy* (Cambridge University Press 2012, with John Buchanan and Dominic Chai). Simon has been a member of the editorial boards of the *British Journal of Industrial Relations*, the *Industrial Law Journal* (UK), and the *Cambridge Journal of Economics* and is currently editor of the *Industrial Law Journal*. He is a recipient of the ECGI and Allen & Overy prizes for corporate governance research and was elected to a Fellowship of the British Academy in 2005.

Riccardo Del Punta

Riccardo Del Punta is Full Professor of Labour Law at the University of Florence, Faculty of Law and has researched and lectured at other universities including Trieste and Siena. He has published one of the leading texts in Italian labour law, *Diritto del lavoro* (5th edn, Giuffrè 2011). He is a member of the Italian Association of Labour and Social Security Law, the Advisory Board of the Italian Society of Law and Economics, and the scientific committee of the most important Italian labour law journals (including *Giornale di diritto del lavoro e delle relazioni industriali* and *Rivista italiana di diritto del lavoro*). Riccardo also practises as a barrister in labour law and is a member of the executive board and of the scientific committee of AGI (Avvocati Giuslavoristi Italiani).

Rochelle Cooper Dreyfuss

Rochelle Dreyfuss is the Pauline Newman Professor of Law at New York University School of Law and Co-Director of the NYU's Engelberg Center on Innovation Law and Policy. She is a member of the American Law Institute and was a Co-Reporter for its Project on Intellectual Property: Principles Governing Jurisdiction, Choice of Law, and Judgments in Transnational Disputes. She was a consultant to the Federal Courts Study Committee and the Presidential Commission on Catastrophic Nuclear Accidents, and a member of the National Academies' committees on Intellectual Property in Genomic and Protein Research and Innovation, on Intellectual Property Rights in the Knowledge-Based Economy and the Secretary of Health and Human Services' Advisory Committee on Genetics Health and Society. She is presently on the Academies' Committee on Science, Technology, and Law. She is the author of *A Neofederalist Vision of TRIPS: The Resilience of the*

International Intellectual Property Regime (Oxford University Press 2012, with Graeme B. Dinwoodie).

Claire T. Driscoll

Claire Driscoll is Director of the National Human Genome Research Institute's (NHGRI) Technology Transfer Office (TTO) at the U.S. National Institutes of Health (NIH) in Bethesda, Maryland. Prior to joining NHGRI in 1999 she was a Senior Technology Development Manager with the NIH's National Institute of Allergy and Infectious Diseases (NIAID). At NHGRI Claire is responsible for the overall oversight of the Institute's intramural patent and licensing portfolio; the TTO also negotiates and manages research collaboration agreements on behalf of NHGRI scientists and advises staff on technology transfer policy matters. Ms Driscoll frequently gives talks on biomedical technology transfer as well as related intellectual property and policy topics at conferences including AusBiotech, New Zealand Bio (NZBio), the Biotechnology Industry Organization (BIO), Association of University Technology Managers (AUTM) and Licensing Executives Society (LES)-sponsored events.

John Duns

John Duns is Associate Professor in the Faculty of Law at Monash University and Convenor, PhD programmes. He teaches competition law and corporations law at undergraduate and postgraduate levels and has written widely in the area. The third edition of *Competition Law: Cases and Materials* (with Arlen Duke) was published by LexisNexis Butterworths in 2011. He is the 'Restrictive Trade Practices' editor of the *Australian Journal of Competition and Consumer Law*. John's other publications include *Corporate Law* (2nd edn, Oxford University Press 2009, with E. Boros) and *Australian Insolvency Law* (LexisNexis 2009; 2nd edition to be published in 2012, with C. Symes) and *Insolvency: Law and Policy* (Oxford University Press 2002).

Ray Finkelstein

The Hon Ray Finkelstein is Adjunct Professor in the Faculty of Law, Monash University and was formerly a Judge of the Federal Court of Australia. He was called to the Bar in 1975, specialising in equity, commercial and corporate law, and was appointed Queen's Counsel in 1986. Thereafter he concentrated on appellate work often acting for State and Federal governments and their instrumentalities. He was acting Solicitor General for the State of Victoria during 1992. He was appointed a Judge of the Federal Court in 1997 and retired from the Court in 2011.

He held additional appointments as Deputy President of the Australian Competition Tribunal and the Copyright Tribunal of Australia. In December 2008 he was appointed part-time President of the Australian Competition Tribunal and held this position until 2011.

Paul Finn

The Hon Justice Paul Finn was a Judge of the Federal Court of Australia from 1995 until 2012. In 2010–2011, he was the Arthur Goodhart Visiting Professor at the University of Cambridge. He has held a number of university positions and was Professor of Law in the Research School of Social Sciences at the Australian National University prior to his judicial appointment. He has been a fellow of the Academy of Social Sciences in Australia since 1990. He has authored a number of books including *Fiduciary Obligations* (Law Book Co 1977) and *Law and Government in Colonial Australia* (Oxford University Press 1987). His edited books include *Equity and Commercial Relationships* (Law Book Co 1987), *Essays on Restitution* (Law Book Co 1990), *Equity and Commercial Relationships* (Law Book Co 1987), *Essays on Contract* (Law Book Co 1987) and *Essays in Equity* (Law Book Co 1990).

Alison Firth

Alison Firth is a Visiting Professor at CCLS, Queen Mary, University of London. She originally read physics at Oxford and, after researching and teaching physics in London and Lima (Peru), she pursued an interest in patents, qualified as a barrister and has practised in intellectual property chambers since 1983. She was a full-time member of the intellectual property law unit at the Centre for Commercial Law Studies, Queen Mary College, University of London (1987–2004); Professor of Commercial Law at Newcastle Law School, Newcastle University (2005–2009), where she is now a visiting professor; and Emeritus Professor of Law at the University of Surrey (2009–2012). Her publications include *Trade Marks: Law and Practice* (3rd edn, Jordan 2012, with G. Lea and P. Cornford). Her research interests involve the law of intellectual property and its interaction with other areas of law, such as contract, competition law, civil and criminal procedure, conflict of laws and human rights.

Catherine L. Fisk

Catherine Fisk is the Chancellor's Professor of Law at the University of California, Irvine. She teaches courses on labour and employment law, the intersection of labour and intellectual property, and the legal profession. She also has appointments in Irvine's departments of Criminology Law and Society, and History and serves as the director of the Center in

Law, Society and Culture. Professor Fisk is the author of three books, including the prize-winning *Working Knowledge: Employee Innovation and the Rise of Corporate Intellectual Property, 1800–1930* (University of North Carolina Press 2009). Catherine has published dozens of articles in leading American law reviews on diverse aspects of labour and employment law, civil rights and legal history. She previously was a chaired Professor of Law at Duke University.

Mark Freedland

Mark Freedland is a Reader in Employment Law with the title of Professor at the University of Oxford and a Fellow and Law Tutor at St John's College, Oxford. His university teaching is in the fields of labour law, international and European employment law, and comparative public law. He has acted as the Director of Graduate Studies for the Law Faculty, as Vice-Chair of the Law Board, and as Director of the Institute of European and Comparative Law. Mark is currently a Deputy Director of the IECL and is the Convenor responsible for organising the Course in Legal Research Method. In recent years he has held visiting professorships at the Universities of Paris I and Paris II. His book publications include *The Personal Employment Contract* (Oxford University Press 2003) and *Towards a Flexible Labour Market – Labour Legislation and Regulation since the 1990s* (Oxford University Press 2007, with P.L. Davies).

Rosa Greaves

Rosa Greaves is Professor and Head of the Law School, the University of Glasgow and a Professor II at the University of Oslo. She specialises in competition and European commercial law in her research and teaching. She has written *Transport Law of the European Community* (Athlone 1991), *EC Competition Law: Banking and Insurance Services* (Wiley 1992), *EEC Block Exemption Regulations* (Wiley 1994), *EC Transport Law* (Pearson 2000) and co-authored *Advocate General and EC Law* (Oxford University Press 2007). Her edited books include: *Protecting and Exploiting Biotechnological Inventions* (Worldwide Information 1991) and a volume for *The International Library of Essays in Law and Legal Theory on Competition Law* (second series, Ashgate 2002). Rosa is Visiting Professor at the Catholic University of Lisbon and has been Visiting Professor at universities in Australia, the US, Europe and the UK. She is a member of the Editorial Advisory Board of the *Journal of Comparative Law*, *Web Journal of Current Legal Issues*, *The Irish Jurist* and *Revista de Concorrencia e Regulacao.*

Carol M. Hayes

Carol Hayes is a graduate of the University of Illinois College of Law, where she received her Juris Doctor degree magna cum laude. She has also served as a Christine Mirzayan Science and Technology Policy Graduate Fellow with the National Academy of Science. She is currently working as a Research Associate through the University of Illinois College of Law, focusing on topics related to cyberlaw. Her article (with Jay P. Kesan), 'Mitigative Counterstriking: Self-Defense and Deterrence in Cyberspace', is published in volume 25 of the *Harvard Journal of Law and Technology* 2012.

John Hull

John Hull is a consultant with the London firm Farrer and Co where he specialises in technology law and intellectual property. His practice covers all aspects of intellectual property including infringement actions, licensing, advisory work on issues such as trade mark portfolio management and the intellectual property aspects of corporate transactions extending to data privacy, freedom of information and to aspects of IT. He is an acknowledged expert in the law relating to trade secrets and confidential information. John is Visiting Professorial Fellow in Intellectual Property at Queen Mary, University of London; Visiting Lecturer at University College London; Visiting Lecturer at the Intellectual Property Academy, Singapore; and Senior Fellow at the Faculty of Law, Monash University. He is the author of *Commercial Secrecy: Law and Practice* (Sweet & Maxwell 1998) and numerous articles and papers in professional and academic journals.

Marie-Christine Janssens

Marie-Christine Janssens is Professor at the Centre for Intellectual Property Rights (CIR), at the University of Leuven (KU Leuven) in Belgium, where she teaches various courses on intellectual property law. Since 2009, she has been a Visiting Professor at the China University of Political Science and Law in Beijing. Previously she acquired experience as a barrister in international law firms in Brussels and Washington DC. Her PhD dissertation was on the legal status of employee and university inventions in the countries of the EU. In 2005 Marie-Christine was appointed President of the High Council for Intellectual Property Rights, which advises the Belgian Minister for Economy. She is also a member of the editorial board of leading Belgian IP journals. Her publications include books (in Dutch) on employee inventions (1996), trade mark law in the Benelux and the EU (2009) and copyright on the Internet (2012).

Jay P. Kesan

Jay Kesan is Professor, H. Ross & Helen Workman Research Scholar and Director of the Program in Intellectual Property and Technology Law at the University of Illinois. After clerking for Judge Patrick Higginbotham in the Fifth Circuit Court of Appeals, he worked as a patent attorney in the former firm of Pennie & Edmonds LLP. Author of several books and numerous articles, his academic interests and writings are in the areas of patent law, cyberlaw, entrepreneurship, and law and technology. Jay continues to be active in the area of patent litigation and he has served as a Special Master in patent lawsuits. He is a registered patent attorney. In addition to legal qualifications, he has a PhD in electrical and computer engineering (University of Texas at Austin) and worked for several years as a research scientist in New York.

Dorothy Livingston

Dorothy Livingston is Consultant, EU/competition with the law firm Herbert Smith Freehills LLP, London. She specialises in all aspects of EU and UK competition law and regulation including mergers, market investigations, anti-competitive practices and agreements and State aids. Dorothy also works on matters involving regulatory law (particularly the interaction of EU and UK law) and her experience spans several fields including finance, transport, the utilities, broadcasting and other media. Dorothy has an extensive background in financial and banking law. She is the Chairman of the Financial Law Committee of the City of London Law Society (CLLS) and represents the Society on the Treasury Banking Liaison Panel appointed to consider important subsidiary legislation and the Code of Practice under the *Banking Act 2009* (UK) related to the Special Resolution Regime for failing banks.

Andrea Mina

Andrea Mina is Senior Research Fellow at the Centre for Business Research at the University of Cambridge. He is also Research Associate of the Business Economics and Management Division of the Judge Business School (Cambridge) and Associate and Co-investigator of the UK Innovation Research Centre at Cambridge University and Imperial College London. His research focuses on the problem of technological, organisational and institutional change with special emphasis on the emergence of new technologies, innovation systems and networks, industrial dynamics and the financing of innovation. He has published in the leading international innovation and science policy journals. Andrea has been Principal and Co-Principal Investigator of several projects funded, among others, by the UK Engineering and Physical Sciences Research Council, the Economic and Social Research Council, the Department of Business Innovation and Skills, and the European Commission.

Chris Molnar

Chris Molnar is a partner at Melbourne law firm McKean Park. He has practised in workplace relations law in Australia for over 15 years. Previously he worked for several major national law firms and has acted for major national corporations, and governments and public sector agencies at federal, state and local levels. His areas of expertise include employment law, industrial relations, anti-discrimination and workplace safety. In addition to his legal qualifications, he has a Master of Business Administration and is a workplace relations specialist accredited by the Law Institute of Victoria. In 2009 Chris was awarded the prestigious President's Award from the Law Institute of Victoria for his contribution to the specialisation scheme. He is a member of the Monash Law Faculty's LLM Workplace and Employment Law advisory panel, a Fellow of the Australian Institute of Company Directors and an accredited mediator.

Ann L. Monotti

Ann Monotti is Professor in the Faculty of Law, Monash University and was Associate Dean, Postgraduate Studies (2006–2011). Her research and teaching interests focus upon intellectual property law. More specifically, she researches issues concerning universities and their ownership and exploitation of intellectual property, employee inventions, commercialising intellectual property and technology transfer and access to and protection of biomedical research materials. Her Monash PhD was awarded on the basis of the book of which she is the principal author: *Universities and Intellectual Property, Ownership and Exploitation* (Oxford University Press 2003, with Sam Ricketson), a book arising from two ARC grants, and influential in developing policy and legal principles in this area. Her other books include two editions of Davison, Monotti and Wiseman, *Australian Intellectual Property Law* (Cambridge University Press 2008 and, 2nd edn, 2012).

Justine Pila

Justine Pila is University Lecturer in Intellectual Property Law at the University of Oxford, and an Official Fellow of St Catherine's College, Oxford. She is also the Convenor of the Law Faculty's Intellectual Property Subject Group, Senior Law Tutor and College Counsel (in-house legal officer) at St Catherine's College, and a Research Fellow at the Oxford Institute of European and Comparative Law. Her primary areas of research are copyright and patent law in all of their historical, doctrinal and theoretical aspects. Her monograph, *The Requirement for an Invention in Patent Law,* was published by Oxford University Press in 2010.

Marilyn Pittard

Marilyn Pittard is Professor of Law, Faculty of Law, Monash University and Associate Dean, International. She has held positions of Associate Dean of Postgraduate Studies and of Research in the faculty. She teaches labour law at undergraduate and postgraduate levels and publishes extensively in labour law journals. Her co-authored books include *Australian Labour Law: Text, Commentary and Cases* (5th edn, LexisNexis 2010 and several previous editions); *Industrial Relations in Australia: Development, Law and Operation* (Longman 1995); and an edited volume arising from an ARC grant, *Public Sector Employment Law in the Twenty-First Century* (ANU EPress 2007, with P. Weeks). Marilyn is a founding and current member of the *Australian Journal of Labour Law*'s editorial board and General Editor of LexisNexis' *Employment Law Bulletin.* By invitation, she presented the Phillipa Weeks Annual Lecture 2010 at the Australian National University. She is Vice President of the Australian Labour Law Association.

Jeremias Prassl

Jeremias Prassl is a Stipendiary Lecturer in Jurisprudence at Jesus College, Oxford. He read law at the Universities of Oxford and Paris II (Panthéon-Assas) and received an LLM at Harvard Law School before returning to work on his doctorate at Magdalen College, Oxford. Jeremias's research focuses on employment and company law aspects of the alternative fund management industry in the United Kingdom and continental Europe, with a particular interest in the relationship between employees of private equity portfolio companies and fund management. He is also interested in the European Union's constitutional relationship with its overseas territories, and the pricing of legal risk in financial markets. Jeremias is Supernumerary Fellow-elect at St John's College, Oxford.

Preface

Our journey to the ultimate destination of publication of this book involved several significant steps. First of all, Ann and John enthusiastically accepted Marilyn's invitation to discuss her concept of a legal inter-disciplinary approach to business innovation; and the genesis of this book arose from our plan for collaborative work on business innovation and law, starting with a conference. Next, we received the support of the Faculty of Law, Monash University in the form of a conference grant and so were able to start planning the conference. Then, as indicated in our chapter 1, this conference, held over three days in May 2011, provided the springboard for this book, enabling the authors to come together to present their papers on business innovation and further discuss the areas from the inter-disciplinary perspectives of intellectual property, labour and employment law and competition and corporate laws. Finally, we were very pleased to secure a book contract with Edward Elgar Publishing.

A book such as this, built upon and substantially developed from a diverse and multi-disciplinary range of papers presented at an international conference, requires whole-hearted commitment and support from many people. We wish to record our gratitude to those people and a number of organisations involved in the publication of this book.

We thank the Faculty of Law, Monash University for its financial support for the conference as well as the small research grant we were awarded to assist with editing. Our marketing and finance sections provided expert assistance for essential aspects of the conference. We are grateful to our conference administrator, Dr Ellen Berah of The Conference Organiser, for her efficient and enthusiastic administration of the conference and for being on the ground at the Monash University Centre, Prato, Italy to undertake the day-to-day running of the conference. The staff at the Monash University Prato Centre cheerfully supported and accommodated our conference needs, and we thank them, in particular Cathy Crupi and the then Director of the Centre, Dr Loretta Baldassar.

The book would not be possible without the authors who have contributed their chapters. They readily accepted our invitations to present their research on this new legal inter-disciplinary perspective in the conference forum; and again they were keen to write and contribute their chapters to this book. They have contributed in so many ways, both scholarly and personal. Many of them have now become our friends, a friendship that goes across international borders and which we value.

Michael Adams undertook editing assistance for us in relation to the chapters. We thank him for that assistance and for continuing to help us (after business hours) once he had commenced full-time employment.

We are grateful to our international publisher, Edward Elgar Publishing and its staff, especially John-Paul McDonald. They have been nothing but professional, helpful and supportive in their dealings with us for which we thank them.

That the conference exploring the legal field of research in this book – innovation and invention – was held in Italy was fitting too, as many great inventions and innovations have emanated from inventors in that country – from Da Vinci to Marconi and beyond.

Professor Marilyn Pittard
Professor Ann L. Monotti
Associate Professor John Duns
Faculty of Law, Monash University
Clayton, Australia
June 2012

PART I

Business innovation: introducing the perspectives

1. Perspectives and themes

John Duns, Ann L. Monotti and Marilyn Pittard

> It is well to observe the force and virtue and consequences of discoveries, and these are to be seen nowhere more conspicuously than in those three which were unknown to the ancients, and of which the origins, though recent, are obscure and inglorious: namely printing, gunpowder, and the magnet [Mariner's Needle]. For these three have changed the whole face and state of things throughout the world.
>
> Bacon, *Novum Organum* (1620) bk 1, *Aphorism 129* (translated by J. Spedding)

1. INTRODUCTION AND CONTEXT

Innovation is a central pillar in government policy agendas that aim to produce a 'resilient economy'[1] through competition and productivity. Through the centuries 'innovation' has been understood to encompass the creation and implementation of new knowledge and invention but the predominant criteria that governments use in the 21st century for its measurement link these requirements directly with entrepreneurial activity that delivers economic benefits to society.[2] Governments have relied upon evidence that 'innovation pre-eminently determines our prosperity'[3] to design policies that aim to foster innovative activities. These policies include support for investment in research and development as well as a range of other programmes, infrastructure and tax incentives. Innovation encompasses a spectrum of activity that extends from development of ideas, frequently within public research institutions, through to their commercial implementation. Hence, a succinct summary of the present concept of 'innovation' may be 'the process by which new ideas are

1 DIISR (2011).
2 E.g., OECD (2011).
3 Cutler & Company (2008), 1.

successfully exploited to create economic, social and environmental value'.[4] A more detailed definition becomes necessary for the purpose of measuring the comparative success of government innovation programmes and policies. This appears in the current (3rd) edition of the OECD *Oslo Manual: Guidelines for Collecting and Interpreting Innovation Data*, a manual that OECD members use to inform their independent evaluations[5] of domestic innovation performance: 'Innovation is the implementation of a new or significantly improved product (good or service), or process, a new marketing method, or a new organisational method in business practices, workplace organisation or external relations.'[6]

History demonstrates that innovation bears some resemblance to a chameleon in that its appearance takes its final form from the environment in which it exists[7] and that environment is fluid. As knowledge and the manner of its creation and dissemination change, we see periodic reappraisal and redesign of innovation policy frameworks to 'revitalise' innovation systems with the aim of enhancing domestic productivity in an increasingly competitive global marketplace.[8]

The impact of business innovation on the national economies is critical. Evidence that innovation has been instrumental in the success of the small number of high-growth businesses[9] is influencing the design of innovation policies in the United Kingdom. Its *Annual Innovation Report* (2011) prepared by the Department for Business Innovation & Skills (BIS) and NESTA, UK's innovation foundation,[10] reported on the impact of innovation on economic growth as follows:

> Innovation drives economic growth – it has accounted for 63 per cent of annual labour productivity growth since 2000, with investments in intangibles accounting for 23 per cent of productivity growth. Investment in intangibles in 2008 also helped reduce the negative impact on productivity of the start of the recession.[11]

---

[4] UK BIS website: <http://www.bis.gov.uk/innovation>.
[5] E.g., DISSR (2011); Commonwealth of Australia (2009).
[6] OECD (2005), [146].
[7] Godin (2008).
[8] Cutler & Company (2008), 4; DIISR (2011).
[9] Anyadike-Danes et al (2009); Mason et al (2009).
[10] Website: <http://www.nesta.org.uk/about_us>.
[11] BIS and NESTA (2011), Key Findings.

However, partnering with universities – 'the strength of UK universities and the wider knowledge base is a national asset'[12] – also represents a key feature for providing benefits for business innovation. BIS observed in its 2011 *Innovation and Research Strategy for Growth* that:

> [Businesses] are more likely to improve the quality of their goods and services, improve their labour productivity, increase their range of goods and services and more than twice as likely to open new markets or increase their market share compared to those businesses that don't interact with [Higher Education Institutions].[13]

Its overall message is that success in the 'global innovation economy' requires that 'the UK must strengthen its ability to accelerate the commercialisation of emerging technologies, and to capture the value chains linked to these. The private sector is always going to be central to innovation'.[14] These sentiments are consistent with the future direction of innovation policy in Australia. Support for business innovation is now identified as an explicit priority for Australian innovation policy alongside the continuing recognition of the need to support knowledge creation that occurs within universities.[15]

Effective innovation policy requires the support of effective legal regimes that are designed to protect new ideas and the rights of all the participants in the innovation system, to enhance effective and competitive marketing of new products and processes and to regulate organisational structures and relationships in ways that maximise the economic and social outcomes of innovation policy. Various laws come into play here. Employment law and intellectual property laws play a part because it is often the employee who is the inventor or innovator and issues arise as to whether the employee has undertaken this innovation or made an invention as part of his or her contract of employment. Competition law may play a role, too, both because market power may be granted by intellectual property laws and, on the other hand, an acknowledged objective of competition law is to promote innovation. And, finally, corporate governance rules may well have a say, along with intellectual property and employment law, in the ownership of business inventions and, more broadly, the nature of corporate governance systems may be a significant factor in promoting or impeding innovation.

---

12 BIS (2011), 1.
13 Ibid, 31, citing Lambert (2003).
14 Ibid, 1.
15 Cutler (2008), 4; DISSR (2011).

Commonly, legal issues arising from business innovation are viewed from the perspective of only one discipline. Hence, a principal objective of this volume is to adopt a more holistic approach and to explore the potential for using these different legal perspectives – intellectual property, employment and labour law, competition law and corporate governance rules – to guide future analysis of emerging issues in this field in order to achieve maximum benefits for all relevant parties from business innovation. These perspectives provided the structure for an international conference conducted by Monash University in May 2011 and held at the Monash University Prato Centre in Prato, Italy. The catalyst for the conference was a high-profile dispute fought out in the Australian Federal Court in *University of Western Australia v Gray*[16] over rights to academic employee inventions. Although the case dealt with the special considerations that apply in academic employment, it highlighted the multiple legal perspectives that inform policy in this area. The conference drew together top international scholars in each of these fields as well as legal practitioners, postgraduate students, policy makers and those responsible for business innovation in both public and private research institutes from around the world. The various papers and discussions evaluated the impact of each of these areas on aspects of business innovation using discipline-specific perspectives, and explored the extent to which such perspectives are influenced by the others. The question whether there could be a more harmonised approach to the legal protection of business innovation was identified and examined with particular reference to some EU jurisdictions.

This volume represents the final scholarly culmination of the investigation of business innovation using varied perspectives, which commenced with the conference in Prato, Italy in 2011. It presents and critiques approaches of the law in Australia, the United Kingdom and the United States and of civil jurisdictions, particularly the EU, in order to inform and provide guidance at an international level for the further analysis of emerging issues in this field. The range and scope of the different perspectives are taken up in the following sections.

2. INTELLECTUAL PROPERTY LAW PERSPECTIVES

One theme that is instrumental for effective business innovation is the protection that intellectual property law in its many guises provides for

---

[16] (2010) 179 FCR 346.

new knowledge. A number of separate legal doctrines and statutory regimes are bundled for simplicity of reference under the umbrella term 'intellectual property' (IP). Each protects a range of rights that for the most part qualify as 'property' rights and that derive from intellectual creative ideas in the fine and useful arts. These rights include copyright, trademarks, geographical indications, registered and unregistered designs, patents for inventions, plant breeders' rights, circuit layouts and protection for confidential information.[17] Although all forms of IP may play a role in innovation, the emphasis in this volume is upon two specific interrelated but independent areas:

(a) the law relating to patents for inventions, which grants limited property rights in return for public disclosure of the invention; and
(b) the legal principles of various doctrines that allow originators of new ideas to keep those ideas secret.

A patent for an invention is available only for subject matter that is a new and inventive product, method or process in any field of technology provided that it is capable of industrial application.[18] In contrast, secret information of all kinds (including patentable inventions) can gain protection under express confidentiality agreements and various legal doctrines that generally appear in treatises on IP law such as the equitable doctrine of breach of confidence in Australia and the United Kingdom and the law of trade secrets[19] in the United States. The owner of a patentable invention that can be kept secret – such as methods and processes that cannot be reverse engineered from the products released into the marketplace – has a choice. She might file for a patent and assume the attendant risks of publication prior to grant together with risks of failure to obtain a granted patent or later invalidation of the patent. Alternatively, she might protect the business asset from appropriation by trade rivals by taking the risk of maintaining its secrecy with the use of business systems and confidentiality agreements. The options are alternatives: it is not possible to use the invention secretly and later seek a patent when the risk of public disclosure is too great.[20] The vehicles

---

[17] Classifications in Agreement on Trade-Related Aspects of Intellectual Property Rights 1994 (TRIPS).
[18] TRIPs art 27(1); e.g., *Patents Act 1990* (Cth) s18 (1990 Act).
[19] E.g., Lemley (2008).
[20] E.g., 1990 Act ss 9, 18(1)(d).

selected to protect inventions will be those which offer greatest protection from competition in the marketplace to protect the value of intellectual assets from free riders.

A business cannot exploit IP rights in the absence of clear entitlement to do so. IP laws generally acknowledge the supremacy of the originators by vesting them with initial ownership. In the case of inventions, the originator is the inventor – broadly the person or persons who have made a material contribution to the inventive concept. The decision to vest property rights in the inventor reflects the early rationales for the grant of monopoly rights in inventions: natural rights theories as well as the need to provide incentives and rewards for individuals to be innovative, to produce services useful to society, and to disclose their secrets. Vesting ownership in the inventors gives them what they believe is their right and entitlement – they generally feel an intense possessiveness for their ideas. Others must derive rights from the inventors and the usual process for this is under an express contract.

Patent laws not only provide an incentive for individuals to invent by vesting initial ownership in the inventor, but they also recognise the need to provide incentives to entice entrepreneurs to develop and commercialise new technologies that those individuals invent. The concern here is to provide incentives for a business to protect and exploit its inventions in ways that maximise their benefits for society without undermining the incentive for individuals to invent. The challenge is to balance the rights of those who perform these two integral and complementary aspects of research and development in ways that further government innovation policies. Hence, any IP perspective of business innovation must consider not only the interests of the individual inventor but also the interests of any business entity that takes the commercial risks in research and development activities. This will usually be an employer that wants to exploit inventions created by its employees during their employment. As explained below, the perspectives of employment and labour law have assisted courts in developing principles that recognise the needs of business without unreasonably eroding rights given to inventors under patent law. The balance struck is one that requires the employee who is employed to invent to assign rights in any invention to the employer. In all other situations, the rights remain with the employee inventor. There are attempts to soften this 'all or nothing' approach with the concept of 'shop-rights' in the United States and rights of compensation for employee inventors in Europe, but an employer's rights to own inventions dominate in standard commercial employment environments. This aims to provide businesses with a degree of certainty that they can invest in the exploitation of inventions created for their business by employees who are paid to invent.

The entry of universities into the world of commercial exploitation of inventions that arise from research conducted within the university has challenged the understanding that these default principles can be applied in all employment contexts. The Australian full federal court in *UWA v Gray* held that the nature of academic employment bears little resemblance to the cases 'that gave rise to the common law implication of employer ownership of employee inventions that were developed in the course of, and as a product of, what the employee was employed actually to do'.[21] Public sector research generally poses special and distinctive issues for intellectual property protection and exploitation. These extend beyond questions of ownership as a matter of law into the fundamental policy issue of the extent to which universities and other public sector research institutes should be involved in protection and exploitation of public sector research. These issues are tackled in some of the contributions to this volume. Irrespective of whether inventions are generated within a business or public sector research environment, the realistic expectation is that employees will be the creators of IP. Hence, the employment and labour law perspective which follows is integral to any evaluation of the legal principles that apply to the management of employee inventions.

3. EMPLOYMENT AND LABOUR LAW PERSPECTIVES

As outlined above, employees are usually critical to businesses in the role they play in inventing. The most common issue presented in this area of law confronting employers and employees is whether an invention or innovation made by an employee is owned by that employee or the employer. This, as indicated above, could be approached from the viewpoint of intellectual property law and its concern with patents, with copyright and with reducing uncertainties through legislative intervention. Frequently, however, the IP law throws the issue back to the common law, so that entitlement to patent rights might really depend on the resolution of concepts such as 'course of employment' and questions such as: What does the contract expressly say? What did the parties to the contract intend? What is the practice or custom in the industry? Is

[21] *UWA v Gray* (2010) 179 FCR 346, [206].

there a term implied in the actual factual circumstances of this particular contract and its negotiations? What does the law imply in contracts of a particular class, that is, contracts of employment?

The focus from the employment or labour side is very particular and it is a focus at the micro level of employer and employee. The starting point in the common law countries has been the model that the employer 'takes all' – the proceeds of invention or innovation will belong to the employer so long as the employee is engaged to invent, or so long as the invention or discovery is within the scope of employment. This micro approach is quite blinkered – it generally takes no account of equitable distribution of profits or royalties, and in reality takes no account of whether, and how, the law should be – or could be – encouraging creativity amongst the employer's workforce and fairly distributing its proceeds, profits or royalties. Ironically, it relies on non-contractual concepts, such as making *ex gratia* payments, to ensure equity. Today, the common law provides arguably a more nuanced approach in that a duty to invent will not always be implied by law in employment contracts, even in the contracts of employment of researchers; the scope of the employment may be more realistically cast so that everything that an employee does at work using the employer's facilities will not automatically belong to an employer. However, the courts have steered away from examining the 'macro picture' of what is a suitable regime or system to put in place for encouragement of innovation and for equitable distribution of proceeds. The common law courts treat each case on its merits in accord with principles relating to the contract of employment – this 'big picture' is not their concern.

Certainly an employer who realises that the fostering of creativity is significant for the business will appropriately draft a contract of employment to put provisions in place to encourage innovation and the commercialisation of the proceeds of the invention or innovation and provide for accompanying rewards for the creative employees. However, the common law also makes it easy for employers to adopt devices to place limits on the utilisation of the invention – for example, the express contractual clause that all inventions made by the employee whilst employed by the employer belong to the employer; post-employment restraints, invoking limitations of use within geographical limits or time periods, thereby restricting competition by the employee with the employer; or confidentiality clauses. Similarly the contract negotiated at a time when the invention was not even an embryonic idea can distort true equitable sharing in the proceeds of the innovation when made and developed and may lead to attempts by the disaffected employee to retrospectively interpret the contract and the scope of employment in a more favourable light to the employee.

Of greater difficulty is the theme taken up in this volume of the occasional inventor or the 'accidental inventor'. This embraces the problem encountered where it was never contemplated at the time the parties entered into the contract of employment that an invention would be made – but the creator, the employee, is later subject to claims from the employer to share in the winnings. Unless the employer can successfully utilise concepts of the duty to obey reasonable orders or the duty of cooperation, the common law tends to regard this in black and white terms as the right of the employee to own the invention, as opposed to approaches in Europe and some jurisdictions of the United States, which acknowledge that the employer may have some option or interest.

The vagaries of utilising employment law in this area are further aggravated by the problems of differentiating the employee from the independent contractor, where quite different principles might apply to ownership. The United Kingdom, Australia and the United States have not at common law satisfactorily resolved the distinction between these two types of worker. In labour markets where workers are increasingly engaged nominally as contractors but the true employment relationship may be that of employer and employee or may change over time to become an employment relationship, the issue becomes even more acute.[22]

Collaborative work, referred to above, or work undertaken in teams, is a modern organisational phenomenon which further complicates the picture of contribution and entitlement and is a theme addressed.[23] The mobility of the workforce, again a modern feature that is significant in certain industries, will additionally present complications about where and when the invention was created – was the invention commenced in employment elsewhere and precisely what did the employee bring to the workplace?

There is also a competition perspective when considering the employment and labour law perspective. Employers may ultimately wish to prevent employees who have knowledge of inventions from competing with their business – and use an array of contractual devices to prevent or restrict such competition.

---

22 E.g., Pittard and Naughton (2010), ch 3.

23 De Botton (2009) at 141–143.

4. COMPETITION LAW AND CORPORATE GOVERNANCE PERSPECTIVES

Unlike the employment and labour law perspective just considered, competition law and policy provides a broad, market-based response to the issue of innovation. That is, competition law relies on market forces to promote innovation and justifies its intervention in the market where, for one reason or another, the market fails in this task.

At one level, the correlation between innovation and competition law and policy is a simple one. Competition law aims to promote conduct that increases economic welfare[24] and innovation is one of the major means by which welfare is advanced. This much seems uncontroversial, as does the link between the conduct of the firm and wider social welfare. As stated by Baker, 'From one generation to the next, innovation is undoubtedly a central determinant of the welfare of humankind. Economists studying individual projects, moreover, routinely find that the benefits of innovation to society as a whole greatly exceed the benefits to the firms that develop the innovation.'[25] Competition policy proposes, and is based on, a clear causal link between the promotion of competition and the welfare generated by innovation. Competition is valued because it promotes efficiency. Firms are forced to be efficient or face the discipline of the market. One type of efficiency that competition is routinely stated to create is 'dynamic' efficiency. Dynamic efficiency is the outcome of innovation and refers to the new products and technologies that competition encourages firms to develop. Indeed dynamic efficiency is commonly touted as the single most important outcome of competition.[26]

---

[24] There is debate over whether competition law should be concerned with 'total' or 'consumer' welfare, i.e. whether the welfare generated by firms needs to be passed on to consumers for it to be counted. Most jurisdictions, including the US and the EU, claim consumer welfare as their aim. There is also a separate debate over whether competition law should properly be confined to economic objectives or whether it should extend to broader social values. Neither of these issues is of concern in the current context.

[25] Baker (2007), 576; Hovencamp (2010–11), 751 ('there seems to be broad consensus that the gains to be had from innovation are larger than the gains from simple production and trading under constant technology'). Compare Glader (2006), 20 ('The predominant role of innovation and technological change in the achievement of economic wealth is both hard to estimate precisely and to overrate').

[26] Glader (2006), 4, states that 'The central position of innovation and dynamic efficiency in achieving continuous economic growth and welfare in

And so, on this view, one of the key roles of competition law becomes to prevent firms from engaging in conduct that interferes with the competitive process – as such conduct would, in turn, impede the important task of promoting innovation. Conduct that might threaten competition in this way includes mergers, anti-competitive agreements or a misuse of any market power held by the firm. Thus competition law will be encouraging innovation, for the benefit of consumers and society generally. This is an objective it has in common with intellectual property law and, in this sense, these two fields of law are often seen as simply employing different means to the same end.[27]

To a considerable extent, as discussed in the competition chapters in Part IV of this volume, *The competition law perspective on protecting business research and development*, competition law can be effective in promoting innovation in this way. However, as these chapters also show, the link between competition and innovation may also be more complex than the above discussion would suggest. In the first place, the relationship between intellectual property law and competition law is not always harmonious. Much has been written on the interaction between the two. It is not so much that intellectual property creates market power in a firm – it may do so, but this is the exception rather than the rule – but that the exercise of intellectual property rights may create or maintain a firm's market power. Market power is the antithesis of competition. Secondly, and even more fundamentally for competition policy, there is debate over whether competition is in fact good for innovation. Schumpeter famously argued that, for a variety of reasons, including the availability of funds and the ability to reap the rewards of innovation, firms with market power are more likely to engage in innovation than those engaged in the heat of competition.[28] Others, most notably Kenneth Arrow, have argued against this and insist that innovation does in fact require competition.[29] Although the weight of opinion may favour the latter view, the issue remains unsettled and this poses serious challenges for competition policy. Thirdly, there may be situations where innovation itself is

---

society has been acknowledged, not only by economists, but also, to an increasing extent, by public policy makers.' The other efficiencies that result from competition are 'technical' and 'allocative' efficiencies. These terms are explained in Part III of the volume.

27 E.g., Hovencamp (2010–11).

28 Schumpeter (1947).

29 Arrow (1962).

anti-competitive.[30] And finally, there are concerns that traditional competition analysis may not be adequate to identify and assess (let alone provide remedies to protect) the benefits of innovation, particularly in the high tech, 'new economy' markets, where innovation is most pronounced. If these concerns are well placed, competition law errors will occur in the very markets where such errors can least be afforded.[31]

There is also a corporate governance perspective in the innovation debate. How do the principles of corporate governance, such as fiduciary and other duties, including statutory duties, required of officers of the corporation have an impact on claims made to business inventions? Can corporate officers claim inventions and innovations for themselves? When are they acting in the company's, as compared to their own, interests? On a broader scale, do particular models or systems of corporate governance affect the creativity within an organisation and promote inventions? This broader question is of interest to policy makers as well as to the corporate sector generally. Policy of governments in Europe, the Commonwealth and the United States endeavours, in varying degrees, to foster innovation, to fund research and development and to encourage research that will lead to innovation. If corporate governance systems do have an effect on this, there may need to be greater public policy emphasis on these structures.

5. THEMES AND STRUCTURE OF THE VOLUME

The above overview of the perspectives demonstrates the tensions that arise when rationales for each area of law conflict to some extent with each other in the design of our laws. In the context of business innovation, it is essential to consider all perspectives if we are to achieve the optimal legal environment, both nationally and internationally, in which innovation can flourish. An initial dilemma in this book has been to select the entry point for this exploration following this introduction to the various themes. Our decision has been to commence with the chapter authored by the Honourable Paul Finn entitled: 'Failed collaborations: the misappropriation of business opportunities, ideas and advantages by prospective co-venturers, financiers and brokers', as it discusses foundational issues about the protection of new ideas at common law and in equity. An idea for an invention or discovery is the first step along the frequently long path to developing that new concept into a more concrete

---

30 E.g., Gilbert (2007).
31 Manne and Wright (2010).

invention or innovation. The idea represents the embryonic stage of invention and the placement of this chapter next in this section, before we analyse the various perspectives, is chronologically apposite.

The contributions are arranged to mirror to some extent the sequential business innovation process. First, there must be something of potential value for a business to develop and exploit. In the context of this volume we are focusing upon inventions that are either patented or kept secret for the purposes of maximising their commercial potential for the business. As mentioned above, patent law vests inventions initially in the inventors and all rights in those inventions, including rights of the employer, must derive from those inventors. Hence, it seems logical to commence in Part II, *Inventions and discoveries in business: intellectual property perspectives,* with the varied perspectives presented by experts in intellectual property law, all of which assume or highlight the central importance to business innovation of the need to avoid ownership disputes. A clear chain of entitlement to employee inventions is fundamental. The chapters in Part II are principally, but not exclusively, focused upon academic employee inventions that are patented and university employers.

Instead of pursuing the IP perspective themes that include protection of secret information and the exploitation of public sector research, we chose to introduce the employment law perspectives in Part III, *The employment and labour law perspective on protecting business research and development*, to reflect the reality that most invention arises in employment. At the heart of most of the cases giving rise to litigation is the issue whether the correct party in the employment relationship has been given appropriate recompense financially for the invention or innovation. Such cases are generally instituted by the employer (or former employer) in order to claim the proceeds of the innovation which it argues have wrongfully accrued (or will accrue) to the employee; with the employee in all likelihood arguing that they were not under a duty to invent or that they were undertaking the development of the innovation in their own time.

The contract of employment is seen as being of the essence in providing the answer to these questions, together with the readiness of the common law courts to imply terms in a contract of that nature. Thus the employment contract and its implied terms are significant in the issue of who is entitled to the proceeds of an invention. Resort to the express terms of the contract often involves reading the original contract, which may not have kept up with the actual changes over time in the role or tasks of the employee at work, and then constructing the current contractual position. The employer strategy may be to attempt to ensure that property in inventions is claimed in the contract by drafting reasonably broad clauses to guard against the possibility that the employee may make an invention, even an accidental or unexpected invention. The lack of clarity in some cases as to the legal status of the worker – are they employees or contractors? – in Commonwealth jurisdictions further complicates an often complex picture of rights and entitlements. The approaches in the United States and in Europe are examined to provide different ways of looking at the issue. Chapters in Part III address these issues, as well as exploring to what extent limits on former employees taking knowledge with them to rival businesses has actually promoted innovation in the United States.

The chapters in Part IV, *The competition law perspective on protecting business research and development*, explore the key themes which the competition law perspective brings to the debate. One theme is the extent to which intellectual property rights may create market power and in this way interfere with the competitive process. Market power is not the inevitable outcome of intellectual property rights but, where it does occur, the question arises as to whether intellectual property and competition laws work effectively together to promote innovation. Accordingly, one of the issues taken up in the Part IV chapters is whether the promotion of intellectual property rights may, in fact, undermine the process of competition and thereby innovation. Another theme is whether competition law, in principle and in practice, is effective in promoting innovation. To explore this theme, not only are different jurisdictions considered, but authors also draw on the experience of competition law in practice, as well as competition theory, to determine where innovation sits in competition law and policy and the extent to which it is effectively promoted and protected.

The IP and employment law-related themes return in Part V, *Devices to protect business research and development from 'internal attack'*, to explore the other side of the invention coin: the protection of secret inventions and other secret research in ways that maintain their confidentiality. The employer can utilise a number of devices to ensure that confidentiality and to prevent competition from the employee. Confidentiality clauses and clauses which address and restrict competition by the employee during the employment relationship and once the employment relationship has ended may be included as express terms in the employment contract. The parties – employer and employee or former employee – struggle with competing and frequently inconsistent notions: even though confidentiality clauses may be part of the contract, the employee is nonetheless able to use any knowledge gained during employment where it is stock-in-trade or certain acquired information which does not cross the border of confidential information. This is difficult to gauge –

and litigation over the classification of the information may ensue. In the anti-compete clauses, courts struggle with the general concept that they will not impede competition through court orders – thus usually an employee can set up in competition with the former employer and any clauses attempting to restrict this will be struck down or not enforced. This approach, however, is ameliorated by the position that where there is a legitimate business interest to protect in the employer's interest, the courts will enforce reasonable non-compete contractual clauses against employees and in favour of employers. It is difficult, as courts acknowledge, to achieve that 'right' balance. The broader issue of what effect this has on innovation or inventions and creativity is yet to be addressed.

Part VI, *Public sector business research and development*, then pursues the next phase in innovation, but in the context of public sector research, much of which is performed within universities and other research institutes such as the National Institutes of Health (NIH) in the United States. Government innovation policies aim to encourage a culture of collaboration between public sector researchers and industry both nationally and internationally to secure value from commercial innovation. Nevertheless, collaborative research involving people within these different sectors and the transfer of technology between them poses special challenges for those who are responsible for these activities. Frequently there are diametrically opposed values and goals that introduce problems in negotiating the terms and conditions for their relationships.[32] On the other hand, we see considerable advances in managing expectations, conflicts and relationships and the NIH is a leader in this field in its development of IP and licensing policies that aim to serve as 'best practice'.[33] These chapters explore barriers to innovation through research collaborations and technology transfer and methods for dealing with managing these relationships by drawing upon people with extensive experience in the practical management and resolution of these and other related issues concerning collaborative research relationships and technology transfer.

The book ends, in Part VII, *Corporate governance issues and innovation*, by bringing a corporate governance perspective to the innovation debate. In particular, there are two quite separate strands taken up in this Part. The first is to consider how the principles of corporate governance may impact on claims made to business inventions. Parts II and III examined how intellectual property and employment laws deal with

---

32 Lambert (2003), [3.34] ff.

33 Lambert Toolkit: <http://www.ipo.gov.uk/lambert>.

competing claims of employer and employee to business inventions. This Part now considers how fiduciary and statutory duties imposed on corporate officers may further affect such claims. The final chapter in the volume ends, fittingly, with a broader, 'macro' examination of the potential relationship between the features of a jurisdiction's corporate governance system, on the one hand, and innovation on the other. It surveys the empirical studies that have sought to test the various academic hypotheses in this field and, importantly, provides a fundamentally new form of empirical research that throws a fresh light on these studies.

REFERENCES

Anyadike-Danes, M., K. Bonner, M. Hart and C. Mason (2009), *Measuring Business Growth: High-Growth Firms and their Contribution to Employment in the UK*, NESTA, <http://www.nesta.org.uk/library/documents/MBG-2010-web.pdf>

Arrow, K. (1962), 'Economic Welfare and the Allocation of Resources for Inventions' in R. Nelson (ed.), *The Rate and Direction of Inventive* Activity, Princeton University Press

Baker, J. (2007), 'Beyond Schumpeter vs Arrow: How Antitrust Fosters Innovation' 74 *Antitrust Law Journal* 575

Commonwealth of Australia (2009), *Powering Ideas: An Innovation Agenda for the 21st Century*, Commonwealth of Australia

Cutler & Company Pty Ltd (2008), *Venturous Australia: Building Strength in Innovation*, <www.innovation.gov.au/Innovation/Policy/Pages/ReviewoftheNational InnovationSystem.aspx>

De Botton, A. (2009), *The Pleasures and Sorrows of Work*, Hamish Hamilton.

Department for Business Innovation & Skills (BIS) (2011), *Innovation and Research Strategy for Growth* (Cm 8239)

Department for Business Innovation & Skills and NESTA (2011), *Annual Innovation Report* 2010, BIS, <http://www.bis.gov.uk/policies/innovation/annual-innovation-report>

Department of Innovation Industry, Science and Research (DIISR) (2011), *Australian Innovation System Report 2011*, Commonwealth of Australia, <http://www.innovation.gov.au/Innovation/Policy/Pages/AustralianInnovationSystemReport2011.aspx>

Gilbert, R. (2007), 'Holding Innovation to an Antitrust Standard' 3 *Competition Policy International* 47

Glader, M. (2006), *Innovation Markets and Competition Analysis; EU Competition Law and US Antitrust* Law, Edward Elgar

Godin, B. (2008), *Innovation: The History of a Category: Project on the Intellectual History of Innovation*, Working Paper No. 1, Canadian Science and Innovation Indicators Consortium, <http://www.csiic.ca/innovation.html>

Hovencamp, H. (2008), 'Innovation and the Domain of Competition Policy' 60 *Alabama Law Review* 105

Hovencamp, H. (2010–11), 'Antitrust Innovation: Where Are We and Where Should We Be Going?' 77 *Antitrust Law Journal* 749

Lambert, R. (2003), *The Lambert Review on Business–University Collaborations*, HMT

Lemley, M. (2008), 'The Surprising Virtues of Treating Trade Secrets as IP Rights' 61 *Stanford Law Review* 311

Manne, G. and J. Wright (2010), 'Innovation and the Limits of Antitrust' 6 *Journal of Competition Law & Economics* 153

Mason, G., K. Bishop and C. Robinson (2009), *Business Growth and Innovation: The Wider Impact of Rapidly Growing Firms in UK City-Regions*, NESTA, <http://www.nesta.org.uk/library/documents/Business-Growth-Innovation-report-v2.pdf>

Monotti, A. (2010), 'Divergent Approaches in Defining the Appropriate Level of Inventiveness in Patent Law' in L. Bently, G. D'Agostino and C. Ng (eds), *The Common Law of Intellectual Property: Essays in Honour of Prof David Vaver*, Hart Publishing

Organisation for Economic Co-operation and Development (2005), *Oslo Manual: Guidelines for Collecting and Interpreting Innovation Data*, 3rd edn, OECD Statistical Office of the European Communities, <http://www.oecd.org/document/33/0,3746,en_2649_34273_35595607_1_1_1_1,00.html>

Organisation for Economic Co-operation and Development (2010), *Science, Technology and Industry Outlook*, <http://www.oecd.org/document/36/0,3746,en_2649_34451_41546660_1_1_1_1,00.html>

Organisation for Economic Co-operation and Development (2011), *Science, Technology and Industry Scoreboard: Innovation and Growth in Knowledge Economies*, OECD, <http://www.oecd.org/document/10/0,3746,en_2649_33703_3949 3962_1_1_1_1,00.html>

Pittard, M. and R. Naughton (2010), *Australian Labour Law: Text, Cases and Commentary*, 5th edn, LexisNexis

Schumpeter, J. (1947), *Capitalism, Socialism and Democracy*, 2nd edn, Harper

2. Failed collaboration: the misappropriation of business opportunities, ideas and advantages by prospective co-venturers, financiers and brokers

Paul Finn

> In a commercial context ... a degree of self-seeking and ruthless behaviour is expected and accepted to a degree.[1]

Unsurprisingly, a deal of our law on the misappropriation of ideas and business opportunities has originated in cases which are variants on a common theme. A person (alone or with others) has developed an idea or identified a business opportunity. To exploit the idea or to realise the opportunity it becomes necessary or desirable to bring in others, be this for venture capital, to provide needed skill, capacity or facilities, to spread risk and so on. And so the search for a financier, a co-venturer, or whoever begins. In negotiations with a prospective collaborator the idea is disclosed, the opportunity revealed. The negotiations fail. The search resumes only for it to emerge that the former prospective collaborator has appropriated the idea, has exploited the opportunity, for its own benefit.

I said 'unsurprisingly' for this reason. The point at which the need arises to involve others is one of considerable vulnerability for the originator of an idea or the proponent of an opportunity. Sometimes circumstances may permit a measure of contractual protection to be secured.[2] But often not, or else contract is not thought of.

To illustrate the basic problem and some of its variations, one can draw very selectively from a large number of recent commercial examples from across the common law world.

1 *Verco v Rutland Fund Management Ltd* [2010] EWHC 424 (Ch), [343].
2 Ibid.

1. *A* discovered gold on its land. It needed a large co-venturer to finance and conduct operations for a mine. It entered into negotiations with *X* for such a joint venture and disclosed its drilling results. From these it was clear that an adjacent property was likely to include mineral-bearing deposits. *A* attempted to buy that property but was trumped covertly by *X* who later developed a mine on it on its own account.[3]
2. *A* and *X* were both potential purchasers of a site which they proposed to acquire and develop together through a joint-venture company. They had not concluded any contract concerning their joint venture but had agreed that *X* only would bid for it. *X* changed its mind about the joint venture; did not tell *A* of this; and acquired the land through a subsidiary.[4]
3. *A* over time formulated a detailed proposal for the development of an island, the development (which involved forestry and the building of a resort) having a number of component parts, each of which required the investment of business judgement, skill and research. It needed to find a party willing to put up venture capital. It approached a broker, *X*, to act as an intermediary. It disclosed the business opportunity it wished to pursue but could not agree the terms of *X*'s retainer. *X* terminated the negotiations. *A* searched elsewhere for venture capital. *X* having been alerted to *A*'s scheme hastily put together its own consortium and bought and developed the island, albeit using a different combination of components to those *A* proposed.[5]
4. *A* spent considerable time and effort to develop a management buy-in of an underperforming chain of pawn shops. It took that proposal to *X*, a venture capital company, which ultimately agreed to implement *A*'s plan. That plan envisaged *A* would have a senior management position and an equity interest in the business. *X* acquired the business but then contrived to freeze *A* out.[6]
5. *A* developed the idea for a series of television programmes depicting the story of how selected millionaires had achieved their success. They were to participate in the programme. *T* entered into negotiations with a television channel, *X*, for the sale of the idea to

---

[3] *Lac Mineral Resources Ltd v International Corona Resources Ltd* (1989) 61 DLR (4th) 14.

[4] *Banner Homes Group Plc v Luff Developments* [2000] Ch 372.

[5] *Arklow Investments Ltd v Maclean* [2000] 2 NZLR 1.

[6] *Verco v Rutland Fund Management Ltd* [2010] EWHC 424 (Ch). See also *Murray v Yorkshire Fund Managers Ltd* [1998] 1 WLR 951.

> it. *T* later provided *X* with a pilot script. *X* ceased to communicate with *T* about the matter. Some months later *X* advertised a forthcoming series in which millionaires would spell out their recipes for success.[7]

A number of bodies of law intersect to deal in a fashion with the claims that may emerge in such cases. That most commonly invoked is the action for breach of confidence. But beyond it are breach of fiduciary duty, the *Pallant v Morgan* constructive trust, s 52 of the *Trade Practices Act 1974* (Cth)[8] and, finally, equitable estoppel. This jigsaw is itself a potential hazard for the prospective litigant.[9] What will become apparent both within and between these discrete principles and doctrines is that contestable policy assumptions are made and that these contrive the tolerable degree of injustice to be endured before relief is granted to the wronged party. Such is the burden of the opening epigraph.

The primary concern of this chapter is to provide a quick overview of the various bodies of law as they may apply to the problem identified and to assess their relative utility in protecting one party from misappropriation by the other.

1. BREACH OF CONFIDENCE

It is noteworthy that so many of the leading cases in this area of law involve failed prospective collaborations. The basic elements of the action, for present purposes,[10] are well known. Contract apart, the information embodying the idea or business opportunity must itself be confidential – ie it must be relatively secret. Secondly, it must have been imparted in circumstances importing an obligation of confidence. And thirdly, there must have been an actual or apprehended unauthorised use of that information.[11]

---

[7] *Talbot v General Television Corp Pty Ltd* [1980] VR 224; *Fraser v Thames Television Ltd* [1984] 1 QB 44.

[8] Now s 18 of the Australian Consumer Law. See n 61.

[9] For an example of where some number of these were run unsuccessfully, see *John Alexander's Clubs Pty Ltd v White City Tennis Club Ltd* (2010) 266 ALR 462.

[10] I leave out of account information obtained by improper or surreptitious means and those classes of case where a duty of confidence is itself an incident of the relationship in question, e.g., solicitor–client or banker–customer.

[11] See *Coco v AN Clark (Engineers) Ltd* (1969) 4 RPC 41, 47 – a failed negotiations case.

There are three aspects of this action which need to be addressed for present purposes. First, the allegedly confidential idea must be able to be identified with particularity and it must not be too vague or general in character. The policy informing the latter of these requirements is obviously to prevent the action from unduly fettering innovation and enterprise. A good, and easy, example is *De Maudsley v Palumbo*,[12] which exhibits a number of recurring elements in failed collaboration cases. It involved the allegation that an idea for a new kind of dance club which had five component elements had been told to the defendant at a dinner party and had later been misappropriated by him. It was said that the defendant was impressed with the idea and offered either to fund it himself or to arrange finance. In the weeks after the dinner party an arrangement was elaborated for a joint venture company to establish the nightclub. The plaintiff was encouraged to believe he would be part of the enterprise. It was established but he was excluded from it.

The five elements of the idea itself that optimistically were said to be confidential were that the club (i) would be open all night; (ii) would be of large size with décor of a 'high tech industrial warehouse' style; (iii) would have separate areas for dancing, resting and socialising and a VIP lounge; (iv) would have an enclosed dance area of acoustic design; and (v) would employ top disc jockeys. The judge emphasised that there was a significant difference between a concept so developed as to be capable of being realised and 'an aspiration' the flavour of which can be captured in the phrase 'wouldn't it be great if … '.[13] As he put it, before the 'status of confidential information can be achieved by a concept or an idea it is necessary to have gone beyond identifying a desirable goal'. All five elements of De Maudsley's idea were found to be too vague and, save one, without novelty. Likewise the claim to confidentiality in relation to the composite of the features also failed.

Though finding that the action failed, the judge went on:[14]

> The fact remains that Mr de Maudsley was … rather shabbily treated in that he was encouraged to think that he would be part of the enterprise but was only told that this would not be so, long after Mr Palumbo and Mr Waterhouse had decided, almost certainly justifiably because of Mr de Maudsley's rather difficult character and limited abilities, that he would not be included in their project. It is the fact that it was Mr de Maudsley who sowed the original seed in Mr Palumbo's mind and he has in the event got very little indeed out of it. It would have been preferable for him to have been

---

12 [1996] FSR 447.

13 Ibid [456].

14 Ibid [459]–[460].

> told a great deal earlier and more clearly that he was being dropped as dropped he was ... It does go some way to explain his being disgruntled.

What needs to be emphasised in light of these observations is that this was an English decision. There is no UK equivalent to the old misleading or deceptive conduct provision of the Trade Practices Act or its new equivalent in s 18 of the Consumer Law. And English Law, unlike most other major common law jurisdictions,[15] has no general action in equitable estoppel in relation to relied-upon promises, representations and assurances.[16] This will be returned to below.

Secondly, obviously in the commercial arena ideas come in all shapes, sizes and subject matters and have and need greater or lesser detail both for their expression and to qualify as confidential information. The required level of definition, before protection will be given, will turn in considerable measure on the character of the idea itself. This can be illustrated in two groups of cases – the one concerning 'concepts' or 'creative ideas'; the other, business opportunities.

Two examples of creative ideas in which breach of confidence was alleged successfully related to proposals for television programmes. In one, *Talbot v General Television Corporation Pty Ltd*[17], a film producer developed a concept for a series of programmes entitled *To Make a Million*. It was about how particular individuals became millionaires and the distinctive feature of it was that actual millionaires would give their own recipes for success in the programmes. In the other, *Fraser v Thames Television Ltd*,[18] the idea was for a series on the lives of a three-girl rock group who would appear in the series. In each case, the idea was disclosed to a television network – in *Talbot's* case for the purpose of its sale to it and a pilot script was prepared for the purpose; in *Fraser* to have the series written and produced. In both cases, the negotiations came to nothing but the television company in each case later produced series embodying the disclosed idea.

In each instance, as in *De Maudsley*, the issue was whether the concept was susceptible of protection. The test of this – derived from *Talbot* –

---

[15] E.g., Australia: *Walton Stores (Interstate) Ltd v Maher* (1988) 164 CLR 387; *EK Nominees Pty Ltd v Woolworths Ltd* [2006] NSWSC 1172; the US, *Hoffman v Red Owl Stores Inc* 133 NW 2d 267 (1965); Farnsworth (2004) § 2.19; New Zealand, see Butler and Clarke (eds) (2009) Ch 19; and India: *Motilal Padampat Sugar Mills Ltd v State of Uttar Pradesh* [1979] 2 SCC 409.

[16] *Baird Textiles Holdings Ltd v Marks and Spencer Plc* [2002] 1 All ER (Comm) 737; *Cobbe v Yeoman's Row Management Ltd* [2008] 1WLR 1752.

[17] [1980] VR 244.

[18] [1984] 1 QB 1.

was: had the concept or idea been so developed that it could be seen to be one which had at least some attractiveness as a television programme and as being something which was capable of being realised as an actuality, even if in some cases it may require extensive development to meet this criteria?[19]

There does seem to be an element of reasoning backwards from the subsequent use of the idea to justify the results here. But provided there is some originality in the idea itself, may not reasoning backwards in the circumstances provide the best justification of the need for protection?

When one turns to business opportunities – a detailed plan for a management buy-in;[20] a composite plan for a property development;[21] or a business plan to invest in, and to resurrect, a company in receivership[22] – somewhat different considerations intrude. I would note three. They are the intrinsically commercial setting and the involvement of business people; the availability of contract protection (whether or not availed of);[23] and how the opportunity actually was realised.[24] The leading cases are recent decisions of English courts or the Privy Council and the three considerations noted probably have far greater salience in English law than in contemporary Australian law.

The issue of secret protection seems to turn first on the question whether what is protectable is the general business idea itself and the opportunities it reveals (ie 'the idea'), or merely such of its particular component parts which individually embody confidential information.

Two contrasting cases illustrate both of these points. First, *Verco v Rutland Fund Management Ltd*.[25] The facts are complex, but the following will suffice for present purposes. The plaintiffs, Verco and Pratt, devoted considerable time to the identification of a target company (H&T) for a management buy-in which in turn required the participation of a venture capital company. The target company carried on business as a pawnbroker. Verco and Pratt did detailed research on the company, its published accounts and its business sector. Over time they developed both a business plan (in which they were both to have management

---

[19] See *Fraser v Thames Television Ltd* [1984] 1 QB 4, 66.

[20] *Verco v Rutland Fund Management Ltd* [2010] EWHC 424 (Ch).

[21] *Arklow Investments Ltd v Maclean* [2000] 2 NZLR 1 (PC).

[22] *Murray v Yorkshire Fund Managers Ltd* [1998] 1 WLR 951.

[23] Contrast *Verco v Rutland Fund Management Ltd* [2010] EWHC 424 (Ch) and *Murray v Yorkshire Fund Managers Ltd* [1998] 1 WLR 951 in this respect.

[24] Cf *Verco v Rutland Fund Management Ltd* [2010] EWHC 424 (Ch) and *Arklow Investments Ltd v Maclean* [2000] 2 NZLR 1 (PC).

[25] [2010] EWHC 424 (Ch).

positions) and a corporate structure in which they were to be equity participants. They took their plan (inter alia) to RFM, a venture capital company. A confidentiality agreement was signed and the plan and associated information was disclosed. RFM was well disposed towards pursuing the opportunity; it assured Verco and Pratt that they would be part of the management team and encouraged their continuing development of the plan. Having decided to pursue the opportunity, RFM secured the freezing out of first Pratt then Verco, in the latter's case by offering wholly unacceptable conditions for his participation in the buy-in. After acquiring H&T, RFM developed and then floated the business. It made 'large profits' in so doing.

Verco and Pratt sued successfully for breach of the confidentiality agreement and were awarded damages calculated on the agreed basis of a sale of their respective rights under that agreement. They also sued for breach of confidence and breach of fiduciary duty. As to the former, the trial judge described the information provided to RFM (and the opportunity associated with it) as a 'huge advantage' to RFM in finding a viable and profitable acquisition target. The judge found a breach of confidence[26] but denied relief by way of an account of profits which he recognised would have given them 'very much more money than the sums payable as damages for breach of contract'.[27]

The test to be applied in determining whether to order an account for breach of confidence[28] was said to be whether 'the claimant's interest in performance of the obligation in question ... makes it just and equitable that the defendant retain no benefit from his breach of that obligation'.[29] Thus it was commented:

> Cases will frequently arise where a significant choice falls to be made between damages calculated by reference to a notional reasonable buy out fee and an account of profits. Then in my judgment, in the light of *Blake*, where one is not dealing with infringement of a right which is clearly proprietary in nature (such as intellectual property in the form of a patent, ...) *and there is nothing exceptional to indicate that the defendant should never have been entitled to adopt a commercial approach in deciding how to behave in relation to that right*, the appropriate remedy is likely to be an award of damages assessed by reference to a reasonable buy out fee rather than an account of profits ... Still more strongly will that be the case as one moves

26 Ibid, [331] but cf [329].

27 Ibid [332].

28 It was adapted from Lord Nicholl's speech in *Attorney-General v Blake* [2001] 1 AC 268, 285.

29 *Verco v Rutland Fund Management Ltd* [2010] EWHC 424 (Ch), [339].

> further away from confidential information in a form resembling classic intellectual property rights towards forms of obligation in respect of confidential information more akin to purely personal obligations in contract and tort.[30]

It was in this context that Sales J made the comment that is the epigraph to this chapter.

Verco is an English decision. It manifestly betrays preoccupations (e.g., the privileging of property) which do not have such deep resonances in our own legal system. I should not be taken as endorsing the views expressed in the above quotation.

The alleged breach of fiduciary duty was rejected on the basis that:[31]

> Where parties do not choose to enter into a partnership to pursue a joint venture, but purport to regulate their relationship on the basis of contract *without any explicit acceptance that fiduciary obligations are to be assumed under that contract*, I consider that it will only be in special circumstances that equity will intervene to impose additional fiduciary obligations on top of the ordinary contractual rights and obligations which the parties have negotiated and agreed.[32]

As the judge himself acknowledged, his view reflected the 'general reluctance' in English law to overlay fiduciary obligations upon ordinary commercial transactions.[33] That reluctance is not necessarily reflected to the same degree in other common law jurisdictions.[34]

The final comment to be made on *Verco* is that, in light of the findings made on RFM's assurances to Verco and Pratt concerning their participation in the buy-in, as also RFM's long-continued deception of them, it is probable that, in Australian law, claims could have been made both under the Consumer Law for contraventions of s 18 and for equitable estoppel. I will return to this.

A contrasting example – and one more adverse to the originator of an idea – is *Arklow Investments Ltd v Maclean*.[35] It can be dealt with briefly. Arklow sought the services of a banker, FAR, to assist in finding investors in a scheme to buy an island for forestry, residential and resort

---

[30] Ibid [341] (emphasis added).

[31] Ibid [351].

[32] Emphasis added; cf the contrasting view of Mason J in *Hospital Products Ltd v United States Surgical Corp* (1984) 156 CLR 41, 97 and 99–100; contrast also *Chirnside v Fay* [2007] 1 NZLR 433.

[33] *Verco v Rutland Fund Management Ltd* [2010] EWHC 424 (Ch), [352].

[34] E.g., Butler and Clarke (eds) (2009), ch 40 ('Joint Ventures').

[35] [2000] 2 NZLR 1.

purposes. It was no secret such was its intention.[36] From what was said and provided (a business plan and related information) to the directors of FAR, it was learned that Arklow had devised 'a complete, workable scheme' by which they could acquire the whole of the assets of the island's owner without putting up any cash of their own, if they could raise £5 million on an immature forest and other assets.

FAR provided Arklow with a written proposal on the terms of which it would accept the broker appointment. Arklow would not agree to those terms. A month later FAR withdrew its offer and accelerated steps (begun shortly after Arklow's initial approach) to broker arrangements with other parties which resulted in the purchase of the island. Arklow sued unsuccessfully both for breach of confidence and breach of fiduciary duty.

At trial, in the Court of Appeal and in the Privy Council it was held that FAR did receive confidential information but this was limited to six specific pieces of information in Arklow's proposed investment scheme. The scheme itself was not treated compositely as a 'confidential idea'. While it was found that FAR was 'galvanised into action'[37] once it learned of Arklow's scheme – there is a resonance here with *De Maudsley* – it was held in the Privy Council (confirming the decision of the majority of the Court of Appeal), that there was no basis for the inference that FAR used any of the six pieces of confidential information.

The fiduciary claim was rejected on the basis that FAR had not undertaken any obligation to act in Arklow's interest and no informal arrangement to this effect had come into existence.

It is clear, I would note in passing, that once FAR was galvanised into action the investment plan it brokered did not draw upon the elements of Arklow's scheme as such, although it did have a forestry component. But should this matter?

It is open to question how comfortably this decision sits with *Verco* and the 'creative ideas' cases. Or does it expose a lacuna between the law of confidence and fiduciary law in which 'ruthlessness' is to be expected and accepted? And was Thomas J so beyond the mark in his dissenting judgment in the Court of Appeal when he said:

> The facts seem to me to support a fiduciary obligation not to act contrary to Arklow's interests by seeking to put together a competing deal of its own appropriating or utilising the business plan provided by Arklow until its contract of service with Arklow had been completed or the mandate had been

---

[36] *Maclean v Arklow Investments Ltd* [1998] 3 NZLR 680, 699.
[37] [2000] 2 NZLR 1, 8.

> withdrawn and its relationship with Arklow brought to an end. In the circumstances, Arklow was vulnerable to FAR appropriating or utilising the business plan and related information. It had no option but to trust FAR and rely on its integrity not to act contrary to its interests. In all, Arklow could reasonably expect FAR to place Arklow's interests ahead of its own, an exclusivity which evokes the core element of a fiduciary relationship, loyalty, on FAR's part.[38]

Likewise, were Thomas J and, for that matter, La Forest J in his dissenting judgment in *Lac Minerals Ltd v International Corona Resources Ltd*,[39] in error in attributing considerable significance to accepted industry practice as to the conduct to be expected of parties while engaged in negotiations? In each case the industry evidence was consistent with a fiduciary responsibility being assumed during the negotiation period.

Thirdly, there is a distinct but subdued theme in the cases on collaboration which emphasises individual responsibility to protect one's own interests. The courts have, for example, shown some disposition to withhold protection to a discloser who makes an unexpected, unsolicited and unwanted communication of confidential information which, if it gave rise to a duty of confidence, would be inimical to the recipient's interests.[40] More positively there is English Court of Appeal authority for the proposition that, absent a contractual, fiduciary or other special relationship, a member of a group who contributed to the preparation of a highly confidential plan could be excluded from the commercial exploitation of it by the others without redress.[41] As one member of the Court said:[42] 'Mr Murray's lack of any remedy arises from the undisputed fact that his relationship with the other five members of the original team was not regulated by contract.'[43] It is to be hoped that the courts in Australia will be slow to embrace this proposition.[44]

---

[38] [1998] 3 NZLR 680, 728.

[39] (1989) 61 DLR (4th) 14, 37–39.

[40] Cf *Carflow Products (UK) Ltd v Linwood Securities (Birmingham) Ltd* [1996] FSR 424, 429.

[41] *Murray v Yorkshire Fund Managers Ltd* [1998] 1 WLR 951.

[42] Ibid, 960.

[43] The irony in this is that Mr Murray's rights against his other team members arose as a result of a purely equitable obligation in any event.

[44] Leave to appeal to the House of Lords was refused. However, it should be noted that the facts of the case were unpromising ones, the plaintiff having received a payment on his exclusion.

It is difficult usefully to generalise from the breach of confidence cases I have considered – especially the business opportunity cases – given they are few in number and almost all English. They do suggest this much. Cases involving the unauthorised use or disclosure of confidential 'inventive' or 'creative' ideas will as of course be protected if the elements of the action for breach of confidence can be established. With confidential 'business opportunities' on the other hand a less protective temper is discernible and the relief given may be more parsimonious.

2. FIDUCIARY DUTY

Here one enters the vexed territory of preliminary dealings or negotiations for a 'joint venture'. I preface what I have to say with two propositions which I consider are unexceptionable statements of present Australian fiduciary law.

The first is that a person will be a fiduciary in relation to another (or others) when and insofar as that other is entitled to expect that the former will act in that other's interest or, as in a partnership, in their joint interest to the exclusion of his or her own self-interest.[45]

The second proposition is that a person in a fiduciary position –

(a) cannot use his or her position to his or her own, or to a third party's, possible advantage; or
(b) cannot, in any matter within the scope of his or her service, have a personal interest or an inconsistent engagement with a third party

unless this is freely and informedly consented to by his or her beneficiary or is authorised by law.[46] A fiduciary relationship is thus a quite distinctive one and it attracts a narrow and strict obligation.

It has often been said in Australian cases that the term 'joint venture' is not a technical one with a settled common law meaning and that '[O]ne would need a more confined and precise notion of what constitutes a "joint venture" than that which the term bears as a matter of ordinary language before it could be said by way of general proposition that the relationship of joint venturers is necessarily a fiduciary one'.[47] It is not

---

[45] See generally the discussion of the cases in Conaglen (2010), 256–258. This definition comes from my 'Fiduciary Principle' in Finn (1989), 1 at 54.

[46] See *Chan v Zacharia* (1984) 154 CLR 178, 198. This again is drawn from my 'Fiduciary Principle' (Finn, 1989), 27. See generally, Conaglen (2010).

[47] *United Dominions Corporation Ltd v Brian Pty Ltd* (1985) 157 CLR 1, 10.

necessary for present purposes to elucidate what that 'more confined and precise notion' might be. My present concern is with action taken prior to the formalisation (if it occurs at all) of a projected 'joint venture'. As a matter of convenience in exposition, I will differentiate between (a) where the projected ultimate relationship being negotiated between the parties will itself be fiduciary in whole or in part (for example, a partnership) and (b) where it will not (for example, in a 'joint venture' company in which the participants are to be shareholders).

2.1 Negotiating for a Fiduciary Relationship

It is well settled that if parties enter upon negotiations for a relationship which will itself be fiduciary and, in anticipation of their agreement being finalised, commence to effectuate their common objective for their mutual benefit, it will be a breach of fiduciary duty for any one of them to misappropriate, or otherwise secretly to exclude the others from, benefits which fall within the scope of their projected common enterprise.[48] The usual case is that of an intending partner misappropriating an opportunity which has been identified as one for the intended partnership.[49] Here the fiduciary character of the relationship being negotiated colours the relationship that precedes it.

2.2 Negotiating for a Non-fiduciary, or a To-be-determined, Relationship

It is commonplace for parties to wish to pursue a common objective collectively (ie a 'joint venture') but through a legal form or forms – for example a company, or several contracts – which does or do not give rise to a fiduciary relationship. Here, fiduciary issues can still arise in respect of action taken during the negotiation phase – but only in quite distinctive circumstances.

In *Gibson Motorsport Merchandise Pty Ltd v Forbes*,[50] for example, the opportunity having arisen to develop a motor racing team 'joint venture' centred on a well-known racing driver, three separate business interests commenced negotiations to effectuate this objective, but in a way that envisaged each having separate interests and asset management in, and deriving individual profits from, the venture. Their relationships *inter se* were to be settled in a series of contracts. Steps in anticipation of

---

48 Ibid, 11–12.

49 *Fraser Edminston Pty Ltd v AGT* (Qld) [1998] 2 Qd R 1.

50 (2006) 149 FCR 569.

final agreements were taken by the participants to establish their respective, separate, participating businesses, before one of them (with the driver) established its own race team enterprise, to the exclusion of the other two interests. The two alleged that the racing team opportunity had been misappropriated in breach of fiduciary duty. The claim was rejected.

There are two aspects of the Full Court judgments that should be emphasised. First, the judges held that the relationship negotiated for was not a fiduciary one and no fiduciary duties arose during the negotiating phase. Secondly, if fiduciary duties were to arise in that phase, it had to be for reasons distinctive to that phase, as I indicated in my judgment. That they reposed trust in each other, that the venture required co-operation and collaboration, and that they commenced their businesses before finalisation of the agreements, did not severally, or together, attract any fiduciary responsibility.[51] Because of what I earlier said of the importance of commencement before finalisation where the intended relationship was fiduciary, I should repeat what I said in *Gibson* about early commencement in this case:

> There is nothing intrinsically fiduciary about this phenomenon. It is a commonplace in business, particularly between parties who trust each other for whatever reason and who are prepared in consequence to assume the risk of embarking upon the projected business because they are confident that their proposed arrangement will not fall apart before finalisation. One need only point by way of illustration to case law on promissory estoppel: cf, *Waltons Stores (Interstate) Ltd v Maher* (1988) 164 CLR 387; implied contract: *Blackpool & Fylde Aero Club Ltd v Blackpool Borough Council* [1990] 1 WLR 1195; *Brewer Street Investments Ltd v Barclays Woollen Co Ltd* [1954] 1 QB 428; and quasi-contract (or restitution): *Sabemo Pty Ltd v North Sydney Municipal Council* [1977] 2 NSWLR 880; where orthodox non-fiduciary relief has in appropriate circumstances been afforded a party where an envisaged business relationship did not eventuate despite work done in anticipation of it: see generally Dietrich, J, *Restitution: A New Perspective* (1998, Federation Press), p 123 ff; see also Farnsworth, EA, 'Precontractual Liability and Preliminary Agreements: Fair Dealing and Failed Negotiations' (1987) 87 Colum L Rev 217.[52]

This said, it is possible for a fiduciary relationship to precede an anticipated or actual business relationship which will not be, or is not itself, fiduciary as several recent decisions of the Supreme Court of New

---

51 Ibid [7]–[17].

52 Ibid [7].

Zealand illustrate. In *Chirnside v Fay*,[53] though the parties' intention was ultimately to form a joint venture company (ie a non-fiduciary vehicle) to undertake a property development, the significant preliminary steps they took were, in effect, taken as partners in a joint enterprise. This constituted them fiduciaries at that time such as to preclude one from buying the target property on his own account. Likewise in *Amaltal Corporation Ltd v Maruha Corporation*,[54] while the 'co-venturers' were fiduciaries when they were in partnership, they lost that character when they adopted both a corporate structure for their business and a supporting shareholders' agreement to define their rights *inter se*.

What the case law so far demonstrates is that fiduciary law offers only a narrow basis for protecting a business opportunity from misappropriation, at least in the types of business setting with which this chapter is concerned. Its one advantage over the action for breach of confidence is that where it can be invoked, it is not required to be shown that the opportunity in question was a confidential one.

There is one final comment I should make. Reference earlier was made to the significance both Thomas J (in *Arklow Investments*) and La Forest J (in *Lac*) gave to industry practices which were inconsistent with the recipient of information taking advantage of the opportunity revealed during the negotiating period. Such practices were regarded as being consistent with 'fiduciary truces'.[55] These, I emphasise, were dissenting judgments. But when negotiations take place in such a commercial context, is it not entirely appropriate to take account of that context in determining what the discloser is reasonably entitled to expect of the other in the negotiation period? If such is the case, fiduciary law could have considerably more significance in preliminary negotiations and dealings cases than it presently enjoys. This leads naturally to the next topic.

3. THE PALLANT V MORGAN CONSTRUCTIVE TRUST

This particular legal creature properly analysed is probably no more than an application both of fiduciary law[56] and/or equitable estoppel[57] – albeit

---

[53] [2007] 1 NZLR 433; see also *Counties Manukau Pacific Trust v Manukau City Council* [2009] 2 NZLR 260.

[54] [2007] 3 NZLR 192.

[55] My term.

[56] See *Chirnside v Fay* [2007] 1 NZLR 443.

limited to the context of one party's covert acquisition of property (usually land) contrary to an agreed understanding that it would be acquired (if at all) for all parties.[58] The most significant explanation of it in English law is in the judgment of Chadwick LJ in *Banner Homes Plc v Luff Development Ltd*[59] – a case in which one of two potential purchasers of a property who proposed to develop it together through a joint venture company purchased it on its own account without notice to the other, but was held in the Court of Appeal to be a constructive trustee of it for both of them.

The Lord Justice's explanation of this liability was crystallised in the following propositions:

(i) It is the fact of a pre-acquisition arrangement or understanding of the parties that the relevant property will be acquired by one which colours the subsequent acquisition by that party and leads to his or her being treated as a trustee if he seeks to act inconsistently with it.
(ii) It is unnecessary that the arrangement or understanding should be contractually enforceable or have the certainty a contract would require.
(iii) It is necessary that the arrangement or understanding should contemplate that one party will take steps to acquire the property and that if he or she does the other will obtain some interest in it.
(iv) It is necessary that, in reliance on the arrangement or understanding, the non-acquiring party should do (or omit to do) something which confers an advantage on the acquiring party in relation to the acquisition of the property; or is detrimental to the ability of the non-acquiring party to acquire the property on equal terms. The usual case of detriment or advantage is one party's agreement not to acquire the property itself. But it may, for example, be the support given by that party to assist the acquirer obtain planning approval.[60]

---

[57] Cf *Banner Homes Plc v Luff Development Ltd* [2000] Ch 372, 390.

[58] While it has been discussed in trusts texts in Australia, Canada and New Zealand: see Young et al (2009), [12.1070]; Waters (2005), 530; Butler and Clarke (eds) (2009), 40.5 and referred to in passing in judicial decision: e.g., *John Alexander's Clubs Pty Ltd v White City Tennis Club Ltd* (2010) 266 ALR 462, [66]–[70], which has only been applied in England. See also *Cobbe v Yeoman's Row Management Ltd* [2008] 1 WLR 1757.

[59] [2000] Ch 372.

[60] E.g., *Holiday Inns Inc v Broadhead* (unreported 1969), discussed in *Banner Homes Plc v Luff Development Ltd* [2000] Ch 372.

There is little further that needs be said about this. Clearly, it exemplifies redress being given to a victim of a misappropriated opportunity. But what is important to notice is this: while the parties may not have formalised their intended relationship (which may or may not itself be fiduciary), they actually have reached the point of an understanding that one party will act for their *mutual benefit* in the acquisition of the property in question and the innocent party has relied upon this. It is this understanding and the consequential reliance that locates this doctrine at the point of overlap of fiduciary law and equitable estoppel.

Representation and reliance (or else acting inconsistently with an understanding or expectation on which the other reasonably relies) loom large in what I have finally to say.

4. THE AUSTRALIAN CONSUMER LAW[61] (THE TRADE PRACTICES ACT) AND EQUITABLE ESTOPPEL

Section 18 of the Consumer Law proscribes a person's engaging in conduct in trade or commerce which is misleading or deceptive or which is likely to mislead or deceive. For their part sections 20 to 22 proscribe in aggregate conduct in trade or commerce which is unconscionable within the meaning of the unwritten law, or which, in relation to the actual or possible supply or acquisition of goods or services, is unconscionable in all the circumstances.[62]

Though the latter provisions do not say so in express terms, their clear effect is to require good faith and fair dealing in contract negotiation. Without elaborating on the point here, I would emphasise that ss 20 to 22 have a large, but relatively untapped potential, in regulating not only contract formation, performance and enforcement but also conduct engaged in anticipation of a contract that does *not* eventuate – hence their present significance.

---

[61] As a matter of convenience in exposition, I will refer here to the provisions of the new Consumer Law, ss 18, 20, 21 and 22, which have supplanted the now well-understood identical provisions of s 52 and ss 51AA, 51AB and 51AC of the *Trade Practices Act 1974*.

[62] There are statutorily a number of exceptions to this general proposition.

Distinctly, equitable estoppel is a general cause of action in Australian, but not in English, law.[63] Put shortly, if one party reasonably relies upon another's promise, assurance or reasonably induced expectation and would suffer detriment if that other were permitted to falsify the promise, assurance or expectation, the former can obtain such remedy as would do practical justice in the circumstances.[64] While in the past this species of estoppel dealt primarily with promises etc relating to land, now, as in the United States,[65] it is being applied increasingly to assurances given as to proposed business relationships.[66]

Given the examples to which I have referred, it hardly needs now to be said that an almost invariable feature of the cases has been the conscious practice of misleading, deceptive or unfair conduct by one party, or else the giving of encouragement and assurances (later falsified) as to one's future intentions with the strategic object in mind of misappropriating an idea, opportunity or advantage provided by the other in circumstances in which it was envisaged by that other that both might collaborate in its realisation or exploitation.

While equitable estoppel and the Consumer Law provisions to which I have referred are not, as such, directed at the taking of another's or of shared ideas, they clearly have some capacity within their respective spheres to provide redress against the conduct commonly engaged in to practise such misappropriations. Their respective strengths compared with breach of confidence and fiduciary law are that in many cases they provided an easier, a surer, route to establishing liability for the reasons I have given. Their limitation, though, is that unlike breach of fiduciary duty and breach of confidence, they do not provide gain-based remedies – and an account of profits in particular – against the wrongdoer.[67]

---

[63] In England the estoppel cause of action (proprietary estoppel) is limited to reliance upon representations etc relating to property: see e.g., *Cobbe v Yeoman's Row Management Ltd* [2008] UKHL 55.

[64] *Walton Stores (Interstate) Ltd v Maker* (1998) 164 CLR 387; Young et al (2009) [12.290] and [12.310]. On remedy see *Delaforce v Simpson-Cook* [2010] NSWCA 84.

[65] E.g., *Hoffman v Red Owl Stores Inc* 133 NW 2d 267 (1965); *Drennan v Star Paving Co* 333 P2d 757 (1958); *Wheeler v White* 308 SW 2d 93 (1965).

[66] E.g., *EK Nominees Pty Ltd v Woolworths Ltd* [2006] NSWSC 1172; *Yarrabee Chicken Co Pty Ltd v Steggles Ltd* [2010] FCA 394.

[67] Australian courts have shown no propensity to follow the lead shown in *Attorney General v Blake* [2001] 1 AC 268 in awarding an account for breach of contract: see *Hospitality Group Pty Ltd v Australian Rugby Union Ltd* (2001) 110 FCR 157, [155]–[159]. On the former *Trade Practices Act 1974*, s 87(2), see *Multigroup Distribution Services Pty Ltd v TNT Australia Pty Ltd* (2001) 109

Commonly enough the innocent party is likely to be left to a damages remedy for reliance losses. At best, damages may be able to be awarded on a 'lost opportunity' basis. But the factual settings in many of the cases considered have not been propitious ones for invoking even this measure. This said, while a damages-only remedy may seem to reward unfair competition, it probably does reflect an appropriate response where the information or opportunity taken does not qualify as confidential.

5. CONCLUSION

What in the end I have been talking about are simply aspects of what can be described as good faith and fair dealing in preliminary negotiations and dealings. As is well known, common law jurisdictions do not characteristically have any single doctrine directed at securing good faith in such settings. Indeed, as the observations made in some of the English cases I have mentioned illustrate, there is a certain hostility to affording protection unless and until a contract is entered into. But despite ourselves, when we aggregate our various doctrines, we in Australia probably have, with legislative help, reached the Canaan of fairness.

By way of postscript, I would note there is surprisingly little Australian case law dealing with the misappropriation of ideas and opportunities in circumstances such as I have described. Perhaps, maybe accidentally, our law has got it right.

REFERENCES

Butler, A.S. and T. Clarke (eds) (2009), *Equity and Trusts in New Zealand*, 2nd edn, Thomson Reuters

Conaglen, M. (2010), *Fiduciary Loyalty: Protecting the Due Performance of Non-Fiduciary Duties*, Hart Publishing

Farnsworth, E.A. (2004), *Contracts*, 4th edn, Aspen

Finn, P. (1989), 'Fiduciary Principle' in T.G. Youdan (ed.), *Equity Fiduciaries and Trusts*, Carswell

Waters, D.W.M. (2005), *Law of Trusts in Canada*, 3rd edn, Thomson Carswell

Young, P.W., C. Croft and M. Smith (2009), *On Equity*, Lawbook

---

FCR 528. Equitable estoppel has some capacity to achieve a gain-based result to the extent that it can in appropriate contexts require the making good of promises made and assurances given.

PART II

Inventions and discoveries in business: intellectual property perspectives

3. Innovation through the lens of intellectual property law: rights in employee inventions

Ann L. Monotti

1. INTRODUCTION

The nature of intellectual property (IP) law is that it provides time-limited protection for a disparate range of intellectual creations from the 'fine arts' end of a spectrum through to all forms of new technology. Intellectual property rights (IPRs) that might be valuable assets in business innovation differ in their scope and purpose according to the nature of the subject matter in which the rights are granted: in particular patents protect inventions, design law protects the appearance of products, copyright protects against copying all manner of output in the area of 'fine arts' and trade marks can provide a business with valuable protection for distinguishing their products and services from those of their competitors. In many instances a business might rely upon internal secrecy to protect its ideas but in others, patent protection might be the only option for protecting useful ideas to avoid 'free riding' by competitors.

Business innovation is associated generally with the continual development and introduction of new and improved products and methods to help businesses build and retain a profitable and competitive position in the marketplace. The types of expenditure involved may be directed at activities such as research and experimental development including design and testing of product prototypes, application for and acquisition of IPRs, and developing operational, managerial and marketing processes to maximise financial returns.[1] A business may have its own skilled workforce, which generates new knowledge and technology and which

[1] OECD (2005) [146].

manages all aspects of the production and marketing processes. Alternatively, it may 'buy in' skills and technologies from other businesses or institutions. In both instances, the intellectual creativity that is contributed to the development of the innovative products or processes will originate in individuals[2] who are likely to be employees of some entity. This might involve research performed in the private sector or in public sector institutions such as universities and research institutes. Irrespective of where the research occurs, its ultimate value as a proprietary asset for a business is dependent upon a clear chain of title passing from the creators to the business entity. Poorly designed laws can make the task of identifying where ownership vests unnecessarily complex and this can obstruct or even prevent the successful exploitation of IPRs.[3]

The fundamental principle of entitlement in patent law, which is the focus of this Part, is that all rights in inventions derive from the inventor. However, if the inventor is an employee, this principle is modified in ways that seek to balance the rights of employees with the rights of employers to the fruits of their employees' labours. The particular themes that emerge in the following chapters relate first to identifying and resolving the tensions that arise between employees and employers when the product of an employee's research is patentable and is subsequently exploited for commercial gain. Secondly, a further dimension arises in the actual transfer of those new inventions for commercial exploitation when government funds are used to perform the research from which the inventions are generated. The US has specific legislation to provide a consistent policy for promoting utilisation of those inventions and Rochelle Dreyfuss explores this dimension in her chapter. A third theme that generally arises in any discussion of employee inventions is the extent to which the employee inventors should be entitled to compensation when their employer owns and exploits the inventions for the benefit of its business. This theme is raised by Marie-Christine Janssens in her examination of EU perspectives on employees' inventions and appears in later chapters by Riccardo Del Punta, Mark Freedland and Jeremias Prassl, also within the context of European perspectives.[4] It does not arise in the other chapters as their focus is upon entitlement to

---

[2] As to complexities with informational products: Ginsburg (1990); Davison (2003); Glasser (2001); Lindsay (2012); Directive 96/9/EC of the European Parliament and of the Council of 11 March 1996 on the Legal Protection of Databases; *IceTV Pty Ltd v Nine Network Australia Pty Ltd* (2009) 239 CLR 458.

[3] E.g., Hargreaves (2011), ch 9.

[4] Part III, this volume.

employee inventions created within universities, where profit sharing among inventors and the institutions is commonplace.[5]

While the themes are common to some extent within the above parameters, there is divergence in the approaches of the courts and legislatures in each jurisdiction and in the perspectives that each author provides. We can learn from this divergence which aspects will improve the innovation process and commercial outcomes for the benefit of the economies of the various jurisdictions. We can also learn which aspects might warrant some reconsideration in light of the approaches of others. At the same time, it is essential to be alert to the many political and other comparative differences among countries that can hinder any attempts at harmonisation. Ultimately, the question might be whether it is desirable and feasible to work towards some minimum level of harmonisation to some aspects of the law in this area of employee inventions.

2. GOVERNMENT POLICY FOR TECHNOLOGY TRANSFER FROM PUBLIC SECTOR RESEARCH

Universities and not-for-profit or public research institutes are not geared for the 'hands-on' development, marketing and distribution of commercial products but play a central role in that innovative process through their discovery of new knowledge. Apart from the obvious educational mission, their primary goals are to perform research and transfer that new knowledge in ways that are appropriate for the particular research outcomes. Some of this research will produce inventions that are suitable for patenting, whose value is enhanced through strategic partnerships with business. This linkage between the research that is undertaken within these institutions and their inherent value for innovation has resulted in different government programmes that aim to encourage an entrepreneurial culture and provide incentives for industry to collaborate in ways that maximise commercial outcomes from suitable technologies. Intellectual property policy is critical here because it is 'an increasingly important tool for stimulating economic growth'.[6]

Two chapters in this Part raise these issues and divergence in the approach of governments is immediately apparent. First, as mentioned above, Dreyfuss explains the approach in the US of using federal

---

[5] Monotti with Ricketson (2003).

[6] Hargreaves (2011), 3.

legislation to regulate the protection and exploitation of federally supported research and examines its effectiveness at the time of its 30th anniversary. The enactment of the Bayh-Dole Act in 1980 aimed at promoting the utilisation of inventions arising from federally supported research or development and gave universities and certain non-profit organisations the power to elect to take title to those inventions.[7] These statutory provisions regulate the transfer of inventions developed with public funding into the community. The legislation provides standards that all recipients of federal research funding must observe. In contrast, Monotti explains that Australian universities might engage in patenting and technology transfer activities but there are no mandated standards in legislation. Rather, the national policies in this area are contained in government grant conditions and national IP guidelines,[8] which universities then implement in their contractual regimes and IP legislation and policies. There is minimal regulation and considerable discretion in how universities can protect, manage and exploit inventions and other IP that their employees create with federal funding.[9] Monotti highlights the significant role that government policies play in promoting innovation and how the effective implementation of those policies can be derailed if inadequate attention is given to such things as the legal framework in which research is performed, the impact that differences in business innovation models might have on existing legal principles, and the need for rewards and incentives for inventors and businesses to ensure that new ideas are carried forward into innovative products and processes that benefit society and the economy.

The divergence in approach is deliberate. Policy makers and Australian universities have regularly monitored what happens in the US[10] and to date there have not been calls for the introduction of a statutory system modelled upon Bayh-Dole despite various investigations into the need to enhance innovation and the recent overhaul of many aspects of patent law. At the time of celebrating the 30th anniversary of the Bayh-Dole Act it is opportune to review whether the US experience offers any new lessons for Australian management of the innovation process. The obvious divergence in approach is the level of regulation that will most effectively promote technology and knowledge transfer from universities and other non-profit research institutions in order to attract commercial

7 35 USC §§ 200, 202(a).

8 ARC et al, *National Principles of IP Management.*

9 Monotti (2009).

10 E.g., Monotti with Ricketson (2003).

support and thus enhance the respective economies and their competitiveness. The same issue arises for other jurisdictions. It can be observed that like Australia, the UK, for example, uses grants and policy guidelines to drive its aim to exploit the value of new knowledge derived with government funding. To illustrate, the Research Councils UK 'positively encourage the exploitation of the results of the research they support, as a contribution to enhanced quality of life, sustainability and competitiveness of the UK'.[11]

Any review of policies that encourage technology transfer and thus increase patenting activity must take account of the relevant existing patent system that is used to protect the inventions that are to be exploited commercially. The system must complement the incentives that governments provide for patenting inventions arising within universities. This is not necessarily the position in the UK. As Ian Hargreaves pointed out in his *Review of Intellectual Property and Growth* there is evidence that the patent system is deficient in some respects in supporting innovation because it struggles to deal with processing the vast numbers of patent applications. He observed: 'Although the UK patent system continues to function as an important core mechanism for incentivising innovation, some aspects of the way the system is currently working are a source of concern, because they appear to be causing barriers rather than incentives to innovation.'[12] He warned that defects in the patent system 'may be particularly problematic for young innovative firms – a group strategically important to the UK's innovation performance'.[13] Some of those young firms will begin life as start-up companies whose assets are the inventions and other IP that resulted from research within universities.

3. OWNERSHIP AND CERTAINTY

Robert Merges has observed that 'the real purpose of property is to regulate the interactions of competing groups of people'.[14] In the case of patents for inventions that are created within the confines of an employment relationship, the interactions involve at a minimum the employee inventors, the employer, and other co-workers who might not have

---

[11] Website: <http://www.rcuk.ac.uk/Pages/Home.aspx>.

[12] Hargreaves (2011), [6.4]; Lambert Review (2003); Monotti with Ricketson (2003), [9.08]–[9.19].

[13] Ibid, [6.7].

[14] Merges (2011), 70.

conceived the invention but may have helped to reduce the invention to practice. The various theories that have been used over the years to support the grant of property rights in intellectual creations mandate that the rights vest initially in the creator. The principal theme that emerges in all chapters in this Part is the pre-eminence accorded to the individuals whose creativity and intellectual effort enabled them to conceive the invention. Entitlement to be registered as the owner of a patent only arises because the person is the inventor or because a person derives title through the inventor. In broad terms, the laws in each jurisdiction recognise that employers are entitled to own employee inventions when they are created in the performance of paid duties that include an inventive role. The derivation of rights from the inventor means that no entitlement claim can proceed without the identification of the inventors who all have a right to be mentioned as such in any patent granted for the invention.[15] Any other competing groups of people, such as employers or co-workers, must secure their rights through an express agreement with the inventors or from some principle of law that arises from the approaches of courts or legislatures. Hence, as a preliminary observation, any investigation or dispute as to entitlement must first identify who are the inventors of the claimed invention. Courts in each jurisdiction establish common principles for that inquiry, but these principles can prove to be problematic in practice in the case of joint inventorship.[16] Assuming that the actual inventors are known, and that some of these will be employees who are conducting research that they are paid to do, the authors tackle various aspects of the management of rights in those inventions.

Janssens observes in her chapter 'EU Perspectives on Employees' Inventions' that the employer may only acquire a derivative right. While some (but not all) EU countries deal with the issue of employee inventions in their legislation, the lack of consistency in their approaches creates a legal framework that she describes as 'characterized by uncertainty'. Janssens considers employee inventions as a broad class and argues that the complications and problems that arise justify the European Commission reinvigorating attempts to introduce a harmonised legal framework to govern employee inventions in Member States. Monotti

[15] Paris Convention for the Protection of Industrial Property 1883 as revised, art 4ter.

[16] E.g., *Polwood Pty Ltd v Foxworth Pty Ltd* (2008) 165 FCR 527; *The Regents of the University of Michigan and Repligen Corp v Bristol-Myers Squibb Co* 301 F Supp 2d 633 (2003); *IDA Ltd v University of Southampton* [2006] EWCA Civ 145.

also develops the theme of the need for certainty but does so in the context of universities, a research environment which provides fertile ground for uncertainty and emotional and impassioned debate as to who should own employee inventions and other forms of intellectual property. The need for certainty is one factor but the difficulties in drafting statutory provisions to provide a high level of certainty of entitlement become evident from Justine Pila's critical interpretation of the express provision for entitlement to employee inventions contained in s 39(1) of the Patents Act 1977 (UK).

Entitlement to inventions created by academics who are employed by universities is a principal focus in the chapters of Pila and Monotti, and to a lesser extent in the Dreyfuss evaluation of the Bayh-Dole Act. As Dreyfuss points out, it became clear following the recent US Supreme Court decision in *Board of Trustees of Leland Stanford Junior University v Roche Molecular Systems Inc*[17] that the Bayh-Dole Act assumes that the inventors are the source for university entitlement to inventions created with federal funding. The legislation itself does not operate to vest ownership of those inventions in the university employer and could do so only with express language to that effect. Hence, entitlement is dependent upon the validity of contractual claims to employee inventions. In a similar vein, the analysis of *University of Western Australia v Gray*[18] – a case centred on whether the university employer had rights in inventions created by an employed professor either under contract or pursuant to common law principles – in the Monotti chapter highlights the need for universities to source their entitlement in express contractual arrangements in the absence of power to expropriate the intellectual property rights of their employees without their express agreement. Monotti notes the principal lesson from the *Gray* litigation is that clarity of ownership is fundamental to successful innovation and commercial success. The legislation in each country leaves the employers with the responsibility to negotiate an agreed position with their employees. Failure to do so effectively can result in no rights for the university, either because a prior assignment of rights has priority over a later interest of the university[19] or because the express claim is unenforceable.[20]

The default ownership position is one that continues to divide commentators. In contrast with patent laws in the US and Australia, the

---

[17] 131 US 2188 (No. 09–1159, June 6, 2011).

[18] (2010) 179 FCR 346.

[19] *Board of Trustees of Leland Stanford Junior University v Roche Molecular Systems Inc* 131 US 2188 (No. 09–1159, June 6, 2011).

[20] *UWA v Gray* (2010) 179 FCR 346; *VUT v Wilson* (2004) 60 IPR 392.

Patents Act 1977 (UK) includes an express provision in s 39(1) for entitlement to employee inventions. In her chapter, Pila argues that there is scope to apply reasoning of the type in the Australian decision of *UWA v Gray* and to consider policy justifications for limiting the application of s 39 to inventions created by academic employees[21] and a limited range of professional employees. A theme running through each chapter is that the distinctiveness of universities and of academic employment within them warrants different legal principles to apply to establish an employer's entitlement to claim an interest in its employee inventions. Ultimately, any entitlement of an employer must have the employment contract as its source but the law must provide a suitable and clear default position that considers the special needs for distinctive types of employment, and especially that of academic employment within universities.[22]

4. REWARDS FOR EMPLOYED INVENTORS

A significant quantity of inventions arises in the performance of an employee's paid work for which she receives a salary. A question that continues to provoke debate is whether an employee who creates an invention for her employer is entitled to a greater financial reward than the regular salary she receives. One justification for compensation appears in the following passage: 'The thinking behind [ss 39–42 of the Patents Act 1977] was in part that employees would have a greater incentive to invent and in part some sort of general equitable fairness.'[23] Some form of compensation is an ingrained feature of most national laws in the EU, but Janssens draws our attention to the divergence in the approaches taken. She identifies the lack of uniformity to the grant of statutory rights to compensation, the conditions on which any rights to compensation will arise and the lack of predictability as to the financial benefit as problematic for business. Legal uncertainty and the impact of differing approaches upon competition are two of a number of reasons that support her argument for some harmonised minimum rights. This European preference for compensation of some kind contrasts starkly with both the US and Australian patent legislation, which is silent on rights to compensation. Any rights must derive from employment contracts.

21 Monotti with Ricketson (2003).
22 Monotti (2009); Pila (2012).
23 Jacob (1997), 7.

The issue of compensation and rewards for employee inventors takes a different turn where academic employee inventions are concerned. Neither Australia nor the US provides statutory rewards for employee inventors as a class. However, they have reward systems established in other ways. The Bayh-Dole Act requires royalties to be shared with inventors and provides for profits to be used for further research purposes. As Dreyfuss observes, these benefits provide faculty members with a financial incentive to develop their inventions and participate in licensing activities. Australian universities which receive national competitive grants are required by Principle 7 of the *National Principles of Intellectual Property Management for Publicly Funded Research* to share benefits with all stakeholders. This underlying policy for revenue sharing is one that is fundamental to university IP legislation and policies and is implemented by university technology transfer departments or companies.[24]

5. CONCLUDING COMMENTS

Business innovation can appear in many forms, and patented inventions are only one of those forms. There are of course other forms of IP that play a significant role in business innovation, such as copyright and trade marks and more particularly the other side of the invention coin: keeping business innovation secret and relying upon a range of laws to protect that information from misuse and misappropriation. Any patented invention will start life as confidential information. The secrecy of that invention must be maintained prior to filing the patent specification if registration is required in jurisdictions – such as the EU – that require absolute secrecy before filing. While other chapters in this volume deal with protection for all kinds of confidential information in business settings, it is appropriate to briefly raise a final theme in the context of this Part: the extent to which academic employees are required by their duty to perform research to keep any inventions in confidence before a patent application is filed. A principal objective of academic research is open dissemination of information and knowledge and this obligation to publish is one of a number of academic freedoms that make it impossible to reconcile a general academic duty to perform research of no specified nature with any obligation to retain research outcomes from the research chosen by the academic in secrecy pending any evaluation of their

24 Monotti with Ricketson (2003), chs 7, 8 and 9.

patentability. Reliance upon absolute secrecy is completely contrary to the scientific norms that require wide dissemination of research.[25] This theme of distinctiveness of universities from other business entities and the freedoms of their academic employees was a central pillar in the reasoning in *UWA v Gray*,[26] the case that provided the initial inspiration for this volume of essays.

REFERENCES

Australian Research Council, The Australian Tertiary Institutions Commercial Companies Association, The Australian Vice-Chancellors' Committee, The Department of Education, Training and Youth Affairs, The Department of Industry, Science and Resources, IP Australia and The National Health and Medical Research Council, *National Principles of Intellectual Property Management for Publicly Funded Research*, <http://www.arc.gov.au/about_arc/national_ip.htm>

Blumenthal, D., E.G. Campbell, M. Anderson, N. Causino and K.S. Louis (1997), 'Withholding Research Results in Academic Life Science: Evidence from a National Survey of Faculty' 277(15) *Journal of the American Medical Association* 1224

Davison, M. (2003), *The Legal Protection of Databases*, Cambridge University Press

Eisenberg, R.S. (1987), 'Proprietary Rights and the Norms of Science in Biotechnology Research' 97 *Yale Law Journal* 177

Ginsburg, J.C. (1990), 'Creation and Commercial Value: Copyright Protection of Works of Information' 90 *Columbia Law Review* 1865

Glasser D. (2001), 'Copyrights in Computer-Generated Works: Whom, if Anyone, do we Reward?' *Duke Law & Technology Review* 24

Hargreaves, I. (2011), *Digital Opportunity: A Review of Intellectual Property and Growth*, May, <http://apo.org.au/node/24870>

Jacob R. (1997), 'The Stephen Stewart Memorial Lecture: Industrial Property – Industry's Enemy?' 1 *Intellectual Property Quarterly* 3

Lambert Review of Business–University Collaboration: Final Report (HMSO, UK 2003)

Lindsay, D. (2012), 'Protection of Compilations and Databases after IceTV: Authorship, Originality and the Transformation of Australian Copyright Law', *Monash University Law* Review, forthcoming

Merges, R.P. (2011), *Justifying Intellectual Property*, Harvard University Press

Merton, R.K. (1973), *The Sociology of Science: Theoretical and Empirical Investigation*, University of Chicago Press

Monotti, A.L. with S. Ricketson (2003), *Universities and Intellectual Property: Ownership and Exploitation*, Oxford University Press

Monotti, A.L. (2009), 'Commercialization of University Research and Free Diffusion – What Does Experience Show Works Best in and for Australia?' in C. Arup and W. van Caenegem (eds), *Intellectual Property Policy Reform*, Edward Elgar

[25] E.g., Merton (1973); Blumenthal et al (1997); Eisenberg (1987).
[26] (2010) 179 FCR 346; Monotti with Ricketson (2003), [6.168]–[6.179].

Organisation for Economic Co-operation and Development (2005), *Oslo Manual: Guidelines for Collecting and Interpreting Innovation Data*, 3rd edn, OECD Statistical Office of the European Communities, <http://www.oecd.org/document/33/0,3746,en_2649_34273_35595607_1_1_1_1,00.html>

Pila, J. (2012), 'Sewing the Fly Buttons on the Statute: Employee Inventions and the Employment Context' 32(2) *Oxford Journal of Legal Studies* 265

4. Double or nothing: technology transfer under the Bayh-Dole Act

Rochelle Cooper Dreyfuss*

1. INTRODUCTION

The United States is fascinated with technology. Prior to the Tea Party (the first one), the colonies angered England by engaging in rampant technological piracy.[1] Thomas Jefferson was an inventor and took a personal interest in the patent system.[2] Many scientific institutions were established in the first century of the nation's existence – the Smithsonian Institute and the American Association for the Advancement of Science in 1850; the National Academy of Sciences and the Department of Agriculture, in 1862. In 1862 and 1890, the Morrill Acts gave birth to the land-grant college system, which focused on innovation in agriculture, science, and engineering.[3] To many Americans, it was technology – advances in aviation, radar, encryption, medicine, and nuclear energy – that won the Great Wars.

Indeed, during World War II, President Roosevelt asked Vannevar Bush, his science advisor, to create a technology plan for the post-war period.[4] The strategy Bush developed was centered on a linear theory of innovation in which development was perceived as moving from 'upstream' discovery of fundamental insights to their 'downstream' commercial application. In Bush's view, upstream research – basic science – was too far removed from application to be an attractive target for commercial investment. At the same time, however, he saw this work

* I thank Jonathan D. Bean, NYU Class of 2012 for research assistance; Jeffrey Lefstin, for the information in section 4.1; and the support of the Filomen D'Agostino and Max E. Greenberg Research Fund.

1 Ben-Atar (2004).

2 *Graham v John Deere Co.*, 383 U.S. 1 (1966).

3 Rhoten & Powell (2010).

4 Bush (1945).

as the wellspring from which multiple technological prospects flow. To assure continuing support for basic science, he recommended – and the U.S. Government pursued – a mixed program of intramural research within Government laboratories and Government funding of extramural research in universities and other nonprofit organizations. Funding agencies either placed the fruits of these efforts into the public domain (through publication) or patented and licensed them out on a non-exclusive basis.[5] The expectation was that industry would adapt the advances, find applications, create new businesses and jobs, enhance productivity, and improve social welfare.

Given its infatuation with science, it is not surprising that when the United States went into a period of stagflation in the late 1970s, it once again hung its hopes on technological development. While the economists of the day certainly agreed with Bush on the relationship between technology, productivity, and social welfare, many were skeptical about his notion of a linear progression from upstream science to downstream technological application. They argued that while upstream researchers may excel at identifying *scientific* and *technological* opportunities, they might lack sufficient understanding of business to recognize *commercial* opportunities. Further, there was concern that the advantages of cheap access to upstream research through nonexclusive licensing were outweighed by the costs associated with free-riding. It can be expensive to move advances from the lab bench to the marketplace: heavy investments could be required to scale up production, take account of user preferences, build distribution systems, and educate consumers about the value of the product. If second-comers can acquire rights equivalent to those of the first mover, they could undermine the first mover's ability to recapture early (and often risky) investments.[6]

To deal with these problems, the United States doubled down. In 1980, it passed the Bayh-Dole Act, which gave universities (and certain other institutions) the authority to patent the fruits of federally supported research.[7] The Act required the public to pay for inventions twice, first through the tax system and later via supracompetitive pricing.[8] Arguably,

---

[5] Funding agencies had their own approach: NRCNA Committee on Management of University Intellectual Property (2010), 69–70 (Managing University IP).

[6] E.g., 126 Cong Rec. 29,898 (1980) (Rep Don Fuqua).

[7] 35 U.S.C. §§ 200–212; 15 U.S.C. §§ 3701–3714 (Stevenson-Wydler Technology Innovation Act 1980).

[8] Managing University IP (2010); Eisenberg (1996).

however, the new regime also doubled the effectiveness of the Government's investment. Universities could grant developers facing high downstream expenses exclusive rights, which would protect them from free-riders. Furthermore, by requiring universities, faculty, and industry to engage in licensing, the new system would expose academia to business problems, and industry to scientific research. Opportunity-recognition skills would improve for all concerned; upstream research would be better attuned to the market and industry would enjoy advanced information on scientific breakthroughs.

But the Act also carried new risks. As Robert Merton has argued, the reward system in basic science is finely attuned to the demands of the research enterprise.[9] Reputational rewards come from publishing early and sharing materials; the commitment to communitarianism ensures that good work is available to continually push the frontiers of knowledge forward. In contrast, concern for financial rewards promotes secrecy, data hoarding, and a focus on targeted projects; it can lead to conflict among faculty, students, and the administration. In fact, the Bayh-Dole approach could backfire. Upstream research could become more costly as research inputs became subject to patent claims. At the same time, downstream progress could falter as greater reliance on exclusive licensing eliminated the possibility for competitive development of fresh prospects.

The Bayh-Dole Act has now been in force for 30 years; we are in yet another recession in which we are looking to technology for solutions. It is therefore fitting to ask how the wager made in 1980 has panned out: did the Bayh-Dole Act increase social welfare, as its supporters hoped, or did its emphasis on patenting poison the wellspring? This chapter begins with a short description of the Act. It next moves to consideration of the evidence. Finally, the chapter turns to the future. There is a strong element of path dependency at work in this arena. Reliance on Bayh-Dole within the research and academic communities make its repeal virtually unthinkable. However, the Act could be modified in light of experience. Furthermore, other countries might learn from the United States experience and enact technology transfer regimes that do better.

2. THE BAYH-DOLE ACT

The stated goals of the Bayh-Dole Act demonstrate the ambivalence that characterized its enactment. On the one hand, the Act seeks to promote

[9] Merton (1973).

the commercialization of federally-supported inventions and collaboration among scientists in universities and industry. On the other hand, the Act warns that the rights created must be 'used in a manner to promote free competition and enterprise without unduly encumbering future research and discovery' and must be interpreted 'to ensure that the Government obtains sufficient rights in federally supported inventions to meet the needs of the Government and protect the public against nonuse.'[10]

The substantive provisions of the enactment reflect these competing concerns. The Act effectuates the goal of bringing academia and industry in closer contact by making government ownership the default position: certain 'contractors' – small businesses and nonprofit organizations (mainly universities) that are parties to Government funding contracts – can elect to retain title to inventions that arise from federally funded research. If neither the funder nor contractor wishes to patent, the inventor may pursue patent rights, subject to various constraints.[11] These limitations are (ostensibly) extensive. Funding agreements can exempt foreign contractors and those under the control of another Government. A funding agency can also deny rights of election when the research is of national interest or when it determines that Government ownership would 'better promote the policy and objectives' of the Act.[12] After transfer, the United States enjoys a non-exclusive, non-transferable license to practice or allow others to practice the invention on its behalf; funders can also demand similar rights under foreign patents.[13] Periodic reporting of commercialization efforts is required;[14] if the funder determines that the invention has been insufficiently exploited, it can 'march in' and acquire rights to the invention.[15] Government retention or reacquisition is not, however, easy: there are cumbersome requirements and a right of review. In fact, the United States has only rarely withheld patent rights and has never successfully marched in, even in situations where the right was clearly underexploited.[16]

The Act imposes certain other safeguards as well. The contractor must ensure that rights can be secured.[17] It must share the royalties received

---

[10] 35 U.S.C. § 200.
[11] § 202 (a), (c) and (d).
[12] § 202(a)(i)–(iv).
[13] § 202(c)(4).
[14] § 202(c)(5).
[15] § 203.
[16] Rai & Eisenberg (2003); Bar-Shalom & Cook-Deegan (2002).
[17] 35 U.S.C. § 202(c)(1) and (2).

with the inventors; in most cases, it must plow its profits back into support for scientific research or education; excess earnings (measured by comparing profits to institutional budgets) must be returned to the U.S. Treasury; licensing programs must prefer small businesses and U.S. industry.[18] If reasonably possible, all exclusive licenses must be to entities that agree to produce products embodying the invention or using the invention 'substantially in the United States'.[19] The Act thus assures that faculty members are motivated to participate in licensing activities, that there is enough contact among the parties to promote a healthy interchange of ideas and skills, and that the public's double expenditures redound to the benefit of the U.S. taxpayer through both better products and better jobs.

3. EXPERIENCE UNDER THE BAYH-DOLE ACT

Measured in terms of university patent applications, licenses granted, companies formed, joint ventures launched, products marketed, inventions disclosed, revenues earned, and technology transfer offices established, the Bayh-Dole Act is a roaring success.[20] Until 2007, patenting and licensing activity increased each year; some institutions have profited considerably.[21] Most universities have established technology transfer offices (TTO) and require faculty to give them notice of patentable inventions.[22] The Association of University Technology Managers (AUTM) has emerged as an important lobbyist.[23] University scientists now act as industry consultants, serve on scientific advisory boards, and some have created spin-off companies (and attendant jobs) in the vicinity of their campuses.[24] Interaction with business has also generated new sources of funding, including direct industrial funding of research and development, as well as collaborations between universities and major industrial players. Examples include the Energy Biosciences Institute

---

18 § 202 (c)(7).

19 § 204.

20 Managing University IP (2010), 23–26. The data largely derives from that provided by the Association of University Technology Managers (AUTM). See also Henderson, Jaffe & Trajtenberg (1998).

21 Managing University IP (2010), 25.

22 E.g., MIT Technology License Office (2010); MIT (2010).

23 Sampat & Nelson (2002).

24 Owen-Smith & Powell (2003); e.g., Massachusetts Institute of Technology MIT (2009) (MIT Report).

created by British Petroleum and the Universities of California and Illinois.[25]

Lurking in these numbers, however, are significant concerns. One issue is whether the new links between university and commerce can be attributed to the Bayh-Dole Act. In fact, many universities were entrepreneurial prior to the Act's passage.[26] Furthermore, Bayh-Dole's passage coincided with the Supreme Court's decision in *Diamond v Chakrabarty*,[27] which spurred commercialization in a sector (biotechnology) in which universities were already involved. Proof of linkage is thus an impossible task. This section puts that issue to one side, and discusses the evidence concerning the effect of the Bayh-Dole Act in two arenas at the focus of this volume: employment (the academic environment) and competition (technology transfer).

3.1 Employment

Passage of the Bayh-Dole Act was not intended to change the nature of the university, but rather to channel the fruits of fundamental research into the commercial pipeline. Academic and commercial cultures are, however, different. Academics are traditionally driven by curiosity and reputation.[28] Curiosity leads to work on deeply fundamental problems – the type of upstream research that Vannevar Bush prized as productive of multiple applications. Reputation requires early publication, which spreads results quickly and promotes rapid progress. In contrast, commercial work can focus on narrow objectives. It requires rights management, including secrecy, delayed publication, refusals to share tangible materials, and patenting. The fear when Bayh-Dole was enacted was that as academics became motivated by financial incentives (and universities would, arguably, start evaluating their performance by the revenues earned from their work), norms would shift and fundamental knowledge production would suffer.

To a large extent, these fears have proved to be overblown. In a series of studies, Jerry and Marie Thursby found little evidence that faculty motivations have changed dramatically; it appears that most faculty research agendas continue to be driven mainly by curiosity.[29] Nor is

[25] Mimura (2010).

[26] Mowery & Ziedonis (2000), 220.

[27] 447 U.S. 303 (1980); Rafferty (2008); Mowery & Sampat (2005), 209–239.

[28] Stern (2004).

[29] Thursby & Thursby (2007).

commercial work crowding out research. If anything, the evidence demonstrates the contrary: the involvement of faculty in industry is generative of fresh ideas; academics who patent more also publish more.[30]

Nonetheless, some question the quality of faculty work in the commercial domain and its ability to stimulate multiple technological applications. Measuring quality is not easy, but a rough estimate can be gleaned from the number of times a patent is later cited (forward citations). Early studies were discouraging, for they suggested that quality was, in fact, declining over time.[31] But there is more recent work suggesting that when a longer time-line is taken into account, citation rates improve. Some work takes time to diffuse. Furthermore, there is a selection effect: in the early years, TTOs tried to patent every invention, including unproductive ones. As TTOs have become more selective, forward citations have increased.[32]

Academic culture may, however, be changing in ways not picked up by these studies. The propensity to patent rises with a researcher's age and contacts with those who patent.[33] In early years under the Act, superstars were unlikely to patent,[34] but the young scientists replacing them are socialized into a more commercial environment and enter academia with expectations of patenting.[35] Accordingly, there may be a continuing shift to more focused work. Moreover, despite university requirements,[36] some faculty patent on their own; others work directly with industry outside the dictates of the Bayh-Dole Act.[37] If the output of this activity were taken into account, the picture on quality might look quite different.[38]

The emphasis on patenting may have other detrimental effects on the workplace. Participation in industrial activities is highly gendered, leading to dissatisfaction among those who are left out.[39] There are continuous allegations that students are assigned work that is in the business interest of the faculty rather than in the pedagogical interest of the

---

30 Thursby & Thursby (2011); Azoulay (2006).

31 Henderson, Jaffe & Trajtenberg (1998).

32 Sampat, Mowery & Ziedonis (2003); Mowery, Sampat & Ziedonis (2002). Also Leydesdorff & Meyer (2010).

33 Azoulay, Ding & Stuart (2007).

34 Calderini, Franzoni & Vezzulli (2007).

35 Yang & Chang (2010).

36 E.g., MIT (2010), § A; Audretsch, Aldridge & Oettl (2006).

37 Owen-Smith & Powell (2001).

38 Hottenrott & Thorwarth (2010).

39 Ding, Murray & Stuart (2006).

student. Since U.S. patent law gives all inventors equal rights to practice the invention, there are strong incentives to eliminate names from the patent application – most often, the losers are graduate students.[40]

The Bayh-Dole Act also breeds tension between faculty and university administrators. A recent Supreme Court case, *Board of Trustees of Leland Stanford Junior University v Roche Molecular Systems Inc.*,[41] may increase the strain. In *Stanford*, a method for detecting HIV was developed as part of serial efforts involving a Stanford research fellow and a commercial entity that was later acquired by Roche. Stanford, which had been promised an assignment of the research fellow's patent rights, patented the invention pursuant to what it regarded as its Bayh-Dole obligations. Roche, relying on a differently worded assignment, commercialized the invention. Stanford sued for infringement. It lost. The Court held that:

> [o]nly when an invention belongs to the contractor does the Bayh-Dole Act come into play. The Act's disposition of rights – like much of the rest of the Bayh-Dole Act – serves to clarify the order of priority of rights between the Federal Government and a federal contractor in a federally funded invention that already belongs to the contractor. Nothing more.[42]

Justice Roberts, writing for the majority, posited that universities could avoid similar results in the future through properly drafted agreements.[43] However, these contracts may be difficult to negotiate now that the Bayh-Dole Act has been deemed avoidable. The result, noted by Justice Breyer in dissent, is that 'the public will pay twice for the same invention' without the assurance that the 'special public policy' the Act sought to further will be attained.[44] Nor will the Act's safeguards (march-in rights, profit sharing, and local exploitation requirements) apply.

Faculty mobility will also suffer. Because scientific knowledge and research skills are field-specific, academics (and graduate students) expect that when they move, they will continue with the same research using the same research materials. But now that universities have a business interest in their output, administrators have conceptualized tangible materials, data, and training as proprietary assets. Grants are now (or after *Stanford*, will certainly be) carefully negotiated to retain

---

40 35 U.S.C. § 116; Dreyfuss (2000).
41 131 U.S. 2188 (No. 09–1159, June 6, 2011).
42 131 U.S. 2188, 2197.
43 131 U.S. 2188, 2199.
44 131 U.S. 2188, 2201.

rights even when the original researcher leaves.[45] Furthermore, if scientists do leave, their continued use of such materials may be regarded as a violation of trade secrecy laws. For example, research scientists who moved to a Japanese university and continued work they began at the Cleveland Clinic were accused of violating the Economic Espionage Act, a criminal statute with penalties that include both fines and imprisonment.[46] Loss of mobility is a private problem for the faculty and students affected. But it is also a social problem. If scientists cannot take the position that makes the highest and best use of their knowledge and skills, the full value of training them (which is often supported by public funds) is lost.

3.2 Technology Transfer

Costs related to employment may not matter if the Bayh-Dole Act increases social welfare overall. As recounted earlier, measured quantitatively, the benefits of the Act are substantial. But not all universities successfully convert their output into assets that can be commercialized. Half of one percent of all university licensing agreements generate as much as $1 million in revenue; annual income earned by university licensing programs amounts to only 2 percent of typical research expenditures.[47] More important, quantitative measurement may be misleading. Not all technology transfer is quantifiable: some occurs through human interaction, such as by hiring a university's graduates or implementing an invention described in a publication.[48] To the extent that Bayh-Dole enables universities to convert free transfers into monetized ones, the measurables – patents, licenses, and revenue – do not represent an increase in social welfare.

Two examples illustrate the point. First, consider the diffusion of two of the most important discoveries in the biotechnology sector, recombinant DNA technology and the method for producing monoclonal antibodies. In both cases, early publication may have rendered the advances unpatentable. However, the inventors of recombinant DNA, Stanley Cohen and Herbert Boyer, persuaded their university (Stanford) to patent. The patent was licensed out nonexclusively at relatively low rates (presumably low enough to deter patent validity challenges). In the other case, Georges Kohler and Cesar Milstein contented themselves with

---

[45] E.g., MIT, Inventions and Proprietary Information Agreement (2010), § B.
[46] 18 U.S.C. §§ 1831–1839; U.S. Department of Justice (2001).
[47] Managing University IP (2010).
[48] MIT Report (2009).

a Nobel Prize. The Cohen/Boyer invention generated record revenues, but it cannot be said that the technology was transferred more effectively than the Kohler/Milstein invention, which earned no profits. Both were equally important to the growth of the biotechnology sector in the 1980s.[49]

Second, a study commissioned by the Secretary [of Health and Human Services]'s Advisory Committee on Genetics, Health and Society (SACGHS) found no case in which the patent holder on a genetic diagnostic (which is typically discovered in universities) was first to market. Rather, exclusive rights holders *cleared* markets, making it harder for patients to find testing facilities.[50] While university revenue may have increased, technology transfer – when evaluated in terms of laboratory, physician and consumer access – actually declined. In other words, the measurables suggestive of Bayh-Dole's success do not tell the whole story.

3.2.1 Upstream technology transfer

As with employment, evidence on the impact of Bayh-Dole is extensive, but mixed. In two studies commissioned by the National Academies of Science, Wesley Cohen found that upstream research is largely unaffected by increased patenting. Scientists claim they have never cancelled or delayed work because of problems in licensing.[51] They had, in Cohen's words, found a 'work around': essentially, they ignored patents.

Nonetheless, there are reasons to be concerned. Cohen found problems in certain fields. He also identified other impediments to upstream research: difficulty in acquiring unique tangibles. Cohen suggested that it is not patents, but rather the need to negotiate material transfer agreements (MTAs), that prove to be the real sticking point. But it is likely that the MTAs are difficult to negotiate because the parties are concerned with patent rights. Indeed, other researchers have found that Bayh-Dole's emphasis on patenting does interfere with upstream research.[52] For example, Fiona Murray found that the forward-citation rate of papers declined after the advances described had been patented.[53] Conversely, she demonstrated that citation rates (and research lines) go up after a

---

[49] Oliver & Liebeskind (2009).

[50] Secretary's Advisory Commission on Genetics, Health and Society (2010) (SACGHS Report).

[51] Cohen & Walsh (2010); Walsh, Arora & Cohen (2003).

[52] Lei, Juneja & Wright (2009).

[53] Murray & Stern (2007).

patented input is released for free use by researchers.[54] In practice, then, scientists do appear to be influenced by patent status, and to avoid projects that require licensing.

3.2.2 Downstream technology transfer

Nor is it clear that exclusivity improves downstream transfers. Heidi Williams compared the rate at which genetic data in exclusively licensed databases were used to generate products with the rate at which genetic data in a public database were so used. She found that product development involving proprietary data lagged far behind products developed with public data. Moreover, the lag persisted even after the private data became publicly available – an effect Williams attributed to the cumulative nature of knowledge production.[55]

In certain situations, the impediments posed by patents may be particularly acute. Not all downstream work is profitable. Work on malaria and other diseases that uniquely afflict nonmarket economies will never earn a return sufficient to pay licensing fees.[56] In the biomedical field where universities have been particularly active, patent thickets are common.[57] Accordingly, developing plants with particular nutritional properties, or multiplex genetic tests, or personalized medicine will require the negotiation of multiple licenses, and therefore high transaction costs and entail the risk of holdouts.[58]

Another problem is exclusivity. Although the Bayh-Dole Act was motivated by concerns about nonexclusive licensing, it does not require exclusivity. Nonetheless, universities tend to license on that basis, even when the cost of commercialization is low. The result can be a social disaster. For instance, SACGHS found that when universities license diagnostic patents exclusively, patients cannot get second opinions and the quality of testing services is unverifiable.[59] Sole providers lack incentives to update procedures and may suppress further innovation by refusing to authorize researchers to use their patents.[60] The Government's failure to monitor these problems and exploit Bayh-Dole march-in rights

---

[54] Huang & Murray (2009).

[55] Williams (2010).

[56] E.g., Kapczynski, Chaifetz, Katz & Benkler (2005).

[57] Jensen & Murray (2005).

[58] Wright (2010).

[59] SACGHS Report (2010).

[60] Dreyfuss & Evans (2011). It can even be difficult to identify the licensee as the reporting required by the Act is treated as confidential: iEdison webpage: <https://s-edison.info.nih.gov/iEdison/>.

led a class of patients to sue, claiming their own right of action under the Act to ensure an adequate supply of an exclusively licensed medicine.[61]

To be sure, universities are learning. Both the National Institutes of Health (NIH) and AUTM have issued guidelines and best practices.[62] Among other things, they advise universities to retain rights to conduct upstream research and research aimed at serving neglected populations, to refrain from licensing exclusively, and to be mindful of conflicts of interest. Still, there are limits on how far guidelines go. They are not firm commitments and not all universities have adopted them. For instance, Johns Hopkins University, which has licensed ineffectually in the past, nonetheless continues to license gene patents exclusively.[63]

Technology transfer is also highly incomplete. Success is mostly in the pharmaceutical and biotechnology sector, even though upstream research occurs in other university departments. A growing literature on the deficiencies in TTO performance suggests why. The differing goals of industry and academia make negotiations difficult.[64] Because TTOs are evaluated by how much they earn, they concentrate on the most remunerative deals. They do not consider other routes for transfer. When they do license, they focus on 'blockbusters' that will earn large returns, rather than engaging in the hard work of finding industrial partners for more prosaic advances.[65] Additionally, technology transfer is much harder than the proponents of Bayh-Dole assumed. Commercial firms specialize; their staffs know the field and enjoy networks of business contacts. But even a well-resourced TTO is unlikely to develop the skills and connections necessary to accurately assess the value of prospects, identify commercial opportunities, and find potential licensees across all the fields where university scientists work.[66] Finally, university output can be extremely far upstream. Prior to obtaining proof that a concept translates into commercial products, it may be hard to interest licensees. Faculty

---

[61] *Hochendoner v Genzyme Corp.*, Civ. Case No. 2:2011 CV 00313 (filed March 9, 2011 W.D. Pa.).

[62] E.g., Principles and Guidelines for Recipients of NIH Research Grants and Contracts on Obtaining and Disseminating Biomedical Research Resources: Final Notice, 64 Fed. Reg. 72,090 (Dec. 23, 1999); AUTM (2007).

[63] Press Release, IntegraGen Announces Exclusive Licensing Agreement with the Johns Hopkins University and Massachusetts General Hospital for the Autism Gene (April 11, 2011).

[64] Eisenberg (2001).

[65] Kesan & Shah (2005).

[66] Tahvanainen & Hermans (2011); Swamidass & Vulasa (2009).

cooperation in transferring tacit knowledge may be required – but difficult to procure.[67]

Vannevar Bush may have been wrong about the linear theory of development. Interaction between academia and industry has made both more vibrant. But he was largely correct about allowing university work to freely spill over. While technology transfer may not have been ideal before Bayh-Dole, the availability of patents does not alone make it easy and the costs associated with licensing can discourage downstream use. Furthermore, noncompetitive development has costs of its own.

4. THE WAY FORWARD

The discussion in section 2 demonstrates that the controversy surrounding the Bayh-Dole Act has not abated. The Act has been influential in bringing industry and academia in closer contact, although that might have occurred anyway. Patenting has earned at least a few schools significant amounts of money, but the quality of technology transfer has not necessarily improved. The direst predictions of Bayh-Dole's opponents have not come to pass, but academic norms may still be changing. Some have suggested that now that academia and industry have begun to work more collaboratively, it is time to repeal the Act.[68] Repeal is, however, highly unlikely. The National Academies of Science has asked three committees to consider it.[69] Although all three identified problems, none suggested dismantling the system. Universities have come to rely on the revenue and incoming faculty now expect to supplement their academic income with the revenue available from commercializing their work. Besides, it is impossible to predict what the next generation of discoveries will require in terms of downstream investment. There are, however, at least three ways to improve technology transfer within the Act's overall framework.

---

[67] Siegel, Veugelers & Wright (2007).

[68] Kenney & Patton (2009).

[69] Managing University IP (2010); NRCNA Committee on Intellectual Property Rights in Genomic and Protein Research and Innovation (2006); NRCNA Committee on Intellectual Property Rights in the Knowledge-Based Economy (2004).

4.1 Modifying University Practices

Dissatisfaction with universities under Bayh-Dole boils down to two critiques: conflation of technology transfer with patenting and inept practices. The source of the first problem is easily identified: as long as TTOs' performance is measured by patents prosecuted, licenses negotiated, and revenues generated, the staff will see its primary role as adding to the university's coffers. To induce TTOs to concentrate on transfer, universities must adopt new metrics of performance. The University of California at Berkeley, for example, now measures success by the social impact of faculty innovations. Patents, licenses, and revenue are still considered, but non-remunerative transactions are also included: free transfers; global outreach; gifts made as a result of efforts to cure neglected diseases; collaborations; and reputational enhancements.[70]

To be sure, metrics will not change unless universities accept the idea that revenues are not the main goal. That may be a hard sell, particularly at state (public) universities where support otherwise falls on local taxpayers. But tweaking the Act would allow the Government to influence university behavior. If march-in were easier, universities would have stronger incentives to develop strategies that transfer technology quickly and effectively. Alternatively, funders could warn universities that poor performance in the past might lead to future decisions that Government ownership would 'better promote the policy and objectives' of the Act.[71] Additionally, funders could condition grants on concrete plans for the dissemination of research.[72]

The more difficult problem lies in improving the efficacy of technology transfer programs. TTOs have begun to hire more patent professionals and are streamlining MTAs to make materials more readily available.[73] These changes are not, however, likely to reach the crux of the problem: effective transfer requires networks of contacts and methods for helping industry understand how early stage research can be translated into commercial products. It requires greater involvement in proving the concept, reducing the invention to practice, developing prototypes, and testing them.[74] In short, it requires new business models and attention to individual technological fields.

---

[70] Mimura (2010).

[71] 35 U.S.C. § 202(a)(i)–(iv).

[72] SACGHS Report (2010), Rec 2; Campbell, Powers, Blumenthal & Biles (2004).

[73] Kesan (2009); Goulding, Marden & Manion (2010).

[74] Markman, Phann, Balkin & Gianiodis (2005).

Some universities have begun to change. The University of California has developed a range of new entities, including strategic alliances, business parks, and incubators; various campuses have taken a proactive role in start-ups, including providing faculty with business advice and capital.[75] The von Liebig Center at the University of California at San Diego provides seed money and advisory services for inventions in the medical devices and diagnostics areas, as well as for software and clean technologies.[76] The California Institute for Quantitative Biosciences (QB3) centers its work on complex biological systems. It supplies collaborative tools, funds competitions, provides advice at the proof-of-concept stage, and matches projects to commercial funders.[77] Similarly, MIT's Deshpande Center for Technological Innovation furnishes advice, seed money, and sustained support for innovations in biotechnology, biomedical devices, information technology, 'tiny tech' (nanotechnology), and energy.[78] Most aggressively, the University of Southern California's Alfred E. Mann Institute takes patent rights in exchange for engaging in full-scale commercialization efforts.[79]

4.2 Faculty Ownership of Intellectual Property Rights

Not every university has the resources, personnel, or imagination to develop new business models. Observers have therefore suggested that faculty members should be permitted to retain the rights to their inventions.[80] While such recommendations are often made in the context of repealing Bayh-Dole, universities and funders could attain the same result by simply waiving their rights of election. TTOs would continue to exist, but faculty would not be wed to the TTO at their school. Instead, they could shop around, paying the TTO of their choice on a fee-for-services basis.

The approach has much to recommend it. Individual academics are far more likely to have the specialized knowledge and array of contacts necessary to evaluate their inventions and transfer them efficiently. Those interested in a less proprietary model of knowledge governance could

---

75 Mimura (2010).

76 <http://www.vonliebig.ucsd.edu/about/mission.shtml>.

77 <http://qb3.org/about-us/>.

78 <http://web.mit.edu/deshpandecenter/about.html>.

79 Mission of AMI U.S.C.; Alfred E. Mann Foundation for Biomedical Engineering.

80 Kenney & Patton (2009); Litan, Mitchell & Reedy (2007).

experiment with open innovation strategies.[81] Faculty would be free to change jobs without worrying about economic espionage or trade secrecy claims. The complexity of allocating rights exemplified by the *Stanford* case might also abate. At the same time, competition would force TTOs to improve their services without the need for Government intervention. Universities could close unproductive offices and use their resources elsewhere. Private firms, on the model of the Alfred Mann Institute, might enter the business and bring a new professionalism to the field.

Faculty ownership of research outputs would, however, have other problems. Not all faculty members are entrepreneurial and the oversight provided by Bayh-Dole may be insufficient to assure that their discoveries will be transferred efficiently. Equally problematically, faculty ownership of patent rights may further weaken or destroy Mertonian norms. If the entrepreneurial spirit dominates, faculty-ownership may lead to more patenting, more exclusive licensing, more employment stratification, less attention to the problems of neglected populations and nonmarket economies, work of lower generative value, and less time spent with students and colleagues. To most observers, the specter of an academy filled with entrepreneurs acting in their private interest is profoundly worrisome.

4.3 Government Re-involvement in Technology Transfer

A better idea might be to re-insert Government into the technology transfer process. This could partly be accomplished by changing the regulatory impediments that currently surround the Bayh-Dole Act and partly by making technology transfer part of the Government's intramural mission. Under this approach, the current system would continue but the Government would step in with new mechanisms in situations where licensing problems are so complex, no single university can hope to solve them.

Gene patents furnish one example. As noted earlier, multiplex testing, personalized medicine, and other applications of genomics will require multiple patented inputs. Acquiring licenses will be expensive and vulnerable to holdouts. In some fields, patent pools answer these concerns. However, pooling largely works in fields like electronics, where no single patentee can bring a product to market.[82] In contrast, gene patents can be exploited individually. The Government is, however, in an excellent position to jump-start pools. As Robert Merges has noted, in the

---

[81] E.g., Endy (2005).

[82] Van Overwalle et al (2006).

past, it has relied on threats of eminent domain.[83] Here, the Government could require contributions to the pool as a condition for funding, or as a condition for permitting the university to retain its patent rights, or through march-in. Along similar lines, the Government might build information commonses, facilitate the screening of small molecules against protein targets (which is another highly problematic area), and intervene in the development of products and processes uniquely needed by nonmarket economies.[84]

Indeed, there is already an indication that the Government understands the need to supplement Bayh-Dole. Recently, the NIH established the National Center for Advancing Translational Sciences. Designed to 'develop and offer innovative services and expertise in moving promising products through the development pipeline, as well as develop novel approaches to therapeutics development, stimulate new avenues for basic scientific discovery,' the Center will provide a locus of access to research materials and expertise, serve as a catalyst for collaborative interactions, and foster partnerships and other alliances among Government laboratories, academia, industry and venture capitalists. It will also create incentives for sharing precompetitive information (including negative results) and conduct some translational research of its own.[85]

5. CONCLUSION

The evidence suggests that what economist Fritz Machlup famously said about the patent system applies equally well to the Bayh-Dole Act:

> If we did not have a … system, it would be irresponsible, on the basis of our present knowledge of its economic consequences, to recommend instituting one. But since we have had a … system for a long time, it would be irresponsible, on the basis of our present knowledge, to recommend abolishing it.[86]

The Bayh-Dole Act did not poison the wellspring, as its opponents feared. However, it has had a damaging effect in academic employment and reduced competition within the system overall. Because universities

---

83 Merges (1996).

84 Reichman & Uhlir (2004); Dedeurwaerdere (2010); Rai et al (2008).

85 FAQ: Proposed National Center for Advancing Translational Sciences (2011).

86 Subcommittee on Patents, Trademarks, and Copyrights of the Senate Commission on the Judiciary, 85th Congress (1958), 80.

tend to license on an exclusive basis, technological prospects are not competitively developed. And because faculty members are captive clients of their own TTOs, there is likewise no competition for managerial services. Despite these problems, it is not likely that this scheme will be altered significantly. However, competition could be restored by making faculty 'free agents,' able to shop for the TTO that best serves their needs. Alternatively, the Government could, in effect, compete with TTOs and inspire better performance. Public discussion of the problems is also helping TTOs differentiate between revenue maximization and technology transfer, leading universities to debate the question of their ultimate responsibility to their faculty, their students, their funders, and society.

Despite these ambiguities, the U.S. Government has been urging other countries to follow its lead and adopt Bayh-Dole acts of their very own. But Machlup also added another sentence: 'This last statement refers to a country such as the United States of America – not to a small country and not a predominantly nonindustrial country, where a different weight of argument might well suggest another conclusion …'[87] The U.S. experience indeed counsels caution, and not merely for small countries. As *Stanford* demonstrates, Bayh-Dole complicates employment relationships. While it interested universities in technology transfer, the Act also increased the cost of technological inputs and made the process for acquiring them difficult to negotiate. A public domain strategy for Government-funded work may be the superior choice for most economies.

REFERENCES

Association of University Technology Managers (2007), 'Nine Points to Consider in Licensing University Technology', http://www.autm.net/Nine_Points_to_Consider.htm

Audretsch D.B., T. Aldridge and A. Oettl (2006), 'The Knowledge Filter and Economic Growth: The Role of Scientist Entrepreneurship', *Kauffman Foundation Large Research Projects Research*, <http://sites.kauffman.org/pdf/scientist_entrepreneurs_audretsch.pdf and http://papers.ssrn.com/sol3/papers.cfm?abstract_id=1456458>

Azoulay, P., W. Ding and T. Stuart (2006), 'The Impact of Academic Patenting on the Rate, Quality, and Direction of (Public) Research', *National Bureau of Economic Research Working Paper Series, Working Paper 11917*, Jan., http://www.nber.org/papers/w11917

---

[87] Ibid, 80.

Azoulay, P, W. Ding and T. Stuart (2007), 'The Determinants of Faculty Patenting Behavior: Demographics or Opportunities' 63 *Journal of Economic Behavior and Organization* 599

Bar-Shalom, A. and R. Cook-Deegan (2002), 'Patents and Innovation in Cancer Therapeutics: Lessons from Cell Pro' 90 *Milbank Quarterly* 637

Ben-Atar, D. (2004), *Trade Secrets: Intellectual Piracy and the Origins of American Industrial Power*, 2nd edn, Yale University Press

Bush, V. (1945), *Science – The Endless Frontier: A Report to the President on a Program for Postwar Scientific Research*, U.S. Government Printing Office

Calderini M, C. Franzoni and A. Vezzulli (2007), 'If Stars do not Patent: An Event History Analysis of Scientific Eminence and the Decision to Patent in the Academic World' 36 *Research Policy* 303

Campbell E.G., J.B. Powers, D. Blumenthal and B. Biles (2004), 'Inside the Triple Helix: Technology Transfer and Commercialization in the Life Sciences' 23(1) *Health Affairs* 64

Dreyfuss, R.C., D.L. Zimmerman and H. First (eds) (2010), *Working Within the Boundaries of Intellectual Property: Innovation Policy for the Knowledge Economy*, Oxford University Press

Dedeurwaerdere, T. (2010), 'Global Microbial Commons: Institutional Challenges for the Global Exchange and Distribution of Microorganisms in the Life Sciences' 161(6) *Research in Microbiology* 414

Ding, W., F. Murray and T. Stuart (2006), 'An Empirical Study of Gender Differences in Patenting among Academic Life Scientists' 313 *Science* 665

Dreyfuss R.C. (2000), 'Collaborative Research: Conflicts on Authorship, Ownership, and Accountability' 53 *Vanderbilt Law Review* 1161

Dreyfuss R.C. and J.P. Evans (2011), 'From Bilski Back to Benson: Preemption, Inventing Around, and the Case of Genetic Diagnostics' 63 *Stanford Law Review* 1349

Eisenberg R.S. (1996), 'Public Research and Private Development: Patents and Technology Transfer in Government Sponsored Research' 82 *Vanderbilt Law Review* 1663

Eisenberg R.S. (2001), 'Bargaining over the Transfer of Proprietary Research Tools: Is the Market Failing or Emerging?' in R.C. Dreyfuss, D.L. Zimmerman and H. First (eds), *Expanding the Boundaries of Intellectual Property*, Oxford University Press

Endy D. (2005), 'Foundations for Engineering Biology' 428 *Nature* 449

FAQ: Proposed National Center for Advancing Translational Sciences (2011), <http://feedback.nih.gov/index.php/faq-ncats/>

Goulding, R., E. Marden and R. Manion (2010), 'Alternative Intellectual Property for Genomics and the Activity of Technology Transfer Offices: Emerging Directions in Research' 16 *Boston University Journal of Science and Technology Law* 194

Henderson R., A. Jaffe and M. Trajtenberg (1998), 'Universities as a Source of Commercial Technology: A Detailed Analysis of University Patenting 1965–1988' 80 *Review of Economics & Statistics* 119

Hottenrott, H. and S. Thorwarth (2010), 'Industry Funding of University Research and Scientific Productivity', <https://lirias.kuleuven.be/bitstream/123456789/300789/1/MSI_1103.pdf>

Huang K.G. and F.E. Murray (2009), 'Does Patent Strategy Shape the Long-Run Supply of Public Knowledge? Evidence from Human Genetics' 52 *Academic Management Journal* 1193

Jensen K.L. and F.E. Murray (2005), 'Intellectual Property Landscape of the Human Genome' 310 *Science* 239

Kapczynski, A., S. Chaifetz, Z. Katz and Y. Benkler (2005), 'Addressing Global Health Inequities: An Open Licensing Approach for University Innovations' 20 *Berkeley Technology Law Journal* 1031

Kenney M. and D. Patton (2009), 'Reconsidering the Bayh-Dole Act and the Current University Invention Ownership Model' 38(9) *Research Policy* 1407

Kesan, J.P. (2009), 'Transferring Innovation' 77 *Fordham Law Review* 2169

Kesan, J.P. and R.C. Shah (2005), 'Shaping Code' 18 *Harvard Journal of Law and Technology* 319

Lei, Z., R. Juneja and B.D. Wright (2009), 'Patents Versus Patenting: Implications of Intellectual Property Protection for Biological Research' 27(1) *Nature Biotechnology* 36

Leydesdorff, L. and M. Meyer (2010), 'The Decline of University Patenting and the End of the Bayh-Dole Act' 83 *Scientometrics* 355

Litan R., L. Mitchell and E.J. Reedy (2007), *Commercializing University Innovations: Alternative Approaches*, National Bureau of Economic Research Working Paper, May, <http://www.visible-cities.net/documents/Commercializing_University_Innovation.pdf>

Markman, G.D., P.H. Phann, D.B. Balkin and P.T. Gianiodis (2005), 'Entrepreneurship and University-Based Technology Transfer' 20(2) *Journal of Business Venturing* 241

Merges, R.P. (1996), 'Contracting into Liability Rules: Intellectual Property Rights and Collective Rights Organizations' 84 *California Law Review* 1293

Merton, R.K. (1973), *The Sociology of Science: Theoretical and Empirical Investigations*, University of Chicago Press

Mimura, C. (2010), 'Nuanced Management of IP Rights: Shaping Industry–University Relationships to Promote Social Impact' in R.C. Dreyfuss, D.L. Zimmerman and H. First (eds), *Working Within the Boundaries of Intellectual Property: Innovation Policy for the Knowledge Economy*, Oxford University Press

Massachusetts Institute of Technology (2009), *Entrepreneurial Impact: The Role of MIT*, <http://www.kauffman.org/uploadedFiles/MIT_impact_full_report.pdf>

MIT (2010), Inventions and Proprietary Information Agreement, <http://web.mit.edu/tlo/www/downloads/doc/IPIA.doc>

MIT Technology License Office (2010), *Guide to the Ownership, Distribution and Commercial Development of MIT Technology*, <http://web.mit.edu/tlo/www/community/policies.html>

Mowery, D.C. and R.R. Nelson (eds) (2005), *The Oxford Handbook of Innovation*, Oxford University Press, p. 209

Mowery D.C., B.N. Sampat and A.A. Ziedonis (2002), 'Learning to Patent: Experience and the Quality of University Patents 1980-–1994' 48(1) *Management Science* 73

Mowery, D.C. and A.A. Ziedonis (2000), 'Numbers, Quality, and Entry: How the Bayh-Dole Act Affected U.S. University Patenting and Licensing?' 1 *Innovation Policy and the Economy* 187

Murray, F. and S. Stern (2007), 'Do Formal Intellectual Property Rights Hinder the Free Flow of Scientific Knowledge? An Empirical Test of the Anti-Commons Hypothesis' 63 *Journal of Economic Behavior and Organization* 648

National Research Council of the National Academies, Committee on Intellectual Property Rights in Genomic and Protein Research and Innovation (2006), *Reaping the Benefits of Genomic and Proteomic Research*, The National Academies Press
National Research Council of the National Academies (2004), Committee on Intellectual Property Rights in the Knowledge-Based Economy, *A Patent System for the 21st Century*, The National Academies Press
National Research Council of the National Academies, Committee on Management of University Intellectual Property (2010), 'Lessons from a Generation of Experience, Research and Dialogue', *Managing University Intellectual Property in the Public Interest*, The National Academies Press
Oliver, A.L. and J.P. Liebeskind (2009), 'Science and Discoveries in the Context of Private and Public Knowledge Creation and Learning in Networks for Learning and Knowledge Creation in Biotechnology' in A.L. Oliver and J.P. Liebeskind (eds), *Networks for Learning and Knowledge Creation in Biotechnology*, Cambridge University Research
Owen-Smith, J. and W.W. Powell (2001), 'To Patent or Not: Faculty Decisions and Institutional Success at Technology Transfer' 26 *Journal of Technology Transfer* 99
Owen-Smith, J. and W.W. Powell (2003), 'The Expanding Role of University Patenting in the Life Sciences: Assessing the Importance of Experience and Conductivity' 32 *Research Policy* 1695
Rafferty M. (2008), 'The Bayh-Dole Act and University Research and Development' 37 *Research Policy* 29
Rai, A.K. and R.E. Eisenberg (2003), 'Bayh-Dole Reform and the Progress of Biomedicine' 66 *Law and Contemporary Problems* 289
Rai, A.K., J.H. Reichman, P.F. Uhlir and C. Crossman (2008), 'Pathways Across the Valley of Death: Novel Intellectual Property Strategies for Accelerated Drug Discovery' 8 *Yale Journal of Health Policy and Ethics* 1
Reichman, J.H. and P.F. Uhlir (2004), 'A Contractually Reconstructed Research Commons for Scientific Data in a Highly Protectionist Intellectual Property Environment' 66 *Law and Contemporary Problems* 315
Rhoten, D.R. and W.W. Powell (2010), 'Public Research Universities: From Land Grant to Federal Grant to Patent Grant Institutions' in D. Rhoten and C. Calhoun (eds), *Knowledge Matters*, Columbia University Press
Sampat, B.N., D.C. Mowery and A.A. Ziedonis (2003), 'Changes in University Patent Quality after the Bayh-Dole Act: A Re-Examination' 21 *International Journal of Industrial Organization* 1371
Sampat, B.N. and R.R. Nelson (2002), 'The Emergence and Standardization of University Technology Transfer Offices: A Case Study of Institutional Change' in P. Ingram and B. Silberman (eds), *The New Institutionalism in Strategic Management*, JAI Press
Secretary's Advisory Commission on Genetics, Health and Society (2010), *Gene Patents and Licensing Practices and their Impact on Patient Access to Genetic Tests*, <http://oba.od.nih.gov/oba/sacghs/reports/SACGHS_patents_report_2010.pdf>
Siegel, D.S., R. Veugelers and M. Wright (2007), 'Technology Transfer Offices and Commercialization of University Intellectual Property: Performance and Policy Implications' 23(4) *Oxford Review of Economic Policy* 640
Stern, S. (2004), 'Do Scientists Pay to be Scientists?' 50(6) *Management Science* 835

Subcommittee on Patents, Trademarks, and Copyrights of the Senate Commission on the Judiciary (1958), 85th Cong, *An Economic Review of the Patent System* (Comm Print) (prepared by Machlup F)

Swamidass, P. and V. Vulasa (2009), 'Why University Inventions Rarely Produce Income? Bottlenecks in University Technology Transfer' 34 *Journal of Technology Transfer* 343

Tahvanainen, A.J. and R. Hermans (2011), *Making Sense of TTO Production Function: University Technology Transfer Offices as Process Catalyst, Knowledge Converters and Impact Amplifiers*, <http://ideas.repec.org/p/rif/dpaper/1236.html>

Thursby, J.G. and M.C. Thursby (2007), 'University Licensing' 23(4) *Oxford Review of Economic Policy* 620

Thursby, J.G. and M.C. Thursby (2011), 'Faculty Participation in Licensing: Implications for Research' 40 *Research Policy* 20

U.S. Department of Justice Press Release (2001), *First Foreign Economic Espionage Indictment; Defendants Steal Trade Secrets from Cleveland Clinic Foundation*, May 8, <http://www.justice.gov/criminal/cybercrime/Okamoto_SerizawaIndict.htm>

Van Overwalle, G., E. van Zimmeren, B. Verbeure and G. Matthijset (2007), 'Models for Facilitating Access to Patents on Genetic Inventions' 7 *Nature Reviews Genetics* 143

Walsh, J.P., A. Arora and W.M. Cohen (2003), 'Effects of Research Tool Patents and Licensing on Biomedical Innovation' in W.M. Cohen and S.A. Merrill (eds), *Patents in The Knowledge-Based Economy*, National Research Council

Williams H.L. (2010), *Intellectual Property Rights and Innovation: Evidence from the Human Genome*, National Bureau of Economic Research, Working Paper No. 16213, <http://www.nber.org/papers/w16213>

Wright, B.D. (2010), 'Agricultural Biotechnology: The Quest to Restore Freedom to Operate in the Public Interest' in R.C. Dreyfuss, D.L. Zimmerman and H. First (eds), *Working Within the Boundaries of Intellectual Property: Innovation Policy for the Knowledge Economy*, Oxford University Press

Yang, P.Y. and Chang Yuan-Chieh (2010), 'Academic Research Commercialization and Knowledge Production and Diffusion: the Moderating Effects of Entrepreneurial Commitment' 83 *Scientometrics* 403

5. Establishing clear rights in academic employee inventions: lessons learnt from *University of Western Australia v Gray*

Ann L. Monotti

1. INTRODUCTION

Researchers in business are likely to be engaged under express contracts to develop new products or processes in secret that will be manufactured and exploited for the sole benefit of their employer's business. In contrast, the standard academic employment contract commonly expresses research duties in broad terms that reflect their right to pursue a freely chosen research question without any direction from an employer as to the nature of the question or the form in which to disseminate its outcomes. Most of this research will be disseminated openly and in ways that encourage public use and further development for the benefit of the community.

However, some academic research will produce inventions with commercial potential that require protection under patent laws to realise that potential effectively. As the Australian Law Reform Commission (ALRC) concluded in the context of publicly funded research in its *Genes and Ingenuity* Report: 'If research results are not protected effectively, they may fail to attract commercial developers and products that require considerable industry development may not be created. If valuable research is not identified and utilised appropriately, its value to the public may not be realised.'[1]

The effective protection and utilisation of the value in patentable inventions requires clear identification of the owner of those inventions.

[1] ALRC (2004), [11.46].

In the case of employee inventions, a variety of legal principles will determine where ownership vests, namely:

1. Section 15 of the *Patents Act 1990* (Cth) vests all property rights in the inventors, thus recognising the pre-eminent position of the individuals whose creativity and intellectual effort enabled them to conceive the invention. The section makes no express provision for an employer's rights but provides in more general terms in s 15(1)(b) and (c) how a person might gain rights from the inventor. An employer's rights could arise from entitlement to have the patent assigned to it or because the employer derives title from the inventor.
2. From an employer's entitlements under employment law, including an implied term in law to vest ownership of employee inventions in the employer and arising under the implied duty of good faith or pursuant to fiduciary obligations.
3. By the operation of other express or implied agreements. These might include agreements that relate to specific research grants, collaborative research relationships and the provision of specific resources to enable those projects to proceed.

The prevailing default policy that Australian universities adopt to achieve predictability is to vest the university with ownership of academic employee inventions.[2] They then regulate the interactions and balance the interests of the competing groups in those inventions in a manner set forth in a specially negotiated agreement or in their Intellectual Property (IP) statute, regulation or policy, the provisions of which are incorporated within the employment contract. This approach follows government recommendations that favour institutional ownership of employee inventions for a variety of reasons that relate principally to achieving greater certainty and efficiency in dealings with third parties.[3]

The following brief review of this policy development explains why universities claim ownership of academic employee inventions and why, until recently, they felt secure in the validity of their claims, even in the absence of any express entitlement.[4] An overview of the impact of the full Federal Court decision in *University of Western Australia v Gray* on university claims is followed with some tentative observations on the

---

[2] Universities unlike private sector employers do not claim all benefits from commercial exploitation.

[3] OECD (2002), 9, 11; DEST (2003), xii; ALRC (2004), [11.51].

[4] Monotti with Ricketson (2003).

lessons to be learned from this case for establishing clear rights in academic employee inventions so that they can be exploited effectively for the benefit of all parties including the university employer.

2. POLICY DEVELOPMENT TO VEST EMPLOYEE INVENTIONS IN THE UNIVERSITY EMPLOYER

There has always been some degree of patenting activity and engagement with industry within Australian universities. However, at least three developments in the latter part of the 20th century alerted both universities and the Australian government to the need to provide a clear framework for ownership of any inventions (and other IP) that arise in the course of academic research. The first was the opportunity for fundamental university research to result in patentable inventions that were suitable for commercial exploitation. This opportunity followed the emergence of new technologies such as biotechnology[5] that blurred the former categories of 'pure' or 'applied' research. The second influence was the perceived social and economic benefit arising from the increase in patenting university research in US universities that followed the enactment of the *US Bayh-Dole Act*.[6] The third was the developing international awareness that innovation played a vital role in enhancing the strength of a country's economy. Increasingly governments recognised that some research outputs would generate social and economic benefits more effectively if they are patented before being placed in the public domain.[7]

A combination of these and other developments led to the design of competitive research grants and programmes which required universities to have policies and procedures in place to protect and deal with any intellectual property rights (IPRs) that resulted from the funded research. These initiatives aimed at encouraging particular behaviour within Australian universities, including (1) their detection and protection of patentable inventions; and (2) the development of collaborative research and other links with industry which were more likely to generate research outcomes with commercial potential. Faced with this relatively unfamiliar challenge of commercial exploitation of university research on a larger scale, the universities sought advice from their national peak body

---

5 *Diamond v Chakrabarty* (1980) 447 US 303.

6 PL 96–517, *Patent and Trademark Act Amendments of 1980*; Dreyfuss, this volume.

7 OECD (2002), Executive Summary, 9.

at the time, the Australian Vice-Chancellors' Committee (AV-CC) 'on how to deal with questions of ownership of IP generated within the institutions by staff, students, and under agreements with outside bodies, and under grants of sponsorship'. A 1993 discussion paper[8] provided this advice in guidelines that recognised the autonomy of each institution. Its approach did not question whether a university employer is different from any other employer, but assumed it is entitled as a matter of law, like other employers, to be the owner of IP that 'is clearly generated by staff in the course of undertaking duties under their contract of employment'.[9] The common law provided that an employer's entitlement in any situation would then turn on 'that which it was the employee's "duty" to do – and for which the employee was paid'.[10] A claim to own inventions would arise when employment duties required or anticipated the exercise of an employee's inventive faculty.[11]

However, while the recommendation in these and other papers supported university claims to the legal rights in an employee invention in any particular case[12] to enhance effective protection and engagement with third parties, it did not support unconditional vesting of the legal title. Rather, it required these rights to be balanced with the obligation to protect and manage those rights for the benefit of the inventors and other relevant parties. The vehicle that universities used to implement this policy was an IP statute, regulation or policy whose terms were to be incorporated by reference into the standard form of academic employment contract for each level of appointment.

In contrast to the entitlement to copyright in course materials and lectures, the assertion of university ownership of patentable inventions in return for a distribution of rights proved to be largely uncontroversial for at least five reasons. First, as discussed above, there was a general expectation that universities were entitled to own academic employee inventions in any event if they were created in the performance of the

---

[8] AV-CC (1993); updated AV-CC (1995), AV-CC (2002). The National Tertiary Education Union published a model IP policy.

[9] AV-CC (2002), [3.2.2(a)].

[10] *UWA v Gray* (2010) 179 FCR 346, [152] (Lindgren, Finn and Bennett JJ).

[11] *Sterling Engineering Co Ltd v Patchett* [1955] AC 534, 544; *Adamson v Kenworthy* (1932) 49 RPC 57; *Fine Industrial Commodities Ltd v Powling* (1954) 71 RPC 253; *Triplex Safety Glass Co Ltd v Scorah* [1938] Ch 211; *Worthington Pumping Engine Co v Moore* (1902) 20 RPC 41; *British Reinforced Concrete Co v Lind* (1917) 34 RPC 101; *Edisonia Ltd v Forse* (1908) 25 RPC 546.

[12] AV-CC (1993); AV-CC (1995); AV-CC (2002), [3.2.2(a)].

duty to research. That expectation continued to underpin policy until the decision in *University of Western Australia v Gray* negated this implied entitlement. For example, Principle 4 of the 2001 National Principles of Intellectual Property Management for Publicly Funded Research, published to provide a consistent national framework for the management and exploitation of IPR generated by publicly funded research, provides: '*Recognising the Common Law rights of research institutions as employers*, the ownership and the associated rights of all IP generated by the NHMRC and the ARC supported research will initially be vested in the research institutions administering the grants' [author emphasis].[13]

Second, institutional ownership was not intended to be absolute: it was always to be balanced in some way with the distribution of rights and obligations in the IP among the competing groups of people with some interest in that IP. Hence, it seemed to observers that the approaches adopted would enable academics to enjoy better rights in their inventions than were available for researchers employed in private business.[14] Third, it would be relatively uncommon for an academic inventor to have the experience, resources and contacts to assume the responsibility for costs involved in protecting and exploiting any inventions. The access to university resources was likely to be welcome in many instances. Fourth, there was, and remains, a general reluctance to accept joint ownership because it is often recognised as 'a barrier to commercialisation, as industry partners are generally unwilling to invest in developing intellectual property where negotiation with multiple parties will be necessary'.[15] Finally, ownership of most inventions created by academic employees would vest in the inventors in practice. Universities would assert rights only in those inventions that were suitable for protection and in which their technology transfer office personnel were skilled in facilitating their further development and exploitation. They would assign on request of the inventor or inventors the rights in those other inventions, while ensuring in appropriate cases and with the grant of a non-exclusive licence to the university that this would not compromise the ability for others to continue their research.

---

13 ARC et al. (2001).

14 AIPPI (2004), 1.4.

15 ALRC (2004), ch 11, [11.45].

3. LACK OF CERTAINTY IN UNIVERSITY OWNERSHIP OF EMPLOYEE INVENTIONS: THE FIRST CHINKS

3.1 Regulatory Failures

Two decisions shook the confidence of Australian universities in the validity of their claims. The first was a decision in the Supreme Court of Victoria in *Victoria University of Technology v Wilson*.[16] The case involved a claim by the university to ownership of an invention of a software design relating to international trade facilitation that was created by two senior academics in the School of Applied Economics. The claim was based upon the express provisions of an IP policy which required employee inventors to assign their rights in the inventions to the university. This claim was unsuccessful because the university had failed to properly promulgate its IP policy. The consequence of the failure was that its invalid provisions could not be incorporated by reference into the employment contract. Following this decision, all Australian universities no doubt checked that their own policies and legislation were validly passed.

The failure of the express obligation to assign inventions forced the university to rely next upon the implication of a term in law into the employment contract to justify its claim to ownership. In line with the AV-CC guidelines and the *National Principles of IP Management*, Nettle J also assumed that the academic employment contract is one into which the term is implied and proceeded to examine the question whether the duties of employment are inconsistent with the implied term. The university was also unsuccessful on this ground, with Nettle J finding that neither academic employee was employed to invent e-commerce systems. Such inventions were never part of the business of the School of Applied Economics. Instead, 'the sort of research which had been undertaken … was confined to academic research of the kind that is directed to the preparation and presentation of peer reviewed learned papers'.[17] While he considered and rejected the implied term in these circumstances, Nettle J accepted that the implied term might apply to academics working in university departments where it was usual practice to create e-commerce inventions in the performance of research.

---

[16] *VUT v Wilson* (2004) 60 IPR 392; Moodie (2004); van Caenegem (2010); Reid (2004); Arup (2008).

[17] *VUT v Wilson* (2004) 60 IPR 392, [110].

Hence, although this decision alerted universities to the need to confirm that their own IP policies or regulations were properly promulgated and enforced, they remained confident that the common law implied term could apply to academic employment in appropriate circumstances when any express terms were unenforceable.

3.2 Regulatory Failures, Lack of Statutory Power, and Negation of Implied Term in Law

The later decisions in *University of Western Australia v Gray*[18] rocked this confidence and the foundations on which university entitlement to academic employee inventions is based. Their vulnerability was more extensive than mere regulatory failures to properly promulgate policies and extended to their contractual arrangements with their employees.

This complex case involved, among other things, a claim by UWA that it had proprietary rights in inventions arising from Dr Gray's employment obligations in the university as a Professor of Surgery. His employment contract contained a duty 'to undertake research, to organise research and generally to stimulate research among the staff and students'. The dispute arose because Dr Gray's research resulted in inventions with potential commercial value. Without seeking the permission of UWA and without its knowledge, he applied during his employment for a number of patents for those inventions and later assigned rights in those inventions to a company that he established for the purpose of their commercial exploitation. The university could have acquired rights through an express covenant in the employment contract to assign all or any subset of defined IPRs which might arise from Dr Gray's employment duties, but it had not done so.[19]

As in *VUT v Wilson,* there were regulatory failures which reinforced the earlier lessons for universities to review the validity of their policies and their practical ability to enforce their provisions.[20] One related to the failure to maintain the appropriate regulatory structures within the university that were required under its 1971 Patent Policy. The other related to the failure to properly promulgate the 1996 Intellectual Property Regulation and this rendered unenforceable any obligation contained in that regulation to assign to UWA all rights in any inventions

---

[18] *UWA v Gray* (2010) 179 FCR 346; Arup (2008); Clark and Stewart (2009); Pittard (2009); van Caenegem (2010).

[19] *UWA v Gray (No 20)* (2008) 246 ALR 603, [12] (French J).

[20] Clark and Stewart (2009), 32.

created during the course of employment.[21] At the trial, French J identified a further impediment that would stifle university claims to ownership made in regulations: a lack of statutory power. He concluded that the *University of Western Australia Act 1911* (WA) (as amended) gave UWA no power to make regulations which alienate or interfere with property rights not vested in UWA.[22] He pointed out that '[a] regulation beyond power could not change contractual arrangements so as to affect a staff member's proprietary rights'.[23] This finding was not challenged on the appeal. The only circumstances in which a regulation would be effective to expropriate IPRs that vested in the inventor would be if UWA 'could be empowered by its Act to make a regulation appropriating rights derived from the Patent Act'.[24] It is likely that the reasoning applied by His Honour is equally applicable when the university uses an IP statute, as opposed to a regulation, as the vehicle for expropriation.[25]

A further ground on which UWA based its entitlement was the implied term in law as to ownership of employee inventions. The court accepted the principle as identified in *Sterling Engineering Co Ltd v Patchett*[26] – 'an employer is entitled to any product of the work which the employee is paid to do' – but derived little assistance from *VUT v Wilson*. They concluded that while Nettle J considered 'the applicability of the implied term relating to employee inventions and rejected it in respect of academic staff members, he was not called upon to consider, and did not consider, the question whether universities were different as a category of employer'.[27]

It was this distinctiveness of a university as an employer and the special and differentiating aspects of academic employment within it that formed a central pillar in their determination that Dr Gray's contract, and academic employment contracts as a sub-class, are not within a 'class, type or kind to which the legal implication applies'.[28] Two distinctive elements of universities as employers were highlighted to demonstrate

21 *VUT v Wilson* (2004) 60 IPR 392; Monotti (2004).

22 *UWA v Gray (No 20)* (2008) 246 ALR 603, [13]; *UWA v Gray* (2010) 179 FCR 346, [53]. It is unlikely a government would grant such wide powers. E.g., Victorian university statutes were replaced in 2009 without the grant of power that would enable claims to be made using internal legislation.

23 *UWA v Gray (No 20)* (2008) 246 ALR 603, [90].

24 Ibid, [89].

25 Monotti (1997).

26 [1955] AC 534, 544; *UWA v Gray* (2010) 179 FCR 346, [158].

27 *UWA v Gray* (2010) 179 FCR 346, [210].

28 *UWA v Gray (No 20)* (2008) 246 ALR 603, [1365]; *UWA v Gray* (2010) 179 FCR 346, [205].

the differences between a university as an employer and any other employer. First, a university is created to serve public purposes and there was no evidence to suggest that the traditional public function as an institution of higher education is replaced by the pursuit of commercial purposes. Dr Gray was not required to advance the commercial purposes of the university when he selected his area of research. Secondly, in some universities, academics are not only employees but also members of the university – membership being 'integral to their status and place in the university'. To focus simply on terms of the contract of employment ignores a distinctive dimension of that relationship and contrives the context in which the issues are to be resolved.[29]

As to the distinctiveness of academic employment, the court drew upon various considerations to reject the UWA contention that 'Dr Gray's duty to undertake research was, in the circumstances, sufficient to bring it within the class of contract attracting the implied term'. A significant consideration – and one which alone may have justified dismissal of UWA's claim – was that Dr Gray had no duty to invent.[30] According to the court, a general duty to research is not transformed into a duty to invent merely because the academic employee chose to explore research from which inventions could result.[31] This finding is consistent also with an approach taken in the UK decision in *Greater Glasgow Health Board's Application* – it can be said that invention could be 'a useful accessory to his contractual work ... but not really part of it'.[32] In addition, the court was emphatic that a deemed contingent duty to invent 'requires an untenable implication. It is not what Dr Gray's terms of employment required; there is no "necessity" for it being implied by law into the employment contracts of university academic staff; and, importantly, it is inconsistent with the researcher's freedom to share and to publish research results.'[33]

Apart from the two-faceted character of an academic staff member's relationship with a university which is referred to above – employee and member – the court highlighted various freedoms that were present in Dr Gray's employment circumstances as further distinguishing features of the regulation of academic employment: freedom to publish (there were

---

[29] *UWA v Gray* (2010) 179 FCR 346, [96], [185]; *UWA v Gray (No 20)* (2008) 246 ALR 603, [1361].

[30] *UWA v Gray* (2010) 179 FCR 346, [206].

[31] Ibid, [194].

[32] *Greater Glasgow Health Board's Application* [1996] RPC 207, 222.

[33] *UWA v Gray* (2010) 179 FCR 346, [197]; Monotti with Ricketson (2003), [6.56]–[6.67]; [6.168]–[6.175].

no constraints to keep anything secret), freedom to choose the subject and manner of research without being subject to the duty to invent, and freedom to collaborate with external organisations distinguished academic employment from commercial research environments. In their view it was impossible to reconcile such freedoms with a duty implied in all academic employment contracts to invent and to maintain secrecy of research outcomes. There would be significant 'collateral impact' on research practices that would arise if the term was implied into all academic contracts. The court explained that the implied term to hold inventions in trust for the employer is underpinned by a duty not to make unauthorised use or disclosure of confidential information generated in the course or conduct of research. A duty – as distinct from a strategic and rational decision – to maintain research results in confidence could prohibit unauthorised publications containing confidential information and impair 'academic collaborations and exchanges because of the potential for participating in breaches of confidence'. The court rejected the suggestion of a 'free standing' implied term that was unsupported by an obligation of confidence. Their reasoning was that the employee could then choose to destroy the patentability of the invention by 'progressively putting the research results into the public domain'.

Two further features of Dr Gray's own circumstances that complete the picture of the regulation of academic employment relationships were the extent to which Dr Gray and his collaborators were expected to and were successful in acting as entrepreneurs in soliciting research funding and the necessity for entering into collaborative research relationships with external organisations. In essence, the circumstances of Dr Gray's employment and of the research environment in which he worked 'were a long way removed from the situations that gave rise to the common law implication of employer ownership of employee inventions that were developed in the course of, and as a product of, what the employee was employed actually to do'.[34]

The failure of the university to satisfy this threshold test of establishing that Dr Gray's contract was within a class of employment contracts to which the legal implication applies meant that the assessment would not proceed to an examination of whether the term was to be implied into the particular employment contract. Nevertheless, the court observed that some classes of academic employment contracts may fall within the class or kind to which the implied term applies. It distinguished the case of an academic who is employed under a special contract 'to produce an

---

[34] Ibid, [206].

invention or to do research directed to producing an invention. Such a contract may well warrant the implication in law of a term that the rights in relation to the invention produced would belong to [the employer]'.[35] Therefore, some academic employment contracts might still be within a class to which the implied term applies; but no one is suggesting that this should form the basis for entitlement.

It is important to highlight in passing the limited grounds on which UWA pleaded its case as this will undoubtedly have some effect upon the precedential value of the decision. For example, the judges noted the claim in contract was almost exclusively focused on the duty to research and felt this 'rather contrives the context in which his function and his responsibilities to UWA fall to be analysed and characterised'.[36] Second, there were no pleadings on breach of the duty of good faith and fidelity or breach of the fiduciary obligations owed by professional employees to their employers not to profit from their position at the expense of their employer and to avoid conflicts of interest and duty.[37] Third, there was no pleading of an implied contractual term in fact. Finally, the lack of argument relating to the significance or otherwise that membership of UWA might have on the employment relationship may 'have contrived the context in which the issues in this proceeding are to be resolved'.[38] For example, would membership have influenced the legal analysis of the employment contract for the purposes of evaluating the necessity or otherwise to imply the term in law? All judges were at pains to make no evaluation or further comment on any of these grounds, so their impact on the outcome of future disputes remains uncertain.

Following this decision, the immediate task facing universities was to ensure both the validity of the claims already made and to examine and confirm their entitlement to enter past agreements with third parties. The next task was to review employment contracts and IP policies to enhance the security of university ownership when this is the agreed default position with respect to academic employee inventions that are patentable and have potential commercial value.[39] In this regard, the full court highlighted the unsatisfactory nature of relying upon implied terms for determining entitlement to employee inventions in either universities or

---

35 Ibid, [178], [163].

36 Ibid, [123].

37 Successfully pleaded: *VUT v Wilson* (2004) 60 IPR 392, [149].

38 *UWA v Gray* (2010) 179 FCR 346, [96]; *UWA v Gray (No 20)* (2008) 246 ALR 603, [1361].

39 Clark and Stewart (2009); van Caenegem (2010); Arup (2008).

private sector employment. They observed within the university employment context:

> If a less crude and more fair and reasonable result is to be achieved which balances the respective interests of a university and its academic staff members, this will need to be done by or under legislation or, if it could be devised, by an express contractual régime appropriate to the circumstances of the individual case.[40]

In contrast with the view of French J that legal title should vest absolutely in the inventors, this passage makes no recommendation as to where legal title should vest. Instead, it endorses the need for the beneficial interests to be balanced in some way that is fair and reasonable. Hence, the first essential feature in developing any regime is to agree upon where legal title should vest as a default position so that title to deal with the rights is clear. A consequence of this decision is the likely re-engagement within university communities with questioning the merits of university claims to entitlement to own academic employee inventions as a default position.[41] The second essential feature is to agree upon what should be the appropriate balance of rights. This question cannot be explored here, but any evaluation should commence with the various formulae for sharing rights and obligations that exist at present in university IP regulations. The third issue is to develop a legal structure that enhances the enforceability of obligations and claims. The aim is to achieve a clear, unambiguous entitlement to ownership.

4. THE WAY FORWARD: SOME THOUGHTS ON AN APPROPRIATE LEGAL STRUCTURE

4.1 Vesting Title and Balancing Rights

A desirable default position for ownership of academic employee inventions is one that facilitates their protection, further development and exploitation so that benefits (and obligations) are balanced in a fair and reasonable way. Therefore, it is unacceptable to vest title absolutely in academic employee inventions in the university employer in the way that might happen in private enterprise either through express contractual provisions or under the operation of the implied term in law. The earlier

---

40 *UWA v Gray* (2010) 179 FCR 346, [211].

41 van Caenegem (2010).

overview of policy development in this area shows that absolute employer ownership of academic employee inventions has never and will never be an option.

Absolute ownership remaining in the employee inventors without any obligation to grant benefits of some kind to the employer and co-workers is consistent with the negation of the implied term in law and with the philosophical underpinning of patent law that vests ownership in the inventors. This option appears to have the support of French J when he suggested that universities might well consider offering expert commercialisation facilities that are then offered to the academic in return for a negotiated share in the IPR.[42] However, experience has identified a number of practical difficulties that arise when specially negotiated agreements are the sole source of university entitlement. First, a balanced outcome is not assured. There is the potential for the university and co-workers to go away empty handed in circumstances that would seem objectively to be unfair and unreasonable. Once the value of an invention is known it would tempt many individuals to retain those benefits for themselves if they have no obligation to provide some share to their employer.[43] While it may be argued that an express agreement should be negotiated, the reality is that the complex nature of universities and of academic employment within them may render it impractical to identify in advance all the particular circumstances that require an express agreement to govern the vesting of interests in inventions.

Second, there is the risk that third parties may insist on dealing with the university rather than with individual inventors.[44] Melbourne University flirted for a brief period with a policy that vested ownership in the inventors but reverted to an assertion of ownership in Statute 14.1 Intellectual Property following difficulties of this nature. Third, a failure of all inventors to agree on the appropriate protection, grant of mutual rights and exploitation of their invention is likely to cause disruption or complete frustration in any continuing research and development. Fourth, it is unresolved whether inventors who are employed in a (partially) publicly funded institution to engage in research should be entitled to own their inventions without an obligation to return some benefits to their institution. This issue cannot be satisfactorily resolved here, but it is suggested a default position may be an acknowledgement that legal

---

42 *UWA v Gray (No 20)* (2008) 246 ALR 603, [14]; van Caenegem (2010); Cornish (1992).

43 *VUT v Wilson* (2004) 60 IPR 392.

44 ALRC (2004), [11.32].

ownership of academic employee inventions is not absolute and that beneficial interests in the invention should be shared in some fashion.

4.2 A Legal Structure that Enhances the Enforceability of Obligations and Claims

One approach that should be rejected is to introduce a duty to invent into the standard academic employment contract. Such a duty may be appropriate in individual circumstances but not as a default clause in all employment contracts. There are several objections to this option, not least of which is the potential for alienating academic staff. More specifically, such a duty would introduce into the employment relationship the 'common law duty of fidelity and the equitable duty of confidence to protect for the employer's benefit confidential (and other) information generated during the course of the employment, which is not, or is not yet, patentable'.[45] This obligation of secrecy would be contrary to the recognised freedom of academics to choose their area of research and the manner in which to pursue that research. Second, a duty to invent imposed on all academic employees would be inconsistent with the statutory objects of Australian universities. For example, a common objective is that which appears in the *Monash University Act 2009* (Vic), namely 'to undertake scholarship, pure and applied research, invention, innovation, education and consultancy of international standing and to apply those matters to the advancement of knowledge and to the benefit of the wellbeing of the Victorian, Australian and international communities'.[46] Third, a duty for all academic employees to invent without discrimination introduces a sense of absurdity into the employment relationship. How does a law academic, a historian, a sculptor, or a musician comply with this obligation? The refinement of the duty to one that requires the academic to pursue practical applications of discoveries that arise from their research and that lend themselves to commercial development may avoid the absurdity of a duty to invent. However, this duty will undermine academic freedom to engage only with pure research and to publish results openly and it cannot be enforced against an unwilling academic.

Another (favoured) approach is to continue to make express ambit claims in employment contracts but to review their scope to (a) avoid the risks of invalidity exposed in the *UWA v Gray* judgment and (b) minimise

---

45 *UWA v Gray* (2010) 179 FCR 346, [207].

46 *Monash University Act 2009* (Vic), s 5(c).

the risk of a challenge on the grounds of being an unreasonable restraint of trade. The broad policy for ambit claims appears in guiding principle 2 of the University of Melbourne Statute 14.1 Intellectual Property:

> As a matter of general principle, the University asserts ownership of intellectual property, other than scholarly works, created by its academic staff. This is congruent with Commonwealth law and reflects the prevailing expectation of national granting bodies. This approach provides clarity and security of ownership rights, thereby promoting the commercialisation of research and the transfer of knowledge to the wider community.[47]

The incorporation of a default ambit claim in the standard employment contract is not incompatible with the design of an express contractual regime appropriate to the circumstances of the individual case: it supports that regime as a 'safety net'. The challenge is to design an express ambit claim that is acceptable to academic employees and enforceable. For example, some commentators have warned of the risks in drafting express terms with a 'one size fits all' approach and of the need to 'take into account the practicalities of their enforcement'.[48] The metes and bounds of the circumstances in which the ambit claims would operate are complex and existing regimes that operate within universities can provide the starting point for a review. Furthermore, it is possible that they might be contentious and limited now that academic employees understand that the common law does not support employer ownership of academic employee inventions that arise from performance of unspecified academic research. The essence of the strategy is to remove the sole focus for entitlement from the uncertain scope of duties of employment to include a range of identified circumstances that are fair and reasonable and that would survive any validity challenge on grounds of unreasonable restraint of trade.[49]

4.3 By or Under Legislation

The Full Court suggested that another vehicle for achieving a balanced and fair result would be legislation,[50] which presumably refers to either the University Acts or the *Patents Act 1990* (Cth). The potential for

---

[47] Made 11/12/06; approved 12/3/07.

[48] Clark and Stewart (2009), 32.

[49] *Herbert Morris Ltd v Saxelby* [1916] 1 AC 688.

[50] *UWA v Gray* (2010) 179 FCR 346, [211]. In the HC proceedings in which UWA unsuccessfully sought special leave to appeal, Gummow J emphasised the need for express arrangements. Also van Caenegem (2010), 163.

legislative reform is too complex a topic for examination in this chapter, but some brief comment is necessary to highlight the limitations that exist here. First, the experience of Victorian universities in 2009 when their Acts were re-enacted suggests that legislative reform will not develop through the expansion of legislative powers to acquire intellectual property by non-consensual means. The re-enacted statutes give the universities express authority to make any statutes and regulations with respect to a variety of matters including intellectual property,[51] but they have no express power to acquire intellectual property by non-consensual means. The application of the 'well established presumption against construing legislation as interfering with vested interests'[52] is likely to limit the power to dealings with intellectual property that is vested in the university by some other means such as express assignment. The second option for legislative change that involves amendment of the *Patents Act 1990* (Cth) to provide expressly for employee inventions including academic employee inventions is also problematic.[53] A provision that merely codifies the common law will take us no further and will not achieve a balanced outcome because it will vest ownership in one party only. A provision that singles out universities for special treatment is one that would require considerable debate, both for including such a provision and identifying its scope. For example, employer entitlement that is based on the creation of inventions in performance of employment duties will be ineffective to vest ownership in the university employer unless the provision is drafted in a way that overcomes the *UWA v Gray* requirement for a 'duty to invent' and clarifies the nature of the duties that will give rise to employer entitlement. The complexity of academic employment suggests that a statutory change is unlikely to happen quickly if at all.

5. CONCLUSION

It is necessary to have clear principles for vesting ownership in inventions to maximise their efficient and effective protection under patent law and their further development and exploitation. As explained earlier in this chapter, the agreed default policy that granting bodies and universities adopted from the early 1990s was one that would vest legal title in

---

51 E.g., *University of Melbourne Act 2009* (Vic), ss 28, 29, 35. *UWA v Gray (No 20)* (2008) 246 ALR 603; Monotti (1997).

52 *UWA v Gray (No 20)* (2008) 246 ALR 603, [86].

53 E.g., *Patents Act 1977* (UK) s 39 and Pila, this volume.

employee inventions in the university on the assumption that it was best placed to protect and manage the rights in a fair and reasonable way for the benefit of all interested parties. This vesting of legal title was not to be absolute: there was a common understanding that the common law implied term would not produce an appropriate outcome for university inventions. The common law implied term no doubt played some part in the largely universal acceptance of this default legal ownership position but the term did not dictate the actual outcomes in terms of vesting of beneficial interests in the invention.

Theoretically the negation of this underlying assumption of university entitlement might reinvigorate the debate as to who should own the inventions that are created by academic employees during their employment.[54] However, in any debate that might ensue it needs to be recalled that the negation of the implied term in law is one factor among many that are relevant to the development of policy in this area. It is expected that express contracts that govern the specific circumstances and that are negotiated within a collegiate and co-operative environment will apply to the vast majority of cases where inventions are patented and exploited. However, a default position that recognises the need for some fair and reasonable balance of beneficial interests is important to protect the rights of all interested parties against the individual who seeks to exclude others from the fruits of commercial exploitation of an invention to which they have contributed in some identifiable way that warrants some tangible recognition.

REFERENCES

AIPPI Australia (2004), *Report Q183: Employers' Rights to Intellectual Property*, <https://www.aippi.org/download/commitees/183/GR183australia.pdf>

Anderson, B. and F. Rossi (2010), *The Flow of Knowledge from the Academic Research Base into the Economy: the Use and Effectiveness of Formal IPRs and 'Soft IP' in UK Universities*, IPO, <http://www.ipo.gov.uk/pro-ipresearch/ipresearch-right/ipresearch-right-gen.htm>

ARC, AVCC, IP Australia, NHMRC, ATICCA, DETYA, DISR (2001), *National Principles of Intellectual Property Management for Publicly Funded Research*, <http://www.arc.gov.au/pdf/01_01.pdf>

Arup, C. (2008), 'Employee Inventions: Labour Law Meets Intellectual Property' 21(2) *Australian Journal of Labour Law* 208

---

[54] The focus in reports had moved from debating vesting of ownership of rights in universities to consideration of models for transferring IPRs from universities to industry, government and other external stakeholders. E.g., Anderson and Rossi (2010).

Australian Law Reform Commission (2004), *Genes and Ingenuity: Gene Patenting and Human Health*, ALRC Report 99

Australian Vice-Chancellors Committee (1993), *Ownership of Intellectual Property in Universities: A Discussion Paper*, AV-CC

Australian Vice-Chancellors Committee (1995), *Ownership of Intellectual Property in Universities: A Discussion Paper*, AV-CC

Australian Vice-Chancellors Committee (2002), *Ownership of Intellectual Property in Universities: Policy and Good Practice Guide*, AV-CC

Clark, T. and A. Stewart (2009), 'Securing Ownership of Employee Inventions' 31(1) *Law Society of South Australia Bulletin* 30

Cornish, W.R. (1992), 'Rights in University Inventions: The Herchel Smith Lecture for 1991', 1 *European Intellectual Property Review* 13

Department of Education Science and Training (2003), *Analysis of the Legal Framework for Patent Ownership in Publicly Funded Research Institutions*, DEST

Monotti, A.L. (1997), 'Who Owns my Research and Teaching Materials – My University or Me?' 19(4) *Sydney Law Review* 425

Monotti, A.L. (2004), 'Ownership of Academic Employee Inventions: Victoria University of Technology v Wilson' 26(8) *European Intellectual Property Review* N-129

Monotti, A.L. with S. Ricketson (2003), *Universities and Intellectual Property: Ownership and Exploitation*, Oxford University Press

Moodie, G. (2004), 'Victoria University of Technology v Wilson & Ors: The Supreme Court of Victoria Tries Some Socio-legal Analysis in Reconceptualising the Role of Academics' 13(2) *Griffith Law Review* 225

Organisation for Economic Co-operation and Development (2002), *Turning Science into Business: Patenting and Licensing at Public Research Organisations*, OECD

Pittard, M. (2009), 'The Contract of Employment and Inventions: Legal Principles for Fleshing out Duties by Implying Terms' *Employment Law Bulletin* 124

Reid T. (2004), 'Academics and Intellectual Property: Treading the Tightrope' 9(2) *Deakin Law Review* 759

van Caenegem, W. (2010), 'VUT v Wilson, UWA v Gray and University Intellectual Property Policies' 21(3) *Australian Intellectual Property Journal* 148

6. Professional and academic employee inventions: looking beyond the UK paradigm

Justine Pila

1. INTRODUCTION

The vast majority of inventions are devised by employees, raising the question, who is entitled to patent them?

Historically, in the United Kingdom, a patent could only validly be granted to a 'true and first inventor'.[1] While employers were not 'true and first inventors' by virtue of their position as such, they did have contractual rights to the benefits of their employees' labour, including their employees' *inventive* labour. Over time this led to a recognition at common law that employers had (equitable) property rights in respect of inventions which their employees had made while performing an employment duty so to make.[2]

That was the position in the 1970s, which the UK government sought to codify in the Patents Act 1977 (UK), subject to the inclusion of certain provisions in favour of employees. The result was sections 39 to 43, which achieve the following three things. First, they create and allocate property rights in employee inventions (made after 1 June 1978) 'as between' the employee and employer,[3] and thereby determine entitlement to patent such inventions and whether a patent might be revoked for having been granted to a non-entitled person.[4] Second, they give an

1 Statute of Monopolies 1623 (21 Jac I, c 3) s 6; An Act to Amend the Law Touching Letters Patent for Inventions 1835 (Eng) s II; Patent Law Amendment Act 1852 (Eng) s X.

2 For a full account: Pila (2012).

3 1977 Act s 39(1) & (2).

4 1977 Act s 72.

employee whose invention is owned by his employer a right to compensation calculated in accordance with section 41 if, having regard to the circumstances of the case, including the size and nature of the employer's undertaking, 'the invention or the patent for it (or the combination of both) is of outstanding benefit to the employer'.[5] And third, they protect (a) employee inventors against the contractual diminution of their rights in (post-contract) inventions and associated patents without 'derogating from any duty of confidentiality' owed to their employers,[6] and (b) employee inventors and third parties against employer uses of copyright and design rights to obstruct the working, performing or patenting of employee-owned inventions.[7] In this chapter I will focus on the first of these things, namely, the allocation of property rights in inventions devised by employees.

The central provision in this regard is section 39(1), which states as follows:

> Notwithstanding anything in any rule of law, an invention made by an employee shall, as between him and his employer, be taken to belong to his employer for the purposes of this Act and all other purposes if –
>
> (a) it was made in the course of the normal duties of the employee or in the course of duties falling outside his normal duties, but specifically assigned to him, and the circumstances in either case were such that an invention might reasonably be expected to result from the carrying out of his duties; or
>
> (b) the invention was made in the course of the duties of the employee and, at the time of making the invention, because of the nature of his duties and the particular responsibilities arising from the nature of his duties he had a special obligation to further the interests of the employer's undertaking.[8]

According to section 39(2), '[a]ny other invention made by an employee shall, as between him and his employer, be taken for those purposes to belong to the employee'.

As section 39 does not differentiate between employees, it has been widely assumed to apply indiscriminately, without regard to employment field. In a recent article,[9] however, I have questioned that assumption, arguing that section 39(1) is built around a private sector paradigm, and

---

5 1977 Act s 40.
6 1977 Act s 42(2) & (3).
7 1977 Act s 39(3).
8 Also s 130(1) (defining 'employee').
9 Pila (2012).

that there exists a 'rational reason' in the sense of *Unilever v Shanks*[10] for departing from that paradigm in certain cases, including those involving academic and professional employees.[11] While that reason derives from legislative intent, and the common law experience which section 39 was enacted to codify, it is supported, I suggested, by policy considerations. They include the special issues raised by the 'propertisation' of the inventions of academic and professional employees, the appropriateness of morality-based limits on conceptions of 'property', and the undesirability of an ownership regime based on a paradigm in which not all employment relationships can be readily or satisfactorily accommodated. I suggested that such considerations have particular weight if the statutory paradigm is to become the means for 'sewing the fly buttons on' a statute regarded by post-1977 courts as having been poorly drafted,[12] as it raises the risk of the common law principles which section 39(1) was intended to enshrine becoming subverted by parliamentary caprice.

In the current chapter I build on this argument by considering its support in modern copyright and post-1977 patent law.

2. COPYRIGHT IN THE WORKS OF ACADEMIC AND PROFESSIONAL EMPLOYEES

Under the Copyright Act 1911 (UK), copyright in a work was first owned by its author[13] except in two specific cases. The first was where the work was an engraving, photograph or portrait, the plate or other original of which had been made for value under a commissioning agreement, in which case copyright was first owned by the commissioner of the original.[14] And the second (contained in section 5(1)(b)) was where the

---

[10] [2010] EWCA Civ 1283.

[11] By 'academics' I mean regular academic employees, as distinct, for example, from contract-based researchers and students. By 'professional employee' I mean a person employed in a 'profession' as commonly defined; namely, in an occupation 'in which a professed knowledge of some subject, field, or science is applied; a vocation or career, especially one that involves prolonged training and a formal qualification' (OED). Also Hughes (1963), 655. On the status of medicine as a profession: Dyer (1985), 72.

[12] E.g., *LIFFE Administration & Management v Pavel Pinkava, De Novo Markets Ltd* [2007] EWCA Civ 217, [102]; *Kelly v GE* [2009] EWHC 181 (PatC), [7]; *Unilever v Shanks* [2010] EWCA Civ 1283, [32].

[13] s 5(1).

[14] s 5(1)(a).

work had been made 'in the course of [the author's] employment' under 'a contract of service or apprenticeship', in which case copyright was first owned by the author's employer 'in the absence of any agreement to the contrary', and subject to a legislative proviso for certain periodical works.[15]

The Copyright Act 1956 (UK) retained both exceptions, the latter in section 4(4). During its passage, an assurance was sought in the House of Commons that whatever the proper application of that section, it would not alter the position of 'university professors'.[16] That position had been considered only once by the courts, in *Stephenson Jordan & Harrison Ltd v MacDonald & Evans*[17] four years previously. There the Court of Appeal had rejected a claim by a corporate employer to the copyright subsisting in certain lectures written by one of its employee engineers. Considering whether the works had been authored under a 'contract of service' within the meaning of section 5(1)(b) of the 1911 Act, Lord Evershed MR distinguished between works of authors 'engaged to do some specific work under a considerable measure of control, extending not only to the work he does but to the way he does it', and works of authors 'engaged more in the capacity of an independent contractor, for example ... a man engaged professionally'. Only the former were within the scope of the section, he said, and they did not include the lectures of people 'employed to give lectures'. The other Judges agreed, with Denning LJ in particular echoing Lord Evershed MR's connection between academic and professional employees in his suggestion that 'a doctor on the staff of a hospital, or a master on the staff of a school' who is employed 'to give lectures or lessons orally to students' and who reduces the lecture or lesson to writing, does so 'for his own convenience' and not as part of his contracted work. The connection was reminiscent of Viscount Hall's explanation of the Development of Inventions Bill 1948 (UK) in the House of Lords, as a means of encouraging 'medical and university researchers' to overcome their 'pride in the disinterestedness of [their] research', and their preference for publishing over commercializing their work, by creating a mechanism for their valuable and patentable ideas to be patented by the National Research Development Corporation 'for other than private profit'.[18]

Central to the reasoning of *Stephenson Jordan* is the idea that employers lack the control over and responsibility for employee lectures

---

[15] Also s 5(2); Copyright Act 1842 (UK) s 18.

[16] HC Deb (5th series) vol 553 cols 801–802 (4 June 1956).

[17] (1952) 69 RPC 10 (CA).

[18] HL Deb (5th series) vol 155 cols 571 (29 April 1948) 573–574.

to justify owning copyright in them. Thus, Lord Evershed MR and Morris LJ emphasized the inability of the plaintiff to 'command' its employees 'to give a lecture to any particular body on any particular topic'. This was notwithstanding that the lectures were of commercial value to the plaintiff as a source of advertisement for its services, that the employer may have had a right to copy and distribute the lectures, and that the lectures were composed (and permitted to be composed) in the plaintiff's time and using its resources. In combination with the legislative exchange above, the result was support for the suggestion that neither section 5(1)(b) nor its succeeding section 4(4) applied to academic or professionally authored works; and that whether a work was made 'in the course of [the author's] employment' under 'a contract of service or apprenticeship' depended in part on the author's field of employment.

Additional insight into the reasoning of the Court in *Stephenson Jordan* may be gleaned from the report of the Whitford Committee in 1977, the same year that section 39 of the 1977 (Patents) Act was introduced. In its report, the Whitford Committee had considered the ownership of copyright in teaching materials, and rejected the possibility of 'any comprehensive' legislative solution due to the variations in the conditions of teachers' employment and the nature of the materials which they produce.[19] Its analysis of the issues is highly instructive in its recognition of the distinctive nature of academic employment to which the Court in *Stephenson Jordan* had earlier alluded. For example, by referring to the suitability of teaching materials 'for use elsewhere', and the question 'whether a lecturer is entitled to take his work with him from one establishment to another', the Committee alluded to the phenomenon of academic staff mobility. Similarly, by referring to teachers producing material 'in their own time, possibly as an extra-curricular activity', and the question 'when a teacher is "off-duty"', it alluded to the vocational nature of academic work, the comparative independence of academic workers, and the difficulty of clearly defining academic obligations. Finally, by referring to the potential suitability of teaching materials 'for independent publication', and the question 'who has the right to sell such work or authorize its use by other authorities', it alluded to the phenomenon of research-led teaching, and the difficulty in general of distinguishing teaching from research. Read in context, these references support an implication that the courts' application of the statutory

[19] Report of the Committee to consider the Law on Copyright and Designs (1977) (Whitford Report), [569].

principles of copyright ownership ought to take account of the distinguishing conventions of academic employment.

In *Stephenson Jordan* and the Whitford Report, consideration was confined to copyright in lectures and other (university) teaching materials.[20] Subsequently, however, in 1991, the reasoning from *Stephenson Jordan* was applied to support a similar result in the context of a professionally authored work. That occurred in *Noah v Shuba*,[21] where copyright in a guide to hygienic skin piercing authored by an employee of the Public Health Laboratory Service (PHLS) was held to be owned by the author and not the PHLS. According to Mummery J, the guide was not written in the course of the author's employment as required under section 4(4), but rather 'at home in the evenings and at weekends and not at the instigation of or on the direction of PHLS'. This finding was notwithstanding: (a) that the author was expected under his employment contract 'to report on research work by means of contributions to appropriate scientific journals and … recognized learned societies'; (b) that the author was entitled to use and did use PHLS resources when writing the guide; (c) that the guide was created with the collaboration of PHLS staff, and marketed as a PHLS publication; and (d) that if copyright were owned by the author, he could prevent the PHLS from reprinting and disseminating the guide without his permission – a surprising outcome, it was suggested, 'in view of the public functions of PHLS and the public interest in the whole question of hygiene and infectious diseases'. In Mummery J's opinion, however, the author's position was 'very similar' to that of the employee in *Stephenson Jordan*. Further, even if he had been persuaded that the guide were written by the author *qua* employee, he would still have decided against PHLS. Specifically, he would have supported the implication of a contractual term excluding the operation of section 4(4) on the basis of the evidence that 'it had for long been the practice at PHLS for employees there to retain the copyright in work written by them, usually in the form of articles, in the course of their employment'.

Overall, the reasoning of Mummery J emphasizes the *Stephenson Jordan* point that in certain professional and academic contexts at least, employers lack sufficient control over and responsibility for their

[20] Also: White Paper (Cmnd 8302, 1981); HL Deb (6th series) vol 428 cols 1430–2 (31 March 1982).

[21] [1991] FSR 14 (HCJ).

employees' acts of authorship to justify owning any resulting copyright.[22] However, it also extends to the field of medical employment the suggestion of the Whitford Committee that principles of copyright ownership ought to respect the conventions of academic employment.[23] One possible implication of that extension and suggestion is a recognition by the courts that the law ought to protect the ability of salaried doctors to 'place concern for the public good ahead of their own [or their employer's] self-interest'.[24] The reason is that if it does not, it will harm the public interest by undermining the ethic that constitutes medicine as a profession. Central in this regard are considerations of trust and trustworthiness, and of morality as a limit on the exclusionary rights of 'property'.[25] According to Dyer, trust and trustworthiness are 'the keystone of medical virtue in the traditional canons of medical ethics', and 'the basis of what it means to be a professional, what it means to be ethical'.[26] If it is true that one function of the law is to facilitate trust in order to encourage human interaction,[27] then, it is submitted, there are strong policy reasons for the extension above.

The conclusion to be drawn from this discussion is that the principle of employer ownership of copyright in employee works may not apply in respect of the lectures and other writings of academic and professional employees,[28] either because such writings are not 'made in the course of their employment', or because to recognize it as applying would be contrary to the public interest in recognizing and supporting their constitutive ethical obligations to knowledge-driven enquiry and patient health, or, and in my suggestion, both. On this view, the reason that recognizing employer ownership of copyright in certain professional and academic works is inappropriate and undesirable lies in the distinctive nature of professional and academic employment, which is the context in which the phrase 'made in the course of ... employment' ought to be read. The implications for patent law are clear: if academic and professional employment is sufficiently distinctive in character to affect the application of statutory principles regarding copyright ownership, so too

---

22 Also Report of the Inter-Departmental Committee Appointed to Consider the Methods of Dealing with Inventions Made by Workers Aided or Maintained from Public Funds (1922) (Lee Report), [34].

23 Further Lee Report, [4].

24 Dyer (1985), 73.

25 Gray (1991), 280 et seq.

26 Dyer (1985), 73.

27 Pila (2009), 1.

28 Cornish (1992), 15.

it ought to affect the statutory principles regarding the ownership of inventions.

3. INVENTIONS OF ACADEMIC AND PROFESSIONAL EMPLOYEES

That academic and professional employees might attract different considerations when determining the ownership of inventions they have devised receives further support from the courts' application of section 39(1) itself; less for their explicit endorsement of differential treatment of employment fields *per se* than for their implicit endorsement of the reasoning above, that academic and professional employment differs from private sector employment in similar, and similarly fundamental, ways, with implications for the allocation of employment-related intellectual property.

To date the meaning of section 39(1) has been considered in four reported cases only.[29] The first of these is *Harris' Patent*,[30] where a slide valve invented by a manager of the Wey Valve Department of Reiss Engineering was held to be owned by its inventor, Mr Harris. According to Falconer J, while an invention made by an employee applying his mind to problems to which he had a duty to apply his mind was within the terms of section 39(1)(a), Mr Harris had no such duty. Rather, his duties were to sell and provide after-sales services for Wey valves, and extended neither to designing nor inventing products themselves, nor to investigating the cause of any technical difficulties with respect to any products. Further, his status and related duties and responsibilities did not support a 'special obligation to further the interests of [Reiss's] undertaking', with the result that section 39(1)(b) also did not apply. In contrast were the facts of *Staeng Ltd's Patents*,[31] decided on the basis of the guidelines from *Harris' Patent*. There, the Patent Office held that a method of securing an electric cable sheathing to the body of a connector backshell adaptor was owned by its inventor's employer, Hellermann Electric. The reason was the inventor's 'wide-ranging brief, *inter alia*, to find new products for Hellermann', and the relation of the invention to Hellermann's commercial undertaking. With *Harris's Patent*, the case suggests an early distinction by decision makers between two clear cases

---

[29] There exist also several unreported decisions of the Hearing Officer, many of which are referred to below.

[30] [1985] RPC 19 (PatC).

[31] [1996] RPC 183 (PO).

of employer and employee ownership: the first involving an employee with a history of research and development whose duties included the development of new products within the field of the employer's business remit; and the second involving an employee with no history of research and development whose duties did not include the development of new products, and who had no history of innovation with his employer.

Both *Harris' Patent* and *Staeng Ltd's Patents* involved private sector employees, and were decided on the basis of the relation of their inventions to their employment duties and the business interests of their employers.[32] Different was the third case of *Greater Glasgow Health Board's Application*,[33] which involved a junior registrar who had invented an optical device while employed at the Western Infirmary Tennent Institute. Considering who owned the device, the Hearing Officer held that the registrar's duty to treat patients implied a further duty to undertake research – namely, to attempt to resolve any problems he encountered while treating patients through 'analysis, experimentation and investigation' – the performance of which could reasonably have been expected to result in 'original ideas and … invention'. The fact that the registrar had made the invention out of hours and at home was, he held, largely irrelevant.

On appeal Jacob J overturned this decision, arriving instead at the 'very, very clear conclusion' that at the time the registrar devised the invention 'he was not acting in the course of his normal duties as a registrar'. Were it otherwise, he said, it would be 'the duty of this doctor, and probably every other registrar in the country, to devise if he can new ways of diagnosing and treating patients'. So too if the Hearing Officer were correct in finding that an invention might reasonably be expected to result from carrying out the registrar's duties, 'considerable complications and difficulties' could arise, including with respect to employees' recognized freedom to publish what they devise. His Lordship's conclusion was that just as justice and commonsense had been held in *Stephenson Jordan* to support academics' ownership of copyright in their lectures, so too they required that employee doctors own their inventions. Implicit was a view of the principle in each case as being the same; namely, the importance of protecting academic and medical professional conventions, including the freedom to teach and publish research without employer-imposed constraints. In supporting this view, Jacob J signalled

---

32 E.g., *Harris' Patent* [1985] RPC 19, 29; *Staeng Ltd's Patents* [1996] RPC 193, 200; *Ancon Ltd v Szewczyk* (O/301/04).

33 [1996] RPC 207 (PatC). The following account follows that in Pila (2012).

a preparedness to use the inventor's field of employment as a basis for rejecting an employer's claim to ownership on policy grounds, rather than merely (as had been suggested in *Harris' Patent* and *Staeng Ltd's Patents*) as a means for determining the limits of the inventor's employment duties. He also raised the possibility of an inventor defending a claim to ownership by showing that at the time of making the invention he had an occupation other than his employment to which his invention is more appropriately attributed,[34] and in doing so suggested an alternative basis for distinguishing the inventions of certain academic and professional employees, namely, that they are more appropriately attributed to their inventors' membership of an academic and professional community than to their employment duties *per se*. Regardless of whether that reading of *Greater Glasgow* is accepted, its result was to vindicate the original argument of Mr Fysh QC for the registrar 'that English law leans against employers', and that the dispute before the Court ought to be approached 'with a liberal pre-disposition towards the employee by applying the philosophy of English law that a professional man in particular is entitled to make use of his expertise unless the law says otherwise'.[35]

Counsel's distinction between private (or at least, non-professional) and professional employees is reminiscent of that drawn by the Court of Appeal and Viscount Hall above, and can be read as alluding to the changing character of medical practice. In the non-legal literature, that change has been associated with a process of deprofessionalization[36] as doctors have moved increasingly from self-employment to salaried employment, and 'to practice in complicated organizations which intervene in many ways between them and their clients'.[37] This process was described as early as 1963 as involving problems of freedom and autonomy: to whom does one owe one's obligations – one's clients or

---

[34] Also *Slack v SCS Consultancy Services* (O/174/00).

[35] [1996] RPC 207, 211. The only case since *Greater Glasgow* involving a s 39 claim of ownership in respect of an invention made by an employee doctor is *Sabanathan v Bradford Hospitals NHS Trust* (O/037/01), where the Hearing Officer applied *Greater Glasgow* to decide that the employment duties of a consultant surgeon to teach and treat patients did not imply a duty to undertake research, notwithstanding his employer's express 'hope' that he would 'promote and initiate research'.

[36] For a definition: Filc (2006), 273. On deprofessionalization and loss of autonomy: e.g., Freidson (1985); McKinlay and Arches (1985); Dyer (1985).

[37] Hughes, (1963), 664; Hoff (2003), 75; Fry (1973), 401–402. The process has been most pronounced in the US (Ferlie and Shortell (2001), 288. Cf Reiss (1955), 697.

employer – and 'what orders does one accept from an employer, especially one who is not a member of one's own profession and whose interests may not always be those of the professional and his clients?'[38] As the author of this passage went on to note,[39] the other side of this coin has been an increasing professionalization of certain businesses, involving their organization 'like a university, with the staff claiming a kind of academic freedom, participating in the formation of policy, and enjoying permanent tenure'.[40] In such statements, one sees again the conjunction of academic and professional employees.

The phenomenon of businesses organizing themselves as universities is well illustrated by the fourth of the section 39(1) cases: *LIFFE Administration & Management v Pavel Pinkava, De Novo Markets Ltd*.[41] In that case a system for trading financial instruments invented by a manager of the London Futures Exchange (LIFFE) was held to be owned by his employer, LIFFE. As the parties accepted, the inventor was a person of 'considerable academic and technical abilities' who was highly valued by LIFFE for his 'ideas', creativity, and problem-solving skills, and who enjoyed considerable intellectual freedom in carrying out his duties. This, in combination with his joint responsibility for developing LIFFE's product range, and his specifically assigned task of developing a new trading system, led the Court unanimously to conclude that section 39(1)(a) applied.

An important point on which their Lordships disagreed in *LIFFE* was the test for determining the second limb of section 39(1)(a): whether the circumstances of the case were 'such that an invention might reasonably be expected to result from the carrying out of [the employee's] duties'. According to the Chancellor, with whom Longmore LJ agreed, the proper test was whether an invention was reasonably expected to result from the carrying out of the inventor's duties, even if the (or a similar) invention was not, having regard to the circumstances in which the invention was made, including the identity and abilities of the inventor. Jacob LJ agreed, though rejecting the relevance of the latter on the ground that allowing them to be considered would discriminate against clever employees. 'I cannot accept that', he said,

---

38 Hughes (1963), 664–665. More recent commentators have also emphasized the increased influence of market forces as central to the process of deprofessionalization; e.g., Persaud (1991); cf Newman (1995).

39 Hughes (1963), 665; Drucker (1988).

40 Hutchins (1947), 135, quoted in Hughes (1963), 665.

41 [2006] EWHC 595; [2007] EWCA Civ 217.

> given all other factors being equal (contract terms, nature of job and so on), there can be a difference as to ownership depending on whether the individual employee is thick or brilliant. Why should an unimaginative employee get the invention because no-one expected him to come up with anything whereas an Edison in exactly the same situation has to hand it to his employer? I do not think Parliament intended an inquiry into the inventiveness of the individual employee or what, if anything, the employer knew about that. I think the last part of the section in its reference to 'the circumstances of the case' is referring just to the objective circumstances in which the invention was made – was the employee in a situation where one could objectively expect him to try to innovate?[42]

Closely related to his Lordship's reasoning on this point were his criticisms of the drafting of section 39(1)(a), and of the idea (which he regarded as implicit in that drafting) that one might ever reasonably expect an invention to result from research. 'Even in research departments', he wrote, 'most researchers do not make inventions, however hard they try.' Rather, they 'conduct research in the hope of making an invention':

> And that, I think, is what this requirement of s.39(1)(a) must be about. It uses 'an invention' not 'the invention' because it is saying that the employer will own any invention made from the carrying out of the employee's duties if the circumstances are such that an invention might result. If the employee is employed to innovate then it will normally follow that the provision is satisfied.[43]

This interpretation of section 39(1) as 'normally' applying to give an employer ownership of *any* inventions devised by a person employed *to innovate* reflects a broad approach to section 39 which is largely detached from the field of the inventor's employ. With respect to its breadth, and as the Hearing Officer had earlier remarked, it all but renders the second limb of section 39(1)(a) redundant. With respect to its detachment from the field of the inventor's employ, it sits uncomfortably with the view from earlier cases that for an invention to lie within section 39(1)(a), it must further the objectives of the employee's duty. This is because it shifts attention away from whether an invention might reasonably have been expected to result from (and in the light of the nature of) such duty to whether the employee performing it was 'an

42 [2007] EWCA Civ 217 [103].
43 Ibid.

intelligent and inventive man'.[44] Thus, it weakens the first limb of section 39(1)(a) as well, in addition to departing from the common law principles which section 39 was intended to codify.[45] As the 1970 Banks Committee's summary of those principles underlines,[46] the focus of the common law enquiry was on *the* invention (or a *similar* invention to that) which was *in fact* devised, and to which the employee inventor's obligations needed to relate. In addition, this focus was regarded by the Banks Committee (on whose Report section 39(1) of the 1977 Act was explicitly based) as consistent with both the contractual basis of the employer's claim, and the fact-intensive nature of the enquiry which that claim entailed.

In conclusion, it is submitted that until the decision of the Court of Appeal in *LIFFE*, the resolution of the ownership of employee inventions under the 1977 Act depended on a fact- and context-specific enquiry which, even if not endorsing a principle of differential treatment of different employment fields *per se*, nonetheless supported the idea of a paradigm case from which academic and professional employment is estranged in similar and similarly fundamental ways.[47]

No discussion of this area of law would be complete without reference to *University of Western Australia v Gray*,[48] which was strongly influenced by UK jurisprudence. The case is well known and I have discussed it elsewhere.[49] Suffice to say for present purposes that its significance lies in the support it offers for the suggestion above, that the policy rationale for section 39(1) – as for the common law principles from which it derived – does not apply in respect of university academics: first, because academics are engaged as members of a community of teachers and scholars, which community is constituted in part by its ethical commitment to the disinterested pursuit of truth; second, because the reality of academic employment is such that academics cannot be assumed to

---

44 Ibid, [78] (Chancellor, responding to an argument of counsel). This effect is apparent from *Ritchie v Envireneer Marine Cranes Ltd* (O/220/06) and *Ancon Ltd v Szewczyk* (O/301/04).

45 E.g., HL Deb (5th series) vol 382, cols 1160–1161 (5 May 1977).

46 Board of Trade (1970) (Banks Report), [442].

47 The ownership of an invention devised by a regular academic employee is yet to be considered by the courts. Note however *Secretary of State for Defence v Young* (O/070/01), where a patent application by two academic employees for jointly devised inventions was disputed by the government as the former employer of one of the inventors without any suggestion that the inventors' employing university might have had any claim to ownership.

48 [2009] FCAFC 116.

49 Pila (2010a); Pila (2010b).

research exclusively in their university's time and with university-provided resources; third, because of universities' lack of control over and responsibility for the authorship of lectures and research; and fourth, because of the effect that applying section 39(1) would have on principles of academic freedom, and through them, on the ethic which constitutes universities *qua* academe.[50] The result is further support in principle for the reading of section 39(1) as not applying where: (a) an employee makes an invention in the course of carrying out duties which he or she is qualified to carry out by virtue of his or her membership of a university or profession; and (b) the application of 39(1) in the context of the invention would significantly undermine the constitutive ethos of that university or profession. In addition it is submitted that such a reading might have additional purchase in the context of the current statutory regime for a combination of reasons. The first is that ownership determinations within that regime are not 'subject to contract'; and indeed, employees are protected against employer attempts to diminish contractually their statutory rights.[51] The second is that at least one Judge has recognised that 'although s.39(1) is a complete code, it lets the common law back in via the concept of duty', albeit in the context of confidentiality;[52] and that where an employee has an occupation other than his employment, that occupation might provide an alternative explanation and context for his act of invention.[53] And the third is the courts' preparedness to use, on some occasions at least, the field of the inventor's employ as a basis for restricting employers' claims to ownership, including with reference to considerations of public policy.[54]

It is important to emphasize the restrictive scope of the employment contexts to which this suggested exclusion applies. For example, by 'profession' is meant those enterprises 'in which standards of good practice are not just technically or contractually but also morally grounded',[55] and in particular, which are not merely subject to but constituted by ethical regulation.[56] Thus defined, the term includes the

---

[50] Cornish (1992), 14 (raising the question whether universities ought through their intellectual property policies to 'desert Academe in favour of ... Technopolis'). On universities qua Technopolis: HC Deb (5th series) vol 474, col 2087 (5 May 1950). Also HC Deb (5th series) vol 399, col 279 (19 April 1944).

[51] 1977 Act s 42(2); *LIFFE* [2007] EWCA Civ 217, [98].

[52] *LIFFE* [2007] EWCA Civ 217, [100] (Jacob LJ).

[53] See discussion at n 64 and associated text.

[54] Carr (2000), and discussion of *Greater Glasgow*.

[55] Carr (2000), 248.

[56] Ibid. Cf Howard (2001), 69–70.

classic professions of law, divinity and medicine,[57] of which medicine is that to which the exclusion is most likely to apply. This is because it is only doctors who might reasonably be expected to make an invention while carrying out their professional (including clinical) duties, and because recognising doctors' employers as owning their inventions would undermine their autonomy and authority, and in doing so, undermine that which constitutes medicine *qua* profession.

4. CONCLUSION

Speaking extra-judicially in 2011, one of the members of the *UWA v Gray* appellate Court suggested in a paper on an unrelated topic that Australian courts are more sensitive to context than their English counterparts when interpreting and applying English common law.[58] On one view, the current law governing the ownership of employee inventions is an example of this, since the introduction of the 1977 Act at least. On another view, however, the logic of the decision in *UWA v Gray* – that public policy may affect the application of those common law principles of invention ownership which section 39(1) was intended to codify, and cast the inventions of academic employees beyond the reach of those principles in certain cases at least – has its basis in English jurisprudence. Thus, if it is true that section 39(1) requires sensitivity to context, including the field of employment as an essential aspect of the facts of a case, then there is plainly scope in the UK for reasoning of the type in *UWA v Gray*.

Several additional points seem important to make. One is the lack of considered legislative attention that has been given to the impact of intellectual property rights on academic and professional employees.[59] A second is the social problems that can arise when a one-dimensional conception of the 'employment contract' is used as the means of resolving issues of invention ownership.[60] Third is the peculiarity of employee authors having a weaker position in law when compared with employee inventors, notwithstanding the legal recognition of authors' moral rights. Beyond the caprice of parliamentary law-making, and the

---

[57] Ibid, 69.

[58] Finn (2011).

[59] By contrast, the legal and non-legal academic attention has been substantial. Influential in *UWA v Gray* were Cornish (1992); Cornish and Llewellyn (2007); Monotti with Ricketson (2003).

[60] Freedland and Prassl, this volume.

view of some law and policy makers that the act of invention is a 'uniquely personal' one,[61] equivalent to a paradigm act of authorship, this peculiarity is difficult to explain. Fourth is the effect of section 39(1) in confirming the existence of 'property' in inventions[62] ('as between' inventors and employers at least), and the 'propertising' effects of the employment contract.[63] And fifth is the uncertainty over what constitutes an 'invention' in this context. In *LIFFE* this issue was important, as the subject matter was a 'business method as such' within the meaning of section 1(2)(c), and thus not an 'invention' for which a patent could validly be granted. Nor was it an 'invention' within the meaning of section 125(1), for it was not the subject of a UK patent or patent application. Nonetheless, the parties agreed that this did not prevent section 39(1) from applying, which agreement the Court accepted without extensive discussion. For the Chancellor, the reason seems to have been that Dr Pinkava's system was the subject of four US patent applications. For Jacob LJ, it was the nature of the system as an 'innovation'. It is submitted that of these two approaches, Jacob LJ's is the appropriate one. The reason is the purpose of section 39(1) in allocating the right to apply for a patent as between the inventor and his or her employer. Given this purpose, the section ought to cover alleged as well as actual 'inventions' within the meaning of section 1(1) of the Act.[64] By focusing on innovations, Jacob LJ achieved this. He also adverted to the definition of 'invention' contained in the Development of Inventions Act 1948 as 'any new process or new technique',[65] and to two of the central elements of inventions within the meaning of section 1(1) itself: their inclusion of a method and claim to advance an art.

However 'inventions' for the purposes of section 39(1) are defined, several consequences flow from their treatment as objects of exclusionary rights. First, such treatment supports the recognition of 'property' in information.[66] Second, it extends yet further the scope of the basic right contained in Article 1 of Protocol 1 of the European Convention on

---

[61] E.g., Banks Report 464; HC Deb (5th series) vol 399, col 276 (19 April 1944). Cf HL Deb (5th series) vol 128, col 631 (20 July 1943).

[62] Also 1977 Act ss 8(1)(a), 8(1)(b), 8(2), 41(1)(c)(i), 41(2)(b), 41(3).

[63] 1977 Act s 39(1); s 30(1); Pila (2012); Gray (1991) 299–300.

[64] *Viziball Ltd's Application* [1988] RPC 213 (PatC) 222 (Whitford J), consistent with 1977 Act s 125(1).

[65] See s 1(2).

[66] E.g., *Oxford v Moss* [1978] 67 Cr App Rep 183. This follows Lord Hoffmann's conception of inventions as 'information' in *Merrell Dow Pharmaceuticals Inc v Norton & Co Ltd* [1995] RPC 76 (HL) 86.

Human Rights, regarding the peaceful enjoyment of a person's possessions. Third, it supports the shift in conceptions of knowledge as process to knowledge as product, which shift has been described as responsible for the erosion of universities as organic communities of scholars.[67] And finally, and relatedly, it facilitates wider control over the transmission of knowledge, the dangers of which are illustrated by the history of the Export Control Bill 2002 (UK). That Bill originally enabled controls to be imposed by the State on the exportation of university teaching, until principles of academic freedom were raised in the House of Lords, and a vote taken to amend its scope.[68] Moving the amendment, Baroness Miller of Hendon described 'freedom of teaching, and freedom of research' as 'fundamental human rights',[69] consistent with the European Charter and Treaty on European Union:[70]

> The extension of the control of export of goods to the control of intangibles – the control of thoughts and ideas – is a radical step, unheard of in a democracy. It has serious constitutional implications. ... It is for that reason that a solid body of academia is totally opposed to some of the Government's proposed provisions, which are inappropriate in a country where universities have been centres of learning, research and discovery for over 900 years.[71]

And this, it is submitted, underlines the fundamental point of current relevance, which is that the two questions at the heart of this discussion – who has rights in employee inventions, and what are the nature and scope of those rights? – arise at the intersection of many different areas of public and private law, including constitutional law, intellectual property, employment law, competition law, personal property, human rights, and the law of obligations, and engage issues of fundamental social as well as industrial importance.

In concluding, it should be acknowledged that interpreting section 39(1) in the manner proposed would have significant consequences for universities and hospitals, and potentially for other employers of professional workers as well, and for their employees. On the other hand, it is unclear what those consequences would be. Partly this is because of the

---

[67] E.g., Scott (1984); Schuller (1990).

[68] HL Deb (6th series) vol 633, col 1128 (18 April 2002).

[69] Also art 13 of the Charter of Fundamental Rights of the European Union (OJ C 83/02).

[70] HL Deb (6th series) vol 633, col 1109; cf, col 1120.

[71] Ibid, col 1109. Generally cols 1108–1128.

uncertainty of the pre-1977 position, including its constitutional validity.[72] However, it is also due partly to the lack of policy attention given to the question what if any rights *ought* to subsist in the products of employees' intellectual efforts, and by whom if anyone ought those rights to be held? If it is true, as Professor Gray has argued, that there exist morally non-excludable resources and thus moral limits on 'property', then these questions are in need of principled, scholarly attention.

REFERENCES

Board of Trade (1970), *Report of the Committee to Examine the Patent System and Patent Law, The British Patent System*, Chair: Banks MAL (Cmnd 4407)

Carr, D. (2000), 'Education, Profession and Culture: Some Conceptual Questions' 48 *British Journal of Education Studies* 248

Cornish, W.R. (1992), 'Rights in University Innovations: The Herchel Smith Lecture for 1991' *European Intellectual Property Review* 13

Cornish, W.R. and D. Llewellyn (2007), *Intellectual Property: Patents, Copyright, Trademarks and Allied Rights*, 6th edn, Sweet and Maxwell

Drucker P. (1988), 'The Coming of the New Organization', *Harvard Business Review*, January/February

Dyer A.R. (1985), 'Ethics, Advertising and the Definition of a Profession' 11 *Journal of Medical Ethics* 72

Ferlie, E.B. and S.M. Shortell (2001), 'Improving the Quality of Health Care in the United Kingdom and the United States: A Framework for Change' 79 *Milbank Quarterly* 281

Filc, D. (2006), 'Physicians as "Organic Intellectuals": A Contribution to the Stratification versus Deprofessionalization Debate' 49 *Acta Sociologica* 273

Finn, P. (2011), 'England, Equity and Statute: the Curious State of Australia's Contract Law' (unpublished paper presented at the University of Oxford, 17 May)

Freidson, E. (1985), 'The Reorganization of the Medical Profession' 42 *Medical Care Review* 11

Fry, J. (1973), 'The General Practitioner in Europe; Great Britain' in 'Inside Europe: Medicine in the Common Market' *British Medical Journal* 396

Gray, K., 'Property in Thin Air' (1991) 50(2) *Cambridge Law Journal* 252

Hoff T.J. (2003), 'How Physician-Employees Experience their Work Lives in a Changing HMO' 44 *Journal of Health and Social Behaviour* 75

Howard, R.A. (2001), 'The Ethical OR/MS Professional' 31 *Interfaces* 69

Hughes, E.C. (1963), 'Professions' 92 *Daedalus* 655

Hutchins R.M. (1947), 'The Administrator' in R.B. Heywood (ed.), *The Works of the Mind*, University of Chicago Press

McKinlay, J.B. and J. Arches (1985), 'Towards the Proletarianization of Physicians' 15 *International Journal of Health Services* 161

Monotti, A.L. with S. Ricketson (2003), *Universities and Intellectual Property: Ownership and Exploitation*, Oxford University Press

---

[72] Pila (2012).

Newman P. (1995), 'Interview with Alain Enthoven: Is there Convergence between Britain and the United States in the Organization of Health Services?' 310 *British Medical Journal* 1652

Persaud, R.D. (1991), 'What Future for Ethical Medical Practice in the new National Health Service?' 17 *Journal of Medical Ethics* 10

Pila, J. (2009), 'Authorship and e-Science: Balancing Epistemological Trust and Skepticism in the Digital Environment' *Social Epistemology* 1

Pila, J. (2010a), 'Academic Freedom and the Courts' 126 *Law Quarterly Review* 347

Pila, J. (2010b), 'Who Owns the Intellectual Property Rights in Academic Works?', *European Intellectual Property Review* 609

Pila, J. (2010c), *The Requirement for an Invention in Patent Law*, Oxford University Press

Pila, J. (2012), '"Sewing the Fly Buttons on the Statute": Employee Inventions and the Employment Context' 32 *Oxford Journal of Legal Studies* 1

Reiss, A.J. (1955), 'Occupational Mobility of Professional Workers', *American Sociological Review* 693

Schuller, T. (1990), 'The Exploding Community? The University Idea and the Smashing of the Academic Atom' 16 *Oxford Review of Education* 3

Scott, P. (1984), *The Crisis of the University*, Croom Helm

United Kingdom (1922), *Report of the Inter-Departmental Committee Appointed to Consider the Methods of Dealing with Inventions Made by Workers Aided or Maintained from Public Funds*, HMSO (Lee Report)

United Kingdom (1977), *Copyright and Designs Law: Report of the Committee to consider the Law on Copyright and Designs*, Whitford Report, Cmnd 6732

7. EU perspectives on employees' inventions

Marie-Christine Janssens

1. INTRODUCTORY REMARKS

Typically, literature dealing with employees' inventions will refer to patent statistics which indicate that the great majority of applications for the protection of inventions are filed today by companies and only very few by individuals. Studies show that today over 90 per cent of patent applications in industrialized countries originate with employed inventors.[1] In view of this reality the lack of any international or European regulations governing this legal area – or even serious attempts in this respect – is all the more remarkable.

Amongst the many reasons that may explain this gap, one often refers to the particular nature of the issue of employees' inventions which is situated at the intersection between patent law and labour law. These two branches of law approach the question relating to the allocation of the rights to an employee's invention in very different ways, which makes the debate highly political.[2] Simply stated,[3] under labour law it is generally accepted that the employer may, in principle, claim and be entitled to the results of his employees' work ('fruits of labour principle'). The employee is compensated for his efforts by means of his salary and possible other advantages or benefits. It is the employment contract that constitutes the legal basis for the employer's ownership rights. The basic principle of intellectual property (IP), on the other hand, mandates that the rights to the creation or invention originate with the original

[1] Vivant (2010), 160; Bartenbach, et al (2009), 308; Trimborn (2009), preface. Some years ago this percentage was estimated at 80–85%; Yossifov (2004), 2.

[2] Bouvet (2006), 1.

[3] For more refined analysis: Drai (2010), 109.

author/inventor. In patent law, the latter rule follows from the 'inventor principle'.[4] Hence the employer may only acquire a derivate right.

Despite the underlying conflict of legal principles, most national legislatures have been able to come up with substantial legal solutions to regulate the matter of employees' inventions. With the aim to reconcile the opposite principles, most jurisdictions adhere to the principle of original inventorship by stipulating that even a service invention originally belongs to the employed inventor, whilst at the same time providing for a mechanism for transferring property rights from the inventor to the employer.[5]

Where national legislators have succeeded in finding a solution, there is no longer an excuse for the European legislator to refrain from action entirely. To the contrary; as I will argue in this chapter, the current socio-economic context – as well as the lack of uniform international regulations – supports the trend towards European harmonization. Before engaging in the debate on the usefulness and feasibility of a harmonized instrument, I will present a brief overview of the current situation.[6]

2. APPRAISAL OF THE CURRENT SITUATION

2.1 International Lacuna

As the major international treaties, and in particular the Paris Convention and the Patent Cooperation Treaty, are silent on the issue of ownership of employees' inventions, the logical starting point is to be found in the European Patent Convention (EPC). Article 60(1) states that the patent shall belong to the inventor but then goes on to make an exception for employees. If the inventor is an employee and a dispute arises as regards the right to the patent, the relevant national law is that of the location *where the employee is mainly employed*. If this law cannot be determined, article 60 refers to the national law of the place of business of the employer to which the employee is attached or, if this does not provide a clear answer, the place where the employee has the centre of his professional life, respectively. Clearly, this provision does not regulate the issue but merely includes a special rule on the applicable law as well

4 Straus (1990), 354; Ahner and Touati (2010), 72.

5 Junghans and Levy (2005), 74.

6 This chapter will not deal with university inventions.

as on the allocation of jurisdiction[7] in relation to disputes over the ownership of patents between an employee and an employer.

Moreover, article 60 is only useful in relation to applications for registrations which are filed under the EPC. For all other applications, the general conflict of law principles are to be applied. Consequently, depending on whether the employer files a European or a national patent application, different rules regulating ownership of the patent might be applicable. The EPC therefore increases legal uncertainty and is not really useful to solve problems in international relationships.[8]

2.2 Multiplicity of National Regulations

Ideally, one first has to learn from the experiences with the existing domestic laws before coming up with a meaningful proposal for a harmonizing instrument. Such an undertaking is far from simple as there are significant differences in the ways in which the 27 member states handle the legal issue of employees' inventions. Countries with very detailed regulations (e.g., Germany), on the one hand, and countries with no regulations at all (e.g., Belgium), on the other hand, offer a complex legal landscape with a patchwork of variances. As it is not the objective of this chapter to present a comprehensive overview of all national laws, the following conclusions are based on a textual check of the various legal texts[9] as well as on existing literature.[10] In sum, the disparities in the individual national regulations range from different legislative tools, terminology and definitions to divergent legal consequences, and in particular to the legal mechanisms that are used to allocate the rights in the invention and the scope of the right to remuneration. Finally, countries also differ as regards the issues of contractual freedom and settlement of disputes.

Looking at the choice of *the legislative instrument*, the vast majority of member states have regulated the issue of employees' inventions in their patent acts or IP codes. Some legislators, however, have enacted a special

---

[7] *Protocol on Jurisdiction and the Recognition of Decisions in Respect of the Right to the Grant of a European Patent* of 5 October 1973, art 4 (jurisdiction allocated to the courts of the contracting state whose law determines the right to the patent pursuant to EPC, art 60(1)).

[8] Cf Bartenbach et al (2009), 308; Villinger (2001), 3.

[9] Most of the texts currently in force in the member states are available at <http://www.jpo.go.jp/shiryou_e/s_sonota_e/fips_e/mokuji_e.htm> and <http://www.wipo.int/wipolex/en/>.

[10] See references at the end of the chapter.

law (Germany, Sweden, Denmark, Finland and Slovenia) whilst the reliance upon contract law or labour law has clearly not appealed to current EU legislators.[11] Technical differences of this kind are unlikely to be problematic in negotiating a harmonizing instrument.

Controversy is likely to occur in relation to the diverging *definitions and categorization of inventions*[12] that can be found in the national laws. Hence, what is deemed a 'service invention' in country B may not necessarily be likewise in country C. These different definitions of an employee's invention partly explain the differences that exist in the extent to which the employer is transferred or is entitled to claim the rights in such inventions. There are of course also policy reasons as well as underlying legal theories (IP approach versus labour law approach) that will explain the different treatment of service inventions. Furthermore there are different *legal mechanisms* that are used *to allocate rights* to the employer. They range from initial ownership (*ab initio*) or joint ownership,[13] a statutory transfer of the rights or presumption in this respect, to the attribution of a right to claim the invention. Such mechanisms may depend upon political, economic and social traditions, motives and aims of the individual state.[14]

The most significant differences between the various national laws turn around the question whether and how much *compensation* is payable to the inventor when a specific right in an employee invention is assigned to the employer. Certain legislation always mandates the payment of remuneration for service inventions while others provide no remuneration for all or certain service inventions. Due to the complexity of the various national laws, there is currently much uncertainty. Even where a right to compensation is recognized, the amount is most often unpredictable.[15]

---

[11] Examples for these latter solutions are found in Switzerland (contract law) and Mexico (labour law).

[12] Most countries distinguish service inventions from other (free) inventions. Often, with regard to service inventions, a distinction is made between 'permanent' and 'occasional' inventive activities. Many countries provide a third (in between) category which is either separately recognized or included in the general category of the service inventions. This category will typically include inventions outside the employee's regular or specifically assigned duties which were created using knowledge, techniques or methods specific to the employer or data provided by the employer or which relate to the employer's activities.

[13] This solution exists in Greece, albeit only in relation to 'dependent inventions' (Patent Act 1987 Article 6 (4)).

[14] Sagar and Nagarsheth (2006), 3.

[15] Peberdy and Strowel (2009–2010), 64.

Some notable decisions of courts in the UK and France[16] as well as in Sweden[17] and Japan[18] have significantly raised the bar by awarding exceptionally large amounts.

Another noticeable point of difference relates to the *admissibility of contractual arrangements* and their ability to override the statutory provisions. In most countries it is not possible to – and contracts are void that – deprive an employee of his statutory compensation rights. However, further contractual arrangements between employee and employer are often allowed to vary the level of compensation (e.g., France) or are permitted on the condition that the terms were agreed to after the invention has been created. (e.g., Germany).

The above disparities should not cast clouds over some important common rules – at least as regards their goal, maybe not their legal-technical implementation – that can be identified in most national legislation. Previous comparative research has shown that – even outside Europe[19] – similar structures exist in most countries as regards the ownership of employees' inventions. As a rule, most countries accept that, while ownership rights to inventions originate with the employee-inventor, employers can usually have access to inventions made within the scope of the employment relationship.[20] This is not surprising when the main justification that underlies national regulation is to stimulate innovation. From a policy viewpoint all jurisdictions compete against one another to receive investment in innovation sectors and therefore aim to provide an attractive, risk-free and cost-effective system for allocating patent rights. The fact that this common goal has resulted in diverging

---

[16] E.g., *Kelly v GE Healthcare Ltd* [2009] EWHC 181 (Pat), [2009] RPC 12 (UK); *PM v Société Nationale des Chemins de fer français (SNCF) et Vape Rail Intern. SAS (VRI)* (TGI Paris, 3e Ch, 19 May 2009) (France).

[17] See cases in Wolk (2008), 33.

[18] E.g., *Hitachi v Yonezawa*, 20 January 2004, Case Hei 14(ne) No 6451 (ordering the payment of 1.4 million dollars as reasonable remuneration to a former employee who had invented an optical disc reader; this decision was confirmed by the Supreme Court on 17 October 2006) and *Nakamura v Nichia Chemical Co Ltd*, 24 February 2004, Case No Heisei 13 (wa) 17772 (awarding 180 million dollars to the employee Nakamura for his invention of the blue light-emitting diode); see comments by Tessensohn and Yamamoto (2004) 63 and Shigetomi (2004) 7.

[19] E.g., von Falck and Schmaltz (2005), 913 (comparing Germany, France, NL, UK, US, Japan).

[20] Green Paper on the Community Patent and the Patent System in Europe, COM (1997) 314 final, 17–18.

statutory rules in individual countries is to be expected, given their often very different political, economic and cultural backgrounds.

3. OLD AND NEW ARGUMENTS IN FAVOUR OF HARMONIZATION

Despite regular discussions at the international,[21] regional (EU) and national level, previous attempts to harmonize the laws on employees' inventions have been unsuccessful. Nevertheless, many of the earlier recommendations remain relevant today, notwithstanding significant changes to economic, political and/or legal backgrounds.[22] Several scholars who have researched the issue in depth have published their valuable suggestions for a harmonizing initiative, including Joseph Straus,[23] Bernhard Villinger[24] and me.[25] It is unfortunate that the European Commission decided to drop the discussions in 1999 in its follow-up to the Green Paper on the Community Patent.[26] The lack of further initiatives suggests that the Commission has lost its appetite for dealing with this thorny issue.[27]

What new reasons can be put forward to justify harmonization of the regulations regarding employees' inventions in the member states? I will argue that the context of the 21st century is significantly different from the conditions which existed in the second half of the 20th century when most of the prior proposals were drafted. While the earlier arguments remain relevant today, new developments can be identified which sustain my call for the European legislator to review the issue.

---

[21] In particular, the ILO, WIPO and the AIPPI organization.

[22] Godenhielm (1966), 128; id (1975); Janssens (1996), 35; Villinger (2001), 10; AIPPI (2004). As regards, in particular, EU attempts: Ramm (1977); Neumeyer (1962), 75; Weinmiller (1975), 383; Cronauer et al (1988), 11; Bartenbach et al (2009), 308; Straus (1990), 364; Joos (1990), 368.

[23] Straus (1990), 353; see also Straus (1984a), 1–7; Straus (1984b), 402–406.

[24] Villinger (1991).

[25] Janssens (1996).

[26] Communication of 5 February 1999 COM (1999) 42, OJ EPO, 1999, 214 ff, in follow-up to *Green Paper on the Community Patent and the Patent System in Europe*, COM (1997) 314 final, 21; Goetzmann (2008), 174.

[27] Questions involving labour law issues are, in general, considered to constitute 'heisse Kastanien' in the process of harmonization; *see* Straus (1990), 355; Cornish (1990), 298.

3.1 Challenges of the Evolving Macro-economic Environment

In the second half of the last century a shift took place, whereby knowledge and IP replaced capital, buildings and machinery as a company's most important assets. This gradual transformation process has contributed today to a new economic reality where so-called non-material or intangible property has a very high value that generally exceeds that of material assets. In the resulting knowledge society, intellectual property rights (IPRs) are exerted in a different way in comparison to earlier decades. It is reasonable to assume that this global trend of amplified importance regarding IPRs also puts the issue of employees' inventions to the forefront.[28] The fact is that in most cases employees are the source of the intangible assets that make up 'the new global currency'.

What most distinguishes the 21st century from the 20th is the phenomenon of *globalization* with its focus on ever stronger global commercial competition. This economic background presents new challenges for companies to remain competitive and has nourished the tendency towards more global company structures that increasingly involve the posting of employees working in R&D to work in companies abroad. The new challenges have also encouraged an increased openness to new concepts such as open innovation which, in turn, has resulted in a greater openness to develop mutual research projects with different partners. The old tradition which saw companies conducting their research 'in house' with their own resources and facilities has changed. In the current globalized market economy, innovation has, in some sectors, become so costly, competitive and complex that collaboration between companies remains the only option. In view of the above, it is difficult if not impossible to maintain that the rules on employees' inventions remain a mere national issue. Rather it should be looked upon as a strategic issue.[29]

Another argument in support of harmonizing initiatives is the need to increase *legal certainty* as regards rules applicable to employees' inventions in Europe.[30] Consequences in respect of both ownership and

---

[28] Briggs (2006), 611. Ying (2007–2008), 763; AIPPI (2004), 1.

[29] Bartenbach et al (2009), 307; AIPPI (2004), 7; Michaux (2010), 8. In *Promoting Innovation through Patents – Green Paper on the Community patent and the patent system in Europe* COM (97) 314, June 1997 (1997 Green Paper), 18, the Commission admitted the impact of different national rules on research work and management. Cf Meier et al (2005), 168.

[30] Michaux (2010), 8.

remuneration constitute a factor that companies must take into consideration when determining their business strategy. These issues are currently governed by conflict of laws rules[31] which are not only difficult to unravel but may also add to already existing legal uncertainty because of the mandatory character of some rules in some countries.[32]

Last but not least, there is the issue of *equal treatment*. In the many transboundary constellations, employees of different subsidiaries may enjoy different protection and compensation. It is unfair for inventors who work in a common project to be subjected to different national rules. The situation is even more inequitable when they are joint inventors of the same invention. Why do national and community legislators advocate equal treatment and reduction of unreasonable distortions in competition but apparently condone inconsistency and possible legal barriers for ownership of employee inventions?

3.2 Stimulating Innovation and Inventiveness

We all know today's economic credo: innovation is the *condition sine qua non* for companies to compete – and even survive – in the current knowledge society. Assuming that there is convincing proof that harmonization has a positive impact on the innovative capacities and the competitive position of European industry[33] it may be possible to get the European legislator 'on board' to develop harmonized legislation. Any initiative contributing to the enhancement of innovation indeed fits nicely in Europe's 2020 strategy (replacing the equally relevant 2012 strategy). This so-called 'major flagship initiative' has placed innovation at the heart of Europe's future research and innovation policies.[34] A good legal solution may encourage (and reward) employed inventors whose inventive activities are at the source of most innovations.

Equally, we should remember that many employed inventors are not *aware* that they have any rights in their inventions and creations (e.g., SMEs). A coherent legal framework will facilitate the application of

---

[31] EPC, art 60.

[32] E.g., Germany; Bartenbach, et al (2009), 307.

[33] This issue requires empirical research, in particular from an economic angle taking into account the current macro-economic environment.

[34] Communication of 6 October 2010, *European 2020 Flagship Initiative Innovation Union*, COM (2010) 546 final.

provisions on inventors' rights and ultimately contribute to the establishment of a regulatory and economic environment that is supportive of invention and innovation.[35]

3.3 Recent Changes in the Legal Environment

As for the current legal environment in the EU, at least three new developments should be noted.

First, there was the *reform of the German Act on Employee Inventions* (ArbEG) in 2009 providing for some sort of automatic transfer of the rights to the employer (more precisely a legal fiction that the rights have been claimed by the latter).[36] This simplified allocation mechanism may have narrowed the 'gap' between the German system and most other systems which, in the past, was diagnosed as a major obstacle.

Second, the *ongoing process of unification of industrial property rights within the EU* has brought to the fore the question of the ownership of the IPRs for the various types of creations. The Commission's current strategy is to realize a seamless, integrated Single Market for IPRs.[37] Some work has already been accomplished here, including the establishment of the community trademark, the community plant variety right and the community design. The developments that are most useful when discussing the situation of employee inventions arise from the negotiations for establishing unitary patent protection in the EU which, as it seems today, will be pursued through an 'enhanced cooperation' between 25 of the 27 member states.[38] The goal of such cooperation is to facilitate the proper functioning of the internal market by, for example, increasing the number of inventors seeking patent protection throughout the Union, providing equal access to unitary patent protection to all inventors, innovative companies and patent-holders, improving the framework conditions for innovative businesses throughout the Union and eliminating, among participating member states the current fragmentation where

---

[35] Yossifov (2004), 3.

[36] *Gesetzs zur Vereinfachung und Modernisierung des Patentrechts* 31 July 2009 (BGBl. I/2009, Nr. 50 4 August 2009, S. 2521 (2526 ff). See particularly ArbEG § 6 (2).

[37] Communication from the Commission of 24 May 2011, *A Single Market for Intellectual Property Rights. Boosting creativity and innovation to provide economic growth, high quality jobs and first class products and services in Europe*, COM (2011) 287 final.

[38] Council Decision 2011/167/EU authorizing enhanced cooperation in the area of the creation of unitary patent protection [2011] OJ L76/53.

patent right 'borders' exist between member states.[39] Current fragmentation of the treatment of employees' inventions in the EU could equally be included in this line of reasoning.

Finally, the coming into force of the *Lisbon Treaty* on 1 December 2009 changed the legal basis for the creation of EU-wide IP rights by introducing the Treaty on the Functioning of the European Union (TFEU). According to article 118 'the European Parliament and the Council … shall establish measures for the creation of European intellectual property rights to provide uniform protection of intellectual property rights throughout the Union'. One may question whether this new article can regulate the issue of employees' inventions, which is situated at the intersection of IP law and labour law. On the other hand, it is worth noting that the European Commission included this issue of employee inventions as the subject of consultations in the framework of the 1997 Green Paper, when the EU had no direct legislative competence in the area of IP.

3.4 Overcoming Sceptical Voices

It is sometimes observed that legislative action at the community level to promote harmonization is neither necessary nor useful. In support of this opinion, reference is usually made to the relatively limited number of legal proceedings commenced by employee inventors. Furthermore, reasonable doubts are expressed as to whether harmonization of laws to increase protection for employee inventors will increase innovation. As was said before, we lack empirical data to substantiate this proposition. New research is necessary to assess the effects of a different (preferential) treatment between employee inventions and creations protected by IP rights, on the one hand, and other work results resulting from the employees' tasks.[40]

The reference to the limited number of reported cases, though correct, is not new and has limited impact on the debate because of the difficulty in determining the exact causes for this restricted litigation. Those who oppose the need for legislative action interpret the limited number of cases as proof that the law operates effectively.[41] This view is contested by supporters of harmonized legislative measures who identify other

---

[39] Recommendation of 2 February 2011 of the European Parliament on Council Decision 2011/167/EU, COM (2010) 0790, Recital T.

[40] Not all scholars are convinced that creations protected by IPRs merit a special allocation of rights treatment; e.g., Orbach (2002), 4.

[41] E.g., Bouvet (2006), 1 (assessing the situation in France only!).

reasons for the low number of disputes. The first is a concern amongst inventors whether the law – provided they are aware of it! – is effective at all.[42] The rise in litigation in Japan after employees became aware of some favourable decisions from courts awarding high amounts of remuneration supports this view.[43] More importantly, there is the indisputable asymmetry of power which implies that employees are economically and sometimes also socially dependent on their employer. This imbalance will in many cases prevent the employees disputing their inventor rights during their employment contract.[44] Not surprisingly, most reported cases were commenced following the termination of the relationship since employees are unlikely to jeopardize their careers by initiating a legal conflict with their employer.[45]

4. FORMAT FOR FUTURE HARMONIZATION

4.1 General Framework

The present chapter does not aim to propose concrete provisions for a European law regulating the issue of employee inventions but rather to reflect upon the challenges, the possible approaches and the scope of a future regulatory intervention. The goals to be pursued are, in essence, to protect employed inventors who work in a position of dependency, to reasonably resolve conflicting interests between the employer and the employee, to provide a high degree of legal certainty and to meet the economic needs for improved dynamics of innovation.

At the outset, the European legislator will have to make a choice as regards the *most appropriate instrument* to achieve the goal of harmonization. Whilst a cautious approach might point to the use of a 'recommendation', past experiences have demonstrated that this tool does not always produce the desired effect.[46] The most far-reaching instrument of a 'regulation', on the other hand, seems too premature (and possibly

---

42 Cf Orkin and Miller (2001), 68.

43 Sagar and Nagarsheth (2006), 8–9.

44 AIPPI (2004), 6; Janssens (1996), 303–304.

45 E.g., *Kelly v GE Healthcare Ltd* [2009] EWHC 181 (Pat), [2009] RPC 12 (UK); *PM v Société Nationale des Chemins de fer français (SNCF) et Vape Rail Intern. SAS (VRI)* (TGI Paris, 3e Ch, 19 May 2009) (France); Manley (1978), 29.

46 E.g., experiences with Recommendation 2005/737/EC of 18 October 2005 on collective cross-border management of copyright and related rights for legitimate online music services.

hasty) in view of the many differences currently existing between the national laws. Considering previous results that have been achieved by the instrument of a 'directive' in the sector of IPRs, I would consider such instrument as the best means to pave the way for a more uniform regulation of the matter of employee inventions. In particular, inspiration can be drawn from the experiences with the Trademark Directive which has proved to be a useful instrument to approximate the divergent domestic trademark laws through the combination of mandatory ('shall') and optional ('may') provisions.[47] In the hypothesis of a directive aiming at approximating the laws of the member states relating to employees' inventions, countries that currently have nearly no legal framework enacted (and which might be afraid to jump into cold water in all details) can restrict themselves to merely transposing the mandatory provisions, while the more sophisticated optional provisions may appeal to countries having already pertinent law in place. Also the review mechanism that a directive typically includes may subsequently be useful to achieve a gradual upward unification, if need be.

Another challenge will be to solve the systematic *conflict between labour law and IP law*. However, when repeating this balancing exercise,[48] the European legislator should refrain from ideological debates regarding a presumed choice that needs to be made between the predominance of IP law or labour law. Such a dogmatic attitude will almost certainly result in sterile discussions. Instead a more pragmatic attitude seeking to create a proper balance between the interests of the industry (easy access to innovations and inventions made by their employees) and the interests of the employee (fair treatment/compensation for their intellectual efforts) will be a more appropriate way to tackle the problem.[49]

As regards the *scope of a future directive*, a political choice will have to be made between two distinct approaches that are currently reflected in the legal frameworks of the member states. Does one intend to impose a fully fledged statutory regime, codifying the level of protection the

---

[47] Directive 2008/95/EC of 22 October 2008 to approximate the laws of the Member States relating to trade marks [2008] OJ L299/25, replacing an earlier version from 1988. Also in the sector of copyright, where disparities amongst EU member states were even more apparent, a high level of harmonization has been achieved through the enactment of (seven) directives in the period 1991–2001 (see the website of the European Commission (DG Internal Market)).

[48] This same objective was the basis of the various national regulations enacted in the EU member states.

[49] Wolk (2010), section 5.4.

legislator considers fair or does one confine oneself to a minimal body of rules, leaving the details to the national legislators? It will probably be the wisest solution to opt for the latter approach providing for a basic minimum layer of clear, simple and precise mandatory principles and allowing national legislators to enact more detailed optional rules if desired. As was explained above, the instrument of a directive is a very suitable legislative tool to include such a double layer of mandatory principles and optional provisions. The suggested minimalist approach does not mean that the directive should be limited to vague concepts. The text should include clear provisions as regards some basic rules (see next section) thus avoiding the possibility that countries might amend their law in different directions or, even worse, in the opposite direction.[50]

Finally, when conceiving the legal framework, consideration should be given to the solutions that are currently prescribed in respect of creations protected by *other IPRs*. Indeed, the expansion of the scope of several forms of IP rights that we have experienced over the last decades has increased *the possibility of an application of multiple rights in one creation*.[51] Against this background, it becomes less obvious to justify a heterogeneous treatment of employees' creations depending upon the IP-scheme that applies.[52]

4.2 Minimal Provisions

In my view the directive should at least contain minimal rules regarding the following five issues: the inventor principle, the ownership issue, the right to compensation, the availability of an alternative dispute settlement mechanism and the enforcement of deviating agreements.[53] Eventually, also definitions of certain concepts, such as what constitutes a fair, equitable or reasonable remuneration, might be useful to avoid misinterpretations by the application of a one-sided understanding in view of the peculiar place of the issue of employee inventions at the intersection between patent law and labour law.[54] It does, on the other hand, not seem necessary to provide definitions for concepts such as 'employee' or

---

50 Villinger (2001), 10.

51 E.g., computer-related-inventions may cumulate copyright and patent protection. Whereas in both cases the economic rights will be attributed to the employer, only in the case of the grant of a patent may the employee possibly have a right to remuneration.

52 Cf Vivant (2010), 160.

53 The two latter issues are not further discussed.

54 Cf Villinger (2001) 3.

'employment contract' the interpretation of which should be left to the domestic (labour) law.

The principle that inventions made by employees first of all belong to their creators seems to be widely accepted.[55] Accordingly, this issue will probably constitute the simplest one to agree upon. This basic principle, that the inventor is the original recipient of the rights, is today confirmed in most national patent laws and sometimes even in constitutions. It has not been disturbed by international conventions that were concluded in the field of industrial property. Article 2 of the Paris Convention for the Protection of Industrial Property as well as articles 2, 4 and 22 of the Patent Cooperation Treaty and article 60 of the European Patent Convention emphasize the rights of inventors in relation to their inventions. It must be admitted that these conventions do not really consider the situation of employed inventors or merely refer this issue to national law. Nevertheless, with the aforementioned national, constitutional and/or international backstops, there seems no justification for the European legislator to take a differing starting point.

Pushing on the logic of this inventor principle, rights to inventions made by employees may only be obtained by the employer by virtue of a special statutory or contractual *mechanism of transfer of rights*. Upon an inquiry by the AIPPI in 2004, all national groups have, in general, expressed their approval of the idea that, whatever the conditions and the procedures chosen, it should ultimately be the employer who must profit from the rights attached to the inventions carried out by his employees within the framework of the contract of employment.[56] A similar solution has, moreover, already been implemented in relation to other IP rights. In particular, that rule is expressed in article 14(3) of Regulation 06/2002 on Community Designs, in article 3(2) of Directive 87/54/EEC on the legal protection of topographies of semiconductor products and in article 2(3) of Directive 91/250/EEC on the legal protection of computer programs. As was observed by Advocate General Mendozzi, this rule in essence serves the requirement to balance the opposing interests at stake: on the one hand, that of the employer in acquiring the product of an activity which he has usually funded and, on the other hand, that of the employee

[55] See Introduction above. The same principle does not seem to be generally accepted in relation to copyrighted works (e.g., the work-for-hire rule in the US and in the Netherlands).

[56] AIPPI (2004), 2–3.

in being adequately remunerated for the work done.[57] Hence, it seems appropriate that a directive on employee inventions codifies this general understanding that the employer shall have the *enjoyment of service inventions de plano*, without the need for an express transfer. This solution is consistent with the goal to increase the level of legal certainty and meets the economic needs of industry. I do realize that the issue of the ownership rights is, however, more complex since it not only involves a decision as regards the ultimate recipient of these rights but also necessitates rules regarding the definition and scope of application of service inventions. The prescribed length of this chapter does, however, not allow us to discuss these issues in more detail.

The establishment of certain *compensation* in addition to wages will undoubtedly provoke much more discussion than the issue of ownership. Yet, the idea of some form of compensation for the employee seems ingrained in most national laws. Clearly such a noble idea was not only borne from the desire to protect the person of the employee but rather to motivate him to innovate and disclose his inventions.[58] Companies must rely on their employees' inventiveness to fuel their R&D efforts and generate patents. This explains why several countries have mandatory provisions regarding an employed inventor's right to reasonable compensation. While I admit that more empirical research is needed to demonstrate that reasonable compensation is (or is not) the best way to increase inventiveness, some studies provide evidence that creative workers are indeed affected by monetary incentives. Harhoff and Hoisl refer to old (1931) and more recent (1990) empirical analyses as well as their own findings (2002) which all confirm in some way the importance of remuneration for inventive activity.[59]

I do not consider, however, that the possible incentive effect should constitute the only decisive element as there are other arguments that support a right to remuneration. First, such a right is, at least in certain circumstances, simply a matter of justice.[60] Secondly, my plea in favour

---

[57] Opinion AG Mendozzi of 26 March 2009 in Case C-32/08 *Fundación Española para la Innovación de la Artesianía v Cul de Sac Espacio Creativo*, [24].

[58] Yossifov (2004) 3 (n° 8).

[59] Harhoff and Hoisl (2006), 11; Cf Orbach (2002), 99. Amendments were introduced in China in 2000 (currently replaced by new rules in 2010) to motivate employees to invent through a compulsory requirement for employers to pay a compensation to their inventive employees; see Sagar and Nagarsheth (2006), 31 and Xiandong (2009), 721.

[60] Vivant (2010), 164; Heath (2002), 398.

of a harmonizing instrument to this effect is motivated by the difficulty in justifying the different treatment of employees depending upon the applicable law in a market where expanding transborder arrangements have become common practice. Such an environment is not conducive to healthy competition. Finally, I believe that harmonized rules will enhance legal certainty. Possible future financial obligations that a right to compensation creates very often entail uncertainty on the side of the employer regarding financial forecasts. For example, the fact that an employee of a UK company was able to succeed in his action against an employer 20 years after the patents were filed[61] has rightly instigated concern among research-based companies because they must henceforth take account of this risk and make financial provision for it.[62] To accommodate these concerns, the European legislator could consider providing compensation consisting in one or more lump-sum payments as a general 'default' rule.[63] The advantage of such lump sum payments is that they need to be calculated only once, whereas remuneration based upon, for example, a licence analogy entails more bureaucracy and unpredictability as it is to be calculated on an ongoing basis.

In my opinion an initial partial solution is the establishment of a clear minimum right to remuneration[64] that leaves open the possibility for member states to extend the provisions of the directive to provide for terms that are more favourable to the employee.[65] Yet, in order to avoid a failure of the directive to produce the desired effect of harmonization, it will be advisable to include clear optional guidelines for *the criteria* to be taken into account for calculating the compensation. Following the

---

[61] *Kelly v GE Healthcare Ltd* [2009] EWHC 181 (Pat), [2009] RPC 12.

[62] Isaac (2009), 384.

[63] Meier et al (2005), 175; Will and Kirstein (2002), 4: 'We derive a unique efficient payment scheme that consists only of a lump-sum payment. We show that freedom to negotiate over compensation after the invention has been done, provides inefficient incentives. Efficient incentives would require the compensation to be fixed ex-ante.' Petersen-Padberg and Müller (2009), 6. The proposed reform in Germany also suggested certain fixed compensations but this part of the reform was unsuccessful. *See* Von Falck and Schmaltz (2005), 18; Sagar and Nagarsheth (2006), 7–8.

[64] It will be useful, albeit not easy, to agree on the choice and definition of concepts as 'fair', 'reasonable', 'adequate', 'remuneration', 'compensation' and similar notions.

[65] Detailed regulations do, anyhow, not seem to guarantee a more significant remuneration; see Sueur (2010) 19, observing that, contrary to what one should expect, French inventors receive higher amounts than their German colleagues in 90 to 95 per cent of the cases.

example in some countries, the directive should also leave room for individual countries to provide additional rules regarding extra remuneration or the method of calculation of the remuneration in labour law instruments such as collective bargaining agreements and company agreements, to the extent that the provisions are more favourable to the employee than the statutory provisions. In general, employers should always be allowed to include more favourable terms for the employee in individual employment contracts.

5. FINAL REMARKS

This chapter has attempted to reanimate discussions at the European Community level for the introduction of a harmonized legal framework regarding employees' inventions, despite the multitude of unsuccessful attempts that have been made in the past. The failure to act implies that the Community adheres to the status quo, which is characterized by uncertainty because companies have to navigate through a labyrinth of different national laws. This situation causes complications and problems for cross-border R&D, both within multinational enterprises and for cooperation between companies. It has been argued that non-action is unjust, expensive and anti-competitive and, hence, irresponsible from a socio-economic viewpoint. In addition, the EU's single market is paved with increasingly harmonized IP rights. There is a widely held notion today that any shifts in normative IP law should take place on a pan-European level or not at all. The lacuna relating to the issue of employees' inventions is in this context not only surprising but also unfortunate. Yet, I am fully aware that any new initiative will involve delicate decisions from a political viewpoint and require preparedness from all national legislators to shift from their existing positions.

REFERENCES

Ahner, F. and J.J. Touati (2010), *Inventions et Créations des Salariés: du Code du Travail au Code de la Propriété Intellectuelle*, Lamy

Association Internationale pour la Protection de la Propriété Intellectuelle (2004), 'Question 183: Employers' Rights to Intellectual Property', AIPPI Congress, <https://www.aippi.org/download/commitees/183/RS183English.pdf>

Bartenbach, K., F.E. Volz and M. Goetzmann (2009), 'Effect of the German Law on Employees' Inventions when Posting Employees within the European Union' in W.P.W. Pyrmont, M.J. Adelman, R. Brauneis, J. Drexl and R. Nack (eds), *Patents and Technological Progress in a Globalized World. Liber Amicorum Joseph Straus*, MPI Studies on Intellectual Property, Competition and Tax Law, Springer

Bouvet T. (2006), 'Employee-Inventor Rights in France', Paper for Loyola Law School IP Special Focus Conference, <http://www.veron.com/publications/Colloques/Employees_inventions.pdf>

Briggs, N. (2006), 'Entitlement', *European Intellectual Property Review* 611

Brune, A. (2010), *Bewährtes Deutsches Arbeitnehmererfindergesetz*, Heymans Verlag

Cornish, W.R. (1990), 'Rights in Employees' Inventions – The United Kingdom Position' 21 *International Review of Industrial Property and Copyright Law* 298

Cronauer, A., F.K. Beier and G. Schricker (1988), *Das Recht auf das Patent im Europaïschen Patentübereinkommen*, Heymans Verlag

Drai, L. (2010), 'La Logique du Droit du Travail versus la Logique du Droit de la Propriété Intellectuelle' in *Créations et Inventions de Salariés – Rompre avec les Schémas Reçus*, Litec

Godenhielm, B. (1966), 'Die Internationalen Bestrebungen zur Vereinheitlichung des Rechts der Arbeitnehmererfindungen', *Gewerblicher Rechtsschutz und Urheberrecht*, Internationaler Teil 125

Godenhielm, B. (1975), 'Employee Inventions' in *International Encyclopedia of Comparative Law, Volume XIV: Copyright and Industrial Property*, Mohr Tübingen

Goetzmann, M.J. (2008), *Die Harmonisiering des Arbeitnehmererfindungsrecht in der Europäischen Union, Probleme der Rechtszuordnung und Vergütung von Arbeitnehmererfindungen in grenzüberschreitenden Forschungs- und Entwicklungskooperationen* (Studien zum Gewerblichen Rechtsschutz und zum Urheberrecht)

Harhoff, D. and K. Hoisl (2006), 'Institutionalized Incentives for Ingenuity – Patent Value and the German Employees' Inventions Act' 36 *Research Policy* 1128

Heath, C. (2002), 'Remuneration of Employees' Inventions in Europe and Japan' (2002) 27(6) *AIPPI: Bimonthly Journal of the International Association for the Protection of the Industrial Property of Japan* 398

Isaac, B. (2009), 'A Fair Reward for Inventors: *Kelly & Chiu v GE Healthcare Ltd* [2009]' 4 *Journal of Intellectual Property Law and Policy* 383

Janssens, M.C. (1996), *Uitvindingen in Dienstverband en aan Universiteiten – Employee and University Inventions*, Bruylant

Joos, U. (1990), 'Grundlagen und Möglichkeiten der Angleichung des Arbeitnehmererfinderrechts (Diskussionsbericht)', *Gewerblicher Rechtsschutz und Urheberrecht, Internationaler Teil*, 366

Junghans, C.I. and A. Levy (2005), *Intellectual Property Management. A Guide for Scientists, Engineers, Financiers, and Managers*, Wiley-VCH

Manly D.G. (1978), 'Inventors, Innovator, Compensation and the Law' 21 *Research Management* 29

Meier J, T. Schubert and H.R. Jaenichen (2005), 'Employees' Invention Remuneration – Money (f)or Nothing?' 24 *Biotechnology Law Report* 168

Michaux, B. (2010), 'La Propriété des Droits Intellectuels sur les Créations du Salarié' in *Le Patrimoine Intellectuel de L'Entreprise*, Larcier

Neumeyer F. (1962), 'Die Arbeitnehmererfindung in rechtsvergleichender Sicht', *GRUR Int* 65

Orbach, B.Y. (2002), 'The Law and Economics of Creativity in the Workplace', Harvard Law School John M. Olin Center for Law, Economics and Business Discussion Paper Series, Paper 356, <http://lsr.nellco.org/harvard_olin/356>

Orkin, N. and E. Miller (2001), 'A Critical Review of the Czech Employee Invention Statute' 83 *Journal of the Patent and Trademark Office Society* 61

Peberdy, M. and A. Strowel (2009–2010), 'Employee's Rights to Compensation for Inventions – a European Perspective' *Life Sciences Handbook* 63

Petersen-Padberg, A. and M. Müller (2009), 'Reform of the German Act on Employees' Inventions: as of 1 October 2009 Companies' Rights to Inventions Have Been Expanded' 5 *Hoffmann-Eitle Newsletter*

Ramm, T. (ed.) (1977), *Vergleichende Untersuchung über das Recht der Arbeitnehmererfindung in den Mitgliedstaaten der Europäischen Gemeenschaften*, Commission of the European Community, July

Sagar R and A. Nagarsheth (2006), *Ownership of Employee Inventions and Remuneration: A Comparative Overview*, Intellectual Property Institute

Shigetomi, T. (2004), 'Two Judgments on Japanese Patent Law Article 35 Amazed Industry All over the World', *CASRIP Newsletter*, <http://www.law.washington.edu/Casrip/Newsletter/2004/newsv11i1Jp1.pdf>

Straus, J. (1990), 'Arbeitnehmererfinderrecht: Grundlagen und Möglichkeiten der Rechtsangleichung', *Gewerblicher Rechtsschutz und Urheberrecht, Internationaler Teil*, 353

Straus, J. (1984a), 'Die International-Privatrechtliche Beurteilung von Arbeitnehmererfindungen im Europäischen Patentrecht', *Gewerblicher Rechtsschutz und Urheberrecht, Internationaler Teil* 1

Straus, J. (1984b), 'Rechtsvergleichende Bemerkungen zum Begriff des Arbeitnehmererfinders', *Gewerblicher Rechtsschutz und Urheberrecht, Internationaler Teil*, 402

Sueur, T. (2010), 'Les Inventions de Salariés: Principes et Pratiques' in *Le droit des Affaires – Propriété Intellectuelle n° 35, Créations et Inventions de Salariés – Rompre avec les Schémas Reçus*, Litec

Tessensohn, J.A. and S. Yamamoto (2004), 'Japan: Patents-Inventor/Ownership Disputes Relating to Ex Employees' 26 *European Intellectual Property Review* 63

Trimborn, M. (2009), *Employees' Inventions in Germany: a Handbook for International Businesses*, Carl Heymanns Verlag

Villinger, B. (2001), 'Legal Framework of the Relationship between Employed Inventors and Employers – Incentive Systems Encouraging Creativity', WIPO Workshop on Innovation Support Services and their Management, WIPO-CDG/INN/DE/01/5

Villinger, B. (1991), *Vorschlag für Europäische Bestimmungen über Rechte an Erfindungen von Arbeitnehmern und deren Vergütung*, DABEI-Forum/Deutsche Aktionsgemeinschaft Bildung – Erfindung – Innovation Heft 15

Vivant, M. (2010), 'Repense la création en entreprise?' in *Le Droit des Affaires – Propriété Intellectuelle n 35, Créations et Inventions de Salariés – Rompre avec les Schémas Reçus*, Litec

Von, Falck A. and C.H. Schmaltz (2005), 'University Inventions: Classification and Remuneration in Germany, the Netherlands, France, the UK, the U.S. and Japan' *European Intellectual Property Review* 912

Weinmiller, J. (1975), 'Bemerkungen zum Arbeitnehmererfinderrecht in der EWG' *Gewerblicher Rechtsschutz und Urheberrecht, Internationaler Teil* 381

Will, B. and R. Kirstein (2002), 'Efficient Compensation for Employees' Inventions: An Economic Analysis of a Legal Reform in Germany' (Paper provided by Saarland University, CSLE – Center for the Study of Law and Economics in its series CSLE Discussion Paper Series with number 2002–08, <http://ideas.repec.org/p/zbw/csledp/200208.html>

Wolk, S. (2008), 'Compensation of Employed Inventors in Sweden', *World Intellectual Property Report (BNA)* 32, <http://ssrn.com/abstract=1557560>

Wolk, S. (2010), 'EU Intellectual Property Law and Ownership in Employment Relations' 56 *Information & Communication Technology Issues, Scandinavian Studies in Law* 4

Xiandong, Y. (2009), 'Case Note to Decision of the Shanghai Higher People's Court of 18 April, Wong Like v. Shanghai 'EV' Fuel Injection Co. Ltd' 40 *International Review of Industrial Property and Copyright Law* 716

Ying, D. (2007–2008), 'A Comparative Study of the Treatment of Employee Inventions, Pre-Invention Assignment Agreements, and Software Rights' *University of Pennsylvania Journal of Business and Employment Law* 763

Yossifov, V. (2004), 'Relationship between Employed Inventors and Employers: Legal, Contractual and Financial Questions' (Document prepared by the International Bureau of WIPO for the WIPO National Workshop on Innovation Support Services and their Management), <http://www.wipo.int/meetings/en/doc_details.jsp?doc_id=33697>

PART III

The employment and labour law perspective on protecting business research and development

8. Innovation through the lens of labour and employment law

Marilyn Pittard

1. HUMAN RESOURCES

Few would dispute that the capacity of the people engaged by any enterprise to learn, adopt and develop and consequently, the capacity of the enterprise to innovate, are essential components of an enterprise, if it is to provide goods or services successfully in any competitive and changing environment. Likewise, few would dispute that the ways in which those people may be engaged by the enterprise are governed primarily by labour and employment law. So, multidimensional as it is, labour and employment law has, as one of its dimensions, its relationship to the broader human resource function in the context of innovation and inventions in business.

In this context, business will endeavour to engage leaders who can promote innovation within the organisation and bring employees through processes of change. Such leaders may also show the way in harnessing the creativity of workers and in turn encouraging the creative thinking of employees as a means of improving enterprise productivity and profitability. Productivity, in the view of Dr John Edwards, member of the Board of the Reserve Bank of Australia, depends on innovation and technology. He said: 'In the longer term, productivity will come back to technology and innovation, to improvements in human capital and to our capacity to invent, or adopt and adapt productivity in enhancing innovations.'[1]

---

1 *Australian Financial Review*, 6 January 2012, 8.

2. THE CURIOUS, DEDICATED AND LOYAL EMPLOYEE

Chapters in this part of the book will discuss the role of the employment and labour laws in resolving disputes arising between employer and inventor employee which often result in litigation – and possibly unsatisfactory outcomes for either or both parties. The squabbles about ownership and the ensuing financial rewards are at the heart of these disputes. Determining who rightfully is entitled to the rewards is a main focus of any litigation initiated and proceedings in the courts may take many years to resolve. It is not in every case, of course, that financial returns and profit are the main motivators of inventors. Sometimes the employee is very driven to invent and wishes to promote the invention without thought of financial gain, being motivated by curiosity and frequently by a belief in the great utility of the invention.

2.1 Case Study: Black Box Recorder Invention

Such was the case of the inventor of the cockpit voice recorder, the forerunner of the modern 'black box' which is now used as a safety device in aeroplanes. The inventor fervently believed that his idea and invention to record the voices of the crew in the final moments of the aircraft operating would be a vital aid in determining the cause of an air crash. Developed initially unofficially as a project of the Aeronautical Research Laboratories ('ARL') in Australia, the idea came to fruition through the determination of the inventor scientist, Dr David Warren. Ultimately, after interest from overseas, the ARL took up the project and assigned a team of scientists to progress its development. It was later brought to full fruition in production by S. Davall and Sons ('Davall'), which manufactured aircraft equipment components and was based in the UK.

The inventor made no additional financial gain from the invention aside from the drawing of his normal salary from ARL: 'Ironically, the concept that began without funding, as an unofficial project of the Aeronautical Research Laboratories, became one of its most famous inventions, and has proved to be invaluable in the air accident investigation process.'[2] Dr Warren persisted with his invention, contributing to its making at home and proceeding unofficially with some ARL internal support, but this work was undertaken in the face of an official minute

[2] Witham (2005), 170.

which recorded ARL's decision not to proceed with his idea. Fortunately there seemed sufficient freedom for Dr Warren to proceed to develop the idea – or at least no orders to refrain from doing so – and ultimately a visiting British scientist to ARL saw its potential and arranged for Dr Warren to be flown to the UK. However, it would be many more turbulent years and many setbacks later before the idea was put in commercial production and became a regular part of the equipment installed in planes.

This case study shows an extraordinary lack of interest in benefiting financially from the outcomes of the invention; certainly the inventor, Dr Warren, seemed to be motivated by a belief and faith in the utility of, and necessity for, the device, rather than by possible financial gain.[3] The ARL, too, later became involved in supporting the invention, brought the device to a certain stage of development and then handed it over to business interests for commercial exploitation. There was no evidence of disputes between ARL and the inventor over financial rewards and ownership, although there were hints at inadequate acknowledgement in the press (and other reports) of the inventor's significant role. Nor was there discussion of ownership of patents or the invention. Perhaps these were more generous days and the role of such organisations as ARL was perceived differently, as its press release on 23 December 1958 revealed. In announcing the details of the aircraft Crash Recorder, the press release stated: '[The black box] has attracted considerable interest overseas and certain prominent organizations are now arranging for its manufacture and installation in important aircraft. Manufacturing rights are available to Australian manufacturers without charge.'[4] Later the recorder was further developed and refined, and in the early 1960s Davall was granted the right to 'manufacture the ARL recorder under licence for a flat payment plus a royalty'.[5]

The invention and its commercialisation as outlined above may reflect now outmoded approaches to commercialisation, and the work of the selfless scientist who believes totally in the invention. The public body (ARL) needed private enterprise to commercialise – and ultimately 'sold' that right to private industry – but did offer it free of charge at one point. Today government or semi-government organisations, responding to their

---

[3] Witham (2005).

[4] Press Release, extracted in Witham (2005), 74.

[5] Telegram from Secretary of the Department of Supply to various government departments, setting out the brief history of the development of the recorder and putting the case for Dr Warren to be granted permission to work with Davall, in Witham (2005), 122.

own financial pressures and needs for accountability and to recoup monetary returns on investments, approach innovation and invention differently and in line with the private sector approach. Inventors and innovators generally need businesses to assist with capital and commercial production; businesses want to retain rights over their investment in resources and hence the employment and labour law come to the fore. The power of businesses to protect their investments in intellectual property and inventions and innovations is vast, but legal issues still arise and there are many uncertainties.

3. LEGAL STATUS OF INVENTORS AND INNOVATORS: EMPLOYEE AND INDEPENDENT CONTRACTOR

Given the above, how might labour and employment law in turn protect and promote innovation and be a driver of productivity growth, or at least aid in achieving those goals, whilst also taking into account the interests of labour providers – whether they be workers or independent contractors?

The element of labour law most germane to this question is the law governing the rights and obligations of individual employees, or contractors, rather than the law governing relations at the collective level. Collective relationships generally focus on the more immediate terms and conditions of employment. However, pay rises and improvement in employment conditions may be linked in negotiations to productivity rises, or at least might be negotiated only on the basis that the employer gains some improvement in productivity. This improvement in productivity might be linked to innovative working practices (such as methods of handling cargoes on the docks); it might be linked to actual innovation in a particular enterprise, such as the development of robots for use in particular production processes; but in many and most instances, it will be linked to gains through restructuring of jobs or introduction of more modern and productive technology. These matters may be negotiated and so be the subject of collective agreements.

Occasionally a collective agreement might include some form of restrictive covenant but, due to historical reasons and traditional approaches, these restrictions on behaviour by a worker during employment or after the cessation of employment would usually be dealt with in the contract of employment between an individual employer and an employee. Certainly in Australia, awards which were the product of arbitrated settlements by the independent tribunal or the modern awards made by Fair Work Australia did not include these matters – rather, the traditional and rather narrow range of matters relating to essential conditions of employment would be within the subject matter set out in awards.[6]

Looking, then, at the individual in his or her relationship with the engaging firm, from the traditional analysis in common law legal systems, at least, and dealing for the moment only with employees, a broad distinction may be perceived between, on the one hand, those employees who are expressly engaged to undertake research and invent and develop new solutions and products and services, compared, on the other hand, to those employees who are engaged more generally to perform other particular and necessary functions but who may actually develop new systems, processes or inventions and who may owe duties to their employer in respect of those developments if they do so in the course of their employment.

In an employment contract where the primary duty of the employee is to innovate and invent, the remuneration commensurate with an activity central to that role should generally be negotiated between employer and employee. The same would be said of contractors who are engaged for such a purpose.

Where the invention or discovery leads ultimately to the hoped-for developments in products or services the subject of the distribution of any benefits (between employer and inventor) may be covered by the contract of employment. By way of contrast, unexpected windfalls can also arise where an idea or development is itself unexpected or has some unforeseen applications and benefits. In either case, issues of who might be entitled to share in those gains are very likely to arise, if the matter was unaddressed in the original contract. Moreover, the contract of employment (i.e. conferring employee status) might have a different approach to this issue than where the inventor is a contractor: the law in many jurisdictions has invoked the notion of the implied terms in the contract of employment which have the effect that the benefit of the invention goes to the employer (in the absence of express terms).

The general obligation of an independent contractor is far less onerous (unless the issue is dealt with expressly in the contract) and he or she may be able to use the idea to benefit themselves without any duties or obligations owed to the principal. This is the subject of discussion in the

---

[6] See Pittard and Naughton (2010), chapter 10, Creighton and Stewart (2010), Deakin and Morris (2009) and Freedland (2003).

chapter by Mark Freedland and Jeremias Prassl, from the UK perspective, and that of Marilyn Pittard from the Australian perspective.

The thorny issue of the division and legal distinction between an employee, on the one hand, and the contractor, on the other hand, still besets many jurisdictions well into the twenty-first century. Certainly, the UK and Australia set much store by the distinction for a variety of legal purposes. Whilst the law is relatively clear as to what count as factors to be considered in determining whether the worker is to be regarded as an 'employee' or as an 'independent contractor', the law offers little assistance with how the relevant criteria and factors are to be weighted. Similarly, it does not enable the parties to predict with any certainty what legal status the worker has where (as is often the case) there are many factors, with some pointing in opposite directions, as to the conclusion about the legal categorisation of the worker. This general and chronic problem explored in chapters dealing with the UK and Australia is an important theme in this Part; the application of the distinction bears on the duties to innovate or invent, to what extent they apply, and how the benefits of innovation and invention are to be distributed between the inventor and the employer.

Yet another aspect of the legal status question is whether the person is indeed working for financial reward – or is he or she truly a volunteer, or honorary worker, thus having no status as an employee? This brings with it another set of problems as to just what was the understanding when they assumed this status. This is addressed particularly in the chapter by Pittard.

4. UNANTICIPATED DISCOVERIES AND THE PROBLEM OF SHARING ECONOMIC BENEFITS OF INNOVATION

More problematic are the unintended, unexpected or 'fluke' discoveries; that is, discoveries which are not expected or addressed at the stage the worker is employed. Frequently, an employee may have an idea and develop an innovation or invention in the course of undertaking his or her work. It might not be an innovation at the heart of the employee's contractual duties, but it may arise out of the employee performing his or her work – say, a new system or approach in the business may be implemented by the employee, leading to a significant saving of costs and augmenting profits. In turn, this innovation may be utilised more broadly in the sector or industry. How does the law handle the consequential economic benefits from the viewpoint of the rights and obligations of employer and employee?

Moreover, how *should* the law handle the consequences of this unexpected creativity? Is it, or should it be, a matter of the terms of the employment contract itself; or is it to be recognised as a 'relational' matter – arising out of the ongoing relationship between employer and employee and which they deal with not as a matter of the particular current contract (which might have been entered into many years ago) but on broader general principles?

Ideally, the law ought not stifle or discourage the innovator. But, on the other hand, broadly accepted notions of equity and balance of benefits between employer and employee may suggest that not all of the benefits of innovation should accrue to one party alone, especially where the employer's time has been used or the facilities of the employer have de facto contributed to the innovation or been a springboard for it.

The approach of some jurisdictions in the US to this issue is one which might inspire other jurisdictions. The concept of 'shop rights' as a method of dealing with rewards and responsibilities is explored in Richard Bales's chapter. 'Shop rights' is a concept which determines how both the employer and employee will benefit from the invention in the event that the contract of employment does not expressly deal with it. This is a default position. This is in contrast to the Australian, UK and European positions as outlined in the chapters by Riccardo Del Punta, Freedland and Prassl, and Pittard.

5. METHODS OF ORGANISING AND UNDERTAKING WORK: TRADITIONAL AND CONTEMPORARY

Where an employee has invented a new implement to aid in the employer's business (or developed some other productive innovation), under the simple model of nineteenth- and early twentieth-century employment (especially in small-scale enterprises), it was relatively easy to ascertain who were the parties involved, in considering and therefore resolving the rights and obligations of the parties. For example, the employee might be working alongside the employer and subject to his or her direction. In the absence of express agreement and where inventing was neither part of the employee's contractual duties nor could be said to be in the course or scope of the employment, under Australian and UK law the employee would generally be able to keep the invention.

By way of contrast, the shop rights doctrine, as explored in Bales's chapter, would come in to play in the US. Conversely, the employee who is under orders from the employer, or is required by the contract, to innovate will generally not be entitled to keep the invention or to keep the proceeds of it (subject to the order being legitimate within the contract) under UK or Australian law. Where the single employer is the 'master' and the inventor 'employee' is the servant, in the old parlance, the principles are relatively clear.

This simple model was no doubt not always fair and just, even in those periods. But if we move forward in time to modern workplaces in the twenty-first century, the old master and servant method of working, with the servant working under the master's direct orders and even side by side with the master, rarely applies. Generally, putting to one side small retailing and like activities, in contemporary times work in production of goods and services is not commonly performed with a model of a single employer with its few employees working singly and directly with that employer. Much work is organised with large numbers of employees in an enterprise who may be physically separated at a range of work sites. Frequently, too, in larger organisations work is undertaken in teams and through the collaborative efforts of groups of employees.

Thus, if a new method or invention is developed through this modern method of working, complications may well arise as to who has been involved in the innovative contribution and therefore complications as to identifying who could, or should, benefit from the economic gains to the enterprise from the innovation. For example, employee A may have contributed most of the work (creativity) to the invention but A may have been aided and assisted by employees B, C and D in various ways. They each may have used the facilities of the employer in varying degrees. The issue then is how to sort out the contributions as between the employer and the four employees. Do they each share equally in the whole – after all, it would not be made (invented) without all four employees' input? Or are the varying contributions to be identified and percentages attributed? Some of the ways in which legal rules can help resolve these potentially competing interests are considered in the chapters by Del Punta and Bales.

6. DISCLOSURE OF INVENTIONS TO THE EMPLOYER

Is the contract of employment an adequate instrument to protect employer and employee interests? In the absence of express agreement, is the employee under a duty to disclose inventions he or she makes to the employer?

Where the employee makes a discovery or invention outside work hours in his or her own time and not using the employer's materials or equipment, there would not seem to be a duty to disclose to the employer. In the UK and Australia, the courts have not identified a duty to invent as an implied duty in law in these circumstances. But if the discovery made in this context enables the employee to enter into competition with the employer, would that contravene the implied duties to act in good faith and to cooperate with the employer – duties which have long been recognised by the common law? This duty as it is generally treated in Europe is also examined in Del Punta's chapter, where the professor examines the way civil law systems deal with these duties, contrasting that approach to the common law.

Certainly, if inventions were not regarded as being 'in the course of employment', in the common law tradition there is no obligation to disclose. However, there are difficult issues, as we know, about 'the course of employment' which are identified and analysed in the Freedland and Prassl, and Pittard chapters and which are also addressed in Chapter 22 by Chris Molnar.

7. THE 'COURSE' OF OR 'SCOPE' OF EMPLOYMENT

At the heart of questions of ownership of innovations and entitlement to own or have a share in their economic proceeds is the notion of what activity is considered to be in the 'course' or 'scope' of employment. May it be argued convincingly that if the innovative activity arises in the context of the employee doing the tasks which he or she is employed to do (even if 'innovation' or 'invention' is not expressly required), then is that not the very thing which the employer is buying with its purchase of the employee's labour?

But that is, in a sense, circumventing the answer: what exactly is the employer 'buying' in terms of the employee's labour? A problem commonly remains to identify the scope of obligations under particular employment contracts. The terms may not be clear; they may be expressed in generalities according to level of position. Further, the employment position of the employee may have changed over time, so that the written contract actually may relate to a former position. In law there may have been either a variation of this contract; or a termination of that original contract with a new contract in effect entered into – but none of that is reduced to a written document or signed by the parties.

And it may take a court some time to sort through the contractual developments' legal sense.[7] An oral agreement has taken over – it then becomes a matter of evidence as to what is constituted by that oral agreement as to the course or scope of employment. This can be a major impediment to determining where the rights in respect of discoveries and innovations lie. But is it artificial to attempt to construct the scope of employment when there is significant doubt about the exact scope in the particular case?

Interestingly, the Italian approach is to distinguish between two different categories: the 'firm invention' and 'the occasional invention'. The former is invention which occurs during the course of employment and this is in turn owned by the employer – however the employee must receive a fair reward. In the other category, 'occasional invention' occurs where the invention relates to the employer's field of activity ('campo di attivata') but is not within the scope of the employment contract; in that case ownership shifts to the employee, but the employer has an option right. These concepts are addressed by Del Punta in his chapter. Contrasts are drawn with situations in Germany and other countries also in this chapter. The possible harmonisation of the variety of approaches is addressed by Marie-Christine Janssens in Part 2.

8. MOBILITY OF EMPLOYEES AND KNOWLEDGE

What impact does permitting mobility of knowledge have on employee inventions? Or what is the impact of permitting restrictions on mobility, so the one employer retains that same employee? Conventional wisdom leads us to believe that long-term employees will be well versed in the employer's business and will be creative and productive in an innovation sense, especially if post-employment competitive conduct by the employee is limited through the use of restrictive covenants. This 'wisdom' turns out to be true in some cases, as discussed in Catherine Fisk's chapter.

This wisdom, though, is also turned on its head in other instances when Fisk explores the position in the US and over time, as for example in the computer technology industry in Silicon Valley, which might have prospered because of the very lack of restriction on employee mobility.

[7] *Quinn v Jack Chia Australia Ltd* (1992) 1 VR 567; Pittard and Naughton (2010), 83.

She states: 'Both knowledge-protective legal regimes and lax legal regimes have existed in places and periods of economic growth.'[8]

9. WHAT IS THE INFLUENCE OF THE LAW?

A vexed question is to what extent does the law, particularly employment and labour law, influence this area? Does the law ensure that innovation and creativity actually occur within an enterprise? To what extent does the law help resolve ownership issues with any clarity and certainty? Certainly Freedland and Prassl argue that there are limitations of the common law of the contract of employment and this theme also emerges in other chapters later in this volume. John Hull espouses the view that the relationship of mutual trust and confidence between employer and employee is far more important. Fisk, in similar vein, observes that one of the main lessons from the US is that 'the norms of the workplace and the industry are more important than the law'.[9] This question is raised in this volume but it cannot be resolved definitively.

REFERENCES

Creighton, B. and A. Stewart (2010), *Labour Law*, 5th edn, Federation Press
Deakin, S. and G. Morris (2009), *Labour Law*, 5th edn, Hart Publishing
Freedland M. (2003), *The Personal Employment Contract*, Oxford University Press
Pittard, M. and R. Naughton (2010), *Australian Labour Law: Text, Cases and Commentary*, 5th edn, LexisNexis
Witham, J.P. (2005), *Black Box: David Warren and the Creation of the Cockpit Voice, Recorder*, Lothian

---

8 Fisk, chapter 13 in this volume.
9 Fisk, chapter 13 in this volume.

9. Resolving invention ownership disputes: limitations of the contract of employment

Mark Freedland and Jeremias Prassl

1. INTRODUCTION

The traditional approach under the English contract of employment is to treat inventions and discoveries as fruits of the employee's labour, thus belonging to the employer as the work-taking counterparty to the contract of employment. The present chapter identifies several key limitations of this approach, beginning with those inherent in the use of the contractual model as the paradigm form of employment relationships: the unclear scope of the contract of employment and its inability to deal with complex employment scenarios are imported into the statutory regimes of the *Patents Act 1977* (UK) and the *Copyright, Designs and Patents Act 1988* (UK). A further set of limitations arises from the common law operating to control the impact of express terms in the contract of employment, and the side effects of non-derogation provisions in the 1977 Act. Implied terms, especially those of fidelity and confidentiality, are the third limitation to be explored. A brief conclusion then turns to how these limitations might be overcome, not least through a broader reconceptualisation of the employment relationship beyond its current contractual framework.

In a volume exploring the ownership of employee inventions and discoveries, a chapter on the contract of employment in English law might at first appear somewhat anachronistic: with the *Patents Act 1977* providing a complete regime of ownership dispute resolution and related compensation mechanisms and similar mechanisms in the *Copyright, Designs and Patents Act 1988* (CDPA), Parliament has occupied the turf, thus drastically curtailing the role of the common law. Upon closer consideration, however, an analysis of the limitations of the contract of employment is crucial to an understanding of the operation of the current statutory regime: a subtle interplay between statute and common law rules determines the allocation of respective rights and duties, particularly in the context of regulating the relationship between employees (wage-takers) and employers (work-takers). Furthermore, whilst employee invention ownership might no longer be regarded as the prime 'battleground upon which is fought [the] conflict of interests of labour and capital',[1] the present subject will nonetheless appear to be a good testing ground for several of the underlying themes employment law is grappling with today.

In order to explore a series of key limitations the chapter is structured as follows: a brief introduction sets out the paradigm solution to ownership disputes surrounding employee inventions, both under the old common law and the 1977 and 1988 Acts, primarily in order to demonstrate how the contract of employment remains crucially important to the operation of the statutory provisions. Discussion then turns to limitations inherent in the use of the contract of employment as a gateway into the regulatory regimes: the classification of limitless varieties of employment relationships into a narrow contractual model is a doctrinal and practical challenge with direct impact on the scope of the provisions, and an approach that is inherently inflexible in dealing with changing circumstances and more complex employment scenarios.

A second cluster of limitations arises from the fact that contracts of employment are in many aspects quite distinct from the general law of contract. Whereas the latter permits free determination of patent ownership and transfer (and indeed is the primary tool to facilitate such transactions), use of the contract of service to regulate ownership of an employee's invention is heavily curtailed both in statute and at common law. Such limitations arise not only in the context of parties' express contractual arrangements, however, and a third section is consequently dedicated to the role of implied terms. Here, the operation of particular terms presents a direct limitation to the statutory resolution of employee invention ownership disputes: an employee's duty of confidentiality may well clash with his ownership rights under the *Patents Act*. The discussion concludes with a brief overview of possible ways to overcome the issues thus identified.

---

1 Phillips and Hoolahan (1982), 1–2.

1.1 Intellectual Property in the Context of the Employment Relationship

One important caveat remains to be made at this juncture: an employee's invention or discovery may fall under a myriad of statutory provisions and regulatory regimes. For present purposes, however, they are a matter primarily for the patent system, with copyright taking a secondary role.[2] From an intellectual property law perspective these two regimes are fundamentally distinct, both in terms of subject matter and objectives.[3] From an employment law perspective, on the other hand, the regimes' limitations to an application only as between employer and employee are materially identical.

Section 130(1) of the *Patents Act 1977* defines employer and employee as 'the person [in relation to an employee] by whom the employee is or was employed' and 'a person who works or (where the employment has ceased) worked under a contract of employment' respectively. The CDPA similarly relies on the employee concept. Defined in section 263(1) as working 'under a contract of employment',[4] this approach is conceptually identical to the employee definition in the 1977 Act, and section 230(1) of the *Employment Rights Act 1996* more generally.

When it comes to the relevance of the contract of employment as a gateway into both statutory regimes it is therefore

> wrong to suggest that [...] context [...] bears on the question whether there exists employment under a contract of service. Where Parliament has used language in its definitions well understood in other contexts it would take clear words to produce a result where those definitions did not retain their well understood meaning.[5]

Patent and copyright cases concerning employee invention ownership are consequently often reasoned by analogy,[6] and in illustrating the

---

[2] Cornish (1992), 14–15 cites the example of a computer program as an employee invention to be dealt with under the copyright system.

[3] Cornish, Llewelyn and Aplin (2010), [1.04].

[4] The provision's extension to additional categories, such as military personnel and apprentices in certain circumstances is beyond the scope of the present discussion.

[5] *Ultraframe UK Ltd v Fielding* [2003] EWCA Civ 1805, [2004] RPC 24 [19] (Waller LJ).

[6] E.g., *Re Greater Glasgow Health Board's Application* [1996] RPC 207 (PC) as application, by analogy, of *Stevenson Jordan & Harrison v McDonnell & Evans* [1952] 1 TLR 101 (CA): Cornish, Llewelyn and Aplin (2010), 532.

limitations of the contract of employment, reference may be made to cases litigated under a variety of Acts going back as far as the *Copyright Act 1911*.[7] The only important point of difference regarding the contract of employment is the extent to which its terms may impact upon the statutory default solution, as discussed below.

The following paragraphs now turn to a brief account of the existing legal regime. Their goal is not so much to provide a comprehensive overview of the topic, but rather to give the necessary context for discussion in the following sections. Coverage will therefore be selective and brief,[8] and structured into three parts: the position under the common law contract of employment as the traditional approach to resolving ownership conflicts, and the two statutory regimes prevalent today.

1.2 The Common Law Position

Less than 50 years ago, it was noted that in the United Kingdom 'the usual procedure [... was] that if anybody invents anything, they get 2d. an hour rise and the sack the following week'.[9] At common law, the position was somewhat more nuanced, if not a lot less drastic. Primacy was given to the effect of express terms, thus leaving employees vulnerable to employer-drafted ownership assignment clauses. In the absence of explicit provisions, an implied term ensured that the employer was entitled to the fruits of his workers' labour. The operation of these implied terms is illustrated in *Sterling Engineering v Patchett*.[10] There, the inventor of several domestic appliances had brought a claim for compensation under section 56(2) of the *Patents Act 1949*. The House of Lords rejected this claim, as the employee had not been able to establish an interest in the invention. Giving the leading judgment, Simonds VC recalled 'the rule that inventions made by an employee belong to the employer [...] as an implied term of the contract of service'.[11] This was to be understood 'in the same sense that it is an implied term, though not written at large, in the contract of service of any workman that what he produces by the strength of his arm [...] become the property of the employer'.[12] It is important to note that this rule was frequently subject

---

7 *Stevenson Jordan & Harrison* [1952] 1 TLR 101 (CA).

8 For specialist discussion see e.g., Phillips and Hoolahan (1982), Saxby (1981) and Chandler and Holland (1993), Part II.

9 White (1962), 279.

10 [1955] AC 534 (HL).

11 [1955] AC 534 (HL) 543.

12 [1955] AC 534 (HL) 544.

to political and academic criticism,[13] and that the particular outcome is not necessarily inherent in the use of the contractual model.[14] The cases' ongoing relevance, even in a statutory regime that is not declaratory of the previous common law position,[15] has been judicially confirmed, albeit with considerable caution.[16]

1.3 Statutory Regimes

The vast majority of employees' inventions today are thought to come under Part I of the *Patents Act 1977*.[17] Section 39(1) of the Act provides a comprehensive set of tests for the allocation of employee-generated patents. In cases where ownership rests with the employer, sections 40 and 41 set out the conditions under which the employee may be granted compensation by the court or comptroller, as well as the amount thereof. Section 42, finally, prohibits the enforceability of contractual clauses relating to employees' inventions if they are designed to diminish the latter's rights under the Statute.

As regards copyright, section 11(2) of the *Copyright, Designs and Patents Act 1988* similarly awards the employer first ownership of copyright if the creator acted in the course of employment under a contract of service, without however offering the Patents Act's statutory compensation and non-derogation provisions. The two regimes are generally designed to operate independently. One important exception to this is section 39(3) of the 1977 Act, inserted by the CDPA to bar employers from using a copyright claim against an employee's ownership of an invention under section 39(2).

2. LIMITATIONS INHERENT IN THE CONTRACT OF EMPLOYMENT

The direct reliance on the common law concept of the contract of employment in the statutory definitions of employees and employers

[13] See Swan (1959), Taylor (1969) and the (failed) attempts at reform in the Patents (Employees Inventions) Bill 1965.

[14] Taylor (1969), 133.

[15] Jacob LJ in *LIFFE Administration & Management v Pinkava* [2007] EWCA Civ 217, [2007] Bus LR 1369 (CA), noting that the Act's provisions were generally more favourable to employees.

[16] *Harris' Patent* [1985] RPC 19, 28.

[17] Phillips (1981), 2.

gives rise to two sets of limitations. A lack of clarity as to the scope of the statutory invention ownership regimes, firstly, can be traced to the gateway function of the contract of service specifically. The difficulty of applying their provisions in complex employment scenarios, secondly, is an incident of the common law's contractual model of employment relationships more generally.

2.1 Unclear Scope of the Statutory Provisions

In order to determine a worker's status, the common law has historically drawn on a series of different tests to analyse the nature of his or her relationship with the employer. Relying thus on the contract of employment as a regulatory gateway means that it may often be unclear whether an inventor working for a company is an employee labouring under a contract of service. A brief examination of frequently used tests such as control and mutuality of obligation will demonstrate this limitation, both in terms of the general consequences of the unclear interaction between open-ended and fact-heavy tests, and the particular problem in the employee invention ownership scenario where there is no coherent link between the statutes' underlying policy goals and the tests used.

Today, no one test is determinative of employment status on its own.[18] The courts apply a multi-pronged test, looking at factors from control and mutuality of obligation to risk allocation and the existence of any contractual terms that could be inconsistent with employee status.[19] In the employee invention ownership setting, the issue was discussed most recently by the Court of Appeal in *Ultraframe Ltd v Fielding*.[20]

There, a series of preliminary questions, including as to the ownership of design rights, had arisen from the bankruptcy of Mr Davies. The Court of Appeal held that his relationship with various companies could not be characterised as a contract of employment, and that the design rights consequently remained in the defendant's ownership.[21] In so doing, the court considered the various elements required for employment to come

---

[18] *WHPT Housing Association v Secretary of State for Social Services* [1981] ICR 737 (HC) (Webster J).

[19] For an early exposition, see *Ready Mixed Concrete Ltd v Minister of Pensions* [1968] 2 QB 497 (MacKenna J).

[20] *Ultraframe* [2003] EWCA Civ 1805, [2004] RPC 24. A full account of the tests can be found, e.g., in Deakin and Morris (2009), 133–144.

[21] *Ultraframe* [2003] EWCA Civ 1805, [2004] RPC 24 [26].

under a contract of service:[22] mutuality of obligation, control and the absence of terms inconsistent with the existence of a contract of service.[23]

As regards mutuality of obligation, this refers to the analysis of an employment relationship as two concurrent layers, exchange transactions and relational contract:[24] there is, on a first level, the straightforward bargain of a set amount of work for a promised wage. On a second, there is the further promise that the employer will continue to offer work, and the employee to accept it. It was this second layer that the Mutuality of Obligation test initially focussed on, its absence often becoming the 'rock on which [...] contracts of employment founder[ed]'.[25] In the context of employee inventions, mutuality of obligation as a test is completely divorced from the statutory regime's underlying policy goals of 'ensur-[ing], in the interests of business and justice, that employers receive the benefits for which they ha[ve] paid'[26] and that these could then be enjoyed without complex contractual arrangements or vulnerability to external claims.[27] The emphasis on a continued multi-level relationship bears little relevance to these underlying goals of employee-generated patent or copyright ownership and leads to an incongruent application of the regulatory framework.

Waller LJ turned next to the control test which dates back to *Yewens v Noakes*, where Bramwell LJ had held that 'a servant is a person subject to the command of his master as to the manner in which he shall do his work'.[28] From approximately 1910 onwards, use of the test was extended into a wide range of other areas, primarily as an innovation designed to inhibit the wider spread of legislative entitlements.[29]

Today, control is only relevant when understood in a 'wider sense, [*viz*] the idea that an employee is one who agrees to serve, as opposed to producing finished goods or supplying a specified service'.[30] This

---

22 Ibid, [21], relying on *Montgomery v Johnson Underwood Ltd* [2001] ICR 819, [18]–[24] (Buckley J).

23 *Ready Mixed Concrete* [1968] 2 QB 497, 515 (MacKenna J).

24 Freedland (2003), 92ff.

25 *Carmichael v National Power plc*, 11 September 1995, [ET 9].

26 HL Deb (5th series) vol 490 cols 879–917 (30 November 1987) and HL Deb (5th series) vol 379 col 255 (24 January 1977) as cited in Pila (2010), 9.

27 Pila (2010), 10; citing Report of the Copyright Committee (Gregory Report) (Cmd 8662, 1952), [268].

28 (1880–81) LR 6 QBD 530, 532–3.

29 Deakin (1998), 218.

30 Deakin and Morris (2009), 135.

understanding of control with less of a personal and thus more bureaucratic dimension of power over the individual has been highlighted by Hugh Collins.[31] In employment law generally control as a sole criterion would be vastly under-inclusive, potentially excluding swathes of professionals whose employment status would today not be thought contentious. This would be similarly true in the intellectual property context, where such differentiation may be called for.[32] Furthermore, the test does again not sit easily with the nature of the underlying question: employee inventions are only very rarely the result of direct employer control or orders.

2.2 Inability to Deal with Complex Situations

The contract of employment originally came to permeate individual employment law by subsuming within it a host of different relationships between wage- and work-takers. As regards form, the paradigm of a bilateral contract has more or less supplanted all other potential explanations of the employment relationship outside certain limited categories such as office holding. In substantive terms, the emphasis on a bilateral relationship is the most significant influence of this contractual analysis: every wage-work bargain is perceived as between two parties, both of which are distinct individuals.

This unification may be useful in terms of designing regulatory frameworks even in seemingly unrelated fields such as intellectual property, but brings with it severe limitations: the paradigm approach imposed is a narrow one, and fails to address ever-increasingly complex scenarios at both ends of the contract of employment. As regards the employer, the statutory regimes are ineffective in terms of taking into account multi-entity structures; as regards the employee, their applicability to non-paradigm employees such as consultants, directors or shareholders is unclear.

The institution of the contract and its connected doctrines have had a fundamental effect on the perception of the employment relationship in general, and the employer as work-taking counterparty to a contract of service in particular. By looking at the vast majority of personal work relationships through the contractual prism, a unitary view of the employing entity emerges near automatically: if the exchange of wage

---

31 Collins (1986).

32 See e.g., Pila (2010).

and work is characterised as a bilateral contractual relationship, emphasis shifts onto a single work-taking counterparty at the non-employee end.

The limitations inherent in this paradigm are highlighted in the recent decision of the Court of Appeal in *Unilever v Shanks*.[33] Professor Shanks had applied for compensation under section 40 of the *Patents Act 1977* for an invention made whilst employed by a non-trading research company within the Unilever group. Pursuant to section 39(1) the resulting patents belonged to his immediate employer, and had subsequently been assigned to other group companies. One of the conditions for (and subsequent factors in assessing the amount of) compensation under the statute is 'outstanding benefit' to the employer. In interpreting the section Jacob LJ held that

> the real actual benefit to the *actual employer* [is] all that matters. [...] The whole scheme is built around a paradigm case, the case where the inventor works for the same company as received all the benefit of the invention. [... It is] unlikely that Parliament intended that where there has been an in-house assignment of a patent, the inventor should be treated wildly differently from an inventor in the paradigm case.[34]

As the issue did not fall to be decided on the facts of the case, the precise impact of this explicit affirmation of the narrow paradigm remains unclear. It is not at all difficult, however, to imagine a corporate structure designed to deny employee inventors compensation:[35] the unitary notion inherent in the use of the contract of employment makes it highly unlikely that an employer other than the actual contractual counterparty would fall to be considered for the purposes of section 40. In a sophisticated group of companies the benefit of an invention could therefore be shifted to an entirely unrelated entity, leaving the actual employer with no more than nominal gain.

The limitations of the contract of employment are equally apparent when looking at complex employment scenarios. Does the statutory regime apply, for example, to a consultant or agency (temp) worker who makes a patentable invention while on assignment to an end-user client?[36] Another much-litigated issue in this context is the role of

---

33 *Unilever Plc v Shanks* [2010] EWCA Civ 1283, (2011) 177 BMLR 176.

34 Ibid, [8]–[9]. Emphasis added.

35 For an early suggestion, see Bercusson (1980), 262.

36 The issue at hand in *Stevenson Jordan* [1952] 1 TLR 101 (CA). In a triangular employment setting (worker-agency-end-user), the absence of a contract of employment may for once benefit the worker.

shareholders[37] and directors:[38] if they are employees of their companies, section 39(1) will apply. The decided cases and patent applications in this area serve as a practical illustration of many of the issues analysed above.[39]

In concluding this section, attention should be drawn to the fact that the limitations discussed are by no means the only ones inherent in the use of the contract of employment in resolving the ownership of employee inventions. The static nature of the contract of employment, for example, has been criticised for its lacking flexibility in adapting to the evolution of employment relationships over time[40] – a challenging question in the context of the employee's normal duties under section 39. The multiple dimensions of the employment relationship are equally difficult to account for: as noted in *UWA v Gray*, a strict contractual analysis ignores other perspectives such as university employees' membership in the larger academic community.[41]

3. LIMITATIONS ARISING FROM EXPRESS TERMS

In *Sterling Engineering v Patchett*, Lord Reid suggested that 'as the relationship of master and servant is constituted by contract the parties can, if they choose, alter or vary the normal incidents of the relationship but they can only do that by express agreement or by an agreement which can be implied from the facts of the case'.[42] This section sets out to examine whether his Lordship's statement reflects current law as regards the particular incident of employee invention ownership. It will become apparent that the extent to which the contract of employment can determine that particular aspect is limited, both at common law and under the *Patents Act 1977*.

---

[37] An individual can be the sole shareholder and an employee of a company: *Lee v Lee's Air Farming Ltd* [1961] AC 12 (HL).

[38] Note the special case of directors, where standard common law principles such as fiduciary obligations, or even express contractual terms will apply. See Chandler and Holland (1993), 119 and section 3, below.

[39] See e.g., *Ultraframe* [2003] EWCA Civ 1805, [2004] RPC 24: shareholder not an employee; *Enston's Application* BL O/206/04: Managing Director not an employee; *Walter's Applications* BL O/272/05: inventor holding himself out to represent company employee.

[40] *LIFFE* [2007] EWCA Civ 217, [2007] Bus LR 1369 (CA) (Jacob LJ).

[41] *University of Western Australia v Gray* (2009) FCAFC 116; Pila (2010a).

[42] *Sterling Engineering* (1955) AC 534 (HL), 547.

In the present context, such limitations are not necessarily problematic. The employment relationship is one of subordination and inherent inequality of bargaining power between employer and employee. There exists therefore a need to balance freedom of contract with the protection of 'employees whose inferior bargaining position leads them to sign away their statutory rights to the benefit of their employers'.[43] In practice, the balancing exercise takes place in two distinct, yet frequently overlapping places: the common law and section 42 of the *Patents Act 1977*. The latter may at first appear to be considerably more worker-protective, as it places a strict limitation on ownership determination via the contract of employment. Upon closer investigation, however, two significant lacunae appear: section 42 only applies to contracts *ex ante*, and the entire statutory regime can in any instance be completely excised by the operation of collective agreements. In both situations, the individual contract of service ceases to play any significant role.

In these respects, the role of the contract of service is very distinct from other contracts. When it comes to 'relationship[s] with outside bodies', express contractual terms are the main tool for determining patent and copyright ownership.[44] Commercial parties are free to use contracts to override the operation of the *Patents Act 1977* as between themselves.[45]

3.1 The Common Law

A limited abrogation of freedom of contract has long been recognised as necessary at common law.[46] In the context of employee inventions, this is illustrated by the courts' approach to two traditional ways of protecting employers' claims to innovations: restraint clauses and pre-assignment clauses. In *Commercial Plastics v Vincent*,[47] a clause in the defendant's contract of service forbade employment with competitors anywhere in the world for one year. Pearson LJ set out the relevant limitations: '[t]he restriction must be no more than is reasonable in the interests of the party in whose favour it is imposed; if it is too wide, it is oppressive to the party who will be subject to the restraint, and [therefore] contrary to the

---

43 Bercusson (1980), 259.

44 Cornish (1992), 17.

45 *Collag Corp v Merck & Co Inc* [2003] FSR 16 (PC) and (in the copyright context) *Cyprotex Discovery Ltd v University of Sheffield* [2004] EWCA Civ 380, [2004] Info TLR 135 (CA).

46 Peel (2007), 2.

47 *Commercial Plastics Ltd v Vincent* [1965] 1 QB 623 (CA).

public interest'.[48] On the facts, the global restriction was too wide, as there was minimal worldwide competition; the restraint clause was therefore void and unenforceable.

The common law's approach to clauses pre-assigning all rights in eventual discoveries to the employer was set out in *Electrolux v Hudson*,[49] a patent case decided shortly before the 1977 Act. The defendant's contract incorporated a sweeping assignment clause which was found void as absurd when applied to all members of staff.

Section 11(2) of the CDPA decrees that where relevant work 'is made by an employee in the course of his employment, his employer is the first owner of any copyright in the work *subject to any agreement to the contrary*'.[50] Whilst the overall operation of this section is 'often obscure in comparison to Patents',[51] it is nonetheless clear that it imports the general common law regime as just set out. An employee can surrender his or her initial copyright without formality, and an agreement to this effect may even be deduced from the parties' conduct or surrounding circumstances.[52]

When measured against the balancing exercise between freedom of contract and inequality of bargaining power delineated in the introduction to this section, the common law limitations of the contract of employment seem doctrinally reasonable. Employers are in a position to protect their legitimate business interests as long as employees are not unreasonably suppressed. Excessively onerous formulations continue to be used as an effective deterrent against ill-advised employees, however,[53] with the courts' blue pencil approach saving whatever parts of pre-assignment clauses are not too wide.[54]

---

48 [1965] 1 QB 623 (CA), 640, quoting the tests in *Nordenfelt v The Maxim Nordenfelt Guns and Ammunition Co Ltd* [1894] AC 535, 565 (Lord MacNaghten) and *Herbert Morris Ltd v Saxelby* [1916] 1 AC 688, 707.

49 *Electrolux v Hudson* [1977] FSR 312 (HC).

50 Emphasis supplied.

51 Cornish, Llewelyn and Aplin (2010), 352 [13–05].

52 Ibid, [13–07]. Note that if an author arranges for another person to have copyright, the formality provision to confer legal title in s 90(3) CDPA 1988 applies (writing, signed by or on behalf of assignor).

53 Gold (1990), 384.

54 Chandler and Holland (1993), 133. Cf the outcome on the facts in *Electrolux* [1977] FSR 312 (HC).

3.2 The Patents Act 1977

In contrast to that regime stand the explicit statutory limitations of the contract of employment in section 42 of the 1977 Act. It applies to employees' contracts with their employer, or contracts made with a third party either at the employer's request or in pursuance of the contract of employment, and stipulates that '[a]ny term in a contract to which this section applies which diminishes the employee's rights in inventions [...] made by him after [...] the date of the contract [...] shall be unenforceable against him to the extent that it diminishes his rights [...]'.

At first glance, this non-derogation provision appears more worker-protective than the common law regime[55] as it allows no modifications through the contract of employment, and any clause drafted to escape section 42 would still be subject to scrutiny at common law.[56] Furthermore, even though the individual opt-out ban provisions are 'beset with uncertainty, [...] given the extension of common law doctrine, [they] may well be generously construed'[57] by the courts. While it could therefore be argued that any private deal struck between employee and employer would be against the spirit of the Act,[58] section 42(2) is nowhere near as all-embracing:[59] its operation can be displaced by collective agreements and *ex post* contracts, both of which are beyond the scope of the individual contract of employment.

The first of these lacunae arises from the fact that section 42(2) only applies to employer–employee contracts entered into before the moment of the invention, *viz* under most circumstances the contract of employment. An *ex post facto* contracting out of the employee's claim in return for a 'fair share' in the proceeds can therefore avoid the provision,[60] as long as its terms are not contrary to public policy, as might be the case if consideration were hopelessly inadequate.[61] Unless the courts take the unlikely step of interpreting the employee's binding choice as diminishing his rights,[62] the statutory regime can be avoided.

---

[55] Bercusson (1980), 257 notes that the opt-out can have positive and negative effects on either party. For illustration, see Jones and Cole (2009), [42.03].

[56] Bercusson (1980), 262.

[57] Cornish, Llewelyn and Aplin (2010), 300 [7–13].

[58] Reid (1979), 355.

[59] Chandler and Holland (1993), 156.

[60] Russel (1978).

[61] Cornish (1977), 89.

[62] Bercusson (1980), 261.

A very different way around its provision can be found in section 40(3), under which a collective agreement can completely oust the operation of the 1977 Act's ownership determination provisions. The potential impact of this should not be understated. The collective agreement, firstly, 'does not have to procure any particular level of benefit to the employee in order to be effective', and '[t]he broad definition of "trade union" allows a temporary group (for example a research team) to negotiate a collective agreement'.[63] Secondly, in an additional lacuna first identified by Reid, an 'unlucky employee inventor may fall between two stools'[64] where the collective agreement is unenforceable,[65] but has nonetheless operated to curtail his entitlements under section 40.

The limitations thus set out raise two important points on the conceptual level. The common law position, firstly, is an interesting example of developments running counter to the tendency identified by Anderman[66] of contractual concepts being used by the courts in interpreting legislation to reduce the latter's employee-protective effect: here, the narrow interpretation of the relevant clauses actually supplements employee protection, for example in the scrutiny of *ex post* contracts for adequate consideration and reasonableness. The opt-out by collective agreement, on the other hand, creates a hierarchy of regulatory norms with collective bargaining operating to oust statutory provisions, which in turn limit the operation of express terms in the parties' individual contract of employment. Whilst the *de facto* role of the exception in industrial relations may have been, at least initially, rather small,[67] it is nonetheless one of the few remaining examples of the historical approach to labour market regulation embodied in Otto Kahn-Freund's theory of collective *laissez-faire*.[68]

---

[63] Cornish, Llewelyn and Aplin (2010), 299 [7–12] and Cornish (1978).
[64] Reid (1979), 357.
[65] Then by virtue of s 18(1) TULRCA 1974. Today's equivalent provision is s 179 TULRCA 1992.
[66] Anderman (2009).
[67] Gold (1990), 383.
[68] Kahn-Freund (1954). And see Davies and Freedland (1993), ch I (8 ff).

4. LIMITATIONS ARISING FROM THE IMPLIED TERM OF CONFIDENTIALITY

The general law of contract knows a wide range of implied terms, the majority of which are specific to the particular type of contract from which they arise.[69] The contract of employment in particular has seen the development of a wide range of such terms, covering both employers' and employees' duties.[70]

In the context of employee invention ownership, the key implied term is that of confidentiality: where an employee is bound by it, ownership of the invention remains with the employing entity. Whereas the operation of the term is generally limited at common law, section 42(3) of the 1977 Act has the potential effect of overriding an employee's patent ownership under section 39(2). This conundrum lies at the heart of the third limitation to be discussed: it is unclear how the implied obligation of confidence interacts with innovation ownership. This problem is illustrative of the larger question of how to reconcile loyalty and economic freedom as directly opposed interests of the employing entity versus those of its workers.[71]

The employee's legal duty not to disclose his employer's confidential information is cloaked in an unclear mix of terminology, ranging from 'fidelity', 'loyalty', 'good faith' and 'faithfulness' to 'confidence' and 'confidentiality'.[72] Despite its potential impact on employees' freedom to trade,[73] the general trend has been one of growth and extension.[74] Confidential information is protected at different levels depending on the status of the employment relationship: as long as it subsists, the implied duty of good faith and fidelity will be considerably more potent.[75]

At common law, the implied duty of confidentiality as a subset of the larger duty of fidelity appears therefore as a fairly uncontroversial limitation of the contract of employment's balancing exercise between loyalty and economic freedom. Problems arise, on the other hand, in the context of patentable innovation: due to the specific wording of the 1977

---

69 Peel (2007), 223 [6–028]; 228 [6–037].

70 Deakin and Morris (2009).

71 Freedland (2003), 171 ff.

72 Ibid, 173–178.

73 Bercusson (1980), 262–263.

74 But note *University of Nottingham v Fishel* [2002] IRLR 120 (CA): no development towards a general fiduciary duty (Elias J).

75 *Brooks v Olyslager Oms (UK) Ltd* [1997] IRLR 453, affirming *Faccenda Chicken v Fowler* [1986] ICR 297 (CA).

Act, the implied term of confidentially may cut straight across the statutory provisions, tilting the balance heavily in the employer's favour.

The problem arises from section 42(3) of the *Patents Act 1977*, which explicitly protects employees' contractual confidentiality obligations, whether express or implied. This could lead to an impasse in an employee's patent application which relies in part on the employer's confidential information, as the employer's right to protect its confidential material overrides the employee's ownership under section 39(2). Early academic discussion of this conundrum suggested that the resulting stalemate might be overcome by an *ex post* sale of the invention or licensing agreement between employer and employee.[76] In the Court of Appeal's decision in *LIFFE v Pinkava*, on the other hand, it was suggested (albeit *obiter*) that where a duty of confidentiality operated, invention ownership would automatically fall to the employer:

> Section 42(3) makes it clear that Parliament was not intending to abrogate this duty [of confidentiality] in relation to employee inventions. So if in the course of his work an employee comes up with an idea which the common law would require him to hold as confidential to his employer, that will be covered by section 39. Any other conclusion leads to the absurd result that an invention would belong to the employee and yet he would owe a duty of confidence to his employer. Parliament cannot have intended such a stalemate.[77]

Assuming that this statement does indeed reflect the current state of the law, the implications of the implied term of confidentiality severely limiting the operation of section 39 fall to be critically evaluated. The resulting position sits most uneasily with the general design of the *Patents Act's* ownership allocation regime, is ill suited to balance an employee's economic freedom with loyalty towards his employer, and is at odds with the realities of the commercial world.

Turning first to the incongruence of the statutory regime, the CDPA made certain amendments to the 1977 *Patents Act*, including the insertion of section 39(3), which stipulates that

> [w]here by virtue of this section an invention belongs, as between him and his employer, to an employee, nothing done –
>
> (a) by or on behalf of the employee or any person claiming under him for the purposes of pursuing an application for a patent, or

---

[76] Hoolahan (1979), 141.

[77] *LIFFE Administration & Management v Pinkava* [2007] EWCA Civ 217, [2007] Bus LR 1369 (CA), [100].

> (b) by any person for the purpose of performing or working the invention,
>
> shall be taken to infringe any copyright or design right to which, as between him and his employer, his employer is entitled in any model or document relating to the invention.[78]

Two connected problems arise from this provision when considered in the light of *LIFFE*. It is difficult to see, firstly, how Parliament would have intended that whilst employees could ignore their employer's statutory copyright, they should be bound by an implied term of confidentiality. Secondly, if an employer's copyright or design rights are still confidential – as they may frequently be – section 39(3) would be rendered entirely pointless by the implied term's operation under section 42(3). With respect, it is submitted that this result would be considerably more absurd than the position envisaged by Jacobs LJ. If the employee's ownership of a particular invention were to clash with his employer's confidential information, both parties have the opportunity to bargain their way out of that position – be it through a licensing agreement and joint exploitation, the sale of the patent or an appropriately priced confidentiality waiver.

> The outcome of the present conundrum betrays the extent to which the law of personal work or employment contracts, on the one hand, requires workers to identify their personal economic interests with the employing entities by which they are employed, and, on the other hand, asserts the freedom of workers to pursue their own personal interests as separate ones in a competitive market economy.[79]

Seen from this perspective, his Lordship's approach tilts the scales too far towards the obligation of loyalty, thus denying employees the chance of independent participation in the market. The practical implications of this point, finally, are not to be underestimated. In commercial reality, 'inventions (particularly improvements) do not sit in isolation and, in order to explain them or even to work them, [...] might require the use of the employer's confidential information'.[80]

---

78 As inserted into the 1977 Act by s 295, Sch 5 para 11(1) CDPA 1988.
79 Freedland (2003), 171 ff.
80 Jones and Cole (2009), [42.04].

5. CONCLUSION

In 1967, Lord Wedderburn famously referred to 'contract as the fundamental legal institution of Labour Law'.[81] Whilst the general discourse of intellectual property law might not see the contract of service in quite those terms, it is hoped that the present chapter has shown that the contract of employment plays a surprisingly important role in the resolution of employee invention ownership disputes. This role, however, is not without problems, as evidenced by the detailed discussion of three key limitations. What appeared initially as a somewhat obscure question has led to the analysis of several difficult themes, which echo in a range of frequently visited issues of broader labour law scholarship.

In concluding the discussion of the contract of employment's limitations, it is important to note that none of the limitations identified are unsurpassable obstacles. In the operation of both express and implied terms such as pre-assignment clauses and the employee's obligation of confidentiality, the limitations arising from the common law control of contractual terms appeared to be the reasonably successful outcome of a subtle balancing exercise between competing interests.

The limitations arising directly from the *Patents Act 1977* are most likely to be left to the domain of Parliament: the collective agreement lacuna in the regulation of employee-generated patent ownership could be addressed by mandatory minimum standards and coverage before a collective agreement can operate to oust the operation of both the statutory regime and the contract of employment. The overly powerful effect given to the implied term of confidentiality by section 42(3), on the other hand, should be addressed by bringing the provision in line with section 39(3): in 1988 Parliament explicitly addressed the question of competing interests, giving priority to the employee's patent ownership where section 39(2) applied. In the absence of statutory reform, meanwhile, the courts should permit the parties to bargain their way out of the impasse, rather than automatically award ownership of the employee's invention to the employer.

As regards the limitations inherent in the use of the contract of employment, finally, a lack of clarity as to the scope of the statutory invention ownership regimes was traced to the gateway function of the contract of service, in particular a series of tests used to establish it. One possibly better-suited strand of criteria might be an economic or business

---

[81] Wedderburn (1967), 1. This is a comparatively recent development: Deakin and Wilkinson (2005), and Deakin (1998).

integration test of 'whether the [employee was] part and parcel of the organization'.[82] The concept, initially highlighted in several decisions by Denning LJ in response to the perceived shortcomings of the control test, was applied in several leading decisions on employee invention ownership.[83] It is, however, no longer in use, and might be of limited utility given its vulnerability to the increasingly vertically disintegrated legal and economic structures of most businesses.[84]

A potential solution to contract of employment's inability to grapple with complex employment scenarios lies in the differentiated regulation of employee invention ownership, depending on the individual circumstances of employment.[85] This approach would be difficult to reconcile with the contract of employment *stricto sensu*, however, as its historical function is the very opposite, drawing a wide range of different categories of employment together rather than distinguishing between them. In finding an effective response to this limitation, a move beyond the narrow paradigm concept might therefore be necessary. Indeed, analysis of the role of the contract of employment in determining the ownership of employee inventions has provided an excellent instance of the necessity to question the extent to which the very notion of the contract of employment should continue to be regarded as the central organising concept of individual employment relationships.[86]

REFERENCES

Anderman, S. (2009), 'The Interpretation of Protective Employment Statutes and Contracts of Employment' 29 *Industrial Law Journal* 223

Bercusson, B. (1980), 'The Contract of Employment and Contracting Out: The UK Patents Act 1977' 2 *European Intellectual Property Review* 257

Chandler, A. and J. Holland (1993), *Information: Protection, Ownership & Rights*, Blackstone Press Ltd

Collins, H. (1986), 'Market Power, Bureaucratic Power, and the Contract of Employment' 15 *Industrial Law Journal* 1

Collins, H. (1990), 'Independent Contractors and the Challenge of Vertical Disintegration to Employment Protection Laws' 10 *Oxford Journal of Legal Studies* 353

---

[82] *Bank voor Handel en Scheepvaart NV v Slatford (No. 2)* [1953] 1 QB 248 (CA) 295.

[83] *Stephenson Jordan* [1952] 1 TLR 101 (CA), *Nora Beloff v Pressdram Ltd* [1973] 1 All ER 241 (HC).

[84] Collins (1990).

[85] Pila (2010).

[86] Freedland (2003).

Cornish, W. (1978), 'Employees' Inventions' in *The Patents Act 1977* Conference at Queen Mary College, University of London, January
Cornish, W. (1978), 'Employee Inventions: the New United Kingdom Patent Law' 1 *European Intellectual Property Review* 4
Cornish W.R. (1992), 'Rights in University Innovations: the Herchel Smith Lecture for 1991' 14(1) *European Intellectual Property Review* 13
Cornish W.R., D. Llewelyn and T. Aplin (2010), *Intellectual Property: Patents, Copyright, Trade Marks and Allied Rights*, 7th edn, Sweet & Maxwell
Davies, P. and M. Freedland (1993), *Labour Legislation and Public Policy: A Contemporary History*, Oxford University Press (Clarendon Law Series)
Deakin, S. (1998), 'The Evolution of the Contract of Employment' in N. Whiteside and R. Salais (eds), *Governance, Industry and Labour Markets in Britain and France*, Routledge
Deakin, S. and G. Morris (2009), *Labour Law*, 5th edn, Hart Publishing
Deakin, S. and F. Wilkinson (2005), *The Law of the Labour Market*, Oxford University Press (Oxford Monographs on Labour Law)
Freedland, M. (2003), *The Personal Employment Contract*, Oxford University Press
Gold, T. (1990), 'Entitlement Disputes: A Case Review' 12 *European Intellectual Property Review* 382
Hoolahan, M.J. (1979), 'Employees' Inventions – the Practical Implications – Ownership and Compensation – the UK Patents Act 1977' 1 *European Intellectual Property Review* 140
Jones, S. and P. Cole (2009), *CIPA Guide to the Patents Acts*, 6th edn, Sweet & Maxwell/Thomson Reuters
Kahn-Freund, O. (1954), 'Legal Framework' in A. Flanders and H. Clegg (eds), *The System of Industrial Relations in Great Britain*, Basil Blackwell
Peel, E. (2007), *Treitel's Law of Contract*, 12th edn, Sweet & Maxwell
Phillips, J. (ed.) (1981), *Employees' Inventions – a Comparative Study*, Fersway Publications
Phillips, J. and M.J. Hoolahan (1982), *Employees' Inventions in the UK: Law and Practice*, ESC Publishing Ltd
Pila, J., 'Revisiting Section 39(1) of the Patents Act 1977: The Ownership of Academic and Professional Employee Inventions', Oxford Legal Research Paper Series 9 No. 40/2010
Pila, J. (2010a), 'Academic Freedom and the Courts' 126 *Law Quarterly Review* 347
Reid, B. (1979), 'Employee Inventions under the Patents Act 1977' 23 *Journal of Business Law* 350
Russel, P. (1978), 'Employee Inventions' 128 *New Law Journal* 800
Saxby, S. (1981), 'Employees' Inventions and English Law' in J. Phillips (ed.), *Employees' Inventions – a Comparative Study*, Fersway Publications
Swan, S.K. (1959), 'Patent Rights in an Employee's Invention' 75 *Law Quarterly Review* 77
Taylor, B.M. (1969), 'The British Patent System. 1. Administration (Book Review)' 27 *Cambridge Law Journal* 131
Wedderburn, K. (1967), *Cases and Materials on Labour Law*, Cambridge University Press
White, T.A.B. (1962), *Patents for Inventions and the Registration of Industrial Designs*, 3rd edn, Stevens

10. The innovative worker: genius, accidental inventor or thief?

Marilyn Pittard

In Australian labour and employment law, both the collective relationship between groups of workers and their employer, as regulated by the legislative framework, and the individual relationship between an employer and employee, governed by the contract of employment, determine, or have the potential to affect, the relative rights and entitlements of innovative workers and their employers. This chapter focuses first on that potential in the collective relationship in Australia, but secondly it particularly addresses what we learn from the contract of employment in relation to employee and employer ownership of inventions in Australia and the impacts of the vagaries of the common law on employee/contractor status.

The chapter will explore issues through the prism of the 'genius' inventor, the 'accidental inventor' and the 'thief'. The genius inventor may be thought of as an inventor who is specifically engaged to invent; whilst the accidental inventor is one who unexpectedly or accidentally makes an invention whilst employed. The thief is an employee who steals knowledge or an invention belonging to the employer (but not necessarily in a criminal sense of being a thief, although there may be theft of materials or documents), and who additionally may attempt to use it in competition with the original employer.

1. A MATTER OF LABOUR RELATIONS? INDIVIDUAL EMPLOYMENT VERSUS COLLECTIVE RELATIONSHIPS

The Australian labour law and employment law perspective on innovation in employment relies essentially on the individual contractual relationship between employer and employee. The traditional common law relating to the individual relationship provides the legal principles, albeit that these principles are not always easy to apply in different and contemporary factual circumstances. Essentially, the individual relationship will be governed by the contract of employment, its express terms and the terms implied in fact or by law. As the contract is substantially a creature of the common law, judicial approaches, then, are influential in Australia, with very little direct intervention of the legislature to assist.

By way of contrast, the collective labour relationship – the relationship between employer and groups of employees or unions – does not have significant bearing in this area, despite Australia having a strong history of minimum conditions being governed by arbitrated awards and/or collective agreements as well as a history of state intervention in industrial relations matters.[1] Yet there is potential for the collective relationship to be influential.

The statutory framework of the federal regulatory regime, the *Fair Work Act 2009* (Cth) (*Fair Work Act*), tends to reinforce the traditional dichotomy between, on the one hand, matters in the individual sphere which are left to the principles of law dealing with the contract of employment and, on the other hand, matters in the collective sphere which fall within the potential scope of the *Fair Work Act*. That Act provides a framework for the making, approval and enforcement of collective agreements, which in Australia are largely agreements at enterprise level, rather than sectoral or industry-wide agreements. They are also usually agreements with a single employer, rather than multi-employers. The scope of the enterprise agreement under the *Fair Work Act* requires the agreement (relevantly) to pertain to the relationship of employer and employees who will be covered by the agreement.[2] Thus there is the strong possibility for such agreements to deal with ownership of inventions and assignment of patent rights and to restrain the employee from competing with the employer post-employment. Any clause about ownership of inventions made during the course of employment would fall within the breadth of that employment relationship. A

---

1 Pittard and Naughton (2010) chapters 1 and 7.

2 *Fair Work Act* Part 2–4 and s 172(1). 'Permitted matters' in an enterprise agreement include not only matters pertaining to the employment relationship as indicated above but also matters pertaining to the employer–union relationship and deductions from wages for purposes authorised by an employee. On collective agreements: Pittard and Naughton (2010) ch 11; Creighton and Stewart (2010) ch 21, Owens, Riley and Murray (2011) ch 11. Cases on 'matters': *Re Manufacturing Grocers' Employees' Federation of Australia; Ex parte Australian Chamber of Manufactures* (1986) 160 CLR 341 and *Electrolux Home Products Pty Ltd v Australian Workers Union* (2004) 221 CLR 309.

restraint clause, however, might be excluded if worded in such a way as to deal with the *former* employment relationship – but if it was grounded, say, in prohibiting the employee from taking away from employment something acquired during the employment relationship, it might meet the employment relationship definition. Any clause not within that Act's notion of employment matters, however, would not be enforceable – even if it were included in an enterprise agreement approved by Fair Work Australia, the tribunal with power to approve agreements.[3]

Despite these possibilities and no doubt grounded in pre-existing attitudes to what has traditionally been regarded as within the scope of the collective relationship, in Australia the approach has been to leave such clauses dealing with invention to the individual employment relationship. The current 2011–2014 enterprise agreement with the Australian scientific research body, the Commonwealth Scientific and Industrial Research Organisation ('CSIRO'), generally provides: 'CSIRO is committed to creating an environment where innovation thrives and everyone is valued and treated fairly and with respect' and 'The parties to this Agreement recognise that CSIRO's objectives are largely dependent on the innovation and creativity of its staff.'[4] Yet this enterprise agreement goes no further to include clauses about ownership of inventions. So, even an organisation whose main purpose is scientific research and innovation does not deal at the collective enterprise level with such matters. Interestingly though, in the context of commercialisation the CSIRO agreement states in clause 53 that 'the parties to this Agreement acknowledge that effective commercialization of research and development outcomes are fundamental to CSIRO's future' but then goes on to provide in clause 53(c), after acknowledging that the parties will be informed of opportunities for involvement and be consulted appropriately where their employment or work is affected:

> (c) Where CSIRO introduces a scheme allowing officers who generate intellectual property to share in the benefits of the commercialization of that intellectual property, the affected officers and where they choose, their representatives, will be informed of the details of the scheme. The details of the scheme and its operation will be determined by CSIRO and may be varied at CSIRO's discretion. CSIRO will consult affected staff and where they choose their representatives, when undertaking subsequent reviews of the scheme. These schemes will include mechanisms for resolving disputes or

[3] *Fair Work Act* s 253.

[4] Clauses 47 and 49 respectively Enterprise Agreement 2011–2014: <http://www.csiro.au/Portals/Careers/Enterprise-Agreement.aspx>

> grievances and therefore will not be subject to the grievance and dispute procedures contained in Schedule 4 and 87 respectively of this Agreement.

Thus the benefits of commercialisation will be determined unilaterally by the CSIRO as employer and it is the collective agreement which acknowledges this retention of discretion by the CSIRO.

The fact remains, however, that it is theoretically and legally possible to include these matters in collective agreements approved under the Australian legislative framework. Collective agreements made at common law, however, and not approved under the Act, can include such clauses but these common law agreements are notoriously difficult, if not impossible, to enforce.[5]

Similarly, awards which resulted from arbitration of industrial claims by the independent tribunal in Australia have not traditionally addressed invention matters and tended to provide for minimum wages and employment conditions in the industry or occupational group.[6] Modern awards, derived from the old arbitrated awards, and now given status under the *Fair Work Act* (with some changed controls on their scope), do not extend to these matters.[7] Modern awards, together with the legislated National Employment Standards, provide minimum conditions of employment and, together with the contract of employment, are sources of employment rights and obligations. No doubt the history of legislative constraints and their interpretation by the High Court of Australia on matters which may be included in awards confined their scope to traditional employment matters and, when the law altered to broaden the scope of these matters, the possibility of pursuing rights and obligations in connection with inventions may not have been seen as sufficiently pressing or of sufficiently widespread concern as to change the previous practice.[8] These issues were just not seen as industrial issues and thus remain within the province of the common law and the contract of employment.

---

5 Pittard and Naughton (2010), 54–69.

6 Ibid [10.1]–[10.16].

7 Ibid [10.17]–[10.29].

8 E.g., *R v Kelly; Ex parte State of Victoria* (1950) 81 CLR 64 for narrow interpretation and *Manufacturing Grocers' Employees Federation of Australia; Ex parte Australian Chamber of Manufacturers* (1986) 160 CLR 341 for broader interpretations of what pertains to the employment relationship. Also Fox, Howard and Pittard (1995), 376–84.

2. THE CONTRACT OF EMPLOYMENT

Issues relating to invention and innovation then generally fall to the employment contract to regulate. The contract was influenced originally by the common law of the United Kingdom – but has taken directions of its own. As Moore J stated in *EdSonic Pty Ltd v Cassidy*:[9] 'There have been "shifts in emphasis and the tensions that have attended the evolution of the principles" of ownership of an invention, with the tendency at common law to increase the presumption of ownership in favour of the employer.'[10]

Whether the employee will be able to keep his/her invention and reap its proceeds depends on the employment contract and its express and implied terms. In *Victoria University of Technology v Wilson,*[11] the court stated the general principle:

> The law is well settled upon the position of an officer or employee who makes an invention affecting the business of his or her employer. It is an implied term of employment that any invention or discovery made in the course of the employment of the employee in doing that which he is engaged and instructed to do during the time of his employment, and during working hours, and using the materials of his employers, is the property of the employer and not of the employee. Having made a discovery or invention in the course of such work, the employee becomes a trustee for the employer of that invention or discovery, and he is therefore as a trustee bound to give the benefit of any such discovery or invention to his employer.

However, the court issued words of warning which set out some limits to the general proposition: 'But the mere existence of the employer/employee relationship will not give the employer ownership of inventions made by the employee during the term of the relationship.'[12] Moreover, this proposition applies even where the invention gives utility to the employer and its business and was created using the employer's time and resources.[13]

Having said that, the scope for the contract to ensure that the employer is the beneficiary of employment inventions is today reasonably strong, given strategies for express terms, for implying terms in fact and law,

---

9 (2010) 272 ALR 589.

10 Ibid para [35], quoting *University of WA v Gray* (2009) 259 ALR 224, [148]–158].

11 [2004] VSC 33, [104].

12 Ibid.

13 Ibid.

including the duty to invent, and interpretations of the content of the course of employment.

This section will discuss the contractual approach and detail the approach to the genius, accidental inventor and thief.

2.1 The Genius, Express Terms of the Contract and the 'Course of Employment'

The employer which specifically engages a person to invent – the person I call the 'genius inventor' – would usually ensure that the contract's express terms specify that there is a duty to invent and make clear what the expectation of the employee is in this regard. The contract might also include a clause requiring that the employer has the right of ownership in the invention and that the employee relinquishes any and all entitlements to financial benefits which may arise from any inventive activity of the employee. This may clarify in large part the contractual position of rights and entitlements of ownership as between employer and employee. And it would also be hoped that there was due financial reward provided in the contract for relinquishing these rights.[14]

The Federal Court case of *EdSonic Pty Ltd v Cassidy*,[15] albeit in the context of ownership of copyright, provides a useful illustration of factual circumstances and a succinct summary of the law, as well as some of the problems following *University of Western Australia v Gray.*[16] In response to EdSonic's claim of ownership in educational course materials, Ms Cassidy claimed to have created these 'works' prior to being engaged by EdSonic. She did additional work to the materials after commencing employment with EdSonic, but argued that this involved largely reformulating the materials to be on-line and so on.

Moore J posed the question to be answered: '[D]id the employee make the work because the contract of employment expressly or impliedly required or at least authorises the work to be made'?[17] The Federal Court concluded that as Ms Cassidy's arguments were upheld, she was the owner of the works.

Perspicacious observations of Moore J in *EdSonic* concerned the lessons which may be derived from *University of Western Australia v*

---

[14] Merges (1999), however, argued that the default position of the employer owning the invention was usually accompanied by some position of internal reward or monetary compensation.

[15] (2010) 272 ALR 589.

[16] (2010) 179 FCR 346. Chapter 5 in this volume undertakes full analysis.

[17] (2010) 272 ALR 589, [35].

Gray. His Honour outlined four main propositions that emerged from that case, including: 'Unless the contract of employment expressly so provides, or an invention is the product of work which the employee was paid to perform, it is unlikely that an invention made by the employee will be held to belong to the employer … .'[18] Nonetheless, questions may arise: Has the employee made the particular invention in the course of that (genius) employee's employment? The court in *Edsonic* also addressed these issues (from the *Gray* case) as follows:

> The question to be answered is 'what is it that [the employee] is paid to do'. Their Honours [in *Gray*] indicated that where the work in issue is the product of what the employee was paid to do, it will belong to the employer unless otherwise agreed.
>
> The task the Court must undertake, namely to define the subject matter over which an employee's responsibility to the employer extends, can be difficult, and care must be taken in fulfilling this function with lessons to be drawn from the 'parallel problem in fiduciary law' of defining the subject matter over which the fiduciary obligations extend.[19]

The genius employee may still be able to claim ownership where it can be established that the invention was not within the course of his/her employment and was not within the scope of what the employee was paid to do. The employer, in such an instance, may nonetheless seek to argue that the invention was in the course of that employee's employment and can be read into the job description (which may well be expressly stated).

Whilst general principles might be clear about the consequences of inventions made in the course of employment, recent Australian cases serve to identify the approach of the courts and the very real problems of actual innovators: the genius employee. Was the invention created during the 'course of the employment'?

In *Austal Ships Pty Ltd v Damien Smith*,[20] Mr Smith, a naval architect, produced innovative design drawings which were the subject of argument as to whether he or Austal Ships owned them. The Australian Patent Office held that, even though he was not engaged to invent, he produced the drawings in the course of his role as naval architect, thus the employer owned them:

> Given that Mr Smith was employed as a naval architect and that the drawing D01286–018 and its creative content was produced in the course of his work,

---

18 Ibid.

19 Ibid.

20 [2011] APO 4.

> and in accordance with the duties of his position, clearly the intellectual property contained in the drawing comes within the implied term of employment referred to in *Victoria University of Technology v Wilson* [namely that any invention or discovery made in the course of the employment of the employee in doing that which he is engaged and instructed to do during the time of his employment, and during working hours, and using the materials of his employers, is the property of the employer and not of the employee].[21]

It is quite possible that the employee may use the employer's materials and even undertake the invention during working hours but the invention is not regarded as created in 'the course of employment'. Where courts rule in such cases that the employee is entitled to ownership/proceeds of the invention, the law is a very blunt instrument – after all, the employee has made use of the employer's facilities.[22] Yet there is no concept of apportioning benefits, taking account of what each party brought in creating the invention.

2.2 Extending the Ambit of Employment to Private Time

To avoid the tricky question of privately undertaken innovations, as compared to employment-related innovations, the employer may provide an express term of the contract to the effect that any innovation made by the employee *during the period of employment* will remain the property of the employer, even where the innovation was made in the employee's private time. Such clauses are used as standard clauses in some industries. Employers endeavour to anticipate such inventions because '[o]ften major breakthroughs come from seemingly little ideas or insights arising from hands-on engagement, and from learning by doing.'[23]

This raises questions: first, does an employee have bargaining strength to negotiate changes to a standard-form contract presented by the employer for signing? And secondly, what is the appropriateness of agreeing, at the outset of the employment relationship, that whatever may be undertaken, even in the employee's private capacity, belongs to the employer simply because it has occurred during the period of employment? Certainly in other instances employers may endeavour to regulate the private life of the employee – for example, conduct outside working hours which reflects on the employer or the business's reputation. In the *James Boag* case, for example, an employee who was relatively low in

---

21 Ibid [39].

22 In *UWA v Gray*, the employee made use of the employer's facilities – although the outcome was different there.

23 Report on the National Innovation System (2008) ch 5, 35.

the employment hierarchy was bound by the 'no drink driving' policy of the brewery employer because it did not want its company's reputation adversely affected by such behaviour by *employees even when they were not on duty or at work.*[24] It is noteworthy that employers, then, may seek, in similar vein, to tie up contractually invention ownership; and employees – the accidental genius – not anticipating they would invent, may agree to the terms. However, the genius employee, if he/she is indeed a true and habitual inventor, might be wiser and, if possible, avoid tying up the ownership of inventions made during the employee's own time.

The fairness of such an agreement *de novo*, before any invention has indeed been dreamed of, may be criticised – the employee seeking the employment may not be well placed to negotiate suitable terms to protect his/her position and negotiate clauses to share royalties or proceeds from the invention. The 'accidental' or unintended discovery, discussed below, is also usually beyond the contemplation of the express terms of the contract.

Whilst in particular cases express terms may provide many answers, they do not provide all the answers. Because express terms reflect a particular bargain (which may or may not be between the parties of equal bargaining strength), express terms may not address either the microeconomic policy questions of promoting creativity or fair return for endeavours by the employee within the enterprise or the macroeconomic policy questions of what is best for productivity and growth in the economy.

Those issues can only adequately be covered either by legislation or by policy choices implicit (or express) in common law principles which determine the content or interpretation of the relative rights of employer and employee to share in the economic benefits of innovation.

3. THE ACCIDENTAL INVENTOR

> Talk about innovation can be very abstract, but tends to become quite specific and stereotypic when talking about the innovator and entrepreneur – the mad inventor in a lab coat, or the white-shoed commercial hustler. Likewise, there is a tendency to imply that a special 'creative class' of people exists to whom the general population should pay due deference.[25]

---

[24] *Kolodjashni v Lion Nathan T/A James Boag and Son Brewing Pty Ltd* [2010] FWAFB 3258; *Farquharson v Qantas Airways Limited* [2005] AIRC 982.

[25] Report on the Review of the National Innovation System, ch 5, 47.

Despite the stereotypes, the invention may be quite accidental – not by the mad inventor or the 'creative class' but by an employee seeing and seizing a creative opportunity. The classic example of what I have categorised as the 'accidental inventor' was litigated in Australia in *Spencer Industries Pty Limited v Collins*[26] when Mr Collins, the Sales Manager, made an invention related to the business of his employer, Spencer Industries Pty Limited ('Spencer Industries'). Spencer Industries made goods which were used to retread tyres; Collins' invention was an efficient rasp blade used to buff down the thread of worn tyres. Collins' employment contract included an obligation to advance sales of Spencer Industries, however, there were no express provisions relating to inventions' ownership. Collins saw the need for the product when performing this role of sales manager. He was, then, an accidental inventor and, at least in terms of his contract of employment, he had no obligation to invent or to assign ownership of inventions made. He refused to assign patent rights to Spencer Industries, even after a threat of dismissal: 'Sign or resign.' Ultimately, he resigned his employment, selling the patent rights to a competitor of Spencer Industries.

In litigation about entitlement to patent rights, Spencer Industries argued that Collins made the invention 'in the course of employment' and thus his employer should benefit from the patent. The answer, ultimately, was not complicated for the Federal Court: 'The invention was not … the product of the work which Mr Collins was paid to do … .'[27] The connection could not be made between, on the one hand, a contract containing a duty on Spencer to advance sales with, on the other hand, any invention which itself would advance sales made within the scope of employment.

The accidental inventor in this case was entitled to the patent rights. That entitlement rested ultimately on the words of the contract; had the contract gone further in general terms to impose obligations on Collins to, say, notify all ideas to the employer for the benefit of the employer, the answer may not have been so clear cut.

The fate, then, of the accidental inventor may be sealed by the job description and scope of employment and the express contractual terms agreed at a time where neither employer nor employee envisages an invention being made. In the UK case of *LIFFE Administration and Management v Pinkava*,[28] the court posited an example: a research

---

[26] (2003) 58 IPR 425.
[27] Ibid [83].
[28] [2007] EWCA Civ 217, [97].

chemist, researching cancer cures, would not own his invention for arthritis cures. The court cautioned that it does not assist to examine only the daily work which an employee is performing as '[h]is duty as a research chemist is wider than his day-to-day work'.[29]

By way of contrast, *Courier Pete Pty Ltd v Metroll Queensland Pty Ltd*[30] permitted the foreman of Metroll Queensland Pty Ltd to retain ownership of designs he had made for increasing the storage capacity for water through a mechanism of modular water tanks. The contract contained no express duty to invent or to create new designs; the contract was general in nature and also was not precise about the scope of employment. The court rejected the employer's argument that the foreman was expressly instructed to create designs for new tanks and accepted the employee's argument that he undertook the relevant work at home and in his own time. Spender J succinctly stated:

> If the employee was employed to make or discover inventions of the type ultimately produced, [by the company], then that is work for which the employer had paid and the employer is entitled to the benefit of the invention. If the employee does not have any general duty to invent ... then the only basis upon which an invention can be said to have been created 'in the course of employment' is if it had been created pursuant to a specific direction by the employee to undertake work which results in the creation of the invention.[31]

Similarly, in *University of WA v Gray*[32] the Court found that no duty to invent could be implied in Professor Gray's contract of employment – so he was an accidental inventor, entitled to the proceeds of his discovery.

The cases do depend on the factual and contractual scenarios. These, too, may be 'accidental' – at least not made in contemplation of a discovery. Hence there is an artificiality about focusing on the contract's terms and the job description which itself may have changed considerably over the employment period.

4. IMPLYING CONTRACTUAL TERMS: ACCIDENTAL INVENTOR AND THIEF

The common law has traditionally provided for a number of obligations of employees, being regarded as duties which arise in any contract of

---

29 Ibid.

30 [2010] 87 IPR 397.

31 Ibid, [19].

32 Chapter 5 in this volume.

employment. The question is what application those duties may have to inventions and innovations made or contributed to by an employee, in the absence of express contractual provisions.

4.1 Implied Duty to Obey Lawful and Reasonable Orders

The implied duty to obey lawful and reasonable orders arising under the contract of employment is relevant to inventiveness in the workplace.[33] An employer may direct an employee to undertake work towards a particular invention or innovation. Certainly, this is part of the expected contractual duties where the position description as encapsulated in the contract (as in the case of our genius employee) embraces it. Thus the chemist at the pharmaceutical company would not be surprised to receive such a direction where she is involved in drug innovation as part of her express duties. But the employee whose duties do not ordinarily include invention, discovery or innovation may wonder at such an order and may not be obliged to obey it – if the employee was summarily dismissed for disobeying the order, in considering the lawfulness of the order and termination, attention would be focused by a court on whether the scope of the employee's employment extended to such creativity.

Problematic, too, is the question of the respective rights and obligations of employer and employee when the employee, not usually inventing, obeys the employer's directive and successfully invents. The employee's rights and entitlements to share the invention's financial rewards are unclear. Again, the question returns to the uncertainty of scope of employment duties: do they encompass such inventive activity?

Conversely, an employer may instruct an employee not to utilise its equipment and facilities for non-work purposes. Thus, the issue of an employee's entitlement to the proceeds of an invention made utilising the employer's facilities in contravention of the order is muddled by the employee's own contractual breach. Presumably, employer and employee may negotiate a resolution, but the legalities of who reaps the rewards are not clear.

The essential point, however, is that the contractual validity of any directions to invent (and related instructions such as to commercialise the invention and/or apply for patents), and the consequences for 'ownership' and entitlement to participate in the economic benefits flowing from any invention, are all resolved by the determination of whether the order was

---

[33] Pittard and Naughton (2010), 190–218; e.g., *Adami v Maison de Luxe* (1924) 35 CLR 143.

reasonable and lawful as being within the scope or course of employment. It goes without saying that express agreement on these points, rather than an investigation of what may fall within the scope of the course of employment (or what was a reasonable order) after the event, would have the great merit of preventing, or at least reducing, uncertainty and disputation.

4.2 Duty to Invent

The courts will imply a duty to invent in certain types of contract.[34] Having said that, even the contract of the research professor in a university in the *Gray* case was not one in which the duty to invent would be implied because of the nature of the employer and employment. That case has now established that the duty to invent is implied in certain classes of contract – e.g., the research scientist employed to carry out certain tasks. In *The Royal Children's Hospital v Robert Alexander*,[35] the Australian Patents Office, considering a case after *Gray,* held that the head of virology at the employer hospital, who invented the viral recovery medium, was not entitled to ownership of the invention as he was under a duty to invent implied in his contract: '[His invention] addressed a recognized problem in the art and was the product of research which a virologist would undertake when trying to optimize the techniques used at the hospital. I therefore accept that the invention was conceived in the course of Dr Alexander's employment.'[36] By way of contrast, another invention by Dr Alexander was not the employer's: his employer did not expect it and it was outside the employment scope.

In general, the concept of the duty to invent, whilst solving the issues in some cases which come before the courts, is a shaky foundation for determining the rights and obligations with its attendant uncertainty of application in particular cases.

4.3 Duty of Fidelity

This implied duty in law ensures that the employee will act in good faith in the employer's interests, retain confidentiality where necessary and

---

[34] Pittard and Naughton (2010), 262–270; Pittard (2009); chapter 5 in this volume.

[35] [2011] APO 94.

[36] Ibid at [73].

faithfully serve the employer.[37] Innovations made by an employee (or contributed to by an employee) which ultimately enable the employee, or more likely the ex-employee, to compete with the employer, have a high probability of leading to questions about whether the employee's duty of fidelity has been breached.

Outright theft of an employer's trade secret or taking away confidential information will contravene the duty of fidelity. The employer's protection against the thief will last beyond the cessation of employment as the obligation to maintain trade secrecy or the confidentiality of innovation binds the employee not only whilst employed, but also whilst an ex-employee.[38] The murky area, where uncertainty resides, relates to whether there was a 'trade secret' created by the innovation made by the employee, or whether the innovation is (or was deemed to be) 'confidential'.[39]

Significantly, where the employee solely created the invention that she is accused of wrongly utilising during or after employment (or contributed to its creation), he/she would no doubt plead his/her possible ownership of the invention in any litigation as a defence to the employer's allegation of breach of the fidelity duty. The legal issue, then, could return to the employee's ownership rights.

4.4 Are the Duties of Cooperation and of Mutual Trust and Confidence Relevant in Australian Contract Law?

Although the existence of the duty of cooperation with the employer in the running of its business has been mooted from cases such as *Secretary of State for Employment v Associated Society of Locomotive Engineers and Firemen (No 2)*,[40] its precise status has not been determined in Australia by superior courts. However, it is possible that this duty may be invoked where an employer wishes to argue that the innovation is part of the contractual arrangement. In today's employment structure, employees

---

[37] Pittard and Naughton (2010), 224–261; Creighton and Stewart (2010), Part 4.

[38] The duty of fidelity might be informed by the equitable obligation of confidence, they may be one and the same or there might be two different sources. This latter view tends to prevail in Australia but Stewart (1988) argues that the two duties – contract and equity – could exist simultaneously.

[39] *Ansell Rubber Co Pty Ltd v Allied Rubber Industries Pty Ltd* [1967] VR 37; *Faccenda Chicken Ltd v Fowler* [1986] 1 All ER 617 (classic example); *Independent Management Resources Pty Ltd v Brown* [1987] VR 605.

[40] [1972] 2 QB 455.

in many fields of endeavour are likely to be involved in furthering their employer's interests. Those on commission for sales or other targets are well-known examples of employment being geared to maximising sales for the employer's benefit. However, many employees would be expected to contribute to the smooth running of the employer's business, to actively recruit customers and clients, and to promote the employer's business and reputation commercially.

It is, then, a very short step to acknowledging that, in complying with this duty of cooperation, an employee could be developing new processes or procedures in business for its efficiency and productivity. And that would fall easily within the duty *of cooperation*. And could it be another small step to say that *an innovation* which aids or promotes the employer's business falls within that duty of cooperation? Surprisingly this duty has received little attention in the courts but there is scope for further development of its application, especially in current employment approaches where senior employees may be expected to be engaged with the employer's business almost as a joint endeavour.

Similarly, the Australian courts have not wholeheartedly and unreservedly adopted the concept developed in the UK of the implied duty where employer and employee owe each other a duty of mutual trust and confidence.[41] Proponents of this duty and its role argue that it leads the way to promoting fair dealing at work; but such a concept, even read at its best, would seem to provide little relief to resolve the issue of entitlement to the proceeds or ownership of inventions.[42]

4.5 Implied Terms in Fact and Workplace Policies

Even where the duty to invent or innovate in an employment contract is not implied in law (that is, as part of the various duties implied by law in employment contracts discussed in 4.1 to 4.4), the particular contractual circumstances may imply a duty to invent. The tests for implication in the contract of terms in fact include identifying whether the term is necessary

---

41 Brodie (1998) for UK law; Pittard and Naughton (2010), 308–348 for Australian cases and developments.

42 Riley (2003); but note Carrigan (2009) who strenuously argues that the duty of mutual trust and confidence cannot and does not address issues of power imbalance between employer and employee but can only provide some procedural relief to employees.

to give business efficacy to the contract and is 'so obvious that "it goes without saying"' that it is in the contract.[43]

Workplace policies which have not been expressly included in the contract of employment may be an important source of attempts to regulate employment relations in respect of inventions at work – and the legal question arising will be whether they form part of the contract. Ultimately, whether that workplace policy is incorporated in the contract, and therefore enforceable, may come down to a matter of evidence and proof about such issues as notification of the policy to employees and conversations at the time of negotiating the contract. These issues are further addressed in Part 6 of this volume.

Negotiations leading up to the formation of the contract may form part of the contract and inform the rights and entitlements too, depending on the particular circumstances. It is significant to note that in *University of WA v Gray* the submissions of the University did not rest upon the implication *in fact* of a contractual term in the particular circumstances.

5. RESTRAINING THE THIEF AND COMPETITOR

Restraint clauses or restrictive covenants are usually standard terms in senior employees' contracts – that the employee cannot carry on a similar business within certain time and geographical constraints, even after the employment relationship has ended and these further restrict utilisation of the invention or aspects of it.[44] Thus the employer may try to restrict a potential thief and competitor by such express clause(s). However, it is becoming more common to provide that even junior employees or trainees are subject to restraint clauses, as in the case of *Birdanco Nominees Pty Ltd v Money*[45] where the Victorian Court of Appeal ordered the trainee accountant to pay the employer considerable compensation for breaching the restraint clause which was held to apply to him.

Once more, the issue is raised of how such employees, even senior ones, have the bargaining strength to resist fairly tightly worded restraint clauses being included in the contract which may limit their ability to trade or compete down the track.

---

[43] *BP Refinery (Westernport) Pty Ltd v Hastings Shire Council* (1977) 180 CLR 266. There are further preconditions relating to the term being reasonable and equitable; having clear expression and not contradicting any express term of the contract. See *Byrne v Australian Airlines Ltd* (1995) 185 CLR 410.

[44] Molnar chapter this volume.

[45] [2012] VSCA 64.

6. LEGAL CONUNDRUM: THE EMPLOYEE/CONTRACTOR DISTINCTION

The discussion so far has focused on rights and obligations arising out of the individual, and possibly the collective, employment relationship. Of course work or labour services may be provided by an individual person (a sole trader) to a party (or principal) under a relationship of principal and independent contractor. At the heart of the application of principles, derived from the implied duties of an employee, that an employer is entitled to the proceeds of inventions or innovations in the course of employment of the employee (barring express or implied agreement to the contrary) is the legal status of the worker. That worker must be an *employee*, as distinct from a contractor, for the implied duties doctrines to apply.

Even more than a decade into the twenty-first century, the distinction between 'employee' and 'independent contractor' is fraught with difficulty in Australia. Whilst the High Court of Australia has established that the totality of factors must be examined to ascertain overall the legal status of the worker, there is room for discretion in the application of those factors in particular cases. Cases invariably differ as to their facts and circumstances: not all factors are present in all cases and their weightings or significance in individual circumstances will vary. Consequently there is room for great uncertainty in those cases which fall between, on the one hand, the clear or obvious case of the traditional employee and, on the other hand, the person who is in business on his/her own account as he/she is conducting a trade or business which is independent of a particular employer.

Three key High Court of Australia decisions inform the law and application to the worker's status:

1. In *Stevens and Gray v Brodribb Sawmilling Co Pty Ltd*,[46] the High Court conferred independent contractor status on a worker who worked under the following circumstances: he was paid by the job completed; there was very little direction and control by the principal; no taxation payments were deducted; the worker had a right to delegate the task to others and not perform it personally, the worker provided equipment to perform the job and maintained that equipment.

[46] (1986) 160 CLR 16.

2 Later, in *Hollis v Vabu Pty Ltd*,[47] the High Court categorised as an employee a bicycle courier who made deliveries of parcels in the city. The main reasoning was that such couriers were not in business on their own account, even where they supplied and used their own bicycles (which were low cost capital items), were not paid annual or sick leave, and were not taxed as employees. It was significant to the court's conclusion that they were employees that they were subject to actual direction and considerable control as to conduct of the work; they wore the jacket supplied by the business and represented the business; they were directed as to when to take (unpaid) holidays and could not refuse work.. The curious consequence of this decision was that other couriers who were not bicycle couriers and used their own cars, remain classified as 'independent contractors' under a previous ruling of the NSW Court of Appeal.[48]

3. In *Sweeney v Boylan Nominee Pty Ltd*,[49] the worker, a refrigerator mechanic, was classified as a contractor because, although working consistently for Boylan Nominee Pty Ltd, he provided his own tools and equipment, and operated business on his own account.

The contrast of cases in which the legal status is in question may be valuable but in all three the issue arose because of issues of liability of a person injured by the worker's negligence. The body of law in Australia has developed in many other contexts: the entitlements of employees to unfair dismissal protection under industrial relations legislation; entitlements of minimum labour standards either through awards, enterprise agreements or the statutory employment standards (National Employment Standards) to employees only; superannuation entitlements to employees under legislative provisions; and implication of terms into employment contracts only.

The question of the worker's legal status also arises in respect of whether the inventor is an employee. Frequently, the legal question is far from easy to resolve. More recently, the Federal Court of Australia, a superior court in the Federal hierarchy of courts, considered aspects of the distinction. In *Ace Insurance Ltd v Trifunovski*,[50] Perram J conducted a review of the principles propounded by the common law courts and

---

[47] (2001) 207 CLR 21.

[48] *Vabu Pty Ltd v Commissioner of Taxation* [1996] 81 IR 150.

[49] (2006) 226 CLR 161.

[50] [2011] FCA 1204. Leave to appeal was refused: [2012] FCA 235. See also *Roy Morgan Research Pty Ltd v Commissioner of Taxation* (1997) 37 ATR 528.

helpfully identified the first issue: 'the distinction between an employee and an independent contractor is "rooted fundamentally in the difference between a person who serves his employer in his, the employer's, business, and a person who carries on a trade or business of his own" ...'.[51] But is this not simply shifting the question to another? In demonstrating the well-established variety of circumstances which may be relevant, Perram J noted that the 'totality' of the worker–entrepreneur relationship must be examined and continued:

> ... a number of indicia have accreted over time in the authorities which are thought to have thrown light to varying degrees on the outcome without being determinative: the terms of the contract; the intention of the parties; whether tax is deducted; whether sub-contracting is permitted; whether uniforms are worn; whether tools are supplied; whether holidays are permitted; the extent of control of, or the right to control, the putative employee whether actual or de jure; whether wages are paid or instead there exists a commission structure; what is disclosed in tax returns; whether one party 'represents' the other; for the benefit of whom does the goodwill in the business inure; how 'business-like' is the alleged business of the punitive employee – are there systems, manuals and invoices; and so on – the list is neither exhaustive nor short.[52]

The mere listing of these factors, so neatly identified in an inclusive but not exhaustive fashion, demonstrates how complex it may be to determine in a particular case whether a particular arrangement constitutes an employment or independent contractor relationship. The difficulty of course is to ascertain the answer to that question. The difficulty presents itself especially in the case of workers who are creative and make inventions, discoveries or innovations – particularly where over time their contractual position and duties have changed. They may have started as contractors but slowly evolved into employees.

Bromberg J was correctly critical of reliance on the unclear distinction at common law of contractors and employees in *On Call Interpreters and Translators Agency Pty Ltd v Commissioner of Taxation (No 3)*.[53] In deciding that interpreters were employees and consequently entitled to superannuation, the judge was concerned by the lack of clarity and the need for parties to seek rulings from superior courts – he stated that 'the

---

[51] Ibid, [29]. Perram J quoted *Hollis v Vabu Pty Ltd* (2001) 207 CLR 21 at 39 [40] (Gleeson CJ, Gaudron, Gummow, Kirby and Hayne JJ) citing *Marshall v Whittaker's Building Supply Co* (1963) 109 CLR 210, 217 (Windeyer J).

[52] Ibid.

[53] (2011) 279 ALR 341.

absence of a simple and clear definition which explains the distinction between an employee and an independent contractor is problematic'.[54] Bromberg J endeavoured to simplify the approach by suggesting two questions should be asked about contractors:

> Simply expressed, the question of whether a person is an independent contractor in relation to the performance of particular work, may be posed and answered as follows:
>
> Viewed as a 'practical matter':
>
> (i) is the person performing the work an entrepreneur who owns and operates a business; and,
> (ii) in performing the work, is that person working in and for that person's business as a representative of that business and not of the business receiving the work?[55]

Consequently, the underlying issue for determination of rights and obligations in relation to innovation – is the innovator an employee? – can itself be very difficult to resolve in particular cases simply because the common law principles are themselves difficult to apply in the many and varied circumstances.

7. COLLABORATION AND TEAMWORK

Even where the employment relationship is clear, and hence that legal issue has been eliminated, the problem of ascertaining the contribution of an employee and employees may be difficult. After all, there are diverse approaches. As stated in the Australian Review of the Innovation System: 'In a globalised knowledge-based economy, patterns of innovation have evolved and shifted beyond the sole gifted inventor or scientist, or the adept researcher and technologist. They are more diverse and complex than just the picture of the creative entrepreneur with proven commercial acumen.'[56] The IT and computing revolutions are such examples. Whilst there are certain persons – Bill Gates and Steve Jobs – who are renowned as inventors and innovators in the field, there are many teams and input from others in such revolutionary inventions and their application to new horizons.

---

[54] Ibid [206].
[55] Ibid [208].
[56] Report on the Review of the National Innovation System, ch 3, 19.

A case which is illuminating as to practical problems is the case which raised the issue whether the person was the sole inventor. In *David Leigh Wake v Soniclean Pty Ltd*,[57] one question, considered in the context of a patent application, was whether Wake was a sole inventor or joint inventor. It had to be determined what relationship there was between Wake's work and what was in the patent application. It was decided on the evidence that he was neither sole inventor nor joint inventor – his contribution did not represent 'a material step towards the development of the subject invention'.[58]

Similarly, any question of entitlement may be overridden by a subsequent commercialisation agreement. This means that if the employee is involved in that commercialisation agreement, any prior rights of the employee might be overridden.[59]

8. 'BEYOND EMPLOYMENT': VOLUNTEERS AND HONORARY CONSULTANTS

The position of a worker whose legal status is that of an employee, by way of contrast to independent contractor, has been discussed. The inventor or innovator may be neither employee nor contractor but wear another status. The most usual of this other category would be 'volunteer' – emeritus professors who remain working in an unpaid capacity in the university laboratory; scientists who are consultants receiving honoraria, actively working with the pharmaceutical company or research organisation after retirement as employees; interns undertaking placements for experience who happen to invent or contribute to an invention in the organisation hosting the internship; university or college students utilising the institution's equipment and facilities to develop an idea with an invention.

All these examples are not far-fetched and they do highlight the limitations of employment law which ordinarily requires, first, a relevant employment contract. The starting point ordinarily would be a consideration of any arrangement or agreement underpinning the voluntary nature of the work. But, in most instances, whether the agreement or arrangement provides any real consideration may be unclear, as may be whether the parties intend their agreement or arrangement to be legally binding

---

[57] [2010] APO 12.

[58] Ibid, [67].

[59] *New South Innovations Pty Ltd v Dr Wieslaw Kaczmarek* [2010] APO 2 and *Polwood Pty Ltd v Foxworth Pty Ltd* (2008) FCAFC 9.

(i.e. whether there is an intention to enter into legal relations). Consequently, there may be no formal or binding contract. Other sources of rights and obligations, such as a licence or permission to be on the premises and use the facilities of the university or other beneficiary of the activities, also may be a starting point but the relevant legal issues would not commonly be addressed. A fundamental issue might naturally be whether the emeritus professor or volunteer, labelled as such, is nonetheless, *legally* an employee. If the innovator is not an employee, then in circumstances summarised above, prima facie the innovator would appear to own the invention as being its primary creator.

Less clear from an equitable viewpoint is the position of the volunteer who works alongside employees to produce the invention at their employer's place of work. Could it be said to be an implied joint venture – that the business provided its facilities in return for the inventor pursuing inventions so that there is joint entitlement to the proceeds? Or a partnership? Murky waters are entered in sorting out ownership and equitable and other interests in these scenarios. Labour and employment law will not, as a general rule, assist the parties in determining or allocating entitlements in such cases, as the key condition of its application – that the worker is an employee – is not satisfied.

9. CONCLUSION

This survey and analysis of labour and employment laws in Australia, as they affect rights and obligations of the parties in respect of innovation, have illustrated a number of propositions:

First, the rights and obligations are broadly covered by the individual contract of employment rather than by collective agreements.

Secondly, the express terms of the contract may effectively deal with ownership (as with the genius inventor), but whether the variable outcomes at that level on a case-by-case basis are fair and equitable as between employer and employee is far from clear.

Thirdly, in the absence of consideration of the content of general duties implied by law in the contract, or express contractual provisions, the creation of an innovation during the currency of the contract may not determine that the innovation belongs to the employer, even where that employer's facilities have been used – and it is more likely to belong to the employee, as in the accidental inventor case.

Fourthly, to the extent that implied duties may be relied on in particular cases, they are most likely to favour ownership of the innovation by the employer.

Fifthly, despite the uncertainties in the law concerning the legal status of workers (either employee or contractor), the duties implied by law in relation to innovation are applicable only to 'employees'.

Finally, the employment contract, via the express or implied terms doctrines, does not easily or clearly resolve all the issues of ownership concerning sharing in the ownership or proceeds of the innovation made by a worker.

The answer to the question 'who obtains or shares the economic benefits of innovation?' may be simply an accidental by-product of the application of legal principles designed to determine who is an employee. Similarly the answer may be determined as a result of the bargaining power and position of the parties – what bargaining power do they have to negotiate in their own best interests? Whether this results in the best policy outcomes in the individual interests of the parties, or is fair and equitable or serves the broader interests of the economy and society at large is beyond the scope of employment and labour law to resolve. The state of the law is unsatisfactory because it does not provide adequate certainty of rights and obligations in relation to the ownership of innovation and consequently the sharing of economic benefits.

REFERENCES

Brodie, D. (1998), 'Beyond Exchange: The New Contract of Employment' 27 *Industrial Law Journal* 79

Carrigan, F. (2009), 'The Implications of Implied Terms in Law in the Common Law Contract of Employment' 9(1) *Oxford University Commonwealth Law Journal* 73

Creighton, B. and A. Stewart (2010), *Labour Law*, 5th edn, Federation Press

Dent C., C. Fenwick and K. Newitt (2011), 'Legal Incentives to Promote Innovation at Work: A Critical Analysis' 21(2) *Economic and Labour Relations Review* 27

Fox, C., W.A. Howard and M. Pittard (1995), *Industrial Relations in Australia: Development, Law and Operation*, Longman

Merges, R.P. (1999–2000), 'The Law and Economics of Employee Inventions' 13 *Harvard Journal of Law and Technology* 1

Owens, R., J. Riley and J. Murray (2011), *The Law of Work*, 2nd edn, Oxford University Press

Pittard, M. (2009), 'The Contract of Employment and Inventions: Legal Principles for Fleshing Out Duties by Implying Terms' 15(8) *Employment Law Bulletin* 124

Pittard, M. and R. Naughton (2010), *Australian Labour Law: Text, Cases and Commentary*, 5th edn, LexisNexis

Report on the National Innovation System, *Venturous Australia – Building Strength in Innovation*, Report to Commonwealth Department of Industry, Innovation, Science and Research on the Review of the National Innovation System (2008), <http://www.innovation.gov.au/Innovation/Policy/Pages/ReviewoftheNationalInnovationSystem.aspx>

Riley, J. (2003), 'Mutual Trust and Good Faith: Can Private Contract Law Guarantee Fair Dealing in the Workplace?' 16 *Australian Journal of Labour Law* 1
Stewart, A. (1988), 'Confidentiality and the Employment Relationship' 1 *Australian Journal of Labour Law* 1

11. Employees' inventions and the employment contract: a European Union perspective

Riccardo Del Punta

1. INTRODUCTION

In European legal systems, norms governing employees' inventions are not fully integrated with labour law systems, as provided either by national patent legislation (France, Italy, the Netherlands, Austria, Spain, Portugal, Hungary) or by special Acts (Germany, Denmark, Finland, Norway, Poland).

Despite this, due to the connection between the employment contract and the intellectual creation in which the invention consists, the protective function which is characteristic of labour law infiltrates into such norms, giving them hybrid features. Nevertheless, from the perspective of a legal system, they fundamentally remain an – albeit particular – branch of patent legislation.

Surprising as it may seem, European patent legislation is still established at national level, since decades of debate about the creation of a *sui generis* patent right for the European market have persisted without result until very recently.[1] This has happened despite the fact that the European Union possesses all the legal instruments necessary to establish a common standard in this field, which would help to reinforce the single market and promote business innovation throughout Europe.

A first cornerstone in the debate about the creation of a European patent protection was laid in 1997 when a Green Paper on the Community Patent and the patent system in Europe was issued. This is significant in relation to the issue under discussion since it recommended,

[1] Jaeger (2010) for this complicated story.

inter alia, that different national regulations governing inventions made by employees should be harmonized.[2]

This recommendation was justified by the fact that the many differences existing between the European legal systems had an impact on research work and management. 'The more the legislation is detailed and complex', the Green Paper observed, 'the more human resources the firm has to devote to the management of such matters.' It could also be 'that differences between national laws on employees' inventions are having an effect on the freedom to provide services in the single market and/or on the conditions of competition'.

More recently, both the Europe 2020 Strategy and the Single Market Act (finally issued in April 2011) identify the creation of an economy based on knowledge and innovation as a European priority. Following a long history of failure to reach agreement among Member States (a first proposal was issued in 2000), and after having been authorized by the European Parliament and the Council, the European Commission finally adopted a proposal for a Regulation implementing 'enhanced cooperation'[3] among 25 Member States[4] in the area of the creation of a unitary patent protection.[5]

However, in this proposal, no mention is made of employees' inventions, the regulation of which remains at national level. This is a serious failure in the integration process (considering the fact that most patents originate from inventions made by employees), since the field of employees' invention regimes appears particularly adapted to European harmonization. A harmonization process would not entail all the highly problematic implications which characterize, for example, the areas of collective bargaining or individual dismissals.

---

[2] Green Paper on the Community Patent and The Patent System in Europe, presented by the European Commission on 24 April 1997, especially §4.3.

[3] 'Enhanced cooperation' is a procedure laid down in the European Treaty, as amended in 1999, whereby a minimum of nine EU Member States are allowed to establish advanced integration in an area covered by EU structures and competences but without the other Members being involved.

[4] With the exception of Italy and Spain, due to a sharp disagreement about the languages to be used for the future European patent, which have been identified by the majority of the Member States in the existing official languages of the European Patent Organisation, that is English, French and German.

[5] See European Commission, Proposal for a Regulation of the European Parliament and the Council, Implementing Enhanced Cooperation in the Area Of a Unitary Patent Protection, 13 April 2011, COM (2011) 216 final, 2011/0093 (COD).

Nevertheless, this is not to say that the European system is totally disparate and chaotic. Although a European Union standard does not yet exist and national laws vary on numerous aspects and details,[6] a significant (albeit limited) level of osmosis among the European legal systems can be observed, deriving from a natural process of reciprocal influence which is quite common in the European legal experience. Consequently, a selective comparison of the solutions adopted in different Member States[7] on the main points of this subject can allow us to identify the potential basis of a feasible common European standard.

2. WHOSE INVENTION IS IT?

Subordination and creation would appear at first glance to be two concepts that are very difficult to reconcile.[8] Effectively, in accordance with a primitive and simplified notion of the work relationship, a 'subordinate' work characterized by intellectual creativity could seem like an oxymoron. The fact of working 'under the direction' of an employer would exclude any individual contribution of applied knowledge, which is a condition for innovation and particularly for industrial inventions or other intellectual creations.

The propensity to innovation has been particularly neglected, or at least not encouraged, in an organizational model of a strict 'Fordist' type, dominated by hierarchy and an extreme fragmentation of employees' tasks, and in which subordination has been emphasized. However, even in such an environment, and to a greater degree within the 'post-Fordist' models that emerged later, subordination has proved to be open to a wide range of interpretations, even – somewhat paradoxically – comprising a 'duty to invent' as the core of the employee's work activity or of a specific task assigned to him/her.

Incidentally, here we need to clarify the fact that the 'invention' obviously cannot be the final aim of the contractual commitment, but only a potential and felicitous outcome of the working activity.

The first, widely accepted implication of the 'contractualization' of the aforementioned duty is that the products of the inventive activity normally belong to the employer, albeit governed by different legal approaches, which will be dealt with below.

---

[6] For a general overview, see Peberdy and Strowel (2010).

[7] With the exception of the solution adopted by the UK, which is addressed in a separate contribution.

[8] See, from an intellectual property perspective, Fin-Langer (2006).

The employer's ownership rule is often explained as a natural employer's privilege, namely by the mere fact that the invention has been made by exploiting all the resources made available by the employer himself. Moreover, it can be justified on a law and economics basis, since all distinct bodies of economic theory point to the conclusion that such a rule is the most efficient, given the condition that a fair reward system for employed inventors is provided (see below) and can be easily enforced.[9]

Furthermore, the priority of the employer's interest is confirmed by the fact that, in all European legislation, subordination also implies a 'duty of fidelity'. Despite the ambiguity of such an expression (given that it could imply a type of personal subjection of the employee to the employer, which is fundamentally excluded by modern labour law systems), this 'duty of fidelity' undoubtedly comprises a 'duty of confidentiality', i.e. the prohibition on disclosing corporate secrets even after the end of the employment relationship.[10] In the case of infringement of this latter duty an employee can be sanctioned or even sacked, being considered responsible for a serious breach of contract.

Given these premises, various mechanisms are provided by European national legal systems by virtue of which the employer becomes the exclusive owner of the invention. These mechanisms cannot be examined here in detail, since analysis of all the different legislation would take too much space and would go beyond the specific purposes of this contribution.

In the first place, we have to consider that each European legal system envisages different notions of inventions as made by the employee. Although such notions are often referred to in the same terms in different systems (service invention, firm invention, occasional invention, etc.) it does not necessarily follow that the precise legal significance is the same everywhere. Consequently the overall picture is very complex, partly as a result of non-coordinated interaction between the various systems.

Generally speaking, the employer's ownership is automatic when the invention is made by the employee in the normal performance of the employment contract. This is the notion of 'service invention', which is defined by French,[11] Italian[12] and Spanish[13] legislation (although this

---

[9] For a complete analysis of the subject under discussion from an L&E perspective, see Merges (1999).

[10] For an example, see Article 2105 of the Italian Civil Code.

[11] Intellectual Property Code 1992, Article L. 611–7, para 1.

[12] Legislative Decree no. 30, 10 February 2005 (amended in 2010), Article 64, [1]. For Italian literature concerning employees' inventions, see Martone (2002); Pellacani (2005).

could be extended, e.g., to the Dutch or – with regard to case law – Belgian systems) as the invention made 'in the course of an employee's normal duties', that is, made either in the course of an inventive mission defined in the employment contract or during studies or research tasks expressly assigned to the employee.

In addition to 'service inventions', which are at the heart of the system, it is often laid down, e.g., by French legislation,[14] that 'all the other inventions belong to the employee', but also that, as soon as an invention is made either in the execution of an employment contract, or within the employer's field of activity (*domaine des activités de l'enterprise*), or using knowledge, techniques or methods specific to the employer, or data provided by the latter, the employer is given the right to acquire the ownership of the invention, which he/she has to exercise within four months (for the remuneration offered in such cases, see below).

Compared to the French system, the Italian system is more complicated as it distinguishes between the notions of 'firm invention'[15] and 'occasional invention'.[16] The former occurs when the invention occurs during the execution of an employment contract, without being additionally compensated: in this case the rule of employer's ownership is maintained, but a fair reward must be paid to the employee (see below).

Instead, in the case ('occasional invention') where the invention is made outside the contract but is related to the field of activity (*campo di attività*) of the employer an option right regime is established: in this case the invention belongs to the employee, but the employer has an option right, which he/she is obliged to exercise within a certain time.

Given this basic framework, it is interesting, also in terms of tracing the evolution of European legislation over time towards a general predominance of the employer's ownership rule, to recall that a different mechanism was laid down by German law[17] – which tends to play a leading role throughout Europe, and where the notion of 'service invention' in itself is used much as in the other European legislation.[18] Before the 2009 amendment of the Act on Employees' Inventions, first

---

13 Patent Act ('Ley de Patentes') 20 March 1986, Article 15.1.

14 Intellectual Property Code 1992, Article L. 611–7, [2].

15 Legislative Decree no. 30, 10 February 2005, Article 64, [2].

16 Legislative Decree no. 30, 10 February 2005, Article 64, [3].

17 Act on Employees' Inventions ('Arbeitnehmerefindungsgesetz') 25 July 1957, as amended by the Act to Simplify and Modernize the Patent Act of 28 May 2009. The reform came into force on 1 October 2009.

18 For a review of the German standard, before and after the 2009 reform, see respectively Deck and Matthes (2005); Petersen-Padberg and Muller (2010).

issued in 1957, the rights to an invention originally belonged to the employed inventor, albeit governed by a process of notification and claim that had to be complied with.

The employed inventor was obliged to give the employer immediate notification of the invention through a specific written document (containing the description of the technical problem, the solution and the process which led to the invention), and the employer had the right to claim the invention within four months of the receipt of its notification, otherwise the invention became 'free'.

The situation described above has been changed by a reform adopted in 2009 in which a reversal of the default rule is established so that an invention cannot 'unintentionally become free': if the employer does not expressly release the invention (making it 'free') within four months after it has been notified and correctly reported, he/she is legally deemed to have claimed the exclusive rights to the invention and thereby becomes the owner of the same.

3. THE INVENTOR'S REWARD

Since, pursuant to European legislation, the employer's ownership of the invention is not essentially under discussion, the focus has to be shifted to the reward system for employed inventors, which is an essential part of the 'deal' with the employee.

A first question can be posed with regard to the type of compensation regime: can the inventive activity simply be one of the various possible aspects of the subordination relationship, without a specific economic reward, or does it have to be separately compensated? Further, in the second place, does any compensation given have to be related to the economic value of the invention?

An extreme example in which an inventive obligation was simply embedded into the subordination was the original version of the Italian legal concept of 'service invention', which was significantly different from the one illustrated above since it simply concerned an invention made under an employment contract where a creative activity is provided, albeit not specifically remunerated.

In effect, in this case Italian law did not entitle the employed inventor to claim any ulterior remuneration in addition to his/her normal salary. This is similar to the Belgian regime, under which service inventions (the inventions made under an employment contract which encompasses an inventive mission or a specific task) simply belong to the employer and do not entail compensation.

However, an evolution has taken place within the Italian legal system, since Italian courts have interpreted the notion of 'service invention' as circumscribed to those cases where not only is an inventive task assigned to the employee but also a specific and additional remuneration is stipulated.[19] According to the Italian courts, this was seen as the necessary condition for the exclusion of a further compensation to the employee ('fair reward').

In the end this was recognized by Italian positive law,[20] which introduced the standard of 'service invention', stating that it can be applied only when a specific remuneration, not for the invention, but for the inventive activity itself, is stipulated on behalf of the employee. This has brought Italian law into line with the principal European legal systems, such as that of France (which demands the provision of a *remuneration supplémentaire*) and Spain.

In France, for example, the law expressly states that the compensation can be calculated on the basis of collective national agreements, company agreements or individual employment contracts[21] (individual stipulations are very common, providing for remuneration from between one to three times the employee's monthly wage).

However, that described above is not the only kind of reward system provided by European legislatures, since the possibility that the invention is made outside the employee's express duties, and hence without an additional compensation, or that it is somehow related to the employer's activity must also be covered. In such cases, as we have seen above, generally the employer simply has an option right on the invention, apart from a regime such as the Italian one, where the intermediate notion of 'firm invention' is also envisaged.

However, what is relevant for our purposes here is that the employed inventor is normally, eventually entitled to a 'fair reward' (*juste prix, equo premio*) as the amount due for the purchase of the right to the invention. This 'fair reward' is related to the economic value of the invention and to other relevant circumstances (in Italy the 'German formula' – see below – is usually referred to by the courts).[22]

---

[19] E.g., Court of Cassation, Labour Section, 17 February 2003, no. 11305, *Rivista Giuridica del Lavoro*, 2004, II, 305–311.

[20] See the aforementioned Article 64 [1] of Legislative Decree no. 30, 10 February 2005.

[21] Intellectual Property Code 1992, Article L. 611–7, para [1].

[22] For a case in which a quota of the reward was also assigned to a student who had participated in the research activity, see Tribunal of Milan, *University of Florence v Papini et alii*, 1 September 2010.

In short, two alternative reward systems appear to exist within European systems: the first, which applies when the invention is made within the employee's contractual duties, simply provides for a specific remuneration in addition to the employee's normal salary, although this extra remuneration is unrelated to the commercial value of the invention; the second system, which applies when the employee was not recruited to perform an inventive activity and therefore not specifically paid for it, entails a specific *ex post* compensation that is dependent on the value of the invention made.

This dualistic regime is resolved, to a degree, in German legislation, which always entitles the inventor to a remuneration determined 'by the economic usability of the invention, the employee's tasks and position within the firm, and the firm's share in the emergence of the invention'.[23] The most common way of determining the 'economic usability of the invention' is to refer to the royalties which would have to be paid on the market for a licence to use the invention. This reward system appears to entitle the employee to a greater participation in the commercial success of the invention.

A further observation has to be made with regard to the sources which regulate this matter within the European systems. The first point is that, since this field is basically regulated by statutory provisions (except in Belgium, Ireland and Sweden), contractual arrangements are not necessary in order to provide for compensation. Moreover, since, as already noted in the Introduction, these provisions are inspired by the protective mission of labour law, they cannot be derogated *in peius* at individual level: in other words, an employee's right to compensation cannot be contracted out in advance.

However, in contrast to other labour law rights deriving from laws or from collective agreements, which are negotiable only to a very limited degree, this area allows considerable scope for individual negotiation, especially with regard to the determination of the 'fair reward' (e.g., expressly in French legislation, and 'de facto' in Italy too).

In Germany, once the invention has been made and reported by the employee, the Act on Employees' Inventions is open to contractual regulation. For example, between individual parties it could be stipulated that the employer pays a first lump sum for: release of the obligation to file an application; remuneration for a certain sphere of use; restriction of employee's information claim (typically in the range between 1,000 and 2,000 EUR). Then the employer might pay a second (final) lump sum:

---

[23] Act on Employees' Inventions, s 9.

after the granting of a patent; in the case of a higher turnover deriving from the commercial use of the invention.

4. UNIVERSITY INVENTIONS

In most European systems (e.g., Germany, France, Austria and Denmark), the rule of employer's ownership also applies to university inventions. For example, under German law[24] the economic rights related to the exploitation of the invention belong to the university, the researcher being entitled to 30 per cent of the turnover deriving from the invention.

By virtue of a reform adopted in 2001, Italian legislation establishes a different regime,[25] which in view of its peculiarities in the European landscape deserves special attention. Under this legislation, when the inventor is employed by a university or a public research centre, the researcher is the exclusive owner of the invention. This standard reflects the idea that academic researchers should be entitled to own and manage their rights on patentable achievements.

A specific procedure is laid down, according to which the inventor files the patent application and notifies the administration. Then the inventor must pay the university a fee related to licences for the use of the invention. It is up to each university to establish the maximum amount of the fee (the default amount is 30 per cent), but the employee is entitled to a minimum of 50 per cent of the revenues deriving from the invention. However, if the inventor has not exploited the invention within five years, the related economic rights are acquired free by the university, without prejudice to the inventor's 'moral' right. This standard does not apply when the research is supported by private funding or implemented within research projects financed by other public administrations: the rule is unclear in these cases but the invention may in some cases belong to the financial backer. The rationale usually invoked for such a regime, which establishes a professor's privilege, is exploiting ownership of the invention to motivate public employees and taking into consideration the freedom which is intrinsic to university research. In a sense, the employee's ownership rule should not be overvalued, as in the end, the Italian legislation also requires the researcher and the university to share the fees deriving from the commercial success of the invention.

---

24 Act on Employees' Inventions, s 42, as amended in 2000. On the German approach to university inventions, before and after the reform adopted in 2000, see Goddar (1999) and (2005).

25 Legislative Decree no. 30, 10 February 2005, Article 65.

Consequently the concrete implications of such a regime are not as different from the mainstream rule as they would initially appear to be. Leaving this aside, the Italian standard has been criticized because it fails to adequately address the economic interests of the three parties involved (universities, researchers, private firms) and is also in conflict with the constitutional principle of equality since it makes a distinction between public and private researchers.[26]

5. CONCLUDING REMARKS

A review of the main European legal systems indicates that:

1. The employer's ownership of all the inventions which are somehow related to the employment contract, even in a very broad sense, is established or made possible (through option rights at the employer's disposal) by the legislation.
2. A statutory right to compensation for the employed inventor is widely recognized, whether the invention is protected by a patent or exploited under a regime of industrial secret.
3. Within the different systems, the compensation can consist either of a simple supplementary remuneration or of a reward linked to the economic value of the invention, the latter (which is always adopted in Germany, for example) appearing to be the most rational solution with a view to stimulating innovation on the part of employees.
4. There is a great deal of scope for individual negotiations a propos the possible compensation schemes.
5. The standard rule is applied, albeit with variations depending on the different countries (and with a problematic exception regarding the Italian standard), also to university inventions, usually with the provision of a minimum fee for the researcher.

The logical conclusion is that, given the many common features which characterize the various European laws regarding employees' inventions, a common European basis, even in terms of a minimal regulation (as is typical of European law, especially after the enlargement of the European Union to 27 Member States), would not be very difficult to achieve. All the more so, bearing in mind that European laws always derive from a synthesis of the main lines of the dominant European legal systems. This further step would be extremely positive, even from a Euro-sceptic

---

26 For a critical review, see Ubertazzi (2004).

viewpoint (to which I do not subscribe), in terms of enhancing the efficiency of the European common market.

Consequently what is to be hoped for is that the possible advent of a European patent, once the linguistic rivalries have been overcome (although this is far from certain), may as a positive side-effect facilitate a revival of interest in the creation of a common European standard for employees' inventions.

REFERENCES

Deck, M. and J. Matthes (2005), 'Employee Inventions in Germany' (June/July) *IP Ownership* 63

Fin-Langer, L. (2006), 'Les statuts de salarié et de crèateur. Sont-ils compatibles?' *Droit et Patrimoine* 147

Goddar, H. (1999), 'Compliance with the German Employees' Inventions Law in the Handling of Inventions Developed by Universities', Symposium: Streamlining International Intellectual Property Enforcement and Prosecution, University Technology Transfer, and Incentives for Inventors, <http://www.law.washington.edu/casrip/symposium/Number5/>

Goddar, H. (2005), 'Making Industry–University Interactions Work – Model Agreements in Germany' 10 *Journal of Intellectual Property Rights* 389

Jaeger, T.H. (2010), 'The EU Patent: Cui Bono et Quo Vadis?' 47 *Common Market Law Review* 63

Martone, M. (2002), *Contratto di Lavoro e Beni Immateriali*, Cedam

Merges, R.P. (1999), 'The Law and Economics of Employee Inventions' 13(1) *Harvard Journal of Law & Technology* 1

Peberdy, M. and A. Strowel (2010), 'Employees' Rights to Compensation for Inventions – A European Perspective', *PLC Multi-Jurisdictional Guide to Life Sciences* 63, <www.practicallaw.com/9–500–8968>

Pellacani, G. (2005), 'Tutela del Lavoro e Tutela della Proprietà Industriale. Per una Lettura Costituzionalmente Orientata della Disciplina delle Invenzioni del Lavoratore', *Annali Italiani Diritto di Autore* 29

Petersen-Padberg, A. and M.G. Muller (2009), 'Reform of the German Act on Employees' Inventions', May, *Hoffman-Eitle Newsletter*

Ubertazzi, L.C. (2004), 'Le Invenzioni dei Ricercatori Universitari' 2 *Studi di Diritto Industriale in onore di Adriano Vanzetti* 1727

12. US employment law perspectives on the issue of who owns an employee's invention

Richard Bales*

1. INTRODUCTION

United States patent law gives an inventor a property right in his or her invention even if the invention was conceived during the inventor's employment.[1] A patent may be obtained only by its inventor, and 'inventor' status has nothing to do with employment. Being an inventor's employer does not give that employer any direct interest in (or priority with respect to) potential patent rights. However, state contract law may, under certain circumstances, require the inventor to assign the patent to the employer upon issuance.

An employer may acquire either the entire patent or property right, or a right to use the invention, in any of three ways. First, the employer is entitled to ownership of the invention when the employee expressly agrees to assign his or her rights to the employer. Second, the employer generally is entitled to ownership of the invention when it has hired the employee for the express purpose of inventing. Third, the employer receives an irrevocable, but non-exclusive and non-assignable, right to use the invention if the invention was developed during working hours with the use of the employer's equipment and materials. This chapter will describe American law governing employee inventions and will compare it to the law of several other countries.

* Special thanks to Richard Graves and Wendy Lane for reviewing drafts of this chapter.

[1] 35 U.S.C. § 102(f).

2. RULES OF INVENTION OWNERSHIP

As described above, an inventor owns his or her invention absent a legal doctrine requiring the transfer of all or part of the ownership rights to the inventor's employer. The three such doctrines are described below.

2.1 Express Assignment[2]

2.1.1 How express assignments are created

One way that an employer may acquire ownership of an employee's invention is if the employee-inventor expressly assigns ownership rights to the employer. General common-law contract rules apply to the assignment. For example, consideration must be given; at-will employment may suffice as the employer's consideration if the assignment agreement is made at the beginning of employment, but if the agreement is made after employment has commenced, additional consideration will be needed.[3] The assignment must be made in clear and unequivocal terms.[4] The assignment must be in writing if ownership already has been established in a patent or patent application.[5] If the invention does not yet exist, the employee can assign only equitable title to the employer; once the invention exists, the employer will acquire a valid legal title and patent rights to the invention.[6]

2.1.2 Future-invention clauses

There are two types of clauses for assigning future inventions.[7] The first type is for 'future improvements'; this grants the employer title to inventions made by the worker while employed, and also grants the employer title to any improvements to those inventions made after employment has ended. The second type is the 'trailer' or 'holdover' clause; this grants the employer title to all post-employment inventions relating to the employer's field of work. Both are governed by common-law restrictions on the clauses.

---

[2] An excellent source on express assignments of rights to an invention from employees to employers is Caldwell (2006), and much of this section of this chapter is derived from this source.

[3] *Mirafi v. Mirafi*, 14 U.S.P.Q.2d (BNA) 1337, 1350 (W.D.N.C. 1989).

[4] *Monsanto Chem. Works v. Jaeger*, 31 F.2d 188 (W.D. Pa. 1929).

[5] 35 U.S.C. § 261.

[6] *Littlefield v. Perry*, 88 U.S. 205, 226 (1874); *Filmtec Corp. v. Allied-Signal*, 939 F.2d 1568 (Fed. Cir. 1991).

[7] Caldwell (2006), 285.

2.1.2.1 Future-improvement clauses The purpose of future-improvement clauses is to grant an employer ownership of any foreseeable inventions and any 'improvements' made to those inventions after employment has ended. Courts have construed these clauses extremely narrowly. For example, even 'where the clauses specifically reference future improvements, the courts have construed these clauses to cover only inventions (and their improvements) which actually existed when the contract was entered into.'[8] Absent more specific language, these clauses will not cover inventions not yet made or improvements not begun when the contract was signed, and will not cover post-employment improvements to those inventions.[9]

Courts interpret the clauses as narrowly as the language of the clause will permit,[10] on the theory that the law should 'not look favorably upon covenants which place a mortgage on a man's brain, to bind all its future products.'[11] These clauses have fallen into disfavor because of how narrowly the courts have construed them.[12]

2.1.2.2 Trailer (holdover) clauses The purpose of invention trailer (also known as 'holdover') clauses is 'to prevent an employee from appropriating to his own use or to the use of a subsequent employer inventions relating to and stemming from work done for a previous employer.'[13] Trailer clauses are more specific than future-improvement clauses because trailer clauses typically contain time and geographic restrictions and are limited to specific types of inventions or subject matters. Because trailer clauses are more specific than future-improvement clauses, they are more likely to be enforced.[14]

The time, geography, and subject-matter restrictions on trailer clauses make those clauses closely resemble employment non-compete agreements. Perhaps for this reason, most courts interpret trailer clauses

---

8 Caldwell (2006); see, e.g., *De Long Corp. v. Lucas*, 176 F. Supp. 104, 127 (S.D.N.Y. 1959).

9 Caldwell (2006), 286; see, e.g., *New Britain Machine Co. v. Yeo*, 358 F.2d 397, 405 (6th Cir. 1966).

10 See, e.g., *Gas Tool Patents Corp. v. Mould*, 133 F.2d 815, 817–18 (7th Cir. 1943).

11 *De Long Corp.*, 176 F. Supp., 127.

12 Caldwell (2006), 285, 287.

13 *Dorr-Oliver, Inc. v. United States*, 432 F.2d 447, 452 (Ct. Cl. 1970).

14 Caldwell (2006), 288.

identically to how they interpret non-compete agreements.[15] Courts enforce both only if they are reasonable.[16]

The purpose of the reasonableness analysis is to balance the interests of the employer in protecting the fruits of an employee's employment,[17] the employee in protecting the fruits of post-employment inventions, and the public in promoting incentives to invent generally.[18] Courts usually do not conduct this balancing test directly, but instead evaluate the reasonableness of the time, geography, and subject-matter restrictions.

The time restriction focuses on how long after employment has ended the trailer clause would require the former employee to assign his or her subsequent inventions to the former employer. Courts have refused to enforce trailer clauses that were indefinite as to time[19] or that were to last ten years after the termination of employment.[20] In the context of non-compete agreements, a general rule of thumb is that two-year to three-year post-employment agreements are considered reasonable, but longer agreements generally are found to be unreasonable and unenforceable.[21] Although there are fewer cases in the trailer-clause context than the non-compete context from which to generalize, courts seem to follow the same rule of thumb.[22]

The geographical restriction focuses on whether the trailer clause is reasonable as to the geographical area that it covers. Few trailer-clause cases have focused on geographical restrictions,[23] so analogy must be

---

[15] E.g., *Ingersoll-Rand Co. v. Ciavatta*, 542 A.2d 879, 888 (N.J. 1988).

[16] *Ingersoll-Rand Co. v. Ciavatta*, 542 A.2d 879, 888 (N.J. 1988); Caldwell (2006), 288.

[17] *Dorr-Oliver, Inc. v. United States*, 432 F.2d 447, 452 (Ct. Cl. 1970).

[18] *Campbell Soup Co. v. ConAgra, Inc.*, 801 F. Supp. 1298, 1306 (D.N.J. 1991); *GTI Corp. v. Calhoon*, 309 F. Supp. 762, 773 (S.D. Ohio 1969).

[19] *Federal Screw Works v. Interface Sys., Inc.*, 569 F. Supp. 1562, 1564 (E.D. Mich. 1983).

[20] *United Shoe Mach. Co. v. La Chappelle*, 99 N.E. 289, 293 (Mass. 1912).

[21] Bales et al (2007); see also Bales et al. (2007), 135 (discussing how, in some fast-paced industries such as the Internet, shorter time periods may be required).

[22] Cf Caldwell (2006), 295 (arguing that courts should not apply the time restriction to trailer clauses because 'assignment of an existing or future invention is generally a thing of permanence.').

[23] Ibid; see also *Aetna-Standard Engineering Co. v. Rowland* 493 A.2d 1375 (Pa. 1985).

made to non-compete agreements.[24] As a general rule of thumb, if the clause is defined commensurately with the employer's region of business, courts are likely to find it reasonable and to enforce it, but if the clause is much broader than the employer's region of business, courts are likely to find it unreasonable and refuse to enforce it.[25] For some jobs (such as Internet jobs), it is possible for an employer's region of business to be global. In such cases, courts have been willing to enforce non-compete agreements without any geographic scope, but only if the agreements are limited in time to a year or less.[26]

The subject-matter restriction focuses on whether the trailer clause is reasonably related to the former employer's area of expertise. A subject-matter restriction tailored to a specific invention will be deemed reasonable and enforceable, whereas a restriction limited to an entire industry or field of inventions is likely to be deemed unreasonable and unenforceable.[27] A trailer clause requiring an employee to assign his or her invention regardless of subject matter, or of indefinite scope, will be deemed categorically unreasonable and unenforceable.[28]

An example of a court refusing to enforce a trailer clause is *Ingersoll-Rand Co. v. Ciavatta.*[29] An Ingersoll-Rand employee was not specifically hired to design or invent, but nonetheless had signed a standard invention agreement requiring him to assign any invention conceived or developed within one year after termination of his employment if such an invention was attributable to work done during his employment. After he was fired, he developed, patented, and marketed (in direct competition with Ingersoll-Rand) a new coal mine stabilization field.

The court found that because there was no evidence that the employee had conceived of the invention while still employed by Ingersoll-Rand, the invention was not covered by the literal terms of the trailer clause. The court further held that even if the clause applied by its terms, it was

---

[24] Cf Caldwell (2006), 296 (arguing that courts should enforce national or even global trailer clauses because patents are national in scope and can be made international in scope by applying for patents in other countries).

[25] Bales et al. (2007), 130.

[26] Ibid, 131; see, e.g., *Briggs v. R.R. Donnelly & Sons*, 446 F. Supp. 153 (D. Mass. 1978) (enforcing non-compete agreement with no geographic limitation where former employee had worldwide customer contacts).

[27] Caldwell (2006), 290.

[28] Ibid; see, e.g., *Guth v. Minnesota Mining & Mfg. Co.*, 72 F.2d 385, 388–89 (7th Cir. 1934).

[29] 542 A.2d 879 (N.J. 1988); this case description is based on Bales et al. (2007), 135.

unreasonable and unenforceable. The court applied a reasonableness test, balancing the employee's interest in using general skills and knowledge against the employer's interest in protecting investment in research and development. Because the employee used no trade secrets and relied upon only publicly known information in designing his invention, the court concluded the balance favored the employee and, therefore, the holdover clause was unreasonable.

2.1.2.3 Statutory restrictions Several American states have statutes regulating future-invention agreements. These statutes restrict the instances in which employers may compel the assignment of employee inventions. An example is California Labor Code § 2870. It states:

> (a) Any provision in an employment agreement which provides that an employee shall assign, or offer to assign, any of his or her rights in an invention to his or her employer shall not apply to an invention that the employee developed entirely on his or her own time without using the employer's equipment, supplies, facilities, or trade secret information except for those inventions that either:
>
> (1) Relate at the time of conception or reduction to practice of the invention to the employer's business, or actual or demonstrably anticipated research or development of the employer; or
> (2) Result from any work performed by the employee for the employer.
>
> (b) To the extent a provision in an employment agreement purports to require an employee to assign an invention otherwise excluded from being required to be assigned under subdivision (a), the provision is against the public policy of this state and is unenforceable.

Thus, statutory restrictions like California's prevent employers from using their disparate bargaining power to require employees to assign inventions under circumstances that might be considered unfair or inequitable.

2.2 Hired-to-Invent

2.2.1 Explanation and rationale

A second way that an employer may acquire ownership of an employee's invention is if the employer has hired an employee with the specific purpose of inventing something. Under these circumstances, courts may imply, as a matter of common-law contract, an agreement between the employer and the employee to assign all resulting inventions to the employer.[30] An employer acquiring rights to an invention under the hired-to-invent doctrine acquires full title to the invention, including any patents already issued on it.[31]

The primary rationale behind the hired-to-invent doctrine is that the employee's salary has fully compensated the employee for his or her inventions: the employee receives a salary in exchange for assigning the inventions to the employer, and the employer pays the employee in exchange for the assignment of the inventive rights.[32] The rationale also is that, under these circumstances, an employee would reasonably expect that inventions resulting from the employment would belong to the employer.[33] If, however, the employee has made it clear that he or she wishes to retain the inventive rights – such as by refusing to sign an express assignment of rights – then courts will not imply an assignment under the hired-to-invent doctrine even if the employee was clearly hired to invent.[34]

An example is *Teets v. Chromalloy Gas Turbine Corp.*,[35] in which an employee spent 70 percent of his work time developing a new turbine engine fan blade for aircraft engines.[36] There was no express agreement assigning invention rights from the employee to the employer. Nonetheless, the court held that an implied-in-fact contract as to inventive rights did exist, based on the policy that employers may claim ownership of an employee's inventive work where the employer specifically hires or directs the employee to invent something.[37]

2.2.2 The 'specific purpose' requirement

The hired-to-invent doctrine applies only if an employee is hired for the specific purpose of inventing or improving something.[38] It does not apply if an employee was hired to perform work which was 'general' in nature,

---

30 Hill (2006); see, e.g., *Standard Parts Co. v. Peck*, 264 U.S. 52, 58–59 (1923); *E.F. Drew & Co., Inc. v. Reinhard*, 170 F.2d 679, 684 (2d Cir. 1948); *Nat'l Dev. Co. v. Gray*, 55 N.E.2d 783, 787 (Mass. 1944); cf *Cahill v. Regan*, 153 N.Y.S.2d 768, 770 (Sup. Ct. 1956).

31 *State v. Neal*, 12 So.2d 590, 591 (Fla. 1943).

32 Hill (2006), 12.

33 *Nat'l Dev.*, 55 N.E.2d,787.

34 Hill (2006), 12; see, e.g., *Banks v. Unisys Corp.*, 228 F.3d 1357, 1359–60 (Fed. Cir. 2000).

35 83 F.3d 403, 408–09 (Fed. Cir. 1996), cert. denied, 519 U.S. 1009 (1996).

36 Ibid, 408.

37 Ibid, 407.

38 See Lieberstein (2005), 185–92 (describing the leading cases).

or if the employee was not hired specifically to invent.[39] In either of these events, the employee will retain all ownership rights to her or his invention.[40]

Whether an employee has been hired for the specific purpose of inventing or improving something depends on a case-by-case analysis. One court has listed the following factors as relevant to the analysis: (1) whether the employee was paid from funds earmarked for the particular invention; (2) whether the employee devoted the majority of his or her work time to the work from which the invention arose; (3) whether the employer paid all expenses associated with obtaining the patent, if one was sought; (4) whether the employer gave the employee the specific task of developing a new method relating to the resulting invention; (5) whether the employer first attempted to obtain a patent in the name of the employer.[41]

Courts often focus on whether the specific purpose of inventing was present *at the time of hire*. For example, in *Aetna-Standard Engineering Co. v. Rowland*,[42] an engineer was hired, then instructed to develop a 'plug mill receiving table' pursuant to a customer contract. The employee did so, and helped prepare the patent application and drawings. The employee was subsequently laid off, and the employer sought assignment of the invention. The court refused, finding that the employee was only 'hired as a general staff engineer; he was not recruited specifically to design the [invention].'[43]

Nonetheless, most courts have held that the hired-to-invent doctrine is triggered if, after an employee has begun working, the employer gives the employee a specific direction to invent something.[44] One commentator explains:

> while the initial scope of a project may only generally deal with designing a new product or machine, one may be able to show that the scope of the project changed as the parties were collaborating on the development of a prototype design of the new product. Over the course of time, a project's scope may evolve to specifically encompass not only the requested items, but

---

[39] Caldwell (2006), 282–83.

[40] Ibid; see, e.g., *Int'l Carrier-Call & Television Corp. v. Radio Corp. of Am.*, 142 F.2d 493, 508 (2d Cir. 1994).

[41] *City of Cocao v. Leffler*, 803 So.2d 869, 873 (Fla. Dist. Ct. App. 2002) (citing *State v. Neal*, 12 So.2d 590, 591 (Fla. 1943)).

[42] 493 A.2d 1375 (Pa. 1985).

[43] Ibid, 1382.

[44] Hill (2006), 12; see, e.g., *Teets v. Chromalloy Gas Turbine Corp.*, 83 F.3d 403, 408–09 (Fed. Cir. 1996), cert. denied, 519 U.S. 1009 (1996).

> also new ideas or processes that may solve the problem in a more efficient manner, even though the idea or process was not contemplated at the time the contract was entered into.[45]

Under such circumstances, courts generally will apply the hired-to-invent doctrine and require the employee-inventor to assign the invention to the employer.

2.2.3 Limits

The hired-to-invent doctrine does not apply to an employee hired to develop an invention that the employee had conceived on her own before she was hired, because there would be no inference that the parties had intended an assignment *ab initio*.[46] Likewise, the hired-to-invent doctrine does not apply to inventions developed after the termination of employment, because such inventions would fall outside the employment relationship.[47] Finally, the hired-to-invent doctrine does not apply to inventions developed by employees at home, without their employer's equipment, supplies, or compensation, because of the disconnect from the employment relationship.[48]

2.3 Shop Right

2.3.1 Generally

A third way that an employer may acquire ownership of an employee's invention is where an employee is not hired specifically to design or invent, but nevertheless develops an invention during working hours with the use of the company's equipment and materials. Under these circumstances, the employer acquires an irrevocable,[49] but non-exclusive and non-assignable, right to use the invention. The employee gets the patent, but the employer gets to use it for free.

This 'shop right' is an equitable principle developed in common law.[50] Some courts characterize a shop right as an implied license, or a royalty or fee that the employer has earned, resulting from the employer's

---

[45] Lieberstein (2005), 191–92 (citing *Teets*, 83 F.3d, 408–09).

[46] Caldwell (2006), 282; see, e.g., *Cahill v. Regan*, 157 N.E.2d 505 (N.Y. 1959).

[47] Caldwell (2006), 282; see, e.g., *Int'l Carrier-Call & Television Corp. v. Radio Corp. of Am.*, 142 F.2d 493, 508 (2d Cir. 1994).

[48] Caldwell (2006), 283; see, e.g., *Teets v. Chromalloy Gas Turbine Corp.*, 83 F.3d 403, 408–09 (Fed. Cir. 1996), cert. denied, 519 U.S. 1009 (1996).

[49] *Thomson v. American Tobacco Co.*, 174 F.2d 773 (4th Cir. 1949).

[50] Hill (2006), 13.

investment in providing the facilities and materials to make the invention possible.[51] Other courts characterize the shop right as a form of equitable estoppel, reasoning that once an employee consents or acquiesces to the employer's use of the invention, the employee is estopped from asserting his or her patent rights against that employer.[52] Whether a shop right exists is determined by courts on a case-by-case basis.[53]

2.3.2 Nature of right[54]

An employer's shop right is irrevocable – it survives both the termination of the inventor-employee's employment and the inventor-employee's obtaining a patent on the invention.[55] The shop right also, however, is non-exclusive and non-transferable, as the case of *Francklyn v. Guilford Packing Co.*[56] makes clear. Employee Gilbert Francklyn, while employed as a clammer and while using his employer's resources, modified a clam harvester and received a patent for his new design. Francklyn had been hired to harvest clams and not to design or invent improvements to a clam harvester. Nevertheless, the court held that because he had used employer materials during his time at work to make the invention, his employer was entitled to a shop right in the new clam harvester invention.[57] Francklyn also had agreed to allow his employer to use the invention without paying royalties. The court, however, forbade the employer from selling its shop right to another concern, which wished to buy the license to the invention so that its product would not infringe Francklyn's patent. Thus, a shop right holder is not free to assign its right to another person, because the right is a limited personal right that can be used only by the employer.[58]

---

[51] Hill (2006), 13; Bales et al. (2007), 134. Additionally, by allowing employers and employees to split ownership of an invention in such instances, shop rights eliminate the possibilities of 'hold outs', who seek to exploit the other party by holding out and demanding a higher price for their part of a multi-component invention. See Mergens (1999).

[52] Hill (2006), 13; Lieberstein (2005), 193; see, e.g., *McElmurry v. Arkansas Power & Light Co.*, 995 F.2d 1576, 1580–81 (Fed. Cir. 1993).

[53] *McElmurry*, 995 F.2d, 1582–83.

[54] Both vertical and horizontal choice-of-law issues can arise in this context. See, e.g., Schroeder v. Tracor, Inc., 217 F.3d 859 (Table), 1999 WL 1021055, *2 (Fed. Cir. 1999).

[55] *Thomson v. American Tobacco Co.*, 174 F.2d 773 (4th Cir. 1949).

[56] 695 F.2d 1158 (9th Cir. 1983); this case description is based on Bales et al. (2007), 134.

[57] 695 F.2d at 1161.

[58] 695 F.2d at 1162–63.

A shop right can apply to any employee, including a general laborer, as the *Francklyn* case illustrates.[59]

3. THE US APPROACH IN COMPARATIVE PERSPECTIVE

Having described each of the three ways that an employer may acquire a patent or property interest in an employee's invention, this chapter now will analyze each of the three from a comparative perspective.

3.1 Express Assignments

An express assignment is a sophisticated employer's first choice of ways to acquire a patent or property interest in an employee's invention. This is so because it gives employers the greatest degree of control and certainty over the acquisition of the interest. American courts will readily enforce express assignments, subject to two important caveats.

The first caveat is that American courts disfavor future-improvement clauses. These clauses are designed to extend indefinitely into the future. Courts are reluctant to give employers a property interest in an employee's invention that might be developed years or even decades after the termination of the employment relationship, and hence tend to interpret these clauses as narrowly as the language of the clause will permit. For this reason, future-improvement clauses are uncommon in the United States.

The second caveat is that trailer (holdover) clauses must be narrowly tailored in time, geography, and subject matter. Courts are reluctant to give employers a property interest in an employee's invention that might be developed years after the termination of the employment relationship, or that geographically will have little or no impact on the employer's business, or that is unrelated to the former employee's employment with the former employer. Subject to these limitations, American courts will readily enforce trailer clauses, using traditional contract-interpretation principles. This gives employers assurances that a written contract assigning the rights of an employee's future invention will be enforced so long as it is narrowly tailored, carefully drafted, and within the reasonable intent of the parties.

---

59 See also *Wommack v. Durham Pecan Co., Inc.*, 715 F.2d 962 (5th Cir. 1983).

US law on express assignments is not unlike the law of other countries. For example, express-term assignments generally are enforceable in the UK, though common-law contract analysis has been replaced by the UK Patents Act.[60] As in the UK, Indian law on employee inventions is governed by statute,[61] but unlike in the UK, there is still room for common-law contract analysis. Indian common-law contract analysis of employee assignments of inventions is very similar to that in the US – assignments of future inventions are enforceable only if reasonable in scope and duration.[62]

In Germany, by contrast, the law assumes that inventions remain the property of the inventing employee until ownership rights are transferred to the employer, and this will only happen if the employer claims the invention in return for monetary compensation.[63]

3.2 Hired-to-Invent

The hired-to-invent doctrine is a second-best way for an employer in the United States to acquire a patent or property interest in an employee's invention. An employer will turn to this doctrine if, during an employee's employment, the employer failed to acquire an express assignment of future patent or property rights, and the employee subsequently has invented something in which the employer believes the employer should have a property interest. It is a second-best way for the employer to acquire a patent or property interest because it gives the employer very little control over the scope of the assignment. Unlike a trailer clause, which the employer can draft itself (subject perhaps to negotiation with an employee-signatory), an employer invoking the hired-to-invent doctrine must rely on a court to define the scope of the purported assignment.

The hired-to-invent doctrine is an implied-by-law contract.[64] A court will imply an employee's agreement to assign future inventions to the employer if the circumstances surrounding the employment suggest that the employer hired the employee for the specific purpose of inventing something, and it would be reasonable for an employee to assume that he

---

[60] Section 39(1) of the UK Patents Act 1977.

[61] Patents Act 1970 (India).

[62] Essenese Obhan & Sumathi Chandrashekaran, Strategies for Assessing Patents, http://www.managingip.com/Article/2282150/Strategies-for-assigning-patents.html.

[63] German Employee's Inventions Act §§ 1–2.

[64] Pittard chapter 10 this volume.

or she had received a salary in exchange for assigning to the employer the rights to the resulting invention.

The rationale for this doctrine is similar to the rationale underlying *Edisonia v. Forse*[65] in the UK. In *Edisonia*, William Forse began working for Edisonia Ltd as an hourly worker, then became the salaried manager of the department for molding cylinders for phonographic records. As manager, Forse developed an improvement to the molding cylinders and obtained two patents, for which Edisonia paid the patent fees. He then quit his employ with Edisonia, became managing director of a competing company, and assigned a license to those patents to the competitor. Edisonia sued Forse and the competitor.

The court acknowledged that the general rule is that absent a contract to the contrary, patents belong to an employee even if made on the employer's time with the employer's materials and at the employer's expense. The court held, however, that an exception exists if it can be inferred from the general contract of employment that the employee was acting as a trustee for the employer. The court found that Forse had become a trustee of Edisonia by using Edisonia's funds to obtain the patents and by acknowledging that the patents were being taken out for the benefit of Edisonia.

US law is similar to that in the UK and India. Under UK statutory law and Indian common law, the general rule is that inventions outside an employee's duties belong to the employee.[66] Inventions made in the course of an employee's duties, however, belong to the employer. For example, in *Harris*,[67] an employee's invention was deemed outside the scope of his duties when he had been hired for the non-inventive duties of sales and after-sales service, whereas in *Staeng*,[68] an employee's invention was deemed within the scope of his duties because his job description assigned him, in addition to his primary duty of marketing, the additional duties of using discussions with customers to generate ideas for new products and of thinking of novel uses for existing products.

3.3 Shop Right

Of the three ways that an employer may acquire a patent or property interest in an employee's invention in the United States, the least

---

65 (1908) 25 RPC 546.

66 Section 39(1) of the UK Patents Act 1977; Rao and Guru (2010).

67 *Harris' Patent* (1985) RPC 19.

68 *Staeng Limited's Patents* (1996) RPC 183.

preferred (from the employer's perspective) is the shop right. Employers disfavor this approach because the right that an employer acquires in this way is a very limited one – it is a right to use the invention; it does not permit the employer to transfer the right to use the invention or to exclude others from using it. The employee retains the patent rights on the invention, and may sell or license those rights to anyone as the employee sees fit. The employer acquires only the right to use the patent without having to pay the employee for the privilege, but may not license or sell this right-to-use to anyone else.

The shop right may be American law's greatest contribution to resolving the issue of who owns an employee's inventions. It is a compromise of sorts, and it uniquely recognizes that both an employer *and* an employee may legitimately claim an interest in an invention created during employment: the employee because he or she was the actual inventor and the employer because the employee used the employer's time, tools, and equipment to create the invention, and may have done so with the intent of furthering the employer's business interests. In any given case, the other American doctrines yield all-or-nothing outcomes: either the employer wins the battle and acquires the patent, or the employee wins the battle and gets the patent. Under the shop right doctrine, both the employer and the employee get some sort of property interest in the patent.

The closest international analog to the American shop right appears to be the German Employee's Inventions Act. Under this model, an employee is presumed to own his or her inventions, subject to a claim that may be made by the employer in return for monetary compensation.[69] If the employer makes a limited claim to the invention, the employer acquires a nonexclusive right to use the invention in return for compensation.

4. CONCLUSION

US law governing employee inventions is governed primarily by common law. At common law, an employee owns his or her invention even if the invention was conceived during the employee's employment. However, an employer may acquire the patent, a property right in, or a right to use the invention in any of three ways: through express assignment, through implication if the employee was hired to invent something, and

[69] German Employee's Inventions Act §§ 1–2.

through the shop-right doctrine if the invention was developed during working hours with the use of the employer's equipment and materials. The first two methods are broadly consistent with the law of most other countries. The shop right, however, appears to be unique to American law, and may offer other countries a concept worth adopting.

REFERENCES

Bales R., J. Hirsch and P. Secunda (2007), *Understanding Employment Law*, LexisNexis

Caldwell P. (2006), 'Employment Agreements for the Inventing Worker: A Proposal for Reforming Trailer Clause Enforceability Guidelines' 13 *Journal of Intellectual Property Law* 279

Hill, S. (2006), 'I Quit and I am Taking My Patents with Me! Who Owns the Patent Rights to Inventions Made in the Course of Employment?' 53 *Federal Lawyer* 12

Lieberstein M. (2005), 'Employers Beware: Will You Own Your Employee's Inventions?' 1 *Hastings Business Law Journal* 183

Mergens, R. (1999), 'The Law and Economics of Employee Inventions' 13 *Harvard Journal of Law & Technology* 1

Rao, M. and M. Guru (2010), *Patent Law in India*, Kluwer

13. Taking the long view on competition and the mobile employee: lessons from the United States history of efforts to regulate employee innovation and the mobility of workplace knowledge

Catherine L. Fisk*

1. INTRODUCTION

An early twenty-first century effort by a national organization of lawyers and scholars in the United States to revise the law of employment provoked bitter disagreement over the proper contours of the law governing employee use of knowledge in competition with current or former employers. The controversy replicates a centuries-old debate over legal restrictions on employee mobility. Since the American colonies first began to recruit skilled British artisans to emigrate in violation of British law, Anglo-American courts and lawyers have disputed whether restrictions on employee mobility help or hinder economic development and free intellectual inquiry. While some uses of confidential workplace knowledge in post-employment competition may be wrongful, many recognize that information flows associated with employee mobility foster innovation. Moreover, as knowledge is inevitably both an attribute of employees and an asset of companies, strong moral as well as practical considerations limit the extent to which companies can and should invoke law to prevent competition from former employees.

* The author gratefully acknowledges research assistance from Joshua Mayer, of the Duke University Law School class of 2010.

Businesses are even less likely than lawyers to reach a consensus about the desirable level of protection against competition from former employees. In cases pitting an enterprising employee against his or her former employer, it is always in the company's interest to restrict employee mobility. In the aggregate, however, companies benefit from employee mobility at least as much as they are harmed by it, for departing employees usually go to work for other companies that recruit employees to gain the benefit of their knowledge. Although some companies may believe they will be net consumers of technology developed by others and thus may want relatively lax restrictions on employee mobility, others may believe they are and will remain industry leaders or technology pioneers and may want stronger protections.

This chapter responds to an invitation to offer lessons from the past to inform debates about the proper scope of legal regulation of post-employment competition. I offer two. The first is that the relationship between law, the rate and direction of innovation, and the welfare of a region or an economy as a whole is difficult to assess objectively and the optimal legal rules are likely to be a matter of substantial controversy. From the persistence of controversy flows the inescapable fact that clarity and precision in the law are unlikely to be obtained. The lack of legal clarity stymies efforts to identify which legal rules are correlated with which patterns of economic development, simply because it will be hard to know what companies and employees actually regarded the law as being and what legal rules actually were enforced.

A second lesson of the past is that the norms of the workplace and the industry have always been as important as the law in determining the transmission of knowledge from employee mobility. In some eras, industries, and companies, employees controlled quite a bit of the intellectual property they produced. In others they did not. Even companies with restrictive policies toward IP ownership and post-employment competition negotiated individual arrangements granting some employees substantial control over their ideas. Moreover, scholarly and trade press literature documenting the twentieth century history of large companies' knowledge management policies suggests that companies with internal labor markets struggled to develop suggestion systems and other policies to motivate their employees to innovate. Thus, companies recognized the importance of norms even as they confronted limits on their power to create or change them.

The conclusion that follows from these two lessons is that robust economic development can occur in legal regimes that treat employee knowledge as mobile and in those that treat it as the property of the employer and restrict knowledge mobility. Relatively little is known about the optimal level of restrictions on knowledge transmission associated with employee mobility. In the US, until the late nineteenth century, companies had few legal rights to restrict competition or use of knowledge by former employees, yet the nineteenth century witnessed rapid economic growth and technological development.[1] Moreover, as scholars who have studied the growth of computer technology in the middle and late part of the twentieth century have shown, Silicon Valley grew notwithstanding, and may even have prospered *precisely because*, California does not enforce non-compete agreements against employees and Silicon Valley employers seldom resorted to trade secret litigation before the 1990s.[2] In the early- and mid-twentieth century, however, some innovative companies did restrict transmission of employee knowledge. Both knowledge-protective legal regimes and lax legal regimes have existed in places and periods of economic growth.

2. LESSON ONE: CLARITY AND HARMONIZATION ARE CHIMERICAL

The American Law Institute (ALI) in the United States – an elite organization of lawyers and judges engaged in law reform – is in the process of adopting a Restatement of Employment Law with a controversial chapter defining when an employee is prohibited from competing with a current or former employer using knowledge or information that the employee developed, used, or acquired in the employment relationship.[3] A Restatement seeks to modernize, organize, and rationalize a body of judicial decisions in order to assist judges and lawyers to identify the most rational law undergirded by the most sensible policy. The Restatement of Employment Law is an ambitious and controversial project, largely owing to a wide divergence of opinion about what rules of employment are rational and supported by wise policy. Chapter 8, which is entitled 'Employee Obligations and Restrictive Covenants,' replicates longstanding vagueness in the law of trade secrets and non-compete agreements. As to the law of trade secrets, sections 8.01 through 8.05 of the Restatement propose to rebrand as a 'duty of loyalty' the obligation not to misappropriate trade secrets. Section 8.01 states that employees 'owe a duty of loyalty to their employer' which is breached by

---

1 Fisk (2008).

2 Saxenian (1996); Hyde (2003); Gilson (1999); Feldman (2006).

3 American Law Institute, Restatement (Third) of Employment Law (hereafter Restatement), Chapter 8 (2011).

'disclosing or using the employer's confidential information (as defined in § 8.02) for any purpose adverse to the employer's interest (including after termination of the employment relationship.'[4] 'Confidential information' is defined as that information having 'economic value because of its secrecy' which the employer has taken 'reasonable measures' to keep secret. This is the conventional and widely accepted legal definition of a trade secret.[5] The Restatement definition specifically excludes information 'generally known to the public or in the employer's industry' or that is 'part of the general experience, knowledge, and skills that its employees acquire in the ordinary course of their employment,'[6] both of which are also conventional exceptions to the definition of trade secrets. Essentially, what the Restatement proposes to do is to incorporate the law of trade secrets into the duty of loyalty, which is a novel change of labels but not a radical redrawing of the rules.

The problem is that the rules have long been difficult to apply. Drawing clear lines between the knowledge and skills employees acquire in the ordinary course of their employment and that which is a company asset is a difficult task when the ordinary course of highly skilled employment requires immersion in technical details. Moreover, in an economy in which employees are hired precisely for their specialized knowledge, to conclude that any use of knowledge for another employer is unlawful would make people with highly specialized knowledge unemployable. It would also undermine the diffusion of knowledge that supported the rapid innovation and start-up culture of Silicon Valley.[7] The proposed Restatement replicates these factual difficulties and the political controversy in distinguishing general knowledge from corporate property.

The Restatement encounters similar difficulty in sections 8.06 through 8.08, which restate the law of employee non-compete agreements. The formulation chosen is that non-competes are enforceable if they are 'reasonably tailored in scope, geography, and time to further a protectable interest of the employer,'[8] the traditional three part reasonableness test under the law of non-competes in Britain and the US. Three of the protectable interests that define reasonableness are uncontroversial: confidential information as defined in § 8.02, customer relationships, and the goodwill of a business owned or managed by the employee. The somewhat novel protectable interest is 'investment in the employee's

---

4 Restatement, § 8.01.

5 *Uniform Trade Secrets Act* § 1(4) (1985).

6 Restatement, § 8.02.

7 Hyde (2007), 330.

8 Restatement, § 8.06.

reputation in the market.'[9] Without explaining how to distinguish the employer's investment from the employee's own efforts to develop her reputation, the concept that an employer owns the employee's professional or business reputation invites litigation.

The statement that an employer has a legitimate interest in enforcing non-compete agreements when it has invested in an employee's reputation begs questions about what is meant by an 'investment,' how much of an investment is required, and how to determine when employers' investments outweighs the employees' own investments such that employees should be deprived of the ability to capitalize on their reputation by obtaining competitive employment.[10] Old cases raise that issue, such as one involving an effort to prevent Frank Rogers, the general manager of a silverware manufacturing company doing business under the name of William Rogers Co., from working for or lending his name to a rival silverware company. The Connecticut Supreme Court held in 1890 that Rogers was free to work for the competitor and refused to enforce a 25-year prohibition on competitive employment, finding no showing that Rogers was a trademark or that Rogers's use of his own name 'would do them any injury other than such as might grow out of a lawful business rivalry.'[11] More recently, the European Court of Justice had to decide whether the English fashion designer Elizabeth Emanuel, who originally made her reputation designing Princess Diana's wedding dress and who had founded an eponymous design company to which she assigned her name as a trademark, could prevent use of her name after leaving the company she founded. The European Court of Justice concluded that Emanuel's name could be used as a trademark, over her objection, by the firm to which she had assigned the mark and business goodwill. The court left open the possibility that Emanuel could prove the use of her name by her former firm was intended to deceive consumers into believing that she was still involved with the firm. But Emanuel's name, and some portion of the credit for her work, the court said, could validly be sold to another.[12] It did not have to decide whether she could be prevented from doing business under her own name.

---

9 Ibid, § 8.07.

10 Scholars using economic analysis to identify the appropriate level of post-employment restraint to reward employer and employee investment in employee human capital have suggested that current law is not optimal. Lester (2001); Lester & Talley (2000).

11 *William Rogers Mfg. Co. v. Rogers*, 20 A. 467, 468, 469 (Conn. 1890).

12 *Elizabeth Florence Emanuel v. Cont'l Shelf 128 Ltd* [2006] ECR I-3089.

Finally, the Restatement proposes to restate the law governing ownership of employee-generated patents. Section 8.09 states that employees are entitled to their patents unless they have been 'hired for inventive work,' in which case the employee 'is deemed to have agreed to assign patents' to the employer. Section 8.10 gives employers a shop right in employee inventions developed using the employer's time or resources. Section 8.11 makes agreements requiring employees to assign patents enforceable if the inventions 'were created during work time or using the employer's resources' or 'relate to the employer's line of business or research.' As with the other sections, these provisions generally restate the law as it has been abstractly stated in the US for nearly a century.[13] These provisions fudge all the hard issues that have vexed the law for just as long, such as defining which employees were 'hired' or 'assigned' to invent and which inventions 'use' the employer's resources or 'relate to the employer's line of business.'

Here, as elsewhere, the difficult questions are ones which the Restatement does not answer. Courts began in the mid-nineteenth century to say that employers may demand assignment of employee inventions related to the employer's line of business, or when an employee was hired to invent, but there has been wide variation in when a court will find an employee was hired to invent and in how broadly courts will construe the employer's line of business. In some cases courts found that employees hired to 'improve' the company's business by innovating in a particular area were hired to invent and in other cases courts found they were not.[14] Thus, for example, in *Hapgood v. Hewitt*, an 1886 US Supreme Court decision, the Court held that a managerial employee who had been hired 'to devote his time and services to getting up, improving, and perfecting plows and other goods, and to introducing the same' was not required to assign to his employer the patent for an improved plow he had conceived and developed while employed by the company and using company resources because he was not hired to 'exercise his inventive faculties for the benefit of the company.'[15] Depending on how a court construes those concepts, the law either allows inventive employees substantial latitude for entrepreneurship or assigns a wide range of employee inventions to the former employer.

---

[13] Fisk (2008).

[14] Fisk (2008).

[15] *Hapgood v. Hewitt*, 119 U.S. 226 (1886). Some of the language quoted above was in the Court of Appeal's decision in the case, 11 F. 422, 424 (C.C.D. Ind. 1882).

The principal practical problem with the Restatement is not that it seeks radically to move the law in one direction or another toward greater restriction or greater freedom, although it does suggest a number of overbroad rules restricting competition by current and former employees that many scholars consider unwise as a matter of innovation policy. Rather, the problem is that the effort to strike a middle ground on the controversial issues leads the Restatement to achieve little clarity. As the Restatement has evolved through successive drafts over the course of the decade it has been in progress, the Reporters have trimmed some of the more controversial anti-competitive provisions contained in early drafts. In particular, later drafts omit a proposed rule that would have limited employee use of 'proprietary information,' a concept with little recognition and no coherent definition in existing law.[16] Similarly, the later drafts omit a hugely controversial rule prohibiting employees not subject to a non-compete agreement from taking competitive employment if the employment would 'inevitably' lead to disclosure of the former employer's trade secrets.[17] In the main, the Restatement is consistent with the majority of states' approach to the laws in these areas, although it overstates certain rules (particularly those pertaining to competition by current employees and those governing non-compete agreements) and it missed a crucial opportunity to modernize the law so as to promote competition and innovation in the contemporary labor market in which employees frequently switch jobs and employers benefit from greater employee mobility. The reason *why* the Restatement is consistent with the law of many states, however, is that it states the law at such a high level of generality and abstraction as to skip over the controversies that have long kept judges and lawyers busy.

3. LESSON TWO: THE NORMS OF THE WORKPLACE AND THE INDUSTRY ARE MORE IMPORTANT THAN THE LAW

Whether or not the law grants employer rights in employee knowledge and restricts competition by former employees, many employers – and many scholars – have discovered that the norms of the workplace and the industry are more important than law in stimulating employee innovation and in controlling the dissemination of workplace knowledge. Not only

16 Montville (2007).

17 *Pepsico, Inc. v. Redmond*, 54 F.3d 1262 (7th Cir. 1995).

do norms explain patterns of knowledge transmission associated with employee mobility among firms,[18] but companies have also attempted to create workplace cultures and employee suggestion systems that stimulate innovation within the firm when bureaucratic employment practices, corporate ownership of workplace knowledge and post-employment restrictions have removed entrepreneurial incentives for employee innovation.

Examples of the significance of industry norms over legal rules stretch back to the earliest period of US history. In Wilmington, Delaware in 1808, the du Pont family gunpowder company (now known as DuPont) enjoyed robust demand for its product and the competitive advantage of extensive knowledge of the chemistry of gunpowder. Competitors wished to lure away workers with knowledge of the techniques for mixing the powder and wanted to get their hands on the devices that were useful. At that time, the law of enticement prohibited recruiting employees under contract, but there was some uncertainty about whether that law could be applied to skilled male labor whose freedom to quit their employ was one of the hallmarks of their distinction from slaves or indentured servants. The various civil and criminal cases filed after an employee was persuaded to leave DuPont and to take some manufacturing devices with him ended inconclusively. But du Pont discovered that the most effective remedy was discouraging employee mobility through persuasion and force.[19] A century later, when a research chemist working on artificial leather left DuPont to join his family textile firm, DuPont sued for misappropriation of trade secrets on the theory that the chemist's knowledge was a product of DuPont research and would enable his family company to be a serious competitor in the artificial leather business. The chemist defended on the ground that the knowledge he proposed to use was only that which was common knowledge among chemists familiar with that arcane branch of materials science.[20] DuPont litigated the case all the way to the US Supreme Court on the issue of how much of the company's alleged trade secret must be revealed in litigation in order to prove misappropriation, a question that remains a hot issue for litigators today.[21] But DuPont never succeeded in proving the chemist had misappropriated company knowledge. Although neither the chemist nor DuPont succeeded in the artificial leather business in that era, the case marked a conceptual transition at the company, as the

---

[18] Feldman (2002; 2003; 2006).

[19] Fisk (2008), 45–54.

[20] Fisk (2008), 196–206.

[21] *E.I. du Pont de Nemours Powder Co. v. Masland*, 244 U.S. 100 (1917).

company insisted that the highly specialized knowledge possessed by its PhD chemists was corporate property rather than the scientific expertise of its research staff.

A company's approach to using innovation to enhance its market position also affects how it manages employees. DuPont believed that rigorous control over the chemical knowledge of its laboratories was necessary to protect its competitive advantage. Kodak took the same position, although it also recognized that aggressive use of trademarks and marketing were as important as controlling its patents and trade secrets. In contrast, many railroads did not regard innovation, or controlling employee innovation, as essential to their market position. Thus, the Reading Railroad did not insist on assignment of all employee patents, and was willing to ask for and pay for the use of technologies incorporating patents that its employees had developed on the job and using company resources. It did not matter that the company could claim either to own the patent outright or to have, at a minimum, a shop right to the patent.[22]

Whatever the default rules of corporate control of employee innovations may be, the historical record of many companies suggests that many employees negotiated specific arrangements that allowed for greater employee control. For example, the high-level employee at the Reading Railroad who owned the patents to an important innovation in locomotive engines may have negotiated more favorable treatment than the default rules of law would have imposed because he was in a position of power within the company. Similarly, the Rand McNally Company may have been willing to share control of copyrights to an innovative map developed by a University of Chicago geography professor who consulted with the company because the professor-cartographer enjoyed status within the firm.[23] The lawyer who advised DuPont about intellectual property issues in the early twentieth century lamented the difficulty of getting every employee in the laboratories to sign invention assignment and trade secret nondisclosure agreements.[24] Even in the middle of the twentieth century, when many large companies had developed bureaucratic legal and personnel policies to govern intellectual property issues, some employees maintained ownership of their patents and copyrights notwithstanding a general company policy asserting ownership of all employee-produced intellectual property. One example is a

---

22 Fisk (2008), 120–125.
23 Fisk (2008), 231.
24 Fisk (2008), 206.

songwriter employed by the J. Walter Thompson advertising agency who copyrighted a song used in a particularly successful advertising campaign (for Kodak, as it happens).[25] Successful companies differed in the degree to which they encouraged employee innovation, recruited talent versus restricted later competition, or urged employees to be entrepreneurial as an incentive to innovate as opposed to allowing them to in fact be entrepreneurial by leaving the firm.

As consolidation of intellectual property rights in the corporation reduced opportunities for individual entrepreneurship, companies began to experiment with using personnel policies to motivate employees to innovate and to capitalize upon employee tacit knowledge. One of the principal lessons to be drawn from the twentieth-century history of business innovation policies is the difficulty companies faced in using financial and other rewards to induce employees to suggest innovations. A major recent study of Bell Laboratories, the research and development arm of AT&T which pioneered the semiconductor and the laser, among other advances, suggests that the physical layout of the workplace and the company's deliberate effort to support a combination of pure science research, engineering, and manufacturing were essential to the production of innovations.[26] The study also shows that AT&T's willingness to disseminate information about and license its inventions was crucial to the revolution in computing. The academic and trade journal literature on employee suggestions programs illustrates the limits of company power to shape the norms governing innovation.

The first study of organized efforts of companies to induce employee innovation through suggestion systems, published in 1927 by the University of Michigan School of Business Administration and based on 60 American and British companies' employee suggestion programs, reported that the earliest known programs (in the 1880s) were a modest form of profit sharing animated by the companies' concern with motivating employees to invent.[27] At the turn of the twentieth century, many large American companies, including the National Cash Register Company, Kodak, and Westinghouse, inaugurated such programs.[28] The Michigan study found disagreement among managers as to whether enhancing employee voice in the workplace or monetary rewards were more effective, but the study concluded that a combination of both was

[25] Fisk (2010).
[26] Gertner (2012).
[27] Dickinson (1927), 56.
[28] Ibid; Mishra (1994), 587.

more effective than either alone.[29] One obstacle to the success of programs, said the study, was complacency among managers. It did no good to induce employees to suggest innovations if executives were unwilling to reconsider 'their own methods and judgments.'[30] Among the plans surveyed, the study found that cash awards generally were approximately 10 percent of the estimated first year's saving attributable to the innovation, although 90 percent of accepted suggestions received close to the minimum award. Successful plans included 'continuous and varied publicity,' 'arrangements which tend to assure fair consideration, such as concealing suggestor's name during investigation,' and prompt reviews.[31] A suggestion's originality or patentability often had little to do with the size of the award, and successful suggestions often were based on better practices observed by employees in other establishments.[32]

In the 1950s and 1960s, a number of trade journals published articles on how to establish an employee suggestion program. They discussed cost reduction measures, the proper design of a suggestion plan manual, and ways for supervisors to stimulate idea submission. Those written by accounting staff focused on how to efficiently process suggestions, report savings, and 'sell' the program to employees.[33] Articles by engineers concentrated more on ensuring that supervisors stimulate idea submission by remaining open to criticism and recognizing the value of employee suggestions.[34] Some companies experimented with variations on employee awards. Following one employee's suggestion, Wisconsin Power & Light created a new system: employees were issued a number of $20 certificates, which they could award to one another as they saw fit.[35] In the 1970s employee suggestion systems became common in clerical and administrative operations, not just in manufacturing firms where they originated.[36] Another study found suggestion systems more prevalent at large companies than at small firms.[37]

A number of studies attempted to document the impact of idea submission programs in the mid-twentieth century. The editor of the journal *Industrial Management* reported that by 1965, the tenth year of

---

29 Dickinson (1927), 2.
30 Ibid.
31 Ibid, 1.
32 Ibid, 13.
33 Sullivan (1949), 30; White (1952), 34.
34 Fehr (1967), 206, 208.
35 Thornburg (1994), 58.
36 Reuter (1977), 78, 81.
37 Reuter (1976), 37, 46.

the Federal Employees' Incentive Awards Act, government employees had made a total of 118,564 suggestions that had returned measurable benefits totalling more than $76 million.[38] At General Electric, the head of employee benefit programs reported that about one of every three suggestions resulted in an award.[39] By 1966, the sixtieth year of GE's plan, more than 34,700 ideas had been adopted for an average award of $32 each.[40] In 1985, members of the National Association of Suggestion Systems reported saving $1.24 billion from employee suggestions and paying out $128 million in awards.[41]

The dominance of Japan as a technological powerhouse in the 1970s and 1980s prompted American management theorists to propose that the US emulate the Japanese approach for encouraging and rewarding innovative employees. In a 1999 study, a team of psychology professors began with the premise that suggestion plans are a key feature of corporate productivity, and that 'Europe in particular should be concerned with this issue because European workers provide very few suggestions in comparison to the Japanese' (0.4 suggestions per year for each worker and 61.6 per year, respectively).[42] They approached employee suggestion rates as an indicator of individual initiative, believing that the 'innovation at work literature should systematically include initiative as important explanatory concept.'[43] By studying suggestions at a Dutch steel company, they concluded that the best way to increase suggestion rates was to focus on 'self-efficacy and doing away with suggestion inhibitors,' but that 'increasing external awards for giving suggestions will probably not result in a large increase.'[44] The authors reached conclusions similar to those of many Japanese companies: high employee participation results more from personal initiative than from the size of cash awards.

Scholars of knowledge management at Japanese firms identified the importance of focusing not only on hugely profitable 'big' ideas, but also on the hidden store of tacit knowledge among employees:

---

38 Burns (1965), 13.
39 Ibid.
40 Burns (1967), 15.
41 *Good Suggestions Bring Good Money* (1987), 14.
42 Frese, Teng, & Wijnen (1999).
43 Ibid, 1151.
44 Ibid.

> The centerpiece of the Japanese approach … depends on tapping the tacit and often highly subjective insights, intuitions, and hunches of individual employees and making those insights available for testing and use by the company as a whole. The key to the process is personal commitment, the employees' sense of identity with the enterprise and its mission.[45]

Japanese productivity experts call this approach 'Kaizen Teian,' or continuous improvement. It depends on employees' willingness to freely contribute even the smallest ideas:

> Kaizen improvement is quite different from innovation, the sort of improvement with which many Westerners are more familiar. Innovation implies significant, breakthrough-level progress by only a limited number of trained professionals such as engineers or managers. Kaizen improvement, on the other hand, means a continual and gradual accumulation of small improvements made by all employees.[46]

Japanese data from 1989 showed more employee participation (75 percent in Japan and 9 percent in America) and more frequent adoption of suggestions (87 percent in Japan and 32 percent in America). The disparity in participation rates was attributed to American systems being designed to promote 'big-result ideas,' with the result that two out of three suggestions are not used, and the Japanese system welcoming even small ideas.[47] Japanese observers noted that the drawback of the Japanese system is that it can create wasteful efforts to collect, collate, and reward inept suggestions. The drawback of the American system, by contrast, is that it rejects most proposals, leading employees to feel frustrated by the system.[48]

The conceptualization, design, and use of employee suggestion systems evolved in the 1980s and 1990s as theories of company management changed and companies began to focus more explicitly on knowledge management rather than just on idea submission. Ever since Peter Drucker declared in 1969 that America had switched from an 'economy of goods' to 'a knowledge economy'[49] and predicted that information-based companies would shift away from command-and-control structures as workers became more knowledgeable within their specialty, scholars and management consultants have pondered how to manage the careers of knowledge workers and to figure out how to

---

45 Nonaka (1996), 19.
46 Japan Human Relations Association (1992), 4.
47 Ibid, 21.
48 Ibid, 22.
49 Drucker (1969).

control the sharing of the knowledge they possess.[50] In order to stay competitive, companies would have to maximize the shared knowledge of their employees. In particular, by conceptualizing employees as capital rather than as labor, Drucker insisted that employee knowledge was crucial to productivity.[51] Based on his study of the McKinsey Consulting Group, Tom Peters also promoted the shift to information-based companies which abandoned centralized management in favor of empowered small teams. These teams would require 'knowledge management,' a deliberate and continuous effort to share knowledge among employees that requires tracking and attributing employee contributions. Successful employees at McKinsey 'contributed to the knowledge base,' and became known for doing so, which made them more valuable in the McKinsey network.[52] Peters insisted that the value of information depended not only on its availability, but also on 'the degree to which it's attached to credible people.'[53] The shift that both Drucker and Peters described – from centralized management to diffuse teams of specialists sharing knowledge throughout the organization – may have been the secret to success at places like Lockheed's Skunk Works, Disney, and Apple.[54] Scholars who studied those organizations emphasized the importance of teambuilding and corporate culture, rather than specifics about how to manage intellectual capital. Those companies, and others with exceptionally creative teams, were held up by management experts as 'organizations of the future' because they 'depend on the creativity of their members to survive. And the leaders of those organizations will be those who find ways both to retain their talented and independent-minded staffs and to set them free to do their best, most imaginative work.'[55]

Growing out of the literature on knowledge management, management scholars began to emphasize the notion that organizations must constantly learn in order to stay competitive. A successful learning organization depends on a framework for bringing organizational patterns into focus, pays attention to the assumptions that expand or limit the goals deemed possible, and shares a vision that galvanizes the organization and teams, rather than just individuals.[56]

---

50 Drucker (1988), 45, 50.
51 Drucker (2002), 70, 76.
52 Peters (1992).
53 Ibid, 390.
54 Bennis & Biederman (1997).
55 Ibid, 8.
56 Senge (1990; 2006), 6–10.

> It is no longer sufficient to have one person learning for the organization, a Ford or a Sloan or a Watson or a Gates. It's just not possible any longer to figure it out from the top, and have everyone else following the orders of the grand strategist. The organizations that will truly excel in the future will be the organizations that discover how to tap people's commitment and capacity to learn at all levels in an organization.[57]

The advent of the Internet prompted some companies to take an open-source approach, allowing employees to post their suggestions in an online forum where others may comment on them.[58]

Although luminaries of the management literature agreed that organizations must learn by attracting ideas from their employees, and suggested the possibility of technology to enhance the process, they offered little in the way of practical guidance for recognizing employee contributions: what types of ideas to solicit and how to reward them. The Employee Involvement Association[59] continues to propose lessons from successful businesses – build an integrated system rather than a stand-alone program; screen out ideas that lack value; put the burden of proof on the employee proposing the suggestion to work out the details of implementation; make the immediate supervisor the first review point; and allow teams to submit suggestions – but remains a bit vague about how exactly to do all those things.[60]

Moreover, for all the cheerleading in trade publications about the savings and innovation made possible through knowledge management and employee suggestions, there have been cautionary voices as well. Two principal lines of criticism emerged. First, systems often failed when they overlooked the morale of those employees who had suggestions rejected and those who did not participate.[61] Without transparent procedures for evaluating ideas, management loses the trust and initiative of its employees. Ideas are submitted only if employees believe that the expected reward equals or exceeds the cost of creation for the individual. '[S]ince expectations regarding reviewer evaluation are based primarily on reviewer actions on previous ideas,' if reviewers are perceived to have rejected too many ideas in the past, employees will believe that there is no point in submitting ideas even if reviewers change their behaviors to become more welcoming.

---

57 Ibid, 4.
58 Nalebuff and Ayres (2004), 18.
59 <http://www.eianet.org>.
60 Darragh-Jeromos (2005), 18.
61 Stranne (1964), 17.

> Thus, expectations regarding organizational rewards for idea flow effort are modified downward … . As new employees enter the organization they learn these low expectations from the veterans who have traversed full cycle. In such an environment it is little wonder that potentially creative employees fail to realize their potential and appear to 'go dry' over time.[62]

A second criticism of corporate efforts to solicit employee innovations focuses on the difficulty of coordination among groups. Although groups of employees working together might be most likely to make the strongest suggestions, the promise of cash rewards can make it difficult for groups to cooperate in the design of the suggestion.[63] One study found that 'individuals often are reluctant to share large rewards, and therefore are less likely to embrace developing their ideas in teams. This means that large rewards actually may inhibit implementation.'[64] Moreover, team members hold back when they lack trust in the organization: 'Potential participants fear the credit for their ideas will be stolen' and 'do not want to become detached from their ideas. They don't want others to work on and implement their ideas without their involvement.'[65] Compared to other types of merit pay, one study found that 'idea generation is not an effective strategy for obtaining organizational rewards because the mechanisms for scheduling review and measuring achievement are less well defined.'[66]

A 1972 study of employee trust in knowledge management used the concept of knowledge 'markets' to explain how ideas are exchanged within a company.[67] The study found that credit and attribution are essential to a successful knowledge market, because they are necessary to establish trust. Trust 'is an essential condition of a functioning knowledge market, as it is of any market that does not depend on binding and enforceable contracts. … [T]he knowledge market – with no written contracts and no court of appeals – is very much based on credit, not cash.'[68] In this analysis, employees will trust the organization enough to transfer knowledge to their colleagues only if trust is 'visible' (people are seen to get credit for knowledge sharing), trust is 'ubiquitous,' and upper management refrains from ever exploiting another's knowledge for

---

62 Baker & Freeland (1972), 105, 110, 111.
63 Stranne (1964), 18.
64 Wood (2003), 22, 26.
65 Ibid, 23.
66 Baker & Freeland (1972), 105, 110.
67 Davenport & Prusak (1998).
68 Ibid, 35.

personal gain without giving credit and reward to the person who shared the knowledge.[69]

At the advent of the twenty-first century, scholars pored over the law and business practices of Silicon Valley, trying to discern the legal regime most conducive to the vibrant innovation and start-up culture of the 1980s and 1990s. One theory was that California does not enforce non-compete agreements, which enables employees to switch jobs and take economically valuable knowledge to places where it will be put to its best use.[70] Other theories focused on trade secret law. Much of the knowledge that employees took with them might be protectable as a trade secret and thus knowledge transfers associated with employee mobility might have been prevented regardless of the existence of non-competes. The similarity between California trade secret law and that of many other states (and that in the Restatement described above) has prompted other scholars to focus on reasons why Silicon Valley employers refused to file trade secret litigation against competitors who lured away valuable employees.[71] Among the theories offered for the reluctance to sue were the possibility that employers thought litigation would be useless and the possibility that they did not want to get the reputation of restraining entrepreneurial employees and they cared more about their reputation for recruiting the best and the brightest than about protecting their trade secrets.[72] Still other scholars have explored the role of social norms in explaining what employees regard as a trade secret and when they divulge information that they might regard as a trade secret.[73]

4. CONCLUSION

Over the last two centuries, companies have pursued a wide array of policies for the management of employee workplace knowledge and mobility, recognizing that the norms of the workplace and the industry were more important for exercising control over employee innovation than were legal rules. Of course, the management of employee knowledge is only part of a company's overall strategy with respect to intellectual property and innovation. Nineteenth-century railroad companies were fairly lax about employee-generated intellectual property, but

---

69 Ibid.
70 Saxenian (1996).
71 Gilson (1999).
72 Hyde (2003, 2007).
73 Feldman (2002, 2003, 2006).

they also did not seek market dominance through innovation. Kodak, on the other hand, was very aggressive about technical innovation and about controlling employee knowledge, but its aggressive pursuit of innovation was also tied to aggressive marketing of its products. Given all the other factors that affect company success, it is difficult to say whether one strategy or another is more or less conducive to economic growth or market dominance. Eventually, of course, technological change left both railroads and Kodak behind. In the aggregate, rigorous protection of corporate property rights in employee-generated innovations is unnecessary for robust economic growth.

Although this chapter was invited to consider the lessons of history for legal scholars interested in business innovation, and it duly offers two, the lessons of history can often be stated with confidence only at such a high level of abstraction as to offer little guidance on the concrete choices facing contemporary actors. The lessons offered here – (1) the law governing ownership of employee innovation and controlling employee mobility will likely remain messy; and (2) the norms of the workplace and the industry may be as important as law in shaping employee innovation – are more in the nature of cautionary notes than they are proposals for action by lawyers or testable hypotheses for scholars.

REFERENCES

Amir, O. and O. Lobel (2011), 'Innovation Motivation: Behavioral Effects of Post-Employment Restrictions', <http://ssrn.com/abstract=1876133> accessed 3 August

Baker, N. and J.R. Freeland (1972), 'Structuring Information Flow to Enhance Innovation' 19 *Management Science* 105

Bennis, W. and P. Biederman (1997), *Organizing Genius: The Secrets of Creative Collaboration*, Addison-Wesley

Burns, J. (1965), 'Cost Cutting Suggestions Catching On With Employees' (March) *Industrial Management* 13

Burns, J. (1967), 'GE Pays Out $1,113,000 in Suggestion Awards' (September) *Industrial Management* 15

Darragh-Jeromos, P. (2005), 'A Suggestion System That Works For You', July, *SuperVision* 18

Davenport, T. and L. Prusak (1998), *Working Knowledge: How Organizations Manage What They Know*, Harvard Business School Press

Dickinson, Z.C. (1927), 'Suggestions from Employees' 1 *Michigan Business Studies* No. 3

Drucker P.F. (1969), *The Age of Discontinuity*, Harper & Row

Drucker P.F. (1988), 'The Coming of the New Organization' (Jan.–Feb.) *Harvard Business Review* 45

Drucker P.F. (2002), 'They're Not Employees, They're People' (Feb.) *Harvard Business Review* 70
Fehr R.B. (1967), 'Supervisors and the Employee Suggestion Plan' (Apr.) *Personnel Journal* 206
Feldman Y. (2002), 'An Experimental Approach to the Study of Social Norms: The Allocation of Intellectual Property Rights in the Workplace' 10 *Journal of Intellectual Property Law* 59
Feldman Y. (2003), 'Experimental Approach to the Study of Normative Failures: Divulging of Trade Secrets by Silicon Valley Employees' *University of Illinois Journal of Law, Technology and Policy* 105
Feldman Y. (2006), 'The Behavioral Foundations of Trade Secrets: Tangibility, Authorship, and Legality' 3 *Journal of Empirical Legal Studies* 197
Fisk C.L. (2008), *Working Knowledge: Employee Innovation and the Rise of Corporate Intellectual Property, 1800–1930*, University of North Carolina Press
Fisk C.L. (2010), 'The Modern Author at Work on Madison Avenue' in Paul Saint Amour (ed.), *Modernism and Copyright*, Oxford University Press
Frese M., E. Teng and C.J.D. Wijnen (1999), 'Helping to Improve Suggestion Systems: Predictors of Making Suggestions in Companies' 20 *Journal of Organizational Behavior* 1139
Gertner, J. (2012), *The Idea Factory: Bell Labs and the Great Age of American Innovation*, Penguin Press
Gilson R. (1999), 'The Legal Infrastructure of High Technology Districts: Silicon Valley, Route 128 and Covenants Not to Compete' 74 *New York University Law Review* 575
'Good Suggestions Bring Good Money' (June 1987) *Management Review* 14
Hyde A. (2003), *Working in Silicon Valley: Economic and Legal Analysis of a High-Velocity Labor Market*, ME Sharpe
Hyde A. (2007), 'Trade Secrets Practice in Silicon Valley' in S. Willborn, S. Schwab, J.F. Burton Jr., and G.L.L. Lester (eds), *Employment Law: Cases and Materials*, LexisNexis
Japan Human Relations Association (1992), *Kaizen Teian 1: Developing Systems for Continuous Improvement through Employee Suggestions*
Lester, G.L.L. and E. Talley (2000), 'Trade Secrets and Mutual Investments' (October), <http://ssrn.com/abstract=246406> accessed 3 August 2011
Lester, G.L.L. (2001), 'Restrictive Covenants, Employee Training, and the Limits of Transaction Cost Analysis' 76 *Indiana Law Review* 49
Mishra, J.M. (1994), 'Employee Suggestion Programs in the Health Care Field: The Rewards of Involvement' (Winter), *Public Personnel Management* 587
Montville, C. (2007), 'Reforming the Law of Proprietary Information' 56 *Duke Law Journal* 1159
Nalebuff, B. and I. Ayres (2004), 'Encouraging Suggestive Behavior' (Dec.) *Harvard Business Review* 18
Nonaka, I. (1996), 'The Knowledge-Creating Company' in K. Starkey (ed.), *How Organizations Learn*, Thomson
Orkin N. (1984), 'Rewarding Employee Invention: Time for Change' (Jan.–Feb.) *Harvard Business Review* 56
Peters, T. (1992), *Liberation Management: Necessary Disorganization for the Nanosecond Nineties*, Knopf
Reuter V.G. (1976), 'Suggestion Systems and the Small Firm' (Oct.) *American Journal of Small Business* 37

Reuter V.G. (1977), 'Suggestion Systems: Utilization, Evaluation, and Implementation' (Spring) *California Management Review* 78
Saxenian, A. (1996), *Regional Advantage: Culture and Competition in Silicon Valley and Route 128*, Harvard University Press
Senge, P. (2006), *The Fifth Discipline: The Art and Practice of the Learning Organization* (first published 1990), Doubleday
Stranne L.V. (1964), 'Morale: The Key Factor in a Suggestion System' (Nov.) *Industrial Management* 17
Sullivan, A.A. (1949), 'Cost Reduction through a Controlled Employee Suggestion Plan' (Mar.), *NACA Bulletin*
Thornburg L. (1994), 'Money Is Still the Best Reward' (Aug.) *HR Magazine* 58
White C.G. (1952), 'How to Devise an Employee Suggestion Plan' (Oct.) *NACA Bulletin* 34
Wood A. (2003), 'Managing Employees' Ideas: From Where Do Ideas Come?' (Summer) *Journal for Quality & Participation* 22

PART IV

The competition law perspective on protecting business research and development

14. Innovation through the lens of competition law

John Duns

1. INNOVATION IN COMPETITION POLICY

Innovation is at the heart of competition policy because of the strong link between innovation and efficiency. Efficiency is the main, some would say the sole, criterion by which competition policy judges and assesses conduct. In the blunt words of economist Philip Williams, 'We should regulate for competition where that regulation enhances the efficiency with which resources are allocated. We should not regulate for competition if that regulation lessens the efficiency with which resources are allocated.'[1] Firms that innovate are efficient in that they develop products to meet the changing demands of their customers. Likewise, firms that fail to innovate are inefficient in this sense, as the resources they employ are not being directed to where they are most demanded. The social benefits of dynamic efficiency are well established.[2]

The efficiency that is generated by innovation (referred to as 'dynamic' efficiency because of its forward-focused, changing nature) is one of the key justifications universally offered for competition law.[3] Dynamic efficiency and innovation are commonly described as being a prized outcome of a competitive market. One review of competition law, for example, described dynamic efficiency as being:

> the need for industries to make timely changes to technology and products in response to changes in consumer tastes and in productive opportunities. Competition in markets for goods and services provides incentives to undertake research and development, effect innovation in product design, reform

[1] Williams 1.

[2] E.g., Abel, Mankiw, Summers and Zeckhauser and, generally, Baumol.

[3] The other efficiencies, so-called 'static' efficiencies are explained in Chapters 15 and 16 below so are not further considered here.

management structures and strategies and create new products and production processes.[4]

2. INNOVATION IN COMPETITION LAW

In light of this established link between competition policy on the one hand, and dynamic efficiency and innovation on the other, we might expect to find that innovation is unambiguously supported in competition law. Certainly some support for innovation can be found. For example, as explained by Rosa Greaves in Chapter 18, European competition law provides broad exemptions from the anticompetitive prohibitions that might otherwise apply to research and development joint ventures. The special role joint venture agreements can play in promoting innovation is explicitly recognized.

However in other respects the relationship is more complex. It is not simply a case of dynamic efficiency being available as a defence to, or even set-off against, an allegation of anticompetitive conduct. The reasons for this, and its ramifications, are explored in the following three chapters. The following discussion makes two general observations on why the relationship between innovation and competition law is not straightforward.[5]

2.1 Locating Dynamic Efficiency in Competition Law

The first difficulty is that competition law does not explicitly acknowledge the objective of efficiency. Indeed, with only minor exceptions, competition statutes invariably make no specific reference to efficiency. The focus of competition law is competition. The assumption is that the promotion of competition will thereby promote efficiency. However, as noted above, there is no general 'defence' that conduct that might otherwise be scrutinized as anticompetitive should be exempt on the ground that it will promote dynamic efficiency. So how do innovation arguments emerge? In Australia and the EU there is more obvious scope to raise efficiency arguments than there is in the US. This is because the former jurisdictions have a process to exempt conduct from the competition prohibitions in specified circumstances. These exemptions allow

---

[4] Report by the Independent Committee of Inquiry, 5.

[5] Another complication is that the 'dynamic' efficiency associated with innovation may clash with the 'static' efficiencies generated by competition. This is considered in Chapter 16.

the parties to argue that conduct should be permitted on efficiency grounds.

In EU law, Article 101 of the Treaty on the Functioning of the EU provides for exemptions to be made from the prohibition against anti-competitive agreements where the relevant concerted practice 'contributes to improving the production or distribution of goods or to promoting technical or economic progress'.[6] As explained by Greaves in Chapter 18, this exemption provision is the basis for 'block exemptions' being given by the regulator.

In Australia there is an even broader exemption process. Under Parts VII and IX of the *Competition and Consumer Act 2010* (Cth), most conduct can be 'authorised' by the regulator where, broadly, it creates sufficient 'public benefit'. It is well established that efficiencies may constitute a public benefit[7] and indeed these are the most commonly argued public benefit.[8] And so the prospect emerges of being able to argue that conduct should be exempt from the anticompetitive prohibitions because it is innovative and thereby promotes dynamic efficiency. This is explained in Chapter 16.

Having an outlet to argue the relevance of dynamic efficiency is of course only the beginning. It can be seen even from this brief outline, for example, that not all conduct can be exempted in this way. Even in Australia conduct that would involve an abuse of market power cannot be authorized. And other issues come into play, such as the weight that should be and is, in practice, given to such efficiency arguments. Nevertheless, it is interesting to contrast such exemption processes with the position in the US.

It is true that case law developed under the Sherman Act has accommodated the relevance of efficiencies to the question of whether conduct is caught by its prohibitions. Section 1, which prohibits 'combinations … in restraint of trade', will generally allow arguments to be made that the relevant agreement is based on efficiency, rather than anticompetitive, considerations.[9] Thus, for example, joint venturers who

---

6 See Article 101(3). There are conditions attached to such exemptions. These are that consumers receive a 'fair share of the resulting benefit', that the restrictions be confined to 'indispensable' restrictions and that the restriction does not create 'the possibility of eliminating competition in respect of a substantial part of the products in question'.

7 E.g., Officer and Williams; Duke; Fels and Grimwade.

8 Duns.

9 This, of course, excludes agreements that are deemed to be per se anticompetitive, such as naked price fixing agreements. If the price-fixing

have entered into an agreement for the purpose of research and development will be able to argue that the agreement is concerned with the creation of efficiencies and that this is appropriately taken into account in determining whether the agreement is an illegal restraint.

Section 2, which prohibits 'monopolization' and 'attempted monopolization', also allows efficiency arguments to justify conduct that may otherwise be seen to be 'exclusionary' and so within the prohibition. This was discussed, for example, in the *Microsoft* case. In that case the Court noted that 'from a century of case law on monopolization under s 2 … several principles do emerge'. After pointing out that a plaintiff in a s 2 action must establish that the relevant conduct has an anticompetitive effect on competition (as opposed to an effect on competitors), the Court went on to state how efficiency arguments become relevant:[10]

> then the monopolist may proffer a 'procompetitive justification' for its conduct … If the monopolist asserts a procompetitive justification – a nonpretextual claim that its conduct is indeed a form of competition on the merits because it involves, for example, greater efficiency or enhanced consumer appeal – then the burden shifts back to the plaintiff to rebut that claim.

And 'if the monopolist's procompetitive justification stands unrebutted, then the plaintiff must demonstrate that the anticompetitive harm of the conduct outweighs the procompetitive benefit'. This balancing exercise was likened to the 'rule of reason' approach taken in s 1 actions.

Less clear, however, is the US position on efficiencies in the Clayton Act, at least where the statute prohibits conduct that 'substantially lessens competition'. The merger provisions of s 7 of the Clayton Act are the obvious example. This section prohibits acquisitions where 'the effect of such acquisition may be substantially to lessen competition or to tend to create a monopoly'. With the focus of s 7 on lessening of competition, it is not obvious how arguments about efficiencies that the merger might create become relevant.[11] The US Merger Guidelines take a pragmatic approach and concede that efficiencies, including dynamic efficiencies, are relevant to a merger assessment.[12] The Guidelines acknowledge that

---

agreement is not 'naked', that is, it is ancillary to some other lawful objective, then efficiency arguments will be relevant in this context also, as demonstrated in the early leading case of *Chicago Board of Trade v US* (1918) 246 US 231.

[10] See *Microsoft Corp v United States* 346 US App D C 330 at [46]–[47].

[11] Compare Williams and Woodbridge.

[12] U.S. Department of Justice and the Federal Trade Commission, *Horizontal Merger Guidelines 2010* at 29–31.

'a primary benefit of mergers to the economy is their potential to generate significant efficiencies'. There is some difficulty in reconciling these efficiency considerations with the terms of s 7:

> In conducting this analysis, the Agencies will not simply compare the magnitude of the cognizable efficiencies with the magnitude of the likely harm to competition absent the efficiencies. The greater the potential adverse competitive effect of a merger, the greater must be the cognizable efficiencies, and the more they must be passed through to customers, for the Agencies to conclude that the merger will not have an anticompetitive effect in the relevant market. When the potential adverse competitive effect of a merger is likely to be particularly substantial, extraordinarily great cognizable efficiencies would be necessary to prevent the merger from being anticompetitive. In adhering to this approach, the Agencies are mindful that the antitrust laws give competition, not internal operational efficiency, primacy in protecting customers.

Nevertheless, it is clear that the regulators accept that relevant efficiencies include dynamic efficiency. After a general statement that 'Efficiencies also may lead to new or improved products, even if they do not immediately and directly affect price', the Guidelines go on to make clear that innovation is relevant to a merger assessment:

> When evaluating the effects of a merger on innovation, the Agencies consider the ability of the merged firm to conduct research or development more effectively. Such efficiencies may spur innovation but not affect short-term pricing. The Agencies also consider the ability of the merged firm to appropriate a greater fraction of the benefits resulting from its innovations. Licensing and intellectual property conditions may be important to this enquiry, as they affect the ability of a firm to appropriate the benefits of its innovation. Research and development cost savings may be substantial and yet not be cognizable efficiencies because they are difficult to verify or result from anticompetitive reductions in innovative activities.

However, it is noteworthy in this context that efficiencies created through innovation seem to carry less weight than other (static) efficiencies. The Guidelines state:

> The Agencies have found that certain types of efficiencies are more likely to be cognizable and substantial than others. For example, efficiencies resulting from shifting production among facilities formerly owned separately, which enable the merging firms to reduce the incremental cost of production, are more likely to be susceptible to verification and are less likely to result from anticompetitive reductions in output. Other efficiencies, such as those relating to research and development, are potentially substantial but are generally less susceptible to verification and may be the result of anticompetitive output

reductions. Yet others, such as those relating to procurement, management, or capital cost, are less likely to be merger-specific or substantial, or may not be cognizable for other reasons.

2.2 Innovation and Market Power

Innovation is often linked with market power and this is the second reason why the relationship between competition law and innovation is not a simple one. This is one of the key themes explored in Chapters 15 to 17. Market power, although not itself prohibited under competition legislation, often provides the gateway to anticompetitive conduct. Ray Finkelstein, in Chapter 15, examines the legal protection offered to owners of business information by a range of laws, most notably by intellectual property laws, and then asks whether these laws are appropriately kept in check by competition law. In particular, he assesses the means by which a balance is attempted between competition and intellectual property laws and whether this balance is appropriately struck. Dorothy Livingston, in Chapter 17, explores EU case law involving a clash between competition and intellectual property rights. This is done in the context of a range of conduct, such as tying and bundling, often engaged in by firms with market power.

REFERENCES

Abel, A., N.G. Mankiw, L. Summers and R. Zeckhauser (1989), 'Assessing Dynamic Efficiency: Theory and Evidence' 56 *Review of Economic Studies* 1

Baumol, W. (2002), *The Free-Market Innovation Machine: Analyzing the Growth Miracle of Capitalism*, Princeton University Press

Duke, A. (2007), 'A More Efficient Use of Efficiencies in Merger Authorisation Determinations' 35 *Australian Business Law Review* 278

Duns, J. (1994), 'Competition Law and Public Benefits' 16 *Adel L Rev* 245

Fels, A. and T. Grimwade (2003), 'Authorisation: Is it Still Relevant to Australian Competition Law?' 11 *Competition and Consumer Law Journal* 187

Officer, R. and P. Williams (1995), 'The Public Benefit Test in an Authorisation Decision' in M. Richardson and P. Williams (eds), *The Law and the Market*, Federation Press

Report by the Independent Committee of Inquiry (1993), *National Competition Policy*, Australian Government Publishing Service

U.S. Department of Justice and the Federal Trade Commission (2010), *Horizontal Merger Guidelines*

Williams, P. (1987), 'Why Regulate for Competition?' in M. James (ed.), *Regulating for Competition? Trade Practices Policy in a Changing Economy*, Centre for Independent Studies

Williams, P. and G. Woodbridge (2002), 'The Relation of Efficiencies to the Substantial Lessening of Competition Test for Mergers: Substitutes or Complements?' 30 *Australian Business Law Review* 435

15. Legal protection of business research and development: can it harm competition?

Ray Finkelstein

1. INTRODUCTION

Innovation enhances social welfare. Firms create wealth and employment by generating new ideas and developing them into new or improved products or processes. Consumers, in turn, benefit from these innovations by access to the products and processes and, often, reduced prices. In the modern economy, which is becoming increasingly information and services based, new ideas that result in slight advances in technology and minor improvements in production, can afford firms significant competitive advantages over rivals. Having exclusive use of those ideas can often mean the difference between maintaining and increasing market share and financial ruin.[1]

The law provides this exclusive use by protecting information owners against unauthorized interference with, or use of, commercially valuable information. This is a broad category of information (called intellectual property) which encompasses data technology, know-how and the narrow field of trade secrets. One result of this protection is that firms have the incentive to develop new and improved products. Another is that allowing firms to limit the use of their new ideas can discourage free market competition by permitting firms to maintain or increase their market power.

I propose to examine how the law enables commercial information owners to prevent competitors making use of their information. I will then consider whether that protection should be cut down by existing competition laws because of an overriding need to maintain competition to ensure social welfare is appropriately advanced.

[1] Pace (1995).

2. WHY PROTECT INTELLECTUAL PROPERTY?

There are several rationales for the protection of intellectual property. The major justification adopted by European jurists is rooted in natural rights thinking.[2] According to this approach an innovator's right to his work is akin to an inherent natural right which the State is obliged to protect because it is either unowned or 'held in common'.[3]

An offshoot of the natural rights theory is favoured by English jurists. It is that the misappropriation of commercial information is offensive to commercial ethics. As Megarry J put it in *Coco v A N Clark (Engineers) Ltd*,[4] whether the claim is in contract or equity, 'a court ... must be ready to make those implications upon which the sane and fair conduct of business is likely to depend'.

The third and most conventional justification for intellectual property protection is the reward theory, and its close cousin, the encouragement of invention. Technological innovations usually require substantial investment of time, money and effort.[5] In a private market economy, if firms cannot be assured they will be rewarded for their effort by being given a competitive advantage to exploit their innovations (ie by exclusive use) and thereby recoup their investment, they may lack the incentive to make the investment in the first place.

None of the rationales require that intellectual property be treated as property strictly so described. No doubt intellectual property rights that are created by statute (patents and copyright) are property rights in the sense that, by reason of the statute creating the right, the 'owner' has the ability to exclude everyone else from using or interfering with it. Non-statutory rights (ie those provided by the common law) do not lend themselves to that type of characterisation and, in any event, the protection conferred is not the same as that given to property owners. Still, while the law may not treat commercial information and trade secrets as property, firms certainly do. The cost is treated as an asset in the firm's accounts; the information is bought and sold as part of, or even separate from, the firm's goodwill.

---

[2] Mossoff (2001), 1257–1258.
[3] Oguamanam (2008–2009), 108.
[4] [1969] 86 RPC 41, 51 (Chancery Division).
[5] Pace (1995), 436.

3. HOW IS INTELLECTUAL PROPERTY PROTECTED?

The law plays an important role in protecting commercially valuable information. The common law provides protection for trade secrets or trade secret-like information by contract, claims in equity for breach of fiduciary duty and breach of confidence and, in some jurisdictions, by actions in tort. Statutes protect information which may become publicly available by copyright, the grant of patents and, in some jurisdictions, by data protection laws.

3.1 Contract

Express contracts, especially in the form of agreements not to compete or to maintain secrecy, are a frequently employed device for the protection of commercially valuable information. In addition, contract law recognizes that a party may have a legitimate interest in protecting business information. So the law will, in such cases, often imply an obligation not to use the information, or to keep it confidential. Sometimes the same result can be achieved by the application of an implied duty of fidelity or good faith.

A contract to maintain secrecy is an interesting concept. To a large extent the law permits a person to sell his silence. Parties are generally free to strike whatever bargain they please. But the right is not unlimited. Sometimes public policy requires that courts not enforce what the parties have agreed. So, courts will not enforce a contract of silence that obstructs justice (e.g., to conceal a crime). Still, it is generally accepted that a contract not to disclose a trade secret or other commercially valuable information will be enforced.[6]

Likewise, post-employment restraints will be enforced, though only if it is reasonable both in the public interest and between the contracting parties. Here the court is required to strike a balance between the interests of the information owner, the need for the ex-employee to find new employment and the public interest in the information being disclosed.

---

6 Garfield (1997–1998), 300–303.

3.2 Equity

From the mid eighteenth century Chancery began to issue injunctions to prevent what came to be referred to as 'breach of confidence'.[7] The doctrine does not depend upon the existence of a contract between the parties or a fiduciary relationship. What the plaintiff must show is: (1) the information is 'confidential in nature' (ie not in the public domain); (2) the information has been imparted 'in circumstances importing an obligation of confidence' (ie the recipient must know, or must be likely to have understood, that information was given in confidence); (3) there has been an unauthorized use of the information, possibly 'to the detriment' of the information owner.[8] The duty can sometimes be enforced against a stranger who steals the secret or acts surreptitiously.

3.3 Tort

Few common law jurisdictions have adopted as a tort the misappropriation of confidential information or a trade secret. Such a tort has, however, developed in the United States. The law is modelled on § 757 of the Restatement of Torts (1939).[9] According to the Restatement of Torts, a trade secret 'may consist of any formula, pattern, device or compilation of information which is used in one's business, and which gives him an opportunity to obtain an advantage over competitors who do not know or use it'.

The Restatement lists factors that are relevant for determining whether given information is a trade secret. The factors are: (1) the extent to which the information is known outside the business; (2) the extent to which it is known by employees; (3) the extent of measures taken to guard the secrecy of the information; (4) the value of the information to the owner and to competitors; (5) the effort expended in developing the information; and (6) the ease or difficulty with which the information could properly be acquired or duplicated by others.[10] To be liable the defendant must have 'misapplied' the trade secret. That is, the trade secret must have been acquired by improper means or with notice of its mistaken or accidental disclosure. In general terms, any exploitation of the trade secret that is likely to result in injury to the trade secret owner or enrichment of the defendant will be actionable.

---

7 Hammond (1979).

8 Some of the cases require detriment to be shown, others do not.

9 Now the Restatement of Unfair Competition, 3d, §§ 39–45 (1995).

10 § 757 of the Restatement.

A model statute, the Uniform Trade Secrets Act (UTSA) has been drafted by the National Conference of Commissioners on Uniform State Laws to codify the basic principles of common law trade secret protection. The definition of trade secrets in the UTSA is similar to that in the Restatement of Torts. Most, but not all, states have enacted versions of the UTSA.

The rights conferred by equitable doctrines in England and Australia and those available under tort theory in the United States have some features in common. They are designed to protect information that is: (1) valuable; (2) derives its value from not being publicly known; and (3) which the owner took reasonable steps to protect. If the information is published through negligence or carelessness it is no longer protectable. The information that is protected is broad. It may be technical or non-technical, scientific or non-scientific. It can include ideas, data and facts. Almost anything not generally known is capable of protection.

The other side of the coin is that protection is limited. The owner does not have exclusive rights to the information, is not protected against independent development and reverse engineering, and does not have rights against good faith purchasers. Only a person who knows or should know that the information is secret may be held liable.[11]

The limitations of common law protection mean that statute law (the grant of patents and copyright) provides the primary means of protection of intellectual property.

3.4 Patents

Modern patent law developed from the letters patent granted by the Tudor monarchs, initially to lure skilled craftsmen to England. The grant of monopolies became the subject of considerable abuse, especially by Queen Elizabeth I. To prevent those abuses the Statute of Monopolies was enacted in 1623 and still applies in Australia.[12] The statute prohibited monopolies in general but, by s 6, preserved patents for an invention that was a 'manner of new manufactures' unless it was 'contrary to the law' or 'mischievous to the state by raising prices … or hurt of trade or generally inconvenient'.

The Patent Acts, both in Australia and abroad, create a form of limited monopoly granted to the inventor of a new manufacture.[13] In order to be patentable, an invention must be a manner of manufacture (a product or

---

[11] Czapracka (2007–2008), 226–227.
[12] Patents Act 1990 (Cth), s 18(1)(a).
[13] For instance Patents Act 1990 (Cth), s13(1).

process that is artificially created) that involves an inventive step (not obvious to a person skilled in the particular art), is novel (not known or used by others) and useful (it must do what it is intended to do) and was not previously used.[14] The requirements act as a filter to remove certain innovations from patent protection. The inventor who meets these criteria obtains the right to exclude all others without licence from making, using or selling the invention in the particular jurisdiction, usually for 20 years.[15]

Much commercial information is not patentable subject matter: it is not usually a method of manufacture. Moreover, ideas and scientific principles that are merely abstract and do not lead to a practical application are not patentable.[16] A physical effect is required.[17]

One important aspect of the patent system (which distinguishes it from the protection afforded by the common law) is that, once granted, the patent must be published and is therefore in the public domain. When the statutory monopoly is over, the invention can then be employed by anyone.

Computer programs raise an interesting issue. They are based on algorithms – ie mathematical formula – and this has given rise to a debate whether they are patentable. The debate arose because patent protection is not available for laws of nature, natural phenomena and abstract ideas. Thus, for example, mathematical algorithms, which are 'abstract ideas', are not patentable subject matter. However, with the advent of computer technology, programs began to be developed to perform the mental steps previously performed by humans. The question was whether those programs, based as they were on mathematical algorithms, were patentable. Different approaches have been taken in different jurisdictions, but they lead to a similar result.

In the US in the well-known *State Street* case[18] a patent was sought in respect of software that provided a method of pooling the assets of mutual funds in an investment portfolio. The patent claims involved a data processing system comprising a computer processor, data storage

---

[14] Ibid, s 18(1).

[15] Ibid, s 67.

[16] *National Research Development Corporation v Commissioner of Patents* [1959] HCA 67, (1959) 102 CLR 252, 264; *Grant v Commissioner of Patents* [2006] FCAFC 120, (2006) 154 FCR 62, 70–71; Beckerman-Rodau (2002), 378.

[17] *Grant v Commissioner of Patents* [2006] FCAFC 120, (2006) 154 FCR 62, 70.

[18] *State Street Bank & Trust Co. v Signature Financial Group Inc.* 149 F 3d 1368 (Fed Cir 1998).

and a series of arithmetic logic means to perform calculations. Patentability was challenged on two grounds: that the mathematical algorithms used in the process were not patentable since they were abstract ideas and that the patent fell within the judicially created 'business method' exception. Previously the United States courts had analogized 'business methods' to abstract ideas and denied patentability on that basis.

The Federal Circuit held that the transformation of data by a machine through mathematical calculations is not simply an abstract idea and therefore unpatentable because it produced a useful, concrete and tangible result (the so called 'machine or transformation' test). As to the second ground, the Federal Circuit held that it was irrelevant that the patent claim involved a business method and, further, that business methods should be subject to the same criteria for patentability as any other process or method: ie the Federal Circuit rejected the 'business method' exception.

The *State Street* decision was seen as allowing virtually anything to be patentable. The decision resulted in a 'legal tsunami'[19] of applications seeking protection for common business practices. Applications for business method patents in the United States increased from fewer than 1,000 in 1997 to more than 11,000 in 2007.[20] Many absurd patents were granted, e.g., a method of training janitors to dust and vacuum using video displays, a method for selling expert advice, and a method of enticing customers to order additional food at a fast food restaurant.[21] One commentator even suggested that under *State Street* his new method for skipping classes would be patentable.[22]

In Australia, the algorithmic processing of information has been held to be patentable, though the reasoning employed is somewhat different from that in *State Street*. In *Welcome Real-Time v Catuity*,[23] the claimed patent involved a method of processing coded information stored on a card with a memory chip to allow consumers to accumulate points for purchases from retailers. In upholding the patent, the Federal Court relied on the principle that patentable subject matter included any mode or manner of achieving an end result which is an artificially created state of

---

[19] *In re Bilski* 545 F 3d 943, 1004 (Fed Cir 2008).

[20] Ibid, 1004.

[21] Ibid, 1004.

[22] Keeley-Domokos (1999).

[23] *Welcome Real-Time SA v Catuity Inc.* [2001] FCA 445, (2001) 113 FCR 110.

affairs of utility in the field of economic endeavour.[24] It held that the loyalty cards produced an artificial state of affairs.[25] The Court referred, with apparent approval, to *State Street*, describing it as an 'analogous' case.[26]

The UK has taken a different path. It has, by statute, excluded from the definition of a patentable invention anything which consists of a scheme, rule or method for performing a mental act, playing a game or doing business, or a program for a computer.[27]

Interestingly, in the US, the status of *State Street* has been put in doubt. In the 2010 decision in *Bilski v Kappos*[28] a patent was sought for an invention that explains how commodities buyers and sellers in the energy market can protect (hedge) against price changes. The key claims described a series of steps including the evaluation of historical costs and weather variables and the use of economic and statistical formulas to analyse these data and estimate the likelihood of certain outcomes.

The Supreme Court denied the application on the basis that the concept of hedging described, and reduced to a mathematical formula, was an unpatentable abstract idea.[29] In the course of its reasons, the Supreme Court by majority held that the 'machine or transformation test' is a relevant but not the sole test governing patentability.[30] The majority said of *State Street* that nothing in its opinion 'should be regarded as endorsing interpretations of [the patentability criteria] that the Court of Appeals for the Federal Circuit has used in the past'.[31]

In this confusing state of affairs, the US Patent and Trademark Office (USPTO) issued a guidance notice[32] to assist in determining the patent-eligibility of process claims. According to the USPTO, an invention is more likely to be patent-eligible if it satisfies the criteria of the machine or transformation test or evidence is provided that the abstract idea has been practically applied. Interestingly, the USPTO listed some examples

---

[24] [2001] FCA 445, (2001) 113 FCR 110, 136 citing *CCOM Pty Ltd v Jiejing Pty Ltd* [1994] FCA 1168, (1994) 51 FCR 260.

[25] [2001] FCA 445, (2001) 113 FCR 110, 137.

[26] Ibid, 136. See also the Full Court decision in *Grant v Commissioner of Patents* [2006] FCAFC 120, (2006) 154 FCR 62.

[27] Patents Act 1977 (UK), s 1(2)(c).

[28] *Bilski et al v Kappos, Under Secretary of Commerce for Intellectual Property and Director, Patent and Trademark Office* US Doc No 08–964, 28 June 2010.

[29] Ibid, 15.

[30] Ibid, 16 of the majority opinion and 2 of the dissenting opinion.

[31] Ibid, 16 of the majority opinion.

[32] US Patents and Trademarks Office, July 27 2010, 43,926.

of general concepts which are unlikely to be patentable. They include basic economic practices of theories (e.g., hedging, insurance, financial transactions, marketing) and mathematical concepts (e.g., algorithms, spatial relationships, geometry). This rather suggests that if a business method such as the one in *State Street* were to come before the USPTO at this time it might well not be patentable.

3.5 Copyright

Copyright is granted principally in respect of original literary, dramatic, musical and artistic works, usually for the life of the author plus 70 years. In most jurisdictions the protection also covers compilations of one kind or another. While there can be no copyright in a fact or idea, the selection and arrangement of those facts and ideas may be copyright. Importantly, in 1984 the Australian Copyright Act was amended to specifically include within the definition of 'literary work' computer programs.[33] Before then, there had been some uncertainty whether computer programs were covered.[34] This led to a concern that 'the absence of legal protection and continued uncertainty as to the state of the law would jeopardise the local software industry'.[35]

There are limits to the protection copyright gives. Unlike patents, there can be more than one valid copyright held in identical works. As long as each author produced the work independently, each is entitled to copyright.

4. THE BENEFITS OF INTELLECTUAL PROPERTY PROTECTION

The principal benefit of intellectual property protection is the encouragement of innovation by increasing the returns from research and development. Absent the protection of commercial information, innovators cannot appropriate the full benefits of their labours; some benefit will go to free riders.

---

[33] Copyright Act 1968 (Cth), s 10(1). This definition was poorly drafted and a new definition was substituted by Act 110 of 2000 s 4 and Sch 1 item 7.

[34] *Apple Computer Inc v Computer Edge Pty Ltd* [1983] FCA 328, (1983) 1 IPR 353.

[35] Second Reading Speech by Senator Gareth Evans on 4 June 1984, Hansard 2421.

The second benefit is that it encourages dissemination. That is, absent protection, innovators would rely on secrecy to obtain their advantage which would limit the flow of information to other would-be inventors and discourage licensing which would be detrimental to society.

The third benefit is that protection will encourage the further development of those inventions which have little value or are not commercially viable until improvements are made. More explicitly, protection will facilitate licensing to firms who would invest in the development work.

Finally, intellectual property protection can encourage the orderly development of technologies that may be inspired by an initial invention. Having an orderly system of follow-on inventions is efficient. Controlled licensing can avoid duplicative efforts. Later innovators are encouraged to invest in research and development by appropriate royalty rights.

5. PROTECTION vs COMPETITION

While there are obvious benefits, protection can adversely affect competition and lead to market distortions and market failure. On one view that may sound surprising because both intellectual property protection and competition laws are aimed at encouraging innovation, industry and competition. So how does this conflict arise?

The goal of competition law is to increase social welfare through competition, ie through rivalry of firms. It is this competition that produces efficient market outcomes. There are different types of efficiencies, some more important than others.

A market achieves allocative efficiency when resources are allocated, through price, to their highest-value use among all competing users. Then price will not rise far above the marginal cost of production. Monopolies cannot achieve allocative efficiency as the monopolist's price will exceed the marginal cost.

Productive efficiency results when all goods are produced at the minimum possible cost under existing technology. This means that the producer is unable to sell above marginal cost because if it does consumers will move to another product. Monopolists, who are free from constraints of competition, may restrict their output and raise prices or in some cases may even be higher cost producers.

Dynamic efficiency arises because rivalry between firms encourages innovation to develop new and improved products. Firms that are insulated from competitive pressures may not undertake substantial research and development programmes, leading to inefficient production and higher costs. Most economists contend that innovative efficiency provides the greatest enhancement of social wealth, suggesting it is the most important factor in the growth of real output in industrial countries.

Intellectual property protection may conflict with competition law and, more particularly, may lead to market failure. At a simple level, there are five problems. The first is that intellectual property protection may create a monopoly. To describe intellectual property rights as monopoly rights is not, however, the same as saying that intellectual property rights confer market power in a relevant market, and it is the existence of market power that is the concern of competition law.

In the area of market power it is important nowadays to draw a distinction between, on the one hand, intellectual property rights covering products and processes in the traditional fields of manufacture (the so called 'smoke-stack industries') and what many economists refer to as the 'new economy' (e.g., the computer software, Internet services and biotechnology industries). In traditional markets intellectual property protection will result in little or no significant market power. Professor Kenneth Dam has pointed out that leading companies may obtain hundreds of patents in a single year and not obtain a single monopoly (in the economic sense) in any market.[36]

But this is unlikely to be true in the new economy. In this economy innovation is often costly, whereas the cost of producing the new product or service is low. So, for example, the cost of developing a new medical treatment can be very significant when compared with the cost of producing the product that is needed for the treatment. Also, developing a new line of computer code may require considerable time and money, but the cost of duplicating that code and making it available to consumers is minimal.

Moreover, products and services in the new economy frequently exhibit 'network effects'. This refers to the situation where a consumer's demand for a product or service is directly related to its widespread use by others.[37] When a significant number of consumers use the product or service, future consumers value it more by virtue of its extensive use and popularity. Thus the supplier gains dominance not because of the inherent merit of its goods or services, but rather because it manages to attain a critical mass which tips consumers towards its products rather than those of other suppliers.[38]

---

[36] Dam (1994), 250.

[37] Pitofsky (2001).

[38] Intellectual Property and Competition Review Committee (2000), 103–104.

Network effects are a feature of communications networks (telephone, facsimile, email and Internet). They also arise when a system consists of two or more distinct components purchased by a single user (e.g., a computer operating system and an application program). When different components can work together they are said to be compatible, and the degree of compatibility will shape the nature of innovation and price competition. Innovators are more likely to design products to work with the existing products of a dominant firm (e.g., 'apps' for iPhones and iPads). This leaves potential challengers of the dominant firm without access to competing goods or with the burden of producing them themselves.[39]

There is, nonetheless, controversy about whether more concentration leads to greater research and development. Joseph Schumpeter is one of the principal economists who stressed the important role innovation plays in market economies. He advanced the proposition that monopoly profits give firms security and therefore freedom to innovate in a manner not available to a non-dominant firm.[40]

Kenneth Arrow is one of Schumpeter's main challengers. He argues that competition is essential to innovation, particularly where intellectual property protection is available and the downstream product would substitute for a product already produced by the monopolist.[41] In his view, if a new product would 'cannibalize' the profit from its present monopoly, the monopolist has no incentive to create the product. In the absence of industry evidence, a useful working premise is that a monopolist (or a firm with substantial market power) that does not face the threat of entry by other firms has little incentive to engage in costly research and development of new products.

The second market problem is that if the new good or service is successful, the intellectual property owner will enjoy economic rent; ie it will be able to charge for the product or service more than the marginal cost of its production.

The third market problem arises from network effects in the new economy. According to network theory, strong network markets will move to a standard technology because consumers benefit from all network users adopting standard (or compatible) technology.[42] Being first in the market in which consumers wish to acquire the standard technology confers advantages over later entrants – the so-called 'first mover

39 Pitofsky (2001), 539.
40 Schumpeter (1950), 106.
41 Arrow (1962), 609.
42 Lemley & McGowan (1998), 721.

advantage'. First, higher returns will result if the firm establishes its goods or services as the standard. Second, higher returns raise the possibility of predation and also the possibility of effective leveraging; ie the firm may use its dominance in the market to require the consumer to acquire the complementary product or service. Third, consumers are unlikely to transfer from the standard. In any event, if there are high switching costs consumers may be locked into the network.

The fourth market problem is the inhibiting effect intellectual property protection has on future research and development. On a simple view of intellectual property protection, innovation is treated as a one-off event. But this is incorrect. It is also commonly assumed that the commercialization of an invention requires access to only one (or perhaps a few) protected rights. Yet more and more industries require access to dozens, even hundreds, of protected rights.

No doubt there are many examples of the innovator with broad intellectual property rights who will himself pursue follow-on inventions. Broad intellectual property protection permits the owner 'to make investments to maximize the value of [his ideas] without fear that the fruits of the investment will produce unpatentable information appropriable by competitors'.[43] This is what is known as the 'prospect theory' of intellectual property rights. It focuses on the efficient coordination of, and incentives for, follow-on developments.[44]

But the theory has its detractors. For example, leading economists question whether the initial innovator can provide the necessary efficient management of future developments.[45] Others say the system really depends on efficient licensing of follow-on opportunities. Licensing negotiations, however, are notoriously difficult, lengthy, costly and likely to break down.[46]

Follow-on inventions are, in reality, often undertaken by independent innovators. However, in the face of intellectual property protection, follow-on innovation can result in substantial duplication of effort, since the independent innovator will attempt to design around the existing intellectual property rights.

If the follow-on innovator requires access to multiple protected technologies, as will usually be the case in the new economy, several problems will arise. The transaction costs of gaining access will be significant. These costs will be passed on to consumers as higher prices.

---

43 Kitch (1977), 276.

44 Scotchmer (1991).

45 Scherer (2002), 1362.

46 Merges & Nelson (1990), 874–875.

If the intellectual property is held by a group of oligopolists, they would probably collectively refuse to license to prevent a new entry.

Another aspect of the inhibition of future development is suppression. The suppression of innovation may occur if the intellectual property owner wishes to limit the availability, use or development of its technology. This can take various forms. An intellectual property owner which develops an innovation may refuse to exploit it to enhance its monopoly position. A classic example is the patenting of solar energy inventions by oil companies.

The fifth market problem is the shared development of intellectual property rights. It is becoming increasingly common for firms to engage in research and development as part of a joint venture. There are many advantages: economies of scale; the avoidance of unnecessary duplicative activities; access to intellectual property rights belonging to the joint venturer without which the research and development may not be possible; and shared risk of failure. So, when firms combine their resources and expertise consumers may benefit from enhanced innovation and lower prices.

Nonetheless these joint ventures are troubling for their possible anti-competitive effects:

1. The joint venture will foreclose actual or potential competition between the firms involved.
2. If the relevant industry is concentrated and the joint venture accounts for a substantial share of the output, new innovations by the joint venture will lead to an increase in market power.
3. In high-tech industries, investing in research and development is itself a form of competition which leads to consumer benefits in the form of new products and lower prices. For example, the advance of computer technology has seen dramatic improvement in products and equally dramatic price falls in a short period.[47] The establishment of joint ventures can eliminate this form of competition.

6. KEEPING INTELLECTUAL PROPERTY IN CHECK

The potential overlap between intellectual property protection and competition laws raises the question whether competition laws are sufficiently flexible to deal with market power based on intellectual property.

---

[47] Rappaport & Halevi (1991).

Judge Richard Posner said that 'antitrust doctrine is subtle enough, and its commitment to economic rationality strong enough, to take in stride the competitive issues presented by the new economy'.[48] It may be true that both intellectual property protection and competition laws encourage competition, but, as has been shown, intellectual property protection, while rewarding innovation, will often inhibit competition.

The apparent tension between intellectual property protection and competition laws is well recognized by US courts, but has received remarkably little interest in other jurisdictions, especially in Australia. For many years the US courts viewed the two sets of laws as being 'in conflict'.[49] In the late 1990s, the US courts downplayed the perceived conflict, stressing the complementary purpose of competition and intellectual property laws in promoting innovation, and treating the intellectual property protection of products, processes and ideas as fundamentally no different from any other property right.[50]

More recently there has been a revival of concern about the potential conflict. The famous *Microsoft* case[51] is regarded by some as a paradigmatic case of the application of antitrust to the new economy.[52] One of the many complaints made against Microsoft was the requirement in its Windows 95 operating system that computer manufacturers could not modify the 'first screen' that users see when turning on the computer for the first time.[53] Microsoft argued that the Copyright Act permitted it to prevent licensees from modifying its product.[54] The DC Circuit found that Microsoft was not entitled to rely on its intellectual property rights to justify its 'first screen' provision. It dismissed Microsoft's copyright

---

48 Cited in Sullivan (2001–2002).

49 E.g., *Data General Corp v Grumman Systems Support Corp* 36 F 3d 1147, 1187 (1st Cir, 1994); *Chrysler Motors Corp v Auto Body Panels of Ohio, Inc* 908 F 2d 951, 954 (Fed Cir, 1990); *International Wood Processors v Power Dry, Inc* 792 F 2d 416, 427 (4th Cir, 1986); *SCM Corp. v Xerox Corp.* 645 F 2d 1195, 1203 (2d Cir, 1981).

50 E.g., *Atari Games Corp. v Nintendo of America, Inc* 897 F 2d 1572, 1576 (Fed Cir, 1990); Hovenkamp, Janis and Lemley (2003), §1.4, 1–11.

51 87 F Supp 2d 30 (DDC 2000) (conclusions of law). Although the appellate court reversed the district court on certain issues, it affirmed on the issue discussed here: 253 F3d 34, 59–64 (DC Cir 2001).

52 Carrier (2002), 784.

53 84 F Supp 2d 9, 61 (DDC 1999) (findings of fact).

54 Carrier (2002), 785.

argument as 'frivolous'[55] and made the blanket assertion that '[i]ntellectual property rights do not confer a privilege to violate the antitrust laws.'[56]

The better view is that intellectual property protection and competition laws not only overlap, but, in certain circumstances, conflict. New economy markets, particularly those with innovations that exhibit network effects, tend towards the emergence of a dominant standard. If this standard can be protected by intellectual property laws, the firm or firms that control it will have significant market power.[57] Competition laws must be enforced to correct the balance.

The difficult issue is how the balance is to be achieved. First, looking at the non-statutory means of protection of business information (contract, tort and equity) there is an issue regarding the extent to which those means should be permitted to hold up competition. The doctrine of reasonableness is of particular interest. Restraints in employment contracts are always looked at from the perspective of reasonableness. In appropriate circumstances, such restraints may be reasonable as employers expend time and money training employees and should be entitled to expect some return on that expenditure.

Yet there are also several respects in which restraints on the use of business information may be unreasonable. For example a promise of silence by an employee who possesses confidential (often secret) business information could diminish competition by slowing down or preventing altogether the dissemination of ideas, processes and methods. It is, therefore, appropriate in such cases that courts consider these issues when asked to grant relief under claims in contract or equity the effect of which would be to keep commercial information secret. The matters the court should take into account include: (1) whether the intellectual property owner has substantial power in a relevant market; (2) the extent to which the relief the intellectual property owner seeks in the litigation will or may harm competition; and (3) whether in all the circumstances that harm is unreasonable.

Turning to the statutory protections, there is an as yet unexplored possibility that a patent will not be granted if the effect of the grant will be to entrench a monopolist or otherwise substantially inhibit competition.

---

55 253 F 3d 34, 63 (DC Cir 2001).
56 Ibid, 63.
57 Sullivan (2001–2002) 43.

So far as Australia is concerned it will be recalled that the proviso to s 6 of the Statute of Monopolies provides that a patent must not be: (1) contrary to law; (2) mischievous to the State by raising the price of commodities; (3) to the hurt of trade; or (4) generally inconvenient.

The precise scope of the proviso is uncertain. Still, in *Bristol-Myers Squibb Co v FH Faulding & Co Ltd*[58] I ventured the view that the effect of the proviso is that if 'for one reason or another, [the grant of a patent would be] contrary to the public interest then the invention is not the proper subject matter for a patent'. This was said in the context of an enquiry whether a method of medical treatment was patentable subject matter. But why, it may be asked, should an innovator be given a monopoly for the use of an invention which would prevent or harm competition in a relevant market. It is difficult, in such a circumstance, to formulate a compelling public policy reason in favour of the grant, though it may be acknowledged that one consequence of this approach may be to deter some innovation.

The position in the United Kingdom may be to a like effect but for different reasons. The 1977 Patents Act prohibits the grant of a patent where its publication or exploitation would be contrary to public policy or morality.[59] The comments I made in *Bristol-Myers Squibb Co* seem to apply with equal force to this statute.

6.1 Licensing

Looking more generally at the statutory protections, an important solution to the potentially anti-competitive effects of those protections is the licensing of intellectual property rights. In Australia there are no compulsory licensing provisions in the Copyright Act. By way of contrast, the UK has made provision for compulsory licences to be imposed if a copyright owner engages in anti-competitive practices or abuses its monopoly position in a relevant market.[60]

Speaking very broadly, the UK legislation works in this way. If there is a merger raising a public interest issue, or the misuse of monopoly power, as a result of a condition in a copyright licence or the refusal to grant a licence, that issue may be investigated by the Competition Commission.[61] The investigation is a formal process which, in a public release, the Commission has indicated will usually take between 12 and

58 [2000] FCA 316, (2000) 46 IPR 553, 589.
59 Patents Act (UK), s 1(3).
60 Copyright, Designs and Patents Act 1988 (UK), s 144(1).
61 Ibid.

15 months.[62] A party dissatisfied with the Competition Commission's finding can appeal to the Competition Appeals Tribunal for judicial review. The High Court also has jurisdiction to review decisions. This is quite unsatisfactory. If the means of correcting market failure can, on an optimistic view, take two to three years, the process is itself a barrier to entry.

The Australian Patents Act, by contrast to the position in relation to copyright in Australia, does make provision for compulsory licensing. The court may order a compulsory licence if:

1. the public need for the invention has not been satisfied and the patentee has not given a satisfactory reason for failing to exploit the patent himself;[63] or
2. the patentee has contravened or is contravening Part IV of the Competition and Consumer Act 2010 (Cth) in connection with the patent.[64]

By providing for compulsory licences in situations involving a breach of the competition laws, the legislature has recognized that although the grant of a patent permits a patentee to enjoy a limited monopoly right, anti-competitive conduct that goes beyond the extent of the granted patent right may occur and should not be allowed.[65]

6.2 Essential Facilities[66]

A non-statutory route to licensing may exist in circumstances where access to intellectual property will either produce or increase competition in a relevant market. The view that, absent some statutory obligation, an intellectual property owner is under no obligation to license its intellectual property to a third party has been eroded. In the United States the courts have developed the so-called 'essential facilities' doctrine. Put rather simply, the doctrine provides that facilities that cannot practically

---

62 <http://www.competition-commission.org.uk/our_role/how_investigate/procedures.htm>

63 Patents Act 1990 (Cth), s 133(2)(a).

64 Ibid, s 133(2)(b).

65 The Parliament of the Commonwealth of Australia, House of Representatives, "Explanatory Memorandum to the Intellectual Property Laws Amendment Bill 2006", 16.

66 The discussion in this section is based on my reasons in Re Fortescue Metals Group Ltd [2010] ACOMPT 2, (2010) 271 ALR 256.

be duplicated by would-be competitors must be shared on fair terms by those in possession of them.[67]

The foundation for the doctrine is § 2 of the Sherman Act,[68] which condemns '[e]very person who shall monopolize … any part of the trade or commerce' (ie unilateral monopoly misuse). What the doctrine prohibits is both concerted and unilateral refusals to give access to a facility.

The most important modern decision on the essential facilities doctrine is *MCI Communications Corp v American Telephone and Telegraph Co.*[69] At issue in that case was the extent to which AT&T had to open up the long-distance telephone market to competitors. MCI had built a long-distance telecommunications network but in order to successfully offer long distance service, it had to be able to interconnect with AT&T's 'local loop' or 'last mile' of wire to reach households and businesses. It also sought access to AT&T's long-distance network for the cities not reached by its own network.

The Seventh Circuit set out a four-part test to deal with the essential facilities claim, which has been followed in many later cases. According to this test, courts must examine the following factors: (1) control of the essential facility by a monopolist; (2) a competitor's inability practicably or reasonably to duplicate the essential facility; (3) the denial of the use of the facility to a competitor; and (4) the feasibility of providing the facility.[70]

The Seventh Circuit accepted as a general proposition that antitrust laws do not require a monopolist to deal with anyone. On the other hand a monopolist controlling an essential facility must make it available to competitors on non-discriminatory terms to prevent the monopolist from extending 'monopoly power from one stage of production to another, and from one market into another'.[71]

The following observations may be made about the *MCI* test. First, there is no definition of 'facility'. Ordinarily one might envisage a structure of some sort. But later cases show that a structure is not necessary.[72], to be essential, a facility need not be indispensable. A facility will be essential if an alternative facility is impossible or unduly

67 Neale (1970), 67. This is where the term 'essential facilities' doctrine is first used.

68 15 USC (1994).

69 708 F 2d 1081 (7th Cir, 1983).

70 Ibid, 1132–1133.

71 Ibid, 1132.

72 See e.g., *Aspen Highlands Skiing Corp v Aspen Skiing Co* 738 F 2d 1509 (10th Cir, 1984).

expensive to construct. Third, the fourth element (the feasibility of providing the service), ensures that the owner is only required to make available to competitors excess capacity.

Despite its apparent entrenchment, in 2004 in *Verizon Communications, Inc v Law Offices of Curtis V Trinko, LLP*[73] the Supreme Court cast doubt on the essential facilities doctrine stating: 'We have never recognized such a doctrine ... and we find no need either to recognize it or to repudiate it here.'[74] It is impossible to predict what the Supreme Court will do in the future. If it does bar antitrust scrutiny of the consequences of intellectual property ownership it will be out of step with both Europe and Australia.

So far as Australia is concerned, Part IIIA of the Competition and Consumer Act provides a regime for providing access to facilities of national significance.[75] Intellectual property rights, however, are specifically excluded from the scope of the Part except to the extent that they are an integral but subsidiary part of the service.[76] But other provisions of the Competition Act may be available. For example, in *NT Power Generation Pty Ltd v Power and Water Authority*,[77] the High Court found that the Power and Water Authority had breached the abuse of market power provision (s 46 of the then Trade Practices Act) by refusing to allow a competitor access to its electricity distribution system. The High Court explicitly declined to apply *Trinko*.

The essential facilities doctrine is also alive and well in the European Union. The leading case (an intellectual property case) is *Radio Telefis Eireann v Independent Television Publications Ltd*.[78] There, Irish television stations refused to license their copyright in the information contained in their respective programme listings to Magill TV Guide Ltd which wanted to publish a comprehensive weekly television guide. The European Court of Justice held that the copyright information had to be licensed on reasonable terms. The Court made that order because three conditions had been satisfied. First, there was no actual or potential substitute for a weekly television guide, despite customer demand. Second, no business justification existed for the refusal. Third, the

---

73 540 US 398 (2004).

74 Ibid, 411.

75 Telecommunications services are dealt with separately in Part XIC of the Act.

76 Competition and Consumer Act 2010 (Cth), s 44B.

77 [2004] HCA 48, (2004) 219 CLR 90.

78 Cases C-241/91P and C-242/91P, [1995] ECR I-743. See also *Microsoft Corp v Commission of the European Communities* Case T-201/04.

owners reserved for themselves a monopoly in the secondary market of weekly television guides by excluding all competition.[79]

While some courts in the US have accepted that there are situations in which a refusal to deal may give rise to antitrust liability,[80] the Federal Circuit has taken a stricter view. *In re Independent Service Organizations Antitrust Litigation*[81] concerned an allegation by CSU that Xerox had violated the Sherman Act by setting the prices of its patented parts much higher for ISOs than for end-users to force ISOs to raise their prices and thus eliminate them from the market. The Federal Circuit applied a narrow test for liability stating: 'In the absence of any indication of illegal tying, fraud in the Patent and Trademark Office, or sham litigation, the patent holder may enforce the statutory right to exclude others from making, using, or selling the claimed invention free from liability under the antitrust laws.'[82]

As a matter of logic, if an essential facilities doctrine is to exist, it is difficult, if not impossible, to justify an approach that would isolate intellectual property from other facilities as *CSU* has done.

6.3 Patent Misuse

There is another, quite distinct, means by which the owner of copyright or a patented invention may be prevented from using its statutory rights to inhibit or harm competition. The means is the so-called 'patent misuse' doctrine.

The patent misuse doctrine is founded on the equitable doctrine of unclean hands 'and relates generally to the use of patent rights to obtain or to coerce an unfair commercial advantage. [It] relates primarily to a patentee's actions that affect competition in unpatented goods or that otherwise extend the economic effect beyond the scope of the patent grant.'[83] Under the doctrine the defendant in an infringement action can claim that the patent owner has 'misused' its patent. If the defence is

---

79 See also *IMS Health GmbH & Co v NDC Health GmbH* Case C-418/01, [2004] ECR I-5039.

80 *Data General Corp v Grumman Systems Support Corp* 36 F 3d 1147 (1st Cir, 1994); *Image Technical Services, Inc v Eastman Kodak Co* 125 F 3d 1195 (9th Cir, 1997).

81 203 F 3d 1322 (Fed Cir 2000) cert denied 121 ST 1097 (2001).

82 Ibid, 1327.

83 *C. R. Bard Inc. v M3 Systems Inc* 157 F 3d 1340, 1372 (Fed Cir 1998) cert denied 526 US 1130 (1998).

successful, the court will not grant equitable relief (e.g., an injunction) or damages for infringement.

The doctrine covers conduct that is wider than competition law violations, but the cases of misuse generally track competition laws quite closely.[84] *Chisum on Patents* states there are three classic acts of misuse: (1) requiring the purchase of unpatented goods for use with patented products; (2) prohibiting the production or sale of competing goods; and (3) conditioning the grant of a licence under the patent upon the acceptance of another and different licence.[85] The patent misuse doctrine has also been applied to copyright misuse.[86]

7. CONCLUSION

The existence of a conflict between the protection of business information and competition law is plain. At its most base, the protection of business information is a system of exclusion: the focus of competition law is, well, competition. At the heart of the conflict is the fact that exclusion-based acts often restrict competition.

It is also true that intellectual property protection plays an important role in the new economy. This has been recognized both by Parliament, which is willing to expand protection by legislation (e.g., the protection of computer programs by copyright) and by common law courts in their relatively unquestioning enforcement of contracts of silence and confidence claims. Yet that very protection can have a significant adverse market impact, both because it may stifle innovation and enable market abuse by dominant firms.

The courts can negate the potential harm. When intellectual property protection relies on contract or equity, the court should be required to consider the reasonableness of the protection sought to be enforced. In that task the court should assess the reward the intellectual property owner receives if permitted to enforce a particular restrictive practice and compare that with the welfare loss that will result from the exploitation of that intellectual property.

When the intellectual property owner relies on copyright or patent protection, the anti-competitive provisions in Part IV of the Competition and Consumer Act may come into play. In particular s 46, which is

---

[84] Lemley (1990), 1611.

[85] Chisum (1974–2011), para [9.04] [3].

[86] E.g., *Lasercomb America Inc v Reynolds* 911 F 2d, 970, 973 (4th Cir 1990); *M Witmark & Sons v Jensen* 80 F Supp 843 (D Minn, 1948).

concerned with the misuse of market power for a proscribed purpose, may need to be applied. The court should not shy away from granting relief under this section simply because the intellectual property owner is exercising property rights.

There are other provisions in Part IV that can be used to overcome market failure: sections which prohibit exclusionary practices, exclusive dealing and mergers that substantially lessen competition.

If properly applied, competition principles and competition laws are up to the task of ensuring that intellectual property owners are prevented from taking excessive advantage of their privileged position. Even in the new economy, a wholesale abandonment of competition principles is neither required nor advisable. What is needed is the careful application of sound and long-established principles to intellectual property issues on a case-by-case basis. The aim of a coherent overall competition policy should be to achieve a sensible balance between intellectual property on the one hand and competition principles on the other.

REFERENCES

Arrow, K. (1962), 'Economic Welfare and the Allocation of Resources for Invention' in *The Rate and Direction of Inventive Activity: Economic and Social Factors: a Conference of the Universities-National Bureau Committee for Economic Growth of the Social Science Research Council*

Beckerman-Rodau, A. (2002), 'The Choice Between Patent Protection and Trade Secret Protection: A Legal and Business Decision' 84 *Journal of the Patent & Trademark Office Society* 371

Carrier, M. (2002), 'Unravelling the Patent-Antitrust Paradox' 150 *University of Pennsylvania Law Review* 761

Chisum, D.S. (1974–2011), *Chisum on Patents,* LexisNexis

Czapracka, K. (2007–2008), 'Antitrust and Trade Secrets: The U.S. and the EU Approach' 24 *Santa Clara Computer and High Technology Law Journal* 207

Dam, K. (1994), 'The Economic Underpinnings of Patent Law' 73 *Journal of Legal Studies* 247

Garfield, A.E. (1997–1998), 'Promises of Silence: Contract Law and Freedom of Speech' 83 *Cornell Law Review* 261

Hammond, R.G. (1979), 'The Origins of the Equitable Duty of Confidence' 8 *Anglo-American Law Review* 71

Hovenkamp, H., M. Janis and M. Lemley (2003), *IP and Antitrust: An analysis of Antitrust Principles Applied to Intellectual Property Law*, Aspen

Intellectual Property and Competition Review Committee (2000), *Review of Intellectual Property Legislation under the Competition Principles Agreement, Final Report*, September

Keeley-Domokos, F. (1999), 'State Street Bank & Trust Co v Signature Financial Group, Inc.' 14 *Berkeley Technology Law Journal* 153

Kitch, E. (1977), 'The Nature and Function of the Patent System' *Journal of Law and Economics* 265
Lemley, M. (1990), 'The Economic Irrationality of the Patent Misuse Doctrine' 78 *Cambridge Law Review* 1599
Lemley, M. and D. McGowan (1998), 'Could Java Change Everything? The Competitive Propriety of a Proprietary Standard' 43 *Antitrust Bulletin* 715
Merges, R. and R. Nelson (1990), 'On the Complex Economics of Patent Scope' 90 *Columbia Law Review* 839
Mossoff, A. (2001), 'Rethinking the Development of Patents: An Intellectual History, 1515–1800' 52 *Hastings Law Journal* 1255
Neale, A.D. (1970), *The Antitrust Law of the United States*, 2nd edn, Cambridge University Press
Oguamanam, C. (2008–2009), 'Beyond Theories: Intellectual Property Dynamics in the Global Knowledge Economy' 9 *Wake Forest Intellectual Property Law Journal* 104
Pace, C.R.J. (1995), 'The Case for a Federal Trade Secrets Act' 8 *Harvard Journal of Law and Technology* 427
Pitofsky, R. (2001), 'Antitrust and Intellectual Property: Unresolved Issues at the Heart of the New Economy' 16 *Berkeley Technology Law Journal* 535
Rappaport, A. and S. Halevi (1991), 'The Computerless Computer Company' *Harvard Business Review* 301
Scherer F. (2002), 'The Economics of Human Gene Patents' 77 *Academic Medicine* 1348
Schumpeter J. (1950), *Capitalism, Socialism and Democracy*, 3rd edn, Harper-Collins
Scotchmer S. (1991), 'Standing on the Shoulders of Giants: Cumulative Research and the Patent Law' 5 *Journal of Economic Perspectives* 29
Sullivan L. (2001–2002), 'Is Competition Policy Possible in High Tech Markets?: An Inquiry into Antitrust, Intellectual Property, and Broadband Regulation as Applied to "the New Economy"' 52 *Case Western Reserve Law Review* 41
United States Patents and Trademarks Office (2010), *Interim Guidance for Determining Subject Matter Eligibility for Process Claims in View of Bilski v Kappos* (July 27)

16. Business innovation and competition law: an Australian perspective

John Duns

1. INTRODUCTION

Innovation is central to competition policy. Indeed, in some industries, it is the primary means by which firms compete. The metaphors are dramatic: innovation is a 'life and death matter for the firm'[1] and 'a weapon in the arms race of competition'.[2] Even more fundamentally, innovation, economists tell us, is pivotal to the capitalist economy as a whole. Baumol, in his book on innovation, declares that it is innovation that drives economic growth and that, without it, economies stagnate.[3]

Despite the well-established role of innovation in competition law and policy, however, the contribution such a perspective brings to the particular innovation issues raised in *Gray's case*,[4] the subject of discussion in other chapters, is limited. A contest between an employer and employee for intellectual property rights to an invention has clearer implications for labour, intellectual property and corporate law. The response of competition law to this issue, it seems to me, is far less clear.

---

1 Baumol (2004), 1.

2 Ibid, 43.

3 See, for example, Baumol (2004), who suggests at *viii*, that 'what may well be the most critical attribute of the free-market economy' is such an economy's 'ability to produce a stream of applied innovations and a rate of growth in living standards far beyond anything that any other type of economy has ever been able to achieve for any protracted period' and at 13, that 'it is reasonable to say not only that innovation has contributed to [the capitalist economy's remarkable record of] growth process ... but that without it the process would have been reduced to insignificance'. The pioneer of this suggestion is, of course, Joseph Schumpeter. See his classic *Capitalism, Socialism and Democracy*. And see generally Scherer (1992).

4 *University of Western Australia v Gray (No 2)* (2008) 246 ALR 603; and on appeal (2009) 259 ALR 224.

In broad terms, competition law and policy is concerned with the promotion of competition or, putting it in the more negative terms of competition legislation, prohibiting conduct that lessens competition.[5] With this focus, competition law would seem to have little interest, in a general sense, in whether intellectual property rights are granted to an employer or an employee.

It is true that there is a well-established interface between competition and intellectual property laws and, in a broad sense, some of this interaction may be relevant. This is because competition law, like intellectual property law, sees innovation as one of its key aims. Much has been written on the different means employed by these two different areas of law to achieve this common end and the potential clashes that result,[6] although it has also been suggested that these differences are less significant than their common goal.[7] There are aspects of this interface between competition and intellectual property law that I will touch on, but it is not my main concern in this chapter. This is essentially because competition law's concern with intellectual property rights generally occurs *after* the creation of such rights – for example, with whether (and on what terms) intellectual property rights should be licensed in order to promote competition. In fact some have gone so far as to suggest that intellectual property law and competition law should have separate spheres, with intellectual property law confining itself to assigning and defending property rights and competition law concerned with the use of such rights.[8] Although the creation of intellectual property may create market power, something competition law is generally suspicious of, it is the misuse of this power that attracts most concern.[9] Thus, at least in the context of the issues raised in *Gray*, it seems to me that competition law has little contribution to make.

Similarly, there may be some relevant overlap between competition and labour law. This is evident in restraint of trade clauses, which are commonly entered into between employer and employee. It is possible that these clauses may have an impact on innovation but for similar

---

[5] The antithesis of competition is market power and so competition law is likewise concerned with the acquisition and maintenance of market power, to the detriment of competition.

[6] See generally Anderman (2007), especially chapters 1 and 10. An Australian perspective on this interface is provided by Frances Hanks in chapter 5.

[7] See, for example, Burtis and Kobayashi (2001), especially at 231.

[8] Regibeau and Rockett (2007), 505.

[9] The acquisition of market power may also create its own issues, either under merger law or for misuse of market power.

reasons to the overlap with intellectual property law, it is unlikely that competition policy would have a general response to this issue.

Despite this view I have taken of the issues raised by *Gray*, there nevertheless remain issues on the topic of innovation that are fundamentally challenging for competition law and policy and it is these I wish to consider in this chapter. These are:

(a) Where does innovation sit in competition law and policy?
(b) What challenges are raised by innovation? and
(c) To what extent should changes be made to competition law in response to these challenges?

The thrust of my argument is that the traditional analysis employed to determine whether conduct is anti-competitive is potentially flawed when applied to an innovative industry. Essentially this is because two of the constants in the traditional analysis, namely (a) reliance on price theory and (b) using market structure as a guide to a firm's market power, may be misleading indicators of market power in an innovative industry. This chapter seeks to make this argument in five steps. First, it is suggested that innovation is rightly recognized as a proper goal of competition law. Secondly, promoting competition will generally, although not always, promote innovation and so jurisdictions are right to prohibit anti-competitive conduct as a means of promoting innovation. Thirdly, in markets where innovation is not fundamental to the way firms compete, as in many low-tech (old economy) markets, the conventional competition analysis that is used to assess whether conduct is anti-competitive will generally be adequate to recognize and promote innovation. Fourthly, however, in some markets, such as high-tech (new economy) markets, conventional analysis may give too much weight to price as a signal of competition and, as a result, may mischaracterize the state of competition in these markets. What is required in such markets is a modification of the traditional analysis and so, finally, suggestions are made as to what form this might take.

My focus is on Australian law[10] and how it is placed to respond to the challenge of innovation, but many of the issues discussed are general. It is an area that indeed has been more pressing in the larger economies of the US and the EU.

---

[10] Australian competition law is contained in the *Competition and Consumer Act 2010* (Cth). (Prior to 2011 the Act was named the *Trade Practices Act 1974* (Cth).) The prohibitions against anti-competitive conduct are in Part IV of the Act, with sanctions and remedies set out in Part VI.

2. INNOVATION: ITS PLACE IN COMPETITION LAW AND POLICY

While there is still some debate about the proper scope of competition law, this debate is generally around the margins of competition policy. It is accepted that the promotion of competition brings with it a range of social benefits. The most commonly cited benefits are the efficiencies that the process of competition generates – efficiencies that may be lost if there is an absence of competition (that is, where one or more firms have market power). There does remain some dispute as to whether competition law should be confined to an efficiency objective,[11] or whether it should also embrace other objectives, such as the protection of small business or other public benefits.[12] This has certainly been an issue in Australia, with a strong small business lobby leading to some odd competition provisions that are directed towards the protection of small business rather than the promotion of efficiency.[13] But this is an issue of priority; it does not deny the significance of efficiency. It is only where efficiency and these other objectives clash that it becomes an issue for competition policy.[14]

The Australia competition statute is broadly based on US antitrust statutes. The prohibitions, which are contained in Part IV of the Act, apply to conduct that lessens competition, or is presumed conclusively to do so. The only reference to the object of the Act is in s 2, which refers in very general terms to the Act's object as being 'to enhance the welfare of Australians through the promotion of competition and fair trading and provision for consumer protection'. The reference to consumer protection

---

[11] E.g., Williams (1989), 13. Contrast Sullivan (1997).

[12] As one example, consider a merger between the only two media firms in a jurisdiction – should competition policy assess this merger solely according to whether it generates net efficiencies (that is, if the productive efficiencies outweigh the allocative inefficiencies, discussed below) or is it appropriate to be concerned about the desirability of a plurality of views?

[13] See, in particular, the 'predatory pricing' provisions in s 46(1AA), considered by most commentators to be inappropriate in a competition statute.

[14] There is no explicit reference to efficiency in the Act other than in the special administrative procedure created by the Act to regulate access to certain infrastructure. The efficient use of infrastructure is a stated objective of these provisions: see s 44AA and, in relation to telecommunication access, ss 152AB and 152AH. The Australian Competition Tribunal recently stated, in the context of the telecommunication access provisions, that this objective includes innovation: *Application by Chime Communications Pty Ltd (No 2)* (2009) 257 ALR 765; [2009] ACompT 2.

reflects the double thrust of the Act: its provisions cover both competition and consumer protection. Thus, the objectives of the Act become a matter of implication, which is in turn influenced by competition policy. The only reference to 'innovation' in the Act is in the merger provisions.[15]

And so it is generally accepted that competition law should be concerned mainly, if not solely, with conduct that promotes efficiency. It is here that innovation emerges. It is commonly stated[16] that there are three types of efficiencies that competition brings (and that the absence of competition will therefore deny). The first of these is 'technical' or 'productive' efficiency. This is straightforward. It refers to the fact that the process of competition forces firms to cut costs (and prices) to competitive levels. Failure by a firm to do so will result in customers choosing to turn to a competitor.[17]

The second type of efficiency generated by competition is referred to as 'allocative' efficiency and this is traditionally given great weight as an objective of competition law. It refers to the efficient allocation of society's resources to meet demands for those resources. Competition promotes allocative efficiency by forcing firms to discover what their customers want and to meet these needs. As with cost-cutting, failure to do so will threaten the firm's survival. Firms with market power, in contrast, may well be able to lift their prices above those in a competitive market and this is likely to force at least some customers to resort to an 'inferior' (in the customer's eyes) product. In terms of allocation of resources this is inefficient.

However it is the third type of efficiency that is of interest in the present context. This is 'dynamic' efficiency. There is less consensus about the definition of dynamic efficiency but the thrust of it is clear enough. A review undertaken of the Australian competition Act described dynamic efficiency in the following terms:

> Dynamic efficiency reflects the need for industries to make timely changes to technology and products in response to changes in consumer tastes and in productive opportunities. Competition in markets for goods and services provides incentives to undertake research and development, effect innovation

---

[15] This reference is considered below under heading 5.

[16] In an Australian context, see for example, National Competition Policy Review Committee (1993) (Hilmer Report), 3.

[17] It is true that even firms with market power will want to cut costs (which will otherwise eat into their profits). However, the sanction for their failing to do so will be generally weaker (referred to as the 'X-inefficiency' of firms with market power) and so deny the full effect of efficiency.

> in product design, reform management structures and strategies and create new products and production processes.[18]

The Australian Competition Tribunal has likewise described dynamic efficiency as

> a concept that involves consideration of adaptation by firms to the evolving supply and demand forces in the market. It is a function of innovation and change, and relates to the search for new ideas, new products and new production methods, all of which can expand consumer choice, raise output levels and lead to cost savings in production.[19]

And so this suggests that one of the key reasons competition is valued is because it forces firms to innovate. The discipline of the market forces firms to change with changing demand patterns. Firms which fail to innovate will be left behind. Conversely, firms with market power will not be under the same pressure to innovate and this creates a social detriment. Of course the significance of the dynamic efficiency that competition generates varies from industry to industry. It is particularly in high-tech industries, where innovation may constitute the very manner in which firms compete, that innovation will be strongest and the benefits of dynamic efficiency the most prominent.

3. DYNAMIC VERSES STATIC EFFICIENCIES: A CLASH?

To the extent that the process of competition promotes all three types of efficiency, no particular issue arises about the distinction between the nature of dynamic and other efficiencies. Competition promotes these efficiencies whereas market power (the absence of competition) may retard them. Further, a firm that has market power may use this to prevent or impede innovation. This, indeed, is how the courts in both the United

[18] Hilmer Report (1993), 4. See generally Ellig and Lin (2001).

[19] *Re Qantas Airways Ltd* [2004] ACompT 9, [159]. See also the ACCC's 'Guide to Authorisation' (March 2007, updated January 2011), [5.15] where dynamic efficiency is referred to in the following terms: 'Dynamic efficiency is a less precisely defined term. It generally refers to the economically efficient use of resources over time – incorporating innovation and responses to changes in the market. Arrangements that provide incentives for efficient investment in research and development will promote dynamic efficiency.' The role of the ACCC and the Tribunal in this context is considered below.

States and Europe viewed the conduct of Microsoft in the well-known litigation.[20] It may also be the case that innovation itself creates market power which in turn may restrict competition and deny efficiencies, at least in the short run. Such market power may result from intellectual property rights an innovator obtains or the extensive sunk costs involved in research and development (as typically occurs in the pharmaceutical industry, for example) or through the so-called 'network effects' an innovator may obtain as the first mover who establishes the industry standard.[21]

Nevertheless, despite the fact that competition is valued because it generates all three types of efficiencies, there is an important difference between allocative and productive efficiencies, on the one hand, and dynamic efficiency, on the other and this has significance for the treatment of innovative industries. This is reflective in the terminology itself. Allocative and productive efficiencies are static concepts. That is, they refer to efficiencies that are generated by competition in an existing market, with existing technologies. The key to determining these efficiencies is price – the price of a firm's product sends a signal to customers and other competitors (and potential competitors) and these groups then make decisions on the basis of this price. It is this price signal in a competitive market that leads to productive and allocative efficiencies. For this reason, as will be elaborated below, price plays a key role in traditional competition analysis. Of particular significance in the current context is that traditional competition analysis uses price to determine the extent of competition.

Dynamic efficiency, in contrast, is concerned with *changes* in existing conditions and technologies and with a predicted response by a firm in the *future*. It is a dynamic, not a static concept. And, importantly, as will be discussed below, price typically plays a much less important role in driving and assessing competition than does innovation.[22]

What has recently received attention from some commentators is that, as a result of these differences, the traditional analysis used to determine whether conduct is anti-competitive may well be inappropriate in a market that is subject to innovation. The concern is that in high-tech

---

20 See *US v Microsoft Corp* 534 US 952 (2001) and *Microsoft v Commission* [2007] ECR II-360. For a general discussion of the issues raised in these two cases (and related actions involving Microsoft) see Rubini (2010). See also Salop and Romaine (1999), 619–623 and generally Glader (2006), chapter 1.

21 E.g., Shelanski and Sidak (2001). For a different perspective on network effects, see Liebowitz and Margolis (2001).

22 Baumol (2004), 15.

industries, where innovation is prominent, the traditional tools of analysis may focus too much on static efficiencies and fail to account for dynamic efficiencies. Given the central role of innovation in these industries, it is critical that dynamic efficiencies be taken into account if we wish to get a balanced picture of whether a firm's conduct is socially beneficial.[23]

There are two areas where the traditional analysis may be deficient – (a) in defining the 'market' i.e. identifying the firms (if any) that are competitors of the relevant firm (referred to here as 'the defendant firm') and (b) in assessing the extent of power a defendant firm has in that market. In traditional product markets, that is, where innovation is not prominent, the conventional analysis employed to determine whether the conduct of the defendant firm is anti-competitive is a three-step process.[24] First, the 'market' in which the defendant firm operates is delineated. This is done as a preliminary step, in order to identify the competitors and potential competitors, if any, the defendant firm has. The second step is the more important one of assessing the state of competition in that market. If the market is competitive, then competition law will generally be unconcerned with the defendant firm's conduct – it will be left to the market to chasten an inefficient firm. If, for example, a firm fails to innovate when its competitors do, then the firm will be left behind. In the final step, a determination is made about whether the defendant firm's conduct substantially alters (or is likely to) the state of competition in that market. Only if the defendant firm's conduct has lessened competition substantially, or is likely to do so, should competition law intervene.

Traditionally, sensitivity of the defendant firm's customers to its price plays an important role in both the first and second steps referred to above. This can be seen with market definition. Conventional analysis suggests that a defendant firm's competitors are identified, in theory at least, by assessing the extent of the responsiveness of customers (and other firms) to price changes in the defendant firm's product. In determining the relevant 'market', a price sensitivity test is used: competitors are identified by asking whether a (hypothetical) small increase in the defendant firm's price would result in customers turning to substitute products (that is, products supplied by the firm's 'competitors') or in potential suppliers stepping in to meet this new demand

---

[23] See Glader (2006), 6–7.

[24] In an Australian context, see *Outboard Marine Australia Pty Ltd v Hecar Investments (No 6) Pty Ltd* (1982) 66 FLR 120. Some conduct, such as price fixing, is prohibited 'per se', that is, without the need to prove that it lessens competition but this is not of present concern.

(potential competitors). In the words of the leading Australian decision on markets,

> Let us suppose that the price of one supplier goes up. Then on the demand side buyers may switch their patronage from this firm's product to another, or from this geographic source of supply to another. As well, on the supply side, sellers can adjust their production plans, substituting one product for another in their output mix, or substituting one geographic source of supply for another … Accordingly, in determining the outer boundaries of the market we ask a quite simple but fundamental question: If the first were to 'give less and charge more' would there be, to put the matter colloquially, much of a reaction? And if so, from whom?[25]

That is, those who react to the defendant's price increase are its competitors.

However, such price sensitivity may not assist in identifying the defendant firm's competitors in an innovative industry. This is so for two reasons. First, consumers of innovative products are often less concerned with price than they are with performance and service.[26] As noted, unresponsiveness by customers or firms with the existing capacity to supply the product in question (or available substitutes) to a price increase would traditionally be seen as an indication of a lack of competitors. However, in the case of firms in an innovative industry, price insensitivity will not be a reliable indicator that the firm has market power (an absence of competitors). Secondly, and more fundamentally, with innovative products competitors may well compete *for* the market, rather than in it. In Schumpeter's famous phrase, innovation is 'creative destruction', creating a new market by destroying an existing one. Again, traditional price theory analysis may not capture these potential competitors, who may 'come from nowhere' so to speak. As a result, conclusions about the market drawn from price sensitivity to existing products may well be too narrow and so give a misleading impression that a firm has market power.[27] This has important implications for the appropriateness of the traditional analysis. As stated in the US *Microsoft* case, there is

> significant debate amongst academics and practitioners over the extent to which 'old economy' s 2 monopolisation doctrines should apply to firms competing in dynamic technological markets … Once a product or standard

---

25 *Re Queensland Co-operative Milling Association Ltd; Re Defiance Holdings Ltd* (1976) 25 FLR 169 at 190.

26 Baumol (2004), 15.

27 See Pleatsikas and Teece (2001).

> achieves wide acceptance, it becomes more or less entrenched. Competition in such industries is 'for the field' rather than 'within the field'... In technologically dynamic markets, however, such entrenchment may be temporary, because innovation may alter the field altogether ... Rapid technological change leads to markets in which 'firms compete through innovation for temporary market dominance, from which they may be displaced by the next wave of product advancements'.[28]

The other problem concerns drawing conclusions about whether a firm has market power. In assessing the state of competition, under the second step referred to above, the courts, regulators and tribunals typically consider the 'structure' of the market identified under the first step. Structure in this context refers primarily to the respective market share of the competitors and the height of any barriers to entry into the market.[29] An uncompetitive market structure will typically be one where market shares are large and barriers to entry are high. In such a case the defendant firm has 'market power'.[30] Market power is defined as existing when a defendant firm has a discretion to 'give less and charge more' to its customers.[31] As noted above, a firm with market power is generally assumed to be less efficient and potentially to be in a position to harm the competitive process.

The traditional analysis employed to determine whether a firm has market power potentially gives rise to two concerns in the context of an innovative industry. The first is that an innovating firm may appear to have market power when, in fact, it does not. If the market is defined too narrowly under the first step in the analysis, then this will create the appearance of market power that does not in reality exist. Barriers to

---

[28] 346 US App DC 330, [18] and [19] references omitted.

[29] See *Re Queensland Co-operative Milling Association Ltd; Re Defiance Holdings Ltd* (1976) 25 FLR 169, 187. Other elements of market structure are also referred to here, namely the extent of 'product differentiation', vertical integration and any arrangements made between competitors. Barriers to entry are the most significant. The definition of a barrier to entry remains contentious but it is generally considered to be a cost borne by a potential entrant that would not be borne by an incumbent of the market: see generally *Queensland Wire Industries Pty Ltd v Broken Hill Proprietary Ltd* (1989) 167 CLR 177.

[30] The structural approach has certainly come under criticism but it is still used by the courts. A good discussion of this, in the US context, occurred in the *Microsoft* decision – see *Microsoft Corp v US* 346 US App DC 330, esp at [22] and [23]. Australia adopts a similar approach: for a helpful summary of the issues see *Application by Chime Communications Pty Ltd (No 3)* [2009] ACompT 4.

[31] See *Re Queensland Co-operative Milling Association Ltd; Re Defiance Holdings Ltd* (1976) 25 FLR 169.

entry to this falsely narrow 'market' will not prevent other firms from competing. Another point is that supra-competitive profits made by an innovating firm, which might be thought to indicate a lack of competitors under price theory and hence suggest market power, may in fact be beneficial to innovation. This is because such profits may be a necessary reward for innovation and constitute the means by which the firm recovers costs incurred in the innovation process.

There is a related, although more contentious, concern here. It was suggested by Schumpeter that 'large firms' are more likely to engage in innovation than smaller firms subjected to competition. That is, firms need some relief from competitive pressures if they are to invest in research and development necessary for innovation. If by 'large' Schumpeter meant firms with market power, this would be another reason for taking a more tolerant view of an innovating firm's market power. However, Schumpeter's claim has not been borne out by subsequent empirical studies.[32]

This point raises the fundamental question of the relationship between market structure and the promotion of dynamic efficiency (innovation). Whereas it is generally considered that a competitive market structure promotes static efficiencies (and market power retards them), it is far less clear what market structure promotes dynamic efficiency.[33] As noted, some evidence suggests that it may be that a less competitive market structure is in fact required for innovation. Baumol states that 'oligopolistic competition' is necessary for innovation to flourish and that neither monopoly nor perfect competition will do.[34] Empirical research in the United States on this issue is inconclusive.[35]

4. A NEW ANALYTICAL FRAMEWORK TO ACCOMMODATE INNOVATION?

Does all this mean that the traditional framework of analysis is inappropriate in markets where innovation is prominent? Given the limitations of traditional analysis to deal with innovative markets, it is not surprising that there have been calls for a new framework to be employed to accommodate innovation, to replace the traditional tools of market and

32 See generally Scherer (1992).
33 This area has been described by Glader as 'murky': Glader (2006), 8.
34 Baumol (2004), 4, 44–45.
35 See generally Scherer (1992) esp at 1421–1423; Shelanski and Sidak (2001), 13; Rubinfeld and Hoven (2001).

market power analysis.[36] For example, it has been suggested that a price sensitivity test measure for markets be increased to 25 per cent over a four-year period instead of the existing 5 per cent over one to two years and that, in an industry with a history of innovation, the burden of proof should shift to the party who wishes to argue for a narrow market on traditional criteria.[37] In relation to market power, it has been suggested that a reconsideration of both the definition of barriers to entry and the reliability of 'excess' profits as indicators of market power require reconsideration in an industry marked out by innovation.[38] Traditional structural barriers to entry to a market may not be significant in an innovative industry. This goes back to the earlier point that innovation may result in the whole market being displaced by a previously unseen competitor. The traditional barriers to entry, such as intellectual property rights in existing products or economies of scale or scope in production and sunk costs may be irrelevant to an innovator. In this sense, what may appear as market power in a defendant firm under traditional analysis may be illusory in an innovative industry. And, as noted, market power, if it does exist, is ambiguous in its relationship with innovation – it may be a necessary reward for firms which have innovated or may be used by a firm to restrict innovation by other firms.[39]

However, an alternative framework is yet to gain broad acceptance and the courts are understandably reluctant to move away from the established analysis. As stated by the Appeals Court decision in the US *Microsoft* case, 'there is no consensus among commentators on the question of whether, and to what extent, current monopolization doctrine should be amended to account for competition in technologically dynamic markets characterized by network effects'.[40]

It seems that a cautious approach is appropriate. This would deal with innovation on a case-by-case basis, adjusting the traditional framework of

---

[36] See generally Teece and Coleman (1998).

[37] Ibid.

[38] Although in Australia at least, profitability is not taken as a reliable guide to market power: see *Trade Practices Commission v Ansett Transport* (1978) 32 FLR 305, 328.

[39] Further, in the United States, and to some extent in the EU, a separate concept of 'innovation markets' has developed in the courts. This refers to competition in innovation itself, at least in the research and development phase. Australia does not appear to have considered this concept yet.

[40] *United States v Microsoft Corp* 534 US 952 (2001) at [18].

analysis where this seems warranted by the nature of the industry.[41] This was the approach in the US *Microsoft* case. In particular, in an innovative industry courts and regulators need to be wary of drawing conclusions about market power and its misuse without taking into account the special features of dynamic efficiency. This may require that a longer time frame be considered and that less emphasis be given to price sensitivity as an indicator of market power. Market forces may be stronger than a static analysis would suggest and so intervention by competition law may do more harm than good.[42]

5. INNOVATION IN AUSTRALIAN COMPETITION LAW

The Australian courts have not yet been called on to deal explicitly with the issue of innovation. The only reference in the Act to innovation is a passing mention in the merger provisions. The Australian merger provisions, contained in s 50 of the Act, are based generally on s 7 of the US Clayton Act. Like s 7, s 50 prohibits an acquisition that has the effect of 'substantially lessening competition'. However, unlike the US section, the Court is directed, by subsection (3), to take various matters into account in determining whether there has been a breach. Paragraph (3)(g) of this rather odd collection of factors requires the court to consider 'the dynamic characteristics of the market, including growth, innovation and product differentiation'. As with other jurisdictions, however, the cost and complexity of merger trials has made them a rarity and so this paragraph has not received particular attention.

The Australian Competition and Consumer Commission (ACCC)'s merger guidelines, in discussing s 50(3)(g), do recognize the broad issue of innovation. The guidelines acknowledge that

> markets that are growing rapidly may offer both greater scope for new entry and the erosion of market shares over time. Similarly markets that are characterized by rapid product innovation may be unstable so that any increased market power gained through a merger is transitory. In general a merger is less likely to substantially lessen competition in a market that is rapidly evolving.

---

41 See generally Glader (2006), esp chapter 2. See also Rubinfeld and Hoven (2001).

42 See generally Teece and Coleman (1998).

However, the guidelines also suggest that the ACCC will require 'robust evidence about likely future developments in the relevant market'.[43]

Of potentially broader interest is the possibility of innovation and dynamic efficiency arguments being raised in Australia's 'authorization' process.[44] There is no equivalent process in US antitrust law but the Australian procedure has some similarities with the EU exemption process.[45] The Act allows the ACCC[46] to 'authorize' future conduct. If authorized, conduct is then immune from liability under the competition provisions of the Act.[47]

The ground for authorization is, in general terms, that the conduct creates a 'public benefit' and that this benefit outweighs any anti-competitive or other detriment the conduct may cause.[48] 'Public benefit' in this context has been held to include 'anything of value to the community generally, any contribution to the aims pursued by the society including as one of its principal elements ... the achievement of the economic goals of efficiency and progress'.[49] The most commonly argued public benefit is efficiency.[50] In principle, therefore, dynamic efficiencies and innovation have a key role in the authorization process. Parties may be able to argue that conduct that may otherwise be in breach of the Act, such as the creation of a joint venture for the purposes of research and development,[51] should be authorized because of the dynamic efficiencies the conduct will generate. A survey of the authorization decisions suggests that this argument has not often been employed in practice.

---

[43] See ACCC *Merger Guidelines*, Nov 2008, at [7.52]–[7.55].

[44] Australia also has a 'notification' process. This is similar to authorization but is limited to non-price vertical restraints and creates an immediate immunity – subject to the ACCC's determination on the 'public benefit' of the conduct. See s 93.

[45] See Article 101(3) of the *Treaty on the Functioning of the European Union*.

[46] See generally Part VII of the Act. Authorization is not available for misuse of market power. In the case of mergers, it is now the Australian Competition Tribunal to which parties must apply for authorization.

[47] Authorization and notification decisions may be reviewed by the Competition Tribunal.

[48] See s 90 and generally *Re Qantas Airways* [2004] ACompT 9.

[49] *Re Queensland Co-operative Milling Association Ltd; Re Defiance Holdings Ltd* (1976) 25 FLR 169, 510.

[50] See Duns (1994).

[51] Such conduct may otherwise be at risk of being in breach of the cartel or anti-competitive agreement provisions.

6. CONCLUSION

Innovation is accepted as one of the key goals of competition law. However, there is a risk that the conventional analysis used by courts and regulators to determine whether conduct is anti-competitive will fail to promote this goal. The most likely risk is that the court or regulator will intervene to prevent conduct that may in fact be promoting innovation and so be socially beneficial. The deficiencies of the traditional analytical framework are clear, a replacement framework less so. In view of this it is likely that an Australian court would continue to use the traditional analysis when faced with conduct in any innovative industry. Courts, regulators and tribunals need to be aware of the deficiencies of the traditional analysis when faced with conduct in an 'innovative industry'. The danger with the traditional analysis is that it may fail to identify competitors and suggest market power where there is none. This may lead to intervention by competition law where it is not warranted and deny the very efficiencies that competition policy seeks. Competition policy suggests that, in certain cases, innovation may need to be encouraged, even at the expense of competition, if social welfare is to be improved. This, after all, is a lesson that can be learnt from intellectual property law.[52]

REFERENCES

Anderman, S. (ed.) (2007), *The Interface between Intellectual Property Rights and Competition Policy*, Cambridge University Press

Baumol, W. (2004), *The Free Market Innovation Machine; Analyzing the Growth Miracle of Capitalism*, Princeton University Press

Burtis, M. and B. Kobayashi (2001), 'Intellectual Property and Antitrust Limitation on Contract' in J. Ellig (ed.), *Dynamic Competition and Public Policy: Technology, Innovation and Antitrust Issues,* Cambridge University Press

Duns, J. (1994), 'Competition Law and Public Benefits' 16 *Adelaide Law Review* 245

Ellig, J. and D. Lin (2001), 'A Taxonomy of Dynamic Competition Theories' in J. Ellig (ed.), *Dynamic Competition and Public Policy: Technology, Innovation and Antitrust Issues*, Cambridge University Press

Fisher, F. (2001), 'Innovation and Monopoly Leveraging' in J. Ellig (ed.), *Dynamic Competition and Public Policy: Technology, Innovation and Antitrust Issues*, Cambridge University Press

Glader, M. (2006), *Innovation Markets and Competition Analysis: EU Competition Law and US Antitrust Law*, Edward Elgar

---

[52] See Fisher (2001).

Liebowitz, S. and S. Margolis (2001), 'Network Effects and the Microsoft Case' in J. Ellig (ed.), *Dynamic Competition and Public Policy: Technology, Innovation and Antitrust Issues*, Cambridge University Press

National Competition Policy Review Committee (1993), *National Competition Policy Report* (*Hilmer Report*), Australian Government Publishing Service

Pleatsikas, C. and D. Teece (2001), 'New Indicia for Antitrust Analysis in Markets Experiencing Rapid Innovation', in J. Ellig (ed.), *Dynamic Competition and Public Policy: Technology, Innovation and Antitrust Issues*, Cambridge University Press

Regibeau, P. and K. Rockett (2007), 'The Relationship between Intellectual Property Law and Competition Law: an Economic Approach' in S. Anderman (ed.), *The Interface between Intellectual Property Rights and Competition Policy*, Cambridge University Press

Rubinfeld, D. and J. Hoven (2001), 'Innovation and Antitrust Enforcement' in J. Ellig (ed.), *Dynamic Competition and Public Policy: Technology, Innovation and Antitrust Issues,* Cambridge University Press

Rubini, L. (ed.) (2010), *Microsoft on Trial; Legal and Economic Analysis of a Transatlantic Antitrust Case*, Edward Elgar

Salop, S. and R. Romaine (1999), 'Preserving Monopoly: Economic Analysis, Legal Standards and Microsoft' 7 *George Mason Law Review* 617

Scherer, F.M. (1992), 'Schumpeter and Plausible Capitalism' 30 *Journal of Economic Literature* 1416

Shelanski, H. and J. Sidak (2001), 'Antitrust Divestiture in Network Industries' 68 *University of Chicago Law Review* 1

Sullivan, L. (1997), 'Economics and More Humanistic Disciplines: What are the Sources of Wisdom for Antitrust?' 125 *University of Pennsylvania Law Review* 1214

Teece, D. and M. Coleman (1998), 'The Meaning of Monopoly: Antitrust Analysis in High-Technology Industries' 43 *Antitrust Bulletin* 801

Williams, P. (1989), 'Why Regulate for Competition?' in M. James (ed.), *Regulating for Competition? Trade Practices in a Changing Economy*, Centre for Independent Studies

17. Perspectives from competition law practice

Dorothy Livingston

1. INTRODUCTION

> … in capitalist reality as distinguished from its textbook picture, it is not that kind of competition [competition in the market] which counts but the competition from the new commodity, the new technology, the new source of supply, the new type of organization (the largest-scale unit of control for instance) – competition which commands a decisive cost or quality advantage and which strikes not at the margins of the profits and the outputs of the existing firms but at their foundations and their very lives.[1]

The 'Schumpeterian' economic school of thought sees the possibility for a successful innovatory business to enjoy a monopoly position (at least for a time, until a new and creative technology comes along to destroy the incumbent's business) as a key driver for successful innovation and sees competition law constraints on the achievement of monopoly as a hindrance to the full realization of efficient 'creative destruction' through innovation.

On the other side of this argument, Kenneth J. Arrow argues that 'the incentive to invent is less under monopolistic than under competitive conditions'.[2] Competition (US 'antitrust') law enforcers agree with the Arrow side of the argument:

> Today, it is widely recognized that patent and antitrust drive innovation in different but complementary ways. Both disciplines promote dynamic efficiency: that is, a system of property rights and market rules that create appropriate incentives for invention, innovation, and risk taking – delivering the greatest returns for society not just for today, but tomorrow as well. The patent grant does this by providing incentives for inventors to take risks and

1 Schumpeter (1975) [orig pub 1942], 82–85.
2 Arrow (1962), 619.

> make investments in research and development. Patents transform a claimed piece of intellectual progress into a property right, allowing the inventor to exclude others from using that invention during the term of the patent. Our intellectual property framework further advances follow-on innovation through public disclosure of the invention. Antitrust's core mission is to appropriately foster and protect the competitive environment by preventing certain conduct that threatens free markets. This environment is what pushes companies to constantly innovate and allows them to profit when they do. Antitrust recognizes the critical role that intellectual property rights play in driving innovation and so values these rights. Yet antitrust applies the same analytical framework to intellectual property as it does to other forms of property, and imposes some rules about how the patent monopoly can – and cannot – be used. Thus, antitrust and patent law work together to create and preserve the appropriate incentives for technological progress by creating property rights and preserving competition around those rights.[3]

Competition law regulators and many practitioners, including myself, see the role of competition law as promoting and safeguarding the conditions of competition both in and for the market. In the context of innovation, competition law does not seek to remove the incentives created by monopoly rights, such as patents. It has to respect the fundamental rights given by patents, copyright and other forms of intellectual property right (IPR); indeed Article 101 TFEU recognizes that technological progress may justify restrictive agreements in some circumstances.[4]

Nevertheless competition law can be applied to prevent a strong incumbent seeking to shut off developments by others from reaching the market; to prevent a rights-holder seeking to kill its old invention when it loses monopoly protection and to assist in providing the conditions in which new technologies and their inventors will flourish and grow.

Competition law is generally accepted to have been born in the USA in 1890 with the passage of the Sherman Act. Since then the law has grown in sophistication and application: the spread of laws on the model of

---

[3] Varney (2010), 2.

[4] Consolidated Version of the Treaty on the Functioning of the European Union [2010] OJ C 83/49 incorporating articles originally in the European Economic Treaty (Treaty of Rome) of 1957, in force from 1962; Article 101 deals with anti-competitive agreements and Article 101(3) provides that certain agreements that do restrict competition may be justified if they meet certain conditions, namely that they contribute to promoting technical or economic progress while providing consumers with a fair share of the resulting benefits, provided that the restrictions are indispensable to the achievement of the objectives of the agreement and do not enable competition to be eliminated in any relevant market.

Articles 101–102 TFEU means that competition law has come to be applied not only to agreements, but to the conduct of individual companies with strong market positions, including many successful technology companies.

During the same 120 years, we have seen the most rapid technological invention in human history. It does not look, certainly at the level of the 'man on the Clapham omnibus', as though the development of competition law has held back innovation: from the telephone, the electric light-bulb and the aeroplane to the computer and the web, it has been non-stop.

I would not pretend that competition law has been perfectly applied. Within the EU, in particular, the subsidiary 'single market' aims of Article 101/102 to promote trade within the EU across national boundaries can be distortive. Also the use of full economic analysis to inform decision making in the EU is a recent development. Nevertheless, competition law and economics together operate to enhance competitive conditions for technological innovation, just as they may enhance innovation in 'low-tech' businesses. Businesses to which technology is central are subject to the same laws as those whose 'innovation' is not technological (e.g., a new package of terms and ancillary benefits for a bank account or a new colour combination for a fabric).

Indeed in the modern world all businesses are likely to have a degree of IPR protection for their innovations: a colour combination may in some circumstances be protected by copyright or be argued to constitute a trade mark. Ephemeral reading matter, such as an article on the latest fashions, is protected by copyright,[5] just as much as works of the leading economists (one a Nobel laureate) quoted at the beginning of this chapter.

I now turn to consider a number of cases where competition law has clashed with the use of IPRs.[6]

---

[5] The *Magill* case, involving listings of future TV programmes, was the EU's first major decision on compulsory licensing affirmed at all levels: *Commission Decision Magill TV Guide/ITP/BBC and RTE* [1989] OJ L78/43, Joined Cases C-241 and 242/91P; *Radio Telefis Eireann and ITP v Commission* [1995] ECR 1- 743.

[6] Cases have been selected largely from EU decisions to illustrate issues. This is not a comprehensive survey and does not have comparative analysis of US and European approaches.

2. CUTTING EDGE – COMPUTER TECHNOLOGY

2.1 Overview

Cases involving the market leader in computer technology are not new – in the 1980s it was IBM[7] and in the first decade of the 21st century, Microsoft[8] and Intel[9] have been fined heavily for abuses of a dominant position, with Microsoft making a further settlement with the EU Commission.[10] Some less high-profile businesses have received similar treatment and Google,[11] the latest technological giant, is coming under scrutiny.

Each of these cases has taken place when the business concerned was a well-established market leader. These are not cases taken when the firms were using their innovatory skills to build their businesses from small beginnings, but when they demonstrably had won competition 'for the market' to the point where a high proportion of customers had little choice, pending some substantial new technological development enabling another business to grow. Because of the nature of the businesses, their products would all be protected by some form of IPR.

In European competition law such businesses are described as having a 'dominant position', that is: '... a position of economic strength enjoyed by an undertaking which enables it to prevent effective competition being maintained on the relevant market by affording it the power to behave to an appreciable extent independently of its competitors, its customers and ultimately of its consumers'.[12] The market will be identified using factual and economic tools and may be broad or narrow. It will consist of some or all of the products or services produced by the party under consideration and its competitors.

Dominance is determined by not just market shares but other factors affecting the relative strengths of market participants, including market structure, the possibilities for new entry and the effects of the control of

---

7 *IBM Undertaking* Case IV/29.479 Bull. EC 7/8 1984.

8 *Commission Decision of 24 May 2004,* [2007] OJ (L 32)23 ; Case 201/04 *Microsoft v Commission* [2007] ECR II-3601, referred to as *Microsoft I.*

9 *Commission Decision of 13 May 2009,* [2009] OJ C227/13, Memo/09/235 for access to fuller non-confidential version.

10 *Commission Decision of 16 December 2009* [2010] OJ C36/8, fuller decision available on-line, referred to as *Microsoft II.*

11 IP/10/1624 (30 November 2010), opening of proceedings against Google: the case is not proven and is only at the investigatory stage.

12 Case 27/76 *United Brands v Commission* [1978] ECR 207, [68].

IPRs. In technological markets, the first mover may have built up a formidable position and even competitors with superior technology may have trouble getting their products into the marketplace.

There is no sign that the cases discussed below had any effect on the successful trajectories of the businesses concerned. These cases were limited interventions to address distinct practices, which appeared either to stifle such competition as remained, or to delay or prevent the emergence of businesses that could be real competitors if able to get enough of their products to market. Given the nature of the businesses, the methods employed in these practices in most cases (though not Intel) involved the management and maintenance of IPRs.

Thus the decisions have been open to criticism as negating the value of IPRs, or at least restricting the means of exploitation of these rights.

2.2 Tying and Bundling

The IBM settlement with the EU Commission was preceded by over a decade of antitrust litigation in the USA, mostly inconclusive. In 1980, the EU Commission started proceedings alleging abuse of dominance by IBM in markets for key products in its System/370 mainframe computer range. Allegations included bundling of main memory and software bundling. The settlement in Summer 1984, by which time the technology was relatively old, included a commitment to make available System/370 CPUs with only essential main memory, thus allowing competitors the possibility of supplying additional memory.

The Microsoft cases again followed on from US action. This had condemned aspects of Microsoft's conduct and led to a settlement with the US authorities with behavioural remedies in 2002.[13] In 2004 the EU Commission fined Microsoft €497m and held that it had abused its dominant position inter alia by tying Media Player software with the Windows Operating System. The decision was upheld by the CFI in 2007 and there was no further appeal on the substance. Microsoft was ordered to unbundle Media Player and offer to end users and OEMs in the EEA a full-function version of Windows that did not include Media Player and to refrain from any conduct of equivalent effect.

---

[13] *United States of America v Microsoft Corporation* Civil Action No 98–1232 (CKK) Final Judgment of November 12, 2002 following from *United States v Microsoft Corp* 353 F 3d 935 (D.C. Cir. 2001).

2.3 Access to Source Code

In the IBM case, it was alleged that lack of access to information about interfaces with its mainframes prevented peripheral manufacturers competing with IBM's products: in its EU settlement, IBM undertook to provide competitors in Europe, at their request, with interface information on its hardware and software for large computer systems, and with the procedures for accessing its systems network architecture.

The *Microsoft* decision in 2004 required Microsoft to disclose protocol specifications, and to take other steps to ensure that third parties had the necessary information to produce interoperable products for use with the Windows operating system. Effectively this was compulsory licensing of some of Microsoft's proprietary IPRs.

2.4 Access to Market: No Clash with the Exercise of IPRs

The *Intel* case, by contrast, related to commercial practices, rather than use of the technology itself to gain commercial advantage. The existence and success of Intel's technology lay behind the finding it was dominant, but were not important in relation to the reasoning in establishing abuse.[14]

The commercial practices found by the Commission to be abusive included price rebates for exclusive supply rights, payment to a major retailer to sell exclusively Intel-based PCs and payment to customers who stopped or delayed their launch of specific products containing CPUs produced by Intel's competitor, AMD. The fine was €1.06 bn.[15]

The condemnation of this type of practice by dominant companies goes back to the *Hoffmann-La Roche* vitamins case[16] (which dealt with loyalty price rebates). The Commission relied also on the *Irish Sugar* case,[17] which involved a commodity product.

3. DISCUSSION

Leaving aside *Intel*, the other decisions do raise questions that have vexed commentators about the balance between incentives to innovate and competition law. Tying and bundling of different forms of IPR goes

---

14 See the analysis in Anderman and Schmidt (2011), 181–187.

15 An appeal is pending.

16 Case 85/76 *Hoffman-La Roche v Commission* [1979] ECR 461, para [91].

17 Case T-228/97 *Irish Sugar v Commission* [1999] ECR II-2969.

to the manner of exploitation. A remedy that orders the owner of an IPR to make information available (even on terms of fair remuneration) in effect negates its right to decide whether and, if so how, to exploit that IPR, a right which many think is integral to the existence of an IPR.

3.1 Tying and Bundling

Tying is one of the examples of abuse given in Article 102, which renders 'the conclusion of contracts subject to the acceptance by the other parties of supplementary obligations which, by their nature or according to commercial usage, have no connection with the subject of such contracts'. Pre-contractual structuring may also be tying: this occurs where two or more products with discrete functions are combined into one product so that it is impractical (if not impossible) for the consumer to separate the components and they cannot be acquired separately. Computer software lends itself to this approach and the owner of the core technology (such as the operating system) is well placed to integrate other software that works with the operating system, so that only a bundle is available to the distributor and the consumer. The *IBM* case involved allegations of memory bundling; the *Microsoft* cases the integration of the Windows Media Player and the Internet Explorer web browser with the operating system.[18]

Of course not every case of tying is harmful: the sale of a Swiss army knife incorporating numerous gadgets has little or no effect on demand for the various gadgets in other convenient portable forms from a wide variety of suppliers, both separately and in different combinations: the option to acquire all these functions in a single portable tool simply adds to diversity. Tying may well have a place in encouraging innovation: the integrated product may offer greater functionality than could be achieved by the elements separately – indeed any complex software will be to some extent itself a bundle or tied group of functions together providing comprehensive functionality for a particular task (e.g., management of digital photographs or the layout of a newspaper).

It is not enough that the business that is tying is dominant in the market. There needs to be something which the European courts characterize as 'exceptional' to justify competition law intervening in relation to IPRs. The decisions focus on whether integration is justified or there is tying of discrete products that need not be bundled and have useful independent functionality which generates discrete consumer demand.

---

18 XIVth Report on Competition Policy, [94].

Almost always in such cases (as in IBM and Microsoft) there will be suppliers of discrete examples of at least one of the bundled products. Also if the dominant party itself supplies part of the bundle separately this is significant: for example in *Microsoft I*, Microsoft sold its Media Player on a stand-alone basis for supply with the Apple operating system. It was also significant that Media Player was based on technology originally separately developed by Vxtreme.[19]

The court[20] in *Microsoft I* recognized, however, that there would be objective justification for integration by a dominant company if it produces a form of technology superior to that consumers would have obtained by adding the separate elements together.

How high the barrier is to establish that there is true integration – and indeed whether that is the only consideration – is a matter for debate. While an operating system may be of very limited value without applications, it seems clear that this does not mean that all these should be regarded as integrated. It is a matter of fact and degree; although the law seems woolly, it strives with careful examination of the facts and circumstances of particularly behaviour, to respect the rights and discretions of a dominant IPR owner save to the extent that its choices in exercising its rights cause consumer harm.[21]

Evidence of intent to damage competitors in adopting the particular integration may be treated as confirmation that the integration is not necessary or consumer welfare enhancing,[22] although objectively integration could be both welfare enhancing and a strong defensive strategy.

3.2 Refusal to Supply/License Data Needed for Production of Interoperable Products

The cases on compulsory licensing, *Magill* and *IMS Health*,[23] which provide the background to the *Microsoft I* decision, involve very different facts. Both were cases in which challenges were raised (and lost) as to whether the data (television programme listings and a methodology for

---

[19] Microsoft acquired VExtreme in 1997.

[20] *Microsoft I* [1057] upholding the Commission decision findings at recitals 948–951.

[21] See also Commission Communication 2009/C 45/02 on the application of article 82 (now Article 102) [2009] OJ C45/7, [47]–[62].

[22] See the discussion of correspondence about countering the threat posed by RealPlayer: *Microsoft I*, [911] and [937].

[23] Case C-418/0 *IIMS Health GMBH v NDC Health GMBH* [2004] ECR 1-5039, particularly [38] and [48–52].

market research analysis) were actually protected by copyright. They are the sort of facts which might have made for bad law, because the conclusion that a long term IPR monopoly attaches to either of these types of material may be surprising. One might be concerned that there would be some 'rule bending' to get round what might be seen as excessive protection.

In *IMS Health*, the ECJ specifically recognized that 'in balancing the interest in the protection of the intellectual property right and the economic freedom of its owner against the interest in protection of free competition, the latter can prevail only where refusal to grant a licence prevents the development of the secondary market to the detriment of consumers'. It held that three cumulative conditions must be present for the situation to be sufficiently exceptional to justify overriding a refusal to supply by a dominant party:

1. The refusal is preventing the emergence of a new product for which there is potential consumer demand.
2. It is not justified
3. It excludes any competition on a secondary market.

These were refined *in Microsoft I* and form the background to the settlement decision in *Microsoft II*. The refinements are that:

1. The 'new product' in condition 1 is simply a product that applies additional or different technology and it need not be new at the time the condition is applied, though it should be expected to develop further. This is to be measured against the general words of the abuse example in Article 102 'to limit technical development'.
2. In relation to the justification condition there need to be compelling arguments and evidence.[24] An assertion that there would be a general effect on incentives to innovate will be rejected and it is necessary to carry out a reasoned balancing act in reaching a decision.
3. In relation to the third condition, changed behaviour, such as withdrawing from licensing which had previously occurred, was just as much capable of eliminating effective competition as never licensing.

---

[24] The evidence and arguments are painstakingly examined over hundreds of paragraphs at Commission level. The CFI largely approved this analysis. At para 659, it decided that effects on Microsoft's incentives to innovate should only be considered in the context of objective justification.

The court has been criticized for being over-formalistic and potentially killing the dominant party's incentives to innovate.[25] An established market leader with core technology has, however, an incentive to innovate to hold that position, even if while it enjoys that position it faces the risk that it may be obliged to disclose interface information to those capable of making interoperable products. One does not doubt that any new entrant with novel technology would be delighted to find itself facing those risks in a few years time; indeed, looking at the procession of successful high-tech businesses that have become embroiled with competition law, one might almost say that these proceedings were a sign of having arrived at the top.

4. PHARMACEUTICALS – 'TRADITIONAL' INNOVATION

4.1 Overview

Patents are the exemplar IPR, in which limited exclusivity is awarded to the holder in return for it publishing its invention, which can then be used by others following the expiry of the patent. The incentive to innovate is created by the award of exclusivity and the right to gain high returns from successful inventions. Of course not all – indeed most – inventions are not successful and pharmaceutical companies need to invest a great deal in research and development.

4.2 Parallel Trade in Pharmaceuticals

Because pharmaceuticals are socially important and expensive, in many countries there is price regulation, so as to ensure widest availability at lowest cost to public and insurance-based health care schemes. Countries without R&D establishments may be particularly aggressive, while those who benefit from the employment and academic side of advanced R&D may be less so.[26]

One feels considerable sympathy for the pharmaceutical companies, faced with national price-control regimes and the demands of EU single market and competition policy to facilitate free trade between Member States. Unlike other manufacturers, they cannot converge pricing across the EU. Distributors in low-price countries have every incentive to sell

---

[25] Tilford (2008).

[26] See the discussion in Tilford (2008).

across frontiers and distributors in high-price countries to buy from them. The cases on this issue in the early decades of EU enforcement are numerous and the attitude of the EU Commission less than sympathetic.

The ECJ in *GlaxoSmithKline*[27] did to some extent address the concerns that the continuation of this situation was damaging innovation, accepting that State intervention was one of the factors creating opportunities for parallel trade and recognizing the risk that products would not be made available at all in low-price jurisdictions. The Court held that the situation would justify a dominant company taking 'steps that are reasonable and in proportion to the need to protect its own commercial interests'. The ECJ went on to say that:

> ... a producer of pharmaceutical products must be in a position to protect its own commercial interests if it is confronted with orders that are out of the ordinary in terms of quantity. Such could be the case, in a given Member State, if certain wholesalers order from that producer medicines in quantities which are out of all proportion to those previously sold by the same wholesalers to meet the needs of the market in the first Member State.

In contrast, a refusal to meet 'ordinary orders' would be an abuse of a dominant position. As this case arose from a reference by a national court, the decision on what was an 'ordinary order' was not a matter for the ECJ. This case will guide the EU Commission, but is a long way from providing a complete answer to this conundrum, which arises from a collision of national regulation and the single market aspect of EU competition law, rather than from a collision of competition law and IPRs.

4.3 Playing Games with Patent Rights and Product Registrations

More recently attention has focused on activity as patents expire and on other aspects of patent and regulatory management. While these issues are not limited to pharmaceutical companies, they have been the centre of activity on both sides of the Atlantic[28] (particularly in the context of patent litigation and settlements, for which the EU Commission has an

---

[27] *Sot. Lelos kai Sia EE and others v GlaxoSmithKline* (joined cases C-468/06 to C-478/06) [2008] EC.R I-7139 at [67] *et seq*, quotes [69], [76] and [77].

[28] Hanks, Jacobson, Musgrove and Shen (2011).

ongoing monitoring exercise, following its Pharmaceuticals Sector Inquiry[29]) and the leading European case is *AstraZeneca*.[30]

This case, which also contains an important review of the establishment of dominance and market definition in relation to pharmaceutical products, finds two practices in relation to the drug Losec to be an abuse of a dominant position: first, a pattern of allegedly misleading representations made to the patent offices and courts in several EU Member States in the context of applications for a supplementary protection certificate (SPC), which would extend the duration of the exclusive right granted for the patent; second, the selective deregistrations of marketing authorizations for Losec capsules which had or were about to lose patent protection, in combination with the substitution, on the market, of Losec MUPs tablets, which had additional patent protection.

4.4 Conduct in Patent Extension Applications

The first of these courses of conduct is intimately connected with patent protection and its duration: under EU law an extension under an SPC would be disallowed or allowed for a shorter period (national practice on these options varies) depending on the date of first marketing authorization in the EU, and in applying for SPCs, it is alleged that inaccurate or incomplete information on this date was supplied to some national authorities.

The decisions go beyond holding that conduct of the nature of that alleged in the course of applying for patent extensions would be abusive only in circumstances where a dominant patent holder has actually obtained an advantage from the misrepresentation; the Court upheld the findings of the Commission that there could also be an abuse even where there was no question that an unwarranted extension had been obtained (e.g., because the application was withdrawn or issued for a period which was not excessive, or the SPC was cancelled before the expiry of the original period of protection). Even in relation to the Member State where the decisions record the fullest possible disclosure to the authorities in the course of the application, an abuse was found based on

---

[29] Commission Communication of 8 July 2009 (Sectoral Investigation) 5 July 2010, IP/10/887 of 5 July 2010 and IP/11/40 of 17 January 2011.

[30] *Commission decision of 19 July 2006* [2006] OJ L199/36, largely upheld in Case T-321/05 *AstraZeneca v European Commission* 1 July 2010 (unreported) (henceforth *AstraZeneca*); this case is under further appeal to the ECJ both as to substance and penalty. It should be made clear that AstraZenaca challenges the characterization of its alleged conduct.

alleged conduct at an early stage in the application process, albeit for a limited period. The Court noted: 'None the less, it is absolutely clear from all the documentary evidence submitted for the Court's attention that [the alleged conduct in that Member State] was part of an overall strategy on SPC applications ... '[31]

In practice, this means that parties who may be dominant are required to adhere to the highest standards of disclosure from the outset in applying for patent extensions. Non-dominant parties may be more cavalier and do not face punishment under competition law; although, of course, the extension process itself may require full disclosure regardless of the market power of the applicant. This case also illustrates the often repeated mantra of courts that changing a law that operates unfairly is a matter for the legislature.

4.5 Deregistration of Marketing Authorizations

The effect of this second course of conduct was allegedly to create difficulties for generic manufacturers in obtaining a valid marketing authorization for a generic version of Losec capsules, when patent exclusivity expired. It also allegedly affected the ability of parallel importers to bring Losec capsules into a market where the authorizations were withdrawn. While the Court accepted that a party in a dominant position has no obligation to protect the interests of competitors, it stated that: 'The mere desire of any undertaking in a dominant position to protect its own commercial interests and to guard against competition from generic products and parallel imports does not justify recourse to practices falling outside the scope of competition on the merits.' It went on to say '... an undertaking in a dominant position cannot use regulatory procedures solely in such a way as to prevent or make more difficult the entry of competitors on the market'.[32]

Although marketing authorizations are regarded as regulatory in the decision and the judgment, it has to be noted that they are in practice for pharmaceuticals a prerequisite to actual marketing. The date of the marketing authorization affects the right of the patent holder to an extension to its patent. However, the marketing authorization is not tied to the existence or not of a patent and this is important to understanding the approach taken in the decisions.

---

[31] Case T-321/05 *AstraZeneca* (unreported), [538]–[549] and [602], quote [548].

[32] Case T-321/05 *AstraZeneca* (unreported), [816]–[817].

In a recent UK case, a variant of 'deregistering' conduct was condemned by the UK authorities in a finding against Reckitt Benckiser.[33] The Office of Fair Trading (OFT) found that Reckitt Benckiser had abused its dominant position by withdrawing National Health Service (NHS) packs of Gaviscon Original Liquid from the UK NHS prescription channel after the product's patent had expired but before the publication of the generic name for it, so that more prescriptions would be issued for its alternative product, Gaviscon Advance Liquid, part of the technology for which was still protected (so that it had no generic equivalents). The OFT found that, had it not been for the potential to reduce competition by withdrawal, it would not have made commercial sense to withdraw the product.[34] The fine was reduced for early co-operation.[35]

5. CONCLUSION

The cases do not show a competition law culture insensitive to the needs of businesses whose key assets are IPRs. There is real recognition of the difficulties. However, these businesses are subject, like others, to competition law: to paraphrase and quote the US judiciary in the *Microsoft* proceedings, the proposition that an intellectual property right confers protection from antitrust scrutiny '... is no more correct than the proposition that use of one's personal property, such as a baseball bat, cannot give rise to tort liability'.[36]

REFERENCES

Anderman, S. and H. Schmidt (2011), *EU Competition Law and Intellectual Property Rights. The Regulation of Innovation*, 2nd edn, Oxford University Press
Arrow, K. (1962), 'Economic Welfare and the Allocation of Resources for Invention' in *The Rate and Direction of Inventive Activity: Economic and Social Factors*, UMI
Hanks, K., S. Jacobson, K. Musgrove and M. Shen (2011), '"Pay-for-Delay" Settlements: Antitrust Violation or Proper Exercise of Pharmaceutical Patent Rights', *Business Law Today*, 27 January, <http://apps.americanbar.org/buslaw/blt/content/2011/01/article-hanks.shtml>

---

[33] Abuse of a dominant position by Reckitt Benckiser Healthcare (UK) Ltd and Reckitt Benckiser Group plc OFT CA98/02/2011.

[34] At [6.163].

[35] At [8.57] et seq.

[36] *United States v. Microsoft Corp.*, 253 F.3d 34, 63 (D.C. Cir. 2001) (en banc) (per curiam, 30)

Office of Fair Trading (2011), *Press Release: OFT Issues Decision in Reckitt Benckiser Case*, 13 April 2011
Schumpeter, J. (2008), *Capitalism, Socialism and Democracy* (first published 1942, Harper 1975)
Tilford, S. (2008), 'Is European Competition Policy an Obstacle to Innovation and Growth?', *Centre for European Reform Essays*, Centre for European Reform
Varney, C.A. (2010), 'Promoting Innovation through Patent and Antitrust, Law and Policy', *Intersection of Patent Policy and Competition Policy: Implications for Promoting Innovation*

18. EU competition law, and research and development agreements

Rosa Greaves

1. INTRODUCTION

Not all forms of horizontal agreement, that is, undertakings operating at the same level of production or distribution, are harmful to competition. For example, cooperation between non-competitors, cooperation between competitors that cannot independently carry out the activity in question, and cooperation concerning an activity far removed from the marketing level such as a pure research and development, are unlikely to be seen as anti-competitive.

Although agreements between actual or potential competitors are generally viewed with suspicion by competition authorities, competing undertakings sometimes pool their resources with multiple aims such as to develop a new product or to engage in research and development that would be impossible without cooperation.

Research and development agreements are a type of horizontal agreement which usually carry long-term risky investments whereby the parties to the agreement decide to carry out jointly a number of tasks which are necessary in order to turn an idea into an industrial product and thus enable more and better products to be brought to the market and facilitate greater consumer choice. Research and development agreements range from outsourcing research and development activities to the marketing of completely new products that resulted from the research and development. The agreements may take the form of a mere cooperation between two or more parties or an agreement to set up a jointly controlled company which will carry out the research and development.

EU competition law is generally supportive of research and development agreements as otherwise innovation may be impeded bearing negative effects on the competitiveness of undertakings, particularly EU undertakings competing on the global market. Nevertheless, the European

Commission (the European competition agency) and the national competition authorities need to assess whether the parties to the agreement may be able to exercise such a degree of substantial market power so as to reduce the level of innovation. The consequences of such conduct may lead to fewer products being placed on the market and thus affecting consumer choice, or to a lowering of the quality of products, or to a delay in products reaching the market. Although concern for potential anti-competitive effects of these types of agreement has been shown by the European Commission, the European courts require that the threat to competition has to be demonstrated for the cooperation to be confirmed as unlawful.

Nevertheless, some research and development agreements[1] have been treated sympathetically by the European Commission when assessing whether the agreements are compatible with Article 101 of the Treaty on the Functioning of the EU (TFEU)[2] which prohibits anti-competitive agreements. The main reason for this approach is that the European Commission recognizes that innovation bears a risk and it is expensive. It would be a waste of effort and resources if duplication took place. Moreover, joint research is likely to stimulate and to facilitate innovation. However, there is concern where the joint research and development is carried out by large firms with significant market power and at the same level of production which may lead to a significant reduction of competition, at least during the early stages of the development cooperation. Thus, a specific legislative measure known as a 'block exemption regulation' (BER)[3] has been adopted by the European Commission to enable some joint and research agreements to benefit from a Treaty exception, the conditions of which are set out in Article 101(3) TFEU.

This chapter focuses on the provisions of the most recent version of the Research and Development Agreements BER which was adopted in 2010. The chapter is structured as follows: first it sets out the scope of

---

[1] E.g., *ElopakMetal Box* [1990] OJ L209/15.

[2] [2010] OJ C83/49.

[3] Block exemption regulations permit agreements which comply with specified conditions and obligations set out in Art 101(3) TFEU to be exempted from the prohibition of Art 101(1) TFEU. These regulations are directly effective in the legal systems of the Member States (equivalent to national laws). They are adopted for a specific number of years. This enables the European Commission to review and replace them regularly, thus responding to changes in market conditions and variations on how market operators conduct themselves.

Article 101 TFEU in the context of research and development agreements; secondly, it examines the conditions of the BER that have to be met for the agreement to benefit from the automatic exemption; and finally, it ends with some concluding observations.

2. THE APPLICATION OF ARTICLE 101 TFEU TO RESEARCH AND DEVELOPMENT AGREEMENTS

Article 101 TFEU plays an important role in ensuring that market operators do not conduct themselves in an anti-competitive manner. All agreements between undertakings that contain restrictions which affect competition and affect trade between EU Member States should be assessed by the parties as to the compatibility of such agreements with Article 101 TFEU. This Treaty provision has direct effect which means that it can be relied on in national litigation either by a third party alleging damages caused by the operation of the agreement or by the parties to the agreement themselves. In parallel with the private enforcement of the EU competition rules, the European Commission has competence under EU legislation[4] to investigate such agreements and impose heavy fines[5] on the undertakings found to have infringed the EU competition rules.

Collaboration agreements, where the parties agree to limit their individual research activities and join forces in order to research and develop a product, are likely to contain clauses which restrict competition. The situation is further complicated where intellectual property rights are licensed or assigned in respect of the research activity, or where the new product is likely to be protected by intellectual property rights which are jointly owned and therefore competition between the former independent undertakings is not likely to arise as a result of the research and development agreement.

However, the European Commission has consistently supported research and development collaboration between small and medium-sized undertakings. Furthermore, in some industries it simply does not make economic sense for undertakings to struggle with their limited resources and attempt to develop a product when, by collaborating with another undertaking, together, they would achieve the result much more quickly and more efficiently. If they produce an excellent product they will be in

---

4 Council Regulation 1/2003 [2003] OJ L1/1.

5 Up to 10% of the annual turnover of all the undertakings involved.

a position to compete with larger undertakings with a greater chance of success than if they operated on their own.

Thus, not all agreements which contain restrictions which affect competition are banned. The drafters of the EU competition provisions were well aware that some anti-competitive restrictions should be allowed for the greater good. Thus Article 101(3) TFEU provides an exception by setting out criteria that enable an agreement to be classified as not being within the scope of Article 101(1) TFEU, and, therefore, not prohibited.

In the early 1970s, the Commission sought delegated legislative powers from the EU Council[6] in order to adopt a block exemption regulation which has direct effect within the national legal order of the EU Member States,[7] to enable some types of research and development agreements to benefit from the Treaty exception. In the context of research and development agreements three generations of BERs have been adopted. The BER is an important legislative measure as it ensures that research and development agreements are legal and enforceable. Thus the parties to such agreements avoid the risk of fines being imposed on them by the European Commission for operating an anti-competitive agreement.

These Commission regulations set out the criteria and conditions that the agreement must meet in order to be categorized as being exempted from the prohibition of Article 101(1) TFEU. Most of the BERs adopted by the Commission concern vertical agreements[8] but there are two BERs which govern horizontal agreements. The Research and Development BER is the object of this chapter.[9]

---

6 Council Regulation 2821/71 [1972] OJ Sp Ed p1032.

7 By special procedure also within the EEA which includes the 27 EU Member States as well as Norway, Iceland and Liechtenstein.

8 The BER for vertical agreements, Commission Regulation 2790/1999 [1999] OJ L336/21 which has now been replaced by Commission Regulation 330/2010 [2010] OJ L102/1; the BER for Transfer of Technology Agreements, Commission Regulation 772/2001 [2004] OJ L123/11, which applies mainly to patent licensing agreements.

9 The other BER governing horizontal agreements is Commission Regulation 1218/2010, [2010] OJ L335/43 which applies to specialization agreements.

3. THE BER FOR RESEARCH AND DEVELOPMENT AGREEMENTS

3.1 Contextual Background

As stated above there have been three generations of research and development BERs. Although the EU Council delegated legislative powers to the Commission in 1971, the first horizontal research and development BER was adopted only in 1985.[10] Until then all such agreements had to be notified individually to the European Commission, which assessed the agreements as to their compatibility with Article 101 TFEU which prohibits anti-competitive agreements that affect trade between Member States. Although in most cases such agreements were found to be incompatible with Article 101(1) TFEU, the Commission often granted them an individual exemption under Article 101(3) TFEU given that the benefit of the agreement in question outweighed its anti-competitive effect. It was considered that, in certain circumstances, the substantial economic benefits that would arise through increased efficiency and the opportunity that these agreements would give to the promotion of innovation and increased competition outweighed the negative short-term effects on competition between the parties to the agreement.

Thus, most research and development agreements were allowed to operate by the grant of an individual exemption under Article 101(3).[11] The first generation BER was of limited scope and only exempted the joint research and development. No joint exploitation of the results was allowed. Once the innovative product was developed and manufactured then the parties were free to exploit the product and to compete with each other. Any intellectual property rights would be jointly owned with each party able to exercise their rights freely.

By the mid-1990s most of the legislative measures to ensure that an internal market was completed by the end of 1992 were in place, including the adoption of the patent, know-how and franchising BERs. So in 1993 the Research and Development BER was amended, extending the scope of the protection to include not just the collaboration but also

---

[10] Commission Regulation 418/85, [1985] OJ L53/5 amended by Regulation 2236/97 [1997] OJ L306/12).

[11] Individual exemptions were exclusively granted by the Commission to notified agreements which came within the scope of Article 101(1) TFEU but met the conditions of Article 101(3) TFEU.

the exploitation of the results of the joint research and development and thus facilitating the transfer of technical knowledge.

At the turn of the century the second generation of the Research and Development BER was adopted.[12] The 2000 BER was accompanied by Guidelines[13] which replaced two Commission Notices[14] and complemented the legislation.[15] The Guidelines provide assistance to the parties and national authorities as to the assessment of most common types of horizontal agreements and set out the basic principles for the assessment of these agreements.[16]

The second generation BER reflected the policy change which has taken place in the assessment of the compatibility of agreements with Article 101(1) TFEU. This was a change from a legalistic approach towards a more economic approach in the assessment of all vertical and horizontal agreements. This new approach allowed collaboration between competitors where this was good for the market without creating a risk for competition. Thus the Research and Development BER followed the model adopted in the assessment of vertical agreements,[17] namely a move away from the clause-based approach to a greater contractual freedom being offered to the parties in such agreements. Instead of prescribing what could be included in an agreement, the BER simply listed certain conditions that the undertakings were required to meet and the hardcore restrictions that must not be included in the agreements for the agreements to be able to benefit from the exemption provided by the BER.

Finally, at the end of 2010, the third generation BER, namely Regulation 1217/2010[18] on the application of Article 101(3) TFEU to certain categories of research and development agreements, was adopted. At the time of its adoption, Commission Vice-President in charge of competition policy, Joaquin Almunia stated:

---

[12] Regulation 2659/2000, [2000] OJ L304/7.

[13] [2001] OJ C3/2.

[14] Co-operation Notice of 1968 and the Co-operative Joint Venture Notice of 1993.

[15] Although Guidelines and Notices are not legislative measures and therefore not binding on the Commission or the courts, nevertheless, they are often followed by the competition enforcement agencies.

[16] Horizontal Guidelines provide a framework for the assessment of common types of horizontal cooperation agreements such as information exchange, research and development, production, purchasing, and commercialization and standardization agreements.

[17] See n 8 for the most recent BER governing vertical agreements.

[18] [2010] OJ L335/36.

> One of the overarching goals of the new rules is to contribute to the Commission's Europe 2020 strategy, in particular by promoting innovation and competitiveness. The new Guidelines and Block Exemption Regulations [Regulation 1216 on specialization agreements] will give companies the necessary freedom to co-operate in a globalised market place, while at the same time minimising the risk of agreements that are harmful to industry and to consumers.[19]

The third generation BER follows the same structure as that introduced in the second generation. It sets out market thresholds below which these categories of agreements may benefit from an automatic exemption; the scope of the exemption and conditions that have to be met; and the hardcore restrictions that, if present, will deny any protection to the agreement under the Regulation. However, if the agreement does not meet these conditions, the agreement is not automatically declared incompatible with Article 101 TFEU. It simply means that the agreement cannot be protected automatically by the BER. The consequences are that the agreement will need to be assessed on a case-by-case basis in line with the Horizontal Guidelines as to whether it is compatible with Article 101(1) TFEU and, if not, whether the conditions of Article 101(3) are met in respect of the specific agreement.

One of the reasons that there are three generations of BERs is that each BER states a specific period of validity which is usually a period between 10 and 15 years.[20] Therefore, every 10 to 15 years it is necessary to adopt a new BER. Initially the period set up for the validity of BERs was primarily to ensure that exemptions granted by category of agreement were similar in length to those granted by individual exemption after an investigation by the European Commission. It is also a wise practice to adapt legislation to market conditions as they change. A requirement for the Commission to focus on these agreements that were exempted by category ensured that changes could be introduced into the Regulation to reflect such market changes.

For example, the 2000 BER deleted the requirement to draw up a framework agreement prior to entering into the research and development agreement, increased the market shares thresholds, and increased the period during which the joint exploitation of jointly developed products could be covered irrespective of market shares.

---

[19] Commission Press Release IP/10/1702, Brussels 14 December 2010.

[20] Like all BERs, transitional arrangements are specified in the Regulation. Article 8 of the BER provides that agreements that were in place at 31 December 2010 and that were exempted under the 2000 BER will continue to receive exemption under the 2000 BER but only until 31 December 2012.

As will be discussed below, the 2010 BER not only updates the text but widens the scope of the exemption, reduces the list of hardcore restrictions and clarifies important aspects of the conditions imposed by the legislation.[21] The Horizontal Guidelines have also been updated and published.[22]

3.2 Scope of BER

The scope of the exemption granted by the 2010 BER has been extended to cover 'paid-for research and development.' This refers to the situation where one undertaking finances the research carried out by another. Some small undertakings in some industries are set up purely to research on behalf of others.

The BER also allows a more flexible joint exploitation of the results of the research and development cooperation by allowing joint exploitation agreements to grant an exclusive licence to one of the parties.[23] The BER therefore permits only one party to sell and distribute in the EU the products subject to the cooperation agreement on the basis of an exclusive licence granted by the other party. However, the other party will often have the right to sell the contract products in areas outside the EU. Again this broadening of joint exploitation is very useful for businesses carrying out 'paid-for' research.

3.3 Thresholds

Where the parties are not competitors, the exemption is available irrespective of market power and for the duration of the research and development agreement. Where the results are jointly exploited the exemption will apply for seven years from the time the products or technologies are first placed on the market in the EU. However, as in the earlier BER, the automatic exemption is not available if the parties are competitors and their combined market share (in either the relevant product market or the relevant technology market), at the time the agreement is entered into, exceeds 25 per cent.[24] The competitors' joint

---

[21] The BER also clarifies the definition of 'potential competitor' which had caused uncertainty. Article 1(1)(t)) provides a three year time frame during which a party would need to be likely to enter a market in order to be considered a potential competitor.

[22] [2011] OJ C11/1.

[23] Article 2(2) BER.

[24] Article 4(2)(a) BER.

market power must be within the 'safe harbour' market share limits in order to benefit from the protection of the BER. In the case of research and development funding agreements or joint exploitation agreements arising from research and development funding agreements, this 25 per cent threshold applies to the combined market share of the funding party and all of the parties with which the funding party has entered into research and development agreements with respect to the same products or technologies.[25] This requirement may be problematic given that the funded party may not have sufficient information about the other funded parties to make the calculation.

Any agreements where the parties' combined market share is above the thresholds are not necessarily incompatible with Article 101 TFEU but the pro- and anti-competitive effects must be assessed in the light of the Horizontal Guidelines to determine whether the positive effects outweigh the negative ones.

Determining the market shares in the relevant market where the parties operate is no simple matter, even with the assistance of the Market Definition Notice,[26] which explains how the Commission determines the relevant market. Article 7 of the BER provides a number of rules as to how to calculate the market shares on the basis of the market sales value. If these are not available, estimates on other reliable market information, including market sales volume may be used to establish the market share of the parties.

3.4 Conditions for Exemption

The conditions for securing an exemption are set out in Article 3 which lists certain clauses that must be included in the agreement. It is specified that a clause must state that all parties have access to the final results of the joint or paid-for research and development including any intellectual property rights and know-how for the purposes of further research and development and exploitation as soon as they are available. However, where the other party is a contract research organization, university or similar body, they need only to have access for research and not development or exploitation. The agreement may however provide for compensation for the access to further research or exploitation.

The parties must also have access for further exploitation but this is subject to several exceptions including where the parties have agreed that

---

[25] Article 4(2)(b) BER.

[26] [1977] OJ C372/5.

one party is exclusively licensed or where one party is a university or contract research organization.[27] Thus it is permitted for the agreement to grant an exclusive licence to one of the parties subject to conditions including the right of each party to have access to the results for the purposes of further research.

This is an important clarification. Although some restrictions had been permitted where there was joint exploitation of the results of a joint research and development agreement, it was not clear whether an arrangement whereby one party received an exclusive, worldwide exploitation licence from the other party amounted to joint exploitation.

Another required clause relates to agreements which provide only for research and development or paid-for research and development but not for joint exploitation. In this case each party must be granted access to pre-existing know-how of the other parties if this know-how is indispensable for the purpose of its exploitation of the results. This access can be on a fee-paying basis as long as this does not impede access.[28]

As for joint exploitation agreements, the condition set out is that this only relates to results that are protected by intellectual property rights or constitute know-how which are indispensable for the manufacture of the product or the application of the technologies.[29]

Finally, in the context of exploitation, if parties are charged with the manufacture of the product by way of specialization, they must be required to fulfil orders for supplies from the other parties. The only exception will arise where the research and development agreement provides for joint distribution or where the parties have agreed that only the party manufacturing the products may distribute them.

3.5 Hardcore Restrictions

The inclusion of a hardcore restriction in any agreement takes the agreement immediately outside the BER and thus subject to an assessment as to whether the agreement is compatible with Article 101 TFEU. As far as hardcore restrictions are concerned the list set out in the BER in Article 5 has been relaxed and slightly shortened as well as introducing additional exceptions to the hardcore restrictions. Article 5 of the BER lists seven hardcore restrictions, three of which are subject to exceptions. The restrictions that are considered to be hardcore and have no exceptions are set out in Article 5(a), (e), (f) and (g). Thus restrictions on the

---

[27] Article 3(2) BER.
[28] Article 3(3) of BER.
[29] Article 3(4) BER.

parties carrying out research independently in unconnected fields or in connected fields after completion of the joint or paid-for research and development[30] and the prohibition on active sales in territories or to customers which have not been exclusively allocated to one of the parties by way of specialization in the context of exploitation[31] have no exceptions. It should also be noted that active sales restrictions are now possible without time limits (previously a seven-year limit existed) for territory or customers which have not been exclusively allocated to the other party to the agreement. The third restriction with no exceptions is a requirement to refuse to meet demand from customers in the parties' respective specializations in the context of exploitation, who would market the contract products in other territories within the internal market.[32] Finally, it is a hardcore restriction to make it difficult for users or resellers to obtain the contract products from other resellers within the internal market[33].

The remaining three hardcore restrictions do have exceptions. Article 5(b) provides that the limitation of output and sales is a hardcore restriction but it provides exceptions where the agreement also covers joint production of the products or joint exploitation. It is also possible to restrict parties from handling competing products or technologies during the period of joint exploitation of the results. Similarly Article 5(c) prohibits price fixing in selling the product or licensing the technology but allows price fixing to immediate customers where the joint exploitation of the results includes joint distribution or joint licensing of the technologies. Finally, passive sales restrictions with regard to both territories and customers are considered to be hardcore restrictions with the exception of the requirement to license exclusively the results to another party.[34]

Thus the new exceptions to the hardcore restrictions basically allow non-compete and price-fixing clauses in certain specified circumstances. Similarly, certain restrictions on the price that may be charged to immediate customers and licensees where the parties to the research and development agreement are jointly distributing or licensing the resulting products or technologies are permitted.

---

30 Article 5(a) BER.
31 Article 5(e) BER.
32 Article 5(f) BER.
33 Article 5(g) BER.
34 Article 5(d) BER.

3.6 Excluded 'Grey' Restrictions

A new feature of the 2010 BER is a list of clauses that are not considered 'hardcore' but do not benefit from an automatic exemption under the BER. These types of clauses were first introduced in the Transfer of Technology BER[35] which governs the licensing of patents and other industrial rights. The major difference between a hardcore and the so-called 'grey restriction' is that the inclusion of the former results in the whole agreement not qualifying for an automatic exemption. The grey clauses are simply unenforceable but do not affect the legality of the rest of the agreement.

The two grey restrictions, namely no-challenge clauses[36] and prohibitions on licensing to third parties[37] are in fact slightly changed clauses that were considered hardcore in the earlier 2000 BER. The 2010 BER specifies that certain obligations not to challenge the validity of the intellectual property rights held by the parties are unenforceable but it permits the termination of the agreement in the event of one of the parties challenging the validity of such intellectual property rights. Similarly, certain obligations not to license third parties to manufacture the contract products or apply the contract technologies are not permitted unless the agreement provides for the exploitation of the results of the joint or paid-for research and development by at least one of the parties and such exploitation takes place in the EU vis-à-vis third parties.

4. CONCLUDING OBSERVATIONS

An interesting aspect of the 2010 BER is that there is no provision to deal with 'patent ambush'. This situation arises where the parties to an agreement do not reveal existing or pending intellectual property rights which may unduly impair the exploitation of the results of a research and development agreement by the other parties. It may appear surprising given that an earlier draft of the BER had proposed that an exemption under the BER should only be available if, prior to starting the research and development, all parties agreed that they would disclose, in an open and transparent manner, their existing and pending intellectual property rights relevant for the exploitation of the results by the other parties. However, during the public consultation it became apparent that there is

35 See the discussion in section 2, above.
36 Article 6(a) BER.
37 Article 6(b) BER.

no practical need for such a disclosure obligation as, in particular, potential ambushes in the context of research and development agreements can be adequately addressed by the parties through private contractual arrangements.

This clearly demonstrates the importance of the obligation imposed on the Commission to review and hold public consultation before the new generation of BERs is adopted. Sometimes theoretical problems simply do not arise in practice and this can only be established by the relevant market operators having a dialogue with the policy and law makers.

The 2010 BER also demonstrates the need to update market regulating instruments to ensure that the legislation is fit for purpose. The extension of the scope of the BER to cover paid-for research and development and the provision to allow the grant of an exclusive exploitation licence to one of the parties to the agreement are solid examples.

In conclusion, it is submitted that the correct solution has been found to encourage joint research and development projects even where there is evidence that the agreement negotiated is caught by Article 101(1) TFEU prohibition. By adopting legislation under Article 101(3) TFEU, the European Commission has adhered to its policy of supporting small and medium-sized undertakings but also has ensured that the contractual restrictions imposed on the parties are essential for these agreements to be successful. The fact that the Commission has adopted the third generation of the Research and Development BER is evidence that both the EU competition enforcement agency and the market are satisfied as to how research and development agreements are regulated in the EU internal market.

PART V

Devices to protect business research and development from 'internal attack'

19. Devices at law to protect employers: a conspectus of approaches

Marilyn Pittard

This chapter sets the stage for the discussion in this Part of the legal devices used by businesses and employers to protect themselves from internal attack, through the unauthorized misappropriation of data, information or innovations, and attempts by business to secure the complete loyalty of their workers to work only for and in the interests of the employer and business.

1. THREATS – REAL AND PERCEIVED – TO THE SAFEGUARDING OF BUSINESS INNOVATION AND INVENTION

Employers who have fostered innovation within their organization may perceive a threat that an employee will take an invention, or otherwise utilize the discovered knowledge and information, for the employee's own benefit: for example, by setting up a company controlled by the employee and realizing the fruits of the invention by effectively competing against his or her former employer. Alternatively, the threat could come from the employee seeking employment with another employer and 'divulging all' – and thereby conferring on the new employer, which has not supported, or invested in, the development of the innovation or invention, the ability to 'reap where they have not sewn'.

The threat may not come from the inventor himself or herself, but from another source internal to the employer's business – perhaps another employee or a contractor who has access to the confidential information, trade secret or relevant knowledge of the device or process. This threat may be particularly real where teams of workers have contributed to the innovation, so that knowledge is not centralized in one inventor but available to many.

John Hull's chapter identifies some case examples of divulging trade secrets and analyses these cases. He argues that, in recent years, misappropriation by employees is increasing, with customer and client lists being most likely to be collected and stolen. He cites the Cyber-Ark survey[1] which revealed that '58% of British workers would take confidential company data if faced with redundancy'[2] and, moreover, that a relatively high proportion, 40 per cent of staff, had already retained data which was confidential to the employer in the expectation of making them more competitive and valuable in the job market. In an interesting juxtaposition, Alison Firth in a section of her chapter entitled 'Court Statistics – Is Litigation on Confidential Information on the Increase?' analyses whether these purported increases have resulted in increased litigation over such 'theft' or internal attacks. She concludes that Hull's assertions as to the increase in misappropriation by employees is supported by court statistics in the United Kingdom.

2. ISSUES OF WRONGFUL USE OF INNOVATION OR INVENTION AND THE IMPACT OF TECHNOLOGY

How are problems or issues about whether there is illegitimate use of business's invention or innovation revealed? How such matters come to light often involve issues around patents. The employee inventor himself or herself may have attempted to take out the patent, and the process of registration may bring forth problems of who is actually entitled to be the registered owner. The reverse, of course, can occur where the business attempts to become the registered owner of the patent which the employee or former employee regards as their rightful entitlement. Where the patent has already been granted, the subsequent yet innocent use by another of the employee's invention might bring about a breach of the patent held by the business.

Even where a patent may not be involved, use of confidential information may come to light, or its future use be suspected, by the very fact that the former employee has started up a business in the same competitive field, or has obtained employment with a rival firm or company. This may prompt the business to seek interlocutory relief to prevent any misuse of such information or a trade secret.

---

[1] This survey was reported in *The Times* in 2009: Hull Chapter 20 this volume.

[2] Hull Chapter 20 this volume.

Contravention of restraint clauses, too, may be feared and a business might seek to prevent this breach through injunctive relief or, where actual breach occurred and financial loss ensued, the business might seek compensation through damages.

The 'attack' on a business innovation or invention in a highly sophisticated operation supported by information technology may be revealed by unauthorized intrusions into the business IT system or transmission of documents and data via that means. Employees may be well placed to access data and download information, as occurred in the following cases:

- *National Surgical Pty Ltd v McPhee*,[3] where an employee accessed the hard drive on which the employer stored data (although it was not clear that it was copied);
- *Woolworths Ltd v Olson*,[4] where the employee emailed the data to their home email accounts; or
- *Luxottica Retail Australia v Grant,* where the employee emailed the data to another (related) person.[5]

The ability to remotely access the workplace from home or off site may also provide a temptation for employees to appropriate such business data for themselves. Some organizations do not provide USB ports on their computers in an endeavour to prevent such downloading. It remains the case, though, that remote access can be easily used (or abused) by the employee; however, it may not go undetected. Increasingly, employers are monitoring their employees' emails and access to data. Whilst it is difficult to ascertain the extent of such actual monitoring by employers, an American survey suggests that it is reasonably widespread. According to the *2005 Electronic Monitoring and Surveillance Survey* which surveyed 526 US employers, 50 per cent of employers store and review employees' computer files;[6] 55 per cent retain and review

---

[3] [2010] FCA 972.

[4] [2004] NSWSC 849. See also *Screwpile Engineering Pty Ltd v Manning* [2010] WASC 317, where the plaintiff alleged that the employee (first defendant) had emailed to his own email address at home details of drawings just before he resigned.

[5] [2009] NSWSC 126 (9 March 2009). The employee emailed documents to her husband, who worked for a competitor.

[6] *Electronic Monitoring and Surveillance Survey, Executive Summary*, 4. To further break down the figures 30% of all forms survey all employees whilst 20%

employees' emails;[7], and 38 per cent of employers track content, keystrokes and time their employees spend at the computer[8]. In a similar survey two years later in 2007,[9] there was an increase (to 45 per cent) of employers which surveyed tracked content, keystrokes and time spent at the computer, with 43 per cent reporting that they stored and reviewed computer files and 43 per cent of employers monitoring emails. Interestingly, 28 per cent of employers reported dismissing employees for misusing email, with 22 per cent of these for breach of rules of confidentiality.[10] Such monitoring by employers is very easy, given current technological advances, and can take place without the employee suspecting, or knowing, that it is occurring. The 2007 survey revealed that: 'To help control the risk of litigation, security breaches and other electronic disasters, employers are taking advantage of monitoring and blocking technology to battle people problems – including the accidental and intentional misuse of computer systems and other electronic resources.'[11] In any event, on the other side of the coin, modern technology has certainly aided the ability of employees to effectively and easily access data and information. No longer does information have to be committed to memory or photocopies of documents made: in many instances, the electronic workplace provides one storage place, the computer, for a vast array of information about business innovations. Employer monitoring of emails can usually easily reveal the source of any leak of business information, data or inventions, as indicated in the cases referred to above where emails were sent to other off-site addresses.

However, as a matter of evidence it may be hard to establish that access by the employee to confidential information held by the employer actually led to wrongful use. In the case of *National Surgical Pty Ltd v McPhee*,[12] for example, the judge was not convinced that the employee's accessing of the employer's hard drive on the eve of the former's resignation meant that the information was used by that employee.

---

survey selected jib categories (including 30% for all employees and 20% for selected employees).

[7] Ibid, 5. This figure can be further broken down – it shows that 38% of firms retain and review all employees' email whilst 17% of firms do this for selected job categories.

[8] Ibid, 4.

[9] 2007 *Electronic Monitoring and Surveillance Survey*.

[10] Ibid.

[11] Ibid, 2.

[12] [2010] FCA 972.

Monitoring of emails and surveillance of computer use may not expressly be undertaken for the purpose of detecting 'internal attack' but for monitoring work productivity and use of employees' time at work. However, monitoring for that other purpose may still reveal the misuse of information.

3. THE RANGE OF LEGAL DEVICES AT THE EMPLOYER'S DISPOSAL

There are a number of devices available to businesses to ensure that businesses do retain their invention or innovation or at least the financial rewards which they might yield. Apart from ensuring that they have rights to become the registered patent owner, businesses may wish to keep exclusive rights over the knowledge and information relating to the inventions. In cases where a person is being engaged as an employee, negotiating express terms to acknowledge the employer's superior rights will always be an option. The devices available to the employer are express confidentiality clauses and clauses that restrict competition, which are entered into at the beginning of the employment relationship and usually contained in the contract of employment; utilising workplace policies to control the flow of information and data and issue instructions about maintaining confidentiality; and Deeds which are entered into upon termination of employment relating to confidentiality and restrictions upon competition by the former employee.

Government policy, reflected in laws of Parliament, may further proscribe issues relating to restraint clauses. The NSW *Restraint of Trade Act 1976*, for example, reinforces the common law position in respect of restraint of trade in employment.

4. CONFIDENTIALITY CLAUSES AND RESTRICTIONS IN COMPETITION

4.1 Clauses to Maintain Confidentiality

Clauses which endeavour to limit the use of information or retain it for the business's sole use are strict confidentiality clauses and express clauses dealing with trade secrets. An example of such an express clause can be found in the contract of employment in *TFS Derivatives Ltd v*

Morgan[13] (although it was not this clause that was the subject of the litigation), encompassing confidential information and trade secrets both during and after the cessation of the employment relationship:

> 8.1 During your employment you will have access to and will be entrusted with confidential information and trade secrets relating to the business of the Group. This includes but is not limited to information and secrets relating to:
>
> (a) corporate and marketing strategy, business development and plans, and research results;
> (b) business methods and processes, and technical information and know-how relating to the Group's business which is not available to the public generally;
> (c) business contacts, current planned transactions, lists of and names of clients and customers and details of terms of business with them and client and customer revenues;
> (d) brokerage rates and pricing policies;
> (e) budgets, management accounts, trading statement and other financial reports;
> (f) any document marked 'confidential'.
>
> 8.2 You may not during your employment (otherwise than in the proper performance of your duties and then only to those who need to know such information or secrets) or afterwards (otherwise than with the prior written consent of the Board or as required by law) use or disclose any confidential information or trade secretes concerning the business of the Group or in respect of which the Group may be bound by an obligation of confidence to any third party. You should also use your best endeavors to prevent the publication or disclosure of such information or secrets. These restrictions will not apply after your employment has terminated to information which has become available to the public generally, otherwise than through unauthorized disclosure.

Even with clearly expressed clauses, the problem may be to distinguish between what an employee could legitimately take with him or her after employment has ceased because it is within that employee's stock of knowledge and skills, on the one hand, and what is truly 'confidential information' which must not be utilized even after the employment relationship has ceased, on the other hand. The classic case of *Faccenda Chicken Ltd v Fowler*[14] shows the difficulty of distinguishing between these two types of information, although not in the context of express clauses, when former employees utilized information and knowledge they

---

13 [2005] IRLR 246; [2004] EWHC 3181 (QB) at para [27].
14 [1987] Ch 117.

had gained during their employment with their former employer to set up their own competing business.

4.2 Restraining the Competition

Another approach is to expressly restrain the employee in his or her work. These include restraining the employee from working during the life of the employment contract for another organization or requiring permission to be given for any outside work by the employer, as well as post employment restraints, that is, clauses restraining former employees from working competitively against their former employer's business. Restrictions can be made as to time (for express periods of time) or for geographical areas (e.g., kilometres from the business; not within the state) and so on. The so called 'non-compete clauses' are prevalent in the United States, as discussed in the chapter by Jay Kesan and Carol Hayes, and also have been the subject of much litigation in Australia and the United Kingdom as evidenced in the chapters in this Part by Chris Molnar, John Hull and Alison Firth.

Of course, the restraint imposed by the employer contractually may go beyond what the law is prepared to enforce. In balancing the need for healthy competition amongst businesses against the special interests for preserving an employer's investment, the common law courts have established clear principles. Generally, restraining trade will be against public policy, and clauses in restraint of trade will be void and unenforceable. In *Marlov Pty Ltd v Murat Col*,[15] the clause which was sought to be enforced by a real estate company against a former employee provided:

> 19. RESTRAINT OF TRADE
>
> 19.1 In consideration of your remuneration and to protect the Company's goodwill, you will not while employed by the Company, or for six (6) months within 7.5 km from the company's office, after your employment with the Company ends, of the following:
>
> a. induce, encourage or solicit any of the Company's employees to resign;
> b. induce, encourage or solicit any of the Company's customers, clients or suppliers with whom you have contact in the preceding 12 months, to end or restrict their trade relationship with the Company;
> c. *carry on or be engaged or interested in any business which competes with the Company* [emphasis added].

---

[15] *Marlov Pty Ltd v Murat Col* [2009] NSWSC 501.

The court held that clause 19.1c was unenforceable and void as in restraint of trade because it is 'a covenant against mere competition. It does not protect any legitimate interest of the plaintiff in its business connection or goodwill. It cannot be read down so as to be valid.'[16]

However, such clauses exceptionally may be able to be enforced in favour of the business where it is in the interests of the parties to the contract and can also be regarded as 'reasonable' in the objective view of the court.[17] Yet the courts generally take a stricter and less favourable view of the covenants on restraint of trade entered into between employer and employee than of covenants in other commercial agreements.[18] It is acknowledged that, whilst employers cannot generally stop an employee becoming a competitor, there may be special interest(s) of the employer to be protected, such as confidential information. The restraint's validity and therefore enforceability 'is tested at the time of entering the contract and by reference to what the restraint entitled or required the parties to do, not what they have actually done.'[19]

Restraint clauses which have come before the courts for consideration as to their validity include:

> [Y]ou must not, either during your employment with the Company and for a period of twelve (12) months thereafter, or such lesser period as may be judged by a court of competent jurisdiction as being reasonable in the circumstances and necessary to protect the Company's goodwill and confidential information:
>
> (a) carry on or otherwise be engaged or involved in any business similar to or competitive with the business of the Company … carried on during the twelve (12) months prior to the termination of your employment … [20].

---

16 Per Debelle AJ in *Marlov Pty Ltd v Murat Col* [2009] NSWSC 501 at [32].

17 *Nordenfelt v Maxim Nordenfelt Guns and Ammunition Co Ltd* [1894] AC 535; *Amaco Australian Pty Ltd v Rocca Bros Metal Engineering Co Pty Ltd* [1973] HCA 40; 133 CLR 288.

18 *Ross and Anor v IccTV* [2010] NSW CA 272 at para [88] acting *Geraghoty v Minter* [1939] HCA 42; 142 CLR 177, 185, per Gibbs J.

19 *Ross and Anor v IccTV* [2010] NSW CA 272 at para [88], citing *Woolworths Ltd v Olson* [2004] NSWCA 372 at para [38], per Mason P.

20 *Ross and Anor v IccTV* [2010] NSW CA 272, although another part of the clause prohibiting soliciting or canvassing of business was the main focus of that case.

The court held that such a clause was valid when the words 'similar to' were omitted, so that the clause was confined to a business which was 'competitive with that of IccTV'.[21]

In *Thomas v Farr Plc*[22] the Court of Appeal in the United Kingdom held that the clause in the managing director's contract which restricted him from competing for a period of 12 months after termination of employment could be enforced, as it was not unreasonable in order to protect the confidential information belonging to his employer, a firm of insurance brokers.

Significantly, the court may tailor the order so that the employee is restricted in his or her duties, but not entirely prevented from working for a competitor organization. In *Reed Business Information v Seymour*, for example, the court did not prevent the former employee working for the rival, but restricted the publications on which she could work, so as not to compete with her former employer, Reed Business Information.[23]

Non-compete clauses in the United States are analysed by Kesan and Hayes in their chapter: significantly there is a range of approaches to these clauses with some states in the US prohibiting the use of such clauses and other states permitting their use. Kesan and Hayes critique the effect on behaviour within the business of banning, or not, the non-compete clause and conclude that, where non-compete clauses are permitted, flexibility is promoted and that:

> This flexibility may be optimal since it minimizes strategic behavior and promotes symmetry between the employer and employee, who are both encouraged to exercise due care. This approach may be seen as striking the right balance between protecting employer investments, promoting long-term job stability, and preserving the state's economy, versus encouraging and vindicating the employee's own personal autonomy and freedom.[24]

Similar restraint clauses in the United Kingdom are discussed by Firth and in Australia by Molnar, and the case law is examined. The impact of EU law and directions is also analysed by Firth, and the basis of EU law identified.

---

21 *Ross and Anor v IccTV* [2010] NSW CA 272, footnote at [125]. Clause in *P & B Engineering Ltd and Anor v Peterson and Anor* [2008] NZ ERA 204.

22 [2007] EWCA Civ 118; [2007] ICR 932; [2007] IRLR 419.

23 *Reed Business Information v Seymour* [2010] NSWSC 790 (23 July 2010).

24 Kesan and Hayes, Chapter 23 this volume.

4.3 Evidentiary Issues

There are evidentiary hurdles that must be met in litigation: a serious question to be tried must be established, and the balance of convenience must favour the business, in order for an interlocutory injunction to be granted. Merely preventing competition, however, is a restriction which the courts are concerned to avoid, as parties in *Screwpile Engineering Pty Ltd v Manning* were reminded:

> [T]he law, from a policy perspective, encourages healthy and fair competition between trade rivals. The law would not, on the basis of a mere expressed fear or concern, lightly injunct a business competitor for engaging in healthy and robust competition – in the absence of a strong evidentiary basis to support its intervention.[25]

The important question of remedies and the evidentiary aspects in litigation are also explored by Firth. Just what do businesses want when they resort to litigation and what do they need to prove in order to substantiate their claims? Similarly, cases discussed in Molnar's chapter on the Australian approach delve into remedies and aspects of litigating in this field.

There is a need for assessment of the effect of restraint clauses on competitiveness, job stability and business investment, together with the freedom of the employee to compete and set up in business on their own account. Little to no data is available on these effects in Australia and the United Kingdom and the impact of laws is consequently hard to assess. Do restraint of trade clauses really achieve what they aim to do? What effect do they have on employee behaviours and actions? To what extent do they truly act as a deterrent to employee conduct? Whilst cases do come to court disputing the validity of a restraint clause or seeking to enforce it against an employee, it is the impact of clauses day to day, and which are not litigated so do not come to court, which tell a bigger and more complete story.

---

[25] Martin J in the Supreme Court of Western Australia in *Screwpile Engineering Pty Ltd v Manning* [2010] WASC 317 (5 November 2010) at [23].

5. WORKPLACE POLICIES

Workplace policies are sometimes an effective mechanism of ensuring up-to-date notification of the culture of the workplace about confidentiality and protecting innovation, in addition to providing a mechanism for flagging changes to that culture. Such policies are commonplace in large and medium-sized workplaces. Whether those workplace policies will be legally binding and enforceable is another matter and will depend ultimately on the terms of the employment contract and whether such policies are effectively incorporated as terms of the contract. Workplace policies are addressed in the chapters by Hull (in the United Kingdom) and Molnar (in Australia)[26] and the problems of their enforcement discussed.

Setting the tone for the culture of the workplace through the development and promulgation of policies may be one matter, but actually devising appropriate terms in the employment contracts and converting such policies to contractual terms that must be complied with or regarded as enforceable orders or directives that the employee must follow, is another. This is not always satisfactorily dealt with, as the litigation that is discussed in the following chapters reveals.

6. DEEDS

Sometimes where termination of employment is not sought by the employee, the employer will seek to lay down the conditions of the termination through a Deed, usually a Deed of Release. Such a Deed typically might contain details not only about prohibitions on litigation by the departing employee, but also about the conditions of restraint in competition for a period or geographical area and maintaining confidentiality. Such Deeds are commonly kept confidential between the parties so they are not a source which is readily available for scrutiny, as to, for example, fairness or equity.

7. DUTIES OF DISCLOSURE AS A CONTROL DEVICE

Duties of disclosure where the employer requires the employ to disclose any invention or innovation made in employment are another control device and may be expressly contained in the employment contract.

[26] Pittard Chapter 10 this volume.

Alternatively the courts may regard the employee as under a fiduciary duty to make such disclosures. These duties are particularly discussed by both Hull and Molnar. The recent Australian decision of the Full Court of the Federal Court of Australia in *Blackmagic Design Pty Ltd v Overliese*[27] is a good illustration of the problems faced by employers endeavouring to utilize fiduciary duties as protection. In that case, the employee was found to be under no duty to disclose information to the employer as the innovation was in reality an idea only. Molnar argues that this reflects the traditional reluctance of the courts to recognize a duty to disclose, yet it was potentially economically valuable information that was withheld from the employer.

8. IDEAS ABOUT THE WAY FORWARD

8.1 Characterizing Trade Secrets as Intellectual Property

In terms of the way forward, after concluding that '[l]itigation to enforce workplace secrets looks to be increasing in volume and cross-border complexity', Firth expresses the view that:

> Substantive laws and enforcement arrangements for trade secrets in Europe are subject to considerable variation. The European Commission is looking into the substantive rules. However, applicable law, particularly in non-contractual claims, is likely to pose continuing problems. Characterizing trade secrets as intellectual property, at least for procedural and remedial purposes, would go some way towards simplifying the task of litigants.[28]

Her proposal is to confer the categorization of intellectual property on trade secrets as a basis for assisting litigants in their disputes which are heard by the courts.

8.2 Trust and Confidence – The Non-law Solution?

Hull argues that legal devices (restraint clauses, confidentiality clauses and so on) can be put in place in an endeavour to protect employers, but that there are other requirements for such a strategy to work. He states in his chapter: 'But a strategy like this is unlikely to succeed if it is imposed without the employees themselves accepting the logic and necessity of

---

[27] [2011] FCAFC 13.
[28] Firth Chapter 21 this volume.

the strategy and its approach. Trust and confidence, the elements which underlie the employment relationship, are reciprocal issues.'[29]

The duty of mutual trust and confidence is recognized as an implied duty in the law of the contract of employment in the United Kingdom, but Australian courts have either adopted or rejected this doctrine in varying ways, with the High Court yet to rule on this definitively.[30] However, whether the doctrine is, or is not, accepted as part of the implied terms in the contract of employment – and therefore whether breach of trust and confidence is actionable – the point remains that trust and confidence on the part of the employer and employee are essential ingredients of a stable relationship between employer and employee. There may be monetary aspects or facets, too, which support or contribute to trust and confidence – fair remuneration for inventive tasks; a share in the proceeds or financial benefits of the invention; or acknowledgement and recognition of the skills of the inventor to name just a few.

In other words, just or fair remuneration and acknowledgment of the inventor's role may forestall many arguments or disputes; and employees may then readily agree to some of the express restraining clauses in the contract. However, it seems that standard clauses in the contracts of employment of new graduates with some large employers provide expressly for ownership of inventions and innovations to be exclusively in the company, without recompense to the employee. Together with the restraining and other control devices available to the employer, the contract has expressly plugged up possible 'leakages' of the information to competitors and misuse of the invention or innovation. The point, however, is that this approach takes no risks – even a new graduate may be a potential inventor, so that possibility must be acknowledged and guarded against contractually by the employer. This contract is finalized, in all likelihood, with little opportunity for the new employee to negotiate a change to the contract as presented, or for there to be remuneration or compensation clauses inserted in the contract.

The recent Australian case *Birdanco Nominees Pty Ltd v Money* underscores the approach of some employers to this question.[31] It was proposed in that case that a junior, relatively inexperienced and not yet qualified, accountant should be subject to the same contractual restraints as senior employees. The junior accountant was held to have breached the employment restraint. The Victorian Court of Appeal did not accept

---

[29] Hull Chapter 20 this volume.

[30] Pittard and Naughton (2010), 308–348.

[31] *Birdanco Nominees Pty Ltd v Money* [2012] VSCA 64.

his argument that, as he was not formally qualified as an accountant, the restraint did not apply to him (or to undergraduates or trainees) but only to professional practitioners. The accountant was ordered to pay damages of $188,000 to the employer (as calculated under the contract)[32] and costs were ordered against him. Is a contractual clause of that nature seeking liquidated damages, which no doubt a prospective employee would be required to sign, setting the environment for trust and confidence? A distinction could be drawn between, on the one hand, the blanket clause which purports to require the employee, whatever his or her tasks in the organization, to give up any interest in any intellectual property, copyright or patent entitlements and, on the other hand, the clause which deals with such intellectual property rights in the contract of an employee who might reasonably be expected to contribute to such intellectual property as a integral part of the contract of employment.[33] In the latter instance, it would be easier to compel willing agreement by the employee where there is a stable and trusting employment relationship and some financial acknowledgement – in the employee's remuneration or extra remuneration – of his or her contribution.

REFERENCES

American Management Association and The e-Policy Institute, *2005 Electronic Monitoring and Surveillance Survey, Executive Summary*, available at <http://www.epolicyinstitute.com/survey2005Summary.pdf>

American Management Association and The e-Policy Institute, *2007 Electronic Monitoring and Surveillance Survey, Executive Summary*, available at <http://www.plattgroupllc.com/jun08/2007ElectronicMonitoringSurveillanceSurvey.pdf>

---

[32] The contract provided for liquidated damages as follows: '(d) Should I breach either of the two covenants in paragraph (a) of this clause, or the covenants in clauses 1 or 2, I agree to pay to the Company as liquidated damages, a sum equal to 75% of the fees incurred by the particular client with the Company for Services rendered in the financial year immediately preceding the breach of such covenant (if, as a result of such breach the Company loses work of that client) without prejudice to the right of the Company's right to claim, in the alternative, such damage as it may establish that it has suffered through loss of the business of the particular client. For the purposes of this clause "fees incurred" means the total amount chargeable to the particular client inclusive of Goods and Services tax.'

[33] For the latter, see *Vladimer Batov v Invensys Rail Pty Ltd* [2010] FCAFB 5552, where the employee was fairly dismissed for breaching his contractual term to forward new technologies for the benefit of the employer only.

Pittard, M. and R. Naughton (2010), *Australian Labour Law: Text, Cases and Commentary*, 5th edn, LexisNexis

20. Devices to restrain competition and protect discoveries and enforcement: workplace policies and confidentiality agreements

John Hull

1. INTRODUCTION

The misappropriation of trade secrets by employees is hardly a modern phenomenon.[1] Some of the early English case law[2] shows that employees were as inclined to misappropriate their employer's confidential information as they are now. The only thing which has changed over the years is that technology has made life both easier and, ironically, more difficult for the employee. Instead of laboriously transcribing documents containing formulae or customer lists,[3] the employee can now download them to a memory stick, or, if he is extremely unwise, simply forward them to his home email address.[4] In doing so, of course, he immediately creates a forensic 'fingerprint' of his activity making apprehension and the attachment of liability a great deal easier.[5]

There are two main ways of dealing with the problem of trade secret misappropriation by insiders. One is by legal action, the determination of liability and the imposition of the appropriate legal remedies – the

[1] Bok (1984), ch X.

[2] *Robb v Green* [1895] 2 QB 315; *Measures Bros Ltd v Measures* [1910] 1 Ch 336; *Merryweather v Moore* [1892] 2 Ch 518; *Wessex Dairies Ltd v Smith* [1935] 2 KB 80.

[3] As the defendant did in *Robb v Green* [1895] 2QB 315.

[4] *First Conference Services Ltd v Bracchi* [2009] EWHC 2176 (Ch); *Brandeaux Advisers (UK) Ltd v Chadwick* [2010] EWHC 3241 (QB); *Churchill Retirement Living v Luard* [2012] EWHC 1479 (Ch).

[5] Generally: Goulding (2010), [9.46]–[9.65] appx 1, Computer Forensic Investigations.

injunction, the order to deliver up and so on. At the other end of the spectrum, however, and as an essentially prophylactic tool, there is the application of policies and protocols to highlight duties and to educate employees about their obligations. It is this latter element with which this chapter is concerned.[6]

2. THE NATURE AND SCALE OF MISAPPROPRIATION: SOME EXAMPLES AND EVIDENCE

What then is the nature and scale of the problem? A brief look at some examples and at some statistical evidence provides an outline picture of what is involved.

Perhaps the best known example in recent years was the *VW – Lopez* case. Jose Lopez, the then head of purchasing for General Motors in Europe, was recruited in 1993 by VW. He left GM with some associates (his 'purchasing warriors'). GM responded to his resignation with allegations of trade secret theft. A subsequent search of one of his purchasing warrior's homes disclosed the removal of a 3,350-page list of 60,000 GM parts including supplier details. Also found were details of GM's future product line and plans for a new manufacturing plant.

Mr Lopez was charged in the US in his absence with wire fraud and the transport of stolen property. But Spain, where Mr Lopez lived, refused to extradite him to the US to face these charges. The case was settled in 1997.[7] But, partly as a result of the *Lopez* case, the US passed the Economic Espionage Act 1996.

A similarly high-profile case in the UK involved two Formula 1 teams – McLaren and Ferrari. It was alleged that the chief designer of McLaren received highly secret details of a new Ferrari Formula 1 car from a Ferrari engineer. Litigation was pursued in the UK and Italy.

The case was, predictably, settled but McLaren was fined US$100 million by the FIA for its part,[8] and the Ferrari employee concerned was later sentenced in September 2010 to 20 months' imprisonment in Italy

---

6 For legal remedies see Firth, Chapter 21 this volume.

7 Articles in the *Los Angeles Times* and the *New York Times* both 10 January 1997.

8 *The Times* 8 July 2007 <www.timesonline.co.uk/tol/sport/formula-1/article 2042025.ece>.

for trade secret theft and related charges.[9] That both cases were settled comes as no surprise. The spectacle of companies such as these, however bitter rivals they may be, engaging in full-scale litigation was unlikely to appeal to senior management. This kind of litigation is attritional and costly. But the damage to the brand and reputation is usually what prompts settlement.

The simple fact remains that employees, particularly those sufficiently senior to be privy to highly sensitive, confidential information, sometimes find the temptation to move to a rival irresistible, even though the price is taking trade secrets with them. Employees have more opportunity and more inclination to switch allegiance and will be tempted to remove some sort of corporate data to enhance their attractiveness in the marketplace.

Not all cases have the profile of the VW or Formula 1 cases, but still disclose the same human frailties. *JN Dairies v Johal Dairies and Singh*,[10] involved two rival Indian-owned dairies operating in the UK Midlands. A trusted employee (Singh) left the Claimant's employment to go the Defendant. He was, however, captured by CCTV entering the Claimant's premises during the middle of the night to remove a batch of invoices which contained details of all of the Claimant's customers. The following day he and representatives of the Defendant were detected making approaches to those customers. The Court held that the invoices had considerable commercial value. They represented far more in terms of detail than Singh could possibly have remembered from his employment. The fact that Singh stole the invoices was sufficient to establish a relationship of confidence between him and the Claimant. The Claimant's loss was clearly established.

The *JN Dairies* case shows that it is often customer, supplier or pricing details which are the most important commercially sensitive information owned by many companies.[11] For many such companies it is their life blood, the loss of which could undermine their entire business future. The evidence of Singh misappropriating the invoices was also critical. Evidence in these cases is particularly important. Courts are rightly sceptical of an ex-employer's allegation of trade secret theft, concluding in many

---

9 See <www.news.bbc.co.uk/sportl/hi/motorsport/formula-one/9045983.stm>.

10 [2009] EWHC 1331 (Ch); [2010] EWCA Civ 34 (Ch).

11 *Lock International v Beswick* [1989] 3 All ER 373; *Lansing Linde Ltd v Kerr* [1991] 1 WLR 251; *Poly Lina v Finch* [1995] FSR 751.

cases that this amounts to little more than harassment.[12] This also explains the need to plead cases of breach of confidence against ex-employees with proper particularity. 'It is therefore of the essence of a claim against an employee for misuse of confidential information that the employer should be able to identify with particularity the trade secret or similar confidential information to which he lays claim.'[13]

First Conference v Bracchi[14] also involved customer details, although this time in the form of an electronic database. The Defendant was an events manager who planned to start a rival business in the same field. A search and seizure (Anton Piller) order had already disclosed that he had downloaded considerable extracts from the database to his personal email account. The judge made the following remark in the *Bracchi* case which has wider application:

> It is becoming increasingly common with the computerisation of information for employees who wish to set up their own competing business to help themselves to their employers' confidential information. Some of this material is not necessarily confidential as such and is capable of being found with hard work. However the employees do not wish to go through the hard work and in effect what they do is they seek to take advantage of their employers' time effort and expense in putting together valuable material which provides a tool to an emerging business. Instead of doing their own work using their own brains they simply hijack the employers' gathered material. This gives them what is called a 'springboard' for their business to be up and running almost immediately at the expense of the former employer.[15]

Finally, *Vestergaard v Bestnet Europe Limited*[16] is one of the most significant trade secrets cases in the UK in recent years. The Claimant's

---

[12] *Vestergaard Frandsen A/S v Bestnet Europe Ltd* [2009] EWHC 657 (Ch) 104 (Arnold J): 'I entirely accept that, as Laddie J said in *Ocular Sciences Ltd v Aspect Vision Care Ltd (No 2)* [1997] RPC 289, 359, "it is well recognised that breach of confidence actions can be used to oppress and harass competitors and ex-employees". It follows that the Courts must scrutinise such claims with care to see if they are well founded …'. Also, *Caterpillar Logistics v de Crean* [2011] EWHC 3154 (QB) and on appeal [2012] EWCA Civ 726.

[13] *Lock International Ltd v Beswick* [1989] 3 All ER 373, 378 (Hoffman J); *Lawrence David v Ashton* [1991] 1 All ER 385; *Ixora Trading Inc v Jones* [1990] FSR 251; *GD Searle v Celltech* [1982] FSR 92; *Caterpillar Logistics Services (UK) Ltd v Paula Huesca de Crean* [2011] EWHC 3154 (QB) and [2012] EWCA Civ 726.

[14] [2009] EWHC 2176 (Ch).

[15] [2009] EWHC 2176 (Ch), [25] (Smith J).

[16] [2009] EWHC 657 (Ch); [2009] EWHC 1456 (Ch); [2009] EWHC 1023 (Pat); [2011] EWHC 277(Ch); [2011] EWCA Civ 424.

case was for misappropriation of technical trade secrets relating to the composition of chemically impregnated anti-mosquito nets. The nets had been subjected to rigorous analysis over a lengthy period and a database of tests had been produced. Two ex-employees, aided by a non-employed consultant, left to start their own rival business. The judge held that the database was confidential and amounted to a trade secret. Applying the classic *Coco v AN Clark Ltd* test,[17] Arnold J held that either express or implied obligations of confidence were in place and had been breached. The evidence established surreptitious plans to compete using this material. The defence that the ex-employees relied on their own skill and experience (know-how) was rejected. The misappropriation had occurred on too wide a scale.

Again, the *Vestergaard* case is a prime example of the evidential picture emerging to trap the ex-employees concerned. The commercial success of the Claimant's business clearly persuaded them that launching a rival business was sufficiently attractive. They simply provided themselves with the technical information to do so by misappropriation rather than by independent creation.

Although examples, these recent cases provide an indication of the nature of the problem faced by employers. There is some alternative evidence to suggest that the scale of the problem is, if anything, increasing, spurred perhaps by a tightening job market.

The results of a Cyber-Ark survey were reported in *The Times* in 2009.[18] The survey disclosed that:

1. 58 per cent of British workers would take confidential company data if faced with redundancy;

---

[17] [2009] EWHC 657 (Ch), [623]: 'First, the information itself … must "have the necessary quality of confidence about it". Secondly, that information must have been communicated in circumstances importing an obligation of confidence. Thirdly, there must have been an unauthorised use of the information to the detriment of the party communicating it.' *Coco v AN Clark (Engineers) Ltd* [1969] RPC 41, 47 (Megarry J). Cited with approval at the highest level: *Attorney General v Guardian Newspapers Ltd (No 2)* [1990] 1 AC 109, 268 (Lord Griffiths); *Campbell v MGN Ltd* [2004] UKHL 22; [2004] AC 457, [13] (Lord Nicholls) and *Douglas v Hello! Ltd (No 3)* [2007] UKHL 21; [2008] AC 1, [111] (Lord Hoffman). See also Arnold J in *Force India Formula One Team Ltd v I Malaysia Racing Team SDN BHD and Others* [2012] EWHC 616 (Ch).

[18] Herman, M, 'Employees facing redundancy are tempted by data theft', *The Times* (3 February 2009) <http://business.timesonline.co.uk/tol/business/management/article 5644325.ec e>.

2. 40 per cent of staff were already retaining confidential data to enhance their value on the job market; and
3. client or customer databases were the most likely form of data to be stolen.

The same article disclosed that between 2006 and 2008 the number of English cases to stop employees using confidential information rose steeply (albeit from a low number of 3 to 23).[19]

3. THE EMERGING PICTURE – A TREND TO MISAPPROPRIATION

What are we to make of this picture? Misappropriation of trade secrets is substantially a function of the employment relationship and that broad picture has not changed over the years. What has changed are the opportunities and pressures to misappropriate. The digitisation of information and the ready access to electronic systems and databases makes the identification and removal of large volumes of data a relatively simple task. The pressure to remove and thus to enhance value in the job market are equally clear. Many employees are hired not so much for their skill and experience as for their inside information. The distinction between using an employer's trade secrets or confidential information and using an employee's innate or acquired 'know-how' is notoriously hard to define.[20] Plainly, however, the existence of established evidential

---

[19] The number rose steeply again in 2009 to 95 according to a law firm survey reported in *The Times*, 22 November 2010, 56. Significant recent cases in this area include: *QBE Management Services v Dymoke* [2012] EWHC 80 (QB); *Landmark Brickwork v Sutcliffe* [2011] EWHC 1239 (QB); *Customer Systems Ltd v Ranson* [2011] EWHC 3304 (QB) and *Clear Edge v Elliot* [2011] EWHC 3376 (QB).

[20] Generally see *Gurry on Breach of Confidence* by T.Aplin, L.Bently, P.Johnson and S.Malynicz (2nd edn, OUP 2012). The classic test is given by Cross J in *Printers and Finishers Ltd v Holloway* [1965] RPC 239 (Ch) 256: 'If the information in question can fairly be regarded as a separate part of the employee's stock of knowledge which a man of ordinary honesty and intelligence would recognise to be the property of his old employer and not his own to do as he likes with, then the court, if it thinks that there is a danger of the information being used or disclosed by the ex-employee to the detriment of the old employer, will do what it can to prevent that result by granting an injunction.'

tools such as the Anton Piller order[21] and the experience of forensic experts able to identify the nature and scale of misuse make such cases easier to uncover.

What, then, should be the reaction or response of businesses to this longstanding problem, recast into a more modern guise as a consequence of technological advances?

The scepticism of the courts as to actions against ex-employees is clear,[22] and the use of restrictive covenants can be a blunt and often unsuccessful tool.

What then can employers do to enhance their position and provide a better level of protection for their valuable confidential information? One evident self-help measure is the use of workplace policies designed to highlight the nature of the employee's obligations and how the employee might fulfil those obligations.

A 'workplace policy' represents, however, a good deal more than a contract of employment setting out contractual obligations or an accompanying written document seeking to explain the nature of those obligations. A policy has to consist of a combination of documentation (usually an employee manual which will deal with confidential information and a wider range of issues such as health and safety and employee benefits) and a process to educate and inform.

An employer needs to focus attention on three phases of the policy: first, a process to deal with the incoming employee; second, implementation of the policy for current employees; and third (possibly the most important part of the policy) departing employees. Each will be considered in turn.

3.1 A Policy for the Incoming Employee

Why is this important? An employer engaging a new employee will usually do so because it wants to take advantage of the employee's skill and experience, or possibly his contacts and knowledge of a particular field in business. These are reasonable business objectives. But they are susceptible to the danger that the new employee will find himself on the

---

21 *Anton Piller KG v Manufacturing Processes Ltd* [1976] FSR 129 (CA): called a Search and Seizure order by the CPR Part 25.

22 *Ocular Sciences Ltd v Aspect Vision Care Ltd (No 2)* [1997] RPC 289 (PatC), 359 (Laddie J). E.g.: *Space Conditioning PLC v Guy* [2011] EWHC 2107 (Ch); *Caterpillar Logistics Services (UK) Ltd v Paula Huesca de Crean* [2011] EWHC 3154 (QB), appeal [2012] EWCA Civ 156; *Caterpillar Logistics v de Crean* [2011] EWHC 3154 (QB) and on appeal [2012] EWCA Civ 726.

receiving end of an action by the old employer seeking to protect its own confidential information from being disclosed to and used by the new employer. A new employer will often be included in any action if there is evidence of inducement to breach or that the new employer will, by accident or design, have the old employer's confidential information disclosed to it.[23]

A policy approach to employer recruitment and induction should therefore encompass the following components:

1. During interviews and any induction process, candidates or new employees should be told specifically not to disclose anything they believe to be their current or ex-employer's confidential information.
2. Recruiting employers should assess any incoming employee's restrictive covenants or written confidentiality obligations. How reasonably enforceable are these likely to be? Should a new employer attempt to 'sanitise' an incoming employee and give him duties which are less likely to infringe any existing restraint?
3. Recruiting employers should put in writing that any incoming employees must not bring anything with them to which they are not entitled, and that they will not, for example, email to their new workplace accounts documents (a database of customers, for example) previously (and illegitimately) downloaded from their employer's system.
4. Recruiting employers should document the process and have employees acknowledge in writing that they understand these obligations and will adhere to them.

It might be asked: What is the point of this activity? Adopting a policy of this sort for incoming employees has three functions. First, it helps to insulate the new employer from an allegation of inducement to breach or participation in an ex-employee's wrong-doing. Second, it lays part of an evidential 'paper trail' which a court is bound to take into account in any subsequent action in evaluating the credibility of the new employer. Third, it helps to generate a culture of confidentiality in the workplace.[24]

---

[23] The UK has not gone as far as the US doctrine of 'inevitable disclosure' which holds that employees cannot 'wipe clean' knowledge of an ex-employer's confidential information, even if they and any new employer are intent on them not disclosing any of this information: *PepsiCo v Redmond* 54 F 3d 1262 (7th Circ 1995); *Lumex v Highsmith* 919 F Supp 624 (EDNY 1996); Row (2005).

[24] Dobrusin and Krasnow (2008), chs 9 and 10.

An employer concerned enough to ensure that it does not want to be tainted by its predecessor's confidential information is likely also to be astute to look after its own.

In *The Trade Secrets Handbook* Dennis Unkovic suggests that pre-employment screening programmes

> serve a threefold purpose. First, a screening of the employee's attitudes towards trade secrets as well as normal job applications is possible before a hiring is made. Second, educating a potential employee from the earliest possible point will reinforce the Corporate Trade Secret Policy particularly if the program is more structured or formalised than those of previous employers. And third the interview will serve as the basis from which the employee secrecy agreement will emerge. The employee will not be able to claim surprise at the explicit nature of the contract.[25]

3.2 Workplace Confidentiality Policies

A workplace policy for current employees must be distinguished from an employee's contract of employment. The contract of employment will normally contain a provision on the protection of confidential information and intellectual property. (Even in the absence of any written terms, it is now well established that an employee owes an implied combined duty of fidelity and good faith (in modern parlance: 'trust and confidence') to his employer.[26] The duty of fidelity in effect means that the employee concerned will devote himself to his employer's business. The implied duty of good faith means that he will use his employer's trade secrets and confidential information only for the purpose of doing his job, and not for some ulterior motive such as engaging in, or preparing himself to engage in competition using that confidential information for his own purposes.)

A standard employee confidentiality provision consists of three elements. First, a statement will outline the basic duty in negative terms. A contract of employment might employ drafting along the following lines: 'The employee shall not … disclose or communicate to any unauthorised person … nor use for his own benefit or of the benefit of any other person … any information which is or which he reasonably ought to know is secret or confidential … .' Second, there will be a definition of what, in this context, 'secret or confidential' means. The drafting of these clauses usually takes the form of giving examples of the kind of information which may have the quality of confidence so that the

---

25 Unkovic (1985), ch 4, 70.

26 *Lamb v Evans* [1893] 1 Ch 218 and *Robb v Green* [1895] 2QB 315.

employee cannot later be taken to say that he had no reasonable indication of what he was supposed to protect: 'lists or details of customers … trade secrets … information relating to any process or invention … database of suppliers, customers/clients, employees … price lists, discounts, mark-ups, marketing plans …' and so on. Third, there will be a standard 'escape clause' which omits anything that is in or enters the public domain (other than as a result of some unauthorised disclosure by the employee himself).

By contrast a policy document will usually provide guidance or prescribe specific rules about issues such as:

1. the use of non-disclosure agreements when disseminating information to third parties;
2. the identification and treatment of confidential documents and materials;
3. the encryption of information contained on laptops and the security of digitally held material;
4. the removal of information from an employer's premises of documents or information for working remotely; and
5. the return of material on termination of employment and the employer's obligations post employment.

But a policy will often go further, and encompass training and education sessions in the practical application of these written policies. Careful employers will make attendance at training sessions such as these compulsory and insist that employees register and record their attendance. Inevitably some policies such as this go into considerable detail. It would be neither feasible nor appropriate to incorporate this much detail into a series of contractual provisions. Policies can, and often do, change to reflect changing workplace circumstances and technology.

The purpose of having a policy is twofold. The first is to educate and remind the employee of his obligations about the use and dissemination of the employer's information. The way in which the courts have approached employee obligations is relevant here and dovetails with a policy-driven approach. The leading English case on employee obligations pre and post termination of employment is *Faccenda Chicken Ltd v Fowler*.[27] In assessing whether any particular item of information fell within the implied term of good faith so as to prevent its use or disclosure by an employee after his employment had ended, the Court of

[27] [1985] 1 All ER 724; on appeal [1986] 1 All ER 617.

Appeal said that it was necessary to consider all the circumstances of the case including the following:

1. the nature of the employment – employment in a capacity where 'confidential' material is habitually handled may impose a higher obligation of confidentiality;
2. the nature of the information itself – information will only be protected if it can properly be classed as a trade secret or information of a highly confidential nature requiring it to be given the same level of protection as a trade secret;
3. whether the employer impressed on the employee the confidentiality of the information; and
4. whether the relevant information can easily be isolated from other information which the employee is free to use or disclose.

Employers who take steps to warn their employees about the secrecy of the information to which they will be given access are more likely to gain the court's sympathy in efforts to protect that information.[28]

The second purpose behind a policy is to support and add detail onto the basic contractual provisions in the contract of employment. If a policy document itself, however, is not a contractual document, what then is its status? To some extent this will depend on the steps taken by the employer to incorporate its terms, such as by reference to it in an employee's written contractual terms themselves. A prudent employer will do so, although it is clear that where a contract of employment expressly incorporates an instrument such as a staff handbook, it does not necessarily follow that all the provisions in that document are apt to the terms of the contract. Some provisions, read in context, may be declarations of an aspiration or a policy falling short of a contractual undertaking. This means, of course, that an employee manual containing important provisions on the security of the employer's confidential information, but which are provided as part of a 'policy' does not preclude their having contractual effect, if by their nature and language, they are apt to the contractual terms.[29]

---

[28] *Amber Size and Chemical Co Ltd v Menzel* [1913] 2 Ch 239; *Reid and Sigrist v Moss and Mechanism Limited* [1932] 49 RPC 461; *Ansell Rubber Co Pty Ltd v Allied Rubber Industries Pty Ltd* [1967] VR 37; *New Zealand Manufacturing Ltd v Taylor* [1975] 2 NZLR 33.

[29] *Keeley v Fosroc International Ltd* [2006] EWCA Civ 1277; [2006] IRLR 961, [31].

In practical terms, therefore, a policy which prohibited employees from removing particularly sensitive documents from the workplace, which required laptops to be passworded and encrypted or which prohibited access to downloading to a personal computer of certain types of information like a customer database for example, would be regarded as 'apt' to the contractual terms in the context of a business where the confidentiality of information was particularly important.

3.3 A Policy Approach to the Departing Employee

Nowhere is a policy more important than with the departing employee. It is assumed that most employers, or at least those with employees having access to commercially valuable confidential information such as customer databases, details of new product developments and the like, will be subject to standard restrictive covenants and 'garden leave' provisions.

The restrictive covenant[30] is a well-established device which recognises the need to insulate employers, at least for a short period, from the inevitability that employees will disclose to a new employer or use confidential information. All such covenants are considered restrictive of trade and therefore void in the absence of special circumstances justifying their existence. One such justification is the protection of the employer's trade secrets.[31] The reality of the employer seeking to rely on a covenant was well expressed by Lord Denning MR in *Littlewoods Organisation Ltd v Harris*:[32]

> It is thus established that an employer can stipulate for protection against having his confidential information passed on to a rival in trade. But experience has shown that it is not satisfactory to have simply a covenant against disclosing confidential information ... it is very difficult to prove a breach when the information is of such a character that a servant can carry it away in his head. The difficulties are such that the only practicable solution is to take a covenant from the servant by which he is not to go to work for a rival in trade. Such a covenant may be held to be reasonable if limited to a short period.

By contrast, the 'garden leave' device has a shorter history but is now a well-established feature of English employment law and a valuable tool

---

30 Goulding (2010), ch 5. The legal position in England is conveniently summarised in *Brake Brothers Ltd v Ungless* [2004] EWHC 2799 (QB), [15]–[16] (Gloster J).

31 *Mason v Provident Clothing Ltd* [1913] AC 724.

32 [1978] 1 All ER 1026 (CA), 1033.

in the employer's armoury.[33] It enables the employer to remove the employee from the workplace and hence the source of information and place him at home with full benefits for the period of notice.

The main function of a trade secrets policy at this stage in the employment relationship is essentially to reinforce the message that the policy should have delivered at its earlier stages – that the employer treats its trade secrets and confidential information as commercially valuable assets of the business and not as a fund of information which the departing employee can treat as his own.

The policy should prescribe an exit interview (which should be carefully recorded) at which the employee should be reminded of his obligations and asked to provide his new employer with a copy of his employment agreement and/or confidentiality agreement. There is nothing to prevent the old employer from writing separately to the new employer (assuming its identity is known) asking for an undertaking that the new employer will not induce or encourage the employee to divulge details of his employer's business. Even if (as will often be the case) the new employer refuses to give the undertaking, the fact that it has been alerted in this way may be enough to give the old employer a level of comfort and protection.

The departing employee should be asked to return any company property – laptops, documents, access keys and the like – and be asked to sign an undertaking that he has read and understood his obligations to the old employer. The purpose of this activity is to establish the employer's position and to lay a paper trail which can be disclosed to the court at a later date if any legal action ensues. As Mark Halligan puts it:

> From the company's point of view the trade secret exit interview protects the company from a later assertion of 'I didn't understand my obligations' or 'I didn't know this was a trade secret'. The ... exit interview ... constitutes contemporaneous evidence that the employee was placed on notice of his trade secret obligations upon departure.[34]

With senior employees or those entrusted with access to particularly sensitive trade secrets an employer might want to adopt a more aggressive form of policy and undertake, during the notice period (assuming there is sound evidence of wrongdoing) a forensic investigation into the employee's recent activities. This may take the form of an analysis of the

---

33 *Evening Standard Ltd v Henderson* [1987] ICR 588; Goulding (2010), ch 4.

34 Halligan and Weyand (2006), 88.

employee's e-mail usage or his access to electronic documentation and databases.[35]

4. CONCLUSION

A business which regards its trade secrets as valuable corporate assets[36] should have a strategy to protect these assets. The strategy will have a number of components. A well-drafted employment contract containing (depending on the seniority of the employee) a clear obligation of confidentiality, restrictive covenants and a 'garden leave' provision is one component. A policy, such as the one outlined above, designed to inform and educate is another. But a strategy like this is unlikely to succeed if it is imposed without the employees themselves accepting the logic and necessity of the strategy and its approach. Trust and confidence, the elements which underlie the employment relationship, are reciprocal issues. As Mark Halligan puts it:

> There is no silver bullet for proprietary information protection, no hardware widget or software program or canned process that can provide proprietary information protection in the absence of employee involvement. A corporate trade secret culture requires both top down communication of goals and bottom up communication of needs to be effective.[37]

REFERENCES

Aplin, T., L. Bentley, L. Johnson and S. Malynicz (2012), *Gurry on Breach of Confidence*, 2nd edn, Oxford University Press.

Bok, S. (1984), *Secrets: On the Ethics of Concealment and Revelation*, Oxford University Press

Dobrusin, E.M. and R.A. Krasnow (2008), *Intellectual Property Culture*, Oxford University Press

Goulding, P. (ed.) (2010), *Employee Competition*, 2nd edn, Oxford University Press

Halligan R.M. (2007), 'Capturing the Value of Trade Secrets' in R. Shearer (ed.), *Business Power: Creating New Wealth from IP Assets*, Wiley

---

[35] Data privacy laws and related statutory obligations (particularly the Regulation of Investigatory Powers Act 2000) need careful observation. The UK Information Commissioner considers that covert monitoring will rarely be justified and should be used in exceptional circumstances only – The Employment Practices Code, [3.4.1].

[36] Halligan (2007), ch 7.

[37] Halligan and Weyand (2006), 103.

Halligan, R.M. and R.F. Weyand (2006), *Trade Secret Asset Management: An Executive's Guide to Information Asset Management, Including Sarbanes-Oxley Accounting Requirements for Trade Secrets*, Aspatore Books
Row E. (2005), 'When Trade Secrets Become Shackles: Fairness and the Inevitable Disclosure Doctrine', 7 *Tulane Journal of Technology and Intellectual Property* 167
Unkovic D. (1985), *The Trade Secrets Handbook: Strategies and Techniques for Safeguarding Corporate Information*, Prentice Hall

21. Devices to restrain competition and protect discoveries and enforcement: confidentiality in the courts and Europe

Alison Firth

1. INTRODUCTION

John Hull's chapter in this volume 'Devices to Restrain Competition and Protect Discoveries and Enforcement: Workplace Policies and Confidentiality Agreements' (Chapter 20) discusses the problem of misappropriation of trade secrets by employees and the precautionary measures which may be taken before, during and after employment. However, policies and contractual provisions can never ensure that workplace secrets are fully secure and that departing employees (and new employers) are properly apprised as to what information can and cannot be used. Indeed, it may not be cost-effective to do so.[1] There comes a point where litigation is necessary to resolve conflicting interests, although workplace policies continue to be important evidentially.

This chapter firstly questions whether available court statistics from England and Wales are consistent with the suggestion that employee confidentiality cases are on the increase, then briefly examines the remedial landscape in the UK and Europe in the light of international obligations. The European Union (EU) as well as its Member States are WTO members and hence bound by the WTO agreement on Trade Related Aspects of Intellectual Property Rights (TRIPS).[2] However, the extent to which the EU's Directive on the enforcement of intellectual

[1] Bone (2011), 65–67.

[2] EU, 1 January 1995: <http://www.wto.org/english/thewto_e/whatis_e/tif_e/org6_e.htm>.

property[3] applies to trade secrets is unclear. Arguably Europe should take its cue from Art 1(2) TRIPS, which characterizes the subject-matter of all sections of Part II as 'intellectual property', including Section 7 on undisclosed information, and from Art 41 which requires the enforcement procedures specified in Part III to be available for 'any act of infringement of intellectual property rights covered by this Agreement'.

The European Commission's Communication 'A Single Market for Intellectual Property Rights: Boosting creativity and innovation to provide economic growth, high quality jobs and first class products and services in Europe'[4] recognizes that trade secrets are valuable intangible assets,[5] but also that their protection may hamper innovation by competitors.[6] It asserts that 'legal regimes in the Member States and the level of protection granted throughout the EU differ considerably' and proposes a study of the situation 'before taking a position on a possible way forward'.[7] If this means harmonization, Marie-Christine Janssens has argued in her chapter in this volume that harmonization (of employee patent rules) is advantageous in furthering innovation in the knowledge economy, cross-border collaboration, legal certainty and equal treatment of employees. These arguments are equally applicable to workplace secrets but the sheer variety of modes of protection in Europe means that harmonization would be an uphill task.[8] This chapter will survey some of the issues, including whether contract can enhance other protection, sampling laws of EU member states.

---

[3] Directive 2004/48/EC on the enforcement of intellectual property rights in the Member States, published in corrected form at [2004] OJ L195/16; in *Vestergaard v Bestnet* [2011] EWCA Civ 424 Jacob LJ, [56] 'it is accepted that a claim for misuse of technical trade secrets such as the present is a claim to enforce an intellectual property right'.

[4] COM(2011) 287 final, 3.4 (Communication).

[5] Cites evidence that attacks on trade secrets from the outside and the inside are increasing, nn 33–4.

[6] Ghidini (2006).

[7] A study is being commissioned with a view to reporting by end 2012: point 13 of Annex to the Communication. A call for tender was issued on 19 September 2011: <http://ec.europa.eu/dgs/internal_market/calls_en.htm>.

[8] The Communication cites the prohibition of unfair competition, tort law, contract law, labour law and criminal law. There seems a reluctance to recognize the action for breach of confidence as a distinct species: it is stated that the UK and Ireland, Cyprus and Malta do not have 'specific provisions of civil law on trade secrets'. This is true if it means legislative provisions, less so if it means civil causes of action.

In the absence of harmonization, rules of private international law identifying forum and applicable law serve to reduce process costs and the rules available in the EU will be briefly outlined at the end of the chapter.

2. COURT STATISTICS – IS LITIGATION ON CONFIDENTIAL INFORMATION ON THE INCREASE?

Unfortunately public domain information is limited, but court statistics available for the High Court of England and Wales[9] appear to be consistent with the observations cited by Hull in his chapter in this volume. Within the High Court, technical trade secret litigation is allocated to the Chancery Division,[10] but cases involving employee restrictive covenants and breach of confidence may also be brought in the Queen's Bench Division,[11] which has general contract and tort jurisdiction, and in the Commercial Court.[12] Numbers of reported decisions suggest that the Chancery Division hears a significant share of employee cases. Statistics from the Queen's Bench Division do not show detail of the cause of action or remedies claimed,[13] but figures for the Chancery

[9] Ministry of Justice *Judicial and Court Statistics 2009* revised October 2010, <http://www.justice.gov.uk/downloads/statistics/mojstats/jcs-stats-2009–211010.pdf>; Ministry of Justice *Judicial and Court Statistics 2010* (Revised July 2011), <http://www.justice.gov.uk/downloads/statistics/courts-and-sentencing/judicial-court-stats.pdf>. The High Court of Northern Ireland has Chancery and Queens Bench Divisions. In Scotland civil claims may be brought in Sheriff Courts and the Court of Session <http://www.scotcourts.gov.uk/session/index.asp>.

[10] Civil Procedure Rules (CPR) Part 63, r 63.13 read in conjunction with para 16.1 of Practice Direction 63. Part 63 claims (but not pure breach of confidence claims) may also be brought in the Patents County Court and certain provincial county courts (local civil courts). <http://www.justice.gov.uk/downloads/guidance/courts-and-tribunals/courts/patents-court/patents-court-guide.pdf>.

[11] E.g., *Hydra Plc v Anatasi* [2005] EWHC 1559 (QB), Royce J: 'In this case men who have for some time worked in harmony now feel great bitterness. The litigation process has not helped. Feelings on both sides run high.'

[12] E.g., *Sectrack NV v Satamatics Limited, Jan Leemans* [2007] EWHC 3003 (Comm); the Commercial Court sits within the Queen's Bench Division.

[13] Thanks are due to the Queen's Bench staff who assisted the author in April 2011 by explaining the forms of search that are, and are not, currently available.

Division[14] show a dramatic increase in 2009 in the number of cases brought in relation to confidential information. This may be partly due to a fashion for celebrity figures to seek privacy injunctions against publication of their misdeeds. However, a committee headed by Lord Neuberger concluded that so-called 'super-injunctions', prohibiting publication even of the existence of the order, were being granted very sparingly.[15] The extent to which privacy[16] can be reconciled with the public interest in open justice[17] and with freedom of expression[18] has taxed the courts.[19]

The Chancery Division also hears claims relating to databases – these would be included in 'copyright and design right' which shows a steady increase. The importance of databases of technical information was highlighted in *Vestergaard Frandsen S/A (MVF3 APS) v Bestnet Europe Ltd.*[20]

Figure 21.1 illustrates the trends. A change in statistical methodology prevents figures from 2010 being compared directly with earlier figures.[21]

---

14 Above n 9, ch 5.

15 Report of the Committee on Super Injunctions: Super Injunctions, Anonymised Injunctions and Open Justice (Chairman, Lord Neuberger 2011) <http://www.judiciary.gov.uk/media/media-releases/2011/committee-reports-findings-super-injunctions-20052011>. Practice Guidance (HC: Interim Non-Disclosure Orders) High Court, 1 August 2011 [2012] EMLR 5 was subsequently issued.

16 Protected by Art 8 of the European Convention on Human Rights (ECHR), implemented in the UK by way of the Human Rights Act 1998, given effect through the action for breach of confidence.

17 Art 6 ECHR.

18 Art 10 ECHR.

19 E.g., *JIH v News Group Newspapers Ltd* [2011] EWCA Civ 42; [2010] EWHC 2818 (QB); judges at both levels were concerned by the possibility of 'jigsaw identification' whereby the identity of the claimant could be ascertained by piecing together individually unobjectionable publications.

20 [2011] EWCA Civ 424. The defendants moved their business from Denmark (where the employees' obligations arose) to England. Also, *Exchange Communications Ltd v Masheder* [2009] CSOH 135.

21 Ministry of Justice *Judicial and Court Statistics 2010* (Revised July 2011), 124, note.

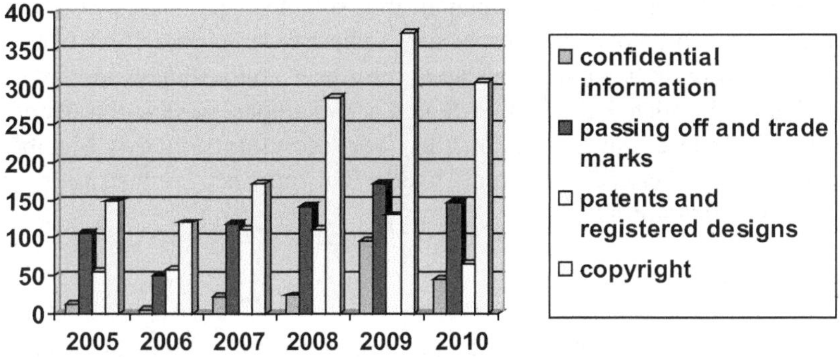

Source: From Ministry of Justice statistics, 2009, 2010, n 9 above.

Figure 21.1 Chancery division claims issued in London, by nature

3. REMEDIES

In cases involving the protection of workplace secrets, injunctions, especially interim injunctions, and interim remedies for the disclosure and preservation of evidence are probably the most important remedies, although pecuniary remedies may also be significant.[22] The interim injunction or interdict is available in all UK courts with jurisdiction over confidential information. Article 9(1)(a) and (b) of Directive 2004/48/EC on the enforcement of intellectual property rights provides for interim injunctions, supported by seizure or delivery up of infringing items.

3.1 Obtaining and Preserving Evidence

The importance of the Anton Piller or 'search and seize' order[23] in gaining evidence of misappropriation of confidential material has been

[22] Damages – *Seager v Copydex Ltd (No 1)* [1967] 1 WLR 923; *(No 2)* [1969] RPC 250 – as well as account of defendant's profits. Article 13(1)(a) of Directive 2004/48/EC includes infringers' profits as a factor in the damages enquiry. This has been transposed verbatim into Reg 3(2) of The Intellectual Property (Enforcement, etc.) Regulations 2006 SI 2006/1028, but as yet 'unjust profits' do not seem to have been used in the UK as a basis for damages – unsurprisingly, since the account of profits is more potent a remedy. In *Force India Formula One Team Ltd v 1 Malaysia Racing Team Sdn Bhd* [2012] EWHC 616 (Ch), [374]–[427], Arnold J undertakes a comprehensive review of the authorities on damages for breach of confidence.

[23] *Anton Piller KG v Manufacturing Processes Ltd* [1976] FSR 129; CPR Part 25.

highlighted by Hull in his chapter in this volume.[24] By the 1990s these orders came to be overused, especially against ex-employees; this excess was curbed by judicial and legislative reforms.[25] Anton-Piller type orders are known in other EU Member States, for example 'saisie-contrafaçon' orders in France, but their availability was not uniform across Member States or as between different intellectual property rights prior to Directive 2004/48/EC.[26]

3.2 Disclosure Orders

Evidence may also be obtained by party or non-party[27] disclosure orders. In *Sectrack NV v Satamatics Limited*,[28] information from a 'Blackberry' mobile telephone returned by an ex-employee showed misuse of information. On the basis of this evidence, the claimant applied (without notice to the defendants) for an injunction and orders for the preservation, disclosure and delivery of other documents and records. Article 6(1) of Directive 2004/48/EC allows for an intellectual property litigant to call for evidence from the other party, such as samples, and Art 6(2) in certain circumstances extends this to financial and commercial documents. Article 8 provides a right of information against parties and non-parties. The Commission's Analysis of implementation suggests that the application and interpretation of these articles has been limited in some Member States.

3.3 Does the EU Enforcement Directive Apply to Workplace Secrets? Should it?

This depends upon whether confidential information from the workplace is 'intellectual property' within the meaning of the Enforcement Directive. As outlined below, in UK jurisdictions and other Member States, confidential information is not regarded as proprietary; many Member States protect trade secrets under unfair competition laws, as envisaged

---

24 Citing *First Conference v Bracchi* [2009] EWHC 2176 (Ch).

25 *Universal Thermosensors Ltd v Hibben* [1992] 1 WLR 840; [1992] 3 All ER 257; [1992] FSR 361. Powers and safeguards are now enshrined in the Civil Procedure Act 1997, s 7; CPR Part 25 and Practice Direction 25A, [7].

26 Analysis of the application of Directive 2004/48/EC on the enforcement of intellectual property rights in the Member States (SEC(2010) (Analysis), [2.3.1].

27 *Norwich Pharmacal Co v Commissioners of Customs & Excise* [1974] AC 133.

28 [2007] EWHC 3003 (Comm).

by TRIPS Art 39 (Part II Section 7). The directive does not define 'intellectual property' but a Statement by the European Commission in 2005 listed a number of exemplary forms, not including confidential information or trade secrets.[29] The Commission admits that there is lack of clarity as to whether the directive covers trade secrets, and comments that it could be useful to 'assess this negative phenomenon'.[30] Is it likely that the Enforcement Directive will be amended to clarify that it applies to trade secret cases? The Synthesis[31] reports that a majority of stakeholders favoured clarification or extension to cover trade secrets, but notes that these were 'mostly rightholders' and five Member States. By contrast, a greater number of Member States, along with academics and others, were against extension 'considering that such an extension was not warranted and that the 'nature' of acts of unfair competition was different from IPR infringements'. The tenor of this suggests that no change will be made.

TRIPS defines undisclosed information as 'intellectual property' for the purposes of the Agreement. It has been argued from TRIPS (above) that the EU and its Member States should make the remedies of Directive 2004/48/EC available to protect workplace secrets as 'intellectual property'; failure clearly to do so may contravene TRIPS obligations of the EU and its Member States. However, it is not argued that TRIPS requires the protection for undisclosed information to be *proprietary* as such. Dessemontet argues that Art 39(2) gives a 'strong hint that the property right theory – leading to the notion of misappropriation – has been generally accepted, when the text mentions the information which is "legitimately under the control" of plaintiffs'.[32] It is submitted that the wording of Art 39(2) is carefully neutral. Article 39 TRIPS places protection firmly within the sphere of unfair competition, consistent with the position in many EU Member States.[33] Lemley has argued that regarding trade secrets as 'intellectual property' (not necessarily having

---

[29] Statement by the Commission concerning Article 2 of Directive 2004/48/EC of the European Parliament and of the Council on the enforcement of intellectual property rights (2005/295/EC) [2005] OJ L94/37.

[30] Synthesis of the Comments on the Commission Report on the Application of Directive 2004/48/EC of the European Parliament and of the Council of 29 April 2004 on the Enforcement of Intellectual Property Rights (Synthesis) COM(2010) 779 final, [3.2].

[31] Ibid, [2.2].

[32] Dessemontet (1998).

[33] Hull (2009); Bruun (2001), [1029]; Bouche (2011): in France, contracts for the communication of know-how are regarded as contracts for services. Ghidini (2006), 112–113.

the character of traditional property) is beneficial not only in terms of remedies, but paradoxically in terms of limiting adverse effects on innovation and competition.[34] Ghidini and Falce have bewailed Italy's recent bestowal of full intellectual property status on trade secrets.[35]

English law appears to be in harmony with that of many other European Member States in resisting a proprietary analysis for confidential information.[36] Scots law on breach of confidence is broadly similar to English law, although Scottish courts do not have equitable jurisdiction.[37] What, then, is the basis for protection in Europe?

4. BASES FOR PROTECTION OF WORKPLACE SECRETS IN EUROPE AND A NOTE ON TERMINOLOGY

Texts at the European level may suggest that, in Lemley's words, there is 'widespread agreement on the basic contours of [trade secret] law'.[38] The 'Technology Transfer Block Exemption', Regulation (EC) No 772/2004, which shields patent and know-how licences from the full force of EU competition law, defines 'know-how' as

> a package of non-patented practical information, resulting from experience and testing, which is:
>
> (i) secret, that is to say, not generally known or easily accessible,
> (ii) substantial, that is to say, significant and useful for the production of the contract products [subject of the licensing agreement], and
> (iii) identified, that is to say, described in a sufficiently comprehensive manner so as to make it possible to verify that it fulfils the criteria of secrecy and substantiality …

'Secret-Substantial-Identified' looks reassuringly like the tests for confidential information under UK law,[39] but the phrase 'mere know-how' has been used historically to denote the skill and knowledge which an ex-employee may take and use, as opposed to trade secrets of the

---

34 Lemley (2011).

35 Ghidini and Falce (2010).

36 *Kitechnology BV v Unicor GmbH Plastmaschinen* [1995] FSR 765 (CA).

37 MacQueen et al (2010), 816–817; SLC Report No 90 (1984); Coleman (1992).

38 Lemley (2011), 107.

39 *Coco v AN Clark (Engineers) Ltd* [1969] RPC 41; *Ocular Sciences Ltd v Aspect Vision Care Ltd (No 2)* [1996] EWHC Patents 1; [1997] RPC 289.

ex-employer.[40] In the UK, trade secrets are therefore a subset of confidential information, along with private information and government secrets, whereas 'know-how' may in some contexts refer to unprotected information.

The European Commission's Communication 'A Single Market for Intellectual Property Rights: Boosting creativity and innovation to provide economic growth, high quality jobs and first class products and services in Europe'[41] defines trade secrets[42] in these terms:

> Trade secrets refer to know-how that has not or not yet been registered as industrial property rights but that is actually or potentially valuable to its owner and not generally known or readily ascertainable by the public, and which the owner has made a reasonable effort to keep secret.

Thus, on this definition, trade secrets are a subset of protectable 'know-how'. However, it is clear from EU procedural rules that at the administrative level, a wider range of 'business secrets' is recognized as deserving of confidentiality.[43]

Bouche notes that in France trade secrets and confidential information are regarded as subsets of 'savoir-faire'[44] or know-how, connoting 'an ensemble of technical info, transmissible, not immediately available to the public; an immaterial asset' which does not include mere personal aptitudes or competence.[45]

De Vrey's comparative study including Dutch, English and German law, suggests that 'trade secrets' and 'know-how' may be used synonymously in the Netherlands to denote 'secret information, applicable in practice (and of general value) and not known to third parties'.[46]

In Finnish law the term translated into English as 'trade secret' seems to be the wider one: 'a business or professional secret of some corresponding info concerning a certain trade or business which the trader

---

40 Hull (this volume Ch 20, n 20), citing *Printers and Finishers Ltd v Holloway* [1965] RPC 239; c.f. unprotectable 'experience, knowledge, memory and skill, which he gained while employed': *Van Products Co v General Welding and Fabrication* Co 419 Pa 248; 213 A2d 769, 776 (1965) (US).

41 Communication (2011) 287 final, 3.4.

42 Ibid, 3.4.1, n 32.

43 E.g., Commission Notice on the rules for access to the Commission file in cases pursuant to Articles 81 and 82 of the EC Treaty, Articles 53, 54 and 57 of the EEA Agreement and Council Regulation (EC) No 139/2004, [18].

44 Bouche (2011), [1027].

45 Bouche (2011), [2017]–[2019] and citations.

46 de Vrey (2008), 142.

keeps confidential and the disclosure of which could cause economic damage either to his trade or to another trader who disclosed the info to him.'[47]

Inconsistent terminology suggests that harmony is lacking, but substance is more important than the labels. There is considerable divergence: the variety of modes of protection is illustrated in Table 21.1, which is exemplary, rather than comprehensive.[48]

5. CONTRACTUAL MEANS FOR PROTECTION OF WORKPLACE SECRETS – CAN THEY PROVIDE MORE EXTENSIVE PROTECTION?

5.1 Express Restraint Clauses

These are seen as a practical mechanism for protecting the ex-employer against misuse of information and unfair competition generally from ex-employees and/or their new employers.[49] English law in this area can be traced particularly to *Nordenfelt v Nordenfelt*,[50] involving a covenant on the sale of a business. To escape invalidity for restraint of trade, restrictions must be necessary to protect a legitimate interest of the person wishing to enforce the covenant, reasonable as between the parties and reasonable in the public interest, 'so framed and so guarded as to afford adequate protection to the party in whose favour it is imposed, while at the same time it is in no way injurious to the public'.[51] Similar principles are applied in the case of employee covenants, except that the public interest in mobility of employment will temper very much what is considered as reasonable between the parties.[52] This is usually assessed in terms of scope of the restriction (limited to competing activity), reasonableness of geographical scope and reasonableness of duration.

Is this still a good legal methodology in the Internet age? As regards scope of activity, the enquiry as to e-commerce is probably the same as for offline business. However, relevant time periods may be shorter; there may be need for greater immediacy in enforcing a restriction, but rapidly changing patterns of trade may suggest a shorter period of restraint. In

47 Bruun (2001), [607] ff, citing ch 30, s11 of Finland's Penal Code.
48 Cook (2010), Ch 9.
49 E.g., *Thermascan v Norman* [2009] EWHC 3694 (Ch).
50 *Nordenfelt v Maxim Nordenfelt Guns & Ammunition Co* [1894] AC 535.
51 Ibid, 565.
52 Fisk, Chapter 13 this volume.

Table 21.1 Protection of trade secrets in selected European countries

Basis jurisdiction	Specific civil legislation/cause of action	General duty of fidelity on employee	Unfair competition	Criminal law
UK	Breach of confidence	Yes, during employment	No	Possibly s4 Fraud Act 2006[a]; Law Commission's recommendation of trade secret offences not enacted to date[b]
France[c]	No; Art L621–1 of IP code protects 'manufacturing secrets' by reference to criminal penalties under Art L152–7 of the Labour Code	Yes	Yes, under damage clauses of Civil Code, e.g., industrial espionage, enticement of competitor's employees, exploitation of info communicated during failed pre-contractual negotiations	Art L152–7 of Labour code – 'revealing or attempting to reveal a manufacturing secret' by director or employee. 'Usurpation of know-how' with intention to harm employer; breach of faith; theft if documents stolen; violation of computer software (Art 323, New Penal code)[d]
Netherlands[e]	No	Yes, but difficult to distinguish trade secrets and professional knowledge of employee	Yes	Offence by employee under ss 272–3 of Criminal code; does not criminalise use by third parties.
Germany[f]	ss 17–19 UWG – comprehensive	Yes		Offence for employee to disclose during employment, not after employment
Finland[g]	Yes		Unfair Trade Practices Acts 1978 s 4	Penal code ch 30, ss 4, 5, 11

Notes: [a] Allgrove and Sellers (2009).
[b] Hull (1998), commenting on Law Commission (1997) and (1981).
[c] Bouche, paras [1026]–[1029].
[d] See, also Kadir (2010).
[e] de Vrey (2006).
[f] de Vrey (2006); Klett, Sonntag and Wilske (2008); Hilty and Henning-Bodewig (2007).
[g] Bruun (2001), ch 9.

Associated Foreign Exchange Ltd v International Foreign Exchange (UK) Ltd[53] the court took into account the speed of change of the business in question in refusing to grant an injunction after a two-month period of garden leave. As for geographical scope, the ease of transmission of information on the Internet and the facilitation of commerce, including cross-border commerce, may suggest that the geographical scope of restraints may need to be wider adequately to protect the claimant's business. Care must also be taken in crafting covenants in the case of non-employee working relationships.[54] For example, in *Swift Technology v Mulcahy*,[55] a non-executive directorship was expressed as a contract for services, not of service. The director was not bound by a covenant referring to period of 'employment'.

5.2 Implied Obligations

Where express contractual arrangements are not in place, courts have enjoined misuse of confidential information by reference to equitable obligations of confidence (together with the notion that a defendant should know that information was confidential), or implied contractual terms. Thus, design information conveyed by the plaintiff in *Coco*,[56] for the purpose of negotiating a hoped-for agreement, was protected; the 'moonlight' employers in *Hivac v Park Royal*[57] were prevented from using information confidential to the main employers; in *ETH Technologies v Rytium*[58] an interim interdict (injunction) was granted to restrain use by an ex-employee of methods for preserving prawns. Cases have shown a set of distinctions in relation to non-express obligations which may or may not remain satisfactory.

---

53 [2010] EWHC 1178 (Ch); [2010] IRLR 964.

54 Freedland and Prassl, Chapter 9 this volume.

55 [2009] EWHC 1485 (QB).

56 *Coco v AN Clark (Engineers) Ltd* [1969] RPC 41.

57 *Hivac Ltd v Park Royal Scientific Instruments Ltd* [1946] Ch 169 (CA).

58 *ETH Technologies v Rytium Technology FZC* [2010] CSOH 143 (Scots Court of Session, Outer House). The action for breach of confidence in Scotland is recognized as closely resembling that in England and Wales: *Lord Advocate v Scotsman Publications* [1990] 1 AC 812; Scottish Law Commission 'Breach of Confidence' (1984) Cmnd 9385 (SCOT LAW COM No 90).

5.3 Categorizing Information

In *Faccenda Chicken*,[59] Goulding J distinguished between three classes of information – unprotectable information which the employee was entitled to take away and use; 'trade secrets' proper, in relation to which the ex-employee owed continuing obligations of confidence; and an intermediate category of information which could be protected by express covenants. This last, pragmatic category was doubted by the Court of Appeal – with good reason – to be valid; a covenant in restraint of trade must reasonably protect a legitimate interest. If the information is not sufficiently confidential to be protected in its own right, how can it be the subject of a valid restraint? However, courts seem subsequently to have recognized that a short-term restrictive covenant may be appropriate to protect information for a limited period and achieve an appropriate balance between the public interest in employee mobility and that in maintaining confidences: *Balston Ltd v Headline Filters Ltd*;[60] *Lancashire Fires Ltd v S.A. Lyons & Co Ltd*.[61] Bently, speaking at the Intellectual Property Institute,[62] suggested that the conundrum may be resolved by taking into account a wider range of factors. Arnold J in *Vestergaard*[63] did consider a number of factors relating to the nature of the information for which protection was sought and relating to the workplace and its ethos:

1. Factors relating to information
   - (a) Nature of the information [654]
   - (b) Separability from general knowledge/skill [657]
   - (c) Commercial value [658]
2. Factors relating to workplace/ethos
   - (a) Nature of work [653]
   - (b) Attitude of employer at the time [655]
   - (c) Steps taken to keep confidential [656]
   - (d) Usage/practices of the trade [659]

---

[59] *Faccenda Chicken Ltd v Fowler* [1987] Ch 117 (CA); judicial citations include Hong Kong, *PCCW-HKT Telephone Ltd v Aitken* [2009] HKCFA 11 (CFA HK) and Ireland, *Visusoft Ltd v Harris* [2009] IEHC 543.

[60] [1990] FSR 385 (Ch).

[61] [1996] FSR 629.

[62] Lionel Bently: <http://www.docstoc.com/docs/47071321/Chicken-Nuggets-Re-reading-Faccenda-Chicken>.

[63] [2011] EWCA Civ 424; figures in square brackets refer to paragraphs of the judgment.

5.4 Duties During and After Employment

Secondly, *Faccenda Chicken* highlighted the distinction between the duty of fidelity owed by employees during employment and the less extensive duty of confidence owed after employment has ended, which is reflected in the examples from other EU Member States given above. Flannigan[64] has argued that this is an erroneous distinction, based upon faulty precedential foundation. Indeed, he posits that the historical separation of breach of confidence into a doctrinal category distinct from fiduciary duty was mistaken and asserts that calibration of the duty of confidence against seniority within an employer's hierarchy was incorrect.

Consistently with these positions, Flannigan also argues against the distinction which may be made between the obligations of an employee and those of an independent contractor.[65] Abolishing this last distinction would certainly lead to convenient uniformity across in-house and outsourced work and in collaborative projects across institutions, such as university/government/industry research projects. However, the current position is probably that in non-employee relationships, the duty of confidence remains constant, whereas with employees there is a step down from the duty of fidelity to a duty of confidence afterwards. The attitude of the courts towards inequalities of bargaining power[66] and mobility of labour may mean that confidential information is in practice less well protected in the hands of ex-employees than in the hands of independent contractors.

5.5 Removal of Information in Physical Form

The final distinction lies between cases in which the departing employee takes away or emails some record of the employer's information, such as the customer list in *Robb v Green*,[67] and cases such as *Faccenda Chicken*, where knowledge of delivery routes and customers is carried in the departing employee's head. This distinction is evidentially convenient,

[64] Flannigan (2008). This approach has been rejected in the English courts: *University of Nottingham v Fishel* [2000] ICR 1462, 22; *Helmet Integrated Systems Ltd v Tunnard* [2007] FSR 16, [36]–[37]; and *Customer Systems plc v Ranson* [2011] EWHC 3304 (QB), [68], citing Millett, P, 'Equity's Place in the Law of Commerce' (1998) 114 *LQR* 214, 217.

[65] Cf *Swift v Mulcahy* [2009] EWHC 1485 (QB).

[66] Finn, Chapter 2 this volume.

[67] *Robb v Green* [1895] 2 QB 315 (CA), stolen invoices in *JN Dairies Ltd v Johal Dairies Ltd* [2009] EWHC 1331 (Ch); [2010] EWCA Civ 348.

but does it remain sound when industries have become much more insistent and reliant upon recorded information – databases, paper trails – than in *Robb v Green* days of horse-drawn milk rounds? Technology has rendered it easier for employees to make away with records,[68] but much of this information might formerly have been lost to the ex-employer as well as gained by a new employer, because a greater proportion of an enterprise's know-how was carried in workers' heads and passed on verbally to junior or incoming colleagues. Removals of information from the workplace may involve unlawful means conspiracy.[69]

Table 21.1 suggests that other European jurisdictions likewise distinguish between obligations during and after employment.

6. CROSS-BORDER CONTRACTUAL AND NON-CONTRACTUAL ISSUES: PRIVATE INTERNATIONAL LAW

Projects like the Lando Commission's Principles of European Contract Law (PECL)[70] have sought to identify common principles in contractual obligations across the laws of European Union Member states. The parties in *Vestergaard* made a breathtakingly practical contribution to commonality. 'It was agreed that although the contract [of employment] was governed by Danish law, it could and should be treated as governed by English law. That includes the law as to implication of terms.'[71] However, not all litigants are as pragmatic and conflict of law rules may be needed.

---

[68] *First Conferences v Bracchi* [2009] EWHC 2176, [26]. In the US *Phonedog* case, noted at <http://www.bbc.co.uk/news/technology-16338040>, ex-employee Noah Kravitz had built up a strong 'following' on his '@Phonedog_Noah' Twitter account. Having changed the account name when he left to join a competitor, he was sued by Phonedog for misuse of the following.

[69] E.g., *Tullett Prebon* [2010] EWHC 484 (QB), appeal dismissed [2010] EWHC 484 (QB); *Berryland Books Ltd v BK Books Ltd* [2009] EWHC 1877 (Ch); [2010] EWCA Civ 1440.

[70] Range of projects: <http://ec.europa.eu/internal_market/contractlaw/links_en.htm>.

[71] *Vestergaard Frandsen S/A (MVF3 APS) v Bestnet Europe Ltd* [2011] EWCA Civ 424, [43].

6.1 Contractual Claims

There is a highly developed private international law regime in Europe, in which the protection of secrets sits rather uneasily.[72] The 'Brussels' Regulation[73] on civil jurisdiction and judgments identifies the courts of the defendant's state of domicile as having general, EU-wide jurisdiction. This forum would be the least oppressive for a defendant[74] and give the claimant the possibility of obtaining an EU-wide injunction. Jurisdiction in contractual disputes generally (including non-employed workers) may also be taken under Art 5(1), which points to the 'characteristic place of performance' of the contract and entitles the court to provide relief only for that state. This place could be difficult to identify in relation to secrecy obligations in the digital age, and is difficult to define for negative obligations generally.[75] In matters relating to individual contracts of employment, Ch II, section 5 of the Brussels Regulation determines jurisdiction: Art 20(1) provides that the employer may bring proceedings only in the courts of the Member State in which the employee is domiciled.[76]

Applicable law in claims under contracts concluded from 17 December 2009 is governed by the 'Rome I' Regulation,[77] which replaced the Rome Convention on applicable law within the EU,[78] apart from Denmark.[79] Article 3 establishes freedom of the parties to choose applicable law; Art 8 protects employees, whose individual contract of employment cannot deprive them of mandatory protections available under the default law. To the extent that the parties have not made a choice, the law of the country

[72] For a full account: Fawcett and Torremans (2011).

[73] Reg 44/2001 on jurisdiction and the recognition and enforcement of judgments in civil and commercial matters. In 2009 the European Commission issued a Green Paper on the Review of Council Regulation (EC) no 44/2001 (COM(2009) 175 final) and in 2010 published a proposal for recasting (COM(2010) 748 final) which does not substantively affect the comments here.

[74] The European Court of Justice in C-462/06 *Laboratoires Glaxosmithkline v Rouard* [2008] ECR I 3965 confirmed that Art 6(1), which allows joinder of multiple defendants in the court of a single Member State, did not apply in the context of employment matters.

[75] Fawcett and Torremans (2011), [9.248].

[76] Subject to the right to file a counterclaim to an action pending in another state: Art 20(2).

[77] Regulation (EC) No 593/2008 on the law applicable to contractual obligations [2008] OJ L177/6 Art 28.

[78] Art 24.

[79] Recital 46.

in or out of which the employee carries out her duties is specified by Art 8(2), failing that the place of business where engaged. Article 8(4) allows another 'proper law' of the contract to be chosen instead. Article 9 permits 'overriding mandatory provisions' of the law of the forum, or the country where the obligations are performed, to be applied. In *BGC Capital Markets (Switzerland) LLC v Rees*,[80] Jack J observed that for a restrictive covenant to be given effect, it would need to be enforceable under both Swiss law (proper law of the contract) and English law (public policy of the forum state).

6.2 Non-contractual Claims

If there is no contractual nexus between the claimant and the defendant, for example a claim against an indirect recipient of confidential information, jurisdiction under the Brussels Regulation is governed by Art 2 (domicile) or Art 5(3), which identifies the state where harm occurs as the jurisdiction.[81] *Mines de Potasse d'Alsace*[82] established that suit may be brought either in the place where the harmful event occurred (which Fawcett and Torremans characterize as the unauthorized use of the information in breach of confidence claims[83]) or the place where the damage occurs (in the sense of direct economic damage to commercial interests).[84]

Applicable law for non-contractual claims is identified by the Rome II Regulation.[85] It is of 'universal application' (Art 3). Rome II excludes claims for violation of privacy[86] or breaches of voluntary trusts[87] but

---

80 *BGC Capital Markets (Switzerland) LLC v Peter Kevin Rees* [2011] EWHC 2009 (QB), [101]. The case arose out of the Tullett Prebon dispute. Jack J applied the equivalent Art 16 of the 1980 Rome Convention on applicable law.

81 Held to be a residual category: Fawcett & Torremans (2011), [9.255], citing *Kalfelis v Schroder* C189/87 [1988] ECR 5565. Although Art 5(3) refers to tort, delict and quasi-delict, Wadlow (2008a) argues persuasively that trade secrets are covered.

82 *Handelswekerij GJ Bier BV v Mines de Potasse d'Alsace SA* (21/76) [1976] ECR 1735.

83 Fawcett and Torremans (2011), [9.266].

84 Ibid, [9.270–9.272].

85 Regulation (EC) No 864/2007 on the law applicable to non-contractual obligations [2007] OJ L199/40, in force from 11 January 2009 with respect to events occurring after this date: Arts 32 and 31.

86 Article 1(2)(g).

87 Article 1(2)(e).

applies to trade secrets.[88] For the purpose of Rome II, trade secrets are probably not categorized as intellectual property, which is governed by Art 8, but under unfair competition.[89] However, for acts of unfair competition that harm only a specific competitor (as is likely to be the case for misuse of workplace secrets) Art 4 applies instead. Article 4 gives the general rule for tort and points to the law of the country in which damage occurs. As Wadlow explains, Rome II in cross-border trade secret cases is 'potentially disastrous in its consequences' and is likely to lead to 'fragmentation of the applicable law'.[90] Some comfort may be gained from Art 4(3), which applies when the tort has a manifestly closer connection with the law of another country. This would at least allow the court seized of the claim to apply a single law. Again, this is an area where regarding workplace secrets as 'intellectual property' would provide greater legal clarity. Although Art 8 of Rome II has its own problems, its *lex loci protectionis* would probably serve trade secret claimants and defendants well, as in *Vestergaard*.[91]

7. CONCLUSION

Litigation to enforce workplace secrets looks to be increasing in volume and cross-border complexity. Substantive laws and enforcement arrangements for trade secrets in Europe are subject to considerable variation. The European Commission is looking into the substantive rules. However, applicable law, particularly in non-contractual claims, is likely to pose continuing problems. Characterizing trade secrets as intellectual property, at least for procedural and remedial purposes, would go some way towards simplifying the task of litigants.

REFERENCES

Allgrove, B. and S. Sellers (2009), 'The Fraud Act 2006: is Breach of Confidence Now a Crime?' 4(4) *Journal of Intellectual Property Law and Practice* 278

---

[88] Wadlow (2008b).

[89] For which Art 6(1) points to the law of the state where competitive relations or the collective interests of consumers are affected. This could give more than one candidate law.

[90] Wadlow (2008b), 313.

[91] *Vestergaard Frandsen S/A (MVF3 APS) v Bestnet Europe Ltd* [2011] EWCA Civ 424.

Bently, L., 'Chicken Nuggets: Re-reading Faccenda Chicken' <http://www.docstoc.com/docs/47071321/Chicken-Nuggets-Re-reading-Faccenda-Chicken>

Bone, R.C. (2011), 'Trade Secrecy, Innovation and the Requirement of Reasonable Secrecy Precautions' in R.C. Dreyfuss, K.J. Strandberg and P. Newman (eds), *The Law and Theory of Trade Secrecy*, Edward Elgar

Bouche, N. (2011), *Intellectual Property Law in France*, Kluwer

Bruun, N. (2001), *Intellectual Property Law in Finland*, Kluwer

Coleman, A. (1992), *The Legal Protection of Trade Secrets*, Sweet & Maxwell

Cook, T. (2010), *EU Intellectual Property Law*, Oxford University Press

de Vrey, R.W. (2006), *Towards a European Law of Unfair Competition: A Clash Between Legal Families*, Martinus Nijhoff, Leiden

Dessemontet, F. (1998), 'Protection of Trade Secrets and Confidential Information' in C.M. Correa and A.A. Yusuf (eds), *Intellectual Property and International Trade: The TRIPS Agreement*, Kluwer

Fawcett, J.J. and P. Torremans (2011), *Intellectual Property and Private International Law*, 2nd edn, Oxford University Press

Flannigan, R. (2008), 'The (Fiduciary) Duty of Fidelity' 124 *Law Quarterly Review* 274

Ghidini, G. (2006), *Intellectual Property and Competition Law*, Edward Elgar

Ghidini, G. and V. Falce (2010), 'Trade Secrets as Intellectual Property Rights: A Disgraceful Upgrading – Notes on an Italian "Reform"' in H. MacQueen, C. Waelde, G. Laurie and A. Brown (eds), *Contemporary Intellectual Property*, 2nd edn, Oxford University Press

Hilty, R.M. and F. Henning-Bodewig (eds) (2007), *Law against Unfair Competition*, Springer

Hull, J. (1998), 'Stealing Secrets: a Review of the Law Commission's Consultation Paper on the Misuse of Trade Secrets' 4 *Intellectual Property Quarterly* 422; 4 *Criminal Law Review* 246

Hull, J. (2009), 'Trade Secret Licensing: the Art of the Possible' 4(3) *Journal of Intellectual Property Law and Practice* 203

Kadir, R.M. (2010), 'The Scope and the Nature of Computer Crimes Statutes – A Critical Comparative Study' 11 *German Law Journal* 609

Klett, A.R., M. Sonntag and S. Wilske (2008), *Intellectual Property Law in Germany*, CH Beck, LexisNexis

Law Commission Consultation Paper No 150, *Legislating the Criminal Code: Misuse of Trade Secrets* (HMSO, 1997)

Law Commission Report on *Breach of Confidence* (No 110 Cmnd 8388, 1981)

Lemley, M. (2011), 'The Surprising Virtues of Treating Trade Secrets as IP Rights' in R.C. Dreyfuss, K.J. Strandberg and P. Newman (eds), *The Law and Theory of Trade Secrecy*, Edward Elgar

MacQueen H., C. Waelde, G. Laurie and A. Brown (2010), *Contemporary Intellectual Property Law and Policy*, Oxford University Press

Scottish Law Commission Report on Breach of Confidence (Scot Law Comm No 90, 1984)

Wadlow, C. (2008a), 'Bugs, Spies and Paparazzi: Jurisdiction over Actions for Breach of Confidence in Private International Law' 30(7) *European Intellectual Property Review* 269

Wadlow C. (2008b), 'Trade Secrets and the Rome II Regulation on the Law Applicable to Non-Contractual Obligations' 30(8) *European Intellectual Property Review* 309

22. Devices to restrain competition and protect confidential information in employment – practical and legal aspects: an Australian perspective

Chris Molnar*

1. INTRODUCTION

The combined operation of the common law, equity and statutory law automatically extend to an employer, without the need for any contractual devices, a range of rights that restrain competition and protect confidential information.[1] However, to the extent that these rights are limited, an employer by contract can augment their scope and application.

An enhanced protective regime based on contractual devices can widen the protection of confidential information, restrain employment and post-employment activities, require an employee not to work (garden leave) during an extended period of notice of termination, assign ownership of intellectual property to the employer and require an employee to disclose conflicts of interest, an interest held in competitors or the development of ideas or concepts for products or services.

---

* The author thanks McKean Park for its assistance and Amy Granger for her comments on a draft of this chapter. All views and any errors belong to the author.

[1] These rights potentially include: the implied duty of good faith and fidelity; implied duty to provide reasonable notice of termination of employment; equitable fiduciary obligations; equitable obligations to maintain confidentiality; s35(6) of the *Copyright Act 1968* (Cth) (employer deemed the owner of copyright); paragraph 13(1)(b) of the *Designs Act 2003* (Cth) (employer entitled to be the registered owner); s182 of the *Corporations Act 2001* (Cth) (officer or employee must not improperly use position) and s183 of the *Corporations Act 2001* (Cth) (officer or employee must not improperly use information).

In Australia there is an important policy debate on the use of devices, which extends to the allocation of the benefits of worker innovation, the ownership of human capital and the *in terrorem* effect of contractual devices.[2] This chapter, however, focuses on the practical legal aspects of the use of devices from an Australian perspective and, in particular, from the point of view of an Australian legal practitioner.

2. PROTECTION OF INTELLECTUAL PROPERTY BY AUSTRALIAN BUSINESSES

2.1 Strategic Approach

A strategic approach assists in assessing whether express contractual terms should be sought that amend or amplify the default common law, equitable and statutory protections. From an employer's perspective, a strategic approach initially requires an audit process to identify which workers may pose a risk, what measures need to be implemented through contracts, deeds and policies to eliminate or minimize the risks; and how the measures need to be maintained through the various phases of a worker's engagement (including changes to the employee's position and duties) and changes to the business itself (including changes to its products, services and markets). On the other hand, an employee may seek to extend or reduce any limitations on their freedom to use and exploit the information acquired or intellectual property created in the course of employment.

Without contractual protection, some categories of employees pose particular risks to an employer. One such category is the employee in possession of sensitive confidential information outside of the area of trade secrets protected by the implied duty of fidelity or equitable obligation of confidence. For example, an employee may be aware of the key capabilities of employees of the employer, which may be useful to a competitor in seeking to employ those persons. Such information is unlikely to be a trade secret and, failing a contractual restraint, is likely to be able to be lawfully disclosed to a competitor immediately after employment. Another category is the employee who has developed a relationship with a client, customer or supplier, often with the marketing support of the employer in the form of lunches, publications, gifts and other promotional devices. Employees in these categories include sales

---

[2] See generally Riley (2005) and Dent, Fenwick and Newitt (2010).

representatives, contract or account managers and professionals who directly service clients. These employees will often possess the most significant intangible asset of the employer, namely, its relationship with customers and suppliers.

A common practical difficulty is the undertaking of a proper assessment of risk by the employer or employee prior to the commencement of the relationship, and the related failure to provide for the adequate protection of interests through enforceable promises.

2.2 Statistical Survey

Some relevant background statistics can be found in the Australian Bureau of Statistics publication *8167.0 – Selected Characteristics of Australian Business* under the intellectual property heading. The statistics were released on 16 September 2010 and are based on a survey of businesses that were asked what methods were used to protect the intellectual property of the business during the year ended 30 June 2009.

The available intellectual property protection methods in the survey were patents, registration of design, copyright or trademark, secrecy or confidentiality agreements (including electronic protection methods) and complexity of product design. Respondents could identify more than one type of method.

Of respondents surveyed, 78 per cent reported that no intellectual property protection methods were in place. Secrecy or confidentiality agreement at 13.6 per cent was reported as the most common intellectual property protection method in place, with copyright or trademark coming in at second place at 9.8 per cent, complexity of product design in third place at 3.7 per cent, and patents and registration of design in equal last place at 2.4 per cent.

It is surprising that 78.4 per cent of businesses reported no methods were in place, although presumably such businesses would have the benefit of any default common law and equitable obligations on employees. Based on this statistic it would appear that an overwhelming number of Australian businesses have an opportunity to significantly enhance the protection of their intellectual property.

The method of secrecy or a confidentiality agreement, whether involving electronic protection methods or not, ultimately relies on an individual person keeping the intellectual property secret and that, in turn, relies on the efficacy of the legal restraints applying to the individual person. However, with only one in ten businesses relying on secrecy or confidentiality agreements, there is a manifest opportunity for businesses to advance the protection of their intellectual property through a number of measures, but at the very least through the means of a confidentiality agreement.

The publication reports that 'Innovation-active businesses were more than three times as likely to use any intellectual property protection methods than non innovation-active businesses'. This outcome accords with what would be expected intuitively and based on experience.

2.3 Use of Devices

In the author's experience, and at a practical level, the Australian legal practitioner, in advising clients on devices restraining competition, faces a client marketplace with uneven interest in the use of devices. Interest in the use of devices mainly varies on the industry and occupation of workers – for example, contract clauses protecting the assets of the employer are more popular in industries with significant research and development components and in occupations which involve or lead to the creation of intellectual property, or involve sales, marketing or business development functions, including professionals such as accountants, stock brokers or lawyers. Interest also varies depending on the type of protection sought – generally employers will invest time and money into confidentiality clauses, but are less likely to do so with clauses deeming or assigning ownership of intellectual property to the employer and are least likely to do so with tailored restraint clauses applying after employment to the activities of the employee.

3. APPLYING DEVICES

3.1 Policies

An employer policy by itself will not create legal obligations. Often, however, a contract of employment will incorporate by reference the policy into the contract and then it will have contractual effect in accordance with its terms. From a contractual point of view it is relatively straightforward – the policy becomes part of the contract. However, it is usually not that simple – either the terms of the incorporation will be ambiguous and subject to dispute, or the incorporated terms are uncertain.

Often a contract will be drafted with terms that 'the employee will adhere to the [name] policy' or 'the employee will comply with the [name] policy'. These phrases are arguably ambiguous as to whether they impose obligations on the employer and have been the subject of litigation.[3] More importantly, there may be evidentiary difficulties in identifying the policy which applied at the time. This is particularly so when the employer is not an effective archivist, as is often the case.

It is the very nature of policies that they change as they are modified to deal with current conditions. For example, it is possible that over the course of an employment period a confidentiality policy is modified a number of times. The employee leaves and it then becomes relevant to identify the contents of the policy at an earlier point of time. It transpires that the policy has been modified twice since that time and a copy is not able to be found. All that can be found is an electronic copy with no record as to whether and, if so, how it became the official policy. The employees who would know, including possibly the HR manager, have left the business and do not return calls or letters. In these circumstances the business is left in a very difficult situation when it comes to establishing that the relevant policy has contractual effect.[4]

It is preferable, given the possibility of these circumstances, for the written contract of employment to contain all relevant terms which restrain competition and protect confidentiality. If, however, policies are to be used to enforce legal obligations, then clear reference should be made in the written contract to their status, and the policies should be communicated and made accessible to employees. A clear and permanent record of the history of the documents and their contents should be maintained.

3.2 Notice Period and Garden Leave

In the absence of circumstances justifying summary dismissal, employment contracts are typically terminable on notice or, if the contract so provides, immediately on payment of an amount in lieu of notice. Failing an express term specifying the period of notice, both the employer and

---

[3] See, e.g., *Riverwood International Australia Pty Ltd v McCormick* (2000) 177 ALR 193; *Goldman Sachs JB Were Services Pty Ltd v Nikolich* (2007) 163 FCR 62; *Yousif v Commonwealth Bank of Australia* [2010] FCAFC 8.

[4] E.g., *Victoria University of Technology v Wilson* [2004] VSC 33, [75]–[102] where the contract referred to 'university policy' but the university failed to establish the existence of an applicable university policy on intellectual property. Similarly, in *University of Western Australia v Gray (No 20)* [2008] FCA 498 at [64]–[83]; [2009] FCAFC 116, (2009) 179 FCR 346 there was difficulty in establishing the promulgation date of university patent regulations.

the employee are required to comply with the implied term that reasonable notice be given.[5]

As the employee is subject to the ordinary duties of an employee during the notice period, including the implied duties of fidelity and the requirement to comply with directions, there are a number of potential opportunities for an employer to manage the exit of an employee during the notice period and therefore protect its interests. For example, the employee could be directed to identify confidential information in the employee's possession in documents and data storage devices and, once identified, provide the information to the employer. Additionally, the employee could be directed to transfer current work to a successor to ensure that there is knowledge transfer, continuation of development and business activities, and preservation of relationships with customers, clients and suppliers. Finally, the employee may be able to be directed not to perform in full or in part their normal duties, and therefore be on what is colloquially known as garden leave. The subsistence of ordinary employee obligations during the notice period means that the notice period may be a more effective tool than post-employment restraints.

The opportunities during the notice period to protect assets tend to favour a lengthy notice period being sought by the employer in the employment contract. From the employer's perspective, weighing against a lengthy notice period is the continuation of normal remuneration at a time when the employee is less, or not at all, productive. Some employers, however, are willing to trade less productivity for more protection.

Whether an employer is entitled to place an employee on garden leave will be a matter of the construction of the employment contract in the surrounding circumstances and in particular, whether there is an obligation to provide work.[6] A majority of the Full Court of the Federal Court in *Ramsey Butchering Services Pty Ltd v Blackadder* stated:

> At common law there is no obligation upon an employer under a contract of employment to provide work unless the contract specifically requires that such work be provided, or unless it is necessary for the employee to be employed in order to maintain a particular profile, such as an actor, or unless the nature of the work for which the employee is employed is such that the

---

[5] On what is reasonable see generally the discussion by Judd J in *Howard v Pilkington (Australia) Ltd* [2008] VSC 491 at [54].

[6] *Wheeler Hill Organisation Ltd v Tucker* [1998] EWCA Civ 615; [1999] ICR 291 at [13] (Morritt LJ), quoted in *Bearing Point Australia Pty Ltd v Hillard* [2008] VSC 115 at [86].

employee's career and future prospects depend upon the extent of the work the employee is able to undertake.[7]

If an employee accepts the ability of an employer to place the employee on garden leave, and otherwise manage the exit of the employee through the notice period, then typically the employer is able to maximize the protection of confidential information and goodwill. However, there will be a significant problem when the employee challenges the imposition of garden leave.

For example, in the recent Victorian Supreme Court case of *Bearing Point Australia Pty Ltd v Hillard*,[8] Mr Hillard, a managing director of information management in a management technology consulting company, claimed that the employer's direction to take garden leave, together with some other acts of the employer, amounted to repudiation of the employment contract, which he was entitled to accept, thus bringing the contract to an end. There was no express provision entitling the employer to put Mr Hillard on garden leave. The court did not accept that directing Mr Hillard not to work was repudiatory. Rather, a term should be implied into the contract entitling Bearing Point to direct Mr Hillard to go on garden leave: 'As counsel submitted, Bearing Point should not be prevented from appointing a successor and progressively giving Mr Hillard's tasks as managing director of the information management team to that person, once Mr Hillard had indicated that he was leaving.'[9]

However, the court was not prepared to issue an injunction restraining Mr Hillard from working other than for Bearing Point because, and consistent with long-standing authority, this would amount to specific performance of an employment contract: 'In practice, Mr Hillard would have no option but to continue to sit out his enforced garden leave, as otherwise he would not be able to earn any income during the balance of his notice period.'[10] The court observed that it was not being asked to enforce the type of restriction enforced in *Lumley v Wagner*,[11] where the person restrained could work elsewhere.[12] Bearing Point was left with its remedy in damages.

---

[7] *Ramsey Butchering Services Pty Ltd v Blackadder* [2003] FCAFC 20 at [65], (2003) 127 FCR 381 at [65] (Tamberlin and Goldberg JJ).

[8] [2008] VSC 115.

[9] *Bearing Point Australia Pty Ltd v Hillard* [2008] VSC 115 at [103].

[10] Ibid [149].

[11] (1852) 1 De GM & G 604; 42 ER 687.

[12] *Bearing Point Australia Pty Ltd v Hillard* [2008] VSC 115 at [144].

Damages in these circumstances are very much a second best outcome – the actual damage may be unknown or difficult to establish. Often for a plaintiff it is a case of injunctive relief or nothing, and as it is difficult to obtain an injunction where it amounts to specific performance of an employment contract, the law may not offer a satisfactory solution in these circumstances.

The use of extensive notice periods should be approached with caution. The restraint of trade doctrine applies during employment, including to a term specifying a notice period, as much as it applies after employment.[13] The currency of the employment supports, but does not conclusively determine, the reasonableness of a restraint operating prior to its termination.[14]

3.3 Restrictions after Employment

3.3.1 Confidentiality

Together, the combined operation of the implied duty of fidelity and the equitable duty of confidence has certain advantages – they operate by default, and, in the case of the equitable duty, equitable remedies such as an account for profits are available and furthermore the obligations extend after the employment has ended. However, a major disadvantage is that the combined duties will not protect information after employment that is not a trade secret[15] or otherwise does not meet the tests for the imposition of the equitable duty of confidence.[16]

An express contractual term prohibiting the disclosure of confidential information has a number of potential advantages:

- it can extend the protection of confidential information beyond the default protection given to trade secrets and in particular, if it is difficult to separate trade secrets from general know how;
- it signals to the employee that particular types of information are

---

13 *Tullett Prebon (Australia) Pty Ltd v Simon Purcell* [2008] NSWSC 852; see generally Coulthard (2009).

14 *Tullett Prebon (Australia) Pty Ltd v Simon Purcell* [2008] NSWSC 852 at [40], [110].

15 See *Faccenda Chicken v Fowler* [1987] Ch 117; [1986] 1 All ER 617 on the distinction between trade secrets and know-how.

16 See the tests identified by Gummow J in *Re Smith Kline and French Laboratories (Australia) Limited and Ors v the Secretary to the Department of Community Services and Health* [1990] FCA 151 at [54].

considered confidential by the employer and therefore have a deterrent effect on the employee; and

- a well drafted express negative covenant to keep certain information confidential can identify precisely the scope of information which is confidential, an important prerequisite in enforcing confidentiality obligations,[17] particularly in seeking injunctive relief.

The weakness in relying on implied or express contractual, or equitable, obligations alone is an evidentiary one. It is often very difficult to know when there has been a breach, particularly post employment. The employee may well be disclosing confidential information to a current employer; there is no interest in the current employer making that fact publicly known.[18] By the time the former employer learns of the breach, if it does at all, it may be too late for injunctive relief.

Confidentiality agreements are at best a supplementary device to be used in conjunction with a clause restraining the former employee from undertaking activities which compete with their former employer (restraint clause). As outlined in the next section the protection of confidential information is considered to be a legitimate interest for the purposes of a valid restraint clause. Prohibiting the employee from engaging in competitive activities offers optimal protection for an employer of its confidential information.

3.3.2 Restraint of trade doctrine

It is trite law that all restraints of trade are void as contrary to public policy, except where the restriction is reasonable by reference to the interests of the parties and the public.[19] For a restraint to be reasonable by reference to the interests of the parties it must afford no more than adequate protection to the party in whose favour it is imposed.[20]

As the New South Wales Supreme Court explained: 'Covenants that restrain competition are invalid unless they are reasonably necessary to

---

17 E.g., *O'Brien v Komesaroff* [1982] HCA 33; (1982) 150 CLR 310 (Mason J).

18 Because of the risk to employers of new employees imparting confidential information, or using intellectual property, of a former employer, it is advisable to have contractual terms that prohibit these acts and, indeed, indemnify the employer for any breach.

19 *Nordenfelt v Maxim Nordenfelt Guns and Ammunition Co Ltd* [1894] AC 535, 565 (Lord Macnaghten).

20 *Herbert Morris Ltd v Saxelby* [1916] 1 AC 688, 707 (Lord Parker).

protect legitimate business interests'[21] and validity is to 'be tested at the time of entering into the contract and by reference to what the Restraint Deed entitled or required the parties to do rather than what they intend to do or have actually done'.[22]

The dimensions of a restraint are typically its scope (what is being restrained?), time (how long is the restraint?) and geography (what area does it cover?). The scope of a restraint can be of different forms. Mr Millar identifies the following types (in descending order of unreasonableness and therefore unenforceability):

- any participation in the former employer's industry;
- any work in a directly competitive capacity;
- any work for clients of the former employer;
- solicitation of clients of the former employer;
- solicitation of employees of the former employer.[23]

A main reason why a particular restraint is unenforceable is that it is unreasonable having regard to the particular interest it seeks to protect, assuming that it is a legitimate interest in the first place. In auditing risk for the purposes of drafting a restraint clause, a key task is to identify what is the legitimate interest to be protected in the circumstances of the employee.

For example, if the interest is confidentiality, then it may be reasonable for a restraint to apply against working post employment in the employer's industry, even though some firms in that industry may not be strictly competitors, because the information held by the employee may enable a firm in the industry to develop products and therefore become a competitor. If the interest is the connection and goodwill of an employee with clients of the employer, then it will be essential that the restriction is limited to competitive conduct. A clause which restricts a sales manager from simply approaching customers of the employer is arguably too wide because it would stop the manager from approaching customers to sell goods not sold by the employer.

It is also trite law that a term of a contract will be unenforceable if it is uncertain, that is, a court cannot determine the meaning the parties intended. Ambiguous restraint clauses carry a high risk of being challenged.

---

21 *OAMPS Insurance Brokers Ltd v Peter Hanna* [2010] NSWSC 781 at [69].

22 Ibid.

23 Millar (2009).

A common method of mitigating risks, but also routinely attacked on the grounds of uncertainty, is the 'ladder' clause or 'cascading' clause. Such a clause sets out a number of combinations of time and area in decreasing extent. Each time and area is combined with each other to provide a number of permutations. Such a clause often contains a term that if one combination is unenforceable then the other clauses are unaffected and also a term that the widest possible combination is intended. In effect, the employer is hedging its bets as to how the court will decide the issue of reasonableness. The decision of the New South Wales Supreme Court in *OAMPS Insurance Brokers Ltd v Peter Hanna*[24] endorsed the line of authority which supports such clauses as being certain and therefore enforceable. This decision was confirmed on appeal in *Hanna v OAMPS Insurance Brokers Ltd.*[25]

The recent decision of the New South Wales Supreme Court in *Seven Network (Operations) Ltd v Warburton (No 2)* (*Seven Network*)[26] typifies the emphasis given to maintaining the integrity of the deal struck between the parties, which is summed up by Pembroke J's adjuration that 'the first duty of the court is to give effect to the parties' contract and not to be too quick to strike it down'.[27]

In this case, a senior media executive entered into post-employment restraints with private equity investors who had an interest in ensuring that their investment was protected from departing executives. He received equity holdings in consideration for the restraint. He was recruited by a rival media organization and placed on garden leave by his employer. The court ultimately granted an injunction to enforce compliance with the restraint clauses.

In emphasizing the importance of the parties' promise, Pembroke J stated:

> One of the abiding principles of a civilized system of law such as ours is that contracts are meant to be observed. Lawyers sometimes use the Latin phrase *pacta sunt servanda* to describe the principle. We make decisions on the assumption that contractual obligations will generally be performed and solemn commitments will not be ignored.[28]

---

24 [2010] NSWSC 781.

25 [2010] NSWCA 267.

26 [2011] NSWSC 386. See Molnar (2011) for more detailed analysis.

27 *Seven Network (Operations) Ltd v Warburton (No 2)* [2011] NSWSC 386 at [39].

28 Ibid at [3].

In determining when the employment ended for the purposes of the commencement of the restraint period, the court interpreted the restraint clause such that the period commenced when the garden leave commenced and not when the contract of employment ended. Once the employee went on garden leave the employee did not have access to confidential information, clients and staff – the relationship had been 'destroyed'.[29] The restraint period of 12 months was reasonable but in exercising its discretion as to the length of the period of the injunction, the court ordered relief for less than 12 months, being the point at which there was no longer a legitimate interest to protect in the form of confidential information. The case illustrates the tailoring of the relief granted to take into account the period of garden leave and the expiration of the legitimate interest forming the basis of the relief.

Not directly explored in *Seven Network*, but a potential issue for consideration in future cases, was whether the nature of the employee's position impacted on the assessment of reasonableness. The employee was highly paid and very senior. As he had agreed to the restraint in exchange for equity holdings, his position arguably was more akin to a purchaser of a business rather than an employee in a disadvantageous bargaining position – in those more commercial circumstances, the court considers that the onus of establishing reasonableness is more easily discharged.[30]

Also not explored in *Seven Network* is the extent to which an express clause enabling an employee to be placed on garden leave may be attacked on the grounds that it is an unreasonable restraint of trade. Clauses that apply during the currency of the employment, such as a garden leave clause, may be void under the restraint of trade doctrine.[31]

3.3.3 *Restraint of Trade Act 1976* (NSW)

In the State of New South Wales the *Restraint of Trade Act 1976* (NSW) empowers a court to adopt a more flexible approach to construing restraint clauses. Subsection 4(1) of the Act provides: '(1) A restraint of trade is valid to the extent to which it is not against public policy, whether it is in severable terms or not.' The approach of the Court is summarized by McLelland J in *Orton v Melman*:[32]

---

[29] Ibid at [28].

[30] E.g., *BDO Group Investments (NSW–Vic) Pty Ltd v Ngo* [2010] VSC 206 at [40].

[31] *Tullett Prebon (Australia) Pty Ltd v Purcell* [2008] NSWSC 852 and see generally Coulthard (2009).

[32] [1981] 1 NSWLR 583.

> In my opinion where the court is to determine, in relation to a restraint to which s 4(1) applies whether (having regard to public policy) the restraint is enforceable in respect of an alleged breach (or threatened breach), it is proper first to determine whether the alleged breach (independently of public policy considerations) does or will infringe the terms of the restraint properly construed, and if so, then to determine whether the restraint, so far as it applies to that breach, is contrary to public policy. If the restraint, so far as it applies to that breach, is not contrary to public policy then by force of s 4(1) the restraint is to that extent valid, subject always of course to any order which may be made under s 4(3).[33]

The court can in effect enforce a reasonable restraint even though the clause is too wide and therefore void as unreasonable. However, the interpretation of subsection 4(1) is not free from difficulty. As Pembroke J opined in *Seven Network*: '... the language of Section 4(1) is enigmatic in its brevity and the explanation in *Orton v Melman* [1981] 1 NSWLR 583 (McLelland J) is neither entirely clear nor, pending an appellate decision, necessarily the last word on the subject'.[34] No other Australian State or Territory has a similar statutory provision. Where restraints are used, the flexibility given to a court makes New South Wales a popular state for employers to choose as the governing law of the contract and as the forum to litigate.

3.4 The Limitations of Fiduciary Obligations

The limitations of the equitable fiduciary obligations were illustrated in the recent case of *Blackmagic Design Pty Ltd v Overliese*,[35] which was the subject of an appeal in *Blackmagic Design Pty Ltd v Overliese*.[36] The employer applicant (Blackmagic) designed, manufactured, marketed and sold hardware and software products for various purposes in television and film markets. The first respondent, Mr Overliese, was the Director of Hardware Engineering of Blackmagic. It was alleged that, unknown to Blackmagic, he and Mr Young, the second respondent, developed a video capture card (Simple Card) for the purpose of establishing a business in competition with Blackmagic. They subsequently left the employment of Blackmagic.

---

33 *Orton v Melman* [1981] 1 NSWLR 583, 587.

34 *Seven Network (Operations) Ltd v Warburton (No 2)* [2011] NSWSC 386 at [91].

35 [2010] FCA 126.

36 [2011] FCAFC 24.

Blackmagic subsequently produced a card similar to Simple Card. The Simple Card was not developed and therefore there was no claim in respect of loss or damage, or an account for profits, related to sales derived from its sale of the Simple Card. Rather, the monetary claims of Blackmagic arose from a loss of opportunity claim that the existence of the Simple Card should have been disclosed and, if that had been done, then Blackmagic's card could have been developed earlier, with consequential profits.

Blackmagic claimed first that there was a duty on Mr Overliese to disclose the details of the Simple Card to Blackmagic. The trial judge dismissed this argument on the basis that fiduciary duties were proscriptive not prescriptive. The Full Court agreed. In other words, there was no positive duty to disclose the Simple Card arising from any fiduciary obligation. There may be a conflict of interest, which there was a duty to avoid, but disclosure was part of a defence that the principal provided fully informed consent based on the disclosure.

Secondly, and this point was pressed on appeal, it was claimed that both Mr Overliese and Mr Young had placed themselves in a position of conflict of interest and duty, and the conflict required disclosure. However, the court ruled that if there was a duty to disclose, the duty did not involve disclosing the details of the Simple Card. The product concept required 'further substantial work'.[37] It was based on hardware and software decided by Mr Overliese and was 'not based on a secret or confidential structure plan'[38] of Blackmagic. It was little more than an idea. It had not been developed in terms of devising a practical way to produce the card, and no customers nor employees had been approached – the card was not a fact which gave rise to a conflict.

The decision reflects the traditional reluctance of the court, whether considering fiduciary duties or the implied duty of fidelity, to find liability where an employee has made only initial steps towards commencing a competitive business. However, the underlying concept behind Simple Card was something of potential value to Blackmagic's business. It was open to Blackmagic to develop a product based on the idea had it known about it. The development of concepts was within Mr Overliese's technical expertise and arguably within the scope of his duties as Director of Hardware Engineering. Mr Overliese gave consideration to developing a competitive business and had taken preliminary steps to that end. It is understandable that Blackmagic would seek to be compensated for

---

37 *Blackmagic Design Pty Ltd v Overliese* [2011] FCAFC 13 at [103].
38 Ibid.

Mr Overliese's failure to disclose the concept and to seek to restrain Mr Overliese from using the concept. However, the best Blackmagic could achieve was to restrain Mr Overliese, Mr Young and Atomos from using or disclosing confidential information of Blackmagic, a not particularly encouraging result for Blackmagic, nor for employers in the business of development and design where it is expected that employees will develop new ideas and concepts. It is difficult to reconcile the court's traditional reluctance to find liability where an employee has taken preliminary steps towards product development with the real prospect that those steps will at least take the employer by surprise.

Blackmagic's position would have been enhanced had it had the benefit of a contractual term requiring Mr Overliese, particularly having regard to his technical duties, to disclose ideas and concepts forming the foundation of a product that Blackmagic may possibly develop. Such a term would be subject to the caveat that it be reasonable, given the possible application of the restraint of trade doctrine.

4. CONCLUDING COMMENTS

Managing the protection of intangible and tangible assets, including goodwill, confidential information and intellectual property, whether during or after employment, sits among the more complex issues that often need to be dealt with between employers and employees. Despite that complexity, contractual devices can offer an opportunity to lawfully restrain competition, protect confidential information and resolve ownership of intellectual property beyond the default operation of the common law, equity and statutory law. The efficacy of such devices is heavily dependent on the extent to which the devices have been customized to the particular circumstances of the employer and the individual employee. Absent customization, the message from Australian cases is clear – the devices will potentially be open to attack on the basis of their limited scope, or the uncertainty or unreasonableness of their terms. The interests of both employers and employees will often be served if there is an investment in time by each party to obtain legal advice, and to negotiate, draft and finalize terms that are enforceable.

REFERENCES

Coulthard, A. (2009), 'Garden Leave, the Right to Work and Restraints on Trade' 22 *Australian Journal of Labour Law* 87

Dent C., C. Fenwick and K. Newitt (2010), 'Legal Incentives to Promote Innovation at Work: A Critical Analysis', *University of Melbourne Law Research Series* 15

Millar, R. (2009), 'Restricting the Activities of Former Employees', *Paper presented at CPDS Seminar* (Brisbane, 1 September)

Molnar, C. (2011), 'Pacta Sunt Servanda – Promises Must Be Kept' 17(3) *Employment Law Bulletin* 42

Riley, J. (2005), 'Who Owns Human Capital? A Critical Appraisal of Legal Techniques for Capturing the Value of Work' 18 *Australian Journal of Labour Law* 1

23. The law and policy of non-compete clauses in the United States and their implications

Jay P. Kesan and Carol M. Hayes

1. NON-COMPETE LAW IN THE UNITED STATES

A person who accepts a job in the United States may be required to sign a contract that includes a covenant not to compete ('non-compete') as a condition of employment. The idea of a non-compete is that it is a contractual term (sometimes presented in a contract by itself or with other employment matters) that serves to protect certain interests of the employer. Non-competes arise in the context of the principal–agent relationship between employer and employee. The employee, or agent, acts on the behalf of the employer (the principal), and the details of the relationship are determined by express or implied agreements between the parties. By requiring the employee to sign a non-compete, the employer puts the employee on notice that the employee will be exposed to confidential information that the employer will trust the employee to keep confidential after the relationship terminates. Non-competes thus act as a signal to the employee, putting him or her on notice about the employer's business interests and intentions. The employee's knowledge of the employer's intentions enables the employee to avoid violating the terms of the relationship, and thus better avoid future conflict with the employer. Non-competes are in this way prophylactic by nature and may serve to reduce future litigation.

A non-compete included in an employment contract may look something like this:

Covenant not to compete

(a) **John Smith** agrees not to compete with **World Services, Inc.** in the practice of **accounting and tax preparation** while working for **World Services, Inc.** and for a period of **18 months** after termination of employment within a radius of **10** miles of **World Services, Inc., Chicago, IL**.

(b) For purposes of this covenant not to compete, competition is defined as soliciting or accepting employment by, or rendering professional services to, any person or organization that is or was a client of **World Services, Inc.** during the term of **John Smith**'s work with **World Services, Inc.**

Because the enforcement of non-competes is governed by contract law, and contract law varies from state to state, there is some variation between approaches to non-competes throughout the country. Some states have explicit statutory regimes that govern non-competes in that state. A list of citations to these statutes is provided in the Appendix.

The substance of these statutory restrictions varies significantly between states. California and North Dakota both have non-compete statutes that bar the enforcement of virtually any non-compete clause in an employment context.[1] On the opposite end of the spectrum is Florida, whose detailed non-compete statute mandates that economic hardship to the covenanting employee not be considered when evaluating a non-compete's enforceability, and also requires that the terms of a non-compete be construed in favor of protecting the covenanting employer's business interests.[2] Most other states take positions counter to Florida's on this, considering economic hardship to an employee when determining enforceability, and construing non-compete terms in favor of the employee instead of the employer.

When the state relies on common law rather than a statute that explicitly sets out the state's policy on non-competes, disputes over non-competes are guided by case law, sometimes taking into consideration the approaches of other states. The Appendix to this chapter also provides a list of case law citations for each state. Between states, there is some degree of consistency, with many states adopting the approach of

---

[1] Cal. Bus. & Prof. Code. § 16600; N.D. Cent. Code § 9–08–06. Montana also has a statute that renders void 'any contract by which anyone is restrained from exercising a lawful profession, trade, or business of any kind.' In practice, though, Montana courts have read this as prohibiting direct restraints on practicing a trade, with indirect restraints on practicing a trade being analyzed under a three-part test. The test looks at the scope of the restriction, whether consideration is present, and whether the restriction is reasonable. Mont. Code Ann. § 28–2-703; *Access Organics v. Hernandez*, 175 P.3d 899 (Mont. 2008). Thus, we consider Montana's position on non-competes to be more in line with that of the rest of the country.

[2] Fla. Stat. Ann. § 542.335.

the Restatement (Second) of Contracts in Section 188. The Restatement, in pertinent part, states the rule that restraints on trade (including non-compete agreements in the employment context) may be unenforceable as against public policy, when:

> (a) the restraint is greater than is needed to protect the promisee's legitimate interest, or
> (b) the promisee's need is outweighed by the hardship to the promisor and the likely injury to the public.[3]

The Restatement test is commonly used to determine whether the various elements of a non-compete are unreasonable. Factors commonly considered in assessing the reasonableness of a restraint on competition include the duration of the restriction, the geographical limitations, and the type of activity restricted. The key question is whether the interests of the covenanting employee and the public outweigh the employer's interests. The trend in case law is that reasonableness is determined as a matter of law dependant on the circumstances at hand. Recent court cases suggest that courts are approaching non-competes with a more restrictive view than in the past. It is unclear what the net effect is of this, however, since the limited empirical data about non-compete litigation also suggests that non-compete agreements themselves have become more narrowly written over the years.[4]

1.1 Legitimate Business Interests

Adjudication of non-compete violations tends to turn on whether the non-compete was protecting a legitimate business interest, so an essential issue is how to determine whether a legitimate business interest is present. By its name, a non-compete's purpose would appear to be to limit the ability of a former employee to compete with his or her former employer. However, many state courts say outright that they refuse to interpret the prevention of ordinary competition as a legitimate business interest.[5] In addition to state disapproval of such use of non-competes, using non-competes to limit ordinary competition may also run afoul of Federal Trade Commission (FTC) regulations.[6] Employers are, however,

---

3 Restatement (Second) of Contracts § 188 (1981).

4 Whitmore (1990).

5 E.g., *All Stainless, Inc. v. Colby*, 308 N.E.2d 481 (Mass. 1974).

6 Federal Trade Commission, 'Dealing with Competitors: Market Division or Customer Allocation' <http://www.ftc.gov/bc/antitrust/market_division.shtm>.

generally permitted to use non-competes to protect against *unfair* competition. A former employee's actions may be considered unfair competition if that individual puts improper use to a business advantage or opportunity that he had gained through his previous employment.[7]

The most common interests that are cited as legitimate business interests are the protection of trade secrets, confidential information, and customer contacts. While California courts have been famously opposed to non-competes in the state, the California Supreme Court has said in hypothetical dicta that non-competes to protect trade secrets would be enforceable.[8] In states that are friendlier towards non-competes, legitimate interests may be supported by restrictions that prohibit a former employee from disclosing confidential information or soliciting customers with whom the employee formerly worked while employed by the covenanting employer. Some states, like Hawaii and Florida, also permit employers to include in the non-compete agreement restrictions pertaining to extraordinary, unique or specialized training that the employee received from the employer.[9]

1.2 Burdens on the Employee and the Public

Leaving aside for a moment the question of what happens if the court does not find a legitimate interest, the next step that most courts would take is to consider the burdens that the non-compete imposes on the employee and the public. These burdens are often evaluated in terms of the reasonableness of the time, place, and activity restrictions, specifically whether any of these factors impose undue burdens on the employee or are injurious to the public.

1.2.1 Burdens on the employee

The terms of a non-compete typically place burdens on the covenanting employee, requiring him or her to refrain from competing in a specific field or region for a specified length of time. Generally, courts evaluate the reasonableness of these burdens based on the circumstances of each case. However, there are some states that set a maximum length of time for a non-compete restriction. The non-compete statutes of Louisiana and Oregon, for instance, limit non-compete agreements to two years after

---

[7] *Cardiovascular Surgical Specialists, Corp. v. Mammana*, 61 P.3d 210 (Okla. 2002).

[8] *Muggill v. Reuben H. Donnelly Corp.*, 398 P.2d 147, 149 (Cal. 1965).

[9] *7's Enterprises Inc. v. Del Rosario*, 143 P.3d 23 (Haw. 2006); Fla. Stat. Ann. § 542.335(1)(b).

employment ends, while the Missouri statute sets a time limit of one year for employment non-competes.[10] If the employer's economic concerns in replacing the employee are considered the primary business interest in favor of the restraint, a court might uphold a restriction that is limited to the length of time that the employer will need to hire and train the employee's replacement.[11]

The question of an appropriate geographical restriction, however, does not lend itself to bright line rules in the same manner as duration. The same distance may be reasonable in one region of the state, but unreasonable in another because of population density. One case in Oklahoma examined a 20-mile non-compete restriction on a cardiovascular surgeon in Tulsa.[12] In practice, however, the closest hospitals where the surgeon could have been employed outside that 20-mile radius were not within 100 miles of his former place of practice, and thus 20 miles was held to be unreasonable.

It is also common for a non-compete to impose restrictions on an employee's ability to hold a job similar to his or her former job. However, these non-competes are often limited insofar as necessary to be tailored to the employer's legitimate interests. A salesman, for example, may be prohibited from taking a sales job with a direct competitor where he solicits business from customers with whom he worked before. An appropriately tailored restriction on an accountant who prepares tax returns might prohibit him from soliciting former clients to his new firm, or might prevent him from preparing tax returns professionally for a period of time if the employer's legitimate interests outweigh the potential harm to the employee. This might be shown by an employer in a situation where the employer's confidential information would be put at risk by the former employee's practice of his trade.

1.2.2 Injury to the public

The second part of the analysis, whether the restriction is injurious to the public, does not get examined as often in courts. The public interest, however, is the primary justification offered by North Dakota courts for why non-competition provisions are almost always invalid in the employment context under the law of that state.[13] The public interest may justify

---

[10] La. Rev. Stat. Ann. § 23:921; 28 Mo. Stat. Ann. § 431.202; Or. Rev. Stat. § 653.295.

[11] *Valley Medical Specialists v. Farber*, 982 P.2d 1277 (Ariz. 1999).

[12] *Cardiovascular Surgical Specialists, Corp. v. Mammana*, 61 P.3d 210 (Okla. 2002).

[13] *Warner and Co. v. Solberg*, 634 N.W.2d 65 (N.D. 2001).

differing approaches based on profession. Some states, such as Massachusetts, have specific statutes or case law explicitly prohibiting non-competes from applying in the medical field.[14] This restriction on non-competes is most commonly justified by pointing to the strong public interest in favor of letting members of the public choose their own physicians. However, courts may be hesitant to read public injury into the restriction of most professions. Recently, a court in Minnesota scoffed at the idea that non-competes applying to hairstylists might be injurious to the public.[15]

1.3 Burden of Proof

When the reasonableness of these factors is in issue, most states will place the burden of establishing reasonableness on the employer. That is, if an employer seeks to enforce the non-compete, that employer must first establish that the terms of the non-compete are reasonable. However, in a small minority of states, including Arkansas, Connecticut, and Kansas, the party challenging the enforceability of the non-compete has the burden of establishing that the non-compete is unreasonable.[16] The question of which party has the burden of proof is very significant. The allocation of the burden of proof determines which party has to be on the offensive and which party needs merely to successfully argue that the other party's arguments are not strong enough.

1.4 Ambiguity in Non-compete Clauses

Sometimes, the language of a non-compete may be unclear in some ways. When that is the case, the court is faced with the problem of how to construe the meaning of the language. Most states, including Alaska, Mississippi, Montana, Tennessee, Virginia, and Wyoming, construe the non-compete in the employee's favor.[17] However, the Florida non-compete statute explicitly provides that vague non-compete language

---

[14] Mass. Gen. Law Ch. 112, § 12X.

[15] *Salon 2000 v. Dauwalter*, 2007 WL 1599223 (Not reported, Minn. App. 2007).

[16] *Environmental Recycling Technologies, Inc. v. Advanced Control Solutions*, 275, S.W.3d 162 (Ark. 2008); *Kim's Hair Study, LLC v. Rogers*, 2005 WL 1971259 (Conn. Super. 2005, July 20, 2005); *Wichita Clinic PA v. Louis*, 185 P.3d 946 (Kan. App. 2008).

[17] E.g., *Omniplex World Services Corp. v. U.S. Investigations Services Inc.*, 618 S.E.2d 340 (Va. 2005).

should be construed in the employer's favor.[18] Florida's statute also contains a provision that employment non-competes are presumed reasonable as to duration if the term is limited to six months or less, and presumed unreasonable as to duration if the term is two years or more.[19] If the non-compete's purpose is to protect trade secrets, under the Florida statute, less than five years is presumed reasonable, and more than ten years is presumed unreasonable.[20]

1.5 Unreasonable Non-compete Clauses

What if some element of the non-compete is found unreasonable by the court? If an element of the non-compete is unreasonable, there are three options available, and which the court follows depends on the jurisdiction. The Appendix lists the current approaches of different states to this question. First, a court may declare the whole non-compete to be void and unenforceable because of the presence of a single unreasonable term. This unforgiving approach is taken by Arkansas, Georgia, Nebraska, Virginia, and Wisconsin.[21]

Because courts tend to favor preserving contracts rather than invalidating them, some courts follow the 'blue pencil doctrine' instead, whereby the court strikes only the offending wording (if it is divisible) and will not add anything to the contract language.[22] A non-compete provision for a company in Indianapolis that says, for example, that the employee agrees to not engage in a competing business 'in Indianapolis *or any other location within the states of Indiana and Illinois*,' might be deemed unreasonably broad in its geographic restriction. Because Indiana is a state that will only amend non-competes using the blue pencil doctrine,

---

18 Fla. Stat. Ann. § 542.335(1)(h).

19 Fla. Stat. Ann. § 542.335(1)(d)(1).

20 Fla. Stat. Ann. § 542.335(1)(e).

21 Vanko (2009).

22 The phrase 'blue pencil doctrine' or 'blue pencil rule' is not used uniformly throughout all jurisdictions. Because this chapter concerns all states, we have adopted a single interpretation of the phrase that appears to follow the majority of readings of the phrase. *Central Adjustment Bureau, Inc. v. Ingram*, 678 S.W.2d 28 (Tenn. 1984) ('The "blue pencil" rule provides that an unreasonable restriction against competition may be modified and enforced to the extent that a grammatically meaningful reasonable restriction remains after the words making the restriction unreasonable are stricken.'); but see *Kegel v. Tillotson*, 297 S.W.3d 908 (Ky. App. 2009) ('In addition, our courts have adopted a "blue pencil" rule, whereby we are empowered to reform or amend restrictions in a non-compete clause if the initial restrictions are overly broad or burdensome.').

an Indiana court might strike everything after the word 'Indianapolis', thus limiting the geographic restriction of the non-compete and making it reasonable, without adding any language to the non-compete. However, many commentators and courts have criticized the blue pencil doctrine as valuing form over substance.[23]

In part due to this criticism, the more common approach in modern state courts is to allow the court to amend the wording of the non-compete to make it reasonable. However, some have criticized non-compete reformation as risky because it removes incentives for employers to narrowly tailor their non-compete clauses.[24] For this reason, before a non-compete is reformed in this way, many courts will require a preliminary conclusion that the employer drafted the non-compete in good faith. Typically, the employer has the burden of establishing that it acted in good faith, but in some states, the employee has the burden of establishing that the employer acted in bad faith.[25]

1.6 Adequate Consideration

Because non-competes are governed by contract law, a non-compete agreement must generally be accompanied by adequate consideration to form a valid contract. If an employee signs the non-compete at the time employment begins as part of the initial employment contract, the beginning of employment is generally viewed as adequate consideration. Some jurisdictions are more flexible on this issue. In the District of Columbia, a non-compete that the employee knew about at the time employment began but did not sign until some later time was considered to be accompanied by consideration.[26] However, if the non-compete is signed at a later time outside of that sort of situation, some states require the non-compete to be accompanied by a promotion or some other change to provide some added obligation on the part of the employer. These states typically do not view a simple promise of continued employment to be adequate consideration.

In contrast, Kentucky does view the promise of continued employment as being adequate consideration, and South Dakota does not require additional consideration if a non-compete is later added to the existing

---

[23] E.g., *Solari Industries, Inc. v. Malady*, A.2d 53 (N.J. 1970).

[24] E.g., Ingram (2002), 77–78.

[25] *Data Management, Inc. v. Greene*, 757 P.2d 62, 64 (Alaska 1988).

[26] *Ellis v. James v. Hurson Associates Inc.*, 565 A.2d 615 (D.C. 1989).

employment contract.[27] A recent change in Texas law now allows non-competes to be formed as unilateral contracts, which means that they are not enforceable at the moment they're made, but later become enforceable through some action by the employer.[28] However, this approach only occurs in a minority of states, with most states being more willing to invalidate a non-compete that is not accompanied by sufficient consideration.

1.7 Limiting Non-competes

In addition to state approaches varying in how non-competes are analyzed, the employee's job title might also affect the enforceability of a non-compete. Most states would treat a non-compete signed by a mailroom clerk in the same way they would treat a non-compete signed by that same company's Vice President of Communications. However, some states have statutory provisions addressing specific professions, either as an exception to non-enforcement or as an exception to enforcement. In Oregon, for instance, there is a statutory exception that specifically permits non-competes in the case of on-air broadcasting personalities.[29] In direct contrast, Arizona, Connecticut, Maine, and Massachusetts specifically prohibit broadcast employers from requiring employees to sign non-competes.[30]

Clearly, state approaches to specific professions can vary widely. Missouri's statute explicitly excludes those performing secretarial or clerical services from entering enforceable non-competes.[31] Contrast that with Colorado's statute, which includes a specific exception permitting non-competes to be enforceable against the 'professional staff' of executive and management personnel.[32] In Minnesota, a court recently considered whether hairstylists are members of a profession where non-competes should be prohibited in the interest of preserving customer

---

[27] *Central Adjustment Bureau Inc. v. Ingram Associates Inc.*, 622 S.W.2d 681 (1981); *Central Monitoring Service Inc. v. Zakinski*, 553 N.W.2d 513 (S.D. 1996).

[28] *Alex Sheshuonoff Management Services LP v. Johnson*, 209 S.W.3d 644 (Tex. 2006).

[29] Or. Rev. Stat. § 653.295.

[30] A.R.S. § 23–494; C.G.S.A. § 31–50b; 26 M.R.S.A. § 599; Mass. Gen. Law Ch. 112, §186.

[31] 28 Mo. Stat. Ann. § 431.202.

[32] Colo. Rev. Stat. § 8–2-113.

choice, but the court dismissed this idea as almost laughable.[33] In Vermont, however, there is a specific statutory provision that prohibits non-competes from being imposed by cosmetology and barbering schools as a condition of training.[34]

Physicians are another group of professionals that are routinely mentioned in the context of non-competes. Colorado, Delaware, and Massachusetts explicitly prohibit non-competes that restrict the employment options of physicians.[35] Massachusetts also includes statutory provisions prohibiting non-competes against nurses and social workers.[36] In contrast, several states without explicit statutory language permit non-compete clauses to be enforceable against physicians. In those states, the medical field is often treated like any other profession, but when the balancing test gets to the question of public policy, the interest of the public in choice of physicians is likely to become a very important factor. Somewhere in the middle between special exclusions for physicians and treating physicians like any other worker, the Texas statute sets out specific conditions that must exist for a non-compete against a physician to be enforceable, including that the physician must still have access to his list of patients and their medical records.[37]

Several states express in their statutes and case law that non-competes are disfavored as restraints of trade. In some cases, this policy position leads to states setting specific standards for applicability of non-competes. Colorado's statute expresses a policy against non-competes, but permits non-competes to be enforceable against executive and management personnel and against their professional staff.[38] Similarly, the Oregon statute on non-competes sets out specific categories of professions to which non-competes may apply.[39] Oregon's law of non-competes thus singles out as eligible for non-competes employees whose tasks are predominantly intellectual, managerial, or creative, where the employee exercises some amount of discretion and independent judgment.

In addition to limiting the application of non-competes based on the job description, some states also promote more concrete limitations. In

---

[33] *Salon 2000 v. Dauwalter*, 2007 WL 1599223 (Minn. App. 2007).

[34] 26 V.S.A. § 281(c).

[35] Colo. Rev. Stat. § 8–2-113; 6 Del. Code Ann. § 2707; Mass. Gen. Law Ch. 112, § 12X.

[36] Mass. Gen. Law Ch. 112, §§ 74D, 135C.

[37] Tex. Bus. & Com. Code § 15.50.

[38] Colo. Rev. Stat. § 8–2-113.

[39] Or. Rev. Stat. § 653.295.

Oregon, the statute declares non-competes unenforceable when the covenanting employee's salary is less than the median family income for a family of four according to the census bureau (approximately $50,000 as of the time of this writing).[40] The Massachusetts legislature also recently attempted to amend its statutory policy on non-competes to exempt all employees making less than $75,000, though this attempt to insert an income threshold was unsuccessful.[41]

1.8 Remedies Available

Having analyzed the various steps in non-compete litigation, the last important consideration is the remedy. Generally, when enforcement of a non-compete is sought by an employer, the employer is seeking an equitable remedy: an injunction barring the covenanting employee from taking action in violation of the non-compete provision. Most states approach non-compete issues from this perspective, though courts may also consider money damages owed by the former employee who breached a non-compete.

Because of the social and moral implications of an injunction limiting a person's ability to earn a livelihood, damages are sometimes more attractive on policy grounds. Non-compete provisions sometimes include language setting forth liquidated damages that will be owed by the covenanting employee in the event of a breach. In Colorado, the statute prohibits using non-competes to enjoin the practice of physicians, but notes that physicians may be liable to their former employer for monetary damages.[42] Put another way, injunctions are not available as a remedy for a violation of a non-compete agreement by a physician in Colorado, but damages may be owed. Similarly, the Texas statutory provision governing non-competes against physicians also includes language permitting the physician to buy out of the non-compete rather than be enjoined from practicing.[43]

1.9 Restatement (Third) of Employment Law

Because of the variety of approaches taken by states, the need has been recognized for a Restatement that explicitly addresses non-compete issues. The American Law Institute (ALI) is currently making efforts to

---

40 Or. Rev. Stat. § 653.295.
41 Rosen (2011).
42 Colo. Rev. Stat. § 8–2-113.
43 Tex. Bus. & Com. Code § 15.50.

address this need by creating the Restatement (Third) of Employment Law, which includes in its tentative draft a chapter about the duty of loyalty and restrictive covenants.[44] As of October 2012, the new Restatement is still being drafted, but the draft language concerning non-compete agreements has been approved by the ALI Council and ALI membership, though it is still subject to editorial changes. The proposed section 8.06 of the Restatement takes the position that non-competes are generally enforceable when reasonably tailored (time, space, and scope) to protect a legitimate interest of the employer, unless outweighed by the public interest or in the event of acts by the employer that would render the non-compete unenforceable.

The approved language of section 8.07 includes four categories of interests considered legitimate interests justifying the use of non-competes: the protection of confidential information, customer relationships, the employer's investment in the employee's reputation, and the employer's investment in purchasing the employee's business. With the possible exception of the business purchase interest (which is likely to be evaluated in a different context from typical employment non-competes), these categories of legitimate interests proposed for the above Restatement language largely echo the categories that are regularly found in non-compete case law and statutes throughout the United States in the context of the employment relationship. New Hampshire case law, for example, lists legitimate interests as including the protection of trade secrets, confidential information, goodwill, and customer contacts,[45] and the Missouri non-compete statute lists situations where non-competes are permitted, including situations involving trade secrets, customer relationships, goodwill, and loyalty.[46]

The language of section 8.07 specifies that the protection of confidential information is a legitimate employer interest. Under the approved language of section 8.02, 'confidential information' is defined as information that has economic value when the employer has made reasonable efforts to keep the information secret. The section further explains that information is not considered confidential if it is generally known, readily obtainable using proper means, or acquired by employees during the ordinary course of employment. This definition of 'confidential information' overlaps significantly with the definition of trade secrets, so

---

[44] The American Law Institute, Restatement (Third) of Employment Law <http://www.ali.org/index.cfm?fuseaction=publications.ppage&node_id=31>.

[45] *National Employment Service Corp. v. Olsten Staffing Service, Inc.* 761 A.2d 401 (N.H. 2000).

[46] 28 Mo. Stat. Ann. § 431.202.

a strict reading of the new Restatement language might restrict non-competes for confidentiality purposes to information that is considered a trade secret. Protecting customer relationships under the Restatement likely includes customer contacts and loyalty concerns as addressed by individual states' case law and statutes. The interest in the investment in the employee's reputation may be interpreted as analogous to goodwill under the current legal language. Accordingly, the proposed language of the Restatement would likely not cause much deviation from the typical balancing test between employee rights and the employer's legitimate business interests in states that adopt this new test, though a shift may be seen in states that previously recognized legitimate business interests in both trade secrets and other confidential information.

The business purchase interest deserves some additional consideration because of the potential effect on competition. A business owner who sells his business to another entity is likely to have a harder time complying with a non-compete, especially if the acquired business and related activities were previously the sole source of the business owner's livelihood. It is harder for the person selling his business to refrain from pursuing activities in the same field, and after the acquisition, he may well be inclined to pursue new activities that may be seen as broadly competing with his former, acquired entity. These business acquisition scenarios are fact intensive and need careful balancing and consideration while deciding whether to enforce a non-compete clause *vel non*.

In addition to these practical considerations, there may also be federal oversight in the context of a non-compete justified by a business purchase interest. The FTC has stated that a non-compete agreement accompanying a business purchase is likely permissible when it is ancillary to the transfer, reasonably necessary, and limited both geographically and temporally.[47] However, the FTC has previously found a business purchase non-compete illegal where an agreement to not compete was accompanied by an agreement by the previous owner to close other existing competing clinics.[48] Accordingly, business purchase non-competes, even if permitted under the proposed language of the Restatement, will likely require careful analysis to avoid unduly oppressive results and potential conflicts with federal law against anti-competitive practices.

---

47 Federal Trade Commission, 'Dealing with Competitors: Market Division or Customer Allocation' <http://www.ftc.gov/bc/antitrust/market_division.shtm>.

48 Federal Trade Commission, 'In the Matter of American Renal Associates and Fresenius Medical Care Holdings' <http://www.ftc.gov/os/caselist/0510234/index.shtm>.

2. TRADE SECRETS

Under the Uniform Trade Secrets Act (UTSA), a 'trade secret' is information, such as a formula, program, method, or process, which the holder takes reasonable steps to keep secret and which 'derives independent economic value, actual or potential, from not being generally known to, and not being readily ascertainable by proper means by, other persons who can obtain economic value from its disclosure or use.'[49] Currently, 46 states, plus the District of Columbia, have adopted the UTSA.[50]

We noted above that protecting trade secrets is regarded by many states as a legitimate business interest that justifies the imposition of a non-compete in the employment context. Because the term 'trade secret' does not encompass all potentially sensitive information, states which recognize protecting trade secrets as an interest justifying non-competes often broaden the interest by referring to the interest as the protection of 'trade secrets and other confidential information.' However, the adoption of the UTSA may also have some effect on a state's interpretation of non-compete law. The UTSA essentially provides an alternative to non-competes for protecting some of an employer's business interests. In part because of the state's adoption of the UTSA, North Dakota does not recognize an exception for protecting trade secrets, and declined to read a trade secret exception into the state's statute which contains a broad prohibition against non-compete agreements.[51]

2.1 Trade Secret Litigation

Trade secret litigation has some advantages over other forms of intellectual property litigation from the perspective of the employer plaintiff. Because of the nature of most businesses, a trade secret is, in a sense, a moving target. Other types of intellectual property (trademarks, copyrights, and patents) are more static, and the protection does not follow new changes, and thus a former employee with bad intentions could potentially make some minor changes to the employer's intellectual property and then pass it off as his own. The same cannot be done with trade secrets, and this flexibility may afford trade secret owners more protection than other forms of intellectual property in certain contexts.

---

[49] Unif. Trade Secrets Act § 1.

[50] Unif. Trade Secrets Act Refs & Annos.

[51] *Warner and Co. v. Solberg*, 634 N.W.2d 65 (N.D. 2001).

In addition to trade secret litigation's advantages over other IP litigation, it also offers an employer plaintiff some advantages over non-compete litigation, including a lesser showing being required to establish a violation. The UTSA allows for injunctive relief against parties in the case of actual *or threatened* trade secret misappropriation, and does not require signed writings or consideration as in the case of a non-compete.[52] Remedies for a UTSA violation are also an important factor. The UTSA provides for injunctions, and also permits an injunction to be extended to eliminate the commercial advantage from the misappropriation. In addition to injunctions, plaintiffs in a trade secret misappropriation suit under the UTSA are also entitled to recover money damages for the misappropriation.[53] The option of money damages under the UTSA is much more favorable to an employer plaintiff than the option of money damages for violation of a non-compete. While a plaintiff is generally not entitled to punitive damages under a contracts cause of action (such as for violation of a non-compete), an action for money damages under the UTSA could potentially include recovery of punitive damages and attorneys' fees.

However, defendants have numerous defenses to a trade secret cause of action, and trade secret law is to an extent murky and idiosyncratic. While the flexibility of trade secret protection does favor the employer to some extent, trade secret law does not include the exclusivity elements of other intellectual property forms. A former employee may use the nature of trade secret protection in this way to claim that there was no misappropriation because the employee either could have arrived at that information by independent discovery or reverse engineering, or because there were not sufficient safeguards in place to protect the trade secret.[54] Nonetheless, a claim of a trade secret violation may offer some protection to an employer who did not have a valid non-compete agreement with the employee.

2.2 Inevitable Disclosure Doctrine

In some jurisdictions, actual or threatened misappropriation may not be required to still find that a former employee violated the state's trade secret act. If actual trade secret misappropriation does not exist and the employee never threatened to disclose trade secrets, courts may turn to the inevitable disclosure doctrine. As its name implies, the inevitable

---

52 Unif. Trade Secrets Act § 2.

53 Unif. Trade Secrets Act § 3.

54 E.g., Saunders (2004), 147.

disclosure doctrine provides protection for the employer holders of trade secrets when disclosure by the former employee will be inevitably necessary to properly perform his new job.[55] Factors that may be considered when applying the inevitable disclosure doctrine may include the extent to which the employee's new and former employers are competitors of each other, how similar the employee's new and former positions are, and the degree to which the employee was exposed to the trade secrets.[56] Some courts, however, require a higher threshold than showing inevitability, such as a finding that the employee is unwilling to preserve confidentiality.[57]

If most employers are already protected from trade secret misappropriation by the UTSA and the inevitable disclosure doctrine, some argue that a non-compete provision aimed at protecting the employer against trade secret misappropriation is unnecessarily duplicative and restrictive of employee mobility. A common criticism of the inevitable disclosure doctrine is that it acts as a non-compete in the absence of a formal contract. This sort of de facto contract is why some courts require actual misappropriation of trade secrets rather than merely a finding that disclosure would be inevitable. This may indicate that courts are, to some extent, more willing to protect employers using non-compete law than trade secret law.

3. NON-COMPETES AND INNOVATION

The US economy has shifted over the last couple of decades towards being based on information and knowledge. In the middle of the century, workers typically joined a company and stayed there more or less permanently. Today, the workforce is more specialized, and rather than a focus being on manufacturing, the focus tends to be on service activities that require problem-solving skills. There is also an increased focus on employee mobility, rather than an expectation that the worker will stay at the same company until retirement. To some extent, this can be translated as decreased job security, but some have observed that increased

---

[55] Ingram (2002), 58–59.

[56] *Proctor & Gamble v. Stoneham*, 747 N.E.2d 268, 279 (Ohio Ct. App. 2000); Garrison & Wendt (2008), 155; Ingram (2002), 59.

[57] *H & R Block Eastern Tax Services, Inc. v. Enchura*, 122 F. Supp. 2d 1067 (W.D. Mo. 2000).

employee mobility leads to knowledge spillovers between firms that result in increased innovation.[58]

Some of the most prominent academic commentary on this topic relies on a comparison between the high technology industrial districts of Silicon Valley, near Stanford, and Route 128, near Harvard and MIT.[59] Route 128 started out ahead of Silicon Valley in the middle of the 20th century, but Silicon Valley quickly overtook Route 128 in terms of innovation. Modern Silicon Valley is a hotbed of technological innovation, rich with established firms and startup companies. The name 'Silicon Valley' has entered the popular lexicon in a way that 'Route 128' has not. Why? What accounts for this significant variation between the two areas? Anna Lee Saxenian attributes the difference to the different job cultures in the two regions, but Ronald Gilson argues that the most important difference between Route 128 and Silicon Valley is the legal infrastructures of the two states, specifically the law of non-competes. Massachusetts, while its law contains a number of statutory exceptions to the application of non-competes, is still largely in line with the rest of the country in viewing non-competes as generally enforceable. California, on the other hand, has a strict statute that explicitly prohibits almost all application of non-competes.[60]

Commentary in favor of non-competes tends to emphasize the degree to which non-competes protect businesses. Some say that the protection of non-competes is important to encourage entrepreneurship. On the other side of the coin, some say that it is important to discourage non-competes to facilitate innovation. As an empirical matter, it is unclear which side has a stronger argument. Non-competes doubtless protect the interests of the employer at the expense of the employee. Some empirical work suggests that non-competition agreements encourage the employer to invest in human capital, while discouraging the employee from investing in his or her own human capital.[61] Thus, any advantage to the employer may be counterbalanced by a decrease in the value of the human capital that the employee is bringing to his or her own position.

The comparison of Silicon Valley with Route 128 suggests that non-competes may facilitate innovation at the expense of long-term job stability. With the current economy being so driven by information and employee mobility, this may be the more desirable outcome, at least in

[58] Bishara (2006), 307.
[59] Gilson (1999).
[60] Ibid, 577.
[61] Garmaise (2011), 379.

appropriate regions. In other regions, however, perhaps it is optimal to continue to focus on protecting the long-term investments of business. In the context of high technology firms, the view of non-competes taken by a region thus may be a function of a tradeoff in the sometimes conflicting views and priorities of business managers and engineers.

4. CONCLUSION

After evaluating the widely differing approaches to non-competes in the US, the reader may be left with more questions than answers. Given California's success in the technology arena in the absence of non-competes, one might expect other high technology regions (like Seattle, Washington and Route 128 in Massachusetts) to take a similar approach, but they do not. It is possible that the variations between non-compete statutory provisions and common law approaches could be understood as products of each state's political economies at work.[62] With the current economy being so driven by information and employee mobility, banning non-competes may be good policy in some states or regions. However, in other regions, it may be optimal to continue to focus on protecting the long-term investments of business. Perhaps the optimality of permitting non-competes is determined by the interaction of the high tech sector and the social capital available, with a ban on non-competes only being desirable when there is both a large number of high tech companies and a large high tech population.

The current approach to non-competes in states that permit them is characterized not by bright line rules, but by a flexible, multi-factor test. This flexibility may be optimal since it minimizes strategic behavior and promotes symmetry between the employer and employee, who are both encouraged to exercise due care. This approach may be seen as striking the right balance between protecting employer investments, promoting long-term job stability, and preserving the state's economy, versus encouraging and vindicating the employee's own personal autonomy and freedom.

---

[62] *See* Ghosh (2011) (referring to California as an example of what Steven Caspar calls a 'liberal market economy').

REFERENCES

Bishara, N. (2006), 'Covenants Not to Compete in a Knowledge Economy: Balancing Innovation from Employee Mobility against Legal Protection for Human Capital Investment' 27 *Berkeley Journal of Employment and Labor Law* 287

Garmaise, M. (2011), 'Ties That Truly Bind: Noncompetition Agreements, Executive Compensation, and Firm Investment' 27 *Journal of Law, Economics and Organization* 376

Garrison, M. and J. Wendt (2008), 'The Evolving Law of Employee Non-compete Agreements: Recent Trends and an Alternative Policy Approach' 45 *American Business Law Journal* 107

Ghosh, S. (2011), 'What the Treatment of Covenants Not to Compete Teaches about Intellectual Property and Competition Norms' (unpublished manuscript on file with the author)

Gilson R. (1999), 'The Legal Infrastructure of High Technology Industrial Districts: Silicon Valley, Route 128, and Covenants not to Compete' 74 *New York University Law Review* 575

Ingram J. (2002), 'Covenants not to Compete' 36 *Akron Law Review* 49

Rosen, M. (2011), 'MA Noncompete Bill Has Been Re-filed', Massachusetts Noncompete Law Jan. 24, <http://www.massachusettsnoncompetelaw.com/2011/01/articles/legislation/ma-noncompete-bill-has-been-refiled/>

Saunders, K. (2004), 'Can You Keep a (Trade) Secret? The Pennsylvania Uniform Trade Secrets Act' 75 *Pennsylvania Bar Association Quarterly* 139

Vanko, K.J. (2009), 'A Quick State-By-State Guide on the Blue Pencil Rule' (*Legal Development in Non-Competition Agreements*, 8 Jan.) <http://www.non-competes.com/2009/01/quick-state-by-state-guide-on-blue.html> accessed Mar. 18, 2012

Whitmore P. (1990), 'A Statistical Analysis of Noncompetition Clauses in Employment Contracts' 15 *Journal of Corporate Law* 483

APPENDIX

STATE BY STATE NON-COMPETE LAW

State	Statute or constitutional provision	State case law	Blue pencil, reformation, or none[63]
Alabama	Ala. Code § 8–1-1	DeVoe v. Cheatham, 413 So.2d 1141 (Ala. 1982).	Equitable reformation
Alaska		Decristofaro v. Security Nat. Bank, 664 P.2d 167 (Alaska 1983).	Equitable reformation
		Data Management, Inc. v. Greene, 757 P.2d 62 (Alaska 1988).	
Arizona	A.R.S. § 23–494	Bed Mart, Inc. v. Kelley, 45 P.3d 1219 (Ariz. App. 2002).	Blue pencil only
Arkansas		Environmental Recycling Technologies, Inc. v. Advanced Control Solutions, 275, S.W.3d 162 (Ark. 2008).	No reform, no blue pencil
California	Cal. Bus. & Prof. Code. §§ 16600–16602.5	Edwards v. Arthur Anderson LLP, 189 P.3d 285 (Cal. 2008).	Non-competes void
Colorado	Colo. Rev. Stat. §8–2-113	Phoenix Capital Inc. v. Dowell, 176 P.3d 835 (Colo. App. 2007).	Equitable reformation
Connecticut	C.G.S.A. § 31–50b	Deming v. Nationwide Mutual Insurance Co., 905 A.2d 623 (Conn. 2006).	Equitable reformation
Delaware	6 Del. Code Ann. § 2707	McCann Surveyors Inc. v. Evans, 611 A.2d 1 (Del. Ch. 1987).	Equitable reformation
District Of Columbia	D.C. Code §28–4502	Ellis v. James V. Hurson Associates Inc., 565 A.2d 615 (D.C. 1989).	Reformation is presumed equitable

[63] Posting of Kenneth J. Vanko to Legal Developments in Non-Competes (Jan. 9, 2009), <http://www.non-competes.com/2009/01/quick-state-by-state-guide-on-blue.html>. 'Blue pencil' and 'equitable reformation' are terms that refer to a state's approach to unreasonable non-compete terms; specifically, whether the courts of that state will strike offending language in a contract (blue pencil), alter the contract by adding new or different terms (equitable reformation), or void the non-compete entirely. Section 1.5 discusses the distinctions further.

State	Statute or constitutional provision	State case law	Blue pencil, reformation, or none
Florida	Fla. Stat. Ann. § 542.335	Miller Mechanical Inc. v. Ruth, 300 So.2d 11 (Fla. 1974).	Reformation required
Georgia	Ga. Const. art. III, § VI, Par. V(c)1	Onbrand Media v. Codex Consulting, Inc., 687 S.E.2d 168 (Ga. App. 2009).	No reformation, no blue pencil
Hawaii	Haw. Rev. Stat. § 480–4(c)	7's Enterprises Inc. v. Del Rosario, 143 P.3d 23 (Haw. 2006).	Undecided
Idaho		Bybee v. Isaac, 178 P.3d 616 (Idaho 2008).	Reformation required
Illinois		Southern Illinois Medical Business Associates v. Camillo, 546 N.E.2d 1059 (Ill. App. 1989).	Equitable reformation
Indiana		MacGill v. Reid, 850 N.E.2d 926 (Ind. App. 2006).	Blue pencil only
Iowa		Ma & Pa, Inc. v. Kelly, 342 N.W.2d 500 (Iowa 1984).	Equitable reformation
Kansas		Wichita Clinic PA v. Louis, 185 P.3d 946 (Kan. App. 2008).	Equitable reformation
Kentucky		Central Adjustment Bureau Inc. v. Ingram Associates Inc., 622 S.W.2d 681 (Ky. 1981).	Equitable reformation
Louisiana	La. Rev. Stat. Ann. § 23:921	Ticheli v. John H. Carter Co., Inc, 996 So.2d 437 (La. 2008).	Reformation permitted for time and activity; not for location.
Maine	26 M.R.S.A. § 599	Roy v. Bolduc, 34 A.2d 479 (Me. 1943).	Equitable reformation
Maryland		Ecology Services Inc. v. Clym Environmental Services LLC, 952 A.2d 999 (Md. App. 2008).	Presumed to follow blue pencil rule
Massachusetts	Mass. Gen. Law Ch. 112, § 12X	Court's focus is on reasonableness. All Stainless, Inc. v. Colby, 308 N.E.2d 481 (Mass. 1974).	Equitable reformation

State	Statute or constitutional provision	State case law	Blue pencil, reformation, or none
Michigan	Mich. Comp. Laws § 445.774a	St. Clair Medical PC v. Borgiel, 715 N.W.2d 914 (Mich. App. 2006).	Equitable reformation
Minnesota		Freeman v. Duluth Clinic Inc. (Minn. 1983).	Equitable reformation
		Overholt Crop Ins. Service Co. Inc. v. Bredeson, 437 N.W.2d 698 (Minn. App. 1989).	
Mississippi		Kennedy v. Metropolitan Life Ins. Co. 759 So.2d 362 (Miss. 2000).	Equitable reformation
Missouri	28 Mo. Stat. Ann. § 431.202	Brown v. Rollet Bros. Trucking Co. Inc., 291 S.W.3d 766 (Mo. App. 2009).	Equitable reformation
Montana	Mont. Code Ann. §§ 28–2-703 and 704	Access Organics v. Hernandez, 175 P.3d 899 (Mont. 2008).	Direct restraints against employees void
Nebraska		Aon Consulting, Inc. v. Midlands Financial Benefits Inc., 748 N.W.2d 626 (Neb. 2008).	No reform, no blue pencil
		Mertz v. Pharmacists Mut. Ins. Co., 625 N.W.2d 197 (Neb. 2001).	
Nevada	Nev. Rev. Stat. § 613.200	Hansen v. Edwards, 426 P.2d 792 (Nev. 1967).	Equitable reformation
New Hampshire		National Employment Service Corp. v. Olsten Staffing Service, Inc. 761 A.2d 401 (N.H. 2000).	Equitable reformation
New Jersey		Whitmyer Bros. Inc. v. Doyle, 274 A.2d 577 (N.J. 1971).	Equitable reformation
		Solari Industries, Inc. v. Malady, A.2d 53 (N.J. 1970).	
New Mexico		Insure New Mexico, LLC v. McGonigle, 995 P.2d 1053 (N.M. App. 2000).	Undecided
New York		Reed, Roberts Associates Inc. v. Strauman, 353 N.E.2d 590 (N.Y. 1976).	Equitable reformation

State	Statute or constitutional provision	State case law	Blue pencil, reformation, or none
North Carolina	N.C. Gen. Stat. § 75–4	Medical Staffing Network Inc. v. Ridgway, 670 S.E.2d 321 (N.C. App. 2009).	Blue pencil only
North Dakota	N.D. Cent. Code § 9–08–06	Warner and Co. v. Solberg, 634 N.W.2d 65 (N.D. 2001).	Non-competes void
Ohio	Ohio Rev. Code Ann. § 1331.02	Raimonde v. Van Vlerah, 325 N.E.2d 544 (Ohio 1975).	Equitable reformation
Oklahoma	15 Okla. Stat. §§ 217–219	Cardiovascular Surgical Specialists, Corp. v. Mammana, 61 P.3d 210 (Okla. 2002).	Blue pencil only
Oregon	Or. Rev. Stat. § 653.295	Kennedy v. Wackenhut Corp., 599 P.2d 1126 (Or. App. 1979).	Equitable reformation
Pennsylvania		J.C. Ehrlich Co. Inc. v. Martin, 979 A.2d 862 (Pa. Super. 2009).	Equitable reformation
Rhode Island		Cranston Print Works Co. v. Pothier, 848 A.2d 213 (R.I. 2004).	Case law conflicts
South Carolina		Milliken & Co. v. Morin, 685 S.E.2d 828 (S.C. App. 2009).	Blue pencil only
South Dakota	S.D. Codified Laws § 53-9-8 through § 53–9-11	Central Monitoring Service Inc. v. Zakinski, 553 N.W.2d 513 (S.D. 1996).	Undecided
Tennessee		Murfreesboro Medical Clinic PA v. Udom, 166 S.W.3d 674 (Tenn. 2005).	Equitable reformation
Texas	Tex. Bus. & Com. Code §§ 15.50–15.52	Alex Sheshuonoff Management Services LP v. Johnson, 209 S.W.3d 644 (Tex. 2006). Mann Frankfort Stein & Lipp Advisors Inc. v. Fielding, 289 S.W.3d 844 (Tex. 2009).	Reformation required
Utah		Robbins v. Finlay, 645 P.2d 623 (Utah 1982).	Undecided

State	Statute or constitutional provision	State case law	Blue pencil, reformation, or none
Vermont	26 V.S.A. § 281(c)	Roy's Orthopedic Inc. v. Lavigne, 454 A.2d 1242 (Vt. 1982).	Equitable reformation
Virginia		Omniplex World Services Corp. v. U.S. Investigations Services Inc., 618 S.E.2d 340 (Va. 2005).	No reform, no blue pencil
Washington		Knight, Vale and Gregory v. McDaniel, 680 P.2d 448 (Wash. App. 1984).	Equitable reformation
West Virginia		Huntington Eye Associates, Inc. v. LoCascio, 553 S.E.2d 773 (W.Va. 2001).	Equitable reformation
Wisconsin	Wis. Stat. Ann. § 103.465	Star Direct, Inc. v. Dal Pra, 767 N.W.2d 898 (Wis. 2009).	Limited blue pencil (divisible covenants in non-compete)
Wyoming		Hopper v. All Pet Animal Clinic, Inc., 861 P.2d 531 (Wyo. 1993).	Equitable reformation

PART VI

Public sector business research and development

24. Innovation in public sector research

Ann L. Monotti

1. INTRODUCTION

1.1 Models for Transferring Public Sector Knowledge to Benefit Innovation

The research performed within universities produces new knowledge that can be disseminated to benefit innovation in at least three broadly defined, but not necessarily mutually exclusive, ways. One is through 'open' dissemination of the ideas for public use. This is the traditional way in which academics engage with their peers and the community at large and is reflected in the oft-used phrase: 'publish or perish'. Dissemination will commonly be in the form of published literature such as books and articles, but may also arise through such activities as conference presentations, interviews, student supervisions and other forms of teaching. As a general principle, the purpose of open dissemination is to share and circulate new ideas widely so that others can use these for their own purposes without having to seek permission. Business innovation in its many forms can benefit from this open dissemination of public sector-generated research provided that the costs and conditions of access do not impede their wide availability on reasonable terms. There have been problems with affordable access to scholarly works in the past[1] and the development of open source licences for software, Creative Commons licences and institutional open access databases for copyright works are initiatives that have helped to makes ideas more widely accessible.[2] In recent years, there has been a move towards modifying this licensing approach so that it can apply to inventions in areas of health and

[1] Monotti with Ricketson (2003), 337–342.

[2] E.g., GPL: <http://www.gnu.org/copyleft/gpl.html>.

biotechnology to enhance their availability and to avoid locking up the rights to exploit the technology in the hands of a few.[3]

The second broad way in which suitable public sector research is disseminated to support business innovation specifically is through 'technology transfer'. This phrase has generally been understood as describing the process of assignment or licensing of intellectual property rights (IPRs), and in particular patented inventions, to existing companies for further research and development in return for a royalty stream.[4] This model is also 'open' in the sense that the details of the invention contained in the patent specification become public but only after a period of secrecy. However, this model is not open in the sense that the ideas are free for people to use. To the contrary, members of the public are limited in the uses to which they can put the knowledge they acquire from reading the specification. A patentee of a granted patent has exclusive rights to exploit the invention and may choose to whom he grants some or all of those rights and upon what terms. In the absence of authorization, a person can use the ideas published in any patent specification but only as long as he does not exercise any of the exclusive rights of the patentee in the process.

A third broad model for disseminating research to support innovation involving new developments in technology has been pursued since the late 1990s in the expectation of generating higher financial returns that will be earned from licensing. This involves the incorporation of a start-up company expressly for the purpose of exploiting the IPRs that are assigned or licensed to the company.[5] A concentration of start-ups appears in the 'high tech' fields of ICT and biotechnology but provides an option for other forms of technology that have a realistic commercial application. The success of these start-ups usually depends upon attracting sufficient venture capital funding to enable further research and development to produce and market the technology and eventually float the company as a public company.[6]

---

3 Kapczynski et al (2005); Hope (2008).

4 E.g., AUTM annual licensing surveys: <http://www.autm.net/Home.htm>.

5 Monotti with Ricketson (2003), 451–456; AUTM US Licensing Activity Survey: FY2010 found 651 start-up companies were formed from research at US universities during 2010.

6 Barkoczy and Sandler (2007); ABS (2011).

1.2 The Changing Nature of Public Sector Research and Incentives for Increased Industry Involvement

In the past, technology transfer related to the IPRs that resulted from academically directed research, much of which is unsuitable for commercial exploitation due to its 'upstream' nature. However, the commercial environment in which universities are required to participate is rapidly expanding beyond working solely with the results of academically directed research. Increasingly government policies in the UK and Australia in particular follow an 'impact agenda' in order to influence the nature of research itself that is performed to increase outcomes suitable for technology transfer. This agenda encourages universities and industry to collaborate in the formulation of the actual research questions and to engage throughout the research process to produce results that have some commercial or social value.[7] At the same time, the role of universities in the innovation process is becoming more important as companies can no longer afford their own research facilities and outsource their R&D activities to universities and others.[8]

1.3 Policy Challenges Facing University–Industry Collaborations

The formation of linkages between business and universities for the purpose of spurring innovation in its many different forms is widely adopted by government policy makers as an essential aspect of public sector research and transfer of technology.[9] Government support and encouragement for such collaborations is long standing and expectations for universities to be involved in the innovation enterprise, and the challenges that this presents, continue appear in policy documents throughout the world despite considerable effort to reduce barriers facing successful collaborations.[10] As the OECD stated in 2010:

> Universities, colleges and vocational training centres are essential nodes in the innovation system, both producing and attracting the human capital needed for innovation. These institutions act as essential bridges between players – businesses, governments and countries – in broader and more open systems of innovation. The major policy challenge is to recognise the essential role of universities in the innovation enterprise rather (than) view them, as is all too

---

[7] Research Councils UK, *Excellence with Impact*; Ternouth and Garner (2011).

[8] Lambert (July 2003b), [1.9].

[9] Lederman (1997), 26; Monotti with Ricketson (2003), 231–243.

[10] Monotti 2009), 221–249.

> commonly the case, simply as providers of essential public goods. This requires a greater focus of policy makers on ensuring independence, competition, excellence, entrepreneurial spirit and flexibility in universities.[11]

The thrust of this passage identifies continuing policy challenges that are not new and identifies *universities* as the actors who must change to become more entrepreneurial and more commercial: two characteristics that frequently sit uncomfortably with the beliefs, practices, attitudes and goals of many researchers in the academic world.[12] It is worth supplementing this passage with observations from the final report of *The Lambert Review on Business-University Collaborations* (2003) that emphasize the roles for both government and business in improving university–business collaborations: 'Government will have to do more to support business–university collaboration. Business will have to learn how to exploit the innovative ideas that are being developed in the university sector.'[13] Finding an appropriate balance between the competing interests of academia, government and business in particular situations enhances successful commercialization of university technologies.

1.4 Emerging Themes

In relation to business innovation generally, the incentive to innovate is likely to be the expectation of increased productivity, competitiveness, profit and growth. However, the degree of uncertainty as to technical and financial outcomes that accompanies innovation means that business will limit investment to acceptable risk levels.[14] The two chapters in this section tackle different aspects of these issues from different perspectives. Noel Byrne highlights the challenges for industry in successfully negotiating patent licences of technologies developed within universities. Although he has observed significant improvement in relationships with 'top level' universities he identifies cultural differences and varying levels of commercial skills that remain as potential obstacles in the wider public research environment. Claire Driscoll's chapter concerns the federal government-funded R&D environment in the US and the leadership role taken by the National Institutes of Health (NIH) to design a mix of grant conditions, guidelines and agreement templates that parties can use to

---

11 OECD (2010b), 11.

12 Monotti with Ricketson (2003), 135–139.

13 Lambert (2003a), Foreword.

14 DIISR (2011), ch 3.

manage their diverse expectations from the transfer of specific technologies. The principal theme that emerges in both chapters concerns the barriers to successful university–industry collaborations and technology transfer and finding means for lowering and removing those barriers in appropriate circumstances.

2. BARRIERS TO INDUSTRY–UNIVERSITY COLLABORATIONS FOR TECHNOLOGY TRANSFER

Innovation involving industry and universities and other public sector research institutions presents its own special set of risks or barriers that can complicate or impede the path to effective collaboration or licensing of technologies.[15] The types of 'barriers' to effective collaborations and commercial transactions that have been identified in the past, and with which policy-makers continue to grapple, include:

1. Inherent differences between universities and the commercial sector.[16] Differences in objectives pursued by industry and public sector institutions can set these parties on a collision course if collaborations are not managed appropriately. Simple differences such as adherence to time-lines can frustrate a more disciplined commercial approach to research.
2. Deficiencies in 'customer service'[17] and 'variable quality' in the university technology transfer offices.[18]
3. Attitudes of inventors – cultural 'problems' of a certain degree of academic lack of enthusiasm for innovation. They may be unaware of the commercial opportunities that may be present in their research or unwilling to be involved in any commercial exploitation.
4. The nature of the research performed within universities, which in many instances is basic or fundamental and thus disconnected from

---

[15] Monotti with Ricketson (2003), 428–434.

[16] *UWA v Gray* (2010) 179 FCR 346, [183]–[185], [206]; Lambert (2003a), [1.25].

[17] Lambert (2003b), [1.16].

[18] Lambert (2003b), Executive Summary 5.

the national innovation system,[19] or 'too general or too fundamental, and thus long term, to be easily usable'.[20] An aligned barrier is the lack of critical mass of IP portfolios and the identified need to establish centres of excellence and entrepreneurship as well as interdisciplinary centres to overcome this barrier.

5. The lack of funds – university research is likely to require a further significant investment in the form of 'pre-seed', 'seed', or 'venture capital' funding to reduce the commercial risk for industry sponsors.[21] This has been referred to progressively by terms such as 'research protection gap', innovation progression gap'.[22] The impact of the global financial crisis in recent times has intensified the shortage of available VC funds.
6. Lack of expertise – the path from disclosure of IP to protection, licensing or other form of exploitation requires extensive skill in a variety of areas that staff in industrial liaison offices might not possess.[23]
7. The patent laws and the conflicts that can arise within a university research setting when academics may want to publish and disseminate results expeditiously to enhance their career progression ('publish or perish') but commercial demands require delays in publication to allow proper development of the invention before patent filing.

3. INITIATIVES TO REMOVE THE BARRIERS FOR INDUSTRY–UNIVERSITY COLLABORATIONS

3.1 A Work in Progress

Governments, industry and universities have worked hard for some decades now to minimize the barriers to effective innovation involving business–university collaborations and have arguably made considerable progress.[24] Nevertheless, as Byrne notes in his chapter, there remains a lot to be done. From his experience in advising and negotiating technology licensing agreements he has observed that 'top universities' have

[19] Kemp D, *Knowledge and Innovation, White Paper* (1999).
[20] Massey, Quintas & Wield (1991), 22; Sherman (1995), 16.
[21] OST (1992), Executive Summary 9, [14(a)].
[22] Monotti with Ricketson (2003), 429.
[23] Rahm et al (2000), ch 5, 83.
[24] E.g., Lambert (2003a); DIISR (2011).

developed their skills to a considerable extent whereas barriers in this area of technology transfer remain in many other academic institutions. These observations are endorsed by the continuing reports issued about performance of universities in technology transfer. Most recently, the OECD observed in its 2010 report on innovation strategy that there remains a need to improve collaborations and technology transfer from research institutions.[25]

> Barriers and regulations that limit effective interaction among universities, firms and public laboratories should be removed and collaborative arrangements that facilitate the formation of networks should be improved. Ensuring that researchers, public research institutes and higher education institutions have incentives and opportunities to collaborate among themselves and with industry is essential. Criteria for evaluating research performance should be adjusted to reflect the multiple missions of research institutions, including knowledge transfer. Clearly defined expectations and boundaries for collaboration and well-trained technology transfer personnel are essential to achieve this goal.[26]

The inherent differences between universities and the private sector raise the particular tension identified above when it comes to patenting and licensing patented technologies: at what point can the academic publish his or her research? As Driscoll notes in her conclusion, potential licensees of technology seek restriction or delay of public disclosure to facilitate their commercial development of that technology. This delay will be important for successful commercialization but the fundamental tension between the public sector research community and commercial interests must be balanced in ways that do not stifle research and development and their contribution towards a country's innovation objectives. The problems are magnified when the inventions are health related.

3.2 Development of Guidelines and Model Agreements

Universities and other public sector research institutes in other jurisdictions generally welcome guidance in managing complex IP, licensing and other complex matters that arise when technologies are commercialized. There is no sense in all having to 'reinvent the wheel' but the areas on which guidelines are required must first be identified. Driscoll focuses specifically in her chapter upon the policies and practices of the NIH in

[25] OECD (2010a), 16; OECD (2010b), 11.
[26] OECD (2010a), 16.

the US. She traces the development of technology transfer in the US and describes the enlightened approaches taken by the NIH from as early as 1994 to provide guidelines and eventually model agreements for its grant recipients.

The important role for such guidelines and precedent materials in lowering barriers was emphasized also by Richard Lambert in *The Lambert Review of Business–University Collaboration* which was released in December 2003. One significant outcome of this review following his recommendations was the drafting of a suite of template agreements – *The Lambert Toolkit* – as a resource for universities and companies that wish to undertake collaborative research projects with each other.[27] These agreements attempt to find a middle ground on the issues that can become stumbling blocks in negotiations and that are discussed in the Byrne chapter – in particular rights in intellectual property generated under the research collaboration and rights to publish research openly. Collaborative research grant schemes from the UK Research Councils now use a template industry funding agreement (MICA) before a project starts so that the parties can agree upon and manage the areas of likely mismatch of interests: including 'relative responsibilities, governance, regulatory approvals, indemnity, intellectual property rights, reporting, and access to data and samples'.[28]

3.3 Tackling Funding Gaps

Lack of funding remains a barrier to creation of knowledge and bringing the ideas to market – there is a finite amount of resources available for R&D activities. Governments use a variety of funding mechanisms to target this lack of funding and to encourage the injection of development funds from venture capitalists. In Australia, lack of venture capital has seen research languish or taken overseas for its further development and the sharp reduction of VC funds generally following the global financial crisis may require innovative programmes to remove heavy reliance upon this source of funds.

A new development is the establishment of programmes that support translational research[29] that aims to accelerate basic medical research to

---

27 See: <http://www.ipo.gov.uk/lambert>.

28 MRC Industry Collaboration Agreement: <http://www.mrc.ac.uk/Funding opportunities/Grants/MICA/Specification/index.htm>.

29 Cancer Council NSW <http://www.register4.org.au/Register4/Our_research/Research_explained/Translational_research/Register4/Our_research/Research_explained/Translational_Research.aspx>.

clinical practice. The programmes generally involve universities and hospitals as the main partners with funding from government and philanthropic organizations. An example in the UK of this development is the Paterson Institute for Cancer Research situated within the University of Manchester.[30] The bulk of the funds are provided by Cancer Research UK, but industry, charitable and government funds also provide research support for additional projects. An Australian example is the Translational Research Institute (TRI), which has been developed in Queensland as a joint initiative of the Australian Government, the Queensland Government, and the Atlantic Philanthropies and involving the University of Queensland, Queensland University of Technology and Mater Medical Research Institute.[31] The aim of TRI is for research on drugs and vaccines to be 'translated' into the final manufacture of those drugs and vaccines within Australia. In the US, the National Institute for Health Research specifically funds translational research involving an NHS provider in collaboration with a university partner.

4. CONCLUDING OBSERVATIONS

An examination of innovation through the lens of industry is complex and requires consideration from multifaceted perspectives. This section is limited to industry innovation that involves some form of collaboration or relationship with a university or a national funding body to develop commercial technologies. Arguably, the principal theme to draw from the two chapters of Byrne and Driscoll is that governments and national funding bodies play a critical role in reducing or removing the barriers that necessarily exist when the objectives of industry and business do not align completely with those of universities and other public research institutes. As long as governments, universities and researchers value openness in science as critical for economic and social development but also recognize the value of technology transfer in appropriate cases there will be barriers to commercial collaboration that require management. The US and UK approach of developing various forms of guidelines, grant conditions and model contracts can help minimize variability in knowledge and skills among universities as well as provide benchmarks for what might represent fair and reasonable terms for commercial collaborations. The Australian government and its public funding bodies

---

[30] Paterson Institute for Cancer Research <http://www.paterson.man.ac.uk/about/funding.stm>.

[31] DIISR (2011).

are less advanced in this regard but they can learn from these resources in the interim until such time as it is necessary to develop an Australian specific set of resources.

REFERENCES

Association of University Technology Managers, *AUTM US Licensing Activity Survey: FY2010*

Australian Bureau of Statistics, *Venture Capital and Later Stage Private Equity Survey 2011*

Barkoczy, S. and D. Sandler (2007), *Government Venture Capital Incentives – A Multi-Jurisdiction Comparative Analysis*, Australian Tax Research Foundation

Department of Innovation Industry (2011), Science and Research, *Australian Innovation System Report 2011*, Commonwealth of Australia

Garner, C. and P. Ternouth, 'ipHandbook of Best Practices' in *New Companies to Commercialize IP: Should You Spinout or Start-up?*, Ch. 13.5, <http://www.iphandbook.org/handbook/ch13/p05/>

Hope, J. (2008), *Biobazaar: the Open Source Revolution and Biotechnology*, Harvard University Press

Kapczynski, A., S. Chaifetz, Z. Katz and Y. Benkler (2005), 'Addressing Global Health Inequities: An Open Licensing Approach for University Innovations' 20 *Berkeley Technology Law Journal* 1031

Kemp, The Hon Dr, MP (1999), Minister for Education, Training and Youth Affairs, Knowledge and Innovation: White Paper, Commonwealth of Australia

Kemp, The Hon Dr (1999), MP, Minister for Education, Training and Youth Affairs, New Knowledge, New Opportunities: Green Paper, Commonwealth of Australia

Lambert, R. (2003a), *The Lambert Review on Business–University Collaborations*, HMT

Lambert, R. (2003b), *The Lambert Review on Business–University Collaborations: Summary of Consultation Responses and Emerging Issues*, HMSO

Lambert Toolkit, <http://www.ipo.gov.uk/lambert>

Massey, D., P. Quintas and D. Wield (1991), *High Tech Fantasies: Science Parks in Society, Space and Time*, Routledge

Monotti, A.L. (2009), 'Commercialization of University Research and Free Diffusion – What Does Experience Show Works Best in and for Australia?' in C. Arup and W. van Caenegem (eds), *Intellectual Property Policy Reform*, Edward Elgar

Monotti, A.L. with S. Ricketson (2003), *Universities and Intellectual Property: Ownership and Exploitation*, Oxford University Press

Office of Science and Technology (1992), *Intellectual Property in the Public Sector Research Base*, HMSO

Organisation for Economic Co-operation and Development (2010a), *Ministerial Report on the OECD Innovation Strategy: Innovation to Strengthen Growth and Address Global and Social Challenges*, <http://www.oecd.org/dataoecd/51/28/45326349.pdf>

Organisation for Economic Co-operation and Development (2010b), *The OECD Innovation Strategy: Getting a Head Start on Tomorrow*, OECD

Rahm, D., J. Kirkland and B. Bozeman (2000), *University–Industry R & D Collaboration in the United States, United Kingdom and Japan*, Kluwer

Research Councils UK, *Excellence with Impact*, <http://www.rcuk.ac.uk/kei/impacts/Pages/home.aspx>

Sherman B. (1995), 'Governing Science: Patents and Public Sector Research in the United Kingdom' 20 *International Review of Industrial Property and Copyright Law* 15

Ternouth, P. and C. Garner (2011), 'What Works in Business–University Knowledge Exchange' *ATSE Focus* 9, <http://www.cihe.co.uk/category/knowledge/publications/>

25. Technology transfer law, policies and practices at the U.S. National Institutes of Health

Claire T. Driscoll

1. INTRODUCTION

The National Institutes of Health (NIH), United States (U.S.) Department of Health and Human Services (DHHS), headquartered in Bethesda, Maryland, is one of the world's largest biomedical research organizations both in terms of the financial support it provides and its research output. Most of the NIH's 27 individual Institutes and Centers have both a funding function (in 2010 \$31.2 billion was distributed in the form of grants and contracts) and a research function (the NIH's 'in-house' or intramural research program, most of which is conducted by U.S. federal employees on its main campus in suburban Washington DC, has a budget of nearly \$3 billion per year).[1] An overview of U.S. government technology transfer statutes will be presented in conjunction with a summary of key federal technology transfer policies. In addition, NIH's intellectual property (IP) and licensing policies as well as several 'best practices' aimed at ensuring that the public derives health benefits from the successful transfer of NIH-supported and NIH-invented biomedical inventions to the private sector will be described.

2. THE AMERICAN TECHNOLOGY TRANSFER LANDSCAPE

2.1 Before Bayh-Dole

The legal basis for the current successful and often imitated U.S. technology transfer system was created in the 1980s and 1990s. Before

[1] NIH (2011 Budget).

1980, technologies discovered in university and government laboratories using federal money were solely owned by the U.S. government (as a whole).[2] Neither the university nor the particular government agency which funded a given research project could seek ownership rights to inventions that arose. If a government-owned invention happened to get licensed then any royalty income earned was deposited directly with the U.S. Treasury. One study estimated that by the 1970s more than 28,000 government-owned patents languished in file cabinets and on shelves – only 5 percent of these inventions were ever licensed and even fewer still resulted in the development of commercial products.[3] The subsequent radical statutory changes were, in part, a response to the realization that government-funded discoveries and inventions, whether made at national laboratories, federal science agency laboratories, or at universities, research institutes and hospitals supported by federal grants and contracts, were not being successfully transferred to or commercialized by companies. This situation was all the more troubling given the fact that during the decades that followed the end of World War II literally hundreds of highly ranked U.S.-based academic and federal research-intensive institutions were expanding and flourishing – a large portion of these entities' research endeavors were funded using U.S. government dollars.[4] The existence of this vast untapped source of technological innovation coupled with growing concerns about waning U.S. competitiveness in the global marketplace sparked Congress to act.

2.2 Summary of Key U.S. Technology Transfer Legislation

One of the first pieces of major technology transfer legislation to be promulgated was the 1980 Patent and Trademark Amendments Act.[5] This law is almost universally referred to by its colloquial name – the Bayh-Dole Act (the bill was originally co-sponsored by Senators Birch Bayh and Bob Dole). Under this Act, all federal grantees and contractors (or 'extramural' entities in NIH jargon), including university recipients of NIH research grants, were for the first time allowed to take title to inventions that arose out of research financed, in whole or in part, by the federal government.[6] Federal agencies that had intramural research

[2] U.S. General Accounting Office Report to Congressional Committees (2003), 3.

[3] Committee on the Judiciary (1998), 3.

[4] Ibid, 2.

[5] Pub. L. No. 96–517.

[6] 35 USC § 201(c)(1)–(3).

laboratories, which are also referred to as government-owned, government-operated (GOGOs) entities such as the NIH, the Food and Drug Administration (FDA) and the Centers for Disease Control and Prevention (CDC), were given the right to elect title to and to make patenting and licensing decisions for inventions made by their employees under the 1980 Stevenson-Wydler Technology Innovation Act.[7] This statute made technology transfer activities, for the first time, a formal part of the mission of federal government agencies.

With the enactment of the Federal Technology Transfer Act (FTTA)[8] in 1986 came several other significant changes to how both GOGOs and government-owned, contractor-operated (GOCO) federal laboratories[9] operated. Federal agencies and national laboratories were allowed to retain royalties and were required to share a portion of their royalty income with their employee inventors. Executive Order 12591[10] reinforced the government's strong support of technology transfer by requiring agencies to identify and empower staff to serve as points of contact for information about federal technologies that were available for licensing and for information about collaborative research opportunities.

2.3 Technology Transfer at NIH: Establishment of Technology Transfer Offices (TTOs) and the Emergence of a New Profession

In 1989 the central NIH Office of Technology Transfer (OTT) was established under the auspices of the NIH Division of Intramural Research.[11] Many of NIH's 27 Institutes and Centers also created dedicated TTOs in the early 1990s and this hybrid centralized-decentralized administrative structure remains in place. OTT has responsibility for managing patent prosecution work performed by more than a dozen contract law firms and OTT licensing and patenting managers have the sole authority to negotiate exclusive licenses on behalf of NIH and the FDA. Institute TTOs are responsible for evaluating all new employee invention disclosures and negotiating most types of technology transfer transactional agreements (except licenses).

After the passage of the FTTA in 1986 NIH TTOs usually hired non-specialized administrative staff – frequently these individuals had

---

[7] Pub. L. No. 96–480.

[8] Pub. L. No. 99–502.

[9] Also referred to as national laboratories or Federally Funded Research and Development Centers (FFRDCs).

[10] (1987) 52 *Federal Register* 13414.

[11] Rohrbaugh and Stanton (2009).

other responsibilities such as grants management, negotiation of government contracts or even human resources-related duties and they were simply asked to 'pitch in' by assisting with technology transfer activities on a part-time basis. Over time NIH TTOs have become primarily staffed by full-time IP, marketing, and business development specialists. In 2012 the majority of NIH technology transfer professionals have advanced degrees in biomedical science and many TTO employees also have business and law degrees as well as have hands-on experience working as patent attorneys, patent examiners, business development experts or researchers with biotechnology and pharmaceutical companies. This same phenomenon has occurred at academic TTOs – administrative generalists have been largely replaced by highly educated and trained specialists.

2.4 Funding Recipients and the Federal Government: a *Quid Pro Quo* Arrangement

The U.S. technology transfer laws described above established, for the first time, a uniform patent policy and straightforward procedures for election of title to IP for U.S.-based recipients of grant and contract funding by U.S. federal government agencies. This new way of doing business was a classic *quid pro quo* arrangement – in exchange for having the right to own and control their own IP and keep all royalty income earned from licensing those inventions, funding recipients and federal laboratories had to abide by some limitations on their activities and they had to adhere to certain reporting requirements.[12]

One Bayh-Dole and FTTA requirement is that the universities and federal agencies, respectively, have to preferentially license to small U.S.-based companies[13] and they must preferentially license to those companies, small or large, that manufacture in the U.S. (e.g., licensee products sold in the U.S. must be manufactured in the U.S. unless a waiver is granted).[14] University patent owners are not allowed to abandon existing pending patent applications or to waive rights to federally funded inventions to inventors in a personal capacity without first giving the funding agency an opportunity to take ownership of the IP.[15] Alternately the funding agency has the right to deny an intellectual property rights (IPR) waiver request from a university inventor and instead place the

[12] 35 USC § 201(c)(1)–(3).
[13] 35 USC § 202(c)(7)(D).
[14] 35 USC § 204.
[15] 35 USC § 202(c)(7)(A).

invention in the public domain if it is felt that this action would best serve the public. Federal funding recipients must report all inventions made using said funds to the government[16] within two months of the filing of a patent application by the grantee institution. Failure to adhere to any of these conditions can result in serious penalties – in theory, a non-compliant grant recipient could be designated as ineligible to receive future governmental funds.

Additional limitations on grantees in the Bayh-Dole Act include the requirement that the federal government retain a perpetual, paid up and royalty-free 'government use' license for all inventions that are made, even only partially, using government funds.[17] The U.S. government also retains what is referred to as a 'march-in' right.[18] The march-in determination process is an administrative proceeding that resembles a trial. The government can initiate such a proceeding under certain narrowly defined circumstances – for example, if an exclusive licensee appears to be unable or unwilling to expeditiously commercialize a given invention then NIH could either require the licensee to sublicense to other companies or it could terminate the license and transfer those same exclusive rights to a more capable company. Another plausible scenario where a march-in might be warranted would be one in which a given licensee company that was the sole supplier of an important drug or vaccine was unable to meet demand in the face of a public health emergency. Any person or company can ask a given government agency to 'march-in' and adjust or even terminate a previously approved license agreement between a licensee and that government agency (note: this march-in right is separate and distinct from proposed commercial development plan milestones and timelines criteria that are often included in exclusive commercial licenses). To date four march-in petitions have been evaluated by the NIH: none of these petitions has been successful.[19]

Finally government agencies are permitted to revoke certain Bayh-Dole rights, namely the right to elect title to inventions, for particular grant and contract solicitations. This administrative tool is called a determination of exceptional circumstances (DEC) and the decision on whether or not one can be used is solely made by the funding agency

---

[16] 35 USC § 202(c)(4); Patents, Trademarks, and Copyrights, 37 CFR § 401 (2002); reporting can be done electronically via the Interagency iEdison website: <http://www.iedison.gov>.

[17] 35 USC § 202(c)(4).

[18] 35 USC § 203.

[19] NIH March-In Response; NIH, *Determination in the Case of Fabrazyme® Manufactured by Genzyme Corporation®*.

itself.[20] The planned use of a DEC must be included in the agency's corresponding Request for Application or Request for Proposal announcement.[21] A DEC is a condition of funding – applicants know upfront that only the funding agency will have the right to elect title to inventions (or to elect not to take title) they may make while carrying out the grant or contract activities. However the NIH, which on average awards more than 50,000 individual research grants and contracts each year,[22] has used a DEC in a specific funding solicitation only a handful of times in the last 30 years. In each instance when a DEC was used the main goal of the particular funded activity was the creation of an important set of valuable biomedical research tools (for example as part of the National Human Genome Research Institute (NHGRI)-funded and managed Mammalian Gene Collection project, the NIH-paid contractors agreed to create physical copies of each and every known mouse, rat and human gene and to make those cDNAs available to researchers worldwide via a central repository; other initiatives that have included a DEC have involved the creation of large collections of transgenic and knockout mice).[23]

3. NIH TECHNOLOGY TRANSFER POLICIES

3.1 Extramural Technology Transfer Policies

Of the large number of federal organizations covered by the Bayh-Dole Act, the FTTA and other related statutes, NIH has issued the largest number of formal technology transfer guidance documents and written policies. Adherence to official NIH policies is a conditional term in most grants and contracts whereas adherence to guidelines or guidance documents is optional though strongly encouraged. By clearly describing its interpretation of how these technology transfer laws should be implemented by its own scientific employees as well as by its extramural funding recipients, NIH has taken a leading role in promoting the transfer of federally funded technologies into real-world applications.

---

[20] 37 CFR § 401.3.

[21] United States Public Health Service Technology Transfer Manual (1999), Chapter No. 607.

[22] NIH Budget (2011).

[23] Thomas (2008).

The first technology transfer-related guidance issued by the NIH came out in 1994 and it was entitled 'Developing Sponsored Research Agreements.'[24] This guidance provided suggested conditions that should be met when a university entered into a broad, often multi-year and potentially financially lucrative sponsored research relationship with a company. NIH's goal was to assist grantees with setting reasonable boundaries so as to ensure that unbiased, independent research continued to be conducted at the institution – for example, the guidance recommended that universities not give any one company decision-making control over the institution's patent decisions nor should the deal block or unduly delay academic scientists' ability to publish.[25]

In the 1990s NIH stepped in to address mounting concerns about lack of access within the scientific community to key research tools such as plasmids, antibodies, cell lines and mouse models – tools that had been created with government money. First NIH authorized the use of a simple, easy-to-execute Material Transfer Agreement (MTA) called the Universal Biological Material Transfer Agreement (UBMTA)[26] to decrease the administrative barriers scientists needed to leap over in order to obtain research tools from colleagues, and then in 1999 NIH issued the now well-known NIH Research Tools Policy (see Table 25.1).[27] In brief this policy made the unrestricted sharing of research reagents for research purposes with third parties, including for-profit entities, a requirement for government grantees.[28] Later in 2004 NIH issued a specialized policy on the sharing of model organisms including mice (see Table 25.1).[29]

Moving beyond the sharing of physical reagents NIH published both a data sharing policy in 2003[30] and an Open Access Policy in 2008[31] (see Table 25.1). The philosophy being espoused by NIH through the enactment of these policies was simple: if a principal investigator used federal money to create a research tool or to generate data then that person must share those materials and data (while allowing for reasonable exceptions and permitting reasonable delays to allow for publishing) with colleagues

---

[24] NIH (1994), 59 *Federal Register* 55673.

[25] Ibid.

[26] NIH (1995), 60 *Federal Register* 12771.

[27] NIH OTT, Policies and Guidelines: Research Tools Archive; NIH (1999) 64 *Federal Register* 72090.

[28] Ferguson (2001).

[29] NIH Statement on Sharing and Distributing Mouse Resources; NIH Policy on Sharing of Model Organisms for Biomedical Research (7 May 2004).

[30] NIH Data Sharing Information.

[31] NIH (2008).

across the globe and with the general public. The 2008 Open Access Policy required all NIH scientists and NIH grantees to make their final author-approved scientific paper manuscripts publicly available on-line at NIH PubMed Central at no cost within six months of when the corresponding journal article was first published.

Although the technology transfer laws and policies discussed in this chapter only apply to research findings and discoveries made with federal financial support, most U.S. universities apply and follow these same policies and practices for all of the research they carry out. In other words the Bayh-Dole Act and NIH policies are adhered to for research that is carried out with donated funds, non-federal grants, fee-for-service arrangements or private sector money received via sponsored research agreements. As a consequence of this practice within the scientific community, U.S. federal law and policy in the area of technology transfer has a disproportionately large impact on academic research activities worldwide.[32]

Table 25.1 NIH technology transfer-related policies and guidelines for grantees and contractors

1994 Developing Sponsored Research Agreements: Considerations for Recipients of NIH Research Grants and Contracts http://www.ott.nih.gov/policy/spons_research.aspx
1995 Universal Biological Material Transfer Agreement (UBMTA) http://www.bioinfo.com/ubmta.html
1999 Research Tool Guidelines http://grants.nih.gov/grants/intell-property_64FR72090.pdf
2003 NIH Data Sharing Policy http://grants.nih.gov/grants/policy/data_sharing
2004 NIH Policy on the Sharing of Model Organisms http://www.nih.gov/science/models/sharingpolicy.html
2004 NIH Best Practices for the Licensing of Genomic Inventions http://www.ott.nih.gov/policy/lic_gen.html#best
2008 NIH Open Access Policy http://publicaccess.nih.gov

32 Rohrbaugh and Stanton (2009).

3.2 Intramural Patenting and Licensing Policies

NIH's patenting and licensing policies are based on the following general premise: the primary reason for undertaking technology transfer and related commercialization activities is as a means to contribute to improving the health and wellbeing of all citizens. The main tenets of NIH's patent policy are straightforward and sensible: NIH will not seek patent protection for a discovery if no further research and development is needed; if the technology addresses a low public health priority and/or if there is a lack of commercial interest in the invention; or if patenting the invention could potentially hinder its transfer to the private sector or block access to the invention to researchers.[33]

Maximizing financial return from licensing activities is not a top priority although NIH does expect to receive a fair return on the American taxpayers' financial support of biomedical research.[34] On average, approximately 85 percent of all licenses executed by NIH in a given year are non-exclusive licenses.[35] This practice is in sharp contrast to how extramural entities handle licensing – the majority of licenses executed by universities are exclusive licenses.[36] Exclusive licenses are only entered into by NIH if there is a compelling case to be made that the invention could not be successfully commercially developed without such a license.[37] For technologies that require little further development, a significant financial investment or for which the market will support more than one supplier only a non-exclusive license will be offered.[38] For the exclusive commercialization licenses that are granted NIH typically does not permit broad fields of uses – the field of use is kept as narrow as is warranted by the capabilities and interests of the licensee and as is warranted by public health concerns. Typically the breath of an NIH exclusive license is narrowed by restricting the fields of use to a particular set of claims in a licensed patent application, to one type of technology platforms, to specific diseases/disorders, or to geographic regions.[39]

---

33 NIH, Patent Policy.

34 Keller (1998).

35 NIH OTT, Commonly Tracked Metrics.

36 Pressman et al (2006).

37 NIH OTT Licensing Policy.

38 Ferguson (2001).

39 Rohrbaugh (2005).

3.3 NIH's Best Practices for the Licensing of Genomic Inventions

In 2004 in response to concerns about an increasing number of disease-specific diagnostic test monopolies the NIH initiated the development of a guidance document that addressed the licensing of genomic inventions. In the 1990s Myriad Genetics executed a broad exclusive license with a U.S. university to two cancer susceptibility genes (BRCA1 and BRCA2) patent. The gene discovery and uncovering of a correlation between the presence of certain mutations in these genes with an increased susceptibility to breast and ovarian cancer was made by an NIH grantee. All clinical BRCA1 and BRAC2 testing in the U.S. is performed by this company as it has refused to sub-license to other testing companies and it also aggressively enforces its patent rights (thereby, in effect, preventing hospitals from developing and using their own less expensive in-house-developed BRCA1 and BRAC2 mutational tests out of a concern about possible infringement law suits).[40] Patients cannot be independently tested by another laboratory since no other company can legally offer a similar test and many believe that the lack of competition means that Myriad has no incentive to keep their prices low. Lastly some scientists and healthcare practitioners have accused Myriad of being slow to incorporate newly discovered mutations into their test and of being resistant to transitioning to newer, improved and less expensive sequencing technologies[41] – all of this translates to a less than optimal situation for patients and the physicians responsible for managing their care.

In the 'NIH Best Practices for the Licensing of Genomics Inventions'[42] document NIH re-emphasized its long-time practice within its intramural research program of only granting exclusive licenses when absolutely necessary for successful commercialization of a given product, usually a therapeutic drug or a vaccine. Importantly, the guidelines encouraged grantees to only grant non-exclusive license rights to prognostic and diagnostic uses of nucleic acid-based inventions. In line with NIH's general licensing policy this best practices directive reminded academic TTOs to include a royalty-free, non-exclusive research use term to the technology in all of their licenses not just for their institution (to comply with the Bayh-Dole Act) but for all other third parties as well.

---

[40] Carbone et al (2010).

[41] Pollack (2011), B1.

[42] NIH (2004), *Federal Register* 13414.

3.4 NIH Intramural Technology Transfer Practices vs. Extramural Grantee Practices

NIH's intramural patent and licensing policies have remained unchanged since 1995 – adhering to a set of general principles as opposed to asking TTOs to comply with specific criteria has served NIH well. In addition, most of NIH's technology transfer policies and practices align with the Association of University Technology Managers (AUTM)'s 2007 'Nine Points to Consider in Licensing University Technology' guidance document.[43] In the 'Nine Points' document AUTM, like NIH, recommends that academic entities reserve research use rights to their technologies. Both AUTM and NIH suggest allowing third parties to use licensed inventions at no cost with zero restrictions for non-commercial purposes. As mentioned above NIH insists on broad access to research tools and it avoids entering into broad exclusive licensing arrangements whenever practicable; AUTM has encouraged a similar approach for the extramural community. Compliance with the 'Nine Points' statement is optional and to date there has been little data available on whether or not signatories to this policy have, in fact, actually modified how they negotiate license terms.

There are several significant differences between licensing and technology transfer practices at extramural institutions and those carried out within NIH. At NIH, TTOs provide a service function only whereas most academic entities have both a technology transfer service function and a significant entrepreneurial function. Universities are legally permitted, unlike NIH, to take equity in lieu of funds as licensing fees and they can also enter into license option agreements. In addition, academia can conduct fee-for-service work and enter into sponsored research agreements. Academic research entities routinely establish startup companies, administer special research funds such as proof-of-concept funds and manage on-campus company incubators. Academic faculty can serve as part-time employees or as paid advisors to companies. None of these activities are permitted within intramural NIH.[44] Lastly, due to strict conflict of interest and ethics rules NIH scientists cannot serve in any sort of paid role for a company; however NIH employees may serve on scientific advisory boards and, of course, they are permitted to enter into collaborative agreements with companies.[45]

---

43 AUTM (2007).

44 Ben-Menachem, Ferguson and Balakrishnan (2005).

45 NIH (2005), 70 *Federal Register* 51559.

3.5 Commercialization of NIH and Federally Funded Inventions

This restructured approach to the management of federally funded research has benefited American citizens and non-Americans by giving them access to new products and services as well as through the creation of new jobs and new companies. By giving control over patent and licensing decisions to funded entities and to funding agencies that carry out independent research supported with government money, by rewarding these invention owners for effectively managing the technology transfer process and by ushering in the hiring and training of a cadre of federal and academic technology transfer practitioners the U.S. government has, in effect, created a new source of technology innovation. Research studies have unequivocally shown that this new technology transfer system has indeed resulted in a number of significant public benefits including numerous medical breakthroughs and increased economic growth in the U.S. and elsewhere.[46] AUTM's 2010 President and the organization's Executive Director describe the impact of the Bayh-Dole Act as follows: 'Data clearly show that it played a critical role in rejuvenating the entire U.S. economic system, transforming it from a manufacturing base to an innovation base.'[47] AUTM licensing survey data collected annually between 1992 and 2008 shows impressive two- to five-fold increases in all standard indices including invention disclosures received, patent applications submitted, patents issued, licenses executed, royalty income, number of university spin-off companies, estimated number of jobs created, and so on.[48]

Due to NIH's focus on carrying out and funding basic biomedical research most NIH inventions are at an early stage of development. Despite being predominantly a 'supermarket for research tools', NIH has had a number of blockbuster inventions – including several first-in-class drugs and vaccines (see Table 25.2).[49] During the past two decades the NIH intramural program has cumulatively received in over U.S.$1 billion in royalty income including U.S.$91.6 million in 2010.[50] That same year annual product sales by NIH licensees were estimated to exceed U.S.$6 billion per year. In an article published in 2011 a group of academic and

---

[46] AUTM (2009).

[47] Loise and Stevens (2010), 1.

[48] Ibid, 53.

[49] FDA approved products developed with technologies from the NIH Intramural Program <http://www.ott.nih.gov/about_nih/fda_approved_products.aspx>.

[50] NIH OTT, 'About NIH OTT'.

federal technology transfer experts analyzed the role of public sector research in the discovery of therapeutic drugs and vaccines.[51] The authors showed that since the early 1970s universities, federal government laboratories, and non-profit research institutions have discovered 153 new FDA-approved vaccines and drugs (this number includes uncovering new uses for existing drugs). The organization which had discovered or co-discovered the largest number of products (approximately 14 percent) among the 75 institutions studied was the intramural research program at NIH with 22 drugs and vaccines.[52]

Table 25.2 Example intramural NIH-developed or co-developed FDA approved drugs and vaccines[a]

Drug/vaccine name	Licensee	Medical use	Year first sold in US
Fludara®	Berlex	B-cell leukemia drug	1991
Videx	Bristol Myers Squibb	Anti-HIV drug	1991
Taxol®	Bristol Myers Squibb	Ovarian and breast cancers drug	1996
Havrix®	GlaxoSmithKline	Hepatitis A vaccine	1997
Synagis®	MedImmune	Respiratory Syncytial Virus (RSV) vaccine	1998
Velcade®	Millennium	Multiple Myeloma drug	2003
TAXUS™ Express2™	Angiotech/Boston Scientific	drug-containing coronary stent for angioplasty	2004
Gardasil®	Merck	Cervical cancer vaccine	2006

Note: [a] FDA Approved Products Developed with Technologies from the NIH Intramural Program http://www.ott.nih.gov/about_nih/fda_approved_products.aspx accessed 21 August 2011.

51 Stevens et al (2010).
52 Ibid, 539.

4. CONCLUSION

Technology transfer professionals, researchers, university administrators, and private sector leaders recognize that there is an inherent tension between the government and academic scientific communities' desire to openly share data and technologies without restriction at low or no cost and NIH's potential licensees' preference for NIH to restrict or delay public disclosure of or access to particular technologies in order to facilitate the commercial development of licensed inventions and generate revenue. As a consequence of the enormous public health and economic ramifications associated with achieving the 'right' balance between these two poles (open versus restricted) it needs to be a top priority for all biomedical research sector stakeholders to identify, implement, and/or enforce practical legal and policy solutions. NIH has crafted numerous patent and licensing guidelines and policies and has implemented best practices that it believes, in concert with innovative federal laws, have allowed it to achieve a reasonable balance between meeting the core needs of the government and academic sectors (pursuing research free of commercial influence, advancing and sharing scientific knowledge, educating and training the next generation of scientists, and so on), while also fostering the efficient commercialization of promising technologies by the private sector.

REFERENCES

Association of University Technology Managers (2007), 'In the Public Interest: Nine Points to Consider in Licensing University Technology', 6 March, <http://www.autm.net/Nine_Points_to_Consider.htm>

Association of University Technology Managers, 'AUTM U.S. Licensing Activity Survey Highlights: Financial Year 2009', <http://www.autm.net/AM/Template.cfm?Section=Documents&Template=/CM/ContentDisplay.cfm&ContentID=5880>

Ben-Menachem, G., S.M. Ferguson and K. Balakrishnan (2005), 'Beyond Patents and Royalties: the Perception and Reality of Doing Business with the NIH' 24 *Nature Biotechnology* 1

Carbone, J., E.R. Gold, B. Sampat, S. Chandrasekharan, L. Knowles, M. Angrist and R. Robert Cook-Deegan (2010), 'DNA Patents and Diagnostics: Not a Pretty Picture' 28 *Nature Biotechnology* 784

Committee on the Judiciary, United States General Accounting Office Report to Congressional Committees, *Technology Transfer: Administration of the Bayh-Dole Act by Research Universities* (Report GAO/RCED-98–126, 1998)

Department of Health and Human Services (2005), 'Supplemental Standards of Ethical Conduct and Financial Disclosure Requirements for Employees of the Department of Health and Human Services', 31 August, 70 *Federal Register* 51559

Executive Order 12591, 'Facilitating Access to Science and Technology', 22 April 1987, 52 *Federal Register* 13414

Ferguson, S.M. (2001), 'Licensing and Distribution of Research Tools: National Institutes of Health Perspective' 41 *Journal of Clinical Pharmacology* 107S

Keller, G.H. (1998), 'Biomedical Technology Transfer in the Government Sector' 64 *American Society of Microbiology News* 454

Loise, V. and A.J. Stevens (2010), 'The Bayh-Dole Act Turns 30' 2 *Science Translational Medicine* 52

'NIH Policy and Procedures on Determinations of Exceptional Circumstances Under NIH Grants, Contracts, and Cooperative Agreements', *United States Public Health Service Technology Transfer Manual Chapter No 607* (9 December 1999)

National Institutes of Health (1994), 'Considerations for Recipients of NIH Research Grants and Contracts' 59 *Federal Register* 55673, 8 November

National Institutes of Health (1995), 'Uniform Biological Material Transfer Agreement: Discussion of Public Comments Received; Publication of the Final Format of the Agreement', 8 March, 60 *Federal Register* 12771

National Institutes of Health (1999), 'Principles and Guidelines for Recipients of NIH Research Grants and Contracts on Obtaining and Disseminating Biomedical Research Resources: Final Notice', 23 December, 64 *Federal Register* 72090

National Institutes of Health (2004), 'Policy on Sharing of Model Organisms for Biomedical Research', 7 May, http://grants.nih.gov/grants/guide/notice-files/NOT-OD-04–042.html

National Institutes of Health (2005), 'Supplemental Standards of Ethical Conduct and Financial Disclosure Requirements for Employees of the Department of Health and Human Services', 70 *Federal Register* 51559, 31 August

National Institutes of Health (2008), 'Revised Policy on Enhancing Public Access to Archived Publications Resulting from NIH-Funded Research', 11 January, *The NIH Guide for Grants and Contracts,* Notice Number: NOT-OD-08–033

National Institutes of Health, 'March-In Response', http://www.ott.nih.gov/policy/Reports.html

National Institutes of Health, 'Patent Policy', <http://www.ott.nih.gov/Policy/phspat_policy.html>

National Institutes of Health, 'Statement on Sharing and Distributing Mouse Resources', <http://www.nih.gov/science/models/mouse/sharing/1.html>

National Institutes of Health, '2011 Budget' <http://www.nih.gov/about/budget.htm>

National Institutes of Health, 'Data Sharing Information', <http://grants.nih.gov/grants/policy/data_sharing/>

National Institutes of Health Office of the Director, 'Determination in the Case of Fabrazyme® Manufactured by Genzyme Corporation®', <http://www.ott.nih.gov/policy/March-in-Fabrazyme.pdf>

National Institutes of Health Office of Technology Transfer, 'About NIH OTT' <http://www.ott.nih.gov/about_nih/statistics.aspx>

National Institute of Health Office of Technology Transfer (2004), 'Best Practices for the Licensing of Genomic Inventions', 19 November, 69 *Federal Register* 13414

National Institutes of Health Office of Technology Transfer, 'Commonly Tracked Metrics', <http://www.ott.nih.gov/ttmetrics/default.aspx>

National Institutes of Health Office of Technology Transfer, 'FDA Approved Products Developed with Technologies from the NIH Intramural Program' <http://www.ott.nih.gov/about_nih/fda_approved_products.aspx>

National Institutes of Health Office of Technology Transfer, 'Licensing Policy' <http://www.ott.nih.gov/policy/phslic_policy.aspx>

National Institutes of Health Office of Technology Transfer, 'Policies and Guidelines: Research Tools Archive' <http://www.ott.nih.gov/policy/reasearch_toolarchive.html>

Pollack, A. (2011), 'Patents Safe, a Company Tries to Keep its Secrets', *The New York Times*, August 25, B1

Pressman, L., R. Burgess, R.M. Cook-Deegan, S.J. McCormack, I. Nami-Wolk, M. Soucy and L. Walters (2006), 'The Licensing of DNA Patents by US Academic Institutions: An Empirical Survey' 24 *Nature Biotechnology* 31

Rohrbaugh, M.L. (2005), 'Distribution of Data and Unique Material Resources Made With NIH Funding' 11 *Journal of Commercial Biotechnology* 249

Rohrbaugh, M.L. and B.R. Stanton (2009), 'Technology Transfer at the National Institutes of Health' in P. Ganguili, R. Khanna and B. Prickril (eds), *Technology Transfer in Biotechnology: A Global Perspective*, Wiley-VCH Verlag Gmbh & Co

Stevens, A.J., J.J. Jensen, K. Wyller, P.C. Kilgore, S. Chatterjee and M.L. Rohrbaugh (2010), 'The Role of Public-Sector Research in the Discovery of Drugs and Vaccines' 364 *The New England Journal of Medicine* 535

Thomas, J.W. (2008), 'Exceptional Circumstances to the Bayh-Dole Act: An NIH Perspective', June 8, Presentation at Federal Laboratory Consortium Annual Meeting, <http://globals.federallabs.org/pdf/2008/Contractors_Thomas.pdf>

United States General Accounting Office Report to Congressional Committees (2003), *Technology Transfer: Agencies' Rights to Federally Sponsored Biomedical Inventions* (Report GAO-03–536, 2003)

26. Licensing university intellectual property: ownership and management of intellectual property in the United Kingdom

Noel Byrne

1. INTRODUCTION

Licensing agreements between commercial enterprises and universities are seen by the universities as a way to enhance their profiles in the commercial world and to earn revenue from their research activities, and by the commercial enterprises as a way to gain access to research expertise or results. For most (if not the vast majority) of universities in the European Union and beyond, those ambitions or aspirations are not (and may never be) realized. Only a relative handful of universities, including the top universities, can hope, let alone expect, to gain financially from licensing their intellectual property to commercial enterprises; and even for this minority the evidence is somewhat thin in so far that the revenue earned from licences outweighs the administrative and legal costs in negotiating, formalizing and managing a licensing agreement.[1] Even the top universities may spend more trying to license or actually licensing their research results than they can expect realistically to gain from licensing, at least in the shorter term.

There is little, if any, 'fast money' to be made by universities from licensing research results. Such information must be transformed into a marketable technology in order to realize a revenue stream. When the research results are a major technological breakthrough (for example the Cohen-Boyer recombinant DNA method in the 1970s) the academic institution may get a significant up-front payment for the grant of a

[1] Anecdotal evidence indicates that far more income comes from sponsored research than from technology licensing.

licence to exploit the results. Beyond such rare exceptions, reward in the form of licence royalties is usually a distant prospect, seldom less than five years away and in some sectors, for example the pharmaceutical sector, usually between eight and ten years from the grant of the licence.

Negotiating a licensing agreement with an academic institution can be a tedious business. As grantor (or would-be grantor) of a licence, the institution(s) and/or the researcher(s) who have (and presumably own) the research results may have an exaggerated view of their potential worth and, in consequence, have unrealistic expectations for what they are offering. Universities in most European countries are funded, wholly or mainly, by the State for teaching purposes. They are not 'commercial enterprises' in the usual sense. They are not established to make a profit. On the other hand, a successful commercial enterprise will know how to evaluate the market prospects for a technology, to take and manage risks associated with placing the technology on the market, to police and if necessary enforce its intellectual property, and to earn a profit and stay in the business. Negotiators representing these two polar opposites may find it extremely difficult to create common ground; and in their efforts to create common ground they must consider and resolve issues relating to ownership of intellectual property.

2. COMMERCIAL RELATIONSHIPS

A commercial relationship between a university and a commercial enterprise may require the university:

1. to undertake research activities
   (a) on behalf of the enterprise and to transfer to the enterprise ownership of or licence rights over the research results arising from the contract;
   (b) as part of a research group or consortium, where each participant licenses its background and/or foreground intellectual property and/or know-how to the other participants (academic institutions or commercial enterprises);
2. to take a licence from a commercial enterprise to exploit (for example in performing a research contract) technology owned by the enterprise;
3. to grant a licence (or equivalent rights) to a commercial enterprise to exploit research results or technology owned by the university or within its rights to license.

The discussion here is limited to certain issues relating to the latter relationship: the grant of a licence by a university that authorizes a commercial enterprise to exploit certain research results or technology that the university owns or has the right to license. The views expressed in relation to these issues may well be pertinent when considering research agreements and inwards licensing.

3. OWNERSHIP OF INTELLECTUAL PROPERTY

The owner of intellectual property can sell, license, mortgage or otherwise dispose of the property (for example on trust) in whole or in part unless the particular transaction would contravene third-party rights. Yet the legal maxim that you cannot give what you do not have applies no less to intellectual property than to other forms of personal property. If the academic institution does not own the intellectual property it purports to license or is not authorized by the owner(s) to license it, any licence which it grants to a commercial enterprise will be legally flawed and exploitation of the intellectual property could expose the enterprise to infringement proceedings by the owner(s). The commercial enterprise may be able to sue the academic institution for damages for breach of warranty of authority, whether or not sued for infringement by the owner.

As a general rule, a would-be licensee must ensure that it (a) takes a licence from the 'right person' (so to speak), (b) provides in the licensing agreement for appropriate warranties as to the licensor's title or authority to grant the licence, and (c) obtains a suitable indemnity from the licensor, as a defence against proceedings for infringement of third parties' intellectual property.

4. JOINT OWNERSHIP OF IPR

It is essential, when negotiating with a university for a technology licence, to investigate title or authorization as far as can reasonably be done. Undue reliance on warranties is imprudent, not least because the licensing agreement will usually exclude or limit the university's liability in damages; and indemnities are rarely given by universities.

Joint ownership, unless there is a clear agreement on it, can create a legal obstacle to the effective exploitation of intellectual property. Most countries (the USA is an exception) regulate the exploitation of jointly owned intellectual property, particularly jointly owned patents for inventions. A jointly owned patent cannot be licensed without the consent of the joint owners – one joint owner cannot grant a valid licence without the consent of the other(s). Joint inventors are presumed to be jointly entitled to any patent granted for the invention.[2]

Inventorship is a prelude to first ownership of an invention. Inventorship asks: who gets credit for an invention, or who must be named in a patent as the inventor or a joint inventor (or co-inventor)? A person need not necessarily make the key inventive step to be classified as an inventor, but he or she must contribute to the inventive concept. If the final concept of the invention would not have come about without that person's involvement then that person is entitled (solely or jointly) to the invention. On the other hand, a person who has made no such contribution cannot be declared (for example by an agreement) to be a joint inventor, and in this respect inventorship differs from ownership: inventorship is not a prerequisite to ownership.[3]

Ownership, as a legal issue, asks: who owns legal title to the subject matter claimed in the patent? An agreement between two parties in dispute cannot attribute inventorship to one who has not made, or contributed to, an invention but it can pass ownership of a patented invention to one who is not an inventor.

Where two or more researchers (R1, R2, R3 …) are working together (collaborating) on a research project, disputes can arise over rights in or to an invention (or other subject matter) apparently made by one of them. R1, R2 and R3 together may be recognized as joint inventors, notwithstanding that one of them may claim to have made the final breakthrough. If R1, R2 and R3 work for the same employer (E), that is to say, the three are employees in a legal sense, then E prima facie is entitled to ownership of any patent granted for the invention; but if they do not, or the employment relationship is unclear, difficult issues arise.[4]

---

[2] E.g., Patents Act 1977 (UK), s 7(2).

[3] E.g., Patents Act 1990 (Cth), s15. A patent application can be filed by the inventor or joint inventors, an employer or other a successor in title. Disputes over inventorship are almost always the prelude to claims for sole or joint ownership of a patent.

[4] In *Pancreas Technologies Pty Ltd v The State of Queensland* [2005] APO 1, the State claimed title to an international patent application relating to treatment of pancreatic disease. The application had been filed by a Research Fellow in their employ. The Deputy Commissioner ruled that although an initial inventive contribution was made by the employee in the course of her employment, later development, although supported by her employer, was not in the course of her employment and therefore the application should proceed in joint names. The Deputy Commissioner's determination regarding entitlement was complicated by the fact that: there was no explicit agreement concerning IP generated by the

If R1 and R2 work for E but R3 does not, then E and R3 are jointly entitled to the invention. Suppose further that E concludes with L a licensing agreement purporting to grant L the right to exploit the invention. Clearly, E can license L to exploit the limited interest that E has in the invention but L cannot exploit the invention effectively without R3's consent.

With registered forms of intellectual property such as a patent for an invention, joint owners of the property must provide for its maintenance and enforcement. Who is responsible for the payment of renewal fees? Who can enforce the jointly owned exclusive rights and who will bear (or share) the costs of enforcing them? A would-be licensee must provide for these issues in a licensing agreement.

When taking a licence under an unregistrable form of intellectual property, such as to works protected by copyright, it is essential to investigate title to the property no less rigorously than has been indicated for a patent of invention.

A work produced by the collaboration of two or more authors (Al, A2, A3 …), in which the contribution of each author is not distinct from that of the other author(s), is a work of joint authorship, and copyright (CR) in the work is owned jointly by the authors or, if they are employed and the work is made in the course of their employment, by their employer (or employers, as the case may be).[5]

A work of joint authorship must not be confused with a work such as a technical manual, a computer program to which two or more authors make separate (distinct) contributions, for example, where two or more researchers each contribute different sections or chapters to a research report. In this case, each author (Al, A2, A3 …) is entitled to a distinct copyright (CR1, CR2, CR3 …), with the result that several copyrights, each owned by a different author, subsist at the same time in the one report. What has been said for copyright is true also for design rights. Again, who can enforce the jointly owned exclusive rights and who will

relevant Research Fellowship; there was an absence of IP management capability and established policies and practices within Queensland Health; it was not clear whether the research fellowship constituted an employment arrangement or a grant; and Queensland Health was unclear and extremely slow in asserting entitlement.

[5] E.g., Copyright, Designs and Patents Act 1988 (UK), ss 9–11.

bear (or share) the costs of enforcing them are issues that should be included in a licensing agreement.[6]

5. MANAGEMENT

Property, including intellectual property, must be managed properly to make the most of the opportunity it offers. Intellectual property must be policed against misuse and misappropriation (infringement). Registered forms of intellectual property – patents for inventions, trade mark registrations and design registrations – must be renewed periodically by timely payment of the renewal fees. Failure to pay renewal fees on time will result in 'deregistration' of the property.

If, due to its failure to manage the licensed property in accordance with the contract terms (express or implied), the licensor causes loss to a licensee, the licensee could claim its loss from the licensor for the latter's breach of the licensing contract,[7] unless the contract excludes liability for such loss. This simple proposition can easily be overlooked by a licensor. If a licensor lacks experience or resources for the effective management of its intellectual property, that task should be given to the licensee (who, no doubt, will want the task reflected in the royalties).

---

6 'University Technology Transfer in the United States, Europe and Asia' <http://www.law.washington.edu/CASRIP/Symposium/Number5/>; specifically Ullrich (2000).

7 Suppose, e.g., that Far West University (FWU) granted Biological Sciences Limited (BSL) a licence to exploit patented enabling technology owned and managed by FWU. BSL built and equipped a new facility (costing €10 million) to develop a marketable product using the licensed technology and, after five years of development (costing €5 million), had a product ready for the market. At that point, the key patents on the licensed technology had 10 years to run. Due to FWU's mismanagement of two key European patents, the renewal fees were not paid on time and these patents were removed from the register. FWU knew that BSL was relying on the licensed patents to amortize the €10 million investment over that 10-year period but due to the loss of the two patents it is likely to take at least five years longer for BSL to recoup its investment. FWU may face a damages action by FSL to recover its loss due to FSL's mismanagement of the licensed patents. Hence, licensees may want to take over the management of key patents for the licensed technology.

6. CONCLUSION

Licensing agreements with universities should be, but may not be, relatively straightforward to negotiate. They may not be easy to negotiate partly because universities in general tend to have unrealistic expectations for what they are offering a commercial enterprise.

Universities in general tend to be extremely cautious when it comes to negotiating licensing agreements with commercial enterprises. The inexperienced or less-experienced ones fear that they 'may be taken for a ride' by a commercial enterprise and this fear may lead an academic institute to seek such wide-ranging, unrealistic assurances in a licensing agreement as to deter an enterprise from concluding the agreement.

Universities tend to be reluctant to enter into licensing alliances with newly formed or 'start-up' companies, other than start-up ventures set up or promoted by the universities themselves, preferring to deal with established businesses with impressive track records and forgetting perhaps that today's 'minnow' may well be tomorrow's Microsoft. A start-up business will involve a greater risk but, if successful, is likely to give a greater reward (and not just in money terms). The top universities are a considerable way up the learning curve when it comes to assessing licensing opportunities and managing the business of licensing their technologies to the commercial world beyond academia. Other academic institutions have yet to grasp the realities involved in the licensing business.

REFERENCES

Ullrich, H., 'Use and Exploitation of Intellectual Property in the Context of Publicly Funded Research and Development: Recent Legal Developments in Germany and in The European Union' (CASRIP Symposium Publication Series Number 5, 2000), <http://www.law.washington.edu/CASRIP/Symposium/Number5/pub5atcl12.pdf>

PART VII

Corporate governance issues and innovation

27. Innovation through the lens of corporate governance

John Duns

1. INTRODUCTION

One of the issues examined in Parts II and III of this book concerned how the law deals with competing claims of the employer and employee to ownership of an invention developed by an employee. Almost invariably in this situation the employer will be a corporation. That fact in itself should introduce no difficulty to the analysis, but if the individual responsible for the invention is a director or other officer of the corporation, whether or not they are also an employee, different legal duties will come into play. It is these duties which are the concern of this chapter. Directors[1] of a corporation are subject to their own particular duties, at both general law and under statute, and these duties will inevitably have an impact on the claims that might otherwise be made to the ownership of business inventions.[2]

To examine these issues, this chapter is structured as follows. The next section considers the fiduciary duties, and their legislative counterparts,

[1] The term 'director' is used here as a general term referring to those who have discretionary powers to make the company act. At equity, fiduciary duties are imposed on those who exercise such powers, whether technically directors or not: e.g., *Canadian Aero Services v O'Malley* (1973) 40 DLR (3d) 371, discussed below. Corporations legislation will invariably define the relevant terms and often in very wide terms: see, for example, the definitions of 'officer' and 'director' in the Australian *Corporations Act 2001* (Cth), s 9. For an illustration of the application of the relevant duties to a person who was bankrupt and thereby disqualified from being a director, see *Dwyer v Lippiatt* [2004] QSC 281.

[2] Directors may also have relevant obligations under their employment contract as well as under the general and statutory law duties considered here. For an example of a director who was sued for breach of both directors' duties and a contract of employment, see *Griffiths & Beerens Pty Ltd v Duggan* [2008] VSC 201.

that are most likely to be relevant to a claim of a director to a business invention. Of particular interest here is the 'corporate opportunities' doctrine. The nature of this doctrine, its limits and how it might apply in the context of business innovations are considered. Next, the chapter outlines the remedies that are likely to apply in the event that a breach of fiduciary duty is established. Finally, the extent to which directors may be able to obtain the company's consent to keep the benefits of an invention is considered.

For the most part Australian law is used to explain these principles but English and Canadian law is similar and so illustrations are also drawn from these jurisdictions. United States law is along similar lines but has some significant differences and these are noted where relevant.

2. FIDUCIARY DUTIES AND THE CORPORATE OPPORTUNITY PRINCIPLE: HOW THEY MIGHT APPLY

Stated in its broadest terms, directors owe a fiduciary duty to the company to act in the company's best interests. This broad duty is generally subdivided into more discrete, but overlapping, strands. One such strand is that the director must not pursue a transaction in which the director has a 'real, sensible possibility of a conflict of interest' ('the conflict rule').[3] Others are that a director must not appropriate property which belongs to the company[4] ('the appropriation rule') nor make a personal profit from their position as director ('the secret profits rule'). It is now accepted that a further strand is that directors must not divert a corporate opportunity for their own, personal benefit ('the corporate opportunities rule').[5] Importantly, in many, but not all, instances the director may be permitted to retain the benefits of an invention without

---

[3] *Boardman v Phipps* [1967] 2 AC 46.

[4] *Cook v Deeks* [1916] 1 AC 554.

[5] There are also statutory equivalents of these duties. In Australia, for example, these can be found in ss 180–183 of the *Corporations Act 2001* (Cth). These statutory duties are generally based on the original equitable duties and so are not separately considered here. A breach of statutory duties is often argued in tandem with a breach of fiduciary duties: see, for example, *Griffiths & Beerens Pty Ltd v Duggan* [2008] VSC 201.

It should be noted, however, that the statutory duties may vary from their equitable counterparts in some respects and that a breach of their provisions will generally have different consequences from a breach of fiduciary duties. See generally Boros and Duns (2010), chs 10–13.

being in breach of these duties if they obtain the company's informed consent to do so. This aspect is taken up in section 7.

A potential overlapping of these categories is apparent. A director who pursues a business invention, either one of their own making or through the opportunity to acquire it from a third party, runs the risk of being in breach of their fiduciary duty and this might variously be analysed as a failure to act bona fide in the interests of the company, a breach of the conflicts rule, a breach of the appropriation rule (if the company already owns the relevant property), a breach of the secret profits rule or, in the appropriate circumstances, a breach of the corporate opportunities rule. Nevertheless, the overlap is not complete and each strand has, in important respects at least, developed along its own distinct lines.[6] The focus of this chapter is the corporate opportunities rule, as it is this rule that directors are most likely to resort to when claiming that they are entitled to ownership of a business invention in their personal capacity. As will be seen, however, these other strands need to be kept in mind, both for their potential relevance and the influence they have had on the corporate opportunities rule itself.[7]

The corporate opportunity rule was described in the following terms by Laskin J of the Canadian Supreme Court:

> Descending from the generality, the fiduciary relationship goes at least this far: a director or a senior officer like [the defendant] is precluded from obtaining for himself, either secretly or without the approval of the company (which would have to be properly manifested on full disclosure of the facts), any property or business advantage either belonging to the company or for which it has been negotiating.[8]

An illustration of this rule in the context of business inventions can be seen in the leading U.S. case of *Guth v Loft, Inc.*[9] Here, the relevant corporation, Loft Inc., was a manufacturer and retailer of a range of products, including Coca Cola, which the corporation sold but did not manufacture. Charles Guth was president and director of Loft Inc. He

---

[6] See Deane J in *Chan v Zacharia* (1984) 154 CLR 178, 198–199.

[7] Other causes of action may also be relevant. For example, a director who fails to develop an opportunity for their company may be in breach of their duty of care. Directors or shareholders may also be vulnerable to claims that they have 'oppressed' minority shareholders: see, for example, *Dwyer v Lippiatt* [2004] QSC 281, although in that case the claim was held to fail on the facts. On this cause of action, see generally Boros and Duns (2010), ch 16.

[8] *Canadian Aero Services v O'Malley* (1973) 40 DLR (3d) 371, 382.

[9] 5 A 2d 503 (Del 1939).

arranged to acquire and then develop, for his own benefit, what was at that stage the more or less unknown Pepsi-Cola Corporation. Loft Inc. successfully sued Guth for breach of his director's duties in diverting what should have been a corporate opportunity to his own benefit.

A particular difficulty with the corporate opportunity rule is to identify its limits. For example, in what circumstances will an opportunity not be a 'corporate opportunity' and so entitle the director to retain the invention personally? Should a distinction be drawn in this context between executive and non-executive directors? Given the breadth with which the rule is stated, inevitably its application in a particular instance will turn on the specific facts of the case. As was stated by one Australian judge,

> It is not, I think, instructive to labor at too great a length attempting to derive some general principle from these cases. The combination of facts and circumstances, for example, the difference between public and private companies, the quasi partnership nature of some of the latter, the variety of relationships encompassed by the designation of fiduciary would expose any attempt to inevitable criticism.[10]

Even in the U.S., where the corporate opportunities doctrine is generally more developed than in Commonwealth jurisdictions, courts have noted the 'often-expressed criticism that the doctrine is vague and subjects today's corporate management to the danger of unpredictable liability'.[11] Despite this, some generalisations about the limits of the rule need to be drawn if the rule is to be useful and this is the task of the following sections.

3. LIMITS TO THE PRINCIPLE: PRIVATE CAPACITY

In principle it might be thought that a distinction would be drawn between a business opportunity that a director acquires or develops in the course of their directorship and, in contrast, an opportunity that arises in the director's private capacity. Only the former, it would seem, should constitute a 'corporate opportunity'. Certainly this factor has been given

---

[10] White J in *Dwyer v Lippiatt* [2004] QSC 281, para [72].

[11] *Miller v Miller* 222 N W 2d 71. For one statement of the U.S. position, see the American Law Institute *Principles of Corporate Governance* s 5.05. See also Bainbridge (2002), [7.3].

weight in the U.S., although it is not decisive.[12] In the Commonwealth jurisdictions there is also some support for the distinction. One of the most commonly cited decisions suggesting a 'private capacity' defence is the well-known decision of the House of Lords in *Regal Hastings Ltd v Gulliver*. In that case, Lord Russell held the directors liable to account but referred to the fact that the directors had obtained their profit 'by reason and only by reason of the fact that they were directors of Regal and in the course of the execution of that office', suggesting that opportunities that arise outside this scope may be safe.[13] Likewise, in *Canadian Aero Services v O'Malley*[14] the court suggested that a director is precluded from pursuing a business opportunity 'where it was his position with the company rather than a fresh initiative that led him to the opportunity which he later acquired'.

Despite this, the courts, at least in Commonwealth jurisdictions, have been unwilling to acknowledge that a director acted in a 'private capacity'. The reason for this appears to derive from a reluctance to separate out the corporate opportunity rule from other, stricter, aspects of a director's fiduciary duty, notably the secret profits rule and the conflict rule. The well-known decision of Roskill J in *Industrial Development v Cooley*[15] is an example. In this case the relevant company was in the business of providing various services, including architectural services, connected with building construction. The company was keen to expand its client base from private industry into the public sector. The defendant was a prominent architect who had been the chief architect of the West Midlands Gas Board and was thus seen as providing an ideal entrée into the public sector for the company. The company accordingly recruited him and appointed him managing director. At the time another Gas Board, the Eastern Gas Board, was considering employing architectural services for the proposed construction of four gas depots. The defendant, in his role as managing director, attempted to persuade the Gas Board to

---

[12] See *Broz v Cellular Information Systems, Inc* 673 A 2d 148 (Del 1996) and the American Law Institute *Principles of Corporate Governance,* s 5.05(b)((1)(A).

[13] [1942] 1 All ER 378, 386. Likewise Lord Wright, at 392, referred to the fact that 'the knowledge and opportunity which enabled them to take the advantage came to them solely by reason of their being directors of the appellant company' and Lord MacMillan, at 392, said that it was necessary to establish that 'what the directors did was so related to the affairs of the company that it can properly be said to have been done in the course of their management and in utilization of their opportunities and special knowledge as directors'.

[14] (1973) 40 DLR (3d) 371, 382.

[15] [1972] 2 All ER 162.

deal with the company but the Gas Board made it clear that it did not wish to deal with the company. However, some 12 months later, the Gas Board contacted the defendant privately, that is at his home, and discussed with him the possibility of working for the Board, essentially on the same job as that which he had unsuccessfully sought for the company. The defendant subsequently resigned as managing director from the company and was employed by the Gas Board. When the company discovered the details of what had occurred, it sued the former director for breach of fiduciary duty.

Not surprisingly, the director 'forcefully' argued that, as the contact from the Gas Board was made to him 'privately', there was no breach of fiduciary duty. However the court dismissed this argument out of hand and held that the defendant had acted in breach of his fiduciary duty:

> The defendant had one capacity and one capacity only in which he was carrying on business at that time. That capacity was as managing director of the plaintiffs. Information which came to him while he was managing director and which was of concern to the plaintiffs and was relevant for the plaintiffs to know, was information which it was his duty to pass on to the plaintiffs because between himself and the plaintiffs a fiduciary relationship existed.[16]

And, in the same vein, 'There can be no doubt that the defendant got this Eastern Gas Board contract for himself and got it as a result of work which he did whilst still the plaintiff's managing director.'[17]

Significantly, Roskill J relied on authorities applying the conflicts rule in rejecting this 'private capacity' argument. The conflicts rule is a prophylactic rule designed to prevent directors from being exposed to temptation. As a result, the rule denies the director the opportunity to argue that any benefit they received was 'reasonable' in the circumstances. As stated in *Boardman v Phipps*, one of the leading cases on the conflicts rule and relied on by Roskill J: 'human nature, being what it is, there is danger, in such circumstances, of the person holding a fiduciary position being swayed by interest rather than by duty, and thus prejudicing those whom he was bound to protect'.[18]

---

16 [1972] 2 All ER 162, 173.

17 [1972] 2 All ER 162, 168.

18 [1967] 2 AC 36, 123. For a similar approach, which applied *Industrial Development v Cooley*, see *Bhullar v Bullhar* [2003] EWCA Civ 424. Likewise, in the Australian case of *Green v Bestobell Industries Pty Ltd* [1982] WAR 1, 5, the link between the corporate opportunities doctrine and the conflict rule was made apparent by Burt CJ: 'It is enough, I think, to show that the fiduciary gains his knowledge or opportunity within the fiduciary relationship; that it was

Is there greater scope for non-executive directors to argue that an opportunity is unrelated to their role as director? Austin has made a case for this. He suggested that while there is a case to be made for a strict approach being taken against full-time executive directors, non-executive directors are arguably entitled to be treated differently.[19] Such a distinction was, however, recently rejected by an Australian court.[20]

4. LIMITS TO THE PRINCIPLE: TIMING

Another potential break in the link between the corporate opportunity rule and a director's liability is the timing of the opportunity. It is well established that simply resigning from a directorship will not enable the (former) director to exploit a corporate opportunity, particularly where the resignation was prompted by the opportunity itself.[21] The reverse situation arose in *S.E.A. Food International Pty Ltd v Lam.* In this case, the defendant argued that the business opportunity exploited by the director personally arose *prior* to him becoming a director. After noting that a director cannot escape liability by resigning after the opportunity has arisen, the Court then asked: 'What of an opportunity for benefit or gain which arises prior to the commencement of any fiduciary relationship but which is pursued whilst such a relationship exists?'[22] In

---

knowledge or an opportunity which could have been used in the sense that it was relevant to the acquisition of the profit or benefit in fact acquired and that by doing what he did to acquire the profit or benefit the fiduciary placed himself in a position where his duty and interest did conflict or in a position where there was a real and sensible possibility that they may conflict.'

[19] Austin (1987), 150 ('the unremunerated part-timer … should be allowed to wear two hats').

[20] *Western Areas Exploration Pty Ltd v Streeter (No 3)* [2009] WASC 213, paras [54]–[72]. See also the English Court of Appeal in *O'Donnell v Shanahan* [2009] EWCA Civ 751.

[21] See the Canadian decision in *Canadian Aero Services Ltd v O'Malley* (1973) 40 DLR (3d) 371. This has been consistently followed. See, for example, *Natural Extracts Pty Ltd v Stotter* (1997) 24 ACSR 110, a decision discussed below under the next heading and *S.E.A. Food International Pty Ltd v Lam* (1998) 16 ACLC 552.

[22] It is accepted that directors may be on competing boards and that this will not, in itself, give rise to a breach of fiduciary duty. See *Bell v Lever Brothers Ltd* [1932] 1 AC 161; *On the Street Pty Ltd v Cott* (1990) 101 FLR 234. Compare, however, *Western Areas Exploration Pty Ltd v Streeter (No 3)* [2009] WASC 213, [76] where the court suggested that this principle seems out of line with the

answering this question, they proposed the following guide as to when an opportunity will be sufficiently linked in time to come within the rule:

> … a director will act in breach of his fiduciary obligations to a company … if he or she takes up an opportunity for profit where there is a sufficient temporal and causal connection between the obligations and the opportunity. What is a sufficient connection will depend, in any particular case, upon a number of factors, including the circumstances in which the opportunity arises and the nature of it and the nature and extent of the company's operations and anticipated future operations.[23]

5. LIMITS TO THE PRINCIPLE: INABILITY OR UNWILLINGNESS OF THE COMPANY TO EXPLOIT

A principle that disallows a director to exploit a corporate opportunity would prima facie seem to be limited to opportunities that the company itself could exploit. Otherwise the director would not be exploiting a 'corporate' opportunity. As stated by Austin, 'There is surely no positive duty to report every business opportunity to the company, however remote it is, from the company's existing and probably future activities.'[24] In *Industrial Development v Cooley* Roskill J referred to the potential unfairness that would otherwise arise: 'The remarkable position then arises that if one applies the equitable doctrine on which the plaintiffs rely to oblige the defendant to account, they will receive a benefit which … it is unlikely they would have got for themselves had the defendant complied with his duty to them.'[25]

The inability or unwillingness of the company to take up the relevant opportunity is a recognised defence in the US. In the celebrated *Meinhard v Salmon* decision, Cardozo J stated that it would be 'a different question … if there were lacking any nexus of relation between the business conducted by the manager and the opportunity brought to him as an incident of management'.[26] Subsequent decisions have confirmed that if the opportunity that arises is not in the company's 'line of business' this will be a significant factor in determining whether the

---

strictness of other fiduciary duties. See also *Manildra Laboratories Ltd v Campbell* [2009] NSWSC 987.

23 (1998) 16 ACLC 552, 557. See also *Dwyer v Lippiatt* [2004] QSC 281.

24 Austin (1987), 147.

25 [1972] 2 All ER 162, 175.

26 *Meinhard v Salmon* 164 N.E. 545, 548 (N.Y. 1928).

director is in breach.[27] There has been academic support for this approach to be taken up by Australian courts.[28]

There is surprisingly little support for this in the Commonwealth cases, however. It is true that in the influential decision of *Peso Silver Mines Ltd (NPL) v Cropper*, the Supreme Court of Canada accepted that, at least where the company explicitly rejects an opportunity, there will no longer be a 'corporate opportunity' and the director will be free to take up the opportunity personally. As stated by Bull JA, 'an out-and-out bona fide rejection by the company would be the best evidence that any later dealings with the property by anyone would not be against its interests'.[29] In *Lee v Futurist Developments Ltd*, the England and Wales High Court of Justice (Chancery Division) accepted the proposition that 'there must be some substance to the alleged opportunity before it can count as a relevant corporate opportunity' and dismissed the allegation of breach of fiduciary duty on that ground.[30]

Nevertheless, the preponderance of case law, at least in England and Australia, is against this factor assisting the director. The reason seems to be that in such situations the courts, as with the 'private capacity' defence, fall back to the stricter profit and conflict rules. Under these rules the fact that the company could not itself have taken up the benefit is given little or no weight. An oft-cited case to support this is *Regal Hastings Ltd v Gulliver*,[31] referred to above. It was accepted in that case that the profits made by the directors (on the sale of shares in the company's subsidiary) could never have been made by the company itself, because the company lacked the funds to exploit the opportunity. The House of Lords, relying on the secret profits rule, rejected the directors' defence that the company's inability therefore meant that there was no breach of duty by them. Lord Russell stated the law as follows:

> The rule of equity which insists on those, who by use of a fiduciary position make a profit, being liable to account for that profit, in no way depends … upon such questions or considerations as whether the profit would or should

---

[27] See, for example, *Miller v Miller* 222 N.W.2d 71 (Minn. 1974); *Broz v Cellular Information Systems, Inc* 673 A.2d 148 (Del. 1996). This is also included in the American Law Institute, *Principles of Corporate Governances* 5.05. And see generally Bainbridge (2002), 333–334.

[28] See, for example, Austin (1987), 158 ff; and Meagher, Heydon and Leeming (2002), para [5–100].

[29] (1966) 58 DLR (2d) 2, 155–156.

[30] [2010] EWHC 2764 (Ch), [53].

[31] [1942] 1 All ER 378.

> otherwise have gone to the plaintiff … or whether the plaintiff has in fact been damaged or benefited from his action.[32]

Likewise Lord Wright stated that 'if a person in a fiduciary relationship makes a secret profit out of the relationship, the court will not inquire whether the other person … has lost a profit which otherwise he would have got'.[33]

This treatment of the corporate opportunities doctrine as being entwined with the secret profits and conflicts rules can be seen in the Australian case of *Natural Extracts Pty Ltd v Stotter*.[34] This case concerned a company established to develop tea tree oil from tea tree plantations. As explained by the court:

> While indigenous Australians have recognised the medicinal qualities of tea tree oil for perhaps tens of thousands of years, commercial exploitation of tea tree oil in modern Australia is a rather more recent phenomenon. There was a cottage industry for tea tree oil in the early 1920's when cutters distilled the oil by crude methods and sold it for use for skin irritations, insect bites, burns etc. There was little or no scientific data to support therapeutic claims for the oil and sales depended largely on folk lore. Interest in tea tree oil lay dormant until the late 1980's. It was probably fed by the general interest at that time in natural alternative medicines … there was a long time when the establishment of a viable tea tree plantation and industry by the individual parties to the present proceedings was as elusive as the finding of a new El Dorado.[35]

The company established to develop this tea tree business was looking to purchase a new property in order to expand its operations. However, it was unable to raise the funds required to make the purchase. One of the directors then resigned from the company and arranged for his family trustee company to take a 50 per cent equity share in a related business which conducted its operations on the relevant property.

In finding the director liable for breach of fiduciary duty, the Court called on a combination of the corporate opportunity and the profit and conflict rules. The court summarised the authorities as follows:

> a fiduciary must account for a profit or benefit if that profit or benefit was obtained either where there was a conflict or possible conflict between his fiduciary duty and his personal interest, or, where that profit or benefit was

---

[32] [1942] 1 All ER 378, 386.

[33] [1942] 1 All ER 378, 392. The Privy Council decision of *Phipps v Boardman* [1967] 2 AC 46 is to similar effect.

[34] (1997) 24 ACSR 110.

[35] *Natural Extracts Pty Ltd v Stotter* (1997) 24 ACSR 110, 112–113.

> obtained, by reason of his fiduciary position or by reason of his taking advantage of an opportunity or knowledge derived from that fiduciary position.[36]

Quoting the High Court decision in *Warman International Ltd v Dwyer*, 'the underlying purpose of the rule' was said to be 'to preclude the fiduciary from being swayed by considerations of personal interest and from accordingly misusing the fiduciary position for personal advantage'.[37]

6. REMEDIES

A director in breach who has diverted a corporate opportunity or made a secret profit will commonly be subjected to an order that the relevant property or profit is to be held on trust for the company.[38] While the director is entitled to be compensated for costs and expenses incurred in developing the opportunity, complications can still arise where the opportunity diverted has expanded in the director's hands. In *Hospital Products Ltd v United States Surgical Corp*, Mason J of the Australian High Court referred to two possible bases for a fiduciary's liability in such circumstances:

> One approach, more favorable to the fiduciary, is that he should be held liable to account as constructive trustee not of the entire business but of the particular benefits which flowed to him in breach of his duty. Another approach, less favorable to the fiduciary, is that he should be held accountable for the entire business and its profits, due allowance being made for the time, energy, skill and financial contribution that he has expended or made … In each case the form of inquiry to be directed is that which will reflect as accurately as possible the true measure of the profit or benefit obtained by the fiduciary in breach of his duty.[39]

---

[36] (1997) 24 ACSR 110, 136.

[37] (1995) 182 CLR 544, 557–58.

[38] Those involved in the breach may also be liable to account under the principle in *Barnes v Addy* (1874) LR 9 Ch App 244. For illustrations of this principle in the current context, see *Natural Extracts Pty Ltd v Stotter* (1997) 24 ACSR 110 and *Western Areas Exploration Pty Ltd v Streeter (No 3)* [2009] WASC 213.

[39] (1984) 156 CLR 41, 110.

It has been held that directors are not entitled to any allowance for the risks they have undertaken or enterprise they have shown in developing the opportunity.[40]

The fiduciary may also be held liable to account for the profit or ordered to compensate the company, as for example in *Griffiths & Beerens Pty Ltd v Duggan*,[41] where the plaintiff companies sought compensation against a director who set up a rival business for the benefit of his children.[42]

7. CORPORATE CONSENT

In many situations the company may be able to consent to the fiduciary's conduct, either by ratification of prior conduct or authorization of future conduct. Where this occurs the fiduciary will be entitled to retain the benefits obtained. The company's consent may be manifested by shareholder approval[43] or through its constitution.[44] The consent must be fully informed and is not available for all types of breaches, such as where the directors have acted in bad faith or have appropriated corporate property. In *Regal Hastings*, the House of Lords appeared to accept that the directors in that case could have obtained approval from shareholders.[45] A virtue of consent being available is that it encourages disclosure by the director, which arguably should be central to this area of the law.[46]

---

40 See *Green v Bestobell Industries Pty Ltd* [1982] WAR 1; *Lym International Pty Ltd v Chen* [2009] NSWSC 167; *Western Areas Exploration Pty Ltd v Streeter (No 3)* [2009] WASC 213.

41 [2008] VSC 201.

42 On equitable compensation generally, including the differences between this and common law damages, see *Gemstone Corporation of Australia Ltd v Grasso* (1994) 13 ACSR 695.

43 Compare *Queensland Mines Ltd v Hudson* (1978) 18 ALR 1, where the court appeared to accept that the company's approval could be given by the board of directors. This case seems to be best explained on the basis that members of the board were also the company's shareholders.

44 See *Whitehouse v Carlton Hotel Pty Ltd* (1987) 162 CLR 285.

45 Compare *Cook v Deeks* [1916] 1 AC 554. It should also be noted that, at least in the Australian context, such ratification may not be effective against a shareholder complaint: see *Corporations Act 2001* (Cth), s 239.

46 Bainbridge (2002), [7.3].

8. CONCLUSION

This chapter has considered some of the corporate law issues that may arise when the person who attempts to claim a business invention or opportunity is a director or officer of the corporation. There are a number of duties that might prevent the director from exploiting the opportunity personally, or at least require the company's consent to do so. In some respects the most interesting, though arguably the least developed, of these duties relates to the corporate opportunity rule. In the Commonwealth jurisdictions at least, this doctrine has struggled to break free of the strict rules against secret profits and conflict of interests. This has arguably resulted in an unfortunate restriction in the scope of the doctrine.[47] While a strict approach encourages disclosure of the opportunity, which may encourage the development of business innovation, an overly strict approach may have the opposite effect.

REFERENCES

Austin, R. (1987), 'Fiduciary Accountability for Business Opportunities' in P. Finn, *Equity and Commercial Relationships*, Law Book Company

Bainbridge, S. (2002), *Corporation Law and Economics*, Foundation Press

Boros, E. and J. Duns (2010), *Corporate Law*, 2nd edn, Oxford University Press

Lowry, J. and R. Edmunds (1998), 'The Corporate Opportunity Doctrine: The Shifting Boundaries of the Duty and Its Remedies' 61 *Modern Law Review* 515

Meagher, R., J.D. Heydon and M. Leeming (2002), *Meagher, Gummow and Lehane's Equity: Doctrine and Remedies*, 4th edn, Lexis Nexis

---

47 See generally Lowry and Edmunds (1998).

28. Institutions and innovation: is corporate governance the missing link?

Simon Deakin and Andrea Mina

1. INTRODUCTION

Innovation has been identified as an engine of growth in different areas of research in economics, business and management, and its positive effects have been theorized and observed at different levels of aggregation. Among the research streams that are most relevant to this theme, evolutionary theories of the firm[1], Schumpeterian frameworks (Old and New, European and North American) and the innovation systems literature[2] have made fundamental contributions to the modern understanding of innovation and economic change. Evolutionary theory has also been discussed in prominent contributions to institutional economics.[3] Many gaps in the literature do, however, remain on (1) the finer mechanisms through which specific institutional arrangements influence and are influenced by innovation, and (2) the policy and business challenge of aligning the legal framework and the needs of innovation-driven growth.

In the field of law and economics, a growing body of work is looking at the relationship between firm-level corporate governance arrangements and the institutional framework at the level of company and employment law. The legal origins hypothesis maintains that the legal infrastructure of a given country – its constitution, its court system, the nature of its legislature, and the structure of the legal professions – shapes the content

[1] Nelson and Winter (1982).

[2] Lundvall (1992); Nelson (1993); Carlsson (1995); Freeman (1995); Edquist (1997).

[3] E.g., Hodgson (1999; 2006).

of its laws on, among other things, corporate governance, with consequences for economic development.[4]

The connection between the two debates – innovation on the one hand, and corporate governance on the other – has been made in the work of William Lazonick and Mary O'Sullivan, but with few other exceptions[5] it has remained vastly under-researched relative to other aspects of the broad legal framework that constrains and enables firm behaviour (for example, in comparison with intellectual property rights). In this chapter we review the theory and evidence of the interaction between corporate governance and innovation. We develop a specific set of hypotheses, illustrate how they can be addressed and suggest avenues for further research which we believe can significantly enrich the current debate of the knowledge (or 'learning') economy.

2. INNOVATION AND INSTITUTIONS

The role played by institutions in the growth process has been explored in some detail within the innovation system framework, which explicitly focussed on innovation and institutions as the cornerstones of economic development, in stark contrast with standard macroeconomic theory at the time of its formulation.[6] In this framework, the quality – not simply the quantity – of capital, user-producer interactions, access to credit, modes of funding and governance of R&D, became crucial co-determinants of growth, together with what later became perhaps the most recurrent feature in the analysis of innovation systems: the science and technology infrastructure underpinning change, generating improved goods and services, fostering competitive advantage, and ultimately pervading the notion of the 'knowledge economy'.

The epistemic component of innovation systems has attracted a great deal of scholarly attention. This is true for all the variants of the literature: national,[7] technological,[8] regional[9] and sectoral.[10] Other

---

4 La Porta et al (1998; 2008).

5 Notably Tylecote (2007).

6 Nelson (1993).

7 The above-cited Lundvall (1992); see also Nelson (1993); Carlsson (1995); Freeman (1995); Edquist (1997).

8 Carlsson and Stankievicz (1995); Carlsson et al (2002).

9 DeBresson (1989); Saxenian (1994); Cooke (2001).

10 Malerba and Orsenigo (1993); Breschi and Malerba (1997); Malerba (2004).

aspects of the original research programme[11] have so far been relatively under-researched.

What formal institutions have been most systematically linked with the study of innovation? First of all, the *higher education system*. As the conduit of formal learning, universities and related organizations (*publicly-funded or 'mixed' public-private research organizations*) are primary determinants of the 'social capability' for growth through the advancement of knowledge.[12] A second broad group of institutional arrangements aimed to the generation and diffusion of new technologies includes instruments of public support to innovation, including *R&D grants, tax incentives, government subsidies and procurement policies*. *Intellectual property rights*, and more generally formal means of appropriating the returns from investments in innovation, are yet another way to remedy under-investment in activities characterized by 'Knightian' uncertainty which the market would not otherwise undertake. This is of course yet another classic example of market failure in the production of knowledge.[13]

While these first three sets of institutions have figured prominently and quite consistently in innovation research throughout the development of the discipline at least from the 1980s, uneven weight has been given to the *sources of investment* and the structure of *financial systems*. With the exception of venture capital in its private, public and hybrid forms, the relationship between finance and innovation has arguably been less central to the study of innovation than the problem of technological know-how, assets and capabilities and their consequences on industry dynamics and structural change. This is surprising considering the emphasis Schumpeter placed, for example, on the investment process and the role of banks in the economy.

Not many quantitative studies have tried to explain the performance of innovation systems in terms of their institutional characteristics on a systematic and comparative basis. One distinguished experiment is the highly cited paper by Furman, Porter and Scott on the determinants of national innovation capacity, defined as 'the ability of a country to produce and commercialize a flow of innovative technology over the long

---

[11] As envisaged, e.g., by Nelson (1993)

[12] See Abramovitz (1986); Freeman (2002). Quite independently from the policy implications discussed, for example, by Nelson (1993) and Lundvall (1992), the role of the university has assumed such prominence that expectations are now higher than ever for universities to engage directly in the commercialisation of results from their fundamental and applied research activities.

[13] Arrow (1962); Nelson (1993).

term'.[14] This framework builds upon research on national innovation systems, ideas-driven growth theory and microeconomics-based models of national competitive advantage and industry organization. The institutional variables taken into account include: openness to international trade and investments, the strength of IP protection, the stringency of antitrust policy and the development of the venture capital market.[15] Openness and IP protection affect innovation (approximated by patent counts) positively and significantly. Results for antitrust and VC development are less significant and less robust.

A few recent contributions have substantially extended the investigation of macroeconomic regularities in the institution–innovation 'nexus'. Fagerberg and Srholec have tried to identify indicators for as many institutional variables as possible and use them to profile macro patterns of innovation that do not depend on firms' atomistic behaviours, but instead on the general and shared institutional properties of the system in which they operate.[16] This kind of inductive search for regularities cannot illuminate the mechanisms through which these are generated but does generate very interesting findings. It also points to novel ways to use available macro data and to identify new areas of research on the role of 'institutional instruments'[17] or 'social capabilities'[18] in economic growth.

In Fagerberg and Srholec's approach, the factors used to capture institutional capabilities are: a set of traditional indicators of *innovation and education* systems (including patents, scientific publications, school enrolment etc.); a set of *governance* indicators (property rights, the quality of the judicial system, corruption and a favourable environment for business); a set of *political* indicators (including indices of democracy and political freedom); and finally a set of indicators or *openness* to trade and foreign capital. The strongest conclusion the authors draw from their result is the importance of innovation system and governance variables, which appear to be more closely related to levels of development (measured by GDP per capita) than the 'Westernization' of the political system and openness to trade and foreign investment, for which empirical support is weak.

---

[14] Furman et al (2002), 899.

[15] The data source for these four variables is the IMD *World Competitiveness Report.*

[16] Fagerberg and Srholec (2008; 2010).

[17] Gerschenkron (1962).

[18] Abramovitz (1986).

3. THE INSTITUTIONAL FRAMEWORK OF CORPORATE GOVERNANCE

The legal origins hypothesis maintains that the legal infrastructure of a given country – its constitution, its court system, the nature of its legislature, and the structure of the legal professions – shapes the content of its laws on, among other things, corporate governance, with consequences for economic development.[19] Most countries in the world have inherited these core features of their legal infrastructure from a small number of parent systems whose laws were diffused through conquest, colonization and transplantation in the course of the eighteenth and nineteenth centuries. Systems with an English common law origin are said to favour the protection of property and contract rights against state intervention, while those with roots in the French or German civil law tend to accommodate the interventions of an activist, developmental state. In the corporate governance field, these different traditions are reflected, it is argued, in the pro-shareholder-value approach of the US and UK, in contrast to the stakeholder-orientated approach of France and Germany and the systems whose laws they have influenced.[20]

The empirical validity of some aspects of the legal origins hypothesis, in particular its account of the common law/civil law divide, has been much disputed, and, in this context, it has been argued that it is implausible to see legal systems as entirely exogenous to economic and political conditions in a given country.[21] In the short run, institutions operate as exogenous constraints on individual behaviour. In the long run, however, institutions are endogenous, in the sense of expressing practices which are widely observed, or of values and beliefs which are widely shared, in a given society. The endogeneity of institutions can be formally modelled using the techniques of evolutionary and epistemic game theory, which views institutions as stable states or equilibria arising from the interaction of agents.

Using this approach, Aoki argues that corporate governance should be seen as a process of interaction between stakeholders which is capable of producing multiple solutions to coordination problems depending on the strategic options available to them, which are shaped, in turn, by the institutional framework. Corporations are understood as self-governing, rule-based associations which operate to distribute cognitive actions

[19] La Porta et al (1998; 2008).
[20] La Porta et al (2008).
[21] Armour et al (2009c).

among their members. They realize surplus value to the extent that as corporate bodies they 'can cognize and store what a mere collection of individuals cannot'.[22] The norms of corporate governance reflect complementarities across the types of cognitive assets deployed within the firm by managers, workers and shareholders. These differ according to context, and are to some degree associated with differences between national systems.

Thus in the hierarchically organized firm, managers' cognitive assets are essential to the returns achieved by workers (in the sense that workers cannot increase their returns without managerial input), but the same is not true in reverse: management can increase its returns by unilaterally extending its use-control rights over the firm's physical assets, and so has no need to share these rights with the wider workforce. This describes the paradigmatic form of the Anglo-American corporation, at least in its mid to late twentieth-century version. By contrast, the 'reciprocal essentialities' or co-dependence of managers' and workers' cognitive assets which operated in German and Japanese firms of the middle decades of the twentieth century found expression in (respectively) the codetermination and lifetime employment models of those countries. External monitoring of reciprocal essentialities through the capital market is, Aoki suggests, an emergent model in a number of countries, including Japan. In this model, shareholders autonomously evaluate the effectiveness of links within the firm between managerial and worker cognitive assets; the capital market supplies a 'cognitive infrastructure' for the evaluation of firm performance.

In Aoki's model, corporate law is endogenous to the emergence of the corporation as an associational entity, or, to put it slightly differently, can be thought of as having co-evolved with it. Inverting the claim that 'corporations' (as opposed to 'firms') must be thought of first and foremost as legal entities, Aoki suggests that the legal features of the corporation should be conceptualized as representations of the corporation's self-organizing form; that is to say, 'business-specific substantive representations of the "unique identity" and "self-organising" dimensions of the corporation'.[23] Legal norms, like other 'public indicators', work by informing agents that they are in a state of play in which common knowledge can be applied with a view to arriving at a coordinated outcome.

The implication of this approach is that cross-national diversity in the rules of company and employment law is a consequence of long-run

[22] Aoki (2010), 5.
[23] Ibid, 9.

divergences between countries in structures of corporate ownership and predominant modes of organization of production, of the kind captured by the idea of 'varieties of capitalism'.[24] 'Coordinated market' systems, which support collective employee voice at the level of the firm, through codetermination or similar institutions, and/or which grant employment protection rights to workers, also tend to limit the scope for hostile takeover bids, thereby restricting shareholder exit. Blockholding, rather than dispersed share ownership, is the norm in such systems. A framework within which both labour and capital are locked into the firm is the result. An insolvency law framework which prioritizes the protection given to secured creditors is another potentially complementary institution, as this empowers the interests of banks which operate as suppliers of long-term 'relational' finance to the firm (see Table 28.1).

In 'liberal market' countries, by contrast, strong legal protection for minority shareholders goes hand in hand with weak employment protection laws, allowing managers to restructure the firm in response to shareholder pressure, not just through takeover bids but also via share buy-backs and high dividend payments which are associated with downsizing. The priority given to the shareholder interest also qualifies the rights of creditors, implying a limit on the protection the law grants to banks as secured lenders. The freedom which shareholders have to exit the firm at short notice in search of higher returns limits the options which management has to incentivize workers to make firm-specific investments (skills and know-how) and to engage creditors in strategic investments which cannot be protected against *ex post* adjustment to the structure of the firm in the interests of shareholder value (banks will be unwilling to lend on a relational basis).

There is of course a very close match between 'liberal market' systems and common law legal origin, and 'coordinated market' systems and civil law origin. La Porta et al argue that legal origin provides the best single explanation for the institutional diversity recognized by the varieties of capitalism literature. They acknowledge that economic and political factors can influence the content of the laws governing the firm, but assert that the essential elements of the legal system, which they refer to as 'legal infrastructure', pre-date industrialization in virtually all countries, and so must be regarded as an exogenous causal variable shaping the long-run path of economic development.[25]

---

[24] Soskice and Hall (2001).
[25] La Porta et al (2008).

Table 28.1 Corporate governance in liberal vs. co-ordinated market systems

	Shareholder protection	*Creditor protection*	*Worker protection*
Liberal market systems	High (legal support for hostile takeover bids, share buy-backs, shareholder activism)	Medium or weak (debtor in possession laws, laws favouring corporate rescue over liquidation)	Weak (minimal legal support for employment protection, no codetermination)
Coordinated market systems	Weak (minimal legal support for market for corporate control, limited minority shareholder rights)	Medium or strong (legal recognition of priority for secured creditors' rights)	Strong (effective legal support for employment protection and codetermination)

An alternative view, which is consistent with the co-evolutionary emphasis in Aoki's model of corporate governance, is that the direction of causation between institutional and behavioural variables runs both ways. Thus the content of corporate governance rules in different national systems is influenced by country-specific variations in corporate ownership structures,[26] political variables such as voting systems,[27] and the composition of interest group coalitions.[28] This is not to deny that institutions, once in place, pose constraints on the strategic options of business actors: firms in different countries are faced with different corporate governance regimes, and, at least in the short run, have to adapt their organizational structures and modes of financing to those constraints.[29] Over the longer run, the legal institutions which shape corporate governance at firm level can be thought of as endogenous in the sense of reflecting the national economic and political contexts in which they operate.

[26] Armour et al (2009c).
[27] Pagano and Volpin (2001).
[28] Roe (2003).
[29] La Porta et al (2008).

4. CORPORATE GOVERNANCE AND INNOVATION

From the viewpoint of agency theory, the economic function of corporate governance is to reduce information asymmetries and associated agency costs which are derived from the separation of ownership from control within business firms. According to Fama and Jensen, corporate forms which designate residual control and income rights to shareholders have 'survival value' because by doing so they reduce the costs associated with contractual monitoring and risk-adjustment. The reduction of agency costs contributes to the firm's competitive survival because it enables it to deliver products at lower prices.[30] In principle, this argument can be extended to cover the case of innovation: shareholder-focused firms are those which are more likely to survive and prosper in environments which offer the possibility of supra-competitive returns from innovation, on the one hand, and the threat of obsolescence, decline and exit under the pressure of 'creative destruction' on the other.

In the context of innovation, the argument for shareholder value also has a macroeconomic dimension. Shareholder pressure, it is argued, operates as a device for releasing capital from under-performing firms and ensuring its reallocation to more profitable and, in principle, innovative ones elsewhere in the economy. Thus it is suggested that the availability of venture capital for start-ups is linked to the ability of shareholders to extract value from companies in mature sectors through takeover bids and direct engagement with companies to increase dividends and engage in share buy-backs ('shareholder activism'). Once the capital is released in this way, the capital market functions to redirect it to growing firms in developing sectors of the economy.[31] More generally, it is argued that a liquid stock market is essential for providing venture capital firms with an exit strategy, via an IPO, which will enable them to cash out their investments.[32]

These approaches see a flexible labour market as complementary to corporate governance mechanisms in various ways. The ability of established firms to downsize at minimal cost is an essential part of the process by which hostile takeovers and shareholder activism work to free up capital for wider circulation in the economy. While downsizing in response to shareholder pressure can be analysed as a breach of implicit

---

[30] Fama and Jensen (1983), 203.
[31] Summers (2001).
[32] Gilson and Black (1997).

contracts between the firm and its core workforce,[33] agency-theoretical approaches see advantages in labour law regimes which give employers the freedom to restructure the enterprise where to do so will enhance shareholder value.[34] This implies a regime of minimal employment protection regulation and limited provision for collective employee voice in the event of redundancies. For start-ups, a minimal labour law regime is argued to provide an important source of flexibility in hiring and firing. Conversely, freedom for employees to move between firms, free of the constraints imposed by non-competition clauses or 'restrictive covenants', is said to be an important dimension of the 'high velocity' labour markets which characterize high-technology clusters.[35]

The agency-theoretical view of the governance–innovation link has however been challenged by the theory of the innovative firm developed by Lazonick[36] and O'Sullivan.[37] In their approach, the firm consists of a set of organizational relations which codetermine the way in which investment decisions are made, what types of investments are made, who makes these decisions and who claims the returns from these investments. The fundamental trade-offs in the investment decision are, first, between the short and the long term, and, secondly, between internal and external mechanisms of financing. The main trade-off in the redistribution of profits is between the claims of shareholders and those of 'residual' stakeholders, above all the employees of the firms who engage in collective learning and by doing so develop the innovative potential of the business. The central conflict of interest for the firm rises from the need to commit to innovation, a source of sustainable growth and continued employment, over a longer period of time than the one that would be sufficient to generate equal amounts of speculative returns for shareholders. The potential consequences include the (mis)use of the stock market to maximize shareholders' returns to the detriment of other stakeholders (workers) as well as investment in innovation. It can also lead, as Lazonick has argued in the case of the US, to inequitable and unstable resource allocation in a number of large corporations governed according to the shareholder value maximization principle,[38] which has had negative effects – Lazonick argues – on workers, firm competitiveness, and macroeconomic growth.

---

33 Shleifer and Summers (1988).
34 Jensen (1993).
35 Saxenian (1994); Hyde (2002).
36 See Lazonick (2000; 2007).
37 See O'Sullivan (2000; 2003).
38 Jensen (1986).

A related critique of the agency-theoretical view has been made by Tylecote and his collaborators. After reviewing the role of finance and corporate governance in a national innovation systems framework,[39] they find that country-specific factors significantly influence the rate and direction of technical change as well as the development path of firms. This suggests that the agency model describes those systems, such as the US and UK, which rely heavily on external finance, supplied through the capital market, to support innovation, but has limited relevance in other contexts.

Table 28.2 associates aspects of corporate governance in liberal vs. coordinated market systems with potential effects on innovation patterns.

5. HYPOTHESES AND THE CURRENT STATE OF EMPIRICAL RESEARCH ON THE LINK BETWEEN GOVERNANCE AND INNOVATION

5.1 Shareholder Protection and Innovation

Within a framework of strong shareholder protection, shareholders are relatively free to enter and exit the firm in rapid response to changes in expected returns on investment among all available investment opportunities at any given time. Thus *strong shareholder protection should exert a positive influence on innovation by providing exit opportunities via IPOs for VC-backed firms.* The positive effect can be associated with a view of innovation that privileges the contribution to technical change by new start-up firms (Schumpeter Mark I) over the contribution of incumbents. The second effect that might be induced by capital market liquidity is mediated by the higher likelihood of takeovers and corporate shake-ups.

Despite numerous theorizations of positive effects of acquisitions on R&D intensity or R&D productivity (both standard microeconomics and the resource base view of the firm argue in this direction), evidence has found that these effects are either neutral or negative. Desyllas and Hughes highlight positive and significant effects conditional on the distance between the knowledge bases of acquirers and acquired firms: related knowledge bases generate positive effects, while the likelihood of negative effects increases as knowledge concentration increases.[40]

---

39 see Tylecote (2007) for comprehensive references.

40 See Desyallas and Hughes (2010).

Table 28.2 Complementarities between corporate governance and modes of innovation

	Shareholder protection	*Creditor protection*	*Worker protection*	*Mode of innovation*
Liberal market systems	High (legal support for hostile takeover bids, share buy-backs, shareholder activism)	Medium or weak (debtor in possession laws, laws favouring corporate rescue over liquidation)	Weak (minimal legal support for employment protection, no codetermination)	• Strong venture capital market • 'Schumpeterian' creative destruction regime • Higher-risk investment • High incidence of radical innovation • Efficient labour market matching
Coordinated market systems	Weak (minimal legal support for market for corporate control, limited minority shareholder rights)	Medium or strong (legal recognition of priority for secured creditors' rights)	Strong (effective legal support for employment protection and codetermination)	• Limited use of venture capital • Slower creative destruction dynamics • Investment risk more spread • Incremental tech development • Continuous staff learning and long-term commitment to innovation

A counter-view is that *strong shareholder protection will impact negatively on innovation by shortening investment time horizons.* There is evidence that firms are less willing to invest in R&D when they come under pressure to prioritize shareholder returns through share buy-backs and higher dividends.[41] Ease of exit at short notice in search of higher returns limits the options which management has to engage workers and creditors in strategic approaches to innovation which imply rent-sharing over the long term. In other words, possible advantages obtained from the freeing up of capital to flow to new firms and emerging industries must be set against the limited capacity of managers to pursue strategies based on long-term investments at firm level with a degree of reciprocity with other shareholders.

5.2 Creditor Protection and Innovation

The protection of creditors' rights can exert direct and significant influences on the capacity of the firm to finance its R&D activities. Strong creditor protection, in particular as it relates to the rights of secured creditors such as banks, reduces the lender's risk, thereby, at least in theory, favouring access to credit by firms that seek external finance. Improved access to credit will provide more and better inputs to be deployed in the R&D process with potentially positive effects on the innovation performance of the firm. Thus *strong protection of secured creditors' rights should favour innovation by firms dependent on bank-led finance.*

The counter-argument is that stronger creditor protection rights will imply stricter control over borrowing and exert a conservative influence over the technological and market risk associated with the innovation investment of the debt-holder. Since innovation can be very sensitive to threshold effects and because its outcomes are systematically and heavily skewed, with the possible (and probable) exception of VC investments, weaker creditors' rights might be more conducive to innovation via a high-risk, high-rewards strategy. If this is so, *stronger creditor protection rights will dampen innovation by allowing banks to impose stricter controls on borrowing and exacerbating the risks of failure for entrepreneurs.* Armour and Cumming (2005) find empirical support for this proposition, using an index which measures the severity of bankruptcy legislation over time. Reductions in the severity of personal bankruptcy law in several European countries in the 1990s were strongly correlated

[41] Graham et al (2005).

with a rise in self-employment in that period. Armour and Cumming also report a stronger effect of bankruptcy law on entrepreneurial activity, so defined, than either real GDP growth or stock market returns.

It may be that the *kind* of innovation activity makes a significant difference in the predicted effects of the strength of creditors' rights. In a high-risk, high-reward scenario, the search for radical innovation might be discouraged by strong creditor protection, which, conversely, will favour incremental innovation in relation to established lines of products, services and businesses. In turn, the type of innovation fostered by different types of creditor protection will be independent of the nature of the relevant technology and its development cycle. Different sectors will host clusters of technologies characterized by different lead development times: these tend to be short for, for example, software, and typically very long for, among other things, new materials.

5.3 Employment Protection and Innovation

Weak employment protection favours higher rates of labour mobility. As a traditional labour economics argument would have it, the firm's capacity rapidly to adjust matching between firms and projects on the one hand and the skill sets of employees on the other favours the search for efficient tasks/skills combinations and reduces the risk of the firm absorbing inflexible labour unable to adapt to new production choices. This could particularly be the case for R&D staff. Moreover, the possibility of workers learning from different firms through different jobs might stimulate the creative (often recombinatorial) processes which are so important for the development of new technologies. Thus *weak employment protection laws should favour innovation based on the capacity of firms to match labour inputs to different combinations of tasks and skills and on the learning effects generated by worker mobility across firms.*

The counter-argument goes as follows: legal frameworks which support collective employee rights at the firm level do not only constrain shareholder exit, but also directly incentivize the long-term pursuit of product, process and organizational innovation by individual workers and teams alike. Workers will only be willing to invest in the development of firm-specific skills and new technical and market knowledge if they are protected against *ex post* adjustment to the structure of the firm in the interests of shareholder value. Thus *strong employment laws should foster innovation based on co-investment by workers and employers in firm-specific human capital and related capabilities of the firm.*

As is the case for the effects of mergers and acquisition on innovation, there is no agreement within the empirical literature on the effects of labour mobility on firms' innovative performance. A recent study by Acharya et al (2009) does, however, find a statistically significant correlation between increasing legal employment protection over time and increases in patenting activity. The authors, who base their research on Centre for Business Research (CBR) data (see section 6 below), explain the link by arguing that employees with a legal measure of job security will be less risk-averse in developing innovative ideas and technologies.

6. OPERATIONALIZING THE STUDY OF THE LEGAL–REGULATORY FRAMEWORK: THE ANALYSIS OF LONGITUDINAL LEGAL DATASETS

As we have seen, a core prediction of the legal origins hypothesis is that common law systems will have relatively high levels of shareholder and creditor protection compared to civil law ones, as well as more flexible labour law regimes. This prediction is largely borne out by the empirical legal origins literature.[42] The empirical basis for the legal origin claim rests on datasets which were constructed so as to quantify the extent of legal variation across systems.[43] However, these data sources, notwithstanding their considerable influence, suffer from a number of methodological limitations; above all, they are (a few exceptions aside) only cross-sectional, and so are unable to capture the dynamics of legal change over time. In an attempt to address this gap, researchers at the CBR in Cambridge have constructed longitudinal datasets covering the period 1970–2005 for a sample of five countries[44] and the period 1995–2005 for a sample of 25 countries.[45] These new datasets are based on coding methods which have sought to address limitations inherent in the early legal origins studies. The main innovations are: the inclusion of data on self-regulatory norms such as corporate governance codes and takeover codes (La Porta et al just coded the formal law); the use of graduated variables to reflect differences between default and mandatory rules and other information concerning the effects of the rules in question

42 La Porta et al (2008).

43 Ibid.

44 Lele and Siems (2007); Armour et al (2008); Deakin, Lele and Siems (2007).

45 Armour et al (2007).

(the early La Porta et al studies mostly used binary variables); and the provision of detailed information on the primary legal sources for all codings (La Porta et al do not provide this information, except in summary form).

The CBR datasets code for legal rules which are directly relevant to the consideration of the relationship between corporate governance and innovation. The five-country shareholder protection index ('SPI') codes for shareholder rights in two main groups: those protecting shareholders against managerial opportunism, and those protecting minority shareholders against dominant majorities.[46] A reduced form of the SPI, used in the 25-country study, contains ten indicators which code for board independence, the regulation of takeover bids, and a number of other indicators of shareholder protection.[47] The creditor protection index (CPI) codes for three areas of corporate insolvency law: the law governing creditors' rights while the company is a going concern; the rights of secured creditors; and the law governing priority of claims and related matters in the event of bankruptcy.[48] A reduced form of this index is used to analyse legal change in the larger sample of 25 countries.[49] The labour regulation index ('LRI') codes for labour laws in five areas: the regulation of atypical employment contracts (including part-time work, fixed-term contracts and agency work), working time, dismissal, employee representation, and the right to strike.[50] The coding of a larger sample of countries using a reduced form of this index is currently being completed.

Figures 28.1–28.3 below illustrate broad trends in the shareholder protection, creditor protection and labour regulation indices respectively for the five systems in the CBR datasets for the period 1970–2005. A strong-form legal origin effect would be time-invariant and constant across closely related areas of law such as these. Neither is the case; the rank order of the countries changes over time and there is a very different picture across the three areas of law concerned. In relation to shareholder protection, we observe a common rising trend rather than the sharp divergence between common and civil law that La Porta et al identified

46 Armour et al (2009b).
47 Armour et al (2009c).
48 Armour et al (2009a); Deakin et al (2012).
49 Deakin et al (2012).
50 Armour et al (2009b); Deakin and Sarkar (2008).

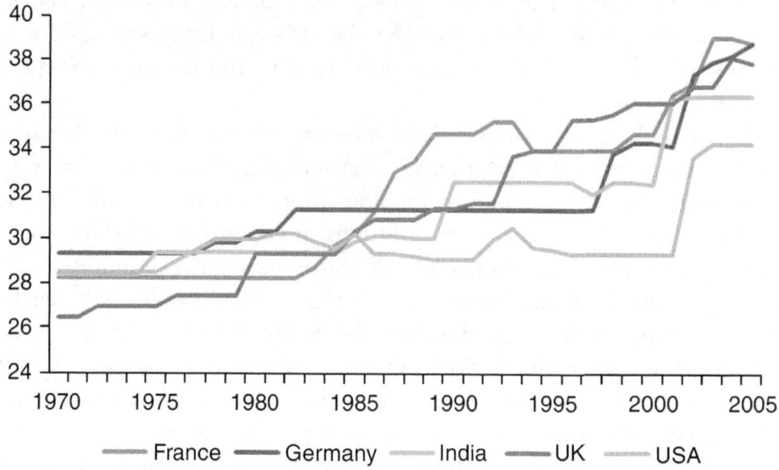

Figure 28.1 Shareholder protection in five countries, 1970–2005 (scale: 0–60)

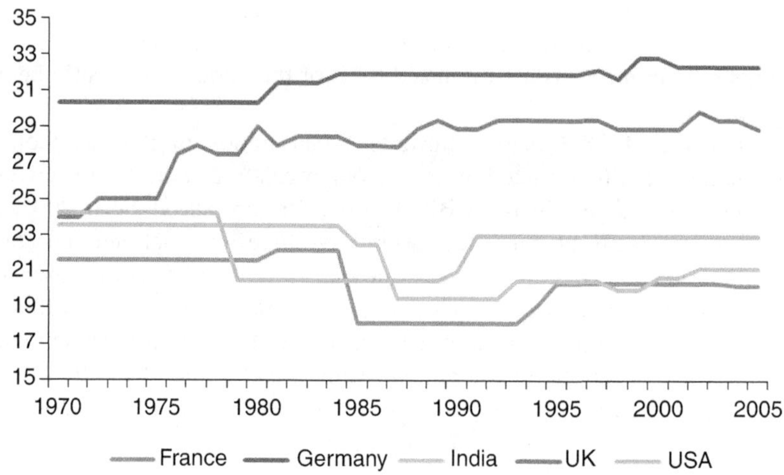

Figure 28.2 Creditor protection in five countries, 1970–2005 (scale: 0–44)

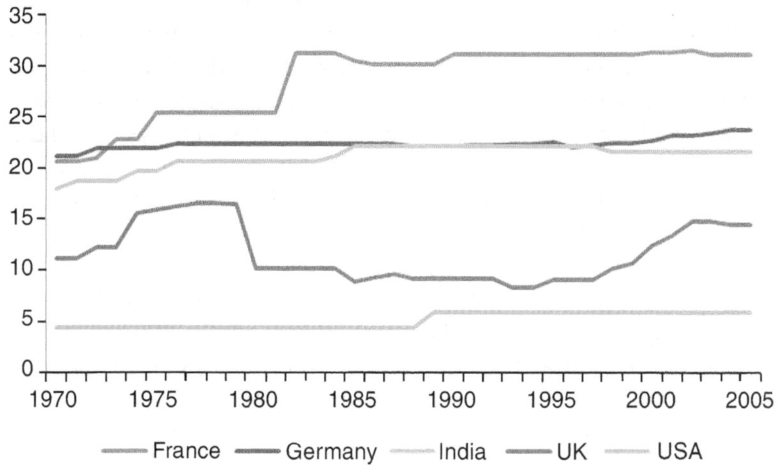

Figure 28.3 Labour regulation in five countries, 1970–2005 (scale: 0–40)

in their cross-sectional studies. For creditor protection, again, for these five countries, we see no clear pattern based on legal origin, and no convergence either. A clearer legal origin effect is visible in the case of labour regulation, but as this is an area in which political factors have played a major role in driving legal change, it is not clear that this is strong evidence in favour of the claim that legal infrastructure, as opposed to politics, is the key driver of change in the content of the law. Figures 28.4–28.7 set out in graphical form the main trends in the 25-year datasets on shareholder protection and creditor protection broken down by reference to state of development and legal origin.[51] As far as the SPI is concerned, nearly all national systems significantly increased

[51] The countries coded are: Argentina (civil law, developing); Brazil (civil law, developing); Canada (common law, developed); Chile (civil law, developing); China (civil law, transition); Czech Republic (civil law, transition); France (civil law, developed); Germany (civil law, developed); India (common law, developing); Italy (civil law, developed); Japan (civil law, developed); Latvia (civil law, transition); Malaysia (common law, developed); Mexico (civil law, developed); the Netherlands (civil law, developed); Pakistan (common law, developing); Russia (civil law, transition); Slovenia (civil law, transition); South Africa (common law, developing); Spain (civil law, developed); Sweden (civil law, developed); Switzerland (civil law, developed); Turkey (civil law, developed); UK (common law, developed); US (common law, developed). The Labour Regulation Index for 25 countries has not yet been completed.

the level of shareholder protection over the period 1995–2005. The two variables which rose most substantially in this period were those relating to independent boards and the mandatory bid rule in takeover bids.[52] There was a steady rise in the score for developed countries over the whole period. Transition systems saw a rapid jump in protection and after 1995 in developed countries there was marked increase after 2000 (Figure 28.3). Developed countries continued to have a higher level of protection throughout, but the gap between them and the rest had narrowed by the end of the period. When the same data are analysed by reference to legal origin, a closing of the gap between common law and civil law systems can also be seen (Figure 28.4). Thus the picture presented by La Porta et al[53] of stronger protection for shareholder rights in the common law world, while true for the start of our period, which is also the point to which their study refers, was not true at the end of it.

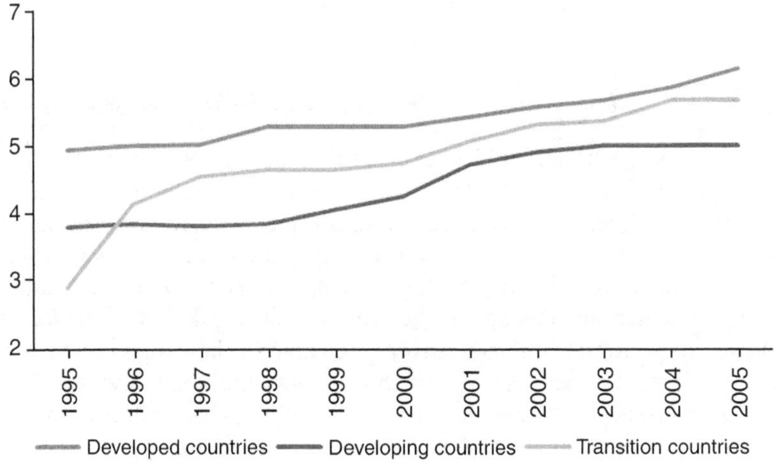

Figure 28.4 Shareholder protection in 25 countries, 1995–2005: developed, developing and transition systems (scale: 0–10)

The charts tracking change in the CPI also show an increase in protection over time. Common law systems and developed systems again have the highest scores, but the gap between the common law and civil law has almost disappeared by the end of the period (Figures 28.5 and 28.6).

[52] For details of these changes see Armour et al (2009c).
[53] La Porta et al (1998).

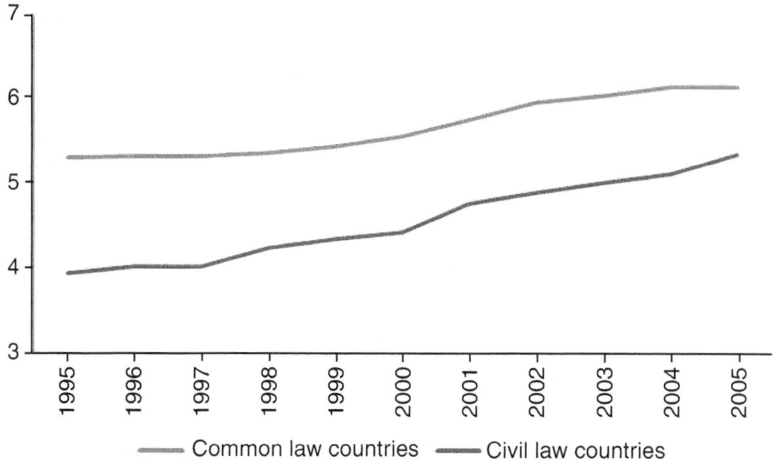

Figure 28.5 Shareholder protection in 25 countries, 1995–2005: common law versus civil law systems (scale: 0–10)

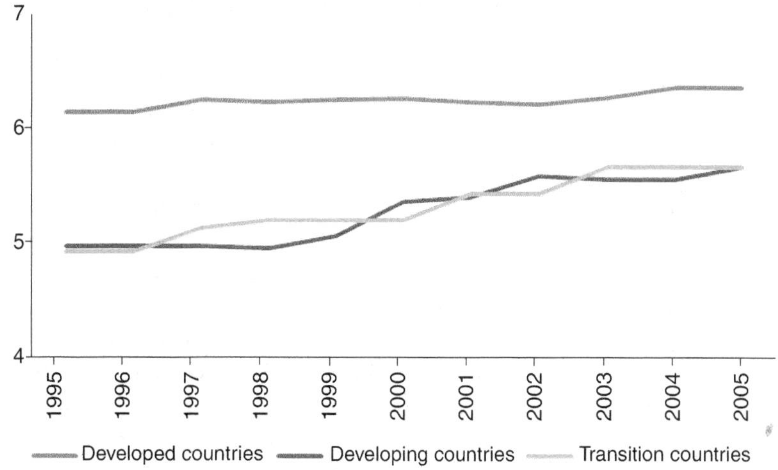

Figure 28.6 Creditor protection in 25 countries, 1995–2005: developed, developing and transition systems (scale: 0–10)

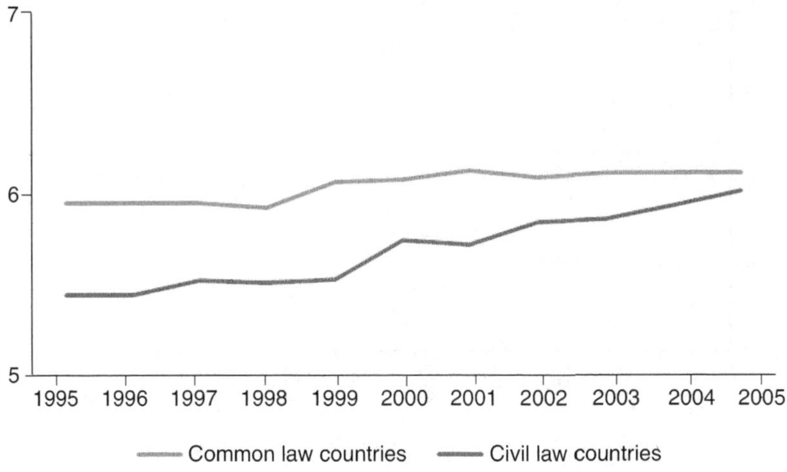

Figure 28.7 Creditor protection in 25 countries, 1995–2005: common law versus civil law systems (scale: 0–10)

Within the civil law group, French-origin systems (a group which includes the southern European and Latin American systems) had lower scores than both the English-origin and German-origin ones, but they also saw some of the greatest increases in protection, suggesting converging on the more protective approaches of the other two legal families. Over the decade to 2005 more or less every country in the sample strengthened protections for secured creditors and took steps to facilitate out-of-court enforcement of security interests.[54]

Two points stand out from this overview of the longitudinal coding of legal change. The first is that the well-known association made by La Porta et al between high levels of shareholder protection and common law legal origin must now be qualified: there is clear evidence of a recent increase in shareholder protection in the civil law world. In the period since La Porta et al's 1998 study, there has been growing convergence between common law and civil law systems, at least at a formal level. There has also been a significant strengthening of creditor rights across all countries, regardless of their legal origin.

The second point relates to the issue of complementarities between shareholder, creditor and worker rights. The CBR datasets show that high and rising levels of shareholder protection can go together not just with

---

[54] See Armour et al (2009c) for details.

strong creditor rights, but with employment protection and codetermination rights.[55] This is particularly the case in many civil law systems. The CBR datasets report formal legal changes; it is not clear how far the enactment of new shareholder rights in the civil law world has been translated into practice. If the effect is more than a formal one, the question raised by the trends in shareholder rights is whether the model of increased investor protection coupled with continuing legal support for job security and collective worker voice is a stable one. It may be compatible with shareholder monitoring of 'reciprocal essentialities' in the sense identified by Aoki, but this is an issue which requires further empirical inquiry.

Thus the CBR datasets present a more variegated picture of legal change than the one which has become familiar from the legal origins literature. This has further repercussions for the way the datasets are used in empirical analysis. A critical issue is how the different legal indicators interact with another in providing the framework for firm-level governance. Increases in shareholder protection may not have the effects intended for them if corresponding increases are taking place in creditor and worker protection. A second point is that formal changes in the law may not translate into new patterns of behaviour at firm level, if complementary institutions are lacking. Thus the enactment of new shareholder rights premised on the need to protect investors as a group against managerial opportunism may have little impact in systems where blockholding is the dominant form of ownership.

From the above we can see that the CBR datasets offer the potential for new insights to be gained into the nature of the link between corporate governance and innovation. By providing a new source of data on legal change over time, they make it possible to test some of the hypotheses to come out of the existing literature on the nature of that link (see section 5 above). However, they will have to be used in a way which makes it possible to analyse the interaction of the legal indicators both with each other and with a number of other variables which are institutional and economic in nature, in particular those relating to ownership structure, forms of financing, and modes of labour contracting.

---

55 Deakin and Sarkar (2008).

7. CONCLUSION

In this chapter we have reviewed the literature on the relationship between corporate governance and innovation, identifying a number of core hypotheses. We have also looked at the coding techniques that make it possible to quantify the extent of legal differences across countries and to map legal changes over time. We have considered the uses that can be made of legal data in exploring the innovation–governance link, and pointed to the need to analyse the role of the legal framework alongside other that of other economic and institutional variables. The next stage in our research will be to operationalize the framework we have set out in this chapter for use in empirical research.

REFERENCES

Abramovitz, M. (1986), 'Catching up, Forging Ahead and Falling Behind' 46(2) *Journal of Economic History* 385

Acharya, V., R. Baghai and K. Subramanian (2009), 'Labor Laws and Innovation', available at SSRN: <http://ssrn.com/abstract=1333621>

Ahlering, B. and S. Deakin (2007), 'Labour Regulation, Corporate Governance and Legal Origin: a Case of Institutional Complementarity?' 41 *Law & Society Review* 865

Aoki, M. (2001), *Towards a Comparative Institutional Analysis*, MIT Press

Aoki, M. (2010), *Corporations in Evolving Diversity*, Oxford University Press

Armour, J. and D. Cumming (2005), 'Bankruptcy Law and Entrepreneurship', CBR Working Paper No. 300

Armour, J., S. Deakin, P. Sarkar, M. Siems and A. Singh (2009a), 'Shareholder Protection and Stock Market Development: An Empirical Test of the Legal Origins Hypothesis' 6 *Journal of Empirical Legal Studies* 343

Armour, J., S. Deakin, P. Lele and M. Siems (2009b), 'How Legal Norms Evolve: Evidence from a Cross-country Comparison of Shareholder, Creditor and Worker Protection' 57 *American Journal of Comparative Law* 579

Armour, J., S. Deakin, V. Mollica and M. Siems (2009c), 'Law and Financial Development: What we are Learning from Time-Series Evidence' *Brigham Young University Law Review* 1435

Arrow, K. (1962), 'The Economic Implications of Learning by Doing' 29(3) *Review of Economic Studies* 155

Breschi, M. and F. Malerba (1997), 'Sectoral Innovation Systems: Technological Regimes, Schumpeterian Dynamics, and Spatial Boundaries' in C. Edquist and M. McKelvey (eds), *Systems of Innovation: Growth, Competitiveness and Employment, Volume 1*, Edward Elgar

Carlsson, B. and R.G. Henriksson (eds) (2002), *Development Blocks and Industrial Transformation: The Dahmenian Approach to Economic Development*, Almqvist and Wiksell International, at 136–48

Carlsson, B. and R. Stankiewicz (1995), 'On the Nature, Function and Composition of Technological Systems' in B. Carlsson (ed.), *Technological Systems and*

Economic Performance: The Case of Factory Automation, Kluwer Academic Publishers

Cooke, P. (2001), 'Regional Innovation Systems, Clusters, and the Knowledge Economy' 10(4) *Industrial and Corporate Change* 945

Cooke, P., M.G. Uranga and G. Etxebarria (1997), 'Regional Innovation Systems: Institutional and Organisational Dimensions' 26(4/5) *Research Policy* 475

Deakin, S., P. Lele and M. Siems (2007), 'The Evolution of Labour Law: Calibrating and Comparing Regulatory Regimes' 146 *International Labour Review* 133

Deakin, S. and P. Sarkar (2008), 'Assessing the Long-Run Economic Impact of Labour Law Systems: a Theoretical Reappraisal and Analysis of New Time Series Data' 39 *Industrial Relations Journal* 453

Deakin, S., P. Demetriades and G. James (2008), 'Creditor Rights and Banking System Development in India' 108 *Economics Letters* 19

Deakin S, P. Sarkar and A. Singh (2012), 'An End to Consensus? The Selective Impact of Corporate Law Reform on Financial Development' in M. Aoki, K. Binmore, S. Deakin and H. Gintis (eds), *Complexity and Institutions: Markets, Norms and Organizations*, Palgrave Macmillan

Debresson, C. (1989), 'Breeding Innovation Clusters: A Source of Dynamic Development' 17(1) *World Development* 1

Desyllas, P. and A. Hughes (2010), 'Do High Technology Acquirers become more Innovative?' 39 *Research Policy* 1105

Edquist, C. (ed.) (1997), *Systems of Innovation: Technologies, Institutions and Organization*, Pinter

Fagerberg J and M. Srholec (2008), 'National Innovation Systems, Capabilities and Economic Development' 37 *Research Policy* 1417

Fagerberg, J., M. Srholec and B. Verspagen (2010), 'Innovation and Economic Development' in B. Hall and N. Rosenberg (eds), *Handbook of the Economics of Innovation*, North Holland

Fama, E. and M. Jensen (1983) 26(2) *Journal of Law and Economics* 301

Freeman, C. (1995), 'The National Systems of Innovation in Historical Perspective' 19(1) *Cambridge Journal of Economics* 5

Freeman, C. (2002), 'Continental, National and Sub-National Innovation Systems: Complementarity and Economic Growth' 31(2) *Research Policy* 191

Furman, J., M.E. Porter and S. Stern (2002), 'The Determinants of National Innovative Capacity' 31 *Research Policy* 899

Gerschenkron, A. (1962), *Economic Backwardness in Historical Perspective*, Belknap Press

Gilson, R. and B. Black (1997), 'Venture Capital and the Structure of Capital Markets: Banks versus Stock Markets' 47 *Journal of Financial Economics* 243

Graham, J., C. Harvey and S. Rajgopal (2005), 'The Economic Implications of Corporate Financial Reporting', NBER Working Paper no. 10050

Hall, P.A. and D. Soskice (2001), *Varieties of Capitalism: The Institutional Foundations of Comparative Advantage*, Oxford University Press

Hodgson, G. (1999), *Evolution and Institutions: On Evolutionary Economics and the Evolution of Economics*, Edward Elgar

Hodgson, G. (2006), *Economics in the Shadows of Darwin and Marx: Essays on Institutional and Evolutionary Themes*, Edward Elgar

Hyde, A. (1998), 'Silicon Valley's High Velocity Labour Market' 11 *Journal of Applied Corporate Finance* 28

Jensen, M. (1986), 'The Agency Costs of Free Cash Flow' 76 *American Economic Review* 323

Jensen, M. (1993), 'The Modern Industrial Revolution, Exit, and the Failure of Internal Control Systems' 48 *Journal of Finance* 831

La Porta, R., F. Lopez-de-Silanes, A. Shleifer and R. Vishny (1998), 'Law and Finance' 106 *Journal of Political Economy* 1113

La Porta, R., F. Lopez-de-Silanes and A. Shleifer (2008), 'The Economic Consequences of Legal Origins' 46 *Journal of Economic Literature* 285

Lacetera, N. (2001), 'Corporate Governance and the Governance of Innovation: the Case of the Pharmaceutical Industry' 5 *Journal of Management and Governance* 29

Lazonick, W. with Mary O'Sullivan (2000), 'Maximizing Shareholder Value: A New Ideology for Corporate Governance' 29(1) *Economy and Society* 13

Lazonick, W. (2004), 'The Innovative Firm' in J. Fagerberg, D. Mowery and R. Nelson (eds), *Oxford Handbook of Innovation*, Oxford University Press

Lazonick, W. (2007), 'The US Stock Market and the Governance of Innovative Enterprise' 16(6) *Industrial and Corporate Change* 983

Lazonick, W. and M. O'Sullivan (1996), 'Organization, Finance and International Competition' 1(1) *Industrial and Corporate Change* 1

Lazonick, W. and M. O'Sullivan (2000), 'Maximizing Shareholder Value: A New Ideology of Corporate Governance' 29(1) *Economy and Society* 13

Lazonick, W. and A. Prencipe (2005), 'Dynamic Capabilities and Sustained Innovation: Strategic Control and Financial Commitment at Rolls-Royce plc' 14(3) *Industrial and Corporate Change* 501

Lele, P. and M. Siems (2007), 'Shareholder Protection: A Leximetric Approach' 7 *Journal of Corporate Law Studies* 17

Lundvall, B.A. (ed.) (1992), *National System of Innovation. Towards a Theory of Innovation and Inter-active Learning*, Pinter

Malerba, F. (ed.) (2004), *Sectoral Systems of Innovation*, Cambridge University Press

Malerba, F. and L. Orsenigo (1993), 'Technological Regimes and Firm Behavior' 2(1) *Industrial and Corporate Change* 45

Metcalfe, J.S. (2001), 'Institutions and Progress' 10(3) *Industrial & Corporate Change* 561

Metcalfe, J.S., A. James and A. Mina (2005), 'Emergent Innovation Systems and the Delivery of Clinical Services: the Case of Intra-Ocular Lenses' 34(9) *Research Policy* 1283

Nelson, R. (1959), 'The Simple Economics of Basic Scientific Research' 67(3) *Journal of Political Economy* 297

Nelson, R. (2003), 'On the Uneven Evolution of Human Know-How' 32 *Research Policy* 909

Nelson, R. (1993), *National Innovation Systems: A Comparative Analysis*, Oxford University Press

Nelson, R.R. and S. Winter (1982), *An Evolutionary Theory of Economic Change*, The Belknap Press

O'Sullivan, M. (2000), 'The Innovative Enterprise and Corporate Governance' 24 *Cambridge Journal of Economics* 393

Pagano, M. and P. Volpin (2001), 'The Political Economy of Finance' 17(4) *Oxford Review of Economic Policy* 502–519

Roe, M. (2003), *Political Determinants of Corporate Governance. Political Context, Corporate Impact*, Oxford University Press

Saxenian, A. (1994), *Regional Advantage: Culture and Competition in Silicon Valley and Route 128*, Harvard University Press

Schumpeter, J.A. (1934), *The Theory of Economic Development*, Oxford University Press

Shleifer, A. and L. Summers (1988), 'Breach of Trust in Hostile Takeovers' in A. Auerbach (ed.), *Corporate Takeovers: Causes and Consequences,* University of Chicago Press

Summers, L. (2001), London Stock Exchange Bicentennial Lecture

Tylecote A. (2007), 'The Role of Finance and Corporate Governance in National Systems of Innovation' 28 (10) *Organization Studies* 1461

Index